David Halberstam was one of America's most distinguished journalists and historians. After graduating from Harvard in 1955, he covered the beginnings of the civil rights movement and was then was sent overseas by the *New York Times* to report on the war in Vietnam. The author of fifteen bestsellers, including *The Best and the Brightest*, he won the Pulitzer Prize for his Vietnam reporting at the age of thirty. He was killed in a car accident on 23 April 2007, while on his way to an interview for what was to be his next book.

'Halberstam is a wonderfully assured portraitist. His depiction of MacArthur the megalomaniac, perceiving a chance to reverse the 1948 "loss" of China to the communists, is superb ... This is a finely crafted story, with a wealth of anecdotage.'   Max Hastings, *Sunday Times*

'The Korean War is now almost completely forgotten. It came a decade too early to be captured on television, while the gruelling nature of the conflict, as well as its inconclusive outcome, has never lent itself to Hollywood melodrama. Yet its extraordinary narrative twists are a gift to the historian, as David Halberstam splendidly proves. One of the greatest American reporters of his generation, Halberstam was killed in a car crash only a few days after finishing the text. This masterfully constructed and grippingly written book is a fitting tribute to his memory – and to the sacrifice of the men who fought and died to save South Korea.'   Dominic Sandbrook, *Daily Telegraph*

'One of Halberstam's greatest strengths was to combine oral history in the manner of Studs Terkel with a grand historical sweep to produce books that illuminate and explain a period of history from the point of view both of policy-makers and the foot soldiers they command.'   *The Times*

Also by DAVID HALBERSTAM

The Noblest Roman
The Making of a Quagmire
One Very Hot Day
The Unfinished Odyssey of Robert Kennedy
Ho
The Best and the Brightest
The Powers That Be
The Reckoning
The Breaks of the Game
The Amateurs
Summer of '49
The Next Century
The Fifties
October 1964
The Children
Playing for Keeps
War in a Time of Peace
Firehouse
The Teammates
The Education of a Coach

The
Coldest
Winter

America and the Korean War

DAVID
HALBERSTAM

PAN BOOKS

First published in Great Britain in 2008 by Macmillan

First published in paperback 2009 by Pan Books
an imprint of Pan Macmillan Ltd
Pan Macmillan, 20 New Wharf Road, London N1 9RR
Basingstoke and Oxford
Associated companies throughout the world
www.panmacmillan.com

ISBN 978-0-330-45850-4

1 3 5 7 9 8 6 4 2

A CIP catalogue record for this book is available
from the British Library.

Printed and bound in the UK by
CPI Mackays, Chatham ME5 8TD

Visit **www.panmacmillan.com** to read more about all our books
and to buy them. You will also find features, author interviews and
news of any author events, and you can sign up for e-newsletters
so that you're always first to hear about our new releases.

For Jean, again

Contents

Glossary of Military Terms

The size, composition, and leadership of military units varies with time, place, and circumstances. In the early fighting in Korea, almost every unit was always understrength. Therefore, these numbers are approximations.

Army	100,000 soldiers
	Comprised of 2 or more Corps
	Normally commanded by a full General
Corps	30,000 soldiers
	Comprised of 2 or more Divisions
	Normally commanded by Lieutenant General
Division	Up to 15,000 soldiers, often only 12,000 in Korea
	Comprised of 3 Regiments
	Commanded by Major General
Regiment	Up to 4,500 men, with affiliated units, such as artillery, armored, and medical units, included
	Comprised of 3 Battalions
	Commanded by Colonel
Battalion	700 to 850 soldiers
	Comprised of 4 or more Companies
	Commanded by Lieutenant Colonel
Company	175 to 240 soldiers
	Comprised of 4 Platoons
	Commanded by Captain

Platoon   45 or more soldiers
                                Comprised of 4 Squads
                                Commanded by Lieutenant

Squad   10 or more soldiers
                                Commanded by Staff Sergeant

WEAPONS AND ARTILLERY

M-1 Rifle   A 9.5-lb. rifle, with an 8-round clip,
  .30-caliber   the basic American infantry weapon.

Carbine   A short-barreled rifle with a 15- or 30-round clip
  .30-caliber   with less range and accuracy.

Browning Automatic   A two-man weapon—one to feed ammunition,
  Rifle, or BAR   one to fire—that was both semi- and fully
  .30-caliber   automatic, capable of firing 500 rounds a
                                  minute.

Machine Guns   The .30-caliber machine guns were capable of
                                  sustained fire of 450 to 500 rounds a minute.

                                The .50-caliber gun was mounted on trucks,
                                  tanks, and other vehicles. It fired 575 rounds
                                  per minute to a range of 2,000 yards.

Rocket Launcher   The ineffective 2.36-inch launcher was
  or Bazooka   replaced by the 3.5-inch in 1950 even as the
  2.36-inch and 3.5-inch   North Koreans drove south. The new
                                  bazooka was capable of penetrating thick
                                  armor plate; it had a range of up to 75 yards.

Infantry Mortars   These front-loaded weapons fired shells at a
  60mm   high angle, able to reach into valleys and
  81mm   trenches, with a range of 1,800 to 4,000 yards.
  42mm

Howitzers   Cannons with a range of 2 to 5 miles.
  105mm
  155mm
  8-inch

List of Maps

Note on Military Map Symbols

Every effort has been made to update the maps in *The Coldest Winter* to a modified version of the standard MIL-STD-2525B common warfighter symbology used by the U.S. Military. This is a comprehensive system that gives a trained interpreter instant information about a military unit's alignment, size, type, and identity.

In some cases, complete information was not available for specific military units, and rather than introduce inaccuracies, an easily legible shorthand has been applied. With clarity in mind, other modifications that aren't standard MIL-STD-2525B have been made to improve readability.

While MIL-STD-2525B accounts for hundreds of military designations, only a few are necessary to understand the units employed in the Korean War.

UNIT ALIGNMENT:	Artillery	●	Division	XX
Friendly Unit ☐	Engineer	⊓	Brigade	X
Hostile Unit ◇	Armor	⬭	Regiment	III
UNIT TYPE:	UNIT SIZES:		Battalion	II
Infantry ⊠	Army	XXXX	Company	I
Cavalry ⧄	Corps	XXX	Platoon	•••

The name of the unit can be displayed to the left of the unit symbol, the name of the larger group it is part of appears to the right of the unit symbol, and the size of the unit is indicated by the marking at the top. For example, the symbol for the Third Battalion of the Eighth Cavalry is:

Unless otherwise noted, a solid black line represents U.N. positions or a defensive perimeter.

The
Coldest
Winter

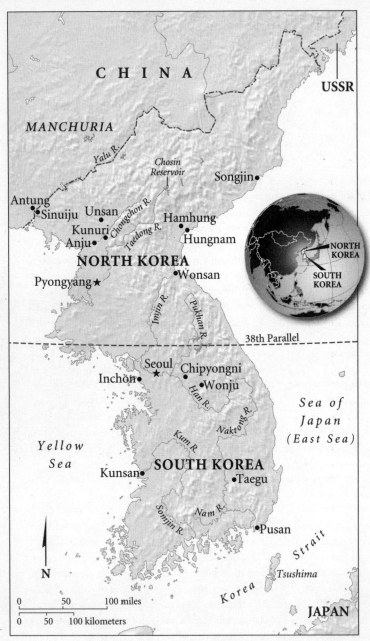

CHINA

USSR

MANCHURIA

Yalu R.

Chosin Reservoir

Songjin

Antung
Sinuiju
Unsan
Chongchon R.
Kunuri
Taedong R.
Hamhung
Anju
Hungnam

NORTH KOREA

NORTH
KOREA

SOUTH
KOREA

Pyongyang ★

Wonsan

Imjin R.
Pukhan R.

38th Parallel

Seoul ★
Chipyongni
Inchon
Wonju

Han R.

Naktong R.

Sea of
Japan
(East Sea)

*Yellow
Sea*

Kum R.

SOUTH KOREA

Kunsan
Taegu

Somjin R.
Nam R.

Pusan

Korea Strait

Tsushima

N

| 0 | 50 | 100 miles |
| 0 | 50 | 100 kilometers |

JAPAN

1. THE KOREAN PENINSULA BEFORE HOSTILITIES, MAY 1950

Introduction

O N JUNE 25, 1950, nearly seven divisions of elite North Korean troops, many of whom had fought for the Communist side in the Chinese civil war, crossed the border into South Korea, with the intention of conquering the entire South in three weeks. Some six months earlier, Secretary of State Dean Acheson, in a colossal gaffe, had neglected to include South Korea in America's Asian defense perimeter, and the only American forces then in the country, part of a tiny advisory mission, were almost completely unprepared for the attack. In the early weeks of the invasion, the Communist offensive was a stunning success. Every bit of news from the battlefield was negative. In Washington, President Harry Truman and his top advisers debated the enemy's intentions. Was this, as they greatly feared, an assault ordered up by the Russians? Were the North Koreans nothing but Moscow's pawns? Or was it a feint, the first in a series of what might be provocative Communist moves around the world? They quickly decided to use United States, and in time United Nations, forces to draw a line against Communist aggression in Korea.

The Korean War would last three years, not three weeks, and it would be the most bitter kind of war, in which relatively small American and United Nations forces worked to neutralize the superior numbers of their adversaries by the use of vastly superior hardware and technology. It was a war fought on strikingly harsh terrain and often in ghastly weather, most particularly a numbing winter cold that often seemed to American troops an even greater enemy than the North Koreans or Chinese. "The century's nastiest little war," the military historian S. L. A. Marshall called it. The Americans and their United Nations allies faced terrible, mountainous terrain, which worked against their advantage in hardware, most notably their armored vehicles, and offered caves and other forms of shelter to the enemy. "If the best minds in the world had set out to find us the worst possible location to fight this damnable war politically and militarily, the unanimous choice would have been Korea," Secretary of State Acheson said years after it was over. "A sour war," Acheson's friend Averell Harriman said of it.

To call it an unwanted war on the part of the United States would be a vast understatement. Even the president who had ordered American troops into battle had not deigned to call it a war. From the start, Harry Truman had been careful to downplay the nature of the conflict because he was intent on limiting any sense of growing confrontation with the Soviet Union. One of the ways he tried to do that was by playing with the terminology. In the late afternoon of June 29, four days after the North Koreans had crossed the border, and even as he was sending Americans into battle, Truman met with the White House press corps. One of the reporters asked if America was actually at war. Truman answered that it was not, even though in fact it was. Then another reporter asked, "Would it be possible to call this a police action under the United Nations?" "Yes," answered Truman. "That is exactly what it amounts to." The implication that U.S. soldiers in Korea were more a police force than an army was a source of considerable bitterness to many of the men who went there. (A similar verbal delicacy would be employed four months later by Chinese leader Mao Zedong when he ordered hundreds of thousands of Chinese soldiers into battle, deciding, for reasons somewhat parallel to Truman's, to call them *volunteers*.)

So, out of a question casually asked and rather casually answered, were policies and even wars defined. The terminology Truman offered that day in some ways endured. Korea would not prove a great national war of unifying singular purpose, as World War II had been, nor would it, like Vietnam a generation later, divide and thus haunt the nation. It was simply a puzzling, gray, very distant conflict, a war that went on and on and on, seemingly without hope or resolution, about which most Americans, save the men who fought there and their immediate families, preferred to know as little as possible. Nearly thirty years after it was over, John Prine caught this spirit exactly in the song "Hello in There," where he sings eloquently of the tragic loss of a young man named Davy, and how he sacrificed himself for no good reason. Over half a century later, the war still remained largely outside American political and cultural consciousness. *The Forgotten War* was the apt title of one of the best books on it. Korea was a war that sometimes seemed to have been orphaned by history.

Many of the men who went to Korea harbored their own personal resentments over being sent there; some had already served once, during World War II, had been in the reserves, had been called away from their civilian jobs most reluctantly and told to serve in a war overseas for the second time within ten years, when all too many of their contemporaries had been called for neither. Others who had served in World War II and had decided to stay in the Army were embittered because of the pathetic state of U.S. forces when the North

Koreans struck. Undermanned, poorly trained American units, with faulty, often outmoded equipment and surprisingly poor high-level command leadership, were an embarrassment. The drop-off between the strength of the Army they had known at the height of World War II, its sheer professionalism and muscularity, and the shabbiness of American forces as they existed at the beginning of the Korean War was nothing less than shocking to these men. The more experienced they were, the more disheartened and appalled they also were by the conditions under which they had to fight.

The worst aspect of the Korean War, wrote Lieutenant Colonel George Russell, a battalion commander with the Twenty-third Regiment of the Second Infantry Division, "was Korea itself." For an army that was so dependent on its industrial production and the resulting military hardware, especially tanks, it was the worst kind of terrain. Countries like Spain and Switzerland had difficult mountain ranges, but these soon opened onto flat areas where industrially powerful nations might send their tanks. To American eyes, however, as Russell put it, in Korea "on the other side of every mountain [was] another mountain." If there was a color to Korea, Russell claimed, "it came in all shades of brown"—and if there was a campaign ribbon given out for service there, he added, all the GIs who fought there would have bet on the color being brown.

Unlike Vietnam, the Korean War took place before television news came into its own and the United States became a communications society. In the days of Korea, television news shows were short, bland, and of marginal influence—fifteen minutes a night. Given the state of the technology, the footage from Korea, usually making it into the network newsrooms back in New York days late, rarely moved the nation. It was still largely a print war, reported in newspapers in black and white, and it remained black and white in the nation's consciousness. In the year 2004, while working on this book, I chanced into the Key West, Florida, library: on its shelves were some eighty-eight books on Vietnam and only four on Korea, which more or less sums up the war's fate in American memory. Arden Rowley, a young engineer with the Second Infantry Division who had spent two and a half years as a POW in a Chinese prison camp, noted somewhat bitterly that, from 2001 to 2002, each year marking a fiftieth anniversary of some major Korean battle, there were three major war movies made in America—*Pearl Harbor, Windtalkers,* and *We Were Soldiers*—the first two about World War II, the third about Vietnam; and if you added *Saving Private Ryan,* produced in 1998, the total was four. No film was made about Korea. The best known movie linked to Korea was 1962's *The Manchurian Candidate,* the story of an American POW who had been brainwashed in a Chinese prison camp and turned into a robotic assassin aimed by the Communists at an American presidential candidate.

To the degree that the Korean War ever had a niche in popular culture, it was through the Robert Altman antiwar movie (and then sitcom) *M*A*S*H,* about a mobile surgical hospital operating during that war. Ostensibly about Korea, the film was really about Vietnam, and came out in 1970, at the high-water mark of popular protest against that war. It was a time when Hollywood executives were still nervous about making an anti-Vietnam movie. As such Korea was a cover from the start for a movie about Vietnam; director Altman and the screenwriter, Ring Lardner, Jr., were focused on Vietnam but thought it was too sensitive a subject to be treated irreverently. Notably, the men and officers in the film wear the shaggy haircuts of the Vietnam years, not the crew cuts of the Korean era.

And so the true brutality of the war never really penetrated the American cultural consciousness. An estimated 33,000 Americans died in it. Another 105,000 were wounded. The South Koreans lost 415,000 killed and had 429,000 wounded. Both the Chinese and North Koreans were exceptionally secretive about their casualties, but American officials put their losses at roughly 1.5 million men killed. The Korean War momentarily turned the Cold War hot, heightening the already considerable (and mounting) tensions between the United States and the Communist world and deepening the chasm between the United States and Communist forces asserting themselves in Asia. Those tensions and divisions between the two sides in the bipolar struggle grew even more serious after American miscalculations brought China into the war. When it was all over and an armed truce ensued, both sides claimed victory, though the final division of the country was no different from the one that had existed when the war began. But the United States was not the same: its strategic vision of Asia had changed, and its domestic political equation had been greatly altered.

THE AMERICANS WHO fought in Korea often felt cut off from their country-men, their sacrifices unappreciated, their faraway war of little importance in the eyes of contemporaries. It had none of the glory and legitimacy of World War II, so recently concluded, in which the entire country had seemed to share in one great purpose and every serviceman was seen to be an extension of the country's democratic spirit and the best of its values, and was so honored. Korea was a grinding, limited war. Nothing very good, the nation quickly decided, was going to come out of it. When servicemen returned from their tours, they found their neighbors generally not very interested in what they had seen and done. The subject of the war was quickly dispensed with in conversation. Events on the home front, promotions at the office, the purchase of a new house or a new car were more compelling subjects. In part this was because the news from Korea was almost always so grim. Even when the war went well, it did not really go *very* well; the possibility of a larger breakthrough seldom seemed near, much less anything approaching victory, especially once the Chinese entered the war in force in late November 1950. Soon after, the sardonic phrase for a stalemate, "die for a tie," became a favorite among the troops.

This vast disconnect between those who fought and the people at home, the sense that no matter the bravery they showed, or the validity of their cause, the soldiers of Korea had been granted a kind of second-class status compared to that of the men who had fought in previous wars, led to a great deal of quiet—and enduring—bitterness.

Part One

===

A Warning at Unsan

I

I T WAS THE warning shot the American commander in the Far East, Douglas MacArthur, did not heed, the one that allowed a smaller war to become a larger war.

On October 20, 1950, the men of the U.S. First Cavalry Division entered Pyongyang, the North Korean capital. Later, there was some controversy over who got there first, elements of the Fifth Regiment of the Cav or men from the South Korean First Division. The truth was the men of the Cav had been slowed because all the bridges in their sector going over the Taedong River had been blown, and so the South Korean troops, or ROKs (for Republic of Korea), beat them into the ruined city. That did not diminish their pleasure. To them, the capture of the city meant the war was almost over. Just to make sure everyone knew that of all American units in country, the Cav got there first, some troopers, armed with paint and brushes, painted the Cav logo all over town.

Small private celebrations were taking place throughout Pyongyang. Lieutenant Phil Peterson, forward observer with the Ninety-ninth Field Artillery Battalion, and his best buddy, Lieutenant Walt Mayo, both working with the Third Battalion of the Eighth Regiment of the Cav, had their own two-person celebration. They could not have been closer as friends, having been through so much together. Peterson thought it an unusual friendship, one only the Army could forge. Walt Mayo was a talented and sophisticated man who had gone to Boston College, where his father taught music, whereas Peterson was a product of Officer Candidate School, and his formal schooling had ended back in Morris, Minnesota, in the ninth grade because they were paying $5 a day for men to work in the fields. In Pyongyang Lieutenant Mayo had managed to procure a bottle of Russian bubbly from a large store of booze liberated from the Russian embassy, and they shared it, drinking the pseudo-champagne, so raw it made you gag, from the metal cups in their mess kits. Vile, but good, they decided.

Sergeant First Class Bill Richardson of Love Company of the Third Battalion felt a wave of relief sweep over him in Pyongyang. The war was virtually over, and the Cav might be getting out of Korea. He knew this, not just because of all the rumors, but because Company headquarters had called asking all men who had experience loading ships to notify their superiors. That was as sure a sign as any that they were going to ship out. Another sign that their days of hard fighting were over was that they had been told to turn in most of their ammo. All the rumors seeping out of the different headquarters must be true.

In his own mind Richardson was the old guy in his unit: almost everyone in his platoon now seemed new. He often thought of the men he had started out with three months earlier, a period that seemed to have lasted longer than the preceding twenty-one years of his life. Some were dead, some wounded, and some missing in action. The only other soldier in Richardson's platoon who had been there from the start was his pal Staff Sergeant Jim Walsh, and Richardson sought him out. "Jesus, we did it, buddy, we made it all the way through," he said, and they congratulated each other, not quite believing their good luck. That mini-celebration took place on one of the last days of October. The very next day they were reissued their ammo and ordered north to save some South Korean outfit that was getting kicked around.

Still, the word was out: there was going to be a victory parade in Tokyo, and the Cav, because it had fought so well for so long in the Korean campaign, and because it was a favorite of Douglas MacArthur's, the overall commander, was going to lead it. They were supposed to have their yellow cavalry scarves back for the parade, and the word coming down was that they better be prepared to look parade-ground sharp, not battlefield grizzled: you couldn't, after all, march down the Ginza in filthy uniforms and filthy helmets. The men of the Cav were planning to strut a bit when they passed MacArthur's headquarters in the Dai Ichi Building. They deserved to strut a bit.

The mood in general among the American troops in Pyongyang just then was a combination of optimism and sheer exhaustion, emotional as well as physical. Betting pools were set up on when they would ship out. For some of the newest men, the replacements, who had only heard tales about how hard the fighting had been from the Pusan Perimeter to Pyongyang, there was relief that the worst of it was past. A young lieutenant named Ben Boyd from Clare-more, Oklahoma, who joined the Cav in Pyongyang, was given a platoon in Baker Company of the First Battalion. Boyd, who had graduated West Point only four years before, wanted this command badly, but he was made nervous by its recent history. "Lieutenant, do you know who you are in terms of this platoon?" one of the senior officers had asked. No, Boyd answered. "Well, Lieu-tenant, just so you don't get too cocky, you're the *thirteenth* platoon leader this unit has had since it's been in Korea." Boyd suddenly decided he didn't feel cocky at all.

On one of their last days in Pyongyang there was another positive sign. Bob

Hope held a show there for the troops. Now, that was really something: the famous comedian, who had done show after show for the troops in World War II, telling his jokes in the North Korean capital. That night many of the men in the Cav gathered to hear Hope, and then, the next morning, with their extra ammo restored, they set out for a place just north of them called Unsan, to protect a ROK unit under fire. Surely, all they would have to do was clean up a small mess, the kind they believed South Korean soldiers were always getting into.

When they headed off, they were not particularly well prepared. Yes, they had gotten some of their ammo back, but there had been the question of uniforms. Should they take the ones they would wear on parade in Tokyo, or winter clothes? Somehow, the choice was made for the dressier ones, even though a Korean winter—this was to be one of the coldest in a hundred years—was fast approaching. And there was their mood: a sense on the part of officers as well as troops, even as they headed for areas perilously close to the Yalu River, the border between Korea and Chinese Manchuria, that they were out of harm's way. Many of them knew a little about the big meeting just two weeks earlier on Wake Island, between Harry Truman and Douglas MacArthur, and the word filtering down was that MacArthur had promised to give Washington back an entire American division then being used in Korea and ticket it for Europe.

MacArthur himself had shown up in Pyongyang right after the First Cav arrived there. "Any celebrities here to greet me?" he had asked when he stepped off his plane. "Where is Kim Buck Tooth?" he joked, in mocking reference to Kim Il Sung, the seemingly defeated North Korean Communist leader. Then he asked anyone in the Cav who had been with the unit from the beginning to step forward. Of the roughly two hundred men assembled, four took that step; each had been wounded at some point. Then MacArthur got back on his plane for the flight back to Tokyo. He did not spend the night in Korea; in fact he did not spend the night there during the entire time he commanded.

AS MACARTHUR HEADED back to Tokyo, it was becoming increasingly clear to some officials in Washington that he was planning to send his troops farther and farther north. He was sure that the Chinese would not enter the war. His troops were encountering very little resistance at that point, and the North Koreans had been in full flight, so he was stretching his orders, which in this case were much fuzzier than they should have been. He obviously intended to go all the way to the Yalu, to China's border, brushing aside the step-by-step limits Washington thought it had imposed but was afraid of really imposing. A prohibition issued by the Joint Chiefs themselves against sending

American troops to any province bordering China seemed not to slow MacArthur down at all. There was no real surprise in that: the only orders Douglas MacArthur had ever followed, it was believed, were his own. His confidence about what the vast Chinese armies everyone knew were poised just beyond the Yalu River would or would not do was far greater than that of top officials of the Truman administration. He had told the president at Wake Island that the Chinese would *not* enter the war. Besides, if they did, he had already boasted of his ability to turn their appearance into one of the great military slaughters in history. To MacArthur and the men on his staff, wonderfully removed from the Alaska-like temperatures and Alaska-like topography of this desolate part of the world, these were to be the final moments of a great victory march north that had begun with the amphibious Inchon landing behind North Korean lines. That had been a great success, perhaps the greatest triumph of a storied career, all the more so because the general had pulled it off against the opposition of much of Washington. Back in Washington most senior people, both civilian and military, were becoming more and more uneasy as MacArthur pushed north. They were not nearly as confident as the general about Chinese (or for that matter Russian) intentions, and they were made uneasy by the extreme vulnerability of the United Nations forces. But they realized that they had very little control over MacArthur himself— they seemed to fear him almost as much as they respected him.

If the balance now favored the UN, the first phase of the war, when the North Koreans had crossed the thirty-eighth parallel back in late June, had decidedly favored the Communists. They had gained victory after victory over weak and ill-prepared American and South Korean forces. But then more and better American troops had arrived, and MacArthur had pulled off his brilliant stroke at Inchon, landing his forces behind the North Korean lines. With that, the North Korean forces had unraveled, and once Seoul had been taken after some very hard fighting, the North Korean resistance had generally vanished. But in Washington many of the top people, though pleased by Inchon, were quite uneasy about the extra leverage it gave MacArthur. The Chinese had warned that they were going to enter the war, and yet MacArthur, difficult to deal with under the best of circumstances, had become even more godlike because of Inchon. He had said the Chinese would not come in, and he liked to think of himself as an expert on what he called the Oriental mind. But he had been wrong before, completely wrong, on Japanese intentions and abilities right before World War II. Later some of the senior people in Washington would look at the moment when the UN troops reached Pyongyang and before they went on to Unsan as the last chance to keep the war from escalating into something larger, a war with China.

* * *

NO LESS NERVOUS were some of the men and officers who were leading the drive north. For experienced officers making the trek as the temperature dropped alarmingly, and the terrain became more mountainous and forbidding, there was an eerie quality to the advance. Years later, General Paik Sun Yup, commander of the South Korean First Division (and considered by the Americans the best of the Korean commanders), remembered his own uneasiness as they moved forward without resistance. There was a sense of almost total isolation, as if they were *too* alone. At first, Paik, a veteran officer who had once fought with the Japanese Army, could not pinpoint what bothered him. Then it struck him: the absolute absence of people, the overwhelming silence that surrounded his troops. In the past, there had always been lots of refugees streaming south. Now the road was empty, as if something important were taking place, just beyond his view and his knowledge. Besides, it was getting colder all the time. Every day the temperature seemed to drop another few degrees.

Certain key intelligence officers were nervous as well. They kept getting small bits of information, from a variety of sources, that made them believe that the Chinese had already entered North Korean territory by late October—and in strength. Colonel Percy Thompson, G-2 (or intelligence officer) for First Corps, under which the Cav operated, and considered one of the ablest intelligence officers in Korea, was very pessimistic. He was quite sure of the Chinese presence, and he tried to warn his superiors. Unfortunately he found himself fighting a sense of euphoria that had permeated some of the upper ranks of the Cav and originated in Tokyo. Thompson had directly warned Colonel Hal Edson, commander of the Eighth Regiment of the First Cavalry Division, that he believed there was a formidable Chinese presence in the area, but Edson and others treated his warnings, he later noted, "with disbelief and indifference." In the days that followed, his daughter Barbara Thompson Eisenhower (married to Dwight Eisenhower's son John) remembered a dramatic change in the tone of her father's letters from Korea. It was as if he were writing to say farewell. "He was absolutely sure they were going to be overrun, and he was going to be killed," she later remembered.

Thompson had good reason to be uneasy. His early intelligence reads were quite accurate: the Chinese *were* already in country, waiting patiently in the mountains of Northern Korea for the ROKs and perhaps other UN units to extend their already strained logistical lines ever farther north. They had not intended to hit an American unit that early in the campaign. They wanted the Americans to be even farther north when they struck; and they knew the difficulty of the march north made their own job easier. "On to the Yalu," General

Paik's soldiers had shouted in late October, "on to the Yalu!" But on October 25, the Chinese struck in force. It was like suddenly hitting a brick wall, Paik later wrote. At first the ROK commanders had no idea what had happened. Paik's Fifteenth Regiment came to a complete halt under a withering barrage of mortar fire, after which the Twelfth Regiment on its left was hammered, and then his Eleventh Regiment, the division reserve, was hit on its flank and attacked from the rear. The enemy was clearly fighting with great skill. Paik thought it must be the Chinese. He reacted by reflex, and thereby probably saved most of his men. He immediately pulled the division back to the village of Unsan. It was, he later said, like a scene from an American Western, when the white folks, hit by Indians and badly outnumbered, circled the wagons. His division had walked into a giant ambush set by the Chinese. Some other ROK units were neither so lucky nor so well led.

That it was the Chinese Paik soon had no doubt. On the first day of battle, some troops from the Fifteenth Regiment had brought in a prisoner. Paik did the interrogation himself. The prisoner was about thirty-five and wore a thick, quilted, reversible winter uniform, khaki on one side, white on the other. It was, Paik wrote, "a simple but effective way to facilitate camouflage in snowy terrain." The prisoner also wore a cap, thick and heavy, with earmuffs of a sort they would soon become all too familiar with, and rubber sneakers. He was low-key but surprisingly forthcoming in the interrogation: he was a regular soldier in the Chinese Communist Army, from Guangdong province. He told Paik in passing that there were tens of thousands of Chinese in the nearby mountains. The entire First ROK Division might be trapped.

Paik immediately called his corps commander, Major General Frank (Shrimp) Milburn, and took the prisoner back to Milburn's headquarters. This time Milburn did the interrogating, while Paik interpreted. It went, he later wrote, like this:

"Where are you from?"

"I'm from South China."

"What's your unit?"

"The Thirty-ninth Army."

"What fighting have you done?"

"I fought in the Hainan Island battle [in the Chinese civil war]."

"Are you a Korean resident of China?"

"No, I'm Chinese."

Paik was absolutely sure that the prisoner was telling the truth. He was without pretension or evasiveness. Of the seriousness of his information there should also have been no doubt. It had long been known that the Chinese had at least three hundred thousand men poised just over the Yalu, ready to come in when they wanted. The only question was whether Beijing was bluffing when it warned the world of its intention to send Chinese troops into battle. Milburn immediately reported the new intelligence to Eighth Army headquarters. From there, it was sent on to Brigadier General Charles Willoughby, Douglas MacArthur's key intelligence chief, a man dedicated to the proposition that there were no Chinese in Korea, and that they were not going to come in, at least not in numbers large enough to matter. That was what his commander believed, and MacArthur's was the kind of headquarters where the G-2's job was first and foremost to prove that the commander was always right. The drive north to the Yalu, involving a limited number of American, South Korean, and other UN troops spread far too thinly over a vast expanse of mountain range, was premised on the idea of Chinese abstinence. If MacArthur's headquarters suddenly started reporting contact with significant Chinese forces, Washington, which had been watching somewhat passively from the sidelines, might bestir itself and demand a major role in the war, and Tokyo headquarters could lose control of its plan and not be able to go all the way to the Yalu. That was most decidedly not what MacArthur wanted to happen, and what MacArthur wanted was what Willoughby always made come true in his intelligence estimates. When the first reports about Chinese forces massing north of the Yalu came in, Willoughby had been typically dismissive. "Probably in the category of diplomatic blackmail," he reported. Now, with the first Chinese prisoner captured, an unusually talkative one at that, the word soon came back from Willoughby's headquarters: the prisoner was a Korean resident of China, who had volunteered to fight. The conclusion was bizarre, and it was deliberately aimed at minimizing the prisoner's significance; it meant that the prisoner did not know who he was, what his nationality was, what unit he was with, or how many fellow soldiers he had arrived with. It was a judgment that would have pleased the Chinese high command—it was exactly what they wanted the Americans to think. The more cavalier the Americans were, the greater the victory the Chinese were sure they were going to reap when they finally closed the trap.

In the coming weeks, American or ROK forces repeatedly took Chinese prisoners who identified their units and confirmed that they had crossed the Yalu with large numbers of their compatriots. Again and again, Willoughby downplayed the field intelligence. But if Division, Corps, Army, and Far East Command were now arguing over whether Chinese prisoners were in fact really Chinese, whether they were part of a division, an army, or an army group, and what this meant for the extremely vulnerable troops of the United Nations force, little of this reached down to the troops themselves. Typical were the men of the Eighth Cavalry Regiment, who had been convinced, as they moved from

Pyongyang to Unsan, that they were pursuing the last ragtag remnants of the North Korean Army and would soon reach the Yalu itself and, if at all possible, piss in it as a personal symbol of triumph.

A very dangerous kind of euphoria had spread through the highest ranks of the Eighth Army, and no one reflected it more than MacArthur himself. As he, the most experienced officer in the American Army, was overwhelmingly confident of the road ahead, so were those in his command, including many of the senior people at Corps and Division. The higher you went in headquarters, especially in Tokyo, the stronger was the feeling that the war was over, and that the only job left was a certain amount of mopping up. There were many telltale signs of this overconfidence. On October 22, three days before the first Chinese prisoner was captured, Lieutenant General Walton Walker, commander of the Eighth Army, had requested authority from MacArthur to divert all further shipments of bulk-loaded ammunition from Korea to Japan. MacArthur approved the request and ordered six ships carrying 105- and 155mm artillery shells diverted to Hawaii. An army that had spent much of the previous four months starved for ammunition now felt it had too much.

In the Eighth Army sector, Major General Laurence (Dutch) Keiser, commander of the famed Second Infantry Division, summoned all his officers for a special staff meeting on October 25. Lieutenant Ralph Hockley, a young forward observer with the Thirty-seventh Field Artillery Battalion, remembered the date and the words precisely. The Second, which had been through much of the heaviest fighting in the war, was going to leave Korea, Keiser said. He was in a wonderful mood. "We're all going home and we're going home soon— before Christmas," he told his officers. "We have our orders." One of the officers asked where they were going. Keiser answered that he couldn't tell them, but it would be a place they would like. The speculation began: Tokyo, Hawaii, perhaps the States, or even some base in Europe.

THE MEN OF the Eighth Regiment of the First Cavalry Division reached Unsan without difficulty. Sergeant Herbert (Pappy) Miller took the news that they had to leave Pyongyang and head north to Unsan to steady the ROKs philosophically. Miller was an assistant platoon sergeant with Love Company of the Third Battalion of the Eighth Cav. He might have liked a few more days in Pyongyang, but these were orders and that was the business they were in, plugging holes. He had never understood why the brass had thought the ROKs could lead the way north in the first place. Miller wasn't worried about the Chinese coming in. What worried him was the cold, because they were still in summer-weight uniforms. Back at Pyongyang they had been told that winter clothes were on their way, already in the trucks, and supposed to arrive the next day, or the one after that. They had been hearing that for several days, but no winter uniforms had arrived. Because Miller's regiment had been in so many battles for so long, the green troops of July and August had, through attrition, been replaced by the green troops of October. He and his close friend Richard Hettinger, from Joplin, Missouri, another World War II veteran, had vowed to keep an eye on each other. There was a lot of talk now about going home by Christmas, but Miller had a somewhat more jaundiced view, which was that you were home when you got home.

Pappy Miller was from the small town of Pulaski, New York. He had served with the Forty-second Division in World War II, gone back to Pulaski, found little in the way of decent employment, and rejoined the Army in 1947. He was part of the Seventh Regiment of the Third Infantry Division, which had been detached and assigned to the First Cavalry, and he had only six months to go on a three-year enlistment when he was ordered to Korea in July 1950. In World War II, he had thought everything was always done right; and in Korea, damn near everything was done wrong. He and his company had arrived in country one morning in mid-July, had been rushed to the front lines near the village and key juncture of Taejon, and had been thrown into the line that first day. He had been through everything ever since, which was why his men called him Pappy, though he was only twenty-four years old.

There had been a lot of bravado on the way up to the line near Taejon that first day, young soldiers who knew battle only through war movies bragging that they were going to kick some Korean ass. Miller had stayed silent while they boasted: better to feel that way *after* the battle was over than before it began. But there was no point in telling them that—it was something you had to learn yourself. And that first battle had been terrible; they were ill-prepared and the North Koreans were very effective, very experienced troops. By the next day, the company had been reduced from about 160 men to 39. "We were damn near annihilated that very first night," Miller said. There was not much talk about kicking Korean ass after that.

It was not that the kids had fought badly. They just weren't ready, not right off the boat, and there were so many North Koreans. No matter how well you fought, there were always more. Always. They would slip behind you, cut off your avenue of retreat, and then they would hit you on the flanks. They were superb at that, Miller thought. The first wave or two would come at you with rifles, and right behind them were soldiers without rifles ready to pick up the weapons of those who had fallen and keep coming. Against an army with that many men, everyone, he thought, needed an automatic weapon. And the American equipment was terrible. Their basic infantry gear was often junk. Back at Fort Devens, they had been given old training rifles in terrible shape, poorly cared for, not worth a damn, which seemed to indicate how the nation felt about its peacetime army.

Once they got to Korea, there was never enough ammo. Miller remembered a bitter fight early in the war when someone had brought over an ammo box and it was all loose. They had to make their own clips. He had wondered what kind of army sent loose ammo to outnumbered infantrymen whose lives were hanging in the balance. It was amateur hour, he thought. The North Koreans were driving good tanks, Russian A-34s, and the sorry old World War II bazookas the Americans had couldn't penetrate their skins. In World War II, you always knew what your objective was and who was fighting on your left and right. In Korea, you were always fighting blind and were never sure of your flanks, because, likely as not, the ROKs were there.

On the day they reached Unsan, Miller took a patrol about five miles north of their base, and they came upon an old farmer, who told them that there were thousands of Chinese in the area, many of whom had arrived on horseback. There was a simplicity and a conviction to the old man that made Miller almost sure he was telling the truth. So he brought him back to his headquarters. But no one at Battalion headquarters seemed very interested. *Chinese? Thousands and thousands of Chinese?* No one had seen any Chinese. On *horseback?* That was absurd. So nothing came of it. Well, Miller thought, they were the intelligence experts. They ought to know.

Of the men in the Eighth Regiment, a young corporal named Lester Urban in Item Company, Third Battalion, was one of the first to sense the danger. He was a runner attached to Headquarters Company, which meant that he was around Battalion headquarters a lot and tended to pick up what the officers were saying. The seventeen-year-old Urban was only five-four, a mere one hundred pounds, too small for the football team at his high school back in the tiny town of Delbarton, West Virginia. His nickname in the Cav was Peanut, but he was tough and fast, and so he had been picked as runner. Given the sorry state of American wire and radio communications in Korea—the equipment rarely functioned properly—it was his job to deliver messages, oral and written, from Battalion to Company. It was exceptionally dangerous duty. Urban was proud of the fact that he knew how to do it and survive. If he made four or five trips to the same place in a day, he *always* varied his route and never got careless. Get predictable and get dead, he thought.

Urban had a sense of unease, because there were no American units on either flank, which maximized your vulnerability. But they had been on such a roll and there had been so little opposition in the last few weeks that he wasn't particularly worried, at least not until they reached Unsan. At Unsan, though, his regiment jutted out, in his words, like nothing so much as a sore thumb, and if you thought about it, then you realized that its three battalions were ill-placed and ill-spaced. The gaps between them, small on a map somewhere back at headquarters, were surprisingly wide if you had to run from one unit to another, as he did.

Urban was near Battalion headquarters on October 31 when Lieutenant Colonel Harold (Johnny) Johnson, until the previous week the battalion commander of Third Battalion of the Eighth Regiment—the 3/8—but recently promoted to the command of his own regiment, the Fifth Cav (also part of the First Cavalry Division), had driven up to check on his old outfit. One of the last things Johnson had done before they all left Pyongyang was hold a memorial service for the men of the Third Battalion who had been lost since the war began—some four hundred of them. He was joined at the service by the soldiers who had been there from the start, "a pitifully small remainder," as Johnson put it.

Johnny Johnson was more than admired, he was loved by most of the men in his old outfit. He had been with them from the day they arrived in country, and they felt he always made the right decisions in battle. He had an unusual sense of loyalty to the men under him, the kind of thing that ordinary soldiers notice and value when they grade an officer—and they were always grading officers, because their lives depended on it. They knew that Johnson had turned down a chance to be a regimental commander early in the fighting in order to stay with the battalion when it was new to combat, because he felt obligated to the men he had brought over.

He was a man who had already been through his own prolonged hell. Captured by the Japanese at Bataan at the start of World War II, he had managed to survive the Bataan Death March and more than three years as a prisoner. Generally, being a prisoner of war did not help an officer's career—this would be especially true in Korea, where the treatment of American prisoners by the Communists was unusually cruel and where, because of the brainwashing, some men had been damaged—but Johnson eventually ended up as chief of staff of the Army. "He was the best," Lester Urban said years later, "someone born to lead men. I think he was always thinking about what was good for us. Nothing ever got by him."

His experience on Bataan had made Johnson less trusting of conventional wisdom, and he knew more about the consequences of undue optimism than most officers. At that moment, he had the Fifth Cav positioned as a reserve force just a few miles south of his old unit, but he was becoming nervous, hearing talk of a large enemy force moving through the area, one that might cut the road, severing the Eighth Regiment from the rest of the division. On his own Johnson had driven north to check the situation out. On the ride, the same stillness that had bothered General Paik, the fact that there was *nothing* moving, upset Johnson too. Something like that, he later said, made the back of your neck prickle. When he finally reached his old battalion, he did not like what he saw at all. His replacement, Robert Ormond, was brand-new to his job and, to Johnson's eye, had dispersed the battalion poorly. Most of the men were positioned in the flat paddy land and not even very well dug in.

Watching the two officers meet, Urban sensed Johnson's distress. Johnson was not, as Urban saw it, a man to chew another officer out, but what he said to Ormond seemed surprisingly tough: "You've got to get these men out of the valley and up on the high ground! They're much too vulnerable where they are! You've got no defense if you're hit!" ("I thought he was going to whip Ormond's butt right then and there," Urban said years later.) Johnson assumed that Ormond would pick up on what he said and was appalled to discover later that his advice had been ignored. Nor was it just the Third Battalion that was poorly positioned. After the entire tragedy was over, many of the more senior officers would admit that the disposition of the entire Eighth Regiment had been very poorly done. The men were arranged as if they had no enemies to fear.

Lieutenant Hewlett (Reb) Rainer joined the regiment immediately after the Unsan battle, and one thing he decided to do was put together in his own mind what had happened. He was shocked at the way the regiment had been positioned: "The first thing was that the battalions could not really support each other. They were not properly linked up. The second thing was that you could drive a division or maybe two divisions of Chinese soldiers through them and the people spending the night there might not even know it. And that was the way the enemy fought—he came up and moved along the flanks, then encircled you, and then squeezed you," Rainer said. "I know Regiment hadn't gotten the word from higher headquarters about the Chinese, but still, they were very far north; it was Indian country; something was clearly up; and there was no point at all in being positioned as if you're back in the States on some kind of war game. To say it was careless—that was an understatement."

Sergeant Bill Richardson, who had a recoilless rifle section of a heavy weapons platoon in Love Company, remembered October 31, 1950, exceptionally well. His section had drawn duty at the south end of the Third Battalion's position, near a place called the Camel's Head Bend, part of a unit guarding a bridge where a small road crossed the Nammyon River. The day before, they had finally received a shipment of what the supply people claimed were winter clothes: some field jackets, fresh socks, and nothing much else. Richardson had told one of his men to distribute the jackets as best he could and skip the sergeants because there just weren't enough to go around. Years later, it infuriated him when he read that the men in his company had been caught asleep in their sleeping bags. It had been bad enough the way they were hit, but they sure as hell weren't in their sleeping bags, because they didn't have any. They had to create do-it-yourself sleeping bags as best they could, wrapping their blankets and shelter halves together.

That day, Richardson had been on duty at the bridge when Lieutenant Colonel Johnson stopped on his way back from the battalion command post. Johnson had wanted to talk, but he was also being somewhat guarded. "Look," he said, "we've had reports of a few minor roadblocks in the area. We think they're remnants of the North Korean Army, and they may be coming up the river bend heading towards you, going north." Richardson was not bothered by the news. He told Johnson ("my famous last words"), "Colonel, if they come up the river bend, they've had it." Then Johnson warned him to be careful and they shook hands. Johnson wished him good luck and Richardson thought to himself—because Johnson was driving through the countryside virtually alone—Colonel, sir, you're the one who needs the luck.

They had been together since training at Fort Devens back in Massachusetts. Richardson had served in Europe at the tail end of World War II, arriving in that war too late to see combat, only the devastation it had wrought. But in Korea, he would eventually be battle-tested far beyond the norm, in combat as difficult and dangerous as any American force had ever been exposed to. He had grown up in Philadelphia and his parents had been entertainers. He was a less than diligent student, and was sent in time to the local industrial school, which was the system's way of telling him to forget about college, in the unlikely event that the idea had ever entered his mind. His formal schooling ended in the ninth grade, and he joined the Army and found he liked it. He had been trained by skilled professionals, men who had been through the worst of World War II and passed on the little things that were most likely to save your life. In the early spring of 1950, Richardson was on the third extension of his enlistment in a period of post–World War II downsizing, and the Army had been trying to force him out. Then the North Koreans moved south, and overnight the people who ran the Army decided they wanted him to stay on.

So instead of mustering out at Fort Devens in late June, he became a charter member of the 3/8. Richardson remembered that immediately after the North Korean invasion, on June 26 or 27, Johnny Johnson had assembled the whole battalion at a post movie house, and the unit was so small that only the first two or three rows were filled. They were shown an infantry propaganda movie that ended with some soldiers being awarded Silver Stars and Bronze Stars. Johnson had told them, "Men, those of you who aren't wearing one of those will be in a few weeks." Richardson had thought he was crazy at the time. Within days men started arriving from every kind of outfit; MPs and cooks and supply men, all infantrymen now, enough to fill any movie theater. Then they shipped out.

Later, after they were hit by the Chinese, Richardson believed that Johnson had been trying to warn him of his concern that the Chinese were in the area and that the approaches to the Eighth Cav were open. Perhaps it was as much of a warning as you could give at a moment when to utter the magic word "Chinese" to an NCO might trigger panic. If Johnson had still been their battalion commander, Richardson was sure, he would have tightened up their positions, moved them to higher ground, and made sure that their firepower was mutually supportive and much more concentrated. Ormond might become a fine officer someday, Richardson thought, but this was neither the time nor the place to make your combat debut.

Major Filmore McAbee, the S-3, or operations chief, of the Third Battalion, like Johnny Johnson, was uneasy with the way the regiment was dispersed, but he would not get a chance to discuss it with Johnson for a long time, because he spent the next two and a half years in a prison camp. McAbee, an experienced combat officer from World War II, had been a company commander with the First Cav from the moment it arrived in country. He was considered an excellent combat leader, but at the moment the Chinese struck he was mainly a frustrated officer. Both Ormond and his exec, Major Veale Moriarty, were new in command, and their experience, as far as McAbee could tell, was primarily as staff men at the regimental level. They knew each other well and left McAbee, the more combat-tested officer, feeling crowded out. "I was the uneasy one, but I was the outsider," he would later say. He had tried to alert Ormond about the battalion's poor positioning, to no avail. Nor did he like the mood of the unit, and he blamed that on the senior officers: too many of the men were becoming far too careless and cocky. There was too much talk about where they were going after Korea. All they talked about was their next two stops—the Yalu and then home. Later, when McAbee found out that some Chinese prisoners had been captured and units like his, up on point, had not been warned, he felt that the decision at headquarters to conceal, if not suppress, this information was one of the most appalling acts he had ever heard of—a complete abdication of military responsibility. After he came to learn much more about Chinese military tactics, it struck him that his regiment, spread out as it was, had presented a particularly enticing target.

WHAT NONE OF them, including Ormond, knew was that, before the Chinese hit, a debate was under way at higher headquarters. The commander of the Eighth Cavalry Regiment, Colonel Hal Edson, wanted to move his troops back. His unit was too exposed, he believed—and there had been enough warnings by then to make a man pay attention. On November 1, when he woke up, the skies were thick with smoke from forest fires. Edson and others suspected that the fires were set by enemy troops eager to shield their movements from American air observation. Major General Hap Gay, the First Cav Division commander, who took the reports of the Chinese in the area more seriously than some of his superiors, was also becoming edgier by the hour. On that first day of November, he had set up his division command post, or CP, at Yongsan-dong, south of Unsan. For some time Gay had been disturbed by the way his division was being split up, with different battalions being shipped off to other divisions, based on the whims of the people at Corps, and not on the integrity of the division itself. He particularly did not like the way the Eighth Regiment was sticking out so nakedly, open to the enemy on all sides.

His aide, Lieutenant William West, believed that Gay had been smoldering all along over the way the Army had been handling the Korean War. Gay, General George Patton's chief of staff in World War II, believed that he had been taught how to do things right and how not to do things wrong, and in Korea they had been doing things wrong from the start. He had been shocked by the terrible state of the Army when the war began; and bothered as well by MacArthur's initial failure to respect the ability of the enemy, his belief that he could handle the North Koreans, as he had said, "with one hand tied behind my back." Gay seemed to think his superiors in Tokyo had little feel for the enemy, or for the terrain, and surprisingly little curiosity about either. "Those goddamn people don't have their feet on the ground—they're living in a goddamn dream world," he told West once after he left MacArthur's headquarters. Nothing angered him more, however, than the way the most talented officers, the kind of men he badly wanted as battalion commanders, always seemed to be siphoned off to staff jobs at MacArthur's headquarters. He was appalled as well by how much larger it had grown than comparable headquarters in the previous war. He would mutter about how Third Army headquarters back in 1945 had only a few hundred officers to deal with thousands of men in the field, but how Tokyo in this war had thousands of men at headquarters to support hundreds of men in the field. There was an officer whose main job, it seemed, was just to fly in from Tokyo to Gay's headquarters periodically to see what he needed. At one point, Gay gave him a list of officers from World War II then assigned to Tokyo whom Gay wanted to command his troops. When the officer next returned, Gay asked where his potential battalion commanders were. "General MacArthur says they're too valuable to be spared," the officer replied.

"Jesus Christ, what in the hell is more valuable than battle-tested officers leading American troops in combat?" Gay muttered.

He was bothered as well by all the talk about being home by Christmas.

"Which Christmas—this year or next?" he would say. "That's stupid talk. All it does is get the troops too excited about going home, and they get careless." Now, fearing the possibility that one of his regiments might soon be encircled, he was pushing hard to pull it back and consolidate the division. But his superior, First Corps commander Frank Milburn, was reluctant to do it. The Army did not like to use the word "retreat" unless it had to; the proper phrase was "retrograde movement"—and Milburn did not want to make a retrograde movement, not after almost six weeks of steady advances and, above all, not with the mounting pressure coming in from MacArthur's headquarters to go all the way to the Yalu as quickly as possible. Gay, West knew, was becoming more and more fearful about losing a regiment to an enemy that Tokyo still insisted did not exist. There was a fault line in this war. On one side was the battlefield reality and the dangers facing the troops themselves, and, on the other side, the world of illusion that existed in Tokyo and from which all these euphoric orders emanated. The fault line often fell between Corps and Division, with Corps feeling the heat from the general in Tokyo, and Division sensing the vulnerability of a regiment of badly exposed troops. More than once when there was still time to move the Eighth Regiment back, Milburn refused to give the order.

On the afternoon of November 1, Hap Gay was in his CP with Brigadier General Charles Palmer, his artillery commander, when a radio report from an observer in an L-5 spotter plane caught their attention: "This is the strangest sight I have ever seen. There are two large columns of enemy infantry moving southeast over the trails in the vicinity of Myongdang-dong and Yonghung-dong. Our shells are landing right in their columns and they keep coming." Those were two tiny villages five or six air miles from Unsan. Palmer immediately ordered additional artillery units to start firing, and Gay nervously called First Corps, once again requesting permission to pull the entire Eighth Cav several miles south of Unsan. His request was again denied.

With that was lost the last real chance to save the Eighth Cavalry and especially its Third Battalion. In some ways, the battle that followed was over almost before it began. Two divisions of elite Chinese Communist regulars, among the most experienced men in their army, were about to strike units of an elite American division that was ill-prepared and ill-positioned for the collision, and commanded in too many instances by men who believed the Korean War was essentially over.

UNITS OF THE Fifth Cavalry under Johnny Johnson, which had been moving north toward Unsan on a relief mission, soon ran into a major Chinese roadblock. Not only would they not be able to help the Eighth Cavalry, but it was touch and go whether they could extricate themselves from a vicious battle with-

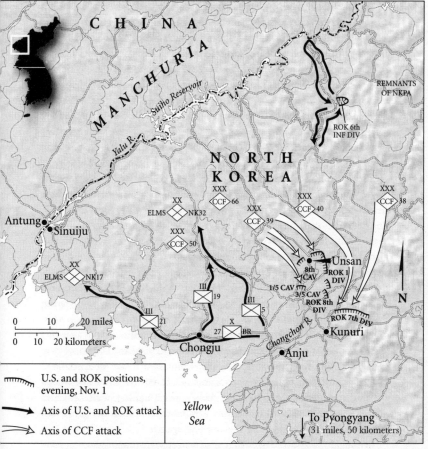

2. First Encounter with Chinese Communist Forces (CCF), November 1, 1950

out being destroyed. As Roy Appleman, an exceptionally careful historian of the Korean War, has pointed out, by nightfall of November 1, the Eighth Cav was encircled on three sides by the Chinese forces. Only on its east, if the Fifteenth ROK Regiment actually stayed in place and fought, might it have any protection.

Lieutenant Ben Boyd was the new platoon leader in Baker Company of the Eighth Cavalry's First Battalion. The First Battalion—with its attached unit of tanks and artillery, in reality a battalion task force—was the most exposed of the regiment's three battalions, positioned about four hundred yards north of the town of Unsan. Boyd's battalion commander, Jack Millikin, Jr., had been his tactical officer at West Point, and Boyd thought him a good, steady man. As far as Boyd knew, their battalion was up there alone—they had been the first of the three battalions out of Pyongyang, and he had no idea whether the rest of the regiment was following. That first afternoon, right after they arrived, they registered their mortars on some surrounding targets, and there were even brief exchanges of fire with the enemy, but the action was light, and everyone had assumed it was North Korean stragglers. That night, though, Boyd was called over by his company commander, who had just been briefed at Battalion. The word Boyd got was: "There are twenty thousand laundry-men in the area." Boyd knew what that meant—twenty thousand Chinese near them.

Then they heard musical instruments, like weird Asian bagpipes. Some of the officers thought for a moment that a British brigade was arriving to help them out. But it was not bagpipes; instead it was an eerie, very foreign sound, perhaps bugles and flutes, a sound many of them would remember for the rest of their lives. It was the sound they would come to recognize as the Chinese about to enter battle, signaling to one another by musical instrument what they were doing, and deliberately striking fear into their enemy as well. Boyd believed his men were in decent positions, though they were not a full platoon in his mind. Nearly half of them were KATUSAs, Korean Augmentation to the U.S. Army, poorly trained Korean soldiers attached to American units who, most American officers believed, could not be relied on if there was a serious fight. They were there to beef up American units, to make the UN forces look larger on paper, if not in battle, than they really were. It was an experiment that no one liked, not the company commanders, not the American troops who fought alongside the Koreans but could not communicate with them, and certainly not the KATUSAs themselves, who more often than not gave every sign of wanting very badly to be almost anywhere else.

At roughly 10:30 P.M., the Chinese struck. It was stunning how quickly something could fall apart, Boyd thought. The American units were so thinly positioned that the Chinese seemed to race right through their fragile lines, al-most like a track meet, some of the men later said. What had once been a well-organized battalion CP (command post) quickly disintegrated. Some of the survivors from different platoons tried to form a makeshift last-second perime-ter, but they were quickly overpowered. There were wounded everywhere. Mil-likin was handling the growing chaos as best he could, Boyd thought, trying to put together a convoy with about ten deuce-and-a-half trucks and loading as many wounded as possible onto them. At that moment, Boyd ran into Captain Emil Kapaun, an Army chaplain who was tending to a number of wounded. Boyd offered to assign the priest to one of the trucks, but Father Kapaun refused.

He planned to stay with the wounded men who would not be able to get out on their own. They would have to surrender, he was sure, but he would do all he could to offer the wounded some modest protection.

The battalion had two tanks, and when the convoy finally took off, it was with Millikin aboard the lead tank and the other tank bringing up the rear with Boyd on top of it. About a mile south of Unsan, the road split, one branch veering southeast, the other in a southwesterly direction, through the edge of the Third Battalion position and over the bridge that Bill Richardson and his weapons section were guarding. Millikin blindly headed them southeast. That any of the men made it out at all came from that choice.

The Chinese had set up a formidable force on both sides of the road, waiting to ambush them. It was hard to measure distance or time in those moments when the enemy was striking with such force, but Boyd thought his convoy got about five or six hundred yards down the road before the Chinese opened up. Their firepower was overwhelming, and the convoy, with so many wounded, had almost no means of fighting back. In the confusion—the vehicles all had their lights off—the driver of Boyd's tank panicked and began to rotate his turret wildly. The dozen or so men on top were all knocked off, and Boyd promptly found himself sprawled in a ditch. Later, he would decide that he survived only by the grace of God.

He could hear the Chinese approaching. His only chance was to play dead. Soon, they started beating on him with their rifle butts and kicking him. Luckily, no one used a bayonet. Finally, they rummaged through his pockets, took his watch and his ring, and left. He waited for what seemed an eternity, hours at least, and then slowly started to crawl away, totally disoriented, suffering from a concussion, among other wounds. In the distance, he could hear artillery fire, and, assuming it was the Americans, he headed that way. He hobbled across a stream, probably the Nammyon, and discovered that his leg was in terrible pain. He realized that he had been badly burned, probably from the white phosphorous the Chinese were firing.

Boyd moved cautiously in the next few days, at night, hiding as best he could during the day. He was out there at least a week, maybe ten days, trying to work his way back to American lines, in constant pain and voraciously hungry. He was helped by one Korean farmer, who fed him and, using primitive hand signals, directed him toward the American positions. He was sure he would not have made it without the farmer's help. Around November 15, after a trek of almost two weeks, Boyd reached an American unit. He was immediately sent to a series of hospitals—his burns were serious indeed. His Korean War was over. He was one of the lucky ones. He had no idea how many of his platoon had died, only that the company commander had been killed. He never saw any of them again.

* * *

AT THE SOUTHERN part of the Eighth Regiment's defenses, at the moment just before the Chinese hit, Bill Richardson of Love Company was still guarding his concrete bridge, a span of about ninety feet over what was alleged to be a river but was essentially a dry creek. He and most of his section were in the flatlands on the north side of the bridge, which itself was technically the southernmost position of the regiment. The battalion headquarters was about 500 yards to the north, and the rest of Love Company about 350 yards to the west. When he first noticed noises coming from a hill just south of them, Richardson asked his pal Jim Walsh, the only other experienced man in the squad, "You hear what I'm hearing?" Richardson knew something was going on out there, but he couldn't spare even the four or five men necessary for a recon. He put in a call to Company headquarters hoping to get some help. It took three tries before Company even picked up. He was furious—how could the people there be so casual? Company then called Battalion, and Battalion finally sent one soldier over from its intelligence and recon section. He came ambling down the road with no sense of urgency at all. Richardson explained the mission, and the soldier disappeared, only to reappear a while later with a squad of four men, who went up the hill making enough noise, Richardson thought, for an entire division.

When the recon patrol returned—just as noisily—the lead soldier said, "There's no one up there." But one of his men was carrying an entrenching tool and a pair of padded gloves that were different from any gloves Richardson had seen so far. More important, they were dry, which, given all the frost and fog, meant they had been left there recently. "Well," the soldier finally admitted, "there are some foxholes, but they've obviously been there a long time." Richardson was quietly furious. The importance of the dry gloves was the kind of thing you were supposed to understand instantly, even if you weren't from the S-2, or a battalion's intelligence section. Richardson insisted he take the gloves and the tool to his boss and tell him that something might be up. Obviously irritated, the soldier said, "Look, if you don't like what we did, then get your own ass up there."

All of this was making Richardson edgier by the minute. Some time after ten that night, he got a call to send some men to Battalion for a recon patrol. That stretched his limits. He had only about fifteen men, and five were KATUSAs, none of whom could speak English. Richardson decided to keep the KATUSAs and send Walsh, his best man, up there with three other Americans. When they reached Battalion, Richardson found out later, they were told just to dig some prone shelters and get some rest. It was still quiet in Richardson's sector, but both the First and the Second Battalions were already being hammered.

Then, about one-thirty in the morning of November 2, it all exploded. The Chinese hit the Third Battalion of the Eighth Cav. Years later, Richardson read

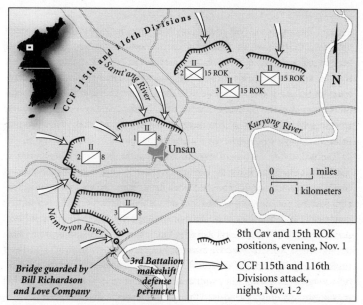

CCF 115th and 116th Divisions

Samt'ang River

2 ⊠ 15 ROK

1 ⊠ 15 ROK

3 ⊠ 15 ROK

Kuryong River

1 ⊠ 8

Unsan

2 ⊠ 8

N

0		1 miles
0		1 kilometers

Nammyon River

3 ⊠ 8

Bridge guarded by
Bill Richardson
and Love Company

3rd Battalion
makeshift
defense
perimeter

8th Cav and 15th ROK
positions, evening, Nov. 1

CCF 115th and 116th
Divisions attack,
night, Nov. 1-2

3. THE UNSAN ENGAGEMENT, NOVEMBER 1–2, 1950

that they had slipped into the area wearing captured ROK uniforms, but he did not believe it. There was no need for disguise. They just poured in from the east, which was completely open. One moment the battalion headquarters was a center of American military activity; the next, it had been completely overrun and was filled with Chinese. At the same time, about 350 yards away on Richardson's left, the Chinese hit Love Company and overran it. That meant that four Chinese machine guns could swing their fire back and forth across Richardson's position, tearing it to pieces.

From the south, a young lieutenant named Robert Kies, a platoon leader in Love Company of the Third Battalion, new to the unit, and Richardson's friend Pappy Miller, the assistant platoon sergeant who had picked up warnings about the Chinese the moment he arrived in Unsan, were pulling back from a position two or three hills to the southeast of Richardson, a place called Hill 904. Richardson barely knew Kies—the Cav went through platoon leaders very quickly—but Kies arrived eager to use Richardson's landline phone to try to find out what was going on. Because of the pathetic state of their communications, Kies and his men were completely cut off. By then Richardson's landline phone was out—the Chinese, Kies decided, had already cut the wires. Kies decided to take his men up the road to Battalion. Miller shook Richardson's hand and wished him good luck. ("The next time I saw him was fifty-two years later at a Cav reunion," Miller said.) By that time, Richardson couldn't even communicate with his own company. He had sent one of his men across the 350-yard gap to Love Company, but the soldier had been hit and had not been able to make it through. He had crawled back toward Richardson, apologizing repeatedly as he got near: "I'm sorry, I'm sorry, I can't make it." When Richardson reached him and opened his jacket, it was completely soaked with blood; the man died in his arms. At that moment, the worst thing, Richardson would recall, was that he could not even remember the soldier's name.

The bridge they were guarding was now open to the Chinese. Richardson took two or three of his remaining men and started north toward Battalion. He was in a ditch alongside the road when he ran into two soldiers coming the other way, part of the team he had sent off with Walsh earlier. "The rest of the squad is all dead! Walsh is dead!" one of the men said. By chance, the soldier added, he himself had gone to take a leak just when the Chinese broke in and shot the others while they were just waiting there. Otherwise he would be dead too. Just a few days earlier Richardson and Walsh, his oldest friend in the unit, had reached Pyongyang and congratulated each other on making it through that far. Now Walsh was dead, and their regiment was being destroyed.

FOR MAJOR FILMORE MCABEE, the Third Battalion S-3, the worst thing was the chaos and confusion. They had no idea who had hit them or with what size force. "Was it ten thousand or was it a hundred or a thousand? Were they Chinese or were they Korean?" he said years later. Soon, there were two other paramount questions: Who was in charge of the American units and what were their orders? Ormond, the battalion commander, had tried to go north to the village of Unsan to check out their positions, had been severely wounded, and was already dying or dead. McAbee never saw him again. Veale Moriarty, the exec officer, went off reconnoitering and McAbee never saw him again either. He remained bitter about Moriarty's disappearance for years afterward—the exec had made it out, but McAbee believed it was his job to stay and help hold the battalion together.

McAbee headed south, to find out what was happening. Along the way, he was overtaken by three Chinese soldiers—he guessed who they were instantly by their padded, quilted jackets and the earflaps on their hats. They seemed as puzzled to stumble upon him as he was them. They raised their rifles and pointed them at him. Communication was impossible, so he just pointed up the road, and remarkably enough, they headed off in that direction without shooting him. Only then did his luck begin to run out. He was hit twice, apparently by Chinese soldiers positioned some distance from the road, whom he never saw. The first bullet struck the side of his head. Then another bullet shattered his shoulder blade and he sensed that it was over: he was bleeding heavily from the head wound and growing weaker by the minute. He knew the terrible cold worked against him, and he was sure he was going to die there when an American soldier found him and somehow guided him back to Battalion headquarters.

LIEUTENANT KIES, WHO had been cut off since he left Richardson at the bridge, was moving his platoon toward Battalion headquarters when the Chinese opened up with machine guns and mortars. He tried to get his platoon to a ditch that ran along the side of the road, but they were caught between the Chinese and the American forces and losing a lot of men. "Lieutenant, I think we've got gooks all around us," Sergeant Luther Wise, one of his squad leaders, said. Just then a mortar round came in and killed Wise and wounded Kies. The lieutenant found that he could not lift one of his arms. But he kept moving what remained of his platoon toward the battalion command post. In the chaos he almost stumbled into a Chinese officer, but saw him first, and quickly moved his men back, and eventually brought them to what was the new CP, which was in effect a battalion aid station. There was a Chinese machine gun that had fairly good coverage of their path back to the battalion, but Kies had checked the way the Chinese gunner fired—a pause and a burst, a pause and a burst, exact increments of firing each time—and it was like breaking a code. He timed each burst and moved his men across in small groups during the pauses. Kies thought they might have gotten some protection from the Chinese machine gun, because the Chinese bodies were beginning to pile up, limiting the gunner's vision. By the time they reached the aid station, Kies estimated that he had only about twelve of the original twenty-eight men in his platoon left. They had been understrength from the start because of the shortage of replacements; now they were more like a squad. He was trying to help Dr. Clarence Anderson, the battalion surgeon, when a grenade landed near his feet, and he was wounded again, what turned out to be four breaks in one leg and some wounds in the other. Even as the grenade landed, a mortar round came in and killed five of the men left in Kies's platoon who could still fight. Kies was absolutely sure that not many more men were going to get out—certainly not him, because he couldn't move either leg.

The battalion command post was a disaster. Men dazed, wounded, completely numbed by what had happened were straggling in from different positions. When Bill Richardson finally reached it, he was shocked by the sheer chaos he found. Americans were mixed in with Chinese, who seemed unable to comprehend their victory, as if they had succeeded beyond their expectations. Now, having taken the CP, it was as if they had no idea what to do next. You could pass a Chinese soldier right in front of the CP at that moment and he would do nothing. A medic told Richardson they had created a small position nearby where they were protecting about forty wounded men. Dr. Anderson was there, along with Father Kapaun. But there was a serious question of who was in charge. Ormond and McAbee were both seriously wounded, and no one knew where Moriarty was. New leadership would have to rise to the surface on its own, Richardson thought.

He decided he would go back to Love Company and see if there were any other men he could help bring back. He started retracing his steps, shouting out his name so his own men wouldn't shoot him. He found Lieutenant Paul Bromser, the commander of Love Company, badly shot up, but the exec, Lieutenant Frederick Giroux, though wounded, was still functioning. It had been awful, Giroux said. The Chinese had swept right through them. Perhaps only 25 of the company's 180 men were left. "Can you get them out?" Giroux asked, and Richardson replied, "Yes, but not over the bridge." He would have to make his own return route, zigzagging back and forth. On the way he ran into two Chinese soldiers with bags of grenades, and shot one. A grenade went off, and then a Chinese machine gun opened up, panicking some of Richardson's men. As they neared the makeshift battalion perimeter, they spotted two American tanks, and, instinctively, some of the men climbed on—Americans always moved to their vehicles, Richardson thought, as if the vehicles could save them. He was sure the Chinese would go after the tanks first. So he and Giroux talked most of the men off.

The perimeter they were creating, about two hundred yards in diameter, abutted the old battalion CP. They dug quickly into the soft loam the river had left behind, with the three tanks inside giving them a little more firepower and some fragile radio links to other units. (Only the tank radios were working by then.) They took fire all the rest of that first night, but miraculously the Chinese, who seemed to have it in their power to overrun them at any point, never made another all-out attack. Probably, Richardson thought, the Chinese were as confused as the Americans on that first night, but their confusion, he remembered, did not last into the second day. When the dawn broke, the Americans relaxed slightly. They had outlasted the first attack. The enemy in this war rarely struck during the day, and even if this was their first battle with the Chinese, they doubted that they would be very different from the Koreans. There was still some vestige of hope. One of the last radio messages they had received was that help was on its way. At one point, Chaplain Kapaun, a man remembered for his remarkable bravery and selflessness (and who would be awarded the Distinguished Service Cross for his heroism), asked Richardson how he was doing. "Do you know what day it is?" the chaplain wondered.

Richardson said he had no idea.

"It's All Souls' Day."

"Father," Richardson answered, "someone better be looking out for our souls because we really need it now."

"Well, He is, He is," the chaplain replied.

FIRST LIEUTENANT PHIL PETERSON, who had shared that bottle of Communist bubbly with Walt Mayo in Pyongyang, was an artillery forward observer with C Battery of the Ninety-ninth Field Artillery Battalion, which supported the Third Battalion of the Eighth Regiment and had been attached to King Company of the Third, which was set up near the battalion CP. Fifty years later, he believed he could still quote almost to the word how the people at Battalion had explained the reports of Chinese being in the area in those hours before the enemy struck: "It is assumed that these Chinese are here to protect the North Korean electrical generators [up along the Yalu], and you are not to fire on them unless they fire on you. No forward observer is to call in any fire on any electrical installation."

It was only after the Chinese hit that Peterson realized how disingenuous the higher headquarters had been in letting them know how dangerous their situation was. "What they gave us," he said angrily many years after, "was a cover story." That night, about 9 P.M., just before the heavy firing began, some men from one of King Company's outposts brought in a prisoner, complete with quilted jacket. The Korean soldiers attached to King Company could not talk to him. Peterson was sure he had encountered his first Chinese soldier. They were ordered off their hilltop position and told to head toward Battalion; it was a confusing maneuver at night, and the company was split up into groups of a dozen or so men each. Then the firing began. Peterson's group was caught in a ditch alongside a rice paddy, with Chinese machine guns hammering away from both ends of the ditch. He hunkered down with a young sergeant who got hit right in the ass and seemed almost amused by it. He told Peterson (the humor was dark, because no one expected to make it out of there alive), "Look, Lieutenant, I got my million-dollar wound!"—the one that would send him home. Home at that moment had never seemed farther away.

While Peterson was trapped in that ditch, others in the company were trying to move the battery's six 105mm howitzers out. The window on saving their pieces from the enemy was closing fast. By the time they decided on an escape route and got together their little convoy (about sixteen vehicles—trucks carrying the howitzers and jeeps carrying some of the men and some food supplies) it was very late. Unbeknownst to them, the Chinese had already cut the road to the south and were waiting on both sides. Many of them were armed with Thompson submachine guns, a weapon no longer favored by the

U.S. Army, but captured or bought by the thousands from their Chinese Nationalist enemies in the recently concluded civil war, and a valuable weapon at this moment.

The fire on the blocked road was withering. Lieutenant Hank Pedicone, one of the best officers in the unit, a man who had won the Silver Star in World War II, was in the convoy that night, one of the few who lived through it. He later told Peterson they hadn't had a chance, that it was a terrible thing to watch an entire company being wiped out. Much earlier that evening, Pedicone had pleaded with his superiors to start moving out, but they had told him they needed to wait on orders. "We can't get any orders," Pedicone had said, "because we don't have any communications. We have to act on our own." A few men, like the battery commander, Captain Jack Bolt, riding in the lead in a jeep, managed to make it out, because the Chinese held their fire—probably waiting to disable a rig carrying a howitzer, not only because it was a bigger prize, but because it might block the road. But of about 180 men in the company, only a handful survived. It was the last convoy that tried to flee the Unsan area. In the meantime, Peterson and his group had retreated slowly toward Battalion headquarters, waiting for morning to come. At dawn, they made it to a flat spot about two hundred yards from the battalion CP and then in small groups raced inside the perimeter.

ON THE NIGHT of November 1, Pappy Miller, his buddy Richard Hettinger, and their platoon were about a mile from Battalion headquarters when they got the call telling them to come back. The battalion, indeed the entire regiment, had been told to pull back, though for them the news came a bit late. They had just passed an outpost near a bridge when they heard the first automatic weapons fire, and then the enemy was all around them, so Miller hustled the platoon under the bridge and across the river—it was nothing but a dry creek by then. Already tracers were lighting up the area. Most of the men were on the other bank when some grenade fragments hit Miller in the hand. What he remembered was how completely disorganized everything was—Chinese everywhere, seemingly coming from all directions, no clear lines for the Americans to fall back to. He had a sense that the enemy troops were close by and then suddenly they were there, right on top of him and his men. By then, his men had reached a ditch alongside the road, and they took cover in it. Almost all of them, Miller remembered, were new men, replacements just arrived, and none of them had ever seen fighting like this. They mistook the ditch for cover, which it was not, and thought they were safe there when they were not. Nothing was going to be truly safe, not even the higher ground, not even at the battalion CP, but Miller knew that the least safe place of all was that ditch, which now held about thirty-five men, some from his platoon, some from others. So he yelled to his friend, "Het, let's get going before we get killed," and they started forcing everyone out. This was about 3 A.M. on November 2, he thought. He was just about to clear the ditch when a Chinese grenade tore his leg apart, shredding muscle and breaking the bones in his foot. He could no longer move.

So he lay there, waiting for daylight, waiting to die. He knew there would be no one to carry him. His only chance was to crawl to a battalion aid station that he thought might be nearby, but even a battalion aid station might be overrun by then. It was so cold his breath was condensing, and he feared that the Chinese, searching the bodies as they were sure to, would be able to tell he was alive from his breath. He tried to cover himself with dead enemy bodies. About 2 P.M. on the afternoon of November 2, five or six Chinese soldiers, moving through the battlefield, methodically checking American and Chinese bodies, found him. One pointed a rifle at his head. Oh, he thought, I've finally bought the big one. Just then, Father Kapaun rushed up, pushed the Chinese soldier aside, and saved his life. Miller waited for the Chinese soldier to shoot both Kapaun and himself, but the chaplain had been so audacious that the soldier seemed in awe of him. Ignoring the enemy soldier, Kapaun pulled Miller up and hoisted him on his back: perhaps they would both be prisoners, but he was going to carry Miller as long as he could.

THE ASSAULT OF the Chinese had come as a complete surprise to the men in the Eighth Regiment's First Battalion. In fact, they had already fought the Chinese in a brief skirmish without knowing they were Chinese. For Ray Davis, a nineteen-year-old corporal with Dog Company in the First Battalion, a heavy weapons company, it was a random firefight, the kind that took place all the time. They had arrived in Unsan on October 31, and he had been part of a company-sized force moving through a rice paddy when they started taking fire from some nearby hills. Davis remembered that he and his men had been rather casual when the firing began. Most of them hadn't even been wearing their helmets. Then both sides had backed off. The real hit came a day and a half later.

Davis was part of a heavy machine gun team, posted on reasonably high ground, on a hill on the south side of a road that wound in an east-west direction. The road was narrow—just wide enough for one oxcart at a time—and it was by then bumper to bumper with the vehicles of the Eighth Cav, a reflection of an Army that did all its movement on wheels and so would prove unusually vulnerable to this new enemy. The Chinese, who moved by foot, invariably had easier access to the high ground, while the Americans were fatefully linked by their vehicles to the roads, which were almost always in the valleys.

A little after midnight, the Chinese struck with full force. For almost four months Davis had been in battles where the enemy always had vastly superior numbers, and where the great problem for those in his squad—like so many other machine gunners—had been the way their machine guns tended to wear out from the heavy use. Davis knew this all too well. As he had moved from being just an ammo bearer when he first arrived in country, to second and then first gunner on the two-man weapon, he had already gone through three or four machine guns. They always needed more firepower because of the sheer numbers of the attacking enemy. The basic infantry weapons they had started out with—the M-1 rifle, the carbine, even the machine guns—had not been designed for the force levels they were encountering. Lieutenant Colonel Bob Kane, his battalion commander, once told Davis that the key to this war was that you had to get one hundred of the enemy before you could go home. Once you got your one hundred, that was that. How you proved that you had your one hundred Kane never quite explained.

Davis had never seen anything quite like this. When the Americans sent up flares, Davis, who had grown up on a farm in upstate New York, saw so many enemy soldiers that he was reminded of nothing so much as wheat waving in a field back home. It was a terrifying sight, all those men, thousands and thousands, it seemed to him at that moment, coming right at him. If you got one, another would come; if you got one hundred, another one hundred would be right behind them. It put a bitter edge on Kane's joke. Then Davis spotted the men on horseback, who seemed to be directing the others. They had bugles, and when the bugles blew, the enemy soldiers would sometimes change the direction of their attack.

Davis knew that the handful of men around him had a limited amount of ammo and thus a limited amount of time left. The Americans fired and fired—often at point-blank range. They had, Davis later figured, an hour, at best two, before they ran out of ammo or the machine guns overheated. About 2 A.M., his platoon sergeant came to get him. Davis destroyed his machine gun with his last thermite grenade, and the two of them managed to make it back to a point where their mortars, firing air bursts against the Chinese, offered them some protection. The first thing was to make it through the night. Then when dawn came, they tried to regroup, somewhat surprised to still be alive. They were completely surrounded.

AT THE HASTILY created perimeter near the battalion CP, Lieutenant Giroux had emerged as the de facto leader of the encircled men, even though he was

seriously wounded. He was a World War II veteran, an experienced infantry
officer, and he seemed to have a sense of how limited their possibilities were—
and how to act as best they could on them while there was still time and still
any degree of choice. Working with him were Lieutenant Peterson and his
friend Walt Mayo, along with Bill Richardson, who was not an officer but had
become in the long trek north from the earliest days of the war a very experienced NCO. From the first hit, they had all understood that it was the Chinese,
and that their entire regiment had become the point unit in what was becoming an entirely new war. The men thrown together inside the perimeter had
managed to make it through the first night, but it looked very bleak. If help
was on the way, as higher headquarters kept saying, there was no sign of it yet.
That day a helicopter tried to land to take out some of the wounded, but the
fire from Chinese positions was so lethal that it had to fly away after dropping
off some medical supplies, mostly small compresses.

The desperate men inside the perimeter now faced a double dilemma: how
to get out and how to deal with all their wounded. They were also in danger of
running out of ammo. In addition, they did not have enough weapons, but a
cold, hard estimate told them that that was probably the least of their problems. Enough men were going to be killed that there would soon be weapons
for all. Their tiny defensive perimeter was about seventy yards—seventy very
flat, very open yards—away from the battalion CP, where most of the wounded
had been moved. On midday of November 3, Peterson, Mayo, Richardson, and
Giroux went over to the CP for a final doomsday kind of meeting. Because he
was not an officer, Richardson did not attend the meeting, but he knew what it
was about. All the officers, many of them wounded themselves, were talking
about a forbidden subject—what to do with the wounded in the terrible final
moment that everyone knew was coming. The wounded officers were going to
have to decide whether to leave themselves behind to the mercies, such as they
were, of the enemy. Bromser and Mayo went over to Lieutenant Kies and said
they were going to try to get out. They asked if he could make it, and Kies answered no, they had to forget about him; he couldn't walk, and he wasn't going
to slow the others down.

What heartbreaking decisions for young men to make, Richardson had
thought at the time and still pondered half a century later. He volunteered to
take some men, stay behind, and protect the bunker with the wounded for as
long as he could, but the offer was turned down by the wounded officers. No
one who was mobile, who might be able to *lead,* was to be wasted, if that was
the word, defending the wounded and the dying. They all knew time was short,
that the next hit would be even harder. They could hear the Chinese digging a
trench from the riverbed directly into their perimeter, which would allow

them to come up right on top of the Americans before they became targets. With Richardson was a particularly tough noncommissioned officer whose name Richardson never learned. Richardson went around collecting grenades from everyone, gave them to the sergeant, and told him that his job was to stop the Chinese dig. The sergeant crawled out there—it was one hell of a brave performance, Richardson thought, the kind of act you're more likely to see in movies than in real life—and personally slowed down the creation of the trench.

But the noose was tightening, and talk of relief missions was dying down. They had gotten an air strike that day, Australians flying B-26s, but time was working against them. There had been one resupply attempt; a small spotter plane had dropped a couple duffel bags about 150 yards beyond the perimeter. Richardson had crawled out and gotten them, but there wasn't much inside, and not what they needed: lots of ammo and lots of morphine.

Relief was not going to come. Hap Gay, the division commander, who had been arguing for a regimental pullback for days, had sent additional forces north to relieve his men, but they had been hammered by the Chinese, who had picked near perfect ambush positions to intercept the inevitable relief forces—it was a basic part of the Chinese MO, to wait for and destroy relief forces. The relief forces were short on both artillery and airpower, the two instruments that might give them an advantage when they assaulted the Chinese positions. One of the units sent to try to break through was Lieutenant Colonel Johnny Johnson's Fifth Regiment of the Cav, and one of his battalions took 250 casualties. On November 3, knowing it was hopeless, Gay, under orders from Milburn at Corps to pull his division back, made what he later called the hardest decision of his career. He ended all relief operations and left the men out there alone.

Later in the day, another spotter plane dropped a message telling the besieged men to try to get out as best they could. It was not exactly a comforting message, but Richardson and most of the other men had already assumed they were on their own. When night finally fell, the Chinese again attacked in full force. The besieged Americans fired their bazookas at some of their own stranded vehicles along the road to the south and southwest, setting them afire. It was like creating your own long-lasting flares, and it helped the defense immensely. Once a vehicle was lit up, it burned for a long time. The number of able-bodied men holding the perimeter continued to drop throughout the night, however. They had started with no more than a hundred men, and there were fewer men by the hour, and little ammo. By November 4, Richardson estimated that a quarter of the Americans still fighting were using Chinese burp guns scrounged off dead bodies. The second full night had been another horror. That night the last tank had departed—some of the men said it had been ordered out, but others be-lieved it had just taken off—and with it, all radio contact with anyone outside the perimeter ended. That in itself was terrifying; somehow it symbolized the fact that they had been abandoned. One thing that Peterson remembered vividly from that day was how American bodies piled up around their last machine gun as the Chinese concentrated their fire on it.

Early on the morning of the fourth, Richardson, Peterson, Mayo, and an-other soldier were chosen to lead a patrol to see if they could find a way out. Rank did not matter very much. Mayo and Peterson were officers, but they were artillery men, forward observers, and Richardson had been reminded by Giroux that, though he was an NCO, he probably had the most experience in infantry tactics and to trust his instincts. Peterson remembered a terrible mo-ment before they left. As he crawled past his radio operator, who was lying there, badly wounded, the man had said, "Lieutenant Peterson, where are you going?" Peterson answered that they were looking for a way out, so they could get help. "Lieutenant Peterson," the man began to plead, "please don't leave me! Please don't leave me! You can't leave me here to them!" A glance at the man and Peterson knew it was only a matter of hours before he would be dead. "I'm sorry. I'm so sorry, but we have to go and get help," he said, and crawled off to join the search party.

Richardson was sure that there was a way out to the east because the Chi-nese assaults were all coming from the other three directions; and, moving very slowly, they eventually found a riverbed littered with wounded Chinese, and knowing how close so many of their own men, especially the wounded, were to becoming prisoners, Richardson told the men with him: Don't even look like you're thinking of pointing a weapon at them, let alone shooting one. Don't think about it. Those are the truest orders you'll ever get. They stopped at one house where American supplies had briefly been stored. Now it was crowded with wounded Chinese. The wounded Chinese in the house kept whispering something eerie that sounded like "Shwee, shwee." The word was *shui,* Richardson was later told, their word for water. They finally reached a riverbed, only to find even more Chinese, perhaps four to five hundred bomb-ing victims, most of them dead but some alive or barely alive, holding out cups and begging for water. The Americans were now convinced that they could get through by heading east, and they slipped back to join the other men at the perimeter.

For Bill Richardson, the decisions they made after he returned to the perimeter proved the most painful he ever experienced. Nothing that hap-pened in the next few days, or for that matter in the rest of his life, measured up to it. There were perhaps 150 wounded men there by then, and there was no way any of them could take the dangerous trip out at night under enemy fire in mountainous terrain, at least not without compromising the able-bodied men. All of the wounded in the perimeter knew what was up. None of them wanted to be left behind for the Chinese. Soon after his return, some of them who were still partially ambulatory, started coming up to Richardson, crying, telling him not to leave them, please, dear God, not to leave them, not for the Chinese, please dear God take them, don't leave them there to die. Was it possible, he wondered, to do your duty, to follow the orders of your superiors, orders you agreed with in the end, and get as many men out as best you could, and yet feel worse about yourself as a human being? Do you ever forgive yourself for some of the things you do in life? It was a question he would still be asking himself a half century later. He was abandoning so many men he knew—who had fought so well.

Giroux had been very good in those first few days, helping create some kind of order, taking care of the more seriously wounded, but he would die in a prison camp. Kies had waited with the other wounded for the Chinese to arrive, sure that it was all over. When the Chinese finally showed up, and one of their men ordered him to stand up, he had tried and fallen over. His legs were useless. He had already cut off his combat boots because his feet were swelling up so badly. He remembered that the Chinese separated the prisoners, putting men like Dr. Anderson and Father Kapaun, who were ambulatory, in one group and the others, men like him who could not walk and needed to be carried—he estimated that there were about thirty such men—in the group to be borne on litters. Five of the men in his group died from their wounds the first night. Over the next few weeks they kept moving the group from house to house. There was almost nothing to eat, and they had to scrounge to get water—one of the men could crawl, and he brought back a little foul-tasting water in a helmet. They got no medical care, not even a Band-Aid or iodine, Kies remembered, for sixteen days, and even then it was the most primitive kind of care. They moved slowly and at night. His memory was of the Chinese taking them north for about two weeks, and he believed after about two weeks he heard the sound of a river, and he was sure it was the Yalu. Then one night, to his surprise, they turned south and headed toward the American lines. Perhaps they were tired of carrying American prisoners, he later thought. They left their prisoners in a house a few miles north of American positions in late November, and one of Kies's group, a newcomer who could walk, managed to go farther south to connect with the Americans, who finally sent vehicles to pick them up. All told, Kies had been a prisoner for just under a month. He was one of the lucky ones, he knew. The men who were ambulatory spent the rest of their time in Korea, more than two years, in brutal captivity, and many of them died. He thought that his original group of thirty men had shrunk to about eight before they were rescued. His left leg was broken in four places and he had fifty-two wounds from a mortar round below his waist. "You look like shit," one of the men who rescued him said. But he went through Army hospitals, got most of his health back, and eventually spent two years as an adviser in Vietnam.

BACK AT THE small American perimeter, those who were going to try to break out made their move a little before 5 P.M. There were about sixty of them, and they made it to the riverbed before cutting south, but it was hard moving. They were behind the Chinese lines now, and the very size of their group made it more likely that they might be spotted. When they reached the main road, known as the MSR, or Main Supply Route, they had to cross it quickly, and Richardson managed to string them out so that they could all do so at once. At one point when they took a break, a sergeant from the intelligence section slipped over and whispered to Richardson that if the two of them took off and just slipped away, they would almost surely make it back to the American lines because they were pros and they would not be slowed down by all these others, some of whom were clearly amateurs. He was right, and probably one of the officers should have made them do just that, but Richardson knew that it was too late for that now, that he could not desert these men, not at this point, even if it cost him his life.

On the morning of November 5, they stumbled into a Chinese outpost and there was an exchange of fire. Now that the Chinese knew where they were, they finally broke up. Richardson was the only soldier in his small group with a weapon, a burp gun. He told the others to take off, and just when he thought he had successfully slipped away himself, the Chinese found him and took him prisoner. He was not, as Tokyo had promised, going to be going home for Christmas. He would spend the next two and a half years instead in a series of brutal prison camps—as would Phil Peterson, who got picked up in a similar fashion.

OF THE EIGHTH CAV when it was all over, there were some eight hundred casualties among the estimated twenty-four hundred men in the regiment; of the ill-fated men of the Third Battalion, eight hundred strong when the battle began, only an estimated two hundred made it out. It was the worst defeat of the Korean War thus far, doubly painful because it had taken place after four months of battle, when, it seemed, the tide had finally turned, when victory was in sight, and it had been inflicted on a much admired American unit. Suddenly, as if out of nowhere, the Chinese Communists had appeared in force and shattered an elite regiment from an elite division. The Eighth Cav had lost half its authorized strength at Unsan, and a good deal of its equipment, including twelve 105mm howitzers, nine tanks, 125 trucks, and a dozen recoilless rifles. A spokesman for the Cav who talked to reporters two days after the Chinese attack was clearly shaken: "We don't know whether they represent the Chinese Communist Government," he said, but it was "a massacre Indian-style, like the one that hit Custer at the Little Big Horn." It was a comparison that would occur to others.

Pappy Miller, wounded, captured, and then carried by the chaplain, was in a small group of prisoners being moved farther north each night. During their trek to a prison camp, they arrived at a place the Chinese were using as a temporary base, and there he saw thousands and thousands of Chinese soldiers, perhaps twenty or thirty thousand. It was like seeing a secret city in North Korea filled with nothing but Chinese soldiers. Privy to a spectacular view of the enemy, he knew how completely the war had changed, but there was no one who mattered whom he could tell. He was on his way to more than two bitter years in a prisoner of war camp in which he would be beaten regularly, denied elemental medical care, and given the barest of rations.

The UN forces, whether they liked retrograde movements or not, quickly moved back to positions on the other side of the Chongchon River. There they prepared for another hit by the Chinese forces. But the Chinese had vanished, as mysteriously as they had appeared. No one knew where they had gone. They had quietly departed the battlefield and become invisible once again. But they had not, as some people in Tokyo wanted to believe, left the country. They had simply moved into positions hidden away, farther north. There they would wait patiently for the Americans to walk into an even bigger trap, one even farther from their main bases. What had happened at Unsan was just the beginning. The real hit would come farther north in even colder weather in about three weeks.

Unsan was a warning, but it was not heeded. In Washington the president and his principal advisers, who had been anxious for weeks about Chinese intentions, became more nervous than ever. The Joint Chiefs of Staff, responding to President Harry Truman's nervousness, cabled MacArthur on November 3, asking him to respond to what "appears to be overt intervention in Korea by Chinese Communist forces." What followed in the next few days reflected the growing schism between what MacArthur wanted to do, which was to drive to the Yalu and unify all of Korea, and what Washington wanted to do, which was to avoid a major war with China.

For the question of what the Chinese were up to had become the central issue before Washington, and once again MacArthur decided to control the decision-making by controlling the intelligence. Here again Brigadier General Charles

Willoughby was the key player. He deliberately minimized both the number and the intentions of the Chinese troops. On November 3 he placed the number of Chinese in country at a minimum of 16,500 and a maximum of 34,500. (Some 20,000 men, or roughly two divisions, had hit the Americans at Unsan alone, and at virtually the same time a comparable number of Chinese had hit a Marine battalion on the east side of the peninsula, causing quite heavy casualties.) In truth there were some 300,000 men, or thirty divisions, already in country. MacArthur, momentarily shaken by the assault, tried to downplay it, and his response to the JCS cable reflected the Willoughby line. The Chinese, he cabled, were there to help the North Koreans "keep a nominal foothold in North Korea" and allowed them to "salvage something from the wreckage."

If he had been somewhat shaken initially by the Chinese attack, now, as they seemed to have vanished, MacArthur became more confident again. General Walton Walker, the commander of the U.S. Eighth Army, whose troops had been hit at Unsan, had cabled back to Tokyo after the attack, "AN AMBUSH AND SURPRISE ATTACK BY FRESH WELL ORGANIZED AND WELL TRAINED UNITS, SOME OF WHICH WERE CHINESE COMMU-NIST FORCES." Blunter than that you could not get. The candor of Walker's message did not please MacArthur's headquarters. The general wanted Walker to minimize the danger of the contact with the Chinese and to continue to push north—business as usual. MacArthur soon came down even harder on Walker, who was increasingly nervous about moving north and who, like the Chiefs back in Washington, had wanted to settle for a line at the narrow neck of the peninsula. Why, MacArthur asked Walker, who already feared he was going to be relieved, had the Eighth Army broken off contact with the enemy after Unsan and retreated behind the Chongchon River—pushed, as he said, by a few Chinese "volunteers"? Clearly Walker was to drive forward and continue north, the pressure on him to go ever faster mounting as the Chinese hid and waited.

On November 6 MacArthur issued a communiqué in Tokyo saying that the Korean War had been brought to a practical end by the way he had closed the trap north of Pyongyang. Not everyone else was that confident. Many of the senior officers in the Eighth Army, aware of what had happened at Unsan, sensed that it had only been a brief flashing of China's potential.

Now more than ever there was plenty of reason for the people back in Washington to be nervous. As Lieutenant General Matthew B. Ridgway noted later, when the Chinese had first struck, MacArthur had seen it as a calamity and had sent a message to Washington protesting any limitations on bombing the bridges over the Yalu. The ability of the Chinese to cross those bridges, he said, "threatens the ultimate destruction of the forces under my command."

When the JCS responded to that message by pointing out that the Chinese intervention seemed, in Ridgway's words, "to be an accomplished fact," which would surely mean a painful reevaluation of all UN movements north, MacArthur sent another message, which seemed in stark contrast to his previous one and in effect told Washington not to worry, that the Air Force could protect his men, and his forces would be able to destroy any enemy in their way. The drive north would continue. It was the ultimate fateful moment of the Korean War: torn between his great dream of conquering all of Korea and the danger to his troops from a formidable new enemy, MacArthur chose to pursue his dream and to put his army at risk.

IN WASHINGTON, THE senior players remained frozen. Control of the war, Dean Acheson, the secretary of state, later wrote, had passed first to the Chinese, then to MacArthur—and it now appeared that Washington had no influence at all on the former and marginal influence on the latter. "And what was General MacArthur up to in the amazing military maneuver that was unfolding before our eyes?" Acheson later wrote. That moment was critical: extremely able troops from a brand-new enemy had shown up on the battlefield, fought well, and then had seemingly "vanished from the earth." "The most elementary caution," he added, "would seem to warn that they might, indeed probably would, reappear as suddenly and harmfully as they had before."

At Sudong, on the other side of the peninsula, the Marines who were part of Tenth Corps had been hit very hard in a parallel battle on November 2–4 and had lost 44 men killed and 162 wounded. They decided that the attack against them had been carefully calculated, as if the Chinese were baiting a trap for them and could not wait for them to push farther north and thus step ever deeper into it. The evidence of Sudong made the developments at Unsan all the more serious and less isolated. This was the last chance to break off the drive north, move back, and avoid a larger war with the Chinese. But Washington did nothing. "We sat around," Acheson noted in his memoir, "like paralyzed rabbits while MacArthur carried out this nightmare."

Part Two

═══════

Bleak Days:
The In Min Gun
Drives South

2

L ESS THAN FIVE months earlier, around June 15, 1950, some six North Korean divisions had moved very quietly into place just above the border with South Korea, joining several units already stationed there. Their training was intensified, but a blackout was placed on all radio transmissions. Quietly and covertly, engineers were put to work reinforcing a number of simple bridges on the main arteries heading south, strengthening them just enough so that they could support the heavy Russian-made T-34 tanks. At the same time, Communist workers were feverishly fixing train tracks, which the North Koreans themselves had disassembled when the country was divided at the end of World War II, on lines that ran on a north-south axis. On the evening of the twenty-fourth, the rains began, and continued into the early morning, as some ninety thousand men, more than seven infantry divisions, and one armored brigade of the North Korean People's Army, or In Min Gun as it was known, crossed the thirty-eighth parallel and headed south. It was an extremely well-planned, multipronged attack. The North Koreans used the main highways, such as they were, and the rail systems to expedite their drive, and in many in- stances they moved so quickly and successfully that they looped around stunned ROK units before anyone realized what had happened. After the first day, one of their Soviet advisers had offered them the ultimate compliment: they had moved even faster than Russian troops.

From the time he was first installed in Pyongyang by the Soviets in 1945, Kim Il Sung, the North Korean leader, had been obsessed with the need to attack the South and unite Korea. He was single-minded on the subject, con- stantly bringing it up with the one man who could give him permission, the Russian dictator Joseph Stalin. He wanted, he told Stalin in a meeting in late 1949, "to touch the South with the point of a bayonet."

The pressure on Stalin from Kim had increased dramatically as Mao Ze- dong came closer to unifying all of China under his revolutionary banner. Mao's successes seemed to heighten Kim's frustrations. Here was Mao about to become a formidable new player on the world stage, and yet Kim was frozen in

place in Pyongyang, unable to send his troops south without Soviet permission. He was the incomplete dictator, the man who ruled only half a country.
So he pushed and pushed with Stalin. What he was selling was simple and
seemingly easy: a Communist assault against the South and an easy victory.
Kim believed that if he struck with a blitzkrieg-like armored assault, the people of the South would rise up to welcome his troops and the war would effectively be over in a few days.

In the past Stalin had always been cautious in response to Kim's entreaties.
The Americans were still in the South, even if only in an advisory capacity, and
Stalin remained wary of directly challenging them. Still, Kim, who believed his
own propaganda and was contemptuous of Syngman Rhee's American-
supported government in the South, proved relentless. He was the most dangerous kind of man, a true believer, absolutely convinced of his own truths. If
the Soviets just got out of the way and let him head south, he could conquer
the region in virtually no time, he believed, just as Syngman Rhee was convinced that if only the Americans, with their own odious restraints, would get
out of *his* way, he could easily conquer the North.

Stalin was not unhappy with a certain level of simmering military tension
between the two Koreas, nothing too large, but enough to keep each other
off balance. On occasion he had encouraged Kim to continue hitting Rhee's
regime. "How is it going, Comrade Kim?" he asked at one meeting in the
spring of 1949. The Southerners, Kim complained, were making things difficult. There were lots of clashes along the border. "What are you talking about?"
Stalin asked him. "Are you short of arms? You must strike the Southerners in
the teeth." He pondered that for a moment, before adding, "Strike them, strike
them."

But permission for an invasion was another matter entirely. The Soviet
leader was in no rush for an open conflict there. Then a number of exterior
developments changed Stalin's attitude, not the least of them the speech Secretary of State Dean Acheson gave on January 12 at the National Press Club
in Washington, which seemed to signal that Korea was not part of America's
Asian defense perimeter and which in Moscow was read as implying that
the Americans might stay out of any conflict in Korea. The speech was a miscalculation of considerable importance on the part of one of the most
tough-minded foreign policy figures of the era, because it so critically affected
judgments on the Communist side. With China having fallen to the Communists, Acheson was trying to explain what American policy in Asia was, and he
had ended up giving a very dangerous signal to the Communist world. "I'm
afraid Dean really blew it on that one," his old friend Averell Harriman said
years later.

In late 1949 and early 1950, Kim apparently made a number of secret trips to Moscow to push for permission, all the while building up his army. The Russians were in those months taking their own cool look at the stakes involved if Kim went south, and they would finally decide that the Americans would not come in. Mao, meeting with Kim, at Stalin's request, on the question of what the Americans might do, also agreed that the Americans were unlikely to enter the war to save "such a small territory." Therefore there appeared to be little need for Chinese help. But if the Japanese, still much feared regionally, were ever to enter the war, Mao promised men and materiel.

Events in China also influenced Stalin in his Korean decision. After all, the Americans had not intervened militarily to save their great ally, the Chinese Nationalist leader, Chiang Kai-shek, to whom they had seemed so heavily committed, when all of mainland China had seemed at stake. If Mao's war—which had gained so much from peasant support—had been so successful, wouldn't the South Korean peasants support Kim in much the same manner? Wasn't there a precedent here? So gradually Kim's plan began to gain support in Moscow. When Mao met with Stalin for the first time in Moscow in late 1949, they had discussed Kim's war plan. Stalin suggested transferring some fourteen thousand soldiers of Korean nationality then serving in the Chinese Communist Army back to the North Koreans, and Mao agreed. The request, wrote the historians Sergei Goncharov, John Lewis, and Litai Xue in their groundbreaking study, *Uncertain Partners: Stalin, Mao, and the Korean War,* showed "that Stalin was thereby backing the Korean enterprise but distancing himself from any direct involvement." Stalin was playing a delicate game, flashing a half-green, half-amber light on the invasion. But since it was still uncertain that everything would go as well as Kim prophesized, he wanted no part of the consequences of a more difficult, costly adventure; nor did he want his fingerprints directly on it.

Mao's final victory in the civil war in October 1949 only intensified Kim's hunger. Now he felt it was his turn. In January 1950, at a luncheon held for a new North Korean ambassador on his way to an assignment in Beijing, Kim again made his pitch to several senior political figures from the Soviet embassy. "Now that China was finishing its liberation," he told them, "it is the turn of the liberation of the Korean people in the South." He could not sleep at night, he added, so fiercely was he struggling to solve the question of how to unify his country. Then Kim pulled aside General Terenti Shtykov, the de facto Russian ruler of North Korea, and asked him to arrange another meeting with Stalin, and afterward with Mao. On January 30, 1950, eighteen days after the Acheson speech, Stalin cabled Shtykov to tell Kim, "I am ready to help in this matter." Shtykov in turn passed the news to Kim, who said he was absolutely delighted.

In April 1950, Kim visited Moscow determined to end Stalin's remaining doubts. He was accompanied by Pak Hon Yong, a Southern Communist leader, who promised the Soviet dictator that the Southerners would rise up en masse "at the first signal from the North." (Eventually Pak paid dearly for his optimism and for an uprising that never took place. Some three years after the end of the war, he was quietly taken out and executed.) Over a fifteen-day period, from April 10 to April 25, Kim and Pak met three times with Stalin. Kim was completely confident of victory. He was, after all, surrounded by people who told him how popular he was and how unpopular Rhee was, and how the people of the South longed for him to invade—just as Rhee was surrounded by people who assured him the reverse was true. But both regimes had been in power for five years, and the Southerners, no matter what their grievances against Rhee, also knew a good deal about the oppressiveness of the Pyongyang regime. That was something Kim did not think about, for he was a true believer as a Communist and did not think of his regime as oppressive. He was convinced that the new Korea rising up in the North was a just, truly democratic country.

Nor would the United States intervene, he assured Stalin, because the Americans would not want to risk a major war with Russia and China. As for Mao, the Chinese leader had always supported the liberation of all Korea and had even offered Chinese troops, though Kim was sure he would not need them. At that point, Stalin said he was on Kim's side but would not be able to help him very much because he had other priorities—especially in Europe. If the Americans came in, Kim should not expect the Russians to send troops: "If you should get kicked in the teeth I shall not lift a finger. You have to ask Mao for all the help." It was Kim's job, Stalin said, to turn to Mao, who had a "good understanding of Oriental matters," for more tangible backing.

It was a classic Stalin move. He had withdrawn his opposition, minimized his own contribution, and passed the buck to a new Communist government, one that had barely taken power but was beholden to him. He knew he had considerable leverage over Mao, who wanted to make his own country whole but was blocked by the Americans on Taiwan, and thus would need Soviet help if he was to move against the last Nationalist redoubt. In fact Mao had already been busy negotiating with the Soviets on his need for the requisite air and sea power. Kim met Mao in a secret session in Beijing on May 13, 1950. His audacity, indeed what the Chinese saw as his brashness, surprised the Chinese leader somewhat. The next day Mao received a cable from Stalin confirming his limited support for Kim's invasion. With that, Mao pledged his own support and asked whether Kim wanted the Chinese to send troops to the Korean border just in case the Americans came in. Kim insisted that there was no need for

that. Indeed, he had answered "arrogantly," Mao later told Shi Zhe, his interpreter. The Chinese were more than a little irritated with him and above all his
manner. They had thought that he would come to them more modestly—a
Korean, a representative of a lesser country dealing with the rulers of mighty
China, men who had just won their own great war—and they would be the senior partner dealing generously with a junior partner. Instead he had treated
them, they believed, with disrespect, as if he were merely going through a formality as promised to Stalin. He clearly wanted as little in the way of Chinese
fingerprints on his great adventure as possible. Kim was confident that it
would be over so quickly—in under a month—that the Americans would be
unable to deploy their troops, even if they wanted to. Mao suggested that because the Americans were already propping up the Rhee regime, and Japan
was critical to American policy in northern Asia, an American entrance should
not be entirely ruled out. But Kim had been unmoved by the suggestion. As for
aid, he was going to get enough from the Soviets. That appeared to be true;
Russian heavy weaponry was already passing through the supply pipeline to
Pyongyang. (On the eve of battle, Kim's forces would be far better equipped,
not only than those of Rhee, but than most units in the Chinese Communist
Army, still using older weapons captured from the Japanese and the Chinese
Nationalists.)

Mao had suggested that Kim fight what the writer Shen Zhihua called "a
quick, decisive war," outflanking the cities, not letting his forces be caught up
in urban warfare, striking instead against Rhee's military strong points. Speed
was of the essence. If the Americans entered the war, Mao pledged fatefully, the
Chinese would send troops. But the Koreans did not think they would need
them. When the meeting with Mao was over, Kim told the Soviet ambassador
to China, N. V. Roshchin, in Mao's presence, that Kim and Mao were in complete agreement on his forthcoming offensive. That was not exactly true, and
Mao was not pleased that this overconfident, younger man, with his limited
record of military success, was treating him in such a high-handed manner
and professed to speak for him.

In those early days, Korea remained very much a Soviet satellite, with the
Russians making a deliberate effort to minimize the influence of the Chinese.
Kim's top advisers as D-day approached were all Russian generals, and they
gradually took over the war planning. They considered Kim's early plans for
the invasion amateurish, and the plans were redrawn to their specifications.
The pro-Chinese members of the Korean politburo and military were carefully excluded from the more sensitive planning sessions. Some of the heavier
weaponry then being moved into the country was sent by sea rather than rail
so that it would not have to go through Chinese territory. It was obvious that

both the Koreans and the Russians wanted to minimize the Chinese role. Kim had suggested that the invasion begin sometime in mid- to late June, before the rainy season hit in full force. Stalin eventually agreed to a date in late June. The last massive shipment of Soviet military gear arrived earlier that month. The closer the North Koreans came to the day of the offensive, the more the Russian hand showed. Kim did not even bother to inform the Chinese authorities that an invasion had begun until June 27, two days after his troops crossed the thirty-eighth parallel. Until then, the Chinese were dependent for news on radio reports. When Kim finally spoke with the Chinese ambassador, he insisted that the South Koreans had attacked first, which the Chinese knew to be a considerable lie. What was interesting about all the positioning in the weeks before the start of the invasion was that even as the forecast was for an easy victory, the tensions and the rivalries between the three nations were very serious, with deep historical roots—and the levels of mutual trust were surprisingly thin.

To the Americans and others in the West, this was not a civil war, but a border crossing, a case of one country invading another, and thus a reminder of how the West had failed to halt Hitler's aggression in the days leading up to World War II. To the Chinese, the Russians, and the North Koreans that was a surprising point of view. They had chosen at that point not to think of the thirty-eighth parallel, selected by the Americans and the Russians back in 1945 as the dividing line between the two Koreas, as a border at all. (That would change a few months later when the American and UN forces crossed the parallel heading north.) What they had done on June 25 was, in their view, just one more act in a long-term struggle on the part of the Korean people, part of an unfinished civil war like the one under way in Indochina and the one just ended in China.

THERE HAD BEEN signs of a buildup in the weeks before the assault, but when the American intelligence reports were checked out daily, the signs had somehow slipped through the cracks, buried among the background noise of countless daily charges and countercharges, of incidents and counterincidents produced by a contested border separating two aggressive, very angry antagonists. Still, had they paid closer attention, the American authorities might have recognized that something quite ominous was beginning to take place. A young American intelligence officer named Jack Singlaub, who served in China with the Office of Strategic Services (OSS), which had now become the CIA, had been training a number of Korean agents to look for indicators that Pyongyang was up to something more than their normal hit-and-run guerrilla raids. Then he had sent his men north as early border crossers. They were new at the game, and their training was hardly of the highest order, so they had been told to look for the simplest of things: first and most important, any up-rooting or displacement of Korean families in the border area, a sign that preparations were under way for which the Communist authorities wanted few witnesses; second, the strengthening or widening of smaller bridges; third, any work that might indicate a reopening of the north-south rail lines.

Singlaub's agents were young, but he thought a number of them were surprisingly good. Late that spring, he received a number of very valuable reports that the North Koreans were moving additional elite units up to the border, and civilians away from it. In addition he was being told that there was a good deal of work taking place on the bridges; and that some railroad lines near the border were being repaired, often at night. Singlaub was sure that buried among all the other bits of intelligence he was getting about endless border incidents, something important was taking place.

Singlaub was working under considerable professional limitations. He could not even operate openly in Korea, because he was a former-OSS-now-CIA agent, and Douglas MacArthur as well as his chief of intelligence, Brigadier General Charles Willoughby, had hated the OSS. They had kept it out of their theater of operations during World War II; now they were intent on doing the same with the CIA. Some of that hatred came from MacArthur's well-known Anglophobia, his dislike of the Eastern Establishment types who had been so influential in the OSS and effectively dominated it; but some of it was a good deal more practical. If his G-2 controlled the intelligence coming out of his theater of operation, then he was more likely to control any decision-making about the theater. He and Willoughby preferred that the Pentagon and the Truman administration be completely dependent upon them for any information about what was going on in their area of Asia—with no countervailing intelligence to limit his hand. Control intelligence, and you control decision-making.

THAT THE TOKYO command was not tuned to what was happening did not surprise George Kennan, who had come away from an earlier trip to Tokyo deeply suspicious of the quality and competence of MacArthur's staff, especially the intelligence people, whom he thought pompous, far too ideological, and dangerously overconfident. When he had mentioned to one senior Air Force officer the geopolitical vulnerability of Korea if American regular ground forces were pulled out, the officer had said there would be no need for ground troops because strategic bombing from Okinawa would take care of any potential enemy. Kennan, who had followed how the Chinese fought in their own civil war, seemingly impervious to enemy airpower, was not so sure. Then in May and June of 1950, some of his people at the State Department's Policy Planning began picking up soundings that something very big was happening in the Communist world and that a large force was going into action soon. At that point the varying American intelligence agencies placed the entire Communist world under intense scrutiny and came away convinced that it was not the Russians nor any of their Eastern European satellites. Perhaps, Kennan thought, it might be Korea. Back from the military came the word that a Communist attack there "was practically out of the question: the South Korean forces were so well armed and trained that they were clearly superior to those of the North."

SO WHEN THE reports of Singlaub's agents were finally integrated into the larger intelligence yield, they came back from Willoughby's shop with an "F-6" label—agents not considered trustworthy, and reports unlikely to be true—the lowest possible rating. And thus when the In Min Gun advanced the morning of June 25, they caught the South Korean troops and their American advisers completely unaware. It was not close to a fair fight. The North Korean troops were very good and very well equipped. In many instances their weapons had been newly manufactured in Russia and shipped to them specifically for use in this offensive. The soldiers were well trained, and they outnumbered the South Korean troops almost two to one. Close to half of them were combat tested, some forty-five thousand Korean nationals who had fought in China having been gradually transferred from the Chinese Communist army to In Min Gun units with Mao's approval. These were men who in many cases had been fighting for more than a decade and had survived a war where the other side *always* had superior weaponry. The In Min Gun was an exceptionally accurate reflection of the authoritarian society just then taking root in the North: a controlled, disciplined, extremely hierarchical, highly indoctrinated army, fighting for a highly controlled, disciplined, hierarchical government. The soldiers were mainly of peasant background and their grievances were very real: they were embittered against their poverty, against the Japanese who had ruled them so cruelly, against the upper-class Koreans who had collaborated with the Japanese; and now they were indoctrinated against the Americans, who in their minds had replaced the Japanese in the South. They were nothing if not hardened: the dogmas they believed had been repeatedly validated by the cruelty of their own and their families' lives.

IN SEOUL THE Americans who were part of the small political and military advisory presence were somewhat slow to react, slow to understand that it was the real thing and that as many as one hundred thousand North Korean soldiers were in play. The North Korean assault had begun at 4 A.M. on Sunday in Korea, or 3 P.M. Saturday in Washington. John Muccio, the American ambassador to South Korea, considered an unusually able State Department official, heard of it four hours after it started, when he got a call from one of his top aides. "Brace yourself for a shock," Everett Drumwright, the American chargé d'affaires in Seoul told Muccio. "The Communists are hitting all along the front." Syngman Rhee heard of it at 6:30 A.M., which means that for at least an hour and a half he did not alert the Americans. After Muccio spoke to Drumwright, they decided to meet at the embassy. On the way over there he ran into Jack James, a United Press reporter who had intended to do some work and then go on a picnic that day. Muccio told James that he was checking out a report that the North Koreans had attacked all along the border. Just as James entered the embassy, he ran into a friend who worked in military intelligence. "What do you hear from the border?" the officer asked James. "Not very much yet," James replied. "What do you hear?" "Hell, they're supposed to have crossed everywhere except in the Eighth Division Area," the officer answered.

With that, James went to a phone and started making calls frantically, trying to piece it all together. A little later, around 8:45 A.M. Seoul time, one of the Marine guards, Sergeant Paul Dupras, asked him what was going on. "The North Koreans have crossed the border," he answered. "That's nothing—that's a common occurrence," Dupras said. "Yeah, but this time they've got tanks," James answered. James kept getting more and more details, and at 9:50 A.M., he sent out his first bulletin. He had been moving around the city, and when he returned to the embassy and one of his friends in military intelligence said something about letting Washington know about it, he decided that if it was good enough for them to go with, then it was good enough for him as well. He was careful, he said later, not to hype it, because it was a question of war and there was no need to make more of it than there was, because surely there would be plenty of details in the hours and days that followed. Though UP was notoriously cheap, he took it on himself to send the bulletin at urgent rates. Because he moved so quickly, his story was the only one to arrive back in America and make the Sunday morning papers. It began in typical wire service fashion: "URGENT UNPRESS NEW YORK 25095 JAMES FRAGMENTARY REPORTS EXTHIRTY EIGHTH PARALLEL INDICATED NORTH KOREANS LAUNCHED SUNDAY MORNING ATTACKS GENERALLY ALONG ENTIRE BORDER PARA REPORTS AT ZERO NINETHIRTY LOCAL TIME INDICATED KAESONG FORTY MILES NORTHWEST SEOUL AND HEADQUARTERS OF KOREAN ARMY'S FIRST DIVISION FELL NINE AYEM STOP ENEMY FORCES REPORTED THREE TO FOUR KILOMETERS SOUTH OF BORDER ON ONJIN PENINSULA STOP TANKS SUPPOSED BROUGHT INTO USE CHUNCHON FIFTY MILES NORTHWEST SEOUL. . . ."

In Washington, there were more and more fragmentary reports coming in from the embassy. But it was James's United Press bulletins that alerted the city. As others in the United Press bureau, and soon other newspaper bureaus, began calling high public officials to get some kind of confirmation, the top people in government were alerted to the fact that a new and very unwanted war had begun on the Korean peninsula.

WHEN THE NORTH KOREANS attacked, Douglas MacArthur was surprisingly slow to respond. He seemed almost indifferent to the early news of the invasion, so much so that he worried some of the men around him. Nor were these witnesses committed liberals, the kind of sworn enemies he believed were always out to undermine him for domestic political reasons; they included one of the most conservative men connected to the U.S. national security apparatus, John Foster Dulles, the shadow Republican secretary of state, then serving as an adviser to the State Department; and John Allison, one of the more hard-line members of the State Department, who was serving as Dulles's aide on a trip to Seoul and Tokyo.

By chance both Dulles and Allison had arrived in Tokyo to discuss a future peace treaty that would formally end the American occupation of Japan, when the North Koreans struck. Just a few days before the attack, both men had visited a South Korean bunker near the thirty-eighth parallel. There they were photographed huddled with ROK troops. Dulles, wearing his signature homburg, looked like he was on his way to a meeting of top Wall Street bankers. "Foster up in a bunker with a homburg on—it was a very amusing picture," said Secretary of State Dean Acheson, who had no fondness for the man who wanted to take his job, and had been sure he was going to get it a mere eighteen months earlier, when Tom Dewey had run for the presidency. The next day Dulles, a man possessed of no small amount of grandiosity, blended as it was with a streak of great personal and religious righteousness, had spoken before the South Korean National Assembly. "You are not alone," he told the assembly. "You will never be alone so long as you continue to play worthily your part in the great design of human freedom." Those words had been specifically written for Dulles and that occasion back in Washington, by men who would in different ways emerge in the coming months as leading hardliners: Dean Rusk, the new assistant secretary of state for the Far East, and Paul Nitze, the head of Policy Planning. Still, for all the intensity of Dulles's rhetoric, there was no real reason to feel that South Korea was in any great danger. Just a few days earlier both Dulles and Allison had been briefed by General Willoughby, and the subject of a potential North Korean attack had never come up.

When the North Koreans struck, Dulles and Allison had an unusually inti-

mate view of MacArthur's headquarters in action—the view of men ideologically sympathetic, but who were not members of MacArthur's inner team.
From the start, the news coming in was very bad, yet MacArthur and his staff
seemed curiously casual about it. There was a briefing that first Sunday night,
June 25, at which MacArthur seemed far too relaxed. The early reports, he told
Dulles and Allison, were inconclusive. "This is probably only a reconnaissance-
in-force. If Washington only will not hobble me, I can handle it with one arm
tied behind my back," he said. Then he added that President Rhee had asked for
some fighter planes, and though he thought the Koreans could not use them
properly, he intended to send a few along, just for morale purposes.

Dulles, Allison thought, seemed momentarily relieved by MacArthur's
aura of confidence, but he still wanted to send a cable to Acheson and Rusk,
urging immediate help for the South Koreans. But the more Allison and
Dulles talked to men outside MacArthur's coterie, the more uneasy they became. That very first night, Allison had gone to dinner with an old friend,
Brigadier General Crump Garvin, commander of the Port of Yokohama.
Garvin startled him by confiding that there had been serious reports coming
through Eighth Army Intelligence for the past two or three weeks indicating
that civilians near the North Korean side of the parallel were being moved
away and that the North Koreans were concentrating large numbers of troops

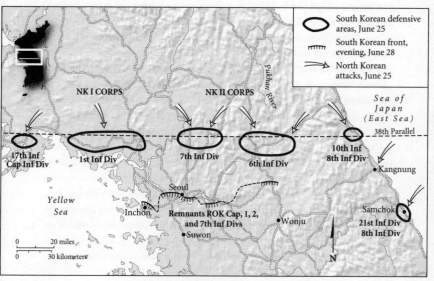

4. THE NORTH KOREAN INVASION, JUNE 25–28, 1950

just above the border. "Anyone who read the reports could see something was going to happen and soon. I don't know what G-2 in Tokyo has been doing," Garvin told Allison.

On Monday, the gap between reality in the field and that in MacArthur's headquarters seemed to grow wider. Ambassador Muccio, the senior American State Department representative in Korea, had ordered the immediate evacuation of American women and children from the country. MacArthur, still on automatic pilot, suggested that it was a premature move. There was, he insisted, "no reason to panic in Korea." Yet the news coming in was uniformly bad. That night the two high-ranking visitors separated, Allison to have dinner with some senior officials in Tokyo, Dulles to attend a private dinner with MacArthur. Allison's dinner party was interrupted by the constant comings and goings of senior journalists and diplomats, all of them checking with their sources during the evening, all coming back with increasingly somber reports—the South Koreans were being routed. At the end of the evening, Allison decided to check in with Dulles, certain that he would know far more from his dinner. "I suppose you've heard the bad news from Korea," he began. Dulles had heard nothing. "But didn't you have dinner with the general?" Yes, Dulles answered, just the two couples, but after dinner they had watched a movie, the general's favorite form of entertainment. No one had interrupted their evening. Dulles thereupon called MacArthur to report on what he had heard about the South Korean collapse. The general said he would look into it. "This may have been one of the few times in American history when representatives of the State Department have had to tell a high American military commander about what was happening in his own backyard," Allison later wrote.

The next day brought yet more signs that a disaster was unfolding in front of them. Ambassador Muccio reported that Seoul was being evacuated, that he and Rhee were about to head south of Taejon, below the Han River. That day Dulles and Allison were scheduled to fly back to the United States. While they were waiting at Haneda Airport, a transformed MacArthur joined them. Allison was shocked by the change in the man. The jaunty, confident figure who only two days earlier had spoken of a recon-in-force in Korea was gone. Now he was completely despondent—as if shrouded in his own darkness. Others in the past had noted the general's tendency toward major mood swings, but Dulles and Allison were nonetheless stunned by the change in his appearance. "All Korea is lost," MacArthur proclaimed. "The only thing we can do is get our people safely out of the country." "I have never seen such a dejected, completely forlorn man as General MacArthur was that Tuesday morning, June 27, 1950," Allison later wrote.

Even more disturbing was MacArthur's behavior when their plane was delayed for mechanical reasons. The farewell ceremony seemed to drag on and on, even when a message arrived that the secretary of the Army wanted a telecom meeting with the general at 1 P.M., Tokyo time. In those days of more primitive communications, a telecom meeting was like a phone conversation done through talking typewriters that conversed with each other. Both Dulles and Allison sensed that the request was an exceptionally important one, Washington desperately needing to talk to its commander in the field to find out what he thought ought to be done in a major crisis. In order to participate, MacArthur needed to leave Haneda immediately. But to their surprise, the general rather airily told his aides that he was busy seeing Dulles off and Washington could talk to his chief of staff. Dulles was appalled, and he used a ploy to get MacArthur back to work: he had his party paged and told to board the plane. Only then did MacArthur leave for headquarters. Thereupon Dulles and his party returned to the VIP room to wait a few hours more. It would be during that teleconference, Allison later learned, that the Truman administration decided to commit U.S. air and sea power to Korea. It was not a comforting beginning.

To some it recalled a comparable lack of preparation in Douglas MacArthur's command before the start of the war with Japan, when he had systematically underestimated the ability of the Japanese to strike at American possessions in the Pacific, and then, because his own command structure was so poorly prepared, had allowed the bombers under his command at Wake Island to be destroyed by Japanese bombers while they sat on the ground *nine* long hours after the Pearl Harbor attack. "Few commanders of any nationality could have borne so large a responsibility for the United States military debacle in the Philippines in 1941–42 yet escaped any share of it," wrote the British historian Max Hastings. "Fewer still could have abandoned his doomed command on Bataan, and escaped to safety with his own court, complete even unto personal servants, and made good the claim that his own value to his country surpassed that of a symbolic sacrifice alongside his men." The rules that governed other men never really applied to Douglas MacArthur.

3

WHEN THE NORTH KOREANS crossed the thirty-eighth parallel in full force, General of the Army Douglas MacArthur's attention was then focused almost exclusively on political developments in Japan, where he was doing an exceptional job trying to shape a defeated country into a more egalitarian, democratic society. Right up to the beginning of World War II, Japan had reflected an odd combination of economic and military modernity blended with social and political feudalism. MacArthur was trying with considerable success to create balancing forces, to bring land reform, labor unions, and rights for women into play. He had been perfectly cast for the occasion—Japan after the defeat in the Pacific was like a nation whose god had failed and now sought a new, more secular one; MacArthur, if nothing else, had always wanted to be idolized, and now he had found an entire nation ready to see him as a kind of deity. His touch, for so instinctively autocratic and self-absorbed a man, had been surprisingly nimble in dealing with a defeated nation. He had been shrewd enough to work through the emperor, thus reinforcing the authority of both of them. Though his own instincts were more conservative than liberal and he was aligned with deeply conservative political elements in America, he had been a surprisingly liberal modern American deity in Japan. Though he had been and would continue to be a serious domestic critic of the New Deal, in Japan he had turned enthusiastically to a group of young liberal New Dealers and given them surprising freedom in shaping postwar Japan. They had had that freedom, their leader Charles Kades believed, in no small part because it was the right thing to do and created a better society, but also in part because the more they changed Japan from the old nation to the new, the greater MacArthur's role in the creation would be, the more it would be *his* Japan.

The changes in Japan, and the coming of a Japanese Peace Treaty, absorbed almost all of the general's working day. He was paying very little attention to the American troops under his command—the occupation army—by then a military force that bore only a passing resemblance to the formidable army that had defeated the Japanese in the Pacific. That his troops were under-strength, poorly equipped, and increasingly poorly trained did not seem to bother MacArthur. He paid even less attention to South Korea, the southern half of the former Japanese colony, liberated and divided by American and Russian troops in 1945, the Americans taking their sphere of influence in the south, the Russians theirs in the north. South Korea interested him so little that he had visited it but once—and then briefly—since it had been created. He had ignored the repeated pleas of General John Hodge, the American commander in South Korea who wanted the Supreme Commander for the Allied Powers (or SCAP), as MacArthur was officially known, far more involved there. Instead, MacArthur ordered the general to use his own best judgment. "I am not sufficiently familiar with the local situation to advise you intelligently, but I will support whatever decision you make in this matter," he said in reply to one of these requests.

It became clear that MacArthur wanted no part of Korea in the period from 1945 to 1950. There were countless cables coming across his desk from Hodge, pleading for his help or his advice: "I urgently request your active participation in my difficult position . . ." Faubion Bowers, who was a principal MacArthur aide in those days because of his ability to speak Japanese, remembered Hodge deciding on his own to come to see MacArthur, and being kept waiting for hours, hoping to see the general, only to be told that he was to take care of Korea himself. "I wouldn't put my foot in Korea. It belongs to the State Department," MacArthur told Bowers later as he was driven home. "They wanted it and got it. They have jurisdiction. I don't. I wouldn't touch it with a ten-foot barge pole. The damn diplomats make the wars and we win them. Why should I save their skin? I won't help Hodge. Let them help themselves." His single visit there had been for the inauguration of the newly installed South Korean president, Syngman Rhee, at which time he had told Rhee rather casually, if grandly—for he had checked with no one in Washington about this pledge—that the United States would defend South Korea if it was attacked, "as we would California."

His admirers and his staff were unanimous in describing his vigor and energy, rare for a man of seventy. Yet among those who were not part of his inner group, there were serious concerns about his age and health. Even as Japan's defeat became apparent in 1945, some senior military men had already begun to worry about him. General Joseph Stilwell, watching MacArthur accept the Japanese surrender aboard the USS *Missouri* in Tokyo Bay that September, had been struck by how badly his hands shook. At first, Stilwell thought it was nerves, but General Walter Krueger, one of MacArthur's senior officers, had assured him it was Parkinson's. Still, thought Stilwell, "it looked like hell." There were other signs that his health might be failing. His attention span seemed limited and sometimes there were significant lapses in it, and he was slow to understand the seriousness of a new challenge. His hearing was known to have slipped badly, and knowledgeable staff aides believed that the supreme commander did not readily hold staff meetings for just that reason. Others believed it was the reason that when visitors were granted audiences with him he tended toward monologues, because he could not hear what others were saying and could not easily engage in two-sided conversations. But older or not, able to work at the level demanded of a combat commander or not, he remained an icon, one with a vast store of political capital. There were all kinds of glitches in his long and often distinguished career, moments when he had been far less than a brilliant commander and his lesser, more vainglorious self had shown too readily, and others had paid a price for his failings, but he was in 1950 still a formidable figure, someone who had been a famous and daring commander as far back as World War I, had conducted his campaign against the Japanese in the Pacific during World War II with shrewd, careful use of his limited forces, and was, on the occasion of the outbreak of the Korean War, doing an admirable job of modernizing Japan.

If MacArthur had little interest in Korea, his attitude toward that unfortunate country was all too typical of his fellow countrymen. Korea was connected neither to the American political process nor to the American psyche. China had long fascinated Americans, many of whom felt a deep, if curious, paternalism toward the poor, struggling Chinese. Japan was alternately admired and feared. Korea, on the other hand, did not fascinate, or even interest, Americans. A missionary named Homer Hulbert wrote in 1906 that the Koreans "have been frequently maligned and seldom appreciated. They are overshadowed by China on the one hand in respect to numbers, and Japan on the other hand in respect to wit. They are neither good merchants like the one, nor good fighters like the other. And yet they are by far the pleasantest people in the East to live amongst. Their failings are such as flow in the wake of ignorance everywhere, and the bettering of their opportunities would bring swift betterment to their condition." In the ensuing four decades American interest in Korea had not increased greatly. The Russians had entered the Pacific War belatedly, and when the war ended abruptly with the use of the atomic bombs, Korea had been divided at the thirty-eighth parallel, almost as an afterthought, the division done in the most casual way at the last minute at the Pentagon. The first American commanders to arrive there, utterly unaware of how much the Koreans loathed their Japanese masters, and how cruel the Japanese occupation had been, had at first been willing to use the Japanese police forces to keep the Koreans in line. General Hodge, the first American general who commanded there after the war, a blunt, raw, direct man, had liked neither Korea nor the Koreans, whom he described as being "the same breed of cat as the Japanese." The American presence in Korea might have begun in the most casual, indeed careless way, but it brought a powerful new player into the orbit of a country whose geography, rather than its natural wealth, had made it for years the target of powerful, aggressive neighbors. What was new in an old equation, as the historian Bruce Cumings has pointed out, was the arrival of a fresh new power, the United States. It was there in no small part in the years after 1945 because the Russians were also there, and then, soon enough, because Korea's security was directly tied to Japan's security.

The marriage of Korea, or more accurately of South Korea, to the Americans, which started in 1945 and was more or less a shotgun affair, a product of the Cold War, was therefore not an easy one. It brought an angry client state, still bitter about its recently ended colonial period and embittered about being severed in half, under the hegemony of an awkward new superpower that was not at all sure it wanted to be in the business of empire. To the Koreans the end of World War II and Japanese colonialism had not brought, as so many had hoped, a great new breath of freedom and a chance to reconstruct their country to their own political contours. That where there had been only one Korea there were now two was a grievous injustice by itself in their eyes; rather than being able to shape their own destiny on their own terms, they had fallen once again under the control of others. The first thing that the people in the South realized was that their country, or more accurately their half country, was controlled by people who lived thousands of miles away across a vast ocean, and had almost no interest or knowledge of the country whose future they would now determine. It was in the beginning a relationship filled with tensions and misunderstandings. Only as the Cold War intensified did the relationship become one of genuine mutual value and interest. Without the threat of global Communism, America cared nothing about Korea; with that threat Americans were willing to fight and die for it.

Korea was a small, proud country that had the misfortune to lie in the path of three infinitely larger, stronger, more ambitious powers—China, Japan, and Russia. Each of them wanted to use it either as an offensive base from which to assault one of the others or as a defensive shield to negate the possible aggressive designs of the other two. Long before June 1950, Korea's formidable neighbors had all at some moment favored the right to invade Korea in what they thought of as a defensive move—a precautionary step—against one of their rivals. As the unfortunate geography of Poland placed it between Germany and Russia, so Korea's geography was to no small degree its fate. Syngman Rhee, the eventual president of South Korea, liked to cite an old Korean proverb that went: "A shrimp is crushed in the battle of the whales."

For much of its history the influence of China had fallen over Korea more heavily than that of other hostile countries, but the Sino-Japanese war of 1894–95 signaled the temporary end of Chinese influence there, as Japan, an ascending power, a nation that was industrializing quickly and was traditionally militaristic, began what was to become a formidable bid for regional domination—in effect the creation of a new Japanese empire. In 1896, Russia—its sheer size concealing a deep social, political, and economic rot—made a compact with an ever more aggressive Japan, dividing their influence over Korea at (ironically) the thirty-eighth parallel. If Russia was a nation that seemed more powerful than it actually was, Japan seemed *less* powerful than *it* was. Their agreement would prove the most temporary of solutions.

In February 1904, the Japanese struck against the Russian fleet, eventually destroying it at the Battle of the Tsushima Straits; that battle took place after the Japanese had inflicted comparable defeats on the Russian army in the Pacific and in parts of Russian-occupied Manchuria. The Japanese later justified their assault on Russia's forces in the Far East by pointing to the danger a Russified Korea held out for them. Rikitaro Fujisawa, a prominent Japanese political figure, quoted a friend as saying that the Japanese *had* to strike against the Russians, because "Korea lies like a dagger, ever pointed towards the heart of Japan," words that could have easily been spoken nearly half a century later, by the most senior American national security officials. Then he added in his own words, "Korea in the possession of Russia, or even a weak and corrupt Korea which might fall any time an easy prey to the Russian Eagle would place Japan's destiny in the hands of the unscrupulous 'Colossus of the North.' Japan could not accept such a fate. That the Russo-Japanese War was not only a defensive war for Japan but Japan's struggle for her very existence as an independent nation is too obvious to require either elucidation or explanation." It was a great way to justify an offensive war—the Koreans, not the devil, made them do it.

It seemed to be part of Korea's national destiny to have little say about its own future. The peacemaker in the Russo-Japanese War was not a Korean but the president of the United States, Theodore Roosevelt, who went on to win a Nobel Prize for his efforts, efforts that had very little to do with any concept of greater good for the Koreans. Roosevelt represented a new, ever more muscular America just beginning to manifest itself in a kind of subconscious imperialist impulse. He had been an enthusiastic advocate of the Spanish-American War in 1898, which had brought the United States the Philippines as a colony. Roosevelt was very much a man of his time: he believed in and in fact popularized the concept of the white man's burden, that is, the obligation of strong, dependable, worthy (Christian) Caucasian powers to rule the less reliable, less worthy non-white world, and he believed in the parallel duty of the non-white world to let itself be ruled. The one country he exempted from his view of Asian nations and peoples as essentially inferior was Japan. "The Japs interest me and I like them," he wrote a friend at the time. After all, they were, except in skin color, size, and shape of eyes, perilously like Anglo-Saxons—hardworking, disciplined, organized, muscular in their own way, and imperially aggressive.

Roosevelt was impressed with the Japanese as being the kind of can-do nation he could admire, "entitled to stand on an absolute equality with all the other peoples of the civilized world." All of this put Korea, in the words of Robert Myers, a writer and former intelligence officer with considerable expertise in Korean affairs, "in a position not unlike that of a newborn calf, defenseless before the Japanese imperial wolf." The only country that might have made a difference, given Korea's unfortunate geography, was the very distant United States. In fact, back in 1882 the kingdom of Korea had made a treaty with the United States (and some European nations as well) that called for them to come to Korea's defense if it was attacked. That aid was to remain altogether theoretical: Korea was too far away; the American Navy at the time of the Russo-Japanese War was pitifully small; and in any case, Teddy Roosevelt had his own priorities for Asia, and Korea was not one of them. The United States was not interested in helping Korea but in securing its own brand-new colonial domain in the Philippines. So with covert American agreement, the Japanese were allowed to control Korea ever more tightly, as a "protectorate" after the Russo-Japanese War, and then, in 1910, by open, brazen annexation—as a full-fledged Japanese colony.

Because he spoke such good English, the young Syngman Rhee had been chosen by some of his countrymen to visit Theodore Roosevelt in the summer of 1905 just as the president was about to negotiate the Russian-Japanese Peace Treaty. Rhee wanted Roosevelt's help in stopping Japan's colonization of his country. In the words of the journalist-historian Joseph Goulden, Roosevelt offered Rhee a dose of "polite and totally misleading doubletalk." He knew that the pro-Japanese elements who ran the Korean embassy in Washington would give Rhee no help; and he did not mention that, even as they were talking, Secretary of State William Howard Taft was on his way to Tokyo to work out a secret treaty giving the Japanese control of Manchuria and Korea, with the Japanese in return pledging the United States a free hand in the Philippines.

No wonder that Rhee eventually became, in the eyes of his American associates, so neurotic and distrustful. America betrayed him more than once and lied to him systematically. Eventually, the Japanese, who renamed Korea *Chosen*, initiated a brutal colonial reign that lasted almost forty years. The United States, Roosevelt later wrote in his memoirs, could not do "for the Koreans what they were utterly unable to do for themselves." The Japanese colonization of Korea would be an unusually cruel one, but it attracted little attention outside Korea's borders.

Rhee himself stayed on in America, received a remarkable education for a Korean of his generation, and became a one-man Korean truth squad, with just enough connections to a few well-placed Americans, many of them church-connected, to reach other, more politically influential figures. If those associations gave him a good deal of access, and allowed him to press the case for his country's freedom, he always fell short of genuine influence. He had attended graduate school at Princeton as a doctoral candidate in political science, becoming a favorite of its then president, Woodrow Wilson. Rhee was a regular at the informal social gatherings the Wilsons held in their home, where students came together around the Wilson family piano and sang. Rhee did not sing, but he liked to share in the warmth of an informal American evening, and Wilson seemed both to like and admire him, introducing him to strangers on occasion as "the future redeemer of Korean independence."

But the Wilson who presided at Princeton and the Wilson who presided over the United States a little later, and who eventually brought America into World War I, proved to be two very different men. The postwar Paris Peace Conference, which was where Wilson hoped to create a new world order, was among other things supposed to grant colonized countries the right of self-determination. No one was more excited about this prospect than Wilson's old friend and protégé Rhee: at this most august gathering the freedom of his country was going to be raised by his old mentor, who had once seemed to anoint him as the leader of a new, independent Korea. To Rhee, this was the moment he had been waiting for. He hoped to leave America for Paris, to lobby on behalf of his countrymen to his great friend, to loosen the Japanese fist. But Wilson wanted no part of him in Paris. The president, as it happened, needed Japan as a player in Asia, and besides, Japan had chosen sides well during the war, and so was one of the victorious allies, ready to inherit German rights in China. Rhee thus learned the first rule of global warfare: nations that ended up on the winning side got to keep their colonies; those on the losing side had to surrender them. The State Department was told not to give Rhee a passport.

*   *   *

IN JUNE 1950, then, there was no small degree of irony in the fact that Americans were now ready to fight and die for Korea. The United States valued Korea, not for its own sake, but because of U.S. fears of what would happen to a neighboring country—Korea's longtime oppressor, Japan—if America did not intervene and answer a Communist challenge. In the whimsical, mischievous way that history moves along, Japan was becoming a new ally, just as China had been a seemingly valiant ally but now was in the process of becoming an enemy.

But the prolonged period of Japanese colonialism had exacted a heavy price from the Koreans. It had destroyed any possibility of normal political evolution and modernization there—not just the sheer cruelty and oppression of the Japanese presence, but the fact that so many talented politicians had been arrested or murdered; while others, like Rhee and his future opponent Kim Il Sung, were driven into exile. Some in the South were contaminated as collaborationists by their connections to the Japanese. During World War II, as Robert Myers has pointed out, the people of the occupied nations of Europe always had the hope that help was coming, that the allies, who were mighty, were gathering and would end German domination on the continent. Koreans held on to no such hopes. Ten years, twenty years, twenty-five years passed, and there was no gathering force of nations determined to rescue the poor, subjugated Korean people and remove the Japanese from their land.

Only in December 1941, when Japan overreached and attacked American, British, and Dutch possessions in South and Southeast Asia, were there the first stirrings of hope, and those were slight, given that most of the early victories in the Pacific War belonged to the Japanese, and when the tide began to turn, little news of it filtered down to the Korean people. The Western allies were coming, if not for the Koreans, then for their own reasons, and in time their success would spell Japan's doom. But by 1945, the cynicism produced by the occupation had done its work: many people in the upper and middle classes had in differing degrees made their accommodations with the colonizers, accepting Japanese rule and becoming powerless, badly compromised parts of the Japanese power structure. Some Koreans had even begun to admire the Japanese, however cynically, for they were, whatever else, the first Asians to defeat the white rulers of much of the rest of Asia.

In 1945, Korea was virtually a country without political institutions, and without indigenous leadership. In the North, when the Red Army swept in, institutions were imposed instantly from the top down by the Russians, as was a new leader, Kim Il Sung. In the South, Rhee, who had spent most of his life in exile, would be the American horse, like it or not. He was then seventy years old, intense, egocentric, volatile, fiercely nationalistic, patriotic, virulently anti-Communist, and no less authoritarian; he was very much a democrat, so long as he had complete control of all the country's democratic institutions and no one else was allowed to challenge his will. He was what the Japanese and the Americans had made him: a lifetime of betrayal, prison sentences, political exile, and broken promises had changed and hardened him. He was one example of what his country's harsh modern history had done to an ambitious young political figure, as Kim Il Sung in a very different way was another example of the same tragic result.

Rhee had been a political prisoner as a young man and had barely missed being executed; he would eventually get a Harvard degree, and the Princeton PhD, but his lifetime was filled with hardships and disappointments that in many ways resembled the hardships and disappointments of his country. His essentially powerless status as an exile paralleled his country's powerless status as an orphaned nation in the eyes of the great powers. After gaining his doctorate, he had returned briefly to Korea, before spending the next thirty-five years in the United States. He became a professional supplicant, not the most healthy of conditions; he had lobbied constantly for a Korea free of colonial bondage with himself at its head. If he was the most passionate kind of nationalist, he was an equally relentless self-promoter: when he finally took power, his success tended to confirm his monomania.

When the war in the Pacific ended in 1945, Rhee had one great ace to play, and he had, by then, waited over three decades to play it—the support of the United States. Since the few Americans who were going to deal with postwar Korea had given almost no thought to the question of its postwar status, Rhee, with his longtime residency in the United States and his long years of lobbying, turned out to be the only Korean candidate with an American constituency. In addition, he had nurtured a long-standing connection to the Chinese Nationalists, who were exceptionally well connected in Washington. In Korea, as in China, the same people seemed to be searching for a leader who was both nationalist and a Christian; their nationalism had to meet Western religious and political standards.

Chiang Kai-shek's backing was the equivalent of a passport to influence in Washington. In fact, Rhee became known, for better or worse, both to admirers of Chiang and those who despised him, as Little Chiang. Unlike Chiang, he was a very serious Christian. Rhee had after all become a Christian in a land that was not Christian, and he had suffered for his faith on many occasions. To some of the Americans who backed him in those early years, his religious beliefs (and those of Chiang) were of great comfort—though Asian, these were men who were very much like them. When, in the years just before the Korean War, an American diplomat had made a critical comment about Chiang and Rhee to the influential John Foster Dulles, later to be Dwight D. Eisenhower's secretary of state, he had answered revealingly, "Well I'll tell you this. No matter what you say about them, these two gentlemen are modern day equivalents of the founders of the church. They are Christian gentlemen who have suffered for their faith."

It was Chiang, among others, who had recommended Rhee to Douglas MacArthur, and when Rhee finally returned to Korea to take up the country's presidency, he arrived in MacArthur's plane, in itself a defining political statement. The Americans, it seemed, had their man—or perhaps more accurately their man had them. Roger Makins, a senior British diplomat friendly to the United States, believed that the Americans in that period, reflecting an isolationist nation being pulled ever so reluctantly into a new role as a world power, always showed a propensity to go for an individual—someone they felt comfortable with. Choosing Rhee, Makins believed, reflected the fact that "Americans have always liked the idea of dealing with a foreign leader who can be identified and perceived as 'their man.' They are much less comfortable with movements." Those most comfortable with Rhee did not, however, include the Americans in Korea who actually had to deal with him on a daily basis, many of whom came to loathe him. General John Hodge, the unusually rough and undiplomatic commander of American troops in South Korea, despised Rhee. He considered him, as Clay Blair, the military historian, wrote, "devious, emotionally unstable, brutal, corrupt, and wildly unpredictable."

4

I N T H E N O R T H, Kim Il Sung had been installed with a good deal more foresight by his sponsors from the Soviet Union, who had had their eye on Korea for a much longer time. He arrived at the end of World War II through the dictate of Joseph Stalin and through the sheer muscle of the occupying Red Army. Because of that, from the start he employed the brutal model of the Soviet system, and was surrounded by Soviet advisers and sponsors. By the spring of 1950, Kim had been in power for almost five years; and, for at least two of them, he had been pushing, with ever greater aggressiveness, for his right to invade the South. That invasion was sure to be supported, so Kim promised the Russians, by a spontaneous national uprising all over the South. Two hundred thousand Southern Communists and patriots would take up arms as one against Syngman Rhee, who was, in a favorite phrase of the Communist vernacular of that era, the running dog of the American imperialists. There was, however, only one person who could give the green light for such an invasion—Stalin himself.

Of the three critical players on the Communist side of the Korean War, Kim Il Sung had the least legitimacy. Stalin, if he had not been the principal architect of the Russian Revolution, had at least been there from the beginning, a harsh, cruel enforcer who had systematically gathered ever greater power from those around him and, by the postwar years, had guided Soviet totalitarianism for almost a quarter of a century. He had gained immense stature from the victory of Russia's armies over Hitler's Germany, despite his own catastrophic miscalculations about Hitler's intentions, and perhaps even worse, his almost suicidal destruction of the Red Army, purging its high command and destroying its officer corps in the months before Hitler launched his invasion. Whatever his miscalculations, Stalin had become the symbolic leader of the Great Patriotic War, as the Russians called it. Those mistakes, which had allowed the Germans to come so close to defeating Russia, had, ironically enough, made him more of a hero to the Russian people, thereby strengthening his personal hold on his nation and melding its spiritual myths with his own myth of leadership. He came to embody not so much Russia's early defeats, but its very survival at Stalingrad, and then the final triumph of the Red Army in Berlin. That victory alone seemed to seal his greatness for ordinary Russians, making him nothing less than a modern incarnation of the legendary tsars and so, for better but mostly for worse, the principal figure of twentieth-century Russia.

Mao Zedong, in 1950 the leader of the revolutionary Chinese government that had come to power after years of oppression, strife, and civil war, might have been if anything an even grander figure on the historical landscape. He was the principal architect of the Chinese revolution and led it through long, difficult days, often against fearsome odds, saving it from the combined forces of Chiang Kai-shek and various warlords. He was both political and military strategist in the Chinese civil war and the creator of a new kind of warfare where politics and war were constantly linked and blended, and where the military side was always an instrument of the political side. His adaptations of Marxist beliefs to a peasant society and his theory of revolution would have a far greater resonance internationally in the second half of the twentieth century than anything Stalin had ever done. By the 1960s, Stalin, his crimes against his own people and against those in Eastern Europe now public, would seem something of an embarrassment to bright, idealistic young leftists in the West and in the underdeveloped world, a leader they preferred to avoid talking about, who represented little but brute power. By contrast Mao, for a long time, until the darker side of his personality and the terror he had let loose on his own people became better known, was a far more romantic figure, more like the personification of *revolution*. In those years, he, far more than Stalin, was seen as the leader of the world of the have-nots against the world of the haves.

Kim Il Sung was something of a contradiction, a fierce nationalist who was the creation of an imperial power, the Soviet Union. He was a man who had seethed with the nationalist fervor produced by Japanese colonization and had become, because of that colonial era, a dedicated Communist and resilient guerrilla fighter, yet he was also from the very beginning almost completely an instrument, and a quite dutiful one at that, of Soviet policy. Others looked at him and saw little but the Soviet hand on his shoulder; he looked at himself and saw the purest embodiment of Korean nationalism. Certainly, the era in which he had come of age helped shape him. To Kim there was no contradiction between being a Korean patriot, a dedicated Communist, and an instrument of the Russians.

All of Korea had been fertile terrain for rebellion because of the Japanese. As their occupation stretched on, a certain fatalism settled in among much of the educated middle class, and many members of the privileged classes reluctantly made their peace with the Japanese and prospered as collaborators.

A large number of them would emerge after the war as influential players in what became South Korea, both in business and the military. By contrast, many Koreans whose roots were in the peasantry, who hated the Japanese and had no economic reason to make accommodations, were pulled toward a deeply alienated left. There was, after all, much to feel alienated about, for the Japanese colonization of Korea had been unusually harsh. The Koreans were regarded by the Japanese as a lower species of humanity, all the more inferior for having been so readily conquered.

The Japanese, sure of their imperial mission and their superiority as a race, had set out to destroy almost all vestiges of Korean independence. What they wanted was nothing less than to obliterate Korean culture, starting with the language. The official language of Korea was proclaimed to be Japanese; in schools, lessons were to be taught in Japanese. The Japanese language test book was called *The Mother-Tongue Reader*. Koreans were to take Japanese names. The Korean language was to become a regional dialect, nothing more. What the Japanese, like so many would-be colonialists, were to learn, of course, was that if you want to make something valuable to a conquered people, you need but suppress it. Only then did such ordinary things—history, language, local religions, things so easy to take for granted—gain real meaning. The divisions caused by the Japanese colonization went much deeper into the society than most foreigners realized. The country was not merely split at the thirty-eighth parallel, but in some ways the separation ran through the entire population—in effect it had to do with which side any Korean had been on in those heartbreaking times. It helped create all kinds of great internal divisions, ones that would collide during the Korean War. It was not only a border crossing war, the North invading the South, but something more as well, for there were ghosts from the recent colonized past there, and so longstanding political struggles that had simmered for decades were at stake too. Both sides were out to settle arguments that had, in different ways and under different labels, been on the table for nearly half a century. The unusual harshness of the Japanese rule had also ensured that the nationalists could barely exist on native soil. In a way, much of the story of contemporary Korea flowed from that fact—those patriots who stayed would generally be tainted in some way or another by association with the Japanese, while those who went into exile were also tainted, or at the very least profoundly affected, by association with the foreign powers—Russian, Chinese, or American—who housed them.

As that hopelessly poor, occupied, and colonized Korea had sent Syngman Rhee into his mendicant's exile in America, so on a very different track it had produced Kim Il Sung, whose own family had suffered because of the economic imbalance of the earlier order. Kim had been politicized in his childhood, gone into exile as a boy, and spent much of what should have been his youth struggling against the Japanese. He represented in his own way the rage and bitterness of the country's recent history.

He was born Kim Song Ju in the village of Nam-ri on April 15, 1912, just two years after the Japanese began their colonial era in Korea. If one imagines some child of modern Europe growing up in Holland or France under a Nazi occupation that lasted for the first thirty-three years of his life, Kim's anger and his rigidity can be better understood. His paternal grandparents lived in a village named Mangeyondai, which eventually became known as his family home. In time he claimed that his great-grandfather had been one of the leaders of an assault on an armed American merchant ship, the *General Sherman*, that had made the mistake of straying too far up the Taedong River in 1866, and then the even bigger mistake of allowing itself to become grounded, whereupon local Koreans stormed the beached boat and hacked the foreigners to pieces. Whether or not Kim's relative was actually involved is another question, for Kim was always exceptionally creative in upgrading his autobiography—a task he took very seriously.

His father, Kim Hyong Jik, came from the peasant class, attending, though not finishing, middle school. At the age of fifteen, the senior Kim married the daughter of the local schoolmaster, then worked as an elementary schoolteacher, an herbal doctor, and on occasion, a grave keeper. His wife, Kang Pan Sok, was seventeen, two years older than her husband. Hers were educated people. There were schoolteachers and Christian ministers in her lineage. Her people were thought to be less than enthusiastic about the wedding because Kim's station was lower and he had only two acres of land to his name. When Kim Il Sung was born, his father was only seventeen and still lived in his own parents' home. There were Christian missionary connections on both sides of Kim's family, though in the cleansing of his curriculum vitae, he later claimed that his family members were nonbelievers and that his father went to church only because the Presbyterians offered a missionary school. "Believe in a Korean God, if you believe in one!" he later quoted his father as saying. While the truth of this is unknowable, it was true that in many underdeveloped places in the world, part of the allure of missionaries was the chance they offered for a better education and in time a certain economic advantage. Of the fact that Kim's family was political there was no doubt; his father and two of his uncles were put in jail at different times for independence activities. In 1919, when he was seven, the family, like thousands of highly nationalistic Koreans, became part of a great migration moving across the country's northern border into

Manchuria, trying to escape Japanese rule. They settled in the town of Jiandao, where there was a large Korean community, and the young Kim attended Chinese schools, learning the language.

When he was eleven, his father sent him back to Korea, so he could have a better sense of his own country and language, even if it was never to be spoken publicly. There he lived for a time with his maternal grandparents, before returning to Manchuria, where he attended a military academy founded by Korean nationalists. Later, he would claim that he was too radical for the school and left after only six months. In any case, he soon moved on to Jilin, a town with a large number of Korean émigrés—and a great many Japanese agents as well. These were fertile times for revolutionaries. He and his friends would argue, Kim later said, about which should come first, the revolution to end the economic cruelty, or the revolution to end the Japanese occupation. They also discussed whether the revolution could come first in Korea, or whether the Koreans would have to wait until Japan itself was taken over by Communist forces. Like so many Koreans of his generation, he became more radical as time passed and the hardships inflicted by the Japanese seemed more permanent. His father died in these years and his mother began to work as a seamstress. Kim himself attended a Chinese middle school, where he encountered Shang Yue, a Communist teacher and party member who took an interest in him, opening his own library to the young man. (Shang was soon fired because of his radical views and eventually became one of the leading historians of Communist China.)

Kim moved steadily to the left, becoming a junior founding member of a Communist youth group. In the fall of 1929, at the age of seventeen, he was arrested by the local Manchurian authorities and imprisoned. He was quite lucky, notes biographer Bradley Martin, that he was not turned over to the Japanese. Six months later, he was released, and the next year he joined the Communist Party—the *Chinese* Communist Party. Somewhere in that period, it was believed, he took the nom de guerre Kim Il Sung. His critics claimed he stole the name from another noted Korean patriot famed for fighting as a guerrilla, and so enjoyed a ready-made reputation as something of a Korean Robin Hood. Because of this alleged switch in identities, some detractors were convinced that Kim's entire service as a guerrilla fighting in Manchuria was a lie. That was not the case: as in all other things, once he came to power, he exaggerated his role as a guerrilla leader, but he had been a serious opponent of the Japanese starting around 1931, and during those years he had lived a difficult, dangerous life as a guerrilla leader, just barely staying ahead of Japanese troops who were intent on hunting him down.

That meant that by the time he was twenty, he had taken up arms against the Japanese, and by the spring of 1932 he had his own guerrilla band. Kim and others like him were part of what was known as the Kapsan Group, named after Manchuria's Kapsan Mountains, where he and other Korean Communists had relocated after fleeing their country. The Japanese, their hunger for domination in East Asia growing with each success, were extending their colonial mandate into Manchuria—giving it the new name, as it was Japanized, of Manchukuo. Kim's was one of many groups fighting the Japanese, some of them Korean and some of them Chinese. The guerrilla struggle against the Japanese went on for much of a decade, a war with few victories for the guerrillas. The Japanese had many more troops, far better weapons, and—so it seemed to the beleaguered Koreans—unlimited supplies of ammunition. They also had the ability to offer the local peasants a painful choice: handsome rewards for information on the guerrillas, who were sometimes their friends and countrymen, or, if they failed to cooperate, death.

From roughly 1934 to 1940, the Japanese brought ever larger forces into the area and used increasingly brutal methods of persuasion on the local population. They finally ground the guerrillas down and drove them into the eastern part of the Soviet Union. During this period, Kim's band joined what was called the Northeast Anti-Japanese United Army, commanded by a Chinese general, Yang Jingyu. The job of the guerrillas was not so much to gain victories as to harass the Japanese, and make each of their moves into China a little more difficult. Kim's men were almost all Korean, but in any real sense he was at first operating under the auspices of the Chinese Communists.

Of the importance of his leadership in that period there was no doubt. His title became grander—battalion and finally division commander—though it is believed that he never led more than three hundred men into battle. But Kim was gaining notoriety. On the Communist side there was growing respect for him as a durable, dependable, and valuable guerrilla leader; from the Japanese perspective, he was one of the most wanted Korean guerrilla leaders of the era; by 1935, the Japanese had put a price on his head, and yet he continued to elude them. He was regarded as tough, pragmatic, and from the viewpoint of his superiors, first the Chinese and later the Russians, ideologically trustworthy. The importance of the last quality could not be underestimated, given the fact that though there were powerful ideological bonds between him and his superiors, there were serious national differences, and thus inevitable suspicions.

When General Yang was finally captured and killed by the Japanese in 1940, Kim became for a brief time the most wanted guerrilla in the region, with the highest price on his head, 200,000 yen. But with the Japanese forces becoming stronger and stronger, it was also time for retreat. Sometime in this period, probably around 1940, he finally came under Soviet command and tutelage.

By 1942, he had been inducted into the Soviet Army and sent to a training camp near the village of Voroshilov in the eastern part of the Soviet Union. He soon became a member of a secret battalion of the Soviet Army, the Eighty-eighth Special Independent Sniper Brigade, its job essentially reconnaissance of those Japanese forces that had moved onto Soviet territory (though the Soviet Union and Japan were not formally in a state of war). He was a captain at the start and later a battalion commander in the brigade. Given how authoritarian their army was, he was in all ways a Soviet soldier and a de facto Soviet citizen. There were about two hundred men in his unit, ethnic Koreans, though some of them had grown up completely under the Russian hand. All of them were very heavily politicized, the process of indoctrination being as important to the Russians as any lessons in military tactics—political truth always preceded military ability. Sometime during World War II, Kim apparently visited Moscow. The Soviets saw his battalion as one not to fight the Japanese head-on, but to be used for various other roles as the war neared its end and their forces moved eastward.

Kim, like any Korean of his generation, knew that the liberation from the Japanese could not be done without outside help. To him—and he now wore the uniform of a Soviet officer—the Russians were a greatly preferred sponsor to the Chinese, for the Chinese had played a larger, unwanted role in Korea's history than the Russians, and Moscow was farther away than Beijing. Besides, by 1944, the Russians looked like sure winners, and to be major postwar players, while Mao Zedong's revolutionary movement was still largely confined to an impoverished region of northwest China. In addition, the Soviet model seemed especially attractive to would-be Communist leaders from the underdeveloped world, because the Russians had actually *done* it, had completed their revolution, defeated their enemies, and in addition had seemingly managed to modernize an archaic state. So Kim became something brand-new, a modern Korean patriot and, at the same time, a dedicated, doctrinaire Soviet loyalist. Others might sense a major contradiction there between nationalism and Soviet authoritarianism, but he did not. He was a man who did not doubt the great Communist cause or, more accurately, *causes*—theirs, and his as well. In the beginning the two were the same for him; what was good for the Soviets was good for him—and for his Korea.

The quick end to the war caught almost everyone by surprise, the Russians as much as the Americans. Korea was instantly and tentatively divided at the thirty-eighth parallel. In came the Red Army—not led by the Eighty-eighth Sniper Brigade, for Russian troops, not Koreans, were to get the credit for the liberation. The Korean wing of the Red Army would be allowed in only a few weeks later. In the beginning, Kim was the ultimate dependent. He had no other ticket to leadership than the Russians, and that was the way Stalin preferred it in the Communist world, all too aware as he was that men with real political constituencies could become difficult and begin to think that they actually were men of true independence. Better to take someone who fit your needs, announce that he was a hero, create a mythic if partially inauthentic history for him, and then install him in power.

That was what they did with Kim Il Sung. He did not need to be charismatic, and he most assuredly was not. The party did not need charismatic figures in its satellite states. Yugoslavia's Communist ruler, Josip Broz Tito, and Mao Zedong, both of whom Stalin was always dubious about because of their considerable achievements, would eventually prove how dangerous it was to back men of exceptional accomplishment who were powerful national figures. There were no ideological problems with Kim: they had been molding him for years, he had passed all kinds of secret tests, and he was a true believer. What the Russians said about the West, about capitalism, and about Korea dovetailed with what Kim knew from personal experience. Years later, long after Stalin's death, after schism upon schism had torn at the Communist world, Kim remained the last great Stalinist in power: rigid, doctrinaire, inflexible, a man who believed all the old truths even as so many of them had turned out to be false. They were not lies, at least not in Korea, because he could, with the hand and the power of the dictator, make them truths. In the end he managed to create one of the most tightly controlled, durable, and draconian societies—one of the most truly *Stalinist* societies—in the world. If Joseph Stalin had been born in Korea and had come to power there in the same era, he would have ruled almost exactly like Kim Il Sung and survived just as Kim did, till death did him part.

North Korea inevitably became a hagiographer's paradise and Kim Il Sung its one modern legend. There would be no flattery too shameless to be used in describing his wartime heroics, no obstacle that he had not overcome almost single-handedly, no Japanese battalion he had not destroyed all by himself, no other guerrilla fighter whose deeds were worthy of recounting, no sun that had ever risen over his country without his own personal assistance. In North Korea there was a revolution, but it had been imposed on the people. The power that had deeded the country over to the Communists was not, as in China (and soon in Indochina), the power of revolutionary ideas executed brilliantly and harshly against a colonial or neocolonial order during a prolonged and exhausting struggle that had demanded the support of the population. It was, instead, the raw power of the Red Army, and the decisions were all made back in Moscow, where Kim fitted his sponsor's needs. He was young; he was brave; he had been well indoctrinated. He had no other sponsors; in blunt terms, he owed them big-time. In his favor was his lack of a political past—there was nothing to undo, and no power base of his own. He could in a sense be created from scratch, made into anything the Soviets wanted him to be. What he became in the end was something almost unique in the world, reflecting the cruelty of a Korean childhood, the colonialism of the Japanese, and the isolation and paranoia that afflicted many of his generation in Korea: a serious if embittered Korean patriot, but a patriot who was also a truly xenophobic, narrow-gauge Korean nationalist, and who by the time of his death was cut off from almost all other world leaders, including those in the Communist world.

Those who might have seemed more likely candidates to lead North Korea, at least to outsiders unfamiliar with how Stalin operated, were in many cases automatically eliminated for their very independence. Some Koreans who had fought alongside Mao's troops for too long a time, no matter how remarkable their wartime activities, were considered tainted by their very closeness to the Chinese. Others were perceived as having ideas and dreams too different from those of the men in the Kremlin. Hyon Chun Hyok, a prominent member of the Korean Communist Party, was soon judged to be too independent and was mysteriously assassinated in late September 1945. He was seated in a truck, beside Cho Man Sik, also a popular figure, when the assassin fired. Clearly one Korean politician was being removed from play and another was being put on warning. It was at virtually the same time as Hyon's assassination that Kim Il Sung was first sighted in Pyongyang, wearing the uniform of a Red Army major.

KIM MIGHT BE their man, but he was quite an unfinished politician, and he cut a disappointing figure to those Koreans who hungered for someone with more obvious credentials to lead them, and did not want any foreign power, no matter how welcome initially for replacing the Japanese, to bestow a leader on them. The Russians apparently chose to unveil Kim Il Sung first at a small dinner party held at a Pyongyang restaurant in early October 1945. Kim was, one Russian general told the assemblage, a great Korean patriot who had fought valiantly against the Japanese. Among others attending was the far better known Cho Man Sik, a nonviolent nationalist, known as the Gandhi of Korea. Aware of just how vulnerable he was, Cho was moving as deftly as he could in a political situation that, once again, the Koreans themselves did not control. He appeared at the dinner as a show of accommodation to the Russians. Part of his job was to welcome Kim. Though he was a figure with a far larger constituency, Cho arrived—in Russian eyes—with too much baggage from the past and was not ideologically trustworthy to the newest occupiers of Korea. Bourgeois nationalist was the category the Russians put him into, and it was not an enviable pigeonhole. A bourgeois nationalist was someone who did not understand that all the important decisions were going to be made in Moscow. Perhaps if he had played it right and been genuinely subservient, Cho might have had some brief value to them as a figurehead at the top, carefully isolated from the real levers of power. But as an independent politician, Cho had no chance. General Terenti Shtykov, Stalin's man on location, the Tsar of Korea as he was then known in Pyongyang, thought Cho too anti-Soviet and anti-Stalin, and reported as much to Moscow.

The dinner in early October was hardly a success. The other Korean politicians present were underwhelmed by Kim's youth and lack of grace. The more crucial introduction—the public one—came in mid-October, at a mass rally in the Northern capital, and the day proved something of a disappointment to a large crowd eager for the introduction of an important Korean nationalist. The people had apparently expected to see and hear a venerable leader, who had served their cause for many years, and who would reflect their own passion for a country now officially free from foreign domination. But it was a Russian show. Kim spoke flatly, in a monotone, in words written by the Russians, and what the crowd heard was a young, rather inarticulate politician with a "plain, duck-like voice." One witness thought his suit too small and his haircut too much like that of "a Chinese waiter." But what really bothered many in the crowd was his adulation of Stalin and the Soviet Union. All praise went to the mighty and wondrous Red Army. Here they were, hoping for distinctly *Korean* words of freedom, and his words were reflecting a new kind of political obedience, Korean words bent to Russian needs, too much of "the monotonous repetitions which had [already] worn the people out." There are two very different photos, each of which tells its own truth about that occasion. In the first, Kim, looking young and anxious, is flanked by at least three senior Soviet generals; in the second, doctored version, produced later as Kim was re-creating his own mythic story, one of greater personal independence, he is on the same podium, the angle is slightly different, and the three Russian generals have magically disappeared. Cho Man Sik's days were already numbered. By early 1946 he had disagreed with the Russians on a number of things important to a Korean nationalist, and had thus become in their eyes even more of a reactionary. General Shtykov had sought and gotten Stalin's permission to purge him. Soon after, he was put under what was ever so gently called protective custody, in a hotel in Pyongyang. No one was allowed to see him. In fact, no one ever saw him again.

Kim Il Sung finally held power over half a nation, but he was hardly that great or commanding a figure on the world stage, or even for that matter the Communist one. He lacked the far greater legitimacy of Mao Zedong, who had come to power on his own with little Soviet help, or of Ho Chi Minh, the

Communist leader in Indochina then mounting a military attack against the French colonialists, the man who became the very embodiment of indigenous Vietnamese nationalism. Instead, for almost a decade after the liberation of Korea, Kim, as Bradley Martin has noted, was "to play for his Russian mentors the role of consummate company man, flattering them and carrying out their instructions as they rewarded him by granting him more and more power and autonomy." Kim came quickly to understand and to use the instruments of the modern totalitarian state, police power and fear. Like Stalin, he knew how to divide and conquer, and how to remove his enemies, and he knew Stalin's great truth: that no one, no matter how seemingly loyal, could ever really be considered trustworthy.

Kim quickly grasped, as Stalin and Mao before him had, the need for a national cult of personality, almost one of worship—and in the future he would rival both men in that department. Already a biography, published in 1948, elevated him above all other Korean guerrilla leaders who fought the Japanese. He was "our nation's greatest patriotic hero, and the sun of our people's hopes." The Japanese imperialists, the biography added, "hated General Kim Il Sung the most among thirty million Koreans." Less than a year after he had first returned to Korea, a poem, "A Song of General Kim Il Sung," was published that signaled what was to come: "The snowy winds of Manchuria/ the long, long nights of the forest/ Who is the timeless partisan, the peerless patriot/ the beneficent liberator of the worthy masses/ Great Sun of democratic new Korea?"

By early 1950, he had systematically taken control of all of the levers of power. The great problem in his mind was that he ruled only half a country. Above all else, he longed to unleash his increasingly powerful, Soviet-trained, Soviet-equipped, well-disciplined army to invade, and to his mind liberate, the South, where hundreds of thousands awaited his strike. He would turn two Koreas into just one. When the North Koreans finally moved on June 25, their early successes seemed to validate his predictions. Because they were doing so well in the beginning, Kim Il Sung and his top officials continued to treat the representatives of Communist China with striking disdain, bordering on contempt. On July 5, Stalin had suggested that the Chinese send nine divisions to the Chinese side of the Yalu River just in case. The Chinese were already thinking the same way; they were not nearly as confident as Kim of what the Americans would do. In fact, a few days earlier Zhou Enlai had assigned one of his most trusted men, Zhai Junwu, to Pyongyang to strengthen China's ties with the North Koreans. Zhai arrived on July 10 and met immediately with Kim, who told him, "If you need anything else just look for me at any time." Kim in turn deputized one of his top people to give Zhai daily briefings, and with that the North Koreans cut Zhai out of the loop. The briefings turned out to be virtually useless, about what you could get from the local foreign news services. A request on the part of the Chinese leadership to send a group of senior Chinese officers to study the battlefield was rejected. Kim was sure there would be no need for their help. Things were going that well.

5

THE SOUTH KOREAN troops were not nearly as well trained or as well prepared. South Korea might well one day be a much stronger, far more dynamic society, but in those first few years, it was a less organized, more chaotic one, and the Army reflected the government. The officer ranks at the top were riddled with corruption. The ROK soldiers lacked motivation and were armed largely with leftover, worn-out World War II weapons. They had little in the way of artillery, almost no armored vehicles, and next to nothing in the way of fighter bombers, because Washington had feared that if it gave Syngman Rhee his weapons wish list, he would order his army to head north the next day. All this reflected the immense uneasiness that existed between Rhee—the most irascible, contentious, and independent of totally dependent clients—and the men who thought of themselves as his sponsors. Almost pathologically anti-Communist, Rhee wanted more than anything to go to war against the North (or, perhaps better still, to bait the richer, more powerful Americans into going to war for him). His goal was the mirror reverse of Kim's: to create by any means a unified, independent, non-Communist Korea that he would rule. It was another version of the difficult and repetitive lessons the United States was to learn in Asia and had learned first with Chiang: with an Asian leader the Americans had helped install in this new postcolonial era, the more he was in all ways dependent on the United States, the more difficult the relationship was likely to be, because as he was dependent, he would ache to make moves that would prove his independence and would resent what might be considered control on the Americans' part.

As the hierarchical and authoritarian In Min Gun reflected the North Korea of 1950, so the ROKs reflected the troubled nation they represented—a subjugated, semifeudal society still struggling with the burdens of a colonial, feudal past, emerging awkwardly, slowly, and seemingly incompetently from that past, under a volatile, authoritarian leader who believed himself the ultimate democrat. The process of modernization in Korea would come, but it would come more slowly at first in the South than the North, where it came quickly but where it was a hollow, soulless kind of modernization, one that was inflicted on the population from the top down, a Sovietization of the nation's political, economic, and security apparatus. In the South, it was an infinitely more difficult, more complicated process. In fact, it took the invasion to help South Korea find both form and purpose. Fifty years later, the South would be an admirable, industrially vibrant, ever more democratic society, while the North remained an arid, authoritarian, Sovietized state, surprisingly like the one that existed when the war started.

In June 1950, what existed in the South was the most marginal kind of army fighting to defend the most marginal kind of country, a nation that did not yet really exist. The South Korean soldiers were mainly raw, illiterate kids pulled more often than not unwillingly off streets and farms and told they were soldiers. Most went into battle almost completely untrained. The level of desertion during that first year of the war was staggering—a battle would begin, and vast numbers of ROKs would simply disappear, presumably killed or missing in action, only to show up weeks or months later, usually without their weapons. The officer corps had some remarkably brave young men, but it also became, as Clay Blair noted, "a haven for too many venal opportunists who used their newly acquired power for personal gain. Among this element, theft, bribery, blackmail and kickbacks were commonplace." As a modern army, the ROKs, like South Korea itself, had a long way to go on that June day.

But in June 1950 no one responsible for the ROK Army was talking about what poor shape it was in. Quite the contrary. The level of self-deception about the quality of this army was surprisingly high among the American advisers and senior people in the Korean Military Advisory Group. (This advisory group had as its formal acronym KMAG, which soon, among American combat troops who fought alongside the ROKs, would be sardonically—and inevitably—retranslated as Kiss My Ass Good-bye.) The same self-deceptions would, a decade later, be repeated in shockingly similar ways in Vietnam as all too many senior American officers, men who knew better, publicly described the indigenous army as the best in Asia. In both Korea and Vietnam, Americans feared in all too many instances that if they told the truth—that they were advisers to a badly trained army whose fighting abilities were at best dubious—they would not get their own promotions.

General William Lynn Roberts, who had finished his tour as the head of KMAG in the weeks just before the war started, was a rare exception, writing a 2,300-word letter to his superior, Lieutenant General Charles Bolté on the Joint Chiefs of Staff, in March 1949, on exactly what dismal shape the ROKs were in. But because the United States was pulling its own combat units out of Korea for budgetary reasons, the public line would be very different: the Korean

Army had turned the corner and its men were better equipped than the In Min Gun. That was how Bolté testified to a congressional committee in June 1949. Things had, he added, progressed to a point where American units could be safely withdrawn. Almost no one involved in training the ROKs believed that. In the weeks before he left for home in June 1950, Roberts himself bowed to the new Pentagon position and started a publicity campaign designed to sell the excellence of the South Korean forces. Most of his subordinates in the KMAG knew it was, sadly, not true. A KMAG report sent to the Pentagon on June 15, 1950, ten days before the invasion, pointed out that the ROKs existed on a bare subsistence level. Much of their gear and many of their weapons were useless. They could defend themselves against attack for at most fifteen days. "Korea is threatened with the same disaster that befell China," the report concluded. How bad the situation was, hardly a secret throughout the Army because of back-channel information networks, caused Major General Frank Keating, ticketed by the Pentagon to replace General Roberts, to retire rather than take the assigned slot.

General Roberts had been especially worried about the North Korean Air Force of more than one hundred Russian planes. But surprisingly, as a former tank commander, he had not worried nearly as much about their armored units, having concluded that tanks were not very important in a country so self-evidently ill-suited to tank warfare. He was right; it *was* poor tank country—and American superiority in tank production and tank warfare would not, later in the war, be as decisive as it might have been elsewhere. But in the immediate term he was wrong, for the North Korean tanks, much more than airpower, proved to be the decisive weapon in those first few weeks, especially against a tankless force armed with impotent, outmoded bazookas. For ordinary infantrymen, no matter how well trained, there was nothing more terrifying than fighting against tanks without tanks of your own or adequate antitank weapons. In that sense, it was not the tanks themselves but simply word that they were coming that spread panic among the South Korean troops in those early critical days. "For an experienced tanker like Roberts, who knew first hand the terror the German panzers had evoked among some tankless infantry in the [Battle of the] Bulge, his apparent indifference to the NKPA [North Korean People's Army] armored forces was simply inexplicable," Clay Blair wrote.

The T-34 was no longer the most modern tank in the Russian arsenal, having been replaced by the Joseph Stalin III, but it was nonetheless an awesome piece of machinery, and the North Koreans had 150 of them. The T-34s had the capacity to dominate any battle in which they appeared in those first few weeks. Some ten years before, the T-34 had played a critical role in the defense of Moscow against the Nazis. General Heinz Guderian, who had commanded the German panzer divisions that had swept so easily across Poland in 1939, had called it "the best tank in the world." When it had first appeared on the battlefields of Russia in 1942, the Russians finally began to gain parity with the Germans. It had a low-sloping silhouette, which often had the effect of deflecting enemy shells; it was durable, and it was fast, with a top speed of thirty-two miles per hour. The T-34 also had an unusually wide tread that kept it from getting stalled in mud and ice, and it possessed an unusually large fuel tank of one hundred gallons that allowed it to go up to 150 miles without refueling. It weighed thirty-two tons, had an 85mm cannon, two 7.62mm machine guns, and very heavy armor plate. Opposing the T-34s, the South Koreans and their American advisers had only old 2.36-inch rocket launchers that had not been particularly good even in World War II. Brigadier General Jim Gavin, who had done a study after the war that cast doubt on their efficiency, thought the basic German rocket launcher infinitely better during that war. Now, five years later, it turned out that the 2.36 bazooka shells not only bounced off the skins of the North Korean tanks, but sometimes did not even explode. No wonder that, in those early days, the T-34 broke the back of any ROK resistance. By chance, the Americans had just finished work on a new, much improved 3.5-inch bazooka. The ammunition for it had gone into production on June 10, 1950. On July 12, the first of the new bazookas and instructors assigned to teach the troops how to use them arrived in Korea. When that happened, the immense advantage the In Min Gun enjoyed began to disappear.

The In Min Gun had struck against the weakest point in the greater defense perimeter of a would-be superpower, one still undecided on what its real national security responsibilities were going to be. Not surprisingly, the ROKs managed to hold few positions against the furious Communist onslaught. It all fell apart very quickly: the In Min Gun took the South Korean capital, Seoul, some sixty miles south of the thirty-eighth parallel on June 27, just two days into their offensive, and the retreating South Korean troops barely had time to blow the bridges over the Han River to give themselves a moment's breathing space.

Part
Three

Washington Goes to War

6

WHEN WORD OF the North Korean invasion reached Washington, it was late Saturday evening and the American government, which did not then operate eighteen hours a day seven days a week, was scattered. The president, a man with a great fondness for train travel, had dedicated a new airport—Baltimore Friendship—on Saturday and then flown home to Independence, Missouri. Dean Acheson, the secretary of state, was on his farm in Maryland, and the other key figures in the government were doing the most banal of weekend things. Acheson had been notified of the North Korean assault by subordinates, and after checking carefully, he alerted Truman. ("Mr. President, I have very serious news. The North Koreans have invaded South Korea.") Truman wanted to return to Washington immediately, but Acheson held him off—the information so far was scant. Besides, a late-night flight to Washington, with its special sense of urgency, could create a sense of alarm in other countries, Acheson believed. Still, Acheson emphasized that this one had the feel of the real thing.

For the next thirty-six hours, news from Korea would reach Washington only in spurts. Perhaps the most important early signal of how serious things were came from John Foster Dulles and John Allison, who cabled Truman and Acheson on Sunday morning from Tokyo to say that if the South Koreans could not hold, then the United States should intervene. "To sit by while Korea is overrun by unprovoked armed attack would start a disastrous chain of events leading most probably to world war." Coming as it did under Dulles's name, the cable was also a reminder that there were always political considerations to these issues, not that Truman needed any political pressure on this one—his responses were instinctive, almost primal, and politics seemed not to matter to him at first.

The moment Truman heard about the invasion, he began to prepare for his return to Washington. Still, he was careful not to vary his schedule. That Sunday morning he visited his brother Vivian's farm as originally planned. Then, in mid-afternoon, he flew back for the first of a series of marathon meetings with his top military and civilian advisers. The first decision—to use American air and sea power in Korea to protect American dependents—would, as the North Koreans continued south at an accelerating pace and as South Korean forces crumbled, culminate in a fateful decision by week's end to send in American ground troops.

The Harry Truman who flew back to Washington on the afternoon of June 25, 1950, was a man of considerable confidence. He was no longer in Franklin Roosevelt's shadow, and he had already tested himself before the American people in the grandest competition of them all, a presidential election, and triumphed in a great upset. He was increasingly confident of his ability to make decisions and he liked most of the men around him—George Catlett Marshall, Dean Acheson, Omar Bradley, and Averell Harriman, who had been running errands for him in Europe but was soon to be a troubleshooter with a wider mandate, a man of exceptional value. He was growing ever closer to Acheson, his secretary of state, and they were soon to forge a relationship virtually unique in modern political annals. He did not doubt that he was up to the job. There was no burden from the past, no inner voice that wondered what Franklin Roosevelt might have done. Harry Truman, whatever else, did not look back.

In a way, the critical decisions on Korea had been made before his plane even landed. Almost all of his top advisers knew which way they were going to come down, as did Truman. To a man, the top people in the National Security Council regarded the North Korean crossing as a flagrant violation of the United Nations charter. One country had invaded another, and if the Communist leaders on the other side of the world thought it would be viewed in Washington the way the civil war in China had been, they were badly mistaken. Instead the reaction was purely generational among these men whose view of national security had been molded by World War II; the North Korean action stirred memories of another moment at the beginning of another war, when the democracies had permitted the crossing of a border and failed to act. Of the many miscalculations made by both sides during the Korean War, perhaps the most egregious on the Communist side was the misunderstanding of how the Western democracies, principally the United States, would respond to a North Korean invasion of the South, that it would be viewed through the prism of Munich. Truman's thoughts while flying back to Washington were, as he recalled, of how the democracies had failed the last time to stop Mussolini in Ethiopia and the Japanese in Manchuria, and of how easily the French and British might have blocked Hitler's moves into Austria and Czechoslovakia. In his mind, the Soviets had pushed—perhaps even ordered—the North Koreans to cross the parallel, and he believed that the only language the Russians understood was force. "We had to meet them on that basis," he later wrote. It was not so much Korea they thought was important—but how America responded to a Communist provocation. America's prestige had been instantly placed at stake when the invasion took place, and prestige, Acheson said, when he heard that the North Koreans had crossed the border, "is the shadow cast by power, which is of great deterrent importance."

Truman was already a hard-liner. The five years since the end of World War II had been difficult ones, as two formidable and excessively anxious nations had faced off, each uncomfortable in its new role as a great power, each in its own way essentially isolationist, each governed by an economic system that saw the other's as its sworn enemy, each with an apocalyptic vision of the other as a relentless predator sworn to its destruction, both of them fearful and anxious in their new roles in a terrifying new atomic age. Each had its own anxieties—indeed, paranoia. A surprisingly cocky, almost ebullient Truman had partially mismeasured Stalin in their first meeting at Potsdam in Germany in late July 1945, after the Allied victory in Europe, and had underestimated his darker side. He had understood some of Stalin's sense of political power ("Stalin is as near like Tom Pendergast as any man I know," he had said right after the meeting, referring to the Kansas City political boss who had given him his start in politics) but had to be disabused of his ideas of being able to deal with Stalin. "And I liked the little son of a bitch," he said later. But at Potsdam he had hoped a certain kind of Midwestern straightness, a kind of let's-get-everyone's-cards-on-the table attitude, could lead to some kind of acceptable and measured accommodation for the postwar period, perhaps even a modest if edgy continuation of the wartime relationship. Those first moves had not worked with Stalin, a man who never put any of *his* cards on the table, most certainly not with the president of the most powerful capitalist nation in the world. (Truman's candor was, of course, not quite as great as he imagined; it was while he was at Potsdam that the first nuclear test took place successfully, something he did not deign to mention, but about which Stalin, because of Soviet spies, knew a great deal.)

Stalin was a new kind of tsar, a people's tsar, driven as much by an age-old paranoia—in his case both national and personal—in dealing with the West, a man with little interest or belief in the possibilities of a postwar alliance. By 1950, the Harry Truman who had made that first rather sympathetic run at Stalin was long gone. He had been replaced by a blunt, considerably more suspicious president who felt that the earlier Truman, the one who had ventured to Potsdam, had been "an innocent idealist." Stalin for his part had gotten Truman as wrong as Truman had gotten him. After they met at Potsdam, Stalin, like various conservative American politicians, had significantly, perhaps dangerously, underestimated the new American president, telling Nikita Khrushchev, then a rising star in the Soviet bureaucracy, that Truman was worthless. A great power chess game had followed the end of the war, inevitably so, given the power vacuum in the world with the collapse of Britain, France, Germany, and Japan, and the disintegration of their empires. By the time of the North Korean invasion, the Cold War had reached its most intense level save for the nuclear abyss the two powers faced during the Cuban Missile Crisis a dozen years later. For the June 25 invasion came four years after Churchill gave his Iron Curtain speech, and two years after the Russian blockade of Berlin and the American airlift to resupply that city. By 1950, the Western allies were well on their way to the completion of the Marshall Plan, and soon the creation of the North Atlantic Treaty Organization (NATO)—which the United States saw as a way of strengthening the still war-ravaged and shaky nations of Europe, but which the Communists viewed as part of an attempt to create a great wall of hostile nations ringing them, armed with nuclear weapons.

When the Truman administration's top officials convened on June 25 to try to figure out what the invasion meant, other than one half of Korea attacking the other half, they were essentially peering into the dark. These were days when everything the Soviet Union did was clouded in the utmost secrecy, when even the Moscow phone book was a classified document. The immediate belief of the people then gathering around the president in Washington was that the invasion was a direct Moscow move, ordered by Stalin and obeyed by his proxies in North Korea. That would turn out not to be true; years later it became clear from the opening of archives in Moscow that the driving force for the invasion was the young and overconfident Kim Il Sung, and that the ever cautious Stalin had somewhat reluctantly gone along with it. At that moment, the administration's Soviet experts considered North Korea simply a Soviet satellite, totally under the Kremlin's thumb, which it largely was, but in this case Stalin was more the accommodator than the instigator. The primary question that concerned Washington at first was: Could the invasion be only a feint, the first move in a larger Russian plan of aggression? And if so, what would Stalin's next move be? Was Stalin secretly eyeing Europe or a target in the Middle East? Acheson thought the invasion was a feint to be followed up by a Soviet-supported Chinese strike at Chiang on Taiwan or, perhaps equally dangerous, a Communist counterstrike after a provocation by Chiang.

Truman, by contrast, thought the next move might come in Iran. So did Douglas MacArthur, with whom he rarely agreed on anything. On June 26, Truman, in the company of a few close staffers, walked over to a globe, spun it to the Middle East, and pointed to Iran. "Here is where they will start trouble if we aren't careful. Korea is the Greece of the Far East. If we are tough enough now, if we stand up to them like we did in Greece three years ago, they won't take any next steps. But if we just stand by, they'll move into Iran and they'll take over the whole Middle East. There's no telling what they'll do if we don't put up a fight now."

When the president had arrived back in Washington in the early evening of the twenty-fifth, he was met at the airport by Acheson, Secretary of Defense Louis Johnson, and Undersecretary of State James Webb. From the moment the three men joined Truman inside his limo, there was no doubt which way the play would go. "By God, I'm going to let them have it!" Truman said. Johnson quickly responded that he was with Truman. Webb said simply that Truman should look at some of the things the people at State had put together for him. They had multiple recommendations as early responses to the still fragmentary reports from Korea, all of which were bad: they wanted the president to authorize General MacArthur to give the South Koreans such arms as they needed; to use American air and sea power to cover evacuation procedures and to hold Korea's ports, lest they fall to the North in the midst of an evacuation. At the same time, based on the president's future decisions, they wanted the Joint Chiefs to come up with what was militarily necessary to stop the North Koreans. They wanted the Seventh Fleet to move into the Straits of Formosa to block any Communist Chinese assault on Taiwan (and also to stop Chiang from doing anything to provoke the new government on the mainland). In addition they believed the United States should initiate military aid programs to support the French in Indochina, and offer military aid to Burma and Thailand. When the limo reached Blair House, where the president was then staying, Webb, in a moment alone with Truman, made one other suggestion: that they consider separating the Taiwan and Korea decisions, especially since Washington intended to take the case of the North Korean invasion to the UN.

If a line was not being crossed on that day, it was most surely being blurred, and it was not necessarily only in Korea. In the years immediately after World War II, there were probably two main issues confronting the policymakers in Washington as they sought to deal with the destruction of the old order and other havoc created by the war. The first and most obvious and most immediate was the need to draw a line against Soviet expansionism in Europe. That was done with great skill and vision, but unfortunately partially at the expense of the other great issue of the era, one seemingly less immediate and more peripheral in terms of sheer power—how to respond to the end of a colonial age, which found the nation's greatest allies being challenged politically and sometimes militarily by their former colonial possessions. On the question of understanding the power of nationalism in the underdeveloped world, cloaked as it sometimes was in a covering of Communism, Washington's record was significantly spottier. There were in fact two very different kinds of Communism posing very different kinds of threats: hard Soviet Communism, driven in Europe by the Red Army, and Communism as it was manifested in the Third World, where it became a convenient instrument of anticolonial forces, who often turned to Moscow (as in Indochina) for help after being rejected by Washington. Whatever else can be said about the North Korean attack, it was an old-fashioned border crossing; but in Indochina, which the United States now began to tie to both Korea and the larger confrontation in Europe, it was a pure colonial war.

That night, all the top military and civilian people dined at Blair House. After dinner they took up the subject of the invasion. Some things were already becoming clear: no one knew how deep the North Korean penetration was, but this was clearly a major invasion and the South Korean forces were not fighting well. They would not be able to hold on their own. After dinner, General Omar Bradley, the chairman of the Joint Chiefs, who had favored pulling American combat troops back from Korea a year earlier because it would be such a terrible place to fight and because it was deemed of so little strategic value, was the first to speak. A line had to be drawn against the Communists, he said, and Korea was as good a place to do so as any. Its value had changed overnight. Truman interrupted to say that he agreed completely. In that moment, the die was cast. Bradley added that, given the size of the attack, the Soviets had to be behind it. Then Admiral Forrest Sherman, the chief of naval operations, and General Hoyt Vandenberg, Air Force chief of staff, spoke. Each reflected the optimism—and dependence—Americans felt about their air and naval superiority, as well as each man's belief in the unique powers of his own service. Neither had very much respect for the fighting abilities of the North Korean Army. Each was confident that air and sea power could turn back the North Koreans. But Joe Collins, the Army chief of staff, said that based on the reports he was getting, it was likely American ground forces would also be necessary. The commitment of ground troops was a very different—much graver—step. Bradley, Collins, and Frank Pace, the secretary of the Army, all insisted that was not a decision the United States ought to rush into. Bradley would soon note, however, that he had underestimated the force and the ability of the North Koreans. "No one believed that the North Koreans were as strong as they turned out to be," he later testified.

Slowly a consensus was building: airpower was needed immediately to slow down the North Korean advance, and the issue should be taken to the UN for its support, though, if need be, the United States would be willing to take unilateral action to stop the invasion. Near the end of the meeting, Webb asked

Truman to discuss the political aspects of the situation. "We're not going to talk about politics!" Truman responded sharply. "I'll handle the political affairs!" Truman then issued orders for airpower to be used to protect the evacuation of American dependents and to contest the North Koreans in the skies above the South. He asked Pace to have MacArthur send a survey team to Korea to find out what was needed militarily, and then, fatefully, he ordered Sherman to send the Seventh Fleet from the Philippines into the Formosa Straits between Taiwan and the mainland of China, now in the hands of Communists. But he said he wanted no announcement made until the fleet was actually in position.

The decision on ground troops remained like a dark storm cloud overhead. None of the president's advisers had any faith in the ability of the South Koreans to hold the line. The next day, Truman wrote his wife, Bess (still in Independence), that it had been a grand trip back once he was in the air. The meeting they had held at Blair House was most successful, but the issue of Korea was a tough one. "Haven't been so upset since Greece and Turkey fell into our lap. Let's hope for the best. . . ." The idea that Stalin had acquiesced to and not driven the invasion was alien, not that it would have made very much difference. Either way, it was viewed as the same thing. "Russians are Said to be Invading; Red Tank units Push on Seoul" was the headline in the influential *New York Herald Tribune*.

To some of the top people in the national security world, like Acheson, the news, however unnerving, was, if not a godsend, then something perilously close, because they had badly wanted a massive increase in the defense budget, and prospects had not been promising. They had in effect been waiting for something like this to happen, fearful of it but also sure it would come, and that when it came it might help wake up the country to the new challenges it faced.

George Kennan, the nation's leading expert on the Soviets, had not, to his immense frustration, made the cut at the Blair House meetings. ("The dinner had the effect of defining—by social invitation, so to speak—the group that would be responsibly engaged in the handling of the Department's decision in the ensuing days," he later wrote.) He was, in his own words, on the sidelines. He had already left behind the job of director of State's Policy Planning staff and was essentially on leave, headed for Princeton, to ponder the past instead of the present and the future. Still, fearing that Korea might be a mere feint, Acheson questioned Kennan closely in the next few days about what the Russians were up to. Kennan did not think that this attack represented anything larger. He wrote Acheson that the Soviets were not looking for a larger war with the United States, but they would be delighted to see the United States either bogged down "in a profitless and discreditable war" or standing on the sidelines doing nothing (and thus be discredited in the region) as the North Koreans conquered the peninsula. The great danger for the United States as it plotted its response, he commented, was not in Europe but in Asia. There, the Russians might try to get the Chinese involved as their proxies. This meant that Kennan did not see a larger war and felt we should be very careful to set limits on it. This turned out to be sobering and largely prophetic advice from the nation's leading Kremlinologist.

When the principals met again at Blair House on the second day, Acheson, already the most important player on Korea except for the president, announced that the Seventh Fleet was now in place and therefore it was time to issue the order for it to protect Taiwan. At the same time, Chiang, he noted, was to be told very bluntly to cease all operations against the mainland. The Seventh Fleet officers were to make sure that he complied. Then Acheson began to outline his recommendations not just for Korea but for all of Asia. The United States would step up aid to the government in the Philippines, now embroiled in a guerrilla war with the Communist-led Huk guerrillas, and do the same for the French, who were fighting the Communist-Nationalist Vietminh in a colonial war in Indochina. In Indochina that was a critical escalation: the United States had originally opposed the idea of the French resuming their colonial rule there, had gone along with it reluctantly under pressure from Paris, and now, four years into that war, just as the French public was beginning to show signs of tiring, the United States was prepared to take on a major share of the financing. Soon the Americans would become the principal backers and financiers of the French. Sending a major military mission to Indochina meant the American toe was being dipped into new waters, those of a bitter colonial war, without anyone imagining, or for that matter very much caring about, the full consequences. Nor was time wasted in doing it. On June 29, four days after the North Korean crossing, eight C-47 cargo planes flew across the Pacific carrying materiel for the French, the beginning of massive military aid and of what would one day become an ever deeper, ever more melancholy adventure for America.

At the Monday night meeting, the Washington policymakers also discussed the possibility of using Chiang's troops in Korea. The Generalissimo had already volunteered some of his best soldiers. Truman was intrigued by the offer and at first leaned toward accepting it. Acheson advised strongly against it. He had been thinking about what he considered the Chiang problem from the moment the Korean crisis began and was not surprised when Chiang's offer came in. He understood that what Chiang wanted (a widening war that would in some way bring in the Chinese Communists) and what the United States wanted (a limited war that China stayed out of) were in no way parallel. The two countries might still be allies, but they wanted very different things. Acheson was absolutely sure he was right on this one. In any case, he had seen quite enough of how Chiang's troops had fought on the mainland to know that he did not want to depend on them in this war, especially against the talented forces who had just defeated them. There were a number of people on the right, including MacArthur, who were fascinated by the idea of using Chiang's troops—unleashing them was the phrase—but Acheson was not among them, nor in the end were most of the Joint Chiefs, who had their own purely military wariness.

But the administration's political opponents wanted to use them and saw the beginning of the Korean War as a way of striking against the president and his secretary of state, and of tying Korea to an issue on which they were already attacking Truman, the loss of China. Their response was immediate and visceral. On the twenty-sixth, Senator Styles Bridges, an extremely well-connected figure in what was called the China Lobby, rose on the Senate floor to ask, "Will we continue appeasement? Will we wait 'for the dust to settle'? [a play on an earlier Acheson phrase of waiting for the dust to settle in China in hope that there might eventually be a chance of separating Russia and China]. Now is the time to draw the line." Bill Knowland of California, so close to the China Lobby that he was known as the Senator from Formosa [Taiwan], added, "If this nation is allowed to succumb to an overt invasion of this kind, there is little chance of stopping Communism anywhere on the continent of Asia." And finally Senator George (Molly) Malone of Nevada tied the situation to the Hiss case, in which a figure in the State Department, Alger Hiss, had just been convicted of perjury on charges of spying for the Soviets. What had happened in China and was happening now in Korea, Malone said, had been brought on by left-wing advisers to the State Department.

While Truman's own response to what had happened when the North Koreans invaded was automatic and almost completely apolitical, it was also true that there were politics at play from the very first. There were in fact some divisions within his own administration over the issue of Chiang, and whether or not to defend him and the island of Taiwan. Not only was continued support of Chiang becoming a major issue employed by the most hostile of the administration's enemies, but even in the administration's most private meetings it festered. Acheson thought Chiang literally a lost cause, and supporting him a dubious policy, one that would work against the United States in the long run, given the changing mood and political face of Asia. But his opposite number at Defense, Louis Johnson, who hoped to succeed Truman as the Democratic candidate for the presidency, was openly pro-Chiang. In the minds of some members of the inner Truman group, he was considered a member of the hostile China Lobby, someone who had promised Chiang's people at the Nationalist embassy in Washington that he was not only going to neutralize Acheson but drive him out of government. (Not only was his top aide, Paul Griffith, in constant touch with Wellington Koo, the Nationalist ambassador and the key figure in the China Lobby, but unbeknownst to the rest of the administration, some nine months earlier Koo had arranged a dinner in Riverdale, New York, for Madame Chiang and Johnson.) Johnson's connection to the Nationalists was a fact of the administration, and it meant that the criticism of the administration's China policy heard constantly from the Republicans was also voiced in-house and that everything said at the top-level meeting was immediately passed on to the Nationalists.

That made for an unpleasant in-house struggle, one that hovered over the administration in the early days of the Korean War as the issue of China itself hovered over every decision. It was not a fight that Johnson could win. In political terms, Truman was much closer to Acheson; the president both admired and trusted him and his political judgment and was eventually wary of anything that might expand the war. But he also owed Johnson, who, almost alone among men with major financial connections, had stood with him in the worst days after the 1948 political convention, when no one thought Truman could win the presidency on his own. Johnson had been Truman's principal fundraiser when the Democratic Party coffers were empty, and as a reward, he had gotten Defense.

From the moment that Truman gathered his team together at Blair House, there had been sharp and unwanted disagreement between Acheson and Johnson over Taiwan, a subject that Johnson had raised. Everyone else at the meeting wanted to concentrate on Korea, but Johnson, who had been trying against the wishes of the president and Acheson to include Taiwan in the American defense perimeter in Asia, now seized on the issue again. American security, he said, was more affected by Taiwan than Korea. Acheson tried to move the subject back to Korea. Finally Truman broke it off and said they would have dinner. After dinner Johnson tried again to raise the question of Taiwan, and again Truman cut him off.

At the Blair House talks, Chiang's troops were then quickly left behind for a more serious consideration of the situation on the ground. Joe Collins pointed out that the ROKs were collapsing. The ROK chief of staff had, in Collins's phrase, "no fight left in him." They all knew what that meant—there would be a need for American combat troops. But even in World War II, it had been American policy to avoid putting combat troops on the mainland of Asia. Omar Bradley suggested that the president wait a few days before making so fateful a decision. Truman then asked the Joint Chiefs to ponder the question.

At one point, reflecting the gravity of the moment, Truman looked at the others with great solemnity and said, "I don't want to go to war." But he was also aware that he was coming closer and closer to making that ultimate decision.

On the morning of June 27, he and Acheson met with congressional leaders and went over his decisions so far. The congressional response was generally very favorable. At one point, Alexander Smith, a Republican senator from New Jersey, asked whether Truman was going to request that Congress pass a joint resolution on military action in Korea. It was a good question, and one that, remarkably enough, in two solid days of meetings no one in the administration had really considered. Politics, they believed, had been put aside, or at least put aside by them. They would take it under advisement, Truman told Smith. Later that day Truman spoke about it with both Acheson and Averell Harriman, who had become a high-level special aide in the hours immediately after the invasion. Though unlike Acheson he came from a background of unparalleled wealth, Harriman was always shrewder about American politics. He strongly advised Truman to go for a congressional resolution. Acheson opposed a resolution; the events, he said, demanded speed. Truman, a man produced by Congress who surely would have been angered had a president gone over *his* head on an issue of war and peace, tended to agree with Acheson. He did not want to slow down the process, and his constant struggles with the Congress over the issue of China and Chiang made him wary of dealing with his enemies in the Senate. Three days later, on the morning of June 30, Truman met again with congressional leaders. This time, Senator Kenneth Wherry of Nebraska, hardly the administration's favorite senator, asked bluntly about congressional approval. (At an earlier hearing Acheson had tried to punch him in the nose, and had had to be restrained by one of his own aides; Truman himself liked to call Wherry "the block headed undertaker from Nebraska.") Truman tried to put him off. "If there is any need for congressional action I will come to you. But I hope we can get those bandits in Korea suppressed without one."

That was the ideal time to get some kind of resolution, but soon the moment passed, and the political unanimity that had existed at the hour of the invasion evaporated. As the war became more difficult than originally imagined, the politics of it became more difficult as well, and the support began to fragment. Because Truman had not tried for congressional support, the opposition was off the hook in terms of accepting any responsibility for America's response. When Secretary of the Army Frank Pace suggested they go for the resolution, Truman had answered, "Frank, it's not necessary. They're all with me." "Yes, Mr. President," Pace answered, "but we can't be sure they'll be with you over a period of time." For the moment everyone seemed to be aboard.

When the word reached the House that the president had decided to send arms to South Korea, virtually the entire House stood to cheer. Joseph Harsch of *The Christian Science Monitor*, one of Washington's best and most experienced reporters, wrote, "Never before have I felt such a sense of relief and unity pass through the city."

The president's advisers all knew that week that they were moving closer and closer to using ground troops on the Asian mainland, the last thing anyone, civilian or military, wanted to do, and it weighed more heavily on them each day. American air and sea power was not going to get it done. MacArthur had been ordered—if he could ever be said to be ordered—to go to Korea and report back on what was needed to hold the line there. Now, very early in the morning of June 30, the word from Tokyo was about to come in and they already knew that it was not going to be good. At about 1:30 A.M., Washington time, John Muccio notified Acheson that MacArthur was going to ask for greater force. Things were desperate on the peninsula, Muccio said. That set the stage for MacArthur's cable asking for troops.

An hour and a half later, MacArthur, who had just returned from his tour of Korea, reported to the Joint Chiefs that the United States needed drastically increased forces there. These were his fateful words: "The only assurance for the holding of the present line, and the ability to regain the lost ground, is through the introduction of U.S. ground forces into the Korean battle area. To continue to utilize the forces of our Air and Navy without an effective ground element cannot be decisive." He wanted, MacArthur said, to introduce a regimental combat team immediately to fight in some already contested areas, and then as quickly as possible to arrange for up to two divisions from his forces in Japan to undertake a counteroffensive. Unless they did this, he said, "our mission will at best be needlessly costly in life, money and prestige. At worse [sic] it might even be doomed to failure."

In Washington, Dean Rusk, the assistant secretary of state for the Far East, and Joe Collins, the Army chief of staff, were working their end of the teleconference between roughly 3 A.M. and 4 A.M. But because they were, relatively speaking, lower-level officials, and the hour was early, it turned out to be a slow and clumsy process. Higher authorization was always needed. These were not minor issues posed by Tokyo: they were about nothing less than war and peace. Answers did not come quickly. There were delays on a number of points and this did not please MacArthur. "This is an outrage! When I was chief of staff I could get Herbert Hoover off the can to talk to me! But here, not just the Chief of Staff of the Army delays, but the Secretary of the Army and the Secretary of Defense. They've got so much lead in there that it's inexcusable."

At about 4:30 A.M. Washington time, MacArthur confirmed his request for ground troops to Collins, and Collins called Pace, who in turn called Truman. Truman was always an early riser. His internal farm-boy clock had never left him. He was shaved by the time he got Pace's call. Just before 5 A.M. on the morning of June 30, 1950, he approved the use of American ground troops in Korea. With that the deed was done. In the very beginning MacArthur had said that he could easily handle the invasion if only Washington would leave him alone. Now he said he needed two divisions to do it. He was, it would turn out, still underrating the enemy, and overrating the forces who would serve under his own command, including American troops.

Truman still wondered if there were a plus side to the offer of Chiang's troops. He then called in Acheson, Harriman, Johnson, and the Joint Chiefs to talk one last time about using them. With the South Korean Army falling apart, Chiang's offer still made some sense to the president as a stopgap measure. Acheson was sure it would bring the Chinese Communists into the war. And the Joint Chiefs wanted no part of it either.

Amid the gloom, there was one upbeat note. U.S. troops would fight under a United Nations flag. Before Truman approved the use of American ground troops, he had already gotten UN authorization—easier then than it would be in any decade to come. The UN of 1950 was still very much a reflection of American and Western European interests, the only significant dissent coming from the Soviets and their satellites. It was in some ways very much a last vestige of a white man's world. On the Security Council vote to authorize the use of force in Korea, the only two abstentions were by non-white countries, India and Egypt. Beginning in the late 1950s and accelerating into the 1960s, the coming of the end of the colonial era, and the arrival of newly independent African and Asian and Middle Eastern nations, would change the UN's makeup dramatically, greatly diminishing Western influence and turning it into an organization that conservative political factions in the United States and Western Europe absolutely scorned. The Russians had foolishly boycotted the Security Council meetings on Korea (ironically because they were protesting the fact that the Chinese Nationalists were still on the council), and with their veto gone, the Americans got the resolution they wanted on Tuesday, June 27, eventually giving the predominantly American force a UN flag under which to fight.

THE UNITED STATES was going to go to war in Korea, and Harry Truman was quite reluctantly going to have to be the commander in chief, dealing with a war he did not want, in a part of the world his national security people had not thought important, and relying from the start on a commander in the field whom he did not like, and who in turn did not respect him. The stars were not properly aligned from the start. Three days after the Korean War broke out, Dwight Eisenhower, then the president of Columbia University, dropped by the Pentagon to talk about the Korean command with Lieutenant General Matt Ridgway, then deputy chief of staff for administration, but the most respected of the new generation of senior officers, and thus the man a number of senior officers thought the ideal candidate to be the battlefield commander in Korea under MacArthur. Few men knew better than Eisenhower how MacArthur operated. He had been MacArthur's aide in both Washington and Manila, and was intimately aware of just how shrewdly MacArthur rationed the truth when he reported back to the civilian and military world in Washington. Eisenhower told Ridgway that they badly needed a younger general out there rather than, as he put it, "an 'untouchable' whose actions you cannot predict and who will himself decide what information he wants Washington to have and what he will withhold." There was, Eisenhower later wrote, a clear line between military and political affairs, which almost all senior officers scrupulously observed, "but if General MacArthur recognized the existence of that line, he usually chose to ignore it." MacArthur had acted throughout his life, as Max Hastings once wrote, "on the assumption that the rules made for lesser men had no relevance to himself."

MacArthur's unsettling performance in those first few days, what Dulles and Allison had witnessed when the North Koreans first struck, was never seen by ordinary Americans. Instead MacArthur's public mystique remained largely unblemished among the senior media people, especially publishers and editors, the men at the top whom he had courted for so long. Four days after the invasion began, the *New York Times,* typically, ran a glowing editorial on the nation's good fortune in having MacArthur on the spot: "Fate could not have chosen a man better qualified to command the unreserved confidence of the people of this country. Here is a superb strategist and an inspired leader; a man of infinite patience and quiet stability under adverse pressures, a man equally capable of bold and decisive action."

He was seventy years old, the senior officer in the American Army—only God, it was said, was senior to MacArthur, the aging wunderkind of West Point. As a young man he had begun his career with scores that were among the highest ever posted there, 98.14 for the four years, and he had more than lived up to the promise of those grades. He had always been the youngest officer to attain whatever position he attained—not just the youngest division commander in France in World War I but also the youngest superintendent of West Point (and a modern liberalizing force there), youngest Army chief of staff, youngest major general, and youngest man ever to be a full general. His good press did not come through happenstance: it was not just the extraordinary career, and the sheer length of it; it was the immense amount of energy he had always put into making sure that his image was the proper one, that he got the maximum amount of credit for any victory, while his subordinates received as little credit as possible. He was the most theatrical of men, busy at all times not merely being a general but doing it in the most dramatic way possible, the Great MacArthur who played in nothing less than the theater of history—as if life were always a stage and the world his audience.

The *Times,* center-liberal in its editorial page, enthusiastic as its homage to MacArthur seemed, was not nearly as fulsome in its praise of the general as *Time* magazine. Given the passion of its founder and editor, Henry Luce, for China and Chiang Kai-shek, *Time* was already closely connected to what was coming to be known as the China Lobby, those Americans who saw China and Chiang Kai-shek as one and the same, and believed the administration was sending inadequate amounts of aid to Chiang. *Time,* at the height of its political and social influence in the late 1940s and 1950s, was far more Asia First in its vision of the world than most other American periodicals of that era, in no small part because Luce himself was a mish-kid; that is, the son of a missionary who had proselytized in China. Chiang, perhaps other than Winston Churchill, was Luce's favorite world leader, while Douglas MacArthur was probably his favorite general, because of their shared belief in the primacy of Asia and their parallel feeling that other internationalists paid too little attention to it. When *Time* put MacArthur on the cover on July 10, 1950, right after the North Koreans struck—and appearing on its cover was extremely important in those years—it was his seventh time, placing him in a dead heat with Chiang himself. The copy for the piece, even for a much favored general, set a new standard in journalistic hagiography: "Inside the Dai Ichi building, once the heart of a Japanese insurance empire, bleary-eyed staff officers looked up from stacks of paper, whispered proudly, 'God, the man is great.' General Almond, his chief of staff, said straight out, 'He's the greatest man alive.' And reverent Air Force General George Stratemeyer put it as strongly as it could be put . . . 'He's the greatest man in history.' "

Not everyone agreed, of course. If he was successful in his courtship of publishers and editors, working reporters were often put off by MacArthur's grandiosity and vainglory, and many of them came to despise the sycophantic ambiance of his staff. A meeting with him was not just a briefing—it was likely to be a performance as well, the energy and care put into it geared to the importance of the visitor. The problem with MacArthur, General Joseph Stilwell told Frank Dorn, one of his top aides, was that he had been "a general too long." Stilwell was speaking in 1944, before MacArthur became the American-approved emperor of an occupied Japan. "He got his first star in 1918 and that means he's had almost thirty years as a general," Stilwell said, "thirty years of people playing to him and kissing his ass, and doing what he wants. That's not good for anyone."

BY 1950 MACARTHUR was so grand a figure that everyone had to play by his rules. In effect he had created not only his own little army within a larger army, which he alone was allowed to command, but his own little world where he alone could govern. Any instructions or orders or even suggestions from Washington were more often than not ignored, even if they came from the general's nominal superiors, men who, in his own view of the hierarchy, were not superior to him, and therefore had no right to question him or give him orders. He had created a dangerously self-isolating little world, one of total social, political, and military separation from everyone and everything else, where no one dared dissent. The men around him were all in awe of him; those who were not in awe of him tended not to last very long in his headquarters. Visitors who arrived at his headquarters at the Dai Ichi building and were deemed worthy of a meeting with him always got The Performance. In the performance—he often practiced that morning in front of a mirror, clad in his bathrobe—he spoke with great confidence and certainty about future events that most men, no matter how knowledgeable, approached with a degree of caution, aware of the tricks that history played. The performances were often quite dazzling, well rehearsed but delivered as if they were impromptu. He was the most gifted of monologuists. But there was an airless quality to it all. Everything was too finely controlled, too carefully calculated and orchestrated, in a world where events could never be controlled and orchestrated, and where many of the forces at play were new and hostile and very different from the forces at play in the earlier century.

Given the unofficial rules of the Dai Ichi—he talked, you listened—no one dared challenge his grandiose statements, his role as a kind of self-proclaimed prophet of what was happening in the world, of what Russia and China were doing and what was happening in America, a country he had largely lost touch with and never entirely understood. There was, sadly, one vital quality for any successful general that he lacked—he did not know how to listen. Nor did he want to. Nothing had revealed that quite so clearly as the moment in 1948 when George Kennan had been sent out from Washington to work on issues of political reform and economic rehabilitation in Japan. At that moment most senior commanders or high-ranking diplomats, especially those operating on the edge of the Soviet Union, would have been thrilled to have Kennan around for even a short period of time, even if they did not always agree with him. He was at the height of his own new fame. He was considered the leading expert in the government on the subject of the Soviet Union and its intentions. Of Kennan's intellect and clarity of mind there could be no doubt. That his knowledge of Russia, the Soviet Union, and China, their histories and their politics, was superb there could also be no doubt. He might still be relatively young, just starting the middle part of his career, but he was obviously a towering figure— with the most practical kind of intellect. But Kennan could never get across the moat with MacArthur—he was too close to people MacArthur loathed. There was to be no give-and-take. In fact Kennan was shocked by what he found in Tokyo. MacArthur, he noted, was "so distant and full of mistrust" toward the incumbent administration that Kennan's own job was "like nothing more than that of an envoy charged with opening up communications and arranging the establishment of diplomatic relations with a hostile and suspicious foreign government."

Harry Truman was the accidental president, but Douglas MacArthur was in no way the accidental general. Far more than most men, Douglas MacArthur was what he had been raised to be. It began with his father, Arthur MacArthur, a formidable figure in his own right, a heroic officer with the Union Army during the Civil War and later a major player during the Philippine Insurrection. Even more important, the elder MacArthur was a towering mythical figure in the eyes of his son—that myth being created and orchestrated shrewdly and constantly by Pinky MacArthur, wife of Arthur and mother of Douglas. She was the principal architect, in the wake of her husband's death and his bitterness over the way his career had ended, of her son's career, his singular, unwavering ambition, and his almost unique self-absorption.

Though much of the drive that Douglas MacArthur eventually exhibited came from his mother, Arthur MacArthur was himself hardly a shy or modest figure. He had a most unfortunate need to be right at all times. He was, in his own view, virtually without peer not just in terms of his military skills but also, hardly less important, in his political judgments. Arthur MacArthur, said his aide Colonel Enoch Crowder, "was the most flamboyantly egotistical man I had ever seen, until I met his son." His career was both brilliant and at times extremely difficult; there were moments when it was meteoric, and moments when it seemed to languish. At the time of his retirement there was almost no Army position of significance he had not filled, no rank he had not gained, no medal offered by his country that he had not won. He had ended his military life a three-star general—the highest rank possible then—a Congressional Medal of Honor winner, but fiercely disappointed with his career, with the Army, and with a political structure he had struggled against for years. By all rights he should have been buried in Arlington National Cemetery, but he was so embittered politically, so alienated from the men running the country at the time of his death, that he refused to be buried there.

Arthur MacArthur was in the end a great American patriot who had become, in some curious twisted way, virtually anti-American. It was as if there were something dark in his soul, something far too focused on self in a profession where great sacrifices are made and risks taken for ideals and concepts much larger than self. His successes and rewards, and there were so many of them, were never enough; it was only what he did *not* attain that he could remember at the end. Of his son, too, many of the same things could also have been said: if he did not control it, if he did not have his way, he was in the end willing to destroy it. Many senior military officers charged with working in difficult situations with civilian authorities have come to dislike or at least to distrust politicians—the two cultures are vastly different, and often the best of our military men are good precisely because they cannot, like politicians, bend with events. In the case of Arthur MacArthur, however, it was far more than the normal wariness and distrust—it was nothing less than a pathology. No matter what any civilian wanted or who he was, Arthur MacArthur seemed compelled to resist. How Washington treated *him* was all that mattered. In his late years, he spoke constantly about the evils of politicians, and it was an attitude he passed on to his son.

Douglas MacArthur, as he began his own career, had a doubly hard race to run: not only would he have to match his father's remarkable accomplishments, but he would also have to gain vengeance for all the disappointments in his father's life, and to even the score with all who might have wounded or slighted him. That was, it would turn out, too much to ask of any man. The lives and careers of father and son stretched over more than an entire century in American life, a critical period in which the size of the country, as well as its military, economic, and political power, grew exponentially. Arthur MacArthur was born in 1845, and became a hero at eighteen in the Civil War; Douglas was born in 1880, became an active commander in the three great wars of the next century, World War I, World War II, and Korea, and died in 1964, a full century after his father's first act of heroism. Both saw their careers end with similar political drama: Arthur MacArthur, then a two-star, was finally pulled back from the Philippine Islands, where he had commanded troops successfully but tangled unnecessarily with civilian authorities; half a century later, and some 105 years after his father's birth, Douglas MacArthur was relieved of his command in the Korean War by a president of the United States for constantly crossing proper military boundaries and becoming too political a player.

Arthur MacArthur was the son of a prominent and properly ambitious judge in Milwaukee. When the Civil War broke out, the judge tried to get his son into West Point. He even had one of Wisconsin's senators take the boy to the White House to meet Abraham Lincoln. But all the slots were filled, and so the judge, using his private network of political connections, got his son a position as the regimental adjutant of the Twenty-fourth Wisconsin Regiment. At eighteen, Arthur MacArthur was an officer, though at first not everyone in the regiment was thrilled to have a boy adjutant. He first came to public prominence in November 1863 at the Battle of Missionary Ridge, near Chattanooga. The Confederates held the high ground there and had been chewing up a large Union force gathered beneath them, at very little cost to themselves. A diversionary attack, ordered by the Union commanders, led to ever heavier casualties among the extremely vulnerable Union troops until, as if reacting in rage to the unspeakable losses they were suffering, the Union soldiers drove recklessly right up the hill, in front of the well-dug-in Southerners, and evicted them.

They had been, it would turn out, led by the Twenty-fourth Wisconsin and the man—or rather the boy—carrying the regimental banner when they finally reached the top, perhaps the third or fourth soldier to pick it up after the others had been hit, Arthur MacArthur. General Phil Sheridan, the Union commander, thrilled by this surprise victory, allegedly said afterward that someone had better take good care of that lad with the banner because he had just won the Congressional Medal of Honor—though, in fact, Arthur

MacArthur did not actually gain that medal for another twenty-seven years. He fought in thirteen separate battles on Sherman's March across Georgia and was wounded four times. He fought so well, in fact, that he was made a colonel at nineteen, the youngest soldier in the Union Army to reach that rank, becoming known as "the boy colonel" of the Civil War. He was brave, intelligent, and had a natural instinct for battle. After the war, he left the Army, but civilian life soon bored him and he returned to the service, though he had to give up his wartime rank.

He quickly made captain, and then went without any additional promotion for the next twenty-three years. Those were hard years of little external reward, save perhaps the experience itself. The country was pushing west, and more often than not he commanded on the country's frontiers. The conditions were always primitive, and he operated in what were often largely lawless regions, or perhaps more accurately regions where the only law was what he said it was. The civilian political presence was often marginal, the restraints on a commander therefore minimal. To the degree that there were restraints, they were imposed upon the men in the field by politicians back in Washington, men who were not only distant but were regarded as innocents, unaware of the real world where the Army was doing the nation's dirty work. To the men in the field the politicians they had to deal with were both compromised and compromising.

Arthur MacArthur was exceptionally successful in this frontier incarnation and confident in his use of troops in battle. Though he had little formal education, he was surprisingly well read and exceptionally confident of his intellectual abilities. His ability to operate without civilian challenge in those years only added to his existing arrogance, making him, as his son's biographer William Manchester noted, particularly contemptuous of civilian authority—an attitude that was to get him into trouble in the Philippines and that, passed on from father to son, would turn the MacArthur family—father, mother, and son—ever more hostile to almost all politicians and yet, in a strange and bitterly ironic, almost unconscious way, ever more political.

In 1889, Arthur finally made major and went to Washington as assistant adjutant general. In 1897, on the eve of the Spanish-American War, he became a lieutenant colonel. When the war began in 1898, he hoped to be promoted to full colonel, and to command troops fighting the Spanish in Cuba, which was presumed to be the focal point of the confrontation between the United States, just beginning to feel its new economic muscle as the leading industrial power in the world, and Spain, a fading imperial power, one that had been in constant decline for much of a century. Instead of being promoted to colonel, Arthur was jumped two grades to brigadier general; instead of commanding troops in Cuba, he was sent to the Philippines.

William McKinley, an Ohio Republican with his own complex and conflicting feelings about America's onrushing new role as an imperial power in the Pacific, was president. He was as surprised as anyone to discover that not only was he dealing with the suppression of a Cuban insurrection but that the United States' easy success there had led to a larger and more complicated additional step in the Pacific. He found himself facing the far more difficult task of imposing America's will on an indigenous uprising in Asia. There the local indigenous leaders wanted one thing—the Spanish imperialists gone. At first they welcomed American help, and then they found—it was part of the age—that the United States intended to do what was good for America and only then, for them as well; that is, create a new political order for them, albeit under U.S. rule and sovereignty.

It was the nation's first real colonial experience and it was not a happy one. The first shots between American troops and Filipino rebels may have been fired in February 1899, eleven months before the millennium, but in terms of American power and ambitions, the brutal counterinsurgency campaign the United States fought in the Philippines heralded much of what was to happen in the coming century. The Americans moved into the archipelago almost casually, more as an adjunct to events in Cuba than anything else. When the fighting in Cuba began, Admiral George Dewey, the commander of the Pacific Fleet, had sailed the American fleet into Manila Bay to destroy the antiquated Spanish one. What he found, in effect, was the feeble remains of the Spanish empire. The Spanish colony of the Philippines, it would turn out, was there more or less for the taking, and so the United States took it.

President McKinley did not particularly want the islands. He could not, he told one friend, "have told where those darned islands were within two thousand miles." But the pressure in the United States for some form of expansion, a continuation of that nineteenth-century sense of an American Manifest Destiny and an expression of the need to display to the rest of the world America's new economic muscle, had its own momentum. If the United States needed some sort of proof of its mounting strength in those years, then it could be gotten from colonial possessions. Two basic impulses in America—one of military and political restraint, the other more bloodthirsty and acquisitive—were, not for the first time, in conflict, and the more hawkish impulse seemed to be winning. As the *Washington Post* noted, "A new consciousness seems to have come upon us—the consciousness of strength—and with it a new appetite, the yearning to show our . . . ambition, interest, land hunger, pride, the mere joy of fighting, whatever it may be, we are animated by a new sensation. . . . The taste of empire is in the mouth of the people even as the taste of blood in the jungle. It means an imperial policy."

America began the Philippine adventure as the ally—indeed almost the partner—of the rebels who were challenging the Spanish colonial regime and were fighting for their post-Spanish independence. The United States had assured them that Americans were noncolonial by their very nature. In time, the United States ended up fighting in a cruel and ugly war of suppression. Again two very powerful American instincts were evident—a missionary drive that demanded the United States assume colonial responsibility over the islands in order to civilize the natives as part of a Christian white man's burden, and at the same time racism of the most virulent kind, so that the guerrillas were called either "niggers" or "gugus" (or "goo-goos"). The latter name came from the bark of a local tree that women used when they shampooed their hair. It was a term that eventually morphed into the more all-purpose word for Asians, *gooks,* that American troops used to identify Asians from World War II right through Korea and Vietnam.

To send in troops or not was the issue McKinley wrestled with, the forces around him always stronger than his own will. He himself appeared to come to the issue without strong convictions. In the end, he told one missionary group, in words that would have considerable resonance in future conflicts, he had sent the troops because he had no other acceptable choice. It had been a very hard decision, he said, and then he noted that he had knelt down in the White House to ask "almighty God for light and guidance." After all, he said, he could not give the archipelago back to the Spaniards. That would be cowardly and dishonorable. Nor could he open it up for two other interested colonial predators, France or Germany. And he *certainly* could not let the Filipinos, childlike as they were, govern themselves. Therefore his only choice was to take them for America, so Americans could "educate the Filipinos, and uplift and Christianize them, and by God's grace do the very best we could by them as our fellow men for whom Christ died."

The war itself was very different from those altruistic words. The Filipinos seemed quite unaware of the favors the United States intended to bestow upon them. The Americans at first tended to underestimate the Filipino insurgents, who knew the country far better than they did, generally had the support of the people, and soon took up arms against the foreigners not as regular infantry, but as guerrillas—and fought surprisingly well. The Americans had a slight superiority in weaponry, thanks to a new Norwegian-made rifle called the Krag-Jorgensen, which had the advantage of a five-round clip and used smokeless powder. That meant it did not give out a small puff of smoke when fired, making it harder for an enemy rifleman to mark the gun. "Underneath the starry flag/ Civilize them with a Krag," went one of the songs sung by the American troops. What happened then was a forerunner of all too many

battles in Asia still to come: Americans who were contemptuous of their adversaries at first because they were not white found themselves quite surprised
and quite embittered by the degree of resistance to their will. After the initial
shots were fired, one American major had called to his superior, Colonel Frederick Funston, "Come on out here, Colonel. The ball has begun." Some ball.
The war turned out to be infinitely harder and more brutal than anyone expected. Like Arthur MacArthur, many of the American troops had come right
off the frontier and out of the Indian wars: there as here the traditional hatred
of an enemy was blended in with racial fears and hatreds. "This country won't
be pacified until the niggers are killed off like the Indians," one soldier told a
reporter. "The only good Filipino is a dead one," another said. Some of the
American commanders were greatly irritated, as their lineal descendants
would be sixty years later in Vietnam, because their adversaries rarely fought
in the open or in daytime where the Americans could see them. They were sly.
They fought at night and they used ambushes. As the rebels took shelter in the
indigenous population, the Americans turned with ever greater violence on
that population, for there was to be no civilian neutrality in a war like this.
What was supposed to be easy and to end quickly stretched on. Before it was
over, some 112,000 American troops, 62,000 regulars and another 50,000 volunteers, were sent there.

The violence not only escalated, but it gradually became more vicious. One
American brigadier general, Jacob (Hell-roaring Jake) Smith, told his subordinates, "I want no prisoners. I wish you to kill and burn, the more you kill and
burn the better you will please me. I want all prisoners killed who are capable
of bearing arms in actual hostilities against the United States." One of his subordinates asked Smith to set an age limit. "Ten years," said Smith. "Ten years?"
asked the subordinate. "People of ten years old are able to bear arms against
America?" "Yes," said Smith. The war went on for three and a half years, less
popular by the day in America. The end was expedited by a daring raid and the
capture of Aguinaldo, the rebel leader, by General Funston in 1901. In the end,
4,200 Americans died in the Philippines and another 2,800 were wounded.
Perhaps 20,000 Filipino soldiers died in the struggle, and as many as 250,000
civilians. "If old Dewey had just sailed away after he smashed that Spanish
fleet, what a lot of trouble he would have saved us," McKinley told a friend afterward.

Major General Arthur MacArthur became the commander of the American forces in the Philippines in May 1900, replacing General Elwell Otis, whom
he regarded with complete contempt. "A locomotive bottom side up on the
track, with its wheels revolving at full speed" was the way he described Otis. He
was more aggressive than Otis, and while he also pushed for political reform,

he was willing to use extreme force to destroy the guerrillas. There were bound to be tensions between him and Washington, given the absolute certitude in his mind-set over what ought to be done, and the comparable ambivalence in Washington. McKinley did not want to be pulled down in an endless, draining, increasingly unpopular war. Thus, he did not want to leave everything to the military on location. He looked instead for some kind of political solution. In 1901, he finally decided to send a five-man commission to the islands to work out a political settlement, and he chose his friend, William Howard Taft, an extremely able Ohio lawyer and judge, to lead it. Taft wanted no part of the Philippines. What he really wanted was a seat on the Supreme Court. If, however, he turned down the first, he feared the second might never come his way. An immense man who weighed some 320 pounds, Taft was in no way enthusiastic about going to Manila. "But Mr. President," he said when they met, "I am sorry we have got the Philippines. I don't want them and I think you ought to have some man who is more in sympathy with the situation." "You don't want them any less than I do," McKinley answered, according to Taft, and then insisted that what he needed was a man he trusted out there representing him.

MacArthur, by then the military governor general of the islands, was furious at this potential challenge to his absolute control, and he never gave Taft a chance. Instead of meeting Taft and the other commissioners when they first arrived in Manila, as protocol required, he sent a deputy to the dock; and, to make things worse, in the words of the diplomat-historian Warren Zimmermann, "he tried to humble the commissioners by keeping them waiting all day in the blistering heat, then receiving them like an Asian potentate." Even meeting with them represented a humiliation for him, he informed them. Neither Taft nor MacArthur had an easy job—and the division of authority between the civilian and military side was never entirely clear—but MacArthur made it much worse with his disrespect for Taft, who was generally regarded as being able and fair-minded. It seemed not to bother MacArthur that in treating Taft with contempt he was treating the president with contempt as well. His struggle was a triumph of ego over common sense: he was setting up himself, not Taft, for a great fall.

Taft's mission was political—more than anything else to protect American future interests and to midwife some distant form of Filipino independence. He would sometimes use phrases like "the Philippines for the Filipinos" or, on occasion, in the style of the times, refer to the Filipinos as "little brown brothers." But the troops fighting under MacArthur did not think of their adversaries as potential siblings. They had a ballad that went: "He may be a brother of William Howard Taft / but he ain't no brother of mine." There was as little informal contact as possible between the general and the lead commissioner;

in order to communicate with MacArthur, Taft had to write him letters. Having dealt with some of the most able men in American politics over the years, Taft was underwhelmed by Arthur MacArthur's inflated ego and wrote home to figures of substance like Secretary of War Elihu Root on the qualities in the general that he did not admire, words that would have an odd resonance half a century later. Arthur MacArthur was lacking in a sense of humor, "rather fond of profound generalizations on the psychological conditions of the people; politely lacking in any great consideration for the views of anyone as to the real situation who is a civilian and who has been here only a comparatively short period of time." He was a man, Taft thought, quick to give lectures and slow to listen.

Given that Taft not only bore the personal imprimatur of the president of the United States but was a close personal friend as well, MacArthur's behavior was not merely petulant, it was shortsighted, and wildly self-destructive. In the process of proving to Taft who was really important in this two-man civilian-military struggle for power, MacArthur quite gratuitously offended the four most important Republican political figures of the era: McKinley; Root; Teddy Roosevelt, who became McKinley's running mate in 1900 (succeeding him the next year when McKinley was assassinated); and Taft himself, who became governor-general of the Philippines in 1902 and then secretary of war, before winning the presidency in 1908. It took thirteen months of MacArthur's constant resistance to Taft before he was recalled. The job in Manila would prove the high-water mark of his career. Eight years passed from the time he was recalled to the moment when Taft assumed the presidency, and when he did, MacArthur quickly resigned his military commission. But it had all been over long before that. Though he became a lieutenant general, then the highest rank in the Army, he was never offered the post of Army chief of staff, the job he wanted more than anything else. Despite his considerable accomplishments, Arthur MacArthur ended his career and life caught up in his own bitterness, a constant rage that was like a self-inflicted virus. In those years, as William Manchester wrote, he planted a terrible seed of conflict between civilian and military authority in his own son: "The seed took a long time to flower—a half century—but in the end its fruit would be extraordinary." To anyone coming somewhat belatedly upon the story of Arthur MacArthur and how he mistreated Taft (and thus his president), and already knowing something of the story of Douglas MacArthur's collision with his president, Harry Truman, it would be an eerie kind of footnote to future events—history not so much repeating itself as preceding itself.

Arthur MacArthur lived for three more years after he resigned in 1909. The real keeper of the flame, the person who kept the myth of him alive, was his widow, Pinky MacArthur. In her mind it would be up to her son, young Douglas, to avenge the family honor. "You must grow up to be a great man," she constantly told him, "like your father," or, she added, "like Robert E. Lee." It would be his job not merely to live up to his father but to exceed his accomplishments, making her the ultimate successful mother. When he was eventually named Army chief of staff, the job his father had been denied, she said, "If only your father could see you now! Douglas, you're everything he wanted to be."

8

WHAT AN ODD thing that a woman born in another century, ninety-eight years before the start of the Korean War, a decade and a half dead by 1950, should have so profound an influence on a battle taking place in the middle of the twentieth century. But there was no way of comprehending Douglas MacArthur without understanding not only his self-absorbed father but his mother as well. For more than any figure of that era, including Franklin Roosevelt, who had his own domineering mother, Douglas MacArthur was a mama's boy. Congressional Medal of Honor winner he might be and brave in the face of enemy fire he certainly was—indeed almost on occasion suicidally so—but he was a mama's boy nonetheless. Of not many American military heroes could it be said that when they left home for West Point, their mothers uprooted themselves and moved to that small town on the Hudson. Pinky MacArthur took a room in the best local hotel, Craney's, in order to stand watch over Douglas for four full years at the academy, lest he fall below her expectations and slough off into mediocrity. West Point might have been the most rigidly demanding four-year institution in America, but Pinky MacArthur was there anyway, just in case the academy's contemporary custodians slipped a bit or did not realize how remarkable a young man she had bequeathed them.

Pinky MacArthur was not just the key architect of Douglas MacArthur's career, but more important, the molder of his psyche, the creator of the almost unique self-absorption that cloaked and on occasion diminished his equally great talent. What she had wrought, all sorts of other talented, devoted public men would struggle with and against for four decades. In contemporary parlance, she would have been known as a stage mother, that is, an immensely ambitious, driven woman who, lacking the outlets for her own ambitions, transferred them to her son and lived through his success. Her career, and she was a world-class careerist, was her son. As MacArthur rose, Pinky MacArthur rose too; as he conquered the varying challenges before him, so did she; as he was honored, so was she. He was raised not just to succeed, but to succeed at the expense of all other human qualities. To be successful you simply could not afford to think of anyone else; if you did, you might be pulled down by them.

In this way, his mother raised him to be the most self-absorbed and thus self-isolated of men. From the start, he was a young man apart in terms of peer relationships. His first wedding—though the weddings of West Point men are normally notable social occasions, reflecting the fierce bonds between the groom and his classmates—was notable for the lack of friends and colleagues. Only one real friend attended. Years later he would end his career very much apart from other officers, save his own staff, one known for its sycophancy. He was a man with no capacity for genuine peer friendships, in no small part because in his own mind he had no peers.

Pinky MacArthur quite deliberately sent him out not merely to avenge the wrongs done to his father but to compete against him. She was raising a gifted, talented, cerebral man cut off from almost anyone else—a kind of military genius/human monster, someone who was never to be wrong. Never. He was never to make a mistake, never to fail. He was a man who for all his very considerable talents was, in some terrible, unrecognized way, incomplete. Perhaps the greatest struggle, as the Korean War began, would not be that of MacArthur against Truman or MacArthur against the Chinese, but MacArthur against MacArthur—the competition between his better self, the side of him that was so truly intelligent, creative, and audacious, and the part of him that was so vainglorious, selfish, and arrogant. The writer Cole Kingseed, a professor of military history at West Point, once noted that a description of Oliver Cromwell, the seventeenth-century Puritan general, was applicable to MacArthur as well in trying to decide whether he was a good man or an evil man: he was "a great bad man."

Much of that came from Pinky MacArthur. From her he learned the need to be perfect or seem perfect, to cover up any sign of weakness or frailty. Perhaps more than anything else, she left him unable to admit to error. From that need to be perfect came inevitably a certain paranoia. People, in his mind, were always out to get him. How could they—there was always a "they," back at headquarters in France when he was younger, in Washington when he became more senior—have done *this* to him? He lived in a world where the only memories, his own and those of his staff members, were of his successes, of the perfection of his deeds. If things had gone wrong, they had gone wrong because of others, enemies surely, not because of his own flaws. About the lack of preparation in the first American troops to enter combat in Korea, he would later write: "How I asked myself could the United States have allowed such a deplorable situation to develop? I thought back to those days, only a short time before, when our country had been militarily more powerful than any nation on the face of the earth. But in the short space of five years this power had been filtered away in a bankruptcy of positive and courageous leadership towards any long range objectives." He did not, of course, mention that he had helped accelerate the forces of demobilization by announcing on his own that he needed fewer than half the troops in Japan originally ticketed for his command; nor did he mention that the garrison-duty soldiers who first went to Korea, and were so ill-prepared, had been under his direct command; that he had rarely deigned to pay attention to them unless they were at intra-Army football games; that, like the country itself, he had essentially been on a peacetime footing.

MARY PINCKNEY HARDY was a Southern belle, back when that mattered a great deal. The daughter of a Norfolk, Virginia, cotton broker, she met Arthur MacArthur in New Orleans during Mardi Gras and they were married in 1873, only eight years after the end of the bloodiest war in American history, when the passions and prejudices it generated were still at their height. Two of her brothers who had fought with the South refused to attend the wedding. Her married life was never easy. She had been born to relative luxury and status, a debutante of her era, but she signed on, for better or for worse, to a harsh life, moving from post to post, turned unwittingly into a pioneer woman, often in godforsaken parts of the West and Southwest where she would be greeted by marginal creature comforts. Given her privileged background, it was amazing that she stuck it out. William Manchester calls it "a tribute, to her courage and perhaps to the strength of social discipline then."

Her first son, Arthur MacArthur III, entered the Navy, and died relatively young in 1923; a second son, Malcolm, died of the measles at the age of five. Douglas was born in 1880 at Fort Dodge, Arkansas, which eventually became Little Rock. How much the death of her second son affected the emotional intensity Pinky MacArthur would focus on her third and last child, one can never know; but surely she had suffered no small amount of emotional damage, and there is no doubt that he was the one on whom she dispensed her very considerable energies—he was the last best hope. If his father, a national hero seventeen years before Douglas was born, was the beau ideal that he was to live up to, a constant almost mythic presence, then his mother was his drill sergeant, reminding him of those deeds of his father's that were still to be matched. On the day that the Japanese Diet passed a land reform act in his years as the unofficial ruler of Japan, MacArthur leaned far back in his chair as if looking up at heaven, though it was actually at a photo of his father, who had pushed unsuccessfully for land reform when he was in the Philippines—and said, "How am I doing, Dad?"

Pinky MacArthur had wanted him to go to West Point, but surprisingly enough, despite the family's political connections, it had been hard for him to

gain an appointment. Finally, she moved them to a district where the congressman was a friend of Douglas's grandfather. He still had problems getting in:
when he flunked his first physical, thanks to curvature of his spine, she went out
and found a doctor who would work on correcting it. When the congressman,
overwhelmed by applicants with comparable connections, set up a special exam,
she immediately hired a high school principal to tutor young Douglas. The
night before the exam, he was nervous and anxious, barely able to sleep. She
rose to the occasion, giving him her most rousing motivational speech: "Doug,
you'll win if you don't lose your nerve. You must believe in yourself, my son, or
no one else will believe in you. Be confident, self-reliant, and even if you don't
make it, you will know that you have done your best. Now go to it." There were
thirteen young men taking the test. MacArthur scored 99.3; the next highest
grade was 77.9.

He excelled at West Point. He was first in his class, of course. That was to
be expected. His grades were for many years the third highest ever recorded,
and of the two men who had done better, one was Pinky's other hero, Robert
E. Lee. Though her son had done brilliantly during World War I and was so
acknowledged by his superiors (seven Silver Stars, and he almost won the
Congressional Medal of Honor), was much recognized for his skilled leadership of the Forty-second or Rainbow Division, and had ended up its commander, the youngest division commander in World War I, it was a meteoric
career that was never quite meteoric enough. Pinky MacArthur was always
there to remind him that there was more to conquer, and just in case others
were not aware of his superior abilities, she was always out there publicizing
them. Her letters to his superiors were coy and manipulative, full of flattery of
the recipients, reminding them not only of his deeds in France but, of course,
of his West Point grades as well, evidence of the old Southern belle at work.
When during World War I she felt that Douglas had been a colonel too long,
she wrote Secretary of War Newton Baker, suggesting he be promoted to general: "This officer is an instrument ready to hand for large things if you see fit
to use him. . . . He is a loyal and devoted officer and I present his name for
consideration as I believe his advancement will serve—not only to benefit his
own interest—but on a much broader scale, the interest of our beloved country in this great hour of her trial." Baker did not respond, but Pinky was not
deterred. Eight months later she wrote him again: "I am taking the liberty of
sending you a few lines in continuation of the little heart-to-heart pen and
ink chat I had with you from California with reference to my son, Douglas,
and my heart's great wish that you might see your way clear to bestow upon
him a Star. . . . Considering the fine work he has done with so much pride
and enthusiasm, and the prominence he has gained in actual fighting, I

believe the entire Army, with few exceptions, would applaud your selecting him as one of your Generals."

Baker quickly passed her on to General John J. (Black Jack) Pershing. Now she had Pershing in her sights—a man who had been a young captain in the Philippines when Arthur MacArthur, then a major general, had befriended him. Pershing soon received what she called a "little heart-to-heart letter emboldened by the thought of old friendship for you and yours and the knowledge of my late husband's great admiration for you. . . . I know the Secretary of War and his family quite intimately and the Secretary is deeply attached to Colonel MacArthur and knows him quite well." Nor, of course, did the letter writing end when MacArthur finally made general in 1917. If anything, the process taught his mother that pressure worked, and when he had been a brigadier general for five years—far too long in her view—she began a new campaign to get him his second star, a campaign in which his first wife, Louise, also participated. Louise MacArthur hired a former Rainbow Division officer who was by then a well-connected lawyer in Washington to lobby for her. ("I don't care what it costs. Just go ahead and send the bill to me personally. Don't tell Douglas.") The lobbyist arranged for a group of men who had been colonels in MacArthur's division in France in World War I to meet with the secretary of war, John Weeks, who told them that MacArthur was too young. Too young, MacArthur later muttered, when he heard what Weeks had said, why, Genghis Khan commanded his hordes at thirteen, Napoleon his armies at twenty-six.

When he was superintendent at West Point, his mother was his hostess. When her son married for the first time—an attractive divorcée—she did not approve; in fact, she immediately took to her bed exhibiting a frailty, never manifested before, but a warning signal that he had better attend to her first, and his wife second. It was a move she would make again and again whenever he seemed to be slipping away from her control. She did not, of course, attend the wedding. To no one's surprise MacArthur's first marriage did not last long, and by the time he was Army chief of staff, Pinky MacArthur was back in charge, serving as his official hostess, and he was returning home every day for lunch. His second marriage, the one that worked, did so in part because Pinky MacArthur handpicked Jean Faircloth for him, and because the second Mrs. MacArthur, herself something of a Southern belle, also revered and idolized him, cherishing her role as the general's lady, referring to him in public as "The General" and calling him in private "Sir Boss."

Pinky MacArthur taught above all else the importance of success, that it validated all the other sacrifices, most especially hers, and that success at a personal level could always be viewed as being good for the country—it was part of her mantra, there in all those obsequious letters she wrote to his superiors: the good of Douglas MacArthur and the good of the United States of America were one and the same thing. As her creation, he was different from other generals of his era, even the most egocentric, like George Patton. Whatever else, the Army, with its great hardships in both peacetime and wartime, served to make the bonds of friendship unusually strong among those who had known one another when they were young and endured together through long and difficult and occasionally arid careers. But MacArthur had none of those bonds, none of those wonderful enduring lifetime friendships. He went through his career as a man with an aura, but almost no real friends. In the Army the needs of self are always to be balanced with a sense of obligation, loyalty, and respect for the institution, and the need to observe orders. Loyalty works two ways; not only to make those beneath you respectful of your orders but to teach you what you owe to those who are your superiors. Here Douglas MacArthur, like his father before him, failed a critical test.

9

MACARTHUR WAS STILL a towering national figure at the start of the Korean War, perhaps by then as much of a political figure as a military one, and a national icon, whether Washington liked it or not, the last active connection to both world wars. His performance as the commander in the Pacific during World War II had been judged as nothing less than brilliant. He had been somewhat behind the curve at the beginning of the war in respecting what the new possibilities were for carrier-propelled airpower, and for what the Japanese as soldiers (and as pilots) would be able to do. When the Japanese planes had struck so successfully against his own planes in the early days of the war, he was convinced—and it was a reflection of both personal and national racism—that their pilots must be white men. In the period before December 7, he had talked far too confidently about what the Japanese could *not* do. He had, for example, told John Hersey, then a talented young writer for *Time* magazine, that if the Japanese entered the war, the British, Dutch, and Americans would be able to stop them with half the forces they had already allotted to the Pacific, and that it would be easy to bottle up the Japanese fleet.

But he came to understand, relatively early in the war, one of the major truths about the Japanese as both a culture and a military force—that when they controlled the agenda, and they were in command, and everything was done according to their schedule, they were formidable, and their rigid command structure seemingly unbeatable. Everything seemed to work as planned; everyone followed the strictest orders faithfully; no mistakes were allowed. But if the tide of battle went the other way, if the Japanese lost the initiative, these very strengths worked against them. They became surprisingly inflexible, skilled in fighting an enemy that behaved only as the Japanese Army itself would behave. Because theirs was so hierarchical and so authoritarian a society, with so little value placed on individual initiative, they were not nearly as imposing a force, and they lacked a critical quality required for the battlefield, an ability to respond to the unknown. As such, they quickly became militarily muscle-bound. "Never let the Jap attack you. When the Japanese soldier has a coordinated plan of attack he works smoothly," MacArthur told his officers. But, he added, "when *he* is attacked—when he doesn't know what is coming—it isn't the same."

He also quickly adapted to a new kind of warfare. If he had not understood the possibilities of airpower in modern warfare, and had been caught with his planes on the ground on Clark Field on December 8, then he was a quick learner and soon rectified that. A skilled and quite forthright young air officer named George Kenney had stood up to him and his bullying chief of staff, Richard Sutherland, and then helped teach him what airpower could do in this immense theater—a theater that was a vast ocean populated, as it was, by occasional islands, among them a certain number of Japanese strongpoints. Out of Kenney's quite practical knowledge of airpower, and MacArthur's originality of mind, they had jointly fashioned a war plan that stripped the Japanese of their strengths. MacArthur's dilemma at the start was obvious: his own ground forces were limited, and the Japanese were capable of fighting ferociously in defense on atolls where it would be hard to apply some of America's technological superiority. The shrewd answer to that dilemma was to avoid confronting the Japanese where they were strongest, and instead he and Kenney concentrated on striking at islands where they were weakest, thereupon creating airfields on other atolls, which in turn allowed them to strike even deeper into Japanese-held territory, and slowly but surely cut off their lines of communication and starve their troops out. They did not so much attack the formidable enemy strongholds as ignore and isolate them. When the Japanese had more than one hundred thousand troops at Rabaul in the Solomons, just aching for a showdown, MacArthur avoided them. "Starve Rabaul! The jungle! Starvation! They're my allies!" It was a military tour de force. John Gunther, one of the best-known journalists of that era, who had his own problems with the darker side of MacArthur, wrote of him in that campaign that "MacArthur took more territory, with less loss of life than any military commander since Darius the Great."

But there was another side of him surfacing at the same time that was far less attractive. Even during World War I there had been signs of the danger of his immense ego. But then he had been young and on the ascent, shrewd enough to button up the other side on most occasions, audacious as a commander and good with his troops, almost always up front with them. In World War II it was different. He was famous by then; he had become politicized, and his ego was constantly in open conflict with his pure military needs. There were more enemies now, and not necessarily the enemy aggressor in the field but civilian and military officials back in Washington; there was an ever greater need for credit, an addiction, really, to fame. In addition, there were fewer restraints on him. By the end of World War II, the part of him that was so talented was in an increasingly fragile balance with the part of him that could be so destructive.

For he was a man who demanded the ultimate in loyalty from those beneath him, and yet to whom the sharing of credit was the most alien of concepts. He had contempt for those like Eisenhower who allowed their subordinate officers any measure of fame. All dispatches emanating from his headquarters were to begin with his name; thus, the dateline for stories filed from the Pacific would always be "MacArthur's Headquarters," implying a dispatch filed from a battlefield headquarters where one man alone made the decisions and did the fighting. All announcements of Pacific victories during the war were to be made in his name. William Manchester once studied the early dispatches from the theater and discovered that in 109 of the first 142 press communiqués sent out in the first three months of the war, no other officer's name was mentioned. General Robert Eichelberger, one of MacArthur's senior Army commanders, once told his own public information officer that he would rather have him place a live rattlesnake in his pocket than mention him prominently in dispatches. When Eichelberger, a talented, extremely aggressive field officer who commanded MacArthur's Eighth Army, was written about in *The Saturday Evening Post* and *Life,* both of them important magazines in that era, MacArthur was not pleased. He called Eichelberger in and told him, "Do you realize I could reduce you to the grade of colonel tomorrow and send you home?" Loyalty with him was a one-way street, and he was capable of being remarkably disloyal to the presidents he served and the senior military men back in Washington. Year by year he had become the most political of men, constantly working on his connections to the Republican Party. Even in the midst of a great global war in 1944, MacArthur, fueled by a relentless ambition and deep personal hatred of Franklin Roosevelt, had seemed to align himself with the president's most bitter political enemies. Then in 1948, he had been part of an attempt to gain the Republican presidential nomination, one that had failed badly, and in 1950, even as he commanded the troops in Korea, it was the general belief in the White House and among some of the Republican presidential candidates that he was thinking of a race in 1952, in the midst of the Korean War, that he still hungered for it.

The conservative wing of the Republican Party thought he was one of them, that his politics were conservative, and that was probably more true than not, though he had proved to be a surprisingly liberal governor-general of Japan. On the Richter scale of American politics he was by the middle of the twentieth

century far more conservative than liberal, his politics and his attitudes shaped
by an entirely different era. But those who knew him well thought that in his
politics ideology was always quite secondary; that he lived, more than anything
else, in the kingdom of self, and that his politics were the politics of self.

Nothing had revealed how political he was, as well as his need to be a
player on the national scene, more than his role in suppressing the Bonus
Army in the early 1930s. The Great Depression had revealed the deepest
chasms in American society, and a profound political, economic, and social
alienation had taken place. MacArthur was the chief of staff of the Army, and
he had aligned himself enthusiastically not merely with the Hoover administration, but with the existing political-economic order, then coming under
fierce challenge on many fronts. That he took the administration's side in that
crisis was not surprising and was perhaps even unavoidable. But the way he
thrust himself into the epicenter went well beyond the requirements of the
job; it was a reflection of his need for fame and glory. The Bonus Army had
arrived in Washington, a group of destitute World War I veterans, desperately
seeking some kind of relief in the form of their bonus for service in the war. It
was 1932, the very height of the Depression. It was a defining political moment for MacArthur; for no matter how famous and celebrated he eventually
became as a general during World War II, the stigma of what he did then
never entirely left him in the minds of many Americans who had come of age
in those years.

Millions of Americans were out of work then and the Bonus Army, or
Bonus Expeditionary Force, as the men in it called their movement, was a ragtag group of veterans who hoped that spring to lobby for a bill sponsored by
Congressman Wright Patman of Texas. The bill would have given them each
an immediate bonus—on average about $1,000 a man, which was very big
money then. Service in World War I was supposed to be rewarded with a
bonus of that size either upon the death of the soldier or in 1945, some twenty-
seven years after the end of the war. Patman's bill was designed to expedite the
process.

Perhaps as many as thirty thousand people, most of them veterans but also
their wives and children, created an instant squatters' village, a pathetic little
camp of cardboard shacks and tents, in the capital, many of them settling in an
area called the Anacostia Flats, just across the Anacostia River, in the southern
part of the city. Few of the men were particularly radical, although there were
some radicals among them, not surprising in a time when more and more ordinary citizens were losing faith in the traditional untempered capitalism
of the era. Courtney Whitney, one of MacArthur's closest aides, and a man
who often spoke for him, later wrote that the Bonus marchers had "a heavy

percentage of criminals, men with prison records for such crimes as murder, manslaughter, rape, robbery, burglary, blackmail and assault." To MacArthur they were nothing but a dangerous anti-American rabble. The Veterans Administration, which kept close records, later reported that 94 percent of them were actual veterans, 67 percent of whom had served the United States overseas. Dwight Eisenhower, then a major and MacArthur's talented young aide, thought the marchers might be mistaken in what they were attempting, but felt there was a poignant quality to them and their demands—"They were ragged, ill-fed, and felt themselves badly abused."

As the political battles in Congress over Patman's bill heated up, the Bonus Army's numbers continued to swell. By summer, the ability of the local police to control them was questionable. Hoover, a man largely paralyzed by the Depression, was at the low ebb of his popularity and becoming increasingly nervous about the threat the marchers posed. That summer Patman's bill was passed by the House only to be defeated by the Senate. Simultaneously, there were several minor skirmishes between Bonus Army members and the local police. Hoover felt it was time to get the veterans out of town and wanted the United States Army to take over the job. At a meeting with top civilian and military officials, including MacArthur, the Bonus Army leaders asked for permission, if the Army were to enter their little encampment, to march out in proper formation and with some measure of dignity. "Yes, my friend, of course!" MacArthur answered. On July 28, the situation came to a head after several scuffles with the marchers. The orders to end the protest came down from Hoover himself. Eisenhower, not wanting the Army too closely associated with what was sure to be, even if carried out skillfully, an odious political act, tried to keep MacArthur somewhat in the background. A brigadier general named Perry Miles, a man of considerable competence, was to lead the troops. A young armored officer, a major named George Patton, Jr., would be in charge of the tanks, a warning of what could happen should the Bonus Army try to resist. Eisenhower was appalled when he realized that MacArthur intended to show up on location to lead the forces of suppression personally. Both he and MacArthur had arrived at their offices that morning in civvies. MacArthur promptly sent Eisenhower home to get his uniform and dispatched his own orderly to his quarters to get his—the one with all the decorations. Eisenhower argued valiantly that this would be a mistake, that a terrible stench would arise from it, and that it would eventually hurt the Army in lobbying on the Hill with Democrats. ("I told that dumb son of a bitch that he had no business going down there. I told him it was no place for a chief of staff," he later said.) The chief of staff, who often spoke of himself in the third person, replied, "MacArthur has decided to go into active command in the field." Then he added, "Incipient revolution is in the air." Eisenhower suggested that if both of them had to visit the scene, they at least do so out of uniform. MacArthur vetoed the suggestion.

So off they went in full uniform to meet the Bonus Army. Their orders from the secretary of the Army were quite specific. Hoover wanted the marchers tamed, but he wanted no riot. The suppression of the protest should be as restrained as possible. The Army troops were not to cross the river or go near the largest encampment of veterans, on the other side of the river. Eisenhower later recounted how he had told MacArthur that there was a messenger there with specific orders from the president. "I don't want to hear them and I don't want to see them. Get him away," MacArthur answered. He had decided that if he did not receive them, then there would be no need to act on them, and thus no limits set on his movements. The river would be crossed, the encampment destroyed.

The scene around them quickly turned ugly. Some of the veterans' pathetic little shacks were soon burning. Eisenhower, aware that there would be considerable press coverage of an event guaranteed to be filled with pathos, tried to get MacArthur out of there. This was, he believed, a civilian matter, ordered by civilians; let them take the responsibility and the heat. Eisenhower might as well have ordered a moth to stay away from a flame. It was as if MacArthur *needed* to be at the center of the coverage. He deliberately held a late evening press conference, where, having exceeded Hoover's orders (and created a political crisis that would greatly help the Democratic candidate Franklin Roosevelt in the forthcoming election), he praised Hoover for being so steadfast: "Had he waited another week, I believe the institutions of our government would have been threatened." In this way did MacArthur present Hoover with a fait accompli. The president could not dissent from what had seemingly been done under his orders. It was a devastating political moment for Hoover. No one understood that more clearly than Franklin Roosevelt, who believed that it would seal his election.

For millions of ordinary Americans, who in hard times sympathized with the marchers, it was a defining moment; MacArthur became forever in their minds the kind of military man who abused the rights of ordinary people, a man who was never to be trusted politically and was too militaristic. In some ways, however, he got just what he thought he wanted, for his actions that day helped connect him ever more tightly to those on the right wing who saw the Bonus Army as part of a larger threat to capitalism. He had made himself the favorite general of a formidable, increasingly frustrated political constituency that resented almost every initiative taken during the New Deal. He had politicized himself more than any general ever should, cut himself off from those who politically were on the ascent, and connected himself to those who were momentarily in decline.

The byplay that day offered a fascinating insight into two Army officers who would play central roles in America's future: Eisenhower with his supple sense of political consequences, his innate political deftness, and his empathy for the difficulties of ordinary people; and MacArthur with his statement that this was a radical moment threatening an entire economic order and, even more important, with his need to be center stage and to receive the full attention of the press, bedecked in full military uniform, medals and all.

MacArthur's own sense of where the country was (and what it was) often seemed badly skewed, especially as he got older and the nation, driven by vast technological breakthroughs, changed at an accelerating rate. He was a distinctly nineteenth-century man, more comfortable with those from an era that was passing than those from an era being fashioned by new political forces, transformed and democratized by dramatic economic changes and changes in communications. That MacArthur dissented from many of the political changes taking place in Washington was not surprising. But with him everything was always more personal; it was as if the men who had arrived with the New Deal were not merely different from those who had preceded them but enemies, usurpers, in no small part because his influence with them was less than it had been with their predecessors. His views of the two Democratic presidents under whom he subsequently served were nothing less than toxic. This was especially true of Roosevelt, who, shrewd and cunning, managed to play the general with exceptional skill, much to the latter's irritation—the irritation of a classic user who finally runs into someone who is even better at it. (Roosevelt's view of MacArthur was almost uniquely cynical. He was to be used but not to be trusted. The president once told his aide Rexford Tugwell that Huey Long was one of the two most dangerous men in the country. Who was the other, asked Tugwell, Father Coughlin, then a fiery hate-spilling radio priest? "Oh, no," Roosevelt answered, "the other is Douglas MacArthur.")

During World War II, he and Roosevelt played the most complicated of games, supremely gifted politician dealing with supremely gifted but deeply antagonistic general. Roosevelt once told the general—it was something MacArthur was fond of quoting, as if to show that he had no political ambitions—"Douglas, I think you are our best general, but I believe you would be our worst politician." Roosevelt, aristocratic and infinitely devious, watched MacArthur like a hawk. Roosevelt understood him (and his burning ambition for the presidency) far better than MacArthur understood Roosevelt. The president never thought the general a serious political threat—he had too little connection to ordinary voters—but just in case, he kept copies of a report MacArthur had submitted just before the outbreak of World War II in which he had insisted he could hold the Philippines and other key points in the Pacific because of "the inability of our enemy to launch his air attacks on our islands" and documentation about the puzzling way MacArthur's command in the Philippines had been caught with its planes on the ground at Clark Field nine hours after his headquarters had learned of the Japanese attack at Pearl Harbor, thus easy prey for the Japanese planes.

Mutual trust was hardly at the core of the relationship. MacArthur, who *always* kept score, sensed that he had met his match and resented it bitterly. In April 1945, when Roosevelt died in office on the very eve of victory in Europe, much of the nation mourned, but Douglas MacArthur most demonstrably did not. Hearing the news, he turned to Bonnie Fellers, a staff officer, and said, "So Roosevelt is dead: a man who would never tell the truth when a lie would serve him just as well." Outsiders being told what he said were shocked; it was hard to imagine any headquarters save this one where a commander would speak like that about a commander in chief who had just died.

What MacArthur remembered about his dealings with Roosevelt was always negative: the grievances, not the successes, not the way Roosevelt had ordered his rescue when in early 1942 he seemed trapped in the Philippines as the Japanese took much of the rest of his command captive, or the fact that the president had come around to MacArthur's side in a crucial dispute with the Navy over the way to conduct the war in the Pacific and approach the Japanese main islands. What was important was not what Roosevelt had done for him, but rather what he had not done for him. Yet nothing had added to his own myth so much as the escape from the Philippines. It was a public relations triumph both for him and for the nation. Arriving in Australia, he had issued his famous "I shall return" statement. Washington had wanted to change it to "We shall return," but the general was having none of it: this was to be the most personal of pledges and missions, and so it went out as he directed. During that dark hour when a hero was needed, he had been lionized for his escape, with the administration an active participant in that lionization. His own significant miscalculations at the start of the war, mistakes that might have ended the career of a lesser general, were covered up, and instead the story became that he had heroically made it out, that *MacArthur had lived to fight another day.* No one had expressed that thought more clearly than William (Wild Bill) Donovan, a man of enormous influence in those days, a Wall Street lawyer with immense ambitions, who would in time head the OSS, the Office of Strategic Services, and its successor, the CIA: "General MacArthur," he said at the time, "a symbol of our nation—outnumbered, outgunned—with the seas around him and the skies above him controlled by the enemy—fighting for freedom." The flattery got him nowhere; MacArthur allowed neither the OSS nor CIA into his command area in both World War II and Korea.

In Europe during World War II, any number of talented younger officers had come into their own under Eisenhower, combat and staff officers alike; but that was not true in MacArthur's command in the Pacific, where no other officer was allowed to make a name for himself and where there would be little turnover in his staff from the beginning of the war to his departure from Tokyo. "There should be newer blood around MacArthur," John Gunther wrote in November 1950, "but he will not tolerate anybody near him being too big. I heard it said, 'None of MacArthur's men can risk being first rate.' "

The Bataan Gang, they were called. The name itself reflected a kind of loyalty test. Were you there at the low point in his career—back in the Philippines with the Japanese closing in, at the moment when he had been forced to leave for Australia? Not many men—Ned Almond, chief of staff in his Tokyo days, was a rare exception—managed to become part of his inner circle if they did not go back to that earlier defining moment. At the start of the Korean War, a disproportionate number of his top men had been with him since the late 1930s. It was the most exclusionary of groups—anyone who was not an insider was suspect. Robert Sherwood, the distinguished author and playwright who represented Roosevelt in an unofficial way during the war, was appalled by the hostility he encountered in that headquarters, the rage against all other instruments of the war and against other theaters. Sherwood arrived there in 1944 and brought with him news of the Allied crossing of the Remagen bridge—a great moment in the drive against Germany. But when he told Charles Willoughby the news, Willoughby snapped at him, "We don't give a damn out here about anything that happens in Europe." There was, Sherwood wrote the president, "unmistakable evidence of an acute persecution complex at work. To hear some of the staff officers talk, one would think that the War Department, the State Department—and possibly the White House itself—are under the domination of 'Communists and British imperialists.' "

MacArthur, Roosevelt always believed, was completely out of touch with domestic American politics, a prisoner of his dreams rather than the country's changing political and economic realities. MacArthur had believed, back in 1936, that Alf Landon was going to beat Roosevelt, and turned angrily on Eisenhower, his chief of staff, and a son of Kansas, who was sure that Landon, a Kansan, had no chance. Eisenhower showed MacArthur a letter from a friend of his in Abilene, suggesting that Landon might not even carry his own state. MacArthur categorized Eisenhower and another staff officer who also doubted Landon's success as "fearful and small minded people who are afraid to express judgments that are obvious from the evidence at hand." Landon carried two states, losing, among forty-six others, Kansas.

By 1944, in the middle of the Pacific war, there was already talk of MacArthur running against Roosevelt. Some of the most passionate Roosevelt-haters on the Republican right were pushing for him to consider the race. One of them, a Republican congressman from Nebraska, A. L. Miller, saw a MacArthur candidacy as the only hope to save the country and wrote him: "I am convinced that unless the New Deal can be stopped this time out, our American way of life is forever doomed." Much that was in Miller's letters—there were several of them—would certainly have struck most political or military figures of the time as the work of a fringe ideologue, a man not to be encouraged. MacArthur, however, began an ongoing exchange with Miller. "I do unreservedly agree with the complete wisdom and statesmanship of your comments," he wrote the congressman, referring darkly to the "sinister drama of our present chaos and confusion." By chance that happened to be the moment when the country was doing exceptionally well for a nation at war, and when ordinary people in all stations of life took on wartime sacrifices with great goodwill and determination.

That did not stop the Miller-MacArthur letters from flying back and forth. "This monarchy," the congressman wrote, "which is being established in America will destroy the rights of common people." Back came MacArthur: "Your description of conditions in the United States is a sobering one indeed, and it is calculated to arouse the thoughtful consideration of every true patriot." What damaged him was the pull of flattery; the need to be revered was too great for him to resist. That was the chink in his armor, and because of it he was sucked in. Miller, thrilled by the fact that a great patriot seemed to see things exactly the way he did, eventually made the letters public, to MacArthur's considerable embarrassment, in the midst of a war. The general then said the letters were private, which was true, and under no condition were they intended to be critical of any political leader or any political philosophy, which, of course, was not. But they were damaging. Pressed by his friend and supporter, Senator Arthur Vandenberg, then still in his isolationist incarnation, MacArthur announced that he did not want his name put into nomination at the Republican convention. Vandenberg sensed that if the general's name were voted on, the results were going to be humiliating. But one delegate slipped through the net, and while Tom Dewey received 1,056 votes, MacArthur got 1 vote. Most assuredly, 1944 had not been a happy year for him politically; just as certainly, the desire to run had not gone away.

*   *   *

IN MAY 1946, Eisenhower, then Army chief of staff, visited the general in Tokyo and they talked of presidential politics. MacArthur pushed Eisenhower to run, and Ike matched that move by suggesting that MacArthur run. At that point MacArthur professed himself too old for a presidential run; but Eisenhower, who understood MacArthur's singular ambition and vanity far better than MacArthur himself, returned to Washington and mentioned to Truman that he might have to face a MacArthur run in 1948. Indeed, with the war over and the democratization of Japan going exceptionally well, the general sent out word to his admirers in 1947 that, though he would not seek the Republican nomination, he would accept a draft if offered. It would be nothing less than his duty, he assured them. The truth was that he had surprisingly high hopes for a run in 1948. But he was badly out of touch with his native land—he had been away for more than a decade, and he was the kind of man who would have been out of touch with his fellow citizens even if he had not left the continental shores.

The journey so many millions of Americans were then making into the middle class would soon have important political consequences for both parties, as former Democratic voters, becoming more affluent, began to think of themselves as independents and to vote more conservatively; but for the moment the New Deal lines, based on elemental economic differences, still held in national elections. The people who were pushing MacArthur to run believed that the New Deal was merely the first step in what was a long and dangerous passage to Communism. His support was strongest in the Midwest, especially in the region served by Colonel Robert McCormick, owner of the *Chicago Tribune* and the leading isolationist of the time. The general's most passionate enthusiasts were isolationists—though MacArthur was not one himself, he was willing to dance with them—nativists, racists, anti-Semites, and labor haters. They were absolutely convinced that they were the truest representatives of what they called Americanism. MacArthur's good friend Major General George Van Horn Moseley, who reflected their attitudes, wrote him on the eve of the 1948 campaign, "There are a great many enemies within our gates who . . . are afraid of you . . . members of the CIO, the Communists, and the Jews, and such skunks as Walter Winchell [a half gossip, half political columnist] and Drew Pearson [a liberal columnist who had tangled with MacArthur earlier on]." As a prominent essayist of the era John McCarten wrote in the *American Mercury,* "It may not be his fault, but it is surely his misfortune that the worst elements on the political Right, including its most blatant lunatic fringe, are whooping it up for MacArthur." Pushed by them to run in 1948, he answered in typical MacArthur prose: "I would say, with all humility that I would be recreant [faithless] to all my concepts of good citizenship were I to shrink because of the hazards and responsibilities involved from any accepting any public duty to which I might be called by the American people." Nobler than that, no man could be.

The people propelling him into the 1948 race were rank political amateurs, filled with their own passion, sense of rectitude, and anger. Everyone they knew agreed with them politically; their worlds, both at the office and at their clubs, were places with few dissenting voices. They knew almost nothing about how to work the machinery of local politics. The test case for MacArthur's run was to be Wisconsin, where he had spent some time as a boy and where his family, as much as any military family can, had roots. It was in the Midwest heartland, and safely within the reach of the *Chicago Tribune*. Robert Wood, an old friend and the dedicated head of the isolationist America First Committee, was his principal supporter and advocate. Wood was sure that MacArthur would win at least twenty of Wisconsin's twenty-seven delegates. Since he was a candidate in absentia, they expected to sell the idea that their patriot-hero was too busy serving his country to run for the office he rightfully deserved. He would do well in Wisconsin, they believed, precisely because he was *not* able to campaign there. Wisconsin would then launch a larger campaign in absentia. But nothing went right—not even with former servicemen. MacArthur had never been known as a soldier's general, and not even the veterans, polls showed, were for him. In fact, those who had served under him tended to favor by a handsome margin a man who now was one of his personal bête noirs, Dwight Eisenhower.

Wisconsin was supposed to launch the campaign, but it effectively ended it. Harold Stassen, the former governor of neighboring Minnesota, won it handily with 40 percent of the vote and nineteen delegates; Thomas Dewey, who went on to win the nomination, got 24 percent and no delegates; MacArthur, on what was supposed to be fertile soil, won 36 percent and only eight delegates. The next day Ambassador William Sebald, the ranking American diplomat in Tokyo, arrived at the Dai Ichi building for a meeting. MacArthur's chief of staff, Major General Paul Mueller, immediately held up a hand to warn Sebald off. "The general is as low as a rug and very disappointed," he told Sebald, who decided to try his luck on another day. But even if the race for the nomination in 1948 had turned into a complete disaster, it had nonetheless proved one thing, which was that late in his career Douglas MacArthur still hoped for the presidency.

THE RELATIONSHIP BETWEEN the president and the general was doomed from the start. The general was disrespectful of the president, and the president, in turn, viscerally disliked and distrusted the general. "And what to do

with Mr. Prima Donna, Brass Hat, Five Star MACARTHUR," the new president wrote in his diary back in 1945. "He's worse than the Cabots and the
Lodges—they at least talked to one another before they told God what to do.
Mac tells God right off. It is a very great pity that we have stuffed shirts like
that in key positions. I don't see why in Hell Roosevelt didn't order Wainwright home [from Corregidor in 1942] and let MacArthur be a martyr. . . .
We'd have a real General and a fighting man if we had Wainwright and not a
play actor and a bunko man such as we have now. Don't see how a country can
produce such men as Robert E. Lee, John J. Pershing, Eisenhower, and Bradley
and at the same time can produce Custers, Pattons, and MacArthurs."

In MacArthur's eyes, Truman's credentials could not have been less imposing. He was a working politician, which was bad enough, but even worse a
Democrat, a liberal Democrat, and he was the designated legatee of the hated
Franklin Roosevelt. How could a man like that, a mere National Guard captain
in World War I and then a politician of marginal abilities, and thus self-
evidently a much, much smaller figure, who had accomplished so little in life,
be above MacArthur in the chain of command? It was in his mind an unanswerable question. Each man was to the other almost an alien being, their
backgrounds were so completely different, their concepts of loyalty and duty
so totally at odds. Almost from the moment in April 1945 that Truman became
president, there were problems between the two men. Senator Tom Connally
of Texas, head of the Senate Foreign Relations Committee, had even warned
Truman against letting MacArthur accept the Japanese surrender. Truman
wrote in his diary: "[Connally] said Doug would run against me in '48 if I built
him up. I told Tom I didn't want to run in '48, and that Doug didn't bother me
that way."

The president and his senior military men believed that MacArthur had
begun behaving badly almost as soon as the war in the Pacific ended. The first
issue that divided them was that of troop levels. In those first months of peace
the president and his top people were trying to slow down the immediate
postwar rush to downsize the Army, fighting the natural urge of American
families to get the boys home and out of uniform. On the issue of troop levels,
MacArthur, in their view, had grandstanded, announcing from Tokyo on September 17, 1945, that, because the occupation of Japan was going so well, he
would need only two hundred thousand troops, not anywhere near the half
million originally ticketed for the job. That had played into the hands of the
administration's domestic critics and had, the people in Washington believed,
been done deliberately, at a time when they were besieged by ever escalating
pressures for demobilization.

In the eyes of Bradley and Eisenhower, this was an example of the general at his absolute worst, never checking in, showing off politically, and putting himself and his own political interests ahead of extremely serious national security concerns. Any other senior officer pulling something like that would have been instantly relieved of his command or at least severely reprimanded. But no one was allowed to move against him. He was always to be treated differently. Even during the war, finalized Pentagon plans were automatically sent out as orders to all headquarters; only to MacArthur were they sent out as a comment. No one even back then had wanted to incur his wrath. But Truman had been furious when he made the demobe harder, and had seriously considered relieving him. Eben Ayers, one of the president's assistants, wrote in his diary at that time, "The president sounded off about Mac and said he was 'going to do something about that fellow,' who he said had been balling things up. He said he was tired of fooling around." Even then, however, the consequences of a major confrontation were too serious. Still, it was an early sign of what would soon be a growing conflict between the two men. In the end, at Truman's request, George Marshall had ever so lightly slapped MacArthur's wrist, sending him a cable indicating that his announcement had made it harder to sustain the draft in peacetime and thus keep adequate American forces overseas. In the future, Marshall wrote, any such statement should be coordinated first with the War Department.

But that incident had helped trigger the back-to-back invitations Truman proffered to MacArthur in September and again October 1945 to come home, consult with the president, be honored by a grateful nation, perhaps be given one more Distinguished Service Cross, and then address a joint session of Congress. A request by a commander in chief, a man newly elevated to the presidency under tragic circumstances in wartime, was never actually a request, though it was masked as one; it was essentially an order. MacArthur nonetheless did not treat it as such and declined, twice. Four-star general he might be, senior American officer he might be, but that was not something any officer should do: if the president summoned, you came. Thus he had been disrespectful to Truman from the start, acting as if they were equals (at best) and there were no chain of command. He was too busy in Tokyo, the general had said, and the dangers of leaving were too great, because of "the extraordinarily dangerous and inherently inflammable situation, which exists here." Truman was livid—this was coming from a man who had only recently said he needed only half the allotted number of troops because things were going so well. MacArthur was very aware of what he was doing. He told one aide, "And I intend to be the first man in our history to refuse to [return home at a presidential request]. I am going to tell them I have work to do and cannot spare the time." What MacArthur told his people privately was even more grandiose.

If he left Japan right now, he insisted, tremors would run through that country as well as other parts of Asia, which would believe themselves abandoned. He also told some of his aides that he would return home on his own terms and when it best suited his own needs. It would perhaps be an emotional return tied to a Republican convention. When one friend suggested to MacArthur that now might be the right time to go, all the anger and paranoia flared: "Don't think for a minute I will go now. At one point I might have done so, but the president, the State Department and Marshall have all been attacking me. They might have won out, but the Reds came out against me and the Communists booed me and that raised me to a pinnacle without which they might have licked me. Thanks to the Soviets I am on top. I would like to pin a medal on their a——."

The two men, president and general, could not have had more contrasting career curves. MacArthur was already a great national hero in those hard pre–World War II years when Truman was still going from failure to failure; in the early 1930s, when MacArthur had exceeded orders and crushed the Bonus Army, it would not have taken a great stretch of the imagination to envision Harry Truman, then at the low point in his own career, as one of its members. The high-water mark of his career at that point, his service in the American Expeditionary Force in France in World War I, as a captain in the Missouri National Guard, seemed hardly a footnote compared to MacArthur's extraordinary exploits in that same war. And yet none of that should have mattered starting in 1945: one was president and the other was a general.

From the beginning, Truman was uneasy with the idea of a commander outside his reach. There was no doubt that he thought frequently of relieving MacArthur. But when someone suggested to Truman, after MacArthur had claimed he didn't need the allotted troops, that perhaps it was time to relieve him, the president answered, "Wait a minute, W-a-i-t a minute." That was MacArthur's great ace in the hole, the fact that the political consequences of removing him were so great because he had a formidable political constituency, one quite deliberately fashioned.

When John Foster Dulles returned to Washington from his meetings with MacArthur in those first grim days of the Korean War and conferred with Truman, he recommended a change of commanders. MacArthur, he said, seemed too old, and he was bothered by the way his attention span seemed to waver. But Truman already felt himself locked in. His hands were tied, he told Dulles, because MacArthur had been so active politically in the country for so long and had even been mentioned, the president noted, as a possible Republican presidential candidate. He could not be recalled, Truman added, "without causing a tremendous reaction in the country," where MacArthur "had been built up to heroic stature." It was a remarkable admission: the president of the United States was about to go to war in a distant land, his armed forces commanded by a general he not only disliked but, more important, distrusted, but whom he feared replacing for political reasons.

MacArthur saw himself as a great surviving link to a magnificent American past; only Washington and Lincoln were his peers. ("My major advisers, now, one founded the United States, the other saved it. If you go back into their lives you can find all the answers," he once said.) When he took over as the supreme commander in the Pacific, one of the first things he did was hang a portrait of Washington behind his desk, and then when the war was done, according to Sidney Mashbir, an intelligence officer, he saluted the portrait of Washington, saying, "Sir, they weren't wearing red coats, but we whipped them just the same." His hatred of the capitol and the men who presided there in those years was palpable. Faubion Bowers, his military secretary in Tokyo and a man privy to his private thoughts as they came pouring out during monologues on rides in his car, thought MacArthur hated *all* presidents. Roosevelt to him was Rosenfeld, and Truman he would refer to as "that Jew in the White House." "Which Jew in the White House?" the puzzled Bowers once asked. "Truman," MacArthur answered. "You can tell by his name. Look at his face." Then one day MacArthur disabused Bowers of the idea that he disliked every president. "Hoover," he said, "wasn't so bad."

MacArthur was given to paranoia anyway, and like most paranoiacs, he quickly made more than his share of enemies. By the spring of 1949, both the State Department and Defense were working on a plan that would effectively diminish a good deal of his power in Japan. Dean Acheson was probably the driving force behind the plans. The idea was to split up the political and military jobs in Tokyo. MacArthur would eventually be brought home to great acclaim, and prominent nonideological replacements would thereupon take up the two jobs, with Maxwell Taylor, a rising star of the Army in World War II, slated to take over the military half. MacArthur, however, got wind of these developments, contacted his own powerful allies in Washington, and brought the plans to the attention of Omar Bradley, the chairman of the Joint Chiefs, in what the latter called "a scathing diatribe, the like of which I have seldom read." The tone of it surprised Bradley, who noted that he had never realized "the deep distrust with which General MacArthur viewed our State Department in general and Dean Acheson in particular." Indeed, noted Bradley, MacArthur must have viewed him as a traitor as well for selling out to State on this issue.

Things never really got any better. Truman and MacArthur were almost never on the same track, with the same aims. They saw the war that they were about to fight in different contexts; they had, it would turn out, quite different ideas of what would constitute an acceptable victory and how much of the nation's resources ought to be committed to attaining it. Yet, starting on June 25, 1950, their lives would be twined together as that of a general and a president rarely had been in American history. Truman would find his presidency severely damaged by his inability to control MacArthur, while the general would find his place in history severely damaged by his failure to respect and to take the full measure of the president.

T HE UNITED STATES would go to war totally unprepared. The first American units thrown into battle were poorly armed, in terrible shape physically, and, more often than not, poorly led. The mighty army that had stood victorious in two great theaters of war, Europe and Asia, just five years earlier was a mere shell of itself. Militarily, America was a country trying to get by on the cheap, and in Korea it showed immediately. The blame for the poor condition of the Army belonged to everyone—the president, who wanted to keep taxes down, pay off the debt from the last war, and keep the defense budget down to a bare-bones level; the Congress, which if anything wanted to cut the budget even more; and the theater commander, MacArthur, under whose aegis the troops had been so poorly trained, and who had only five years earlier said that he did not really need all the troops Washington had assigned him. But mostly it was Truman—the president has to take full responsibility in a matter like this: the Army of this immensely prosperous country, rich now in a world that was still poor and war-ravaged, was threadbare. It had been on such short rations, so desperately underfinanced, that artillery units had not been able to practice adequately because there was no ammo; armored groups had done a kind of faux training because they lacked gas for real maneuvers; and troops at famed bases like Fort Lewis were being told to use only two sheets of toilet paper each time they visited the latrine. There were so few spare parts for vehicles that some enlisted men went out and bought war surplus equipment at very low prices, using their own money, in order to break it down for spare parts. If there was any upgrade in weaponry, it was almost exclusively in the planes and weapons being designed for the Air Force, not in the weapons employed by infantrymen.

World War II had dragged a sleepy, isolationist nation to superpower status. Out of the reach of enemy bombs, the United States had become the great arsenal of democracy. Its awesome factories, their modernity then the envy of the developed world, produced formidable weapons of war at a stunning rate. Many critics at the start of World War II had feared that Americans would not be good soldiers, that they had grown soft because of the nation's material successes. Worse, there was the question of whether because America was so democratic, its men would be able to stand up to soldiers from mighty totalitarian countries like Germany and Japan. But American troops had proved first-rate soldiers, and the country had produced an enviable army from a democratic society, built as much as anything else around the toughness, shrewdness, and skills of its noncommissioned officers, an army that reflected well on the democratic process, where the ability to think for yourself and accept responsibility were valuable assets. In the European theater, the mighty Wehrmacht had been matched by ordinary kids from ordinary American homes, coupled with the growing U.S. technological advantage; that and the sheer ferocity of the Red Army assaulting the Germans on the eastern front had doomed the Third Reich. In the Pacific, the Japanese had fought tenaciously, but again the combination of force, superior American technology, MacArthur's shrewd campaign designed to isolate rather than confront the enemy's strongest positions, and finally Japan's own limited resources had doomed their forces.

But now, almost daily, there were stories of American units being driven back, of constant North Korean advances. Had Americans in this new postwar era too casually overestimated the ability of U.S. troops? Had they thought that the kind of fighting force the United States had produced by early 1944 was somehow a permanent condition, that America was ipso facto such a powerful—indeed superior—nation that it would always produce better weapons and tougher troops? Did America believe that other nations would know this and deal with it accordingly, always keeping their distance? Certainly there was a sense of that at the beginning of the Korean War, even among those senior military men who knew that the Army was too small and not in very good shape. U.S. expectations of how well the Army would fight greatly exceeded its abilities. The Americans had expected when the North Koreans crossed the border that, whatever the Army's multitude of flaws, it would not take much to end the incursion. As soon as they knew that they were fighting *Americans,* the war would turn around, and good news would replace bad news from the front. For it was not just Douglas MacArthur who thought that he could fight the North Koreans with a limited number of troops, it was much of the top military and political establishment, and regrettably altogether too many of the troops themselves.

Much of that reflected a certain kind of racism, a belief in the superiority of Caucasians over Asians on the battlefield. This was a judgment from which the Japanese with their victories at the very beginning of World War II had been quickly exempted, their triumphs explained in American minds not because they were Asians, but because they were fanatics. These, however, were merely Koreans. How could *Koreans* defeat Americans? The answer for some of the commanders in those early days was very disturbing. In late July, Major General Bill Dean was reported missing and was eventually captured by the North Koreans after personally leading the defense of Taejon. But a few days before his capture, Keyes Beech of the *Chicago Daily News* had run into him at a small airstrip. "Let's face it," Dean told Beech, "the enemy has something that our men don't have and that's the willingness to die." Beech agreed with him. Himself a Marine veteran of World War II, Beech later wrote that the first American troops sent to Korea were "spiritually, mentally, morally, and physically unprepared for war." Ordinary troops, pulled from their very comfortable peacetime existences in Tokyo, many of them poor boys back home who now lived with servants and had undergone only the most minimal training, were rushed into combat and had spoken arrogantly of what a piece of cake it would be and how soon they would be back in Japan. And then almost overnight it had turned into a disaster of the first magnitude. The American forces had not been able to hold terrain. The North Korean spearhead units had been very good and were better armed than the Americans. Again and again, the Americans had retreated. The war, by the end of July, was turning into a disaster even as the United States raced to get up to speed, to form new units bound for Korea, and to speed up the deliveries of aircraft, tanks, and bazookas that could stop a T-34 tank.

In Korea itself, the first big surprise had been how well the North Korean troops fought in those first few days; the second had been how poorly the ROKs had done. They had suffered what seemed like an almost complete collapse on most fronts. The next big surprise—for Americans anyway—was just how poorly the first American troops sent to the Korean mainland did during their initiation into battle. It was more than a surprise; it was nothing less than a shock. The first plan for the use of American troops, Operation Bluehearts, drawn up by Major General Ned Almond, MacArthur's chief of staff and closest military associate, reflected a wildly optimistic view of how well American troops would fare. It featured MacArthur's preference for an immediate amphibious strike behind North Korean lines at a place called Inchon, and it was planned as if the North Korean assault was nothing more than the arrival of a few mosquitoes who could easily be swatted away. The landing was to take place on July 16, barely two weeks after the moment when the first American troops made their awkward, clumsy landing on Korean soil. Given the pathetic condition of the American troops in Japan, it was completely undoable at a moment when mere survival was very much in doubt. But it reflected the almost supreme self-confidence of the Tokyo command about what any American troops could accomplish against Korean troops.

Bluehearts was very quickly discarded, the troops too desperately needed for a much more immediate task—keeping the North Koreans from running American forces right off the peninsula. That it had even been considered reflected how little attention the command had paid to the respective forces gathering in the two Koreas; nor were any of the subsequent plans being put together in Tokyo much better. Much of the decision-making in those early days reflected the essential racism of the moment. Any experienced officer knew that for psychological reasons it was important for the first American troops to be at their best in their initial encounter with the North Korean troops, to fight well from strong positions, and to maximize their potential superiority in hardware. Yet at a moment when shrewd planning was critical, it proved not just careless but clueless. The headquarters sent the Twenty-fourth Division, acknowledged by consensus to be the weakest and least well prepared of the four divisions in Japan, into Korea first because it was based at Kyushu, which was closest to the peninsula. Because it had been stationed farthest from Tokyo, on the southernmost island of Japan, the Twenty-fourth had gotten the last pick of everything coming in country—officers, men, and equipment. Its regimental and battalion officers—this would be a major problem with all units in the early months of the war—were largely second- and even third-rate. It was, said one of its platoon leaders, "literally at the end of the supply line." Its equipment, an operations officer for the Thirty-fourth Regiment said, "was a national disgrace." A good deal of the ammo for its mortars was faulty. Its .30-caliber machine guns were worn down and not very accurate. It had the old 2.36 bazookas. Later one of its officers would write that it was "rather sad, almost criminal that such understrength, ill equipped and poorly trained units were committed."

The World War II veterans were gone. They had been replaced by troops who, as T. R. Fehrenbach, a commander of a company in Korea, noted, were fighting a war they did not understand. They knew neither their ally nor their enemy, and hated the country they were in. The men volunteering for the military in the period right after World War II had enlisted, in Fehrenbach's words, "for every reason known to man except to fight." The Army the United States sent to Korea in those early days was, Ned Almond thought, about 40 percent combat effective. That estimate, Clay Blair noted, was on the rosy side. Like most American units in Tokyo, instead of having three battalions to a regiment, the Twenty-fourth Division had only two. Worse, the division commander, disrespectful of his enemy, initially sent in only two regiments, both of them badly understrength—a third was on maneuvers elsewhere in Japan, and instead of feeding all his troops into one area where they could concentrate their efforts and their fire, he broke them down into three smaller units and placed them so that they would almost instantly find themselves badly outnumbered, easily encircled, and incapable of holding off the massive In Min Gun assault. Given the force they were up against, despite some moments of exceptional bravery, they were bound not only to fail but to fail quickly, their battles all too often turning into routs—something that greatly encouraged the North Koreans and discouraged other American units just then starting to arrive.

None of this was by happenstance. It was the direct product of the great victory that had taken place five years earlier and the desire to disarm overnight. When Bob Eichelberger turned the Eighth Army over to Walton Walker, he was all too aware of its weakness—"it is already nothing but a supply organization with no combat soldiers, just a cadre." Whatever hard-won respect for an Asian army that had been gained while fighting against the Japanese during World War II had disappeared. Duty in Tokyo had been considered a very good deal, with all the pleasures of being a victor and living exceptionally well in a very poor Asian country, and little in the way of military responsibility. Newcomers arriving from the States were welcomed, told that Japan was a great place, that if you knew how to play the game, you could get laid easily and cheaply, and you could make a nice bit of change on the side dealing in the black market. Each GI was living much better than he ever had at home. Most had, in the vernacular of the time, a "shack girl." In a devastated, impoverished, burned-out Japan, everyone, even the lowest private it sometimes seemed, could find a houseboy who took care of his uniforms and shined up his boots. The imbalance of personal power in Japan, of an American private or corporal who was momentarily rich (or at least richer than he had ever hoped to be back in Ohio or Tennessee) living among Japanese who were now all supplicants, seemed only to underline an innate American racism and prove that the white world was superior in all ways. The men of the white world won wars; the men of the non-white world shined their shoes, and the women of the non-white world became their girlfriends. In this army of easy occupation, soldiers did not necessarily show up for roll call on a Monday, and it was often the responsibility of the company clerks to work wonders to make sure that units still appeared combat effective.

That these troops were not battle ready was hardly a great secret. Major General Tony McAuliffe, who in 1945 had been the commander at Bastogne during the Battle of the Bulge, had been given the command of the troops in southern Japan in 1948 and he had hated every minute of it. Keyes Beech had visited him and asked him if he liked the duty. McAuliffe answered that he liked it fine, "but they [the troops] don't like me. In fact, I'm just about the biggest sonofabitch in these parts. The only excuse for an army in peace or war is that it be ready to fight. This army here is no damn good. . . . I'm turning the place upside down and seeing that all the men get out in the field on maneuvers. I want them to sleep on the ground and get their feet wet." His tour did not last long, and his spirit, as Beech added, was not contagious.

These were the troops who first set foot in Korea so sure they would readily defeat the In Min Gun. Colonel John (Mike) Michaelis, the first regimental commander to lead his troops well there, was appalled by the performance of most of them in those early months. He told Robert (Pepper) Martin from the *Saturday Evening Post* in early October: "When they started out, they couldn't shoot. They didn't know their weapons. They had not had enough training in plain old-fashioned musketry. They'd spent a lot of time listening to lectures on the differences between communism and Americanism and not enough time crawling on their bellies on maneuvers with live ammunition singing over them. They'd been nursed and coddled, told to drive safely, to buy War Bonds, to give to the Red Cross, to avoid VD, to write home to mother—when someone ought to have been telling them how to clean a machine gun when it jams." They were, he added, so roadbound that they had almost lost the use of their legs—"Send out a patrol on a scouting mission and they load up in a three quarter ton truck and start riding down the highway."

If troops like this were an all too accurate reflection of the mood of the country back home, then so were the North Korean troops a reflection of their country—trying to make the jump overnight from an oppressed, colonized society to instant modernity by using their own crude replica of the Soviet model. They were tough, angry, battle-hardened, elite troops. They carried very little extra gear, were in much better physical shape than the Americans, and could live far better off the land than their American adversaries. Roy Appleman, the studious Army historian, estimated that nearly one-third of them, and certainly most of their officers and NCOs—had fought with the Chinese Communists in the difficult battles against the Nationalists. In their mind this war was an extension of the war that they had been a part of earlier, the war against the Japanese. They were exceptionally well—in fact frighteningly well—indoctrinated; there was an almost robotic quality to their certitude and the way that many of them, when captured, voiced their political beliefs; it exceeded even that of their Chinese Communist colleagues, even some of those Chinese who were true believers.

They came from peasant backgrounds, had hated the Japanese colonization of Korea, and believed that the Americans and their proxies in Seoul were agents of the past, not enablers of the future; the Americans were now the allies of the Japanese, as well as the old Korean ruling class, and thus this was a continuation of the struggle that had forced them to leave their native soil years earlier. The leadership of the South Korean Army was in their minds a reflection of those Koreans who had fought alongside the Japanese, and in the upper-level ranks this was often true. The North Koreans troops had trained hard and were extremely well disciplined and motivated. They camouflaged themselves exceptionally well, stayed off the roads, and often moved over the harsh terrain by foot, as the Americans did not. Like the Chinese Communists who had trained them and with whom they had fought, they tended to avoid all-out frontal battle. They preferred to make early contact, then slide along the flank of their adversaries, hitting the badly outnumbered South Koreans or Americans from the side or the rear. They also sent small parties ahead, disguised as peasants fleeing the In Min Gun, to recon American positions and call in strikingly accurate artillery fire.

They were absolutely sure in the beginning of whom they were fighting and why. They were fighting white foreigners, imperialists, and capitalists, the children of Wall Street, and of course their puppet allies in the South. The Americans were not so sure, despite periodic lectures on the evils of Communism, whom they were fighting, or for that matter why they were fighting them. They might be soldiers stationed in Japan, but they'd had no expectation of going to war, especially in a place called Korea. "When word reached my unit that Sunday," a corporal in the Thirty-fourth Infantry Regiment named Larry Barnett said, "the reaction in my company was 'Where is Korea?'" The next, he added, was "Let the gooks kill each other off." That was too bad because the Thirty-fourth, and its sister regiment the Twenty-first, were slated to be the first units to fight in Korea. They were both part of the ill-fated Twenty-fourth Division. The Twenty-fourth was ordered to get to Korea as quickly as possible and move up the west side of the peninsula, until it met up with the onrushing enemy. That appeared likely to happen near the village of Suwon, just south of Seoul. But then the Twenty-fourth Division commander, Major General William Dean, made his critical mistake and, instead of concentrating his limited forces in one strong position where they might be able to maximize their firepower, unwisely decided to split his units. In this, his orders once again reflected the cavalier attitude of the American commanders toward their new enemy. The lead unit, the first to leave Japan and go into battle in Korea, was Task Force Smith, led by Lieutenant Colonel Brad Smith. Transport planes brought the men to Pusan, a port at the southeast end of the country. Because of bad weather and the limited number of planes available, the airlift took two days. The last of Smith's men landed in Pusan on the morning of July 2. On the evening of July 2, the men of Task Force Smith boarded a train, and they arrived at Taejon, a little more than halfway between Pusan and what was believed to be the front, on the morning of July 3. At Taejon, Lieutenant Colonel Smith met with Brigadier General John Church. Church was an elderly officer hardly known for his vitality who had been put in charge of the survey team sent to Korea by MacArthur to find out what was needed, and where.

Church's recon had not gone especially well in the face of the exceptionally well-coordinated, very cohesive North Korean attack, and the massive, chaotic South Korean retreat. But even the fact that he himself had instantly moved his headquarters back from Suwon to Taejon, a distance of some ninety miles, because the In Min Gun had been bearing down on him, had not diminished his personal cockiness. All they needed, Church told Smith, was a few GIs to make a stand, men who would not fear tanks. That would stiffen the spine of the ROKs. He pointed at a map and told Smith to make his stand near Osan, just south of Suwon. So Smith took his men and headed north by train toward Ansong. At the Ansong train station, they were cheered by Koreans, which momentarily made them feel proud, for it showed they were the good guys, heroes come to rescue a scared people. Later one officer, Lieutenant William Wyrick, decided that the Koreans—there were thousands and thousands fleeing south—were cheering not so much the appearance of the Americans but the arrival of a train, which they quickly boarded for a trip south toward Pusan.

At almost the same time, Major General Dean arrived in Taejon and took command of American forces in Korea from Church. He thereupon assigned the Thirty-fourth Regiment to Pyongtaek, just south and west of Osan on the Seoul-Pusan highway. With that, the Thirty-fourth, its own resources limited, was split off from the men of the Twenty-first Regiment, some ten miles away. Others thought keeping the American troops together and concentrating them about forty miles farther south, using the natural barrier of the Kum River, made more sense. But Dean believed that his mission was going to be, in his own words, "short and easy"; that the North Koreans would not be anxious to fight Americans. Because of that he broke his force down into three groups, the fateful mistake.

Back in Japan, the men of the Thirty-fourth Regiment, shipping out for Korea, had been ordered to pack their summer dress uniforms—for the victory parade that was soon to come in Seoul. Lieutenant Colonel Harold (Red) Ayres, who commanded a battalion from the Thirty-fourth Infantry, had told his men, "There are supposed to be North Korean soldiers north of us. These men are poorly trained. Only about half of them have weapons and we'll have no difficulty stopping them." The ordinary soldiers were equally cocky: they were on their way to fight some gooks, in the language of the time, teach them a lesson or two; and then get back to the good life in Tokyo. Again, there was, thought Captain Fred Ladd, then an aide to Major General Ned Almond, a deep and pervasive racism that ran through the American Army—"a belief that gooks could not stand up to Americans." "It was hard," he added, "to tell whether it ran from top to bottom, or bottom to top, or both." (He would, he noted, see almost exact manifestations of it again when he was a division adviser in Vietnam thirteen years later.) As the Thirty-fourth Regiment moved toward its positions at Pyongtaek, it came across some ROK engineers about to blow bridges: the Americans scolded the ROKs for their lack of spirit and threw the explosives away.

What was about to unfold, as the Americans and the North Koreans rushed toward their initial meeting, was an American disaster of the first magnitude, a textbook example of what happens when a nation, filled with the arrogance of power, meets a new reality. On July 4, Smith took about 540 men, what was effectively an understrength battalion—more like two reinforced companies—a few miles north of Osan. Most of their artillery support was still back at Pusan. They reached their positions about 3 A.M. on July 5. It was raining and they were all tired and cold. A little later the same morning, Sergeant Loren Chambers, an assistant platoon leader, spotted eight T-34 tanks moving down the road from Suwon. His platoon leader, Lieutenant Philip Day, asked what they were. "Those are T-34 tanks, sir," he replied, "and I don't think they're going to be friendly to us."

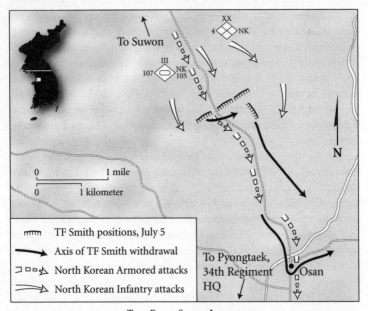

5. TASK FORCE SMITH, JULY 5, 1950

The tanks kept coming—followed by a long line of infantrymen and then an even more terrifying sight, another twenty-five North Korean tanks. When the lead edge of the enemy column, later estimated to be about six miles long, closed to within a mile, the Americans started firing their mortars. There were a few hits, but the tanks kept coming. The Americans waited until the tanks were only about seven hundred yards away and then fired their recoilless rifles, which scored several hits, but again the tanks kept coming. Then the bazookas failed. At one point Sergeant Chambers called on the phone for some 60mm mortar fire. The answer came back that they would not reach that far. "Well, what about the 81mm mortars?" he asked. "They didn't come over with us" was the answer. He then asked for the 4.2 mortars. They couldn't fire, he was told. "How about the artillery?" he asked. There was no communication with it yet. "What about the Air Force?" The Air Force didn't know where Task Force Smith was. Well, Chambers finally said, what about a camera so he could at least take a picture of this? They were in grave danger of being surrounded, he warned. With that the Americans began to fall back as quickly as they could, many simply fleeing, some throwing down their weapons, some even taking off their boots because they could move more quickly through the rice paddies barefoot.

The Thirty-fourth Regiment had established its headquarters not far from Smith's forward unit. Now the North Koreans were moving down on them. Denis Warner, an Australian correspondent for both the London *Telegraph* and the Melbourne *Herald,* had managed to attach himself to the First Battalion of the Thirty-fourth Regiment near Pyongtaek, the unit commanded by Red Ayres. He was there with Ayres on the morning of July 5, when Brigadier General George Barth, who was supposed to be the division artillery officer, arrived. As they had no artillery up front, Dean had put him in charge of the forward areas. Warner watched Barth get out of his jeep, turn to the reporters gathered there, and say, "Well, boys, it's on. I've got the first shell out there for General MacArthur." Barth said he had given orders to fire when the North Koreans closed to within fifteen hundred yards. The American officers, Warner remembered, all seemed exceptionally optimistic about what was going to happen next. "Those Commie bastards will turn and run when they find they're up against our boys," Ayres said. "We'll be back in Seoul by the weekend." Warner wondered, like so many war correspondents before him in situations like this, whether to stay for the action still to come or race back and file a story that American troops were now engaged in battle with the North Koreans.

He decided to stay around for the action. He watched a grim sight, an almost classic warning signal: an endless parade of peasants moving south on

clogged roads, instant refugees fleeing the In Min Gun. The sight of the peasants fleeing south was a telltale one for anyone who knew something about
combat, a kind of straw in the wind. What disturbed Warner even more was
the fact that the number of South Korean troops who were also fleeing far outnumbered the peasants. He started walking north with a few other correspondents, but they quickly ran into a South Korean cavalryman on what looked
to Warner like a Shetland pony, shouting in Korean, "*Tanku! Tanku!*" Then
Warner saw his first enemy tank, "moving steadily and majestically forward."
He immediately turned around and headed back to Ayres's headquarters. But
Ayres seemed to doubt what Warner had just seen with his own eyes. "We
don't have any tanks," he said.

"Not ours, theirs," Warner answered.

"The bridges around here wouldn't take a tank of that size," Ayres insisted.
So back Warner went with a bazooka team sent by Ayres ("perhaps to humor
me"). Soon, two North Korean tanks showed up. The American bazooka men
moved as close as they could and fired away, only to see their shells bounce off
the tanks.

At that point, word had still not reached Ayres's headquarters of the destruction of Task Force Smith. Only then did a few of the survivors begin to
straggle in and report that most of the battalion had been lost. "Soon thereafter," Warner wrote, "Ayres and his men were on the run. Barth's headquarters
also broke during the night, minutes before tanks burst through it. By dawn,
July 6, the tanks were in Pyongtaek, five miles down the road. By breakfast they
were in Songwan, and before the day was over, they had advanced to Chonan,
36 miles in 36 hours." By the end of the next day, with the American troops still
in precipitous retreat, General Dean had dismissed Barth as his forward commander and fired one of his regimental commanders as well.

IT WAS A very bad beginning. Poorly prepared troops poorly deployed had
barely slowed down the ferocious drive south of the North Koreans—at best
by a few days. In the first week of combat the North Koreans had virtually destroyed two American regiments; some three thousand men were either killed,
wounded, or missing in action, and enough weapons had been left behind to
outfit one or two North Korean regiments.

Those were terrible days. The mood in both Washington and Tokyo was increasingly grim. A fear grew that American troops in a limited war might not
be able to hold and that pressure would gradually rise for the use of the atomic
weapon. This was aptly caught in a *New York Times* editorial on July 16: "Our
emotions, as we watch our outnumbered, out-weaponed soldiers in Korea,
must be a mingling of pity, sorrow and admiration. This is the sacrifice we

asked of them, justified only by the hope that what they are now doing will keep this war a small war, and that the death of a small number will prevent the slaughter of millions. The choice has been a terrible one. We cannot be cheerful about it, or even serene. But we need not be hysterical. We need not accept a greater war and the collapse of civilization."

Of the many American illusions that died in those first few weeks of the Korean War, perhaps the most important was the belief in the atomic bomb as the ultimate weapon, in effect the only weapon we needed. That was an idea that had taken serious root in the national security mentality immediately after World War II, in part because it was so formidable a weapon, and in part because it meant that the defense bill could be done on the cheap. Just a year earlier, Omar Bradley, normally a man of exceptional common sense, had testified before the Congress that the day of the amphibious landing was essentially over. "Frankly, the atomic bomb, properly delivered, almost precludes such a possibility [as an amphibious invasion]," he said. In those early painful defeats, the nation learned that its entire defense system was an illusion, that the bomb was the most limited kind of weapon in any kind of limited war, and that the great power stalemate with the Russians might produce on the peripheries of the two superpowers areas where it was harder to control indigenous tensions. There was also this new truth: the atomic weapon was so powerful and so awesome a weapon, that it was in many situations morally abhorrent. It was the great almost unusable weapon. It was the ultimate deterrent, awesome really, for no nation would lightly strike against a member of the atomic club without a good deal of thought. But the early American monopoly of it, the quick, instantaneous way it had seemed to end the Pacific War, had created an illusion when it came to America's defense budget: that it could develop a military arsenal on the cheap, with only one kind of arrow in it. If the bombs dropped on Hiroshima and Nagasaki had seemed to inaugurate a brand-new chapter in the history of warfare, supposedly making all other weapons obsolete and creating a world where military power rested only with the richest, most technologically advanced nations, then the Korean battlefield defeats of early July 1950 shattered that belief. The world of the military had seemed to change completely back in August 1945; but now it was clear it might not have changed that much. As the country realized the limits of the atomic weapon, the popularity of both the Korean War and of the Truman administration began a steady decline. Perhaps not that many people would want to exchange this new, not yet rooted internationalism for the old isolationism, but that did not mean they liked the way things were going nor the men in Washington who were in charge. If this was America's new international fate they were being confronted with, it was hardly a fate they would have chosen.

*   *   *

JULY 1950 WAS one of the worst months in American military history: one long ignominious retreat filled with terrible small battles and occasional moments of great gallantry by outnumbered and outgunned American units who were again and again overwhelmed by the sheer force, size, and skill of the North Korean assault. The American troops were invariably positioned too thinly at critical junctions, trying with limited numbers to slow down the North Koreans until other units by then gathering in the United States and ticketed for Korea could get there; it was an army trying to buy time in precious increments with the most precious coin of all, the lives of its young men. Back home, the country was just beginning to mobilize for this newest war. The manpower situation in Japan on the eve of the war had been so desperate that when the war broke out, soldiers in Japan who had been convicted of relatively serious crimes, and were on their way back to stockades in the States in handcuffs, were given an alternative—fight in Korea and their records would be cleaned. If you had been an officer in an American division in Tokyo in the days before the Korean War broke out, a vast percentage of your time, said Lieutenant William West, an aide to Major General Hap Gay, the commander of the First Cav, was spent arranging for all too many of your men to get ready for their courts-martial.

In early July, MacArthur told the Joint Chiefs he needed eleven battalions simply to hold the line. There was a certain desperation to the way that need was translated back in America: Uncle Sam wants you, now (or yesterday) for the Korean War. Marines who had fought in World War II and had gone happily back to their civilian lives were finding to their extreme displeasure that, though they had not volunteered for the Marine Reserves and thought themselves civilians, they were available nonetheless to the Corps, based on their old contracts with Uncle Sam. They were being rousted from their civilian incarnations for a second tour in less than a decade. In the meantime, draft calls were on the rise for the Army, since not many young men had rushed down to recruiting centers to volunteer as they had back in December 1941 after Pearl Harbor. Men already in the service were herded into combat units and to Korea without much training. When the North Koreans struck, noted an officer named Captain Frank Munoz, who commanded a company in the early fighting, "We turned the vacuum cleaner on. It sucked up men from everywhere, behind desks, out of hospitals, from depots. We filled up fast." At first there was talk of six weeks of combat training before the men were shipped out, but there turned out to be no time for that; then there was talk of ten days of training once they arrived in Korea, but that too was discarded; finally, there was talk of three days of special training once they got to Pusan, but there was no time for that either, as the North Koreans pushed closer and closer. So men arrived in the port directly from the States, drew their gear, and more often than not were immediately shipped up to combat positions, often without having ze- roed in their rifles or calibrated and test-fired their mortars, and with the Cos- moline on their .50-caliber machine guns barely rubbed off.

In the Pentagon, there was a growing nervousness about the effectiveness of the leadership, especially about Lieutenant General Walton Walker, the com- mander of the Eighth Army, which meant, at that time, the commander of all Americans (and soon all United Nations ground forces) in Korea. So it was that, in the terrible days of early August, the Army dispatched its ascending star, Lieutenant General Matthew Bunker Ridgway, as part of a special, high- level, three-man team to meet with MacArthur, listen to him, and go over his needs, while expressing Washington's own anxieties, especially about MacArthur's relationship with Chiang Kai-shek.

While Averell Harriman, the leader of Ridgway's group, was busy measuring MacArthur and trying to bridge the gap between him and the administration on the issue of Chiang and China, Ridgway's most important job was to inspect Walton Walker and his Korean command. Ridgway, who had last witnessed a headquarters in the heady final days of World War II, commanding airborne troops, the elite of the elite, was appalled by what he saw in Korea. All too many of Walker's key officers, he believed, were men who had not done well in that war and were being given one last opportunity to serve so that they could retire at a slightly higher rank and pay level. It was as if the people who had been in charge back in Washington and Tokyo were allowing tickets to be punched for old times' sake, not sending or demanding the best of a new generation of offi- cers. Walker could not have agreed more and was furious with the quality of men he had been getting, and the fact that so many of the better officers seemed to be siphoned off once they reached Asia, to serve in the headquarters in Tokyo rather than in the field commanding troops in battle. Walker was a good and decent officer, Ridgway thought; give him a tank unit and specific orders and no one would be better. But nonetheless he believed Walker was in way over his head in this assignment, and the Eighth Army staff around him was visibly weak and badly organized. The passivity of Walker's chief of staff shocked him. Some of the regimental commanders were older men lacking in combat experi- ence. As for the fighting men themselves, they were not, he reported, by a very long shot up to the standards of their World War II predecessors.

Just about everything in his report was negative. The troops all too often lacked infantry fundamentals and were not aggressive. They had become prison- ers of their machinery, most particularly their vehicles, and thus of Korea's poor and limited system of roads. They did not counterattack; they did not dig in properly; attempts at camouflage were careless, fields of fire poorly drawn up, communications between units weak. Ridgway was shocked—here the United States was, sending young men out into combat in a way that greatly endangered them. That to him violated the most elemental tenet of an infantry commander's creed. Ridgway felt strongly that Walker should be relieved, because in his estimation he lacked the larger command skills and the vision necessary to change things. Ridgway was, however, wary of making that recommendation too forcefully. He was naturally uneasy about relieving an already desperately embattled commander, one whose troops were threatened with being pushed into the sea. Might such a move damage the already fragile morale of our fighting men? he wondered. He was no less uneasy about looking like an opportunist, someone critical of Walker because he wanted the command for himself. Not knowing the deep chasm that already existed between MacArthur and Walker, he worried about MacArthur's reaction if he suggested Walker's relief. Would MacArthur, always so sensitive to Washington, see him as a spear carrier for Truman or just another opportunist? He decided to talk with Harriman, who had been running difficult, sensitive, high-level missions since the 1930s. Harriman, like General Lauris Norstad, an Air Force officer and the third member of their team, believed that Walker had to go, but was wary of broaching it at that moment unless, in their final talks, MacArthur opened the subject himself: any discussion, Norstad believed, should be initiated by the commander. They were not to look like they had come out from Washington to attack his command.

Better, Harriman suggested, for Ridgway to discuss the Walker matter with senior officials in Washington, including the president himself, and then make the suggestion through proper channels. Ironically, as Clay Blair later pointed out, MacArthur himself had already lost confidence in Walker, was thinking of relieving him, and believed that Ridgway was the best man for the job. Had Ridgway actually replaced Walker at that moment, Blair wrote, "events in Korea would very likely have taken a different and more favorable course for the American Army." For Ridgway would have been able to stand up to MacArthur as Walker never could, would have been far more independent of Tokyo than Walker, would have been far better connected back in Washington, and almost surely would have been more cautious in moving north after the thirty-eighth parallel was crossed.

On their way back to Washington, Larry Norstad pushed Ridgway on the subject of the Eighth Army command. "I think you ought to be in command there." But Ridgway, extremely sensitive to the idea that he might use his superior position and great Pentagon leverage to usurp another man's command, resisted. "Please don't mention that. It will look as though I was coming over here looking for a job and I'm not." There was one other thing that Ridgway noted, but he was reluctant to talk about it. Much as he was thrilled by a brief-ing MacArthur had given about his plans for an amphibious landing behind the enemy's lines at a place called Inchon—Ridgway was, after all, an airborne man and he liked the idea of surprise assaults away from the main strength of the enemy—he worried about the difficulties that came from dealing with so senior an officer as MacArthur, so physically distanced from a cruel, bitter, and alien battlefield.

In fact, the command was almost turned over to Ridgway at that moment. Harriman pushed hard for it. His recommendation was made to Truman; Louis Johnson, the secretary of defense; Omar Bradley, the chairman of the JCS; and Joe Collins, the Army chief of staff. It was an ideal move, everyone agreed, because it would put in play the Army's best younger commander and might have the side advantage—though no one ever actually said this—of lessening MacArthur's ability to act on his own. Ridgway was so forceful an of-ficer that even someone as lofty as Douglas MacArthur would find it harder to do end runs around him. But Joe Collins had already ticketed Ridgway for pro-motion to vice chief of staff in 1951 and feared that, in Korea, "you might be so involved I couldn't get you out." It was a curious way to look at command in the only shooting war America was involved in; it undoubtedly reflected a deep-seated belief in Washington that this still might be only the preliminary round, that the really big enemy strike might soon come in Europe. Among those who thought this was true was Ridgway himself.

11

───────────

So WALTON WALKER would not be replaced at that moment, even though he had no important defenders either in Washington or Tokyo, where he was often out of the play on vital command decisions and where MacArthur's people made fun of him in private. Walker was fighting, as his pilot, Mike Lynch, who was also his great confidant, put it, a two-front war—against the North Koreans and the Tokyo high command. Walton (Johnnie) Walker knew what was up, knew that he was perilously close to being relieved. Yet there was one exceptional quality Ridgway had sensed in him, whatever he believed were Walker's limitations, and that was his bulldog tenacity. The two generals had conferred as Walker's troops were being systematically pushed back to the Naktong River. The great question in those gloomy days was whether they could hold in the Pusan Perimeter at all, or might simply be pushed off the peninsula altogether. At their meeting Ridgway had asked Walker what he would do if he were driven back any farther. He would not be driven back any farther, Walker had answered. "That's what you tell the troops," Ridgway said, "but what will you really do if you are driven from the Naktong Line?" "General," Walker had answered defiantly, "I will not be driven from the Naktong Line."

In at least one way Walker was fortunate—he did not have much time to worry about what Washington or Tokyo thought of him. He was too busy each day desperately moving troops around, trying to head off the latest North Korean advance. As such, he had little time for self-pity. Crisis followed crisis. Every division commander, every regimental commander, every company commander was short of troops. Each night in July, the In Min Gun seemed ready to break through American lines at four or five different places. Walker's job was always to plug the next leak—to try to decide which of the many places was most important. Rarely had an American commander been dealt such a bad hand. That his troops were poorly prepared was partly his own fault, for he had been one of the commanders in Tokyo in those pre–June 25 days, but in the early days they were also badly outnumbered by an enemy

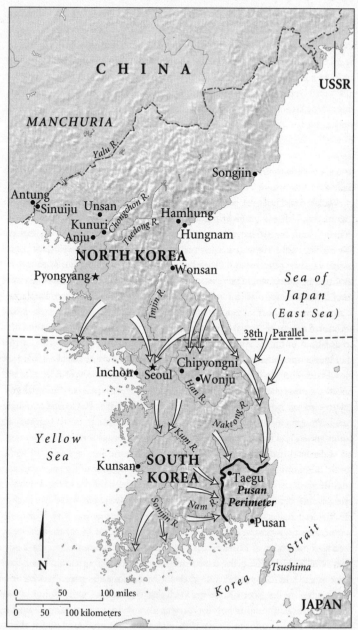

6. Height of North Korean Advance, Late August 1950

fighting on its own terrain. Walker's supply line was hopelessly long, extending all the way back to California. There were shortages of everything: troops, commanders, and sometimes most important of all, ammunition. He was in hostile territory, a tank commander in predominantly mountainous country, and when it came to tanks, the other side had more and better ones than he did. Worse yet, even in his own command he was to no small degree an outsider: MacArthur and his ever more powerful chief of staff, Ned Almond, viewed him with condescension, if not with open contempt. Sometimes it seemed to Walker that he was the last American in the Far East to hear of vital decisions. The entire Tokyo staff under MacArthur and Almond grasped the disrespect shown him by its two superiors and, as so often happens, parroted their attitudes.

Walker could not even get the field officers he wanted. Others back in Washington, and Ridgway on his trip out, had complained about the poor quality of Walker's staff, but whenever a troopship docked in Yokohama, Japan, before any officers could disembark, their records were screened by the Far East command. The best officers would then be skimmed off by MacArthur's headquarters, and the others would be released to the Eighth Army. It was a pipeline to be sure, but a corrupt one, for it was delivering talent to all the wrong places. Walker was not normally a man to complain. He had always accepted the whimsical nature of Army decision-making for what it was, but he would later complain to intimates about how headquarters made fun of the quality of his staff and commanders but then refused to send him the rising stars he asked for. He wanted Slim Jim Gavin, a famed airborne commander in World War II and one of the most talented, charismatic younger officers in the Army, and was angry to discover he could not get him. During World War II, George Marshall had been appalled by the relatively advanced age of many of his regimental commanders and had demanded younger, more vigorous men; he had wanted no regimental commander over the age of forty-five. But in Korea, in what would be an unusually taxing command physically because of the cruel climate and the nature of the war, it was the same old story. On the eve of the war, only one of nine regimental commanders, thirty-seven-year-old Mike Michaelis, met the Marshall test: of the others, one was fifty-five, one was fifty, four were forty-nine, and two were forty-seven. Michaelis was far and away the best regimental commander in Korea in the beginning, and his Twenty-seventh Regiment Wolfhounds were being used in almost every critical situation, much like a fire brigade. In those early days, when the American units were, on occasion, surrounded by the North Koreans, Michaelis was so successful (some of his contemporaries thought) because he was an airborne officer, and airborne people were taught not to worry if they found themselves surrounded. That was in a sense their natural habitat, and they always expected to be resupplied from the air. Officers in other units, surrounded and cut off, had a tendency to panic and fall back too quickly, their unit discipline unraveling as they pulled back, all too often into well-prepared North Korean ambushes. Michaelis and his men worried first and foremost about unit integrity. The ability of his men to protect one another and use their weaponry to create protective fields of fire was considered more important than whether or not they were momentarily encircled.

For Walker, the war was turning into a bitter culmination to a surprisingly rich military career in which, like many other gifted officers, he had defied his academic background and class standing. He had grown up in Belton in central Texas, one more of those boys, in an era when there was so much less choice, who had decided soldiering was his way of getting out of a small town and having a life with some greater measure of meaning. He had gone to a local military academy, and on graduation had wanted to go to West Point. But he was too young at fifteen and had entered VMI instead. He had hardly been brilliant there—fifty-second in a class of ninety-two—but in June 1907 he managed to get a congressional appointment to West Point anyway, and he entered the academy with the class of 1911. But times in Texas were hard; his father wrote him a letter asking him to come home and assist in running the family dry goods store. In October, he left West Point, then reentered with the class of 1912. Again he was more plodder than comet; he graduated seventy-first in a class of ninety-six, into a tiny Army about to become larger because of World War I. In the years just before that war, he was part of the Nineteenth Regiment, which spent a good deal of its time sparring with only marginal success against Pancho Villa during a series of skirmishes on the Mexican border.

In World War I, as a young captain, Walker had led a machine gun company against the Germans and won two Silver Stars in the Meuse-Argonne fighting. It had jump-started what had seemed until then a rather ordinary career. Walker had been an intense, aggressive line officer. His superiors were impressed; they thought of him as a man who was never going to let them down, not brilliant but a damn good man, one you could always rely on. You could build a fine army with men like him. Class standing, what had seemed so important back at West Point, mattered so much less on the battlefield, where it was all about instinct and courage and a sense of duty. He was good with his peers, one of whom was Leonard (Gee) Gerow, himself the best friend of a rising young star of that era named Dwight Eisenhower. In 1925, Walker was picked to attend the Command and General Staff School at Fort Leavenworth, established after the war to help the Army choose which officers were destined to become generals, and if need be to expedite their careers. In those days, no one talked about something called the fast track, but if there was one in a peacetime institution with a snail-like career pace, it began at Leavenworth. With him at Leavenworth were Gee Gerow and Eisenhower, first in the class of 245, and just beginning to break out of the pack. Walker was 117th, but he was getting good assignments. In 1935, even as the Army was thinning out its officer ranks, Walker was admitted to the Army War College. Graduating in 1936, he received what seemed a very ordinary assignment, executive officer of the Fifth Infantry Brigade at Vancouver Barracks in the state of Washington. In reality, he had lucked out, because the commanding officer there was a young brigadier named George Catlett Marshall. The cerebral, austere Marshall, seemingly the quintessential staff officer but quite possibly a superb combat officer as well—no one knew because he had not been given a chance—seemed to take to the intense, aggressive, obviously fearless Walker. Out of that grew a genuine friendship, and in 1939 when Marshall, about to emerge as the single most important officer in the entire Army, arrived in Washington to take up his job as head of War Plans, he stayed for a time with the Walker family. That was both a plus and a minus, a plus for Walker's career, because he was something of a Marshall man, but a minus later when he arrived in Japan and Korea, because of MacArthur's phobic feelings about Marshall left over from World War II.

Whatever else Johnnie Walker was, he was not charismatic. He was about five-five, short and stubby. "He's a little fat, isn't he?" someone once said to George Patton, under whom Walker had served with distinction in World War II. "Yes he is," Patton answered, "but he's a fighting little son of a bitch." His chin was soft and round, his face and body in no way sculpted. He was always more than a little overweight, 165 pounds on a short frame. He looked, noted one British writer, all too much like the man from the Michelin tire advertisements. If Hollywood had been doing the casting, it would have added several inches to his height or, failing that, slimmed him down and broadened his shoulders. The Army, all things considered, prefers its generals to be tall, believing that helps command function, that taller is always better, but failing that, its generals should at least be feisty little gamecocks, out to even the score with all those bigger, taller men who had once made the mistake of lording it over them. In full battle rig, Walker looked nothing like a commander, more like someone just pulled from civilian life and destined to be the company misfit.

What made his way even more difficult was that he was terrible with the press, distrusting and wary, even with reporters who rather liked him and sensed that he was operating in unusually difficult circumstances. On occasion with a journalist he trusted, like Frank Gibney of *Time*, Walker would talk about how hard it was, about the poor quality of his troops—"what they're giving me to fight." The rest of the time he kept his anger and his frustrations buttoned up. He had complete control of his ego, which his son, Sam Wilson Walker (who was awarded a Silver Star in Korea as a young officer), once noted, "was a damn good thing—because he served under two of the greatest egomaniacs the American Army ever produced, George Patton and Douglas MacArthur." He accepted the hand he was dealt, the battlefield as it was. He did not complain. In World War II, he had been first a division and then a corps commander in the Third Army under Patton—"Georgie" in Walker's letters home to his wife, the only time he dared be sardonic about his famed superior. In fact the job as a senior commander under Patton was the one Eisenhower had originally wanted, but when Eisenhower—talented, gifted, charming— was pulled into the world of planning under Marshall, Walker had gotten the prized armored assignment.

He had been a great Patton favorite, in no small part because of his aggressiveness. "Of all the corps I have commanded yours has always been the most eager to attack," Patton, who was never known to be excessive with compliments, once wrote Walker. He had been fearless and relentless in command, his tactics as audacious as those of his superior, but he cut no wide swath, nor did he try to create a cult of his own. He was smart enough to know that there was room for only one superstar in the world of George Smith Patton, Jr. When members of the press showed up, looking to lionize him just a little as Patton's Patton, he invariably blew them off. Nonetheless, Eisenhower had rated him almost on a level with Matt Ridgway and "Lightning" Joe Collins in the war, and when it ended, he was in line to get a major command in the Pacific. He had no illusions about himself; he was a good soldier who did his job, and he had excelled under a truly gifted superior.

The Korean post had originally been ticketed for John Hodge, but he had offended Syngman Rhee and other Koreans with his almost unique insensitivity to their condition and the Japanese occupation. Instead Walker had arrived in Tokyo as Eighth Army commander in September 1948. Even before the Korean War began, he existed in Tokyo on a kind of sufferance. Because MacArthur and his top people considered the generals who had commanded in Europe (who had gotten the men and materiel they believed should have been ticketed for the Pacific) enemies, Walker had arrived with several invisible marks against him among the Bataan Gang. First off, he was not a MacArthur man. Then he had fought in the wrong theater. Then he had the wrong friends, Marshall as a sponsor, Gerow and Eisenhower as pals. He had been one of the few military men invited to the wedding of Eisenhower's son John in 1947.

In Tokyo he never fit in and was never accepted. The old-timers in the inner circle knew that they need not take him seriously. This was especially true of MacArthur's new chief of staff, Major General Edward Almond, for whom World War II had been a distinct disappointment, and for whom this was undoubtedly the last major assignment. Almond was to be a major player in the Korean War, and his singularly unfortunate rivalry with Walker left an indelible stamp on what happened there. He too had not been a MacArthur man; if anything he had been closer to Marshall, and late in his career, he was trying to prove to the Pacific commander, and the men around him, that he was the ultimate MacArthur loyalist, like a convert to the Catholic Church trying to show that he was more Catholic than the pope. Almond was every bit as driven as Walker and far more of a gamesman. In addition he was trying to make up for lost time—he had had, in the way military men talked about these things, a bad war in Europe. For in World War II, he had commanded the Ninety-second Division, an all-black unit in a still segregated army, all of whose officers were white Southerners (because they were believed to know how to, as the Southern saying went, handle blacks). That had turned out to be one of the last great military manifestations of an archaic, feudal relationship in what was supposed to be a modern, egalitarian, democratic institution. Eleanor Roosevelt's Running Riflemen, the men of his division had been called sardonically in the Army, after the then first lady who had a special interest in their welfare and performance. Treated as second-class citizens, more often than not by officers whom they saw as the bane of their existence back home, they had often performed as second-class soldiers.

Almond, a Southerner born in December 1892 with all the traditional prejudices of both the region and the era, had ended the war even more racist than when he started. His command in Korea would later be marked by all kinds of gratuitous instances of racism on his personal part, as if he were some kind of political dinosaur in an Army otherwise just beginning to integrate. Before World War II had started, he had ironically enough been a Marshall short-list man, and the command of the Ninety-second had been a reflection of Marshall's faith in him—that if anyone could take such a difficult assignment and make it work, it would be Ned Almond. He had started the war as a peer—at least in his own mind—of men like Bradley, Collins, Patton, and Ridgway and felt quite bitter about his fate when the war was over, that he had been sabotaged by the luck of the draw.

His ego had always been enormous, right up there, friends thought, with that of Patton. In truth, he had never really thought anyone else was a better commander. To believe that you are among the best of the best, and then have such a troubled command at so critical a professional moment, was a profound disappointment, and he was sure he had been cheated. Whatever happened in Tokyo or Korea, he once told MacArthur, would never bother him, because he had already dealt with the worst situation that any commander in the Army had ever had—he had commanded the Ninety-second Division. Supremely ambitious men in the Army, graduates of West Point or, in Almond's case, VMI, are always measuring themselves against their contemporaries: who gets to be bird colonel first, who gets a battalion first, who gets a star first, and, of course, who gets a division first. The others, his peers, had come of age in that epic war, gotten the great commands, performed as everyone expected, and become part of the collective memory of the nation's proud victory, while he had commanded troops who were part of a social experiment, one that had failed badly, and he was embittered by it. He did not see himself sharing any blame with his troops—in his mind the fault was completely theirs.

Almond was stoic, overly self-confident, absolutely fearless, a man who on occasion seemed to dare death to strike him, and in fact some of the men who served under him in Korea thought he had a death wish. There was, his friends believed, a certain deeply tragic quality to him by the time he arrived in the Tokyo headquarters. It was not just that his great hopes to be an important commander in World War II had crashed because of the nature of the command he had been given; it was something much more cruel, that he sealed away deep inside himself. For in personal terms, he had paid a terrible price during World War II. There had been one horrendous day in 1944 when he learned in a letter from his wife that he had lost both his son and his son-in-law in combat. Young Ned, class of '43 at West Point, had been killed with the Forty-fifth Division in the Po Valley in Italy, and Thomas Galloway, class of '42 at West Point, a fighter pilot married to Almond's only daughter, had been missing over Normandy during the invasion, and the letter represented the confirmation of his death. The news was especially hard for Almond because he had always pushed his son so hard, first to go to West Point and then to go into the infantry. When young Ned had arrived in the combat zone, Almond had written his son's commander saying don't make him a staff officer, give him a rifle company.

The night the letter had arrived, Bill McCaffrey, one of Almond's top staff officers, had asked if he wanted a sedative. McCaffrey had dealt with a situation like this once before, when Townsend Crittenberger, the son of McCaffrey's corps commander, Lieutenant General Willis Crittenberger, had been killed during the Rhine crossing. Crittenberger had closed himself off in his room for two days and let his subordinates run the unit. Perhaps, McCaffrey thought, Ned Almond would need some comparable break and perhaps something to help him sleep. "No, no sedative," Almond had answered. "And, Bill, I'll command the division tomorrow." Under no circumstances was McCaffrey to tell Corps what had happened. He wanted no one monkeying with his division, and no sympathy for himself.

Ned Almond had ended that war as a two-star, when most of the men he thought of as peers had three or four stars. Yet even then, at the lowest point in his career, no one dealing with Almond would underestimate him. He was, like it or not, a force. Everything he did had to be done quickly and perfectly. For the men working under him, there was always one more order to obey, one more squad to be moved, and one more piece of paper to be typed, and typed perfectly, or it would have to be done again. Each soldier in each distant squad had to be perfectly placed, and each commander had to know every soldier's name, no matter how newly arrived the GI might be. Yet in 1945, that kind of drive and ambition had seemed almost pointless. The war was over, the Army shrinking; commands were few, and if an enemy aggressor threatened America, there was always the atomic bomb. What need was there for a used two-star who had already had his great chance? Though he was a man of Europe, in 1946 he had asked for an assignment to MacArthur's headquarters. The alternative was to serve as military attaché in Moscow, which held little attraction for him. The slot in Tokyo was as the G-1, or personnel chief, not normally a springboard to power, but in that pathetically weak headquarters he proved a standout from the moment he arrived, a man of unusual competence in a staff of second-rate hacks. It did not take long for MacArthur to understand that Almond, Europe or no, Marshall man or no, was more effective than anyone else around, and also that he hungered for one last career boost. Almond was his for the taking, MacArthur realized, someone who could, even without Bataan, become a MacArthur man. In early 1949, when MacArthur's chief of staff Paul Mueller was rotated home, Almond, who had already made himself incalculably valuable to his commander, got the job. A combat command it was not, but perhaps one day that too would come. The real job of the chief of staff in the Army is often to be the commander's son of a bitch. Everyone should go away feeling that the commander was a good guy who would make fair (and favorable) decisions on matters both large and infinitesimally small, if only he could be reached. Thus a great chief of staff was there to say no to all the requests demanding things that MacArthur did not want to do or deal with, and make everyone feel that the more benign MacArthur would have approved them if only they could have gotten past the evil Almond.

ALMOND WAS TO be an important player in the months to come. The politics of the command were very important as the war effort and the strategy unfolded, not just Tokyo against Washington, but the ferocious politics within the Tokyo command itself, the constant struggle to be the favored aide; and Almond turned out to be a vastly superior player of headquarters politics than Walton Walker was. In a way the constant struggle between him and Walker was a miniature of a larger struggle that was always taking place, the United States Army against Douglas MacArthur's Army. Of Almond's many nicknames (the Big-A, Ned the Dread), probably the most important among high-level officers in Tokyo was that of Ned the Anointed, which meant that MacArthur's arm was always on his shoulder and he was the commander's principal man, never to be challenged, as he never challenged his superior. It was assumed that he *always* spoke for MacArthur—or at least spoke for him often enough that you did not want to be the one who discovered when he wasn't speaking for him. Almond in time became MacArthur's MacArthur, the man who took MacArthur's vision of what was supposed to happen and brought it directly to Korea, where he employed it, whether it fitted the Korean reality or not.

Almond was much shrewder and infinitely more political than Walton Walker. Walker was a representative of one American Army, commanded by Omar Bradley back in Washington, and Almond had in his time in Tokyo quite deftly become the number two figure in the other American Army, the more or less autonomous one commanded by Douglas MacArthur. He understood from the start that, given the lack of talent among his senior staff (viewed as a bunch of Humpty Dumptys by the rest of the Army), MacArthur needed at least one high-level professional to make the headquarters work. The headquarters was a hothouse of political cronyism and sycophancy, at the center of which was the general himself. Some relatively senior staff members literally used the phrase "Close to the Throne," to designate one's standing with the general. Within a year of his arrival in Tokyo, Almond was the man closest to the throne.

Almond was smart enough *never* to get caught up in any of the many cliques, or to take one side against the other. Most important of all, he realized that a genuine connection to MacArthur could only be attained through complete devotion, loyalty, and obedience. MacArthur's enemies had to become his own enemies. Nothing could be held back. Nothing. And every move had to be the right one. No doubt of his about MacArthur's greatness could ever be revealed. He had to be a more perfect extension of MacArthur than MacArthur himself. He was ready for the test. "He had," wrote J. D. Coleman, an officer and a historian who had served under him, "an instinctive knack of ingratiation." By that Coleman meant that in addition to playing back to his superior what his superior wanted to hear, he had a brilliant ability to anticipate what MacArthur wanted even before the general himself knew that he wanted it.

One of the things that Bill McCaffrey had liked about Almond in his earlier incarnation was his irreverence, but he shed that with MacArthur. Once during World War II, he had been so blunt speaking with Willis Crittenberger, their corps commander, over the phone that McCaffrey had become fearful for his fate. McCaffrey had virtually grabbed the phone away from Almond, because you simply could not speak to a superior that way. But this, McCaffrey thought, was a new Almond, a man who had fallen in love with his commander. If anything bothered some of those who served under him in Tokyo and later Korea, it was his total subservience to MacArthur, along with his gamesmanship, his cool condescension to his peers, and his harshness to those under him—except for a handful of special favorites, his boys, as he was now MacArthur's boy. Even some of those boys—and no one benefited more from his friendship than Jack Chiles, who went from S-3 to regimental commander under him—knew how difficult and explosive he was. "He could precipitate a crisis on a desert island with no one else around," Chiles once said. Few neutral observers were fond of him. "He was mean and vindictive and not very talented—one of the biggest sons of bitches I've ever met, in uniform or out," said Keyes Beech, who won the Pulitzer Prize for his Korean War reporting and was a reporter who generally liked military men.

The problem with playing to MacArthur was that it was all or nothing and you had to play to his entire team. Soon enough, Almond found himself swallowing some of his old opinions simply in order to accommodate the Bataan Gang. In the years before World War II, he had often complained to McCaffrey about an officer working as an attaché in Latin America named Charles Willoughby, whom he had quickly come to despise. A pompous, self-important fool, he had often said, always wrong on everything he reported, a judgment shared by many other professional officers. Now, overnight, Almond started defending Willoughby to others as brilliant. McCaffrey watched this rehabilitation process and just shook his head.

Knowing Walker's vulnerability, Almond set out to diminish his influence further in Tokyo. Although Almond was a mere two-star, he was deft at implying to Walker, a three-star, that he was a de facto five-star, speaking for MacArthur and not for himself, in effect wearing MacArthur's stars. The phone would ring in Walker's headquarters, and it would be Almond talking in a peremptory way. Walker did his best to hold his turf and occasionally would say, "Is this Almond speaking or Almond speaking for MacArthur?" But it was a losing struggle. Walker had very little time on his own with MacArthur. He always had to go through Almond. Walker was aware that none of this would be happening without MacArthur's essential approval, and so he bore his frustrations as best he could. He never challenged Almond, never demanded a better hearing for

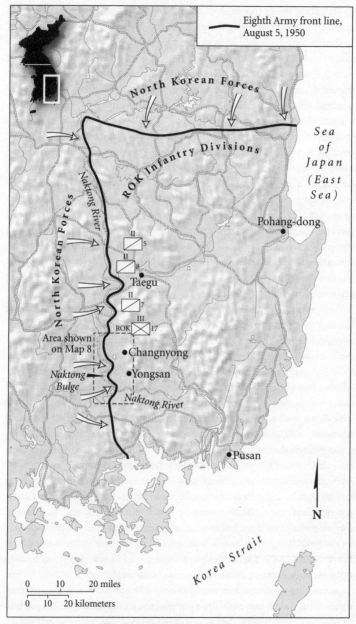

7. THE PUSAN PERIMETER, AUGUST 4, 1950

his ideas, and never complained through back-channel sources to friends in Washington about the difficulty of his situation.

Every day in all kinds of ways, Walker's aide Joe Tyner believed, Ned Almond worked to make Walton Walker's life a kind of hell. Mostly he took it, but there were the rare occasions when Walker's anger at his treatment came through. Tyner remembered one occasion when Walker simply blew up. It was a year before the war started. There had been a dinner party at Almond's house. Just before dinner, Walker took a quick glance at the table and discovered that there was a snub built into the way the seating was done. Military protocol dictated that Walker be seated at the place of honor. Instead, Almond had given it to Lord Alvary Gascoigne, the British ambassador to Japan and a man MacArthur seemed to like. Walker had quickly grabbed Tyner. "Get the car!" he said. "We're getting out of here!" Tyner, realizing why his general was so angry and seeing the potential for a serious breach that could not be healed quickly, bought some time. "General, I've already released the driver," he replied. Then he quickly found one of Almond's aides. He explained the problem with the seating and informed him that his general, a very angry general, was about to leave. The seating was immediately redone, and Walker stayed; he had won a tiny battle, albeit in a losing war.

So it was that in those days, as America raced to build up its forces back home, Walker commanded an understrength army that was trying against great odds to slow down a formidable enemy force. As July turned into August, the battlefield began to change, to become one that favored Walker. The In Min Gun were driving the Americans and their South Korean allies into a tiny corner of the country where, with a great deal less terrain to defend, their lines of communication and supply finally started to stabilize. The North Koreans were giving Walker, by dint of their victories, an ever more compact battlefield where he could more readily summon his strengths and exploit his superior military intelligence and American firepower. At the same time, the North Korean lines of communication and supply, hopelessly extended, were increasingly vulnerable to air attack, even as the Americans were pouring more aircraft into the battle. The relentless pounding from American airpower was already taking its toll. Captured Communist soldiers told of mounting shortages of equipment, ammunition, and medical supplies, and experienced troops. Green troops were filling the slots not long ago held by veterans in some elite North Korean units. Day by day, there were still Communist advances, but each victorious moment seemed increasingly pyrrhic in nature.

More elite American and some other UN troops were now also on their way to what was known as the Pusan Perimeter. For the first time, if American troops stood and fought, they would know which units were on their flanks.

The real battle, Johnnie Walker was telling his commanders and his troops in those dark days, was one of trading distance for time, hoping to slow down the In Min Gun until more American and allied troops could arrive. The only question was: Could his shaky, understrength, exhausted forces hold out long enough on this new shorter battlefield for fresher American troops from elite units to arrive, and until—though he did not talk about it—MacArthur made his daring strike, his great gamble at Inchon now scheduled for September 15? In late July, as the last of his units crossed the Naktong River and began to develop positions there, Walker told some of them: "There will be no more retreating, withdrawal or readjustment of the lines or whatever you call it. There are no lines behind which we can retreat. There is not going to be a Dunkirk or Bataan. A retreat to [the port of] Pusan would be one of the greatest butcheries in history. We must fight to the end. We must fight as a team. If some of us die, we will die fighting together."

Walker himself had been against Inchon as a landing spot: he thought it was too large a gamble and drained too many troops from his understrength defenders. His opposition in some ways sealed his fate with his superior—to be openly against Inchon was to be seen as disloyal to MacArthur, and added to the latter's contempt for Walker. As much as anything else it was the numbers that bothered Walker: for six crucial weeks, the mission might deprive his already depleted forces, trying desperately not to be driven off the peninsula, of two valuable American divisions, plus much of that supporting air and naval power. Unfortunately for Walker, Inchon was not merely a plan for a breathtaking amphibious landing, it was a test of faith and loyalty, which everyone who served under MacArthur had to take. There was no middle ground. Walker's position—he favored an amphibious landing at a spot not so far up the Korean shore—was not good enough. His dissent strengthened Ned Almond's position. Almond became the driving force within the command, organizing the planning for Inchon, fighting off when need be the Navy's senior commanders, including men expert on amphibious landings who had their own considerable doubts about such a dangerous landing in so spectacularly difficult a location.

Few men pass a loyalty test with such flying colors as Almond did then with MacArthur, or fail it as completely as Walton Walker did. With Inchon, Almond became ever closer to MacArthur, and would in fact, to the surprise (and anger) of the Joint Chiefs, be handed something almost unheard of in the Army: command of the Inchon amphibious force, which allowed him to wear two hats—commander of Tenth Corps, the landing force at Inchon, and chief of staff of the Far East command. Walker, the man whose command had just been split and a large slice of it given over to a sworn adversary, knew that in some way he had failed in his commander's eyes. "I'm just a defeated Confederate general," he said.

While the Inchon planning went on feverishly in Tokyo, the Pusan Perimeter battlefield was turning out to be one of the bloodiest of this or any other war fought by Americans. It would rank right up there with the worst of Civil War battles and some of the terrible island-hopping campaigns in the Pacific. The pressure for victory was mounting on both sides as August began; the Americans rushed fresh forces to the contested, shrinking battlefield, and the North Koreans, aware that they had not, as Kim Il Sung had promised Stalin, gone all the way to Pusan in three weeks, felt the pressure to gain their final victory before the American buildup could take full effect. The American entry into the war had caught Kim by surprise, yet he still continued to overestimate the abilities of his own troops and underestimate the advantage superior weaponry would sooner or later give the Americans, and the hardships it would inflict on his troops. The battle slogans issued by the North Korean leadership to its commanders in the field reflected Kim's view that the war had reached a critical point. "Solve the problem before August" and "August is the month of victory" became the newest political slogans, and reflected a growing fear that the war might turn into a stalemate or a defeat. But Kim still remained optimistic. His Chinese peers, however, were far more worried. In their eyes, the In Min Gun's drive south had in the end failed and the tide of battle was about to turn. Kim was still talking victory—while the Chinese were increasingly sure that he had already been defeated. They were far more sophisticated about things like this and had been skeptical of Kim's leadership from the start. In their mind, not only had the North Korean drive already been stopped, but the Americans were growing stronger, rushing more and better troops into the country along with more equipment. They were about to take the offensive. If that happened, and they were sure it would, then it would involve them in some way.

Part
Four

---

*The Politics
of Two Continents*

12

E VEN BEFORE THE Korean War began, the Truman administration had
been operating in something of a crisis mode over two main issues. The
first and less politically explosive was what a considerable number of the administration's senior officials believed was a seriously inadequate defense budget, a feeling that America's recently inherited global responsibilities were far
greater than the country's willingness to pay for them, and that there was a
need to double that budget—at a minimum—and quite possibly triple it. So
far, the president, a fiscal conservative, had stood against those increases. The
other, far more volatile issue was the rapid deterioration of the bipartisan wartime political alliance, along with the decline of Chiang's China and in time
the question of whether someone, in the phrase then being used, had managed
to lose China, if a nation can be lost. The issue of China—whether the Democrats had lost it—would hang over not merely the Truman administration but
the Democratic Party for the next two political generations.

It was one of the enduring myths of American politics in the 1950s and 1960s
that politics stopped at the water's edge, as if the foreign policy of the United
States were some kind of sacrosanct area, separated from and placed above the
normal meanness and conflicting interests of domestic constituencies and the
passions they engendered. Nothing was further from the truth. There had been
considerable (if, on occasion, reluctant) bipartisanship during the war years, a
bipartisanship that was in some ways involuntary, given the very considerable
dangers posed by Germany and Japan, but it began to unravel almost as soon as
the war ended. If anything, that very quality of wartime suppression, in which
one party, out of power for a generation, had felt both voiceless and powerless,
created a political force all its own and would finally lead to a serious, if belated,
backlash against the party that had ruled for so long. There is no way to understand the mean season just beginning in American politics, and which formed
the critical political backdrop to the Korean War—one wing of the opposition
political party accusing the principal architects of both America's victorious
war effort and its postwar foreign policy of acting in concert with the country's

enemies—without grasping the totality with which Franklin Roosevelt had transformed the political landscape during his singular four-term presidency, and thus the degree to which his economic and social revolution had transformed the country and, momentarily at least, marginalized the Republican Party.

Part of what had swept the Republicans away as a majority party was the sheer charismatic quality of Roosevelt himself and his extraordinary ability, far ahead of any other major politician in the nation, to exploit the newest technological instrument of the era—radio. His mastery of radio, his ability to use it in the most intimate manner imaginable to reach the electorate, had proved a stunning political asset. With it he transformed the very nature of the presidency by creating a direct, previously unknown emotional connection to the populace. No longer was the president an aloof figure, formal, distant, and unreachable, a man in some stiff, uncomfortable pose in an occasional photo in a daily newspaper; now there was a new one-way intimacy; in his new incarnation he was a friend of ordinary people, a warm and caring political figure who made house calls over the airwaves, as attuned to the needs and fears of Americans as the favored family doctor, who also made house calls. He did not, it appeared, even need to make speeches—rather they were called fireside chats. *My friends,* was how he would begin one of his radio talks, and as he did, he forged a brand-new connection with millions of voters. He was, in essence, the first media president, the creator of what became known as media politics, which would some thirty years later produce a television presidency.

The cumulative effect of the man—his voice, his unmatched political skills, the bitter Depression that had plunged so many Americans into misery and had catapulted him into office, his seemingly revolutionary New Deal economic and political programs, and of course the galvanizing effect of World War II—simply overwhelmed the Republicans, who had been associated with the forces of the very rich in an era of economic catastrophe. No other American president had served more than two terms, but Franklin Roosevelt, because of the special confluence of very different forces, had run four times and won. His New Deal legislation empowered the more vulnerable in the society and made unionization easier in the workplace. With that he became the head of a political party sympathetic to the needs and rights of labor in what was still very much a blue collar economy. He strengthened his hold on the country thanks to the political leverage offered by the approach of global war during the 1940 campaign, which helped give him his third term, and in 1944, as a wartime president, he won again, despite severely failing health, his physical decline carefully masked from the people. The combination of *two* transcending events—depression and war—had meant he could extend his remarkable hold on the political scene long after the moment when, in normal political times, his fortunes would certainly have begun to ebb. To the Republicans, by 1944, it seemed that he had been president forever and might remain president forever. By the time of his third run, the approach of a world war had not only severely damaged the opposition party, but made it somewhat schizophrenic. Roosevelt, after all, was an internationalist, gradually preparing the nation for entry into a terrifying new global conflict, most assuredly on the side of embattled England, the nation's closest ally.

On such matters, the Republican Party was badly split, caught in divisions that were deep, unhealable, and profoundly geographic. Part of its leadership represented a wing of the traditional internationalist elite, reflecting the views of Wall Street and State Street financiers, transatlantic men all. They believed that, like it or not, America could not sit on the sidelines in such a war, that it must choose—and must choose the side of the Western democracies. That placed much of the Republican leadership in the position of endorsing Roosevelt's internationalism or supporting a slightly more conservative figure who seemed on many of the great issues of the era to sound very much like the president himself. But the other wing of the Republican Party was very different: it was essentially more grassroots; it reflected old, abiding, small-town American isolationist fears of being pulled into the constant squabbles and wars of a corrupt Europe, and worse, doing it for the British. These feelings were rooted primarily in the Midwest, where among the governing circles in many small towns and cities there was a fundamental hatred of almost everything Roosevelt was doing on the domestic scene, of his New Deal, which these critics passionately believed was, to use their favored word, socialistic. Within the party, this isolationist wing might well have been numerically greater than the internationalist wing, and it was surely significantly more influential at the local level, but it had lost out to the Eastern elite, the internationalist wing, at the 1940 convention, principally because of the rise of Hitler. Wendell Willkie, the barefoot lawyer from Wall Street, as he was called, was nominated, a major triumph of the internationalists. That had been bad enough, but the small-town Midwestern wing, the people who *knew* that they were the real Republicans and that the party should be theirs, and that their values were the truer ones because they were the more *American* ones, had lost again at the convention in 1944, this time to Tom Dewey, the governor of New York, and would eventually be beaten once more by Dewey in 1948. To the core Republican leadership in the heartland, the voice of their presidential candidates in all those elections had sounded too much like that of men unable to separate themselves from the Democrats, a thin echo first of Roosevelt and then of Truman. "If you read the *Chicago Tribune*, you'd know I'm a direct lineal descendant of FDR," Dewey once said of the paper that was the central media instrument and voice of the isolationists.

While that amazing Roosevelt run had taken place, the Republican right wing had raged impotently. The more it lost, the angrier it became. Each time, its representatives had come to the national conventions confident of their greater truths, only to see the nomination hijacked by an elite from the big industrial states backed up by a few powerful internationalist publishers, most notably Henry Luce, the head of *Time* and *Life,* a man then at the very peak of his media power. The residual bitterness from the 1940 and 1944 conventions was very real; it was hard to tell who the right wingers were angrier at, FDR and the Democrats or the internationalist wing of their own party. To them, the internationalists were fake Republicans, Eastern snobs, who had just enough skill to steal the nomination but never enough to win an election.

With World War II over and Roosevelt dead, the right wing finally believed it was regaining power, both within the party itself and nationally. The 1946 off-year election had given the right-wingers their first chance to strike back. Their cause, as they saw it, was nothing less than simple Americanism, or the protection of an America of sturdy old-fashioned values, which had produced people exactly like them, against the America of their enemies, which had produced people who favored what they saw as socialism or Communism or, in their minds, people whose lives were too heavily subsidized by the government. "The choice which confronts Americans this year is between Communism and Republicanism," said B. Carroll Reece, the Tennessee congressman and chairman of the Republican Party, just before the election. Nebraska's Senator Kenneth Wherry added: "The coming campaign is not just another election. It is a crusade." And in some ways, and in some parts of the country, it was nothing less.

Harry Truman, the accidental president, the unlikely heir to the mighty Roosevelt presidency, was probably lucky indeed that 1946 was *not* a presidential election year, given the general unhappiness in the country, and the anxieties that lay just under the surface. Unlike its allies (and enemies) whose lands lay in ruins, the United States had emerged from the war as the sole global economic powerhouse, a nation rich in a world that was poor, its allies and adversaries alike ground down by fighting suicidal wars twice within twenty-five years. America, protected in that era by its two great oceans, untouched on its mainland by enemy bombs, had emerged infinitely more muscular than when it had gone in; the country had been dragged by exterior forces, kicking and screaming, to the zenith of its power. But there was a surprising degree of anxiety as well as stored up resentments just underneath the surface, most notably over dealing with the increasingly difficult and complex peace that the United

States had inherited and over accepting the great jump in global responsibility that came with the peace. The new threat of Soviet Communism—the fact that an ally had suddenly become an adversary—was just beginning to fall over American politics. To some of those who had been out of power there was little surprise in this—the Soviets had been an unlikely ally in the first place, and to some of them the war had been the wrong one from the beginning; we had once again fought to save the British. With the war over, not that many Americans were eager to take on these great new unwanted international obligations—and risks—that went with becoming a superpower and replacing imperial Britain as the leader of the Western alliance, nor were many necessarily thrilled to become, as the architects of foreign policy in Washington seemed to be demanding, part of Europe's endless political-military struggles on a long-term basis. Many Americans wanted less, not more, of a connection with the European democracies.

And so the Republicans did very well in the congressional election of 1946. The wartime pressure to support the incumbent president—don't change horses in midstream—had been a very successful Democratic slogan, but it was gone. The Republicans, running on a program of a 20 percent across-the-board tax cut, gained eleven seats in the Senate and fifty-four in the House. The Roosevelt coalition of Northern labor unions and big city machines combined with conservative Southern oligarchs looked like it might be coming apart, replaced by what the Republicans hoped was a return to old-fashioned American normalcy. "The United States is now a Republican country," said Senator Styles Bridges of New Hampshire, soon to be a major player in what would be known as the China Lobby. Some of the newly elected Republicans had campaigned not so much against the Democratic Party as against Communism and subversion. The election added to the party's senatorial ranks Joseph McCarthy of Wisconsin, Bill Jenner of Indiana, John Bricker of Ohio, Harry Cain of Washington, and James Kem of Missouri. Some of them, joining up with conservatives already in the Senate, like Kenneth Wherry, were to turn out to be obsessive on the subject of Communists and subversion in our own government, a wonderful new issue that tended to neutralize their vulnerability on economic matters. "Bow your heads folks, conservatism has hit America. All the rest of the world is moving Left, America is moving Right," wrote T.R.B. after the election in *The New Republic,* then a traditionally liberal magazine.

In play was nothing less than the issue of America's role in the postwar world. Was it willing to accept the global leadership of the Western democracies? And how much in terms of sheer dollars—in terms of taxes—would this cost? On this issue the leadership of both parties was uncertain. Neither party was in any rush to pay the economic price demanded of a nation that was going to lead the West. The Republican Party, the more virulently anti-Communist, was, if anything, in a greater rush to disarm, more willing to depend on the nation's nuclear monopoly, and warier of accepting a role in building up a badly damaged Europe, one dangerously vulnerable, it was believed, to internal Communist subversion. The truth was that on the eve of the Korean War, America's defense posture was a shambles. Its defense budgets had been slashed; its armed forces were far too small; and its weaponry and equipment—the most advanced in the world only five years earlier—was increasingly inferior. The top people concerned with what was already coming to be known as the country's national security were seriously divided over how much was enough. At the moment that the North Korean Army crossed the thirty-eighth parallel, Secretary of State Dean Acheson, already under virulent attack from the Republican right wing for being, as it was said, soft on Communism, was trying as deftly as possible to maneuver a new, dramatically elevated commitment to defense spending through the bureaucracy. Though Acheson had already become the most influential member of the president's top national security team, by no means was this attempt a guaranteed success.

Part of the reason was Truman himself. If Harry Truman was a hawk on most Cold War issues, he was also a hard-liner on budgets, and he hated deficit spending. "A hard money man if I ever saw one," James Forrestal, the conservative Wall Street man who was an early hawk, once said of him, "believing as I do that we can't wreck our economy in the process of trying to fight the 'cold war.' " Truman was by nature an innately skeptical Midwestern populist, wary of men with big titles and those who put on airs, which, he decided, all too many senior military men tended to do. The military, he had always believed, was unusually given to wasting the taxpayers' money. His own experience as an artillery captain during World War I had made him wary of the brass, especially West Pointers, who, in his mind, took themselves far too seriously. He was a small-town boy who had grown up in draconian economic times, and that had made him a serious fiscal conservative—you did not spend it unless you had it. His views had only hardened during his time as a senator, when he headed the Truman Committee, which had focused on mismanagement by the military at the start of World War II: "No military man knows anything at all about money. All they know how to do is spend it, and they don't give a goddamn whether they're getting their money's worth or not," he once said. In time he became extremely close to a few senior officers, like Omar Bradley, but his general attitude never changed. As he told the writer Merle Miller, "They're most of them like horses with blinders on. They can't see beyond the ends of their noses."

Harry Truman hated debt with a personal passion. His family had been burdened with it back in Independence, Missouri, and it had helped cost them their family farm. What he had wanted to do at the end of the war was start paying off the immense—at least so it seemed at the time—$250 billion debt the country had incurred over the previous four years. As soon as the war ended, he had gotten the defense budget down from about $91 billion to a point between $10 and $11 billion a year, and he hoped soon to get it even lower, to $6 or $7 billion a year. Truman, in other words, would need a lot of convincing if military budgets were to be adjusted for the new role that most of his top national security people wanted. Certainly Marshall and Acheson wanted larger military budgets. Normally the secretary of defense should have been an ally of men like Acheson on an issue like this, but in this case, the secretary of defense, Louis Johnson, who had replaced James Forrestal when Forrestal's health broke down, had proved the exception. He had turned out to be a sworn enemy of Acheson, both professionally and personally, jealous of his power and influence with Truman and determined to destroy him politically even if his own budget suffered. The key to Louis Johnson at that point was his own political ambition. He dreamed of succeeding Truman as the Democratic candidate for the presidency in 1952, and he intended to do it by portraying himself as the secretary of defense who had held military spending down. That meant that as the winter ended in 1950, Acheson had become the point man for greater spending on defense, and his critics in the other party, who were enjoying attacking the administration for its failures in foreign policy, especially in China, were in no rush to accede. The United States was supposed to be tougher in dealing with its enemies in the world, but there was no rush to discuss how to pay for it.

That placed Dean Acheson in the rare position of being attacked for being soft on Communism, yet cut off from the kind of spending he believed was needed to stave off a Communist threat in Europe and elsewhere. Because increased military spending was a political minefield—for it would surely demand higher taxes—he pursued it cautiously. His key assistant was a young man named Paul Nitze who was just beginning to ascend in the national security world and was in the process of replacing George Kennan as the head of State's Policy Planning staff, the department's own think tank, because he seemed to Acheson to be more of a hard-liner than Kennan and thus more in tune with Acheson's policies. (Nitze would actually take over Policy Planning from Kennan in January 1950, but he had been the de facto head of it for several months before.) Acheson and Nitze were virtually tiptoeing through the bureaucracy with their plan for a complete overhaul of defense policies—a document that would be known as National Security Council Paper 68, or

NSC 68, a seminal paper that completely redefined America's defense needs. They were trying to keep the magnitude of the change they were planning secret from Johnson and his potential allies for as long as they could, particularly the prospective price. Acheson wanted to get as much support as possible for the principle of an expanded defense commitment from the upper levels of the bureaucracy before anyone talked about price, and he did not want a meeting with Louis Johnson before he was ready. As such he was going behind his back. Ironically, Acheson, the secretary of state, would end up with almost the complete support of the Joint Chiefs in trying to upgrade the budget—for the military had been restless with bare-bones budgets for five years. At the core of these defense budgets on the cheap was the belief that America's nuclear monopoly allowed it to cut corners on every other defense issue. The American atomic monopoly had ended in the fall of 1949, and therefore long-delayed issues were coming to the fore.

The struggle between the military and the civilians over the budget had been going on since 1945. The entire nation, with both political parties eagerly participating, had been in an indecent rush to cut the armed forces when World War II ended. Everyone in politics, both right and left, had favored the demobe, preferably done yesterday rather than tomorrow. The nation at war, which almost overnight created the mightiest military arsenal in the history of mankind, reflected one America; the demobe reflected another—except that they were one and the same country. The problem with a great democracy like the United States, George Kennan once noted, was that it was almost always like a sleeping giant, impervious to its surroundings until suddenly and belatedly awoken, when it proved so angry about what it discovered that it started lashing out wildly.

In 1946, Dwight Eisenhower, by then Army chief of staff, had been invited up to Capitol Hill to meet with J. Parnell Thomas, one of the era's foremost congressional rogues, and at that moment chairman of the House Military Affairs Committee. Thomas was a Republican from New Jersey, a fascinating reflection of the era, a virulent anti-Communist who had often talked about Roosevelt and the New Deal sabotaging the capitalist system. As the head of the House Un-American Activities Committee, he eventually gained some fame hunting Communists in Hollywood, but he would soon enough end up in prison in Danbury, Connecticut, for putting ghost figures on his office payroll and keeping the salaries himself. (There, two of his fellow inmates were Hollywood writers imprisoned because they had refused to testify before his committee.) Preparing to meet with Thomas, Eisenhower had expected a serious discussion with an important member of Congress about how to bring down American force levels with minimal damage to the country. Instead he walked into a world-class ambush. There was Thomas, surrounded by a group of attractive young women, the wives of servicemen anxious to have their husbands shipped home—and on a table a large number of baby shoes. A photographer soon appeared, and a photo of the wives, the baby shoes, a smiling Thomas, and a furious Eisenhower soon went hurtling over the wires.

At the end of the war, the United States had had 12 million men and women in uniform. The rate of the demobe was overwhelming; fifteen thousand military personnel a *day* were processed out of the services. If there were logistical problems in bringing troops back from abroad, there was a new public outcry, "no boats, no votes." By early 1947, the services were down to 1.5 million members, and the annual military budget, which had reached a wartime high of $90.9 billion, had plummeted to $10.3. In addition, the awesome hardware of World War II was not being modernized. Within years, much of it was outdated, some of it useless. At the moment when North Korean divisions first pushed into the South, the Army's studies later showed that 43 percent of the enlisted men in the Far East Command rated in terms of ability and intelligence as either Class IV or Class V, the two lowest categories in the Army's general classification tests. It was a country, in the eyes of the senior military men, that had simply walked away from its responsibilities. "America fought [World War II] like a football game after which the winner leaves the field and celebrates," General Albert Wedemeyer said, as he watched the rush to demobilize. "It was no demobilization," commented George Marshall, "it was a rout." The Army had, said General Omar Bradley, "only one division—the Eighty-second Airborne—that could be remotely described as combat ready." In those years after it downsized so rapidly and just before Korea, America had, in Bradley's words, an army at the start of the Korean War that "could not fight its way out of a paper bag."

The military budgets were becoming increasingly brutal documents. What was being cut, as Cabell Phillips, a national security correspondent for the *New York Times,* noted, was not fat but muscle and bone. In late 1948, preparing for the fiscal 1950 budget year, the three services submitted their tentative budgets. The total was $30 billion. James Forrestal, the first secretary of defense, working exhausting hours, got it down to $17 billion. But Harry Truman, more concerned with the domestic economy than military spending (and all too aware of the disastrous political consequences of any tax increase), decided it could not go over $15 billion. It finally came in at $14.2. The interservice competition for the limited funds available was savage. The role of the Marines was being sharply curtailed; military men like Bradley were talking about there being no future need for amphibious missions, which would limit the role of the Navy as well. If any branch of the service seemed favored at that moment it was the

Air Force, which had the atomic bomb in its arsenal. It was something that seemed endemic to this particular democratic society, one that had built into its psyche a sense of protection based on the two great oceans. Even during Korea, George Marshall, the man who had been the most important figure in rushing the country to readiness at the start of World War II, was sure that America had not yet learned its lesson. When Truman met with MacArthur at Wake Island in mid-October 1950, Marshall did not make the trip, but he was shocked by the euphoria that seemed to have gripped the returning party. Frank Pace, the secretary of the Army, enthusiastically told him of MacArthur's optimistic talk about the war being virtually over and how soon the troops would return. "General Marshall," he had said, "General MacArthur says the war will be over by Thanksgiving and the troops home by Christmas."

To Pace's surprise, Marshall did not seemed pleased: "Pace, that's troublesome."

Pace thought Marshall had misunderstood, so he repeated the good news that the end of the war was at hand. "I heard you," Marshall said, "but too precipitate an end to the war would not permit us to have a full understanding of the problems we face ahead of us." Still puzzled, Pace asked if Marshall meant that the American people needed to better understand the full implications of the Cold War. That, said Marshall, was exactly what he meant. "General Marshall, this has been a very difficult and extensive war from the American people's point of view," Pace said. But Marshall was having none of it. He had been through it before at the end of World War II; the moment it was over, the tanks rotting in the Pacific, the boys rushing home to their civilian jobs, the military strength that had been built up had been allowed in his words just "to fade away."

But that was then and this was now, Pace argued, and "a great deal of water has passed under the bridge since then. Would you say I was naïve if I said that the American people had learned their lesson?"

"No, Pace, I wouldn't say you were naïve. I'd say you were *incredibly* naïve," Marshall answered.

THE PERSON IN the high-level bureaucracy pushing hardest to make an adjustment to changing needs in the early part of the Cold War had been Forrestal, and under the pressure of cutbacks, his own wariness of Soviet intentions, and surely out of some personal psychological disorder, his mental health had begun to deteriorate. He was working man-killing hours that would, Eisenhower said, "kill a horse." Forrestal had been an early hard-liner in dealing with the Soviets, and he had even raised the question, hardly a popular one, in July 1945 of how complete a defeat the United States should inflict on Japan.

He feared that if the victory were too complete, if too little of the old Japan were left, there would be a political vacuum in Northeast Asia that might be filled all too quickly, not just by the Soviets but perhaps by the rising power of the Chinese Communists, who he was sure were going to win their civil war. Did we really want to destroy Japan's industrial base, as so many of our top strategists intended? he wondered. Forrestal grew increasingly melancholy in his belief that our defense budget did not match a realistic view of the Russians, or for that matter, our own rhetoric, that our voice exceeded our military capabilities. His political melancholia was coupled with a serious decline in his mental health, and by late 1948, his close friends had become ever more concerned about him. He grew more and more paranoid, and looked gaunt and haunted. His shirt collars seemed to be several sizes too big. He could no longer sleep; his face was ashen. He was absolutely sure the Russians were tapping his phone. In the final few weeks of his service, he was calling a baffled Truman several times a day to bring up the same subject. He was, it became obvious, in the midst of a full-blown nervous breakdown. Forrestal himself sensed that he was coming apart. In early February 1949, he told Truman that he would leave his post by June 1. But Truman knew he would not last even that long. On March 1, 1949, he called Forrestal in and asked for his resignation. Four weeks later, Louis Johnson, who had been so valuable as a fundraiser for Truman in 1948, replaced Forrestal, and Forrestal was hospitalized. In late May, he took his own life, jumping out of a sixteenth-floor window at the Bethesda Naval Hospital, one of the early victims of, among other things, the pressures of the Cold War atmosphere. Louis Johnson's appointment proved one of Truman's worst and most political. Johnson was a bully, full of certitude if not nuance, who in his own way was hardly less emotionally out of control than Forrestal. He managed to earn the enduring hatred of the senior uniformed military, not only because he kept slashing their budgets, but because he treated them so crudely and with such uncommon disrespect.

What would become ever more clear in retrospect about those years was that Truman and his administration had spanned a critical moment in American history. America was changing, like it or not, from the America that had been, that is, the America that was powerful but did not yet know it and was hesitant to use its industrial muscularity internationally, to the America that would be America the superpower. The ongoing debates over the future, the battle within the administration over NSC 68, and even the ugliness of the McCarthy period itself were in a way manifestations of that dramatic change. These were caused in effect by growing pains. Franklin Roosevelt had been president during the climb to power, and he had died on the cusp of the final moment, the victory over Germany. The Truman years, with all the conflict

over defense spending, with in the beginning only a relatively small elite pushing for a new kind of military and economic alliance with the Western democracies in Europe, and with an ever more powerful domestic undertow pulling
against that same internationalism, were when it had all been fought out.
Truman was the first president who had to deal with the consequences and
contradictions of the great victory in World War II, and the power (and responsibility) it bequeathed to his country. He not only had to marshal the
government behind a new kind of internationalism but had to deal with a
volatile, sometimes hostile, domestic political reaction as the nation slowly began to accept its new responsibilities. The choice was a basic one, between
greater internationalism or continued isolation—and, perhaps equally important, how much the country was willing to pay. It is against that background,
and Truman's belief in the primacy of a strong, democratic Europe allied with
the United States, that the fall of China, the rise of Mao, and in time the Korean
War, and the political forces they unleashed at home, should be viewed.

Dean Acheson was the most important player in the debate over NSC 68,
the man at the center of it all. It was a debate that was not really a debate in any
larger public sense, but more of a struggle of different forces colliding within
the bureaucracy on the question of what America should do in its postwar
incarnation—how great a power it should become and how much of the traditional British role of the leader of the West it should take over. Even before he
became secretary of state, Acheson was in the process of becoming the most
important national security player of the era, quite possibly of the next fifty
years, and the single most important architect of the policies that became central to America's leadership of the Western powers, as well as its containment
of and coexistence with the Soviet Union. Some four decades later, when the
Soviet Union collapsed, largely of its own weight and the failure of its economy to function in any modern capacity, there was in the media an immediate
instinct to give most of the credit to Ronald Reagan, who had helped push a
partially bankrupt adversary to the brink of economic collapse. But more
properly the credit for the policies of the West belonged to a long line of American political leaders who had helped hold off Soviet advances in Europe,
principal among them Acheson.

The era in which he served, the most critical and important years of the
Cold War, in which America's principal postwar alliances were formed, driven
by a formidable new need for collective security, could easily and without exaggeration be known as the Age of Acheson. No non-president dominated
American foreign policy decision-making in that period as he did. George
Marshall had given his greatest years to the period that ended with World War II,
and was exhausted in the years immediately following, his health beginning

to decline. After the death of Forrestal, no one from the Defense Department loomed as large on the landscape. Acheson, more than anyone else, with the debacle of the post–World War I policies fresh in his mind, was vital to creating the military and economic alliances that solidified the West, linking the United States with Europe as never before. Not by chance did he, somewhat immodestly, title his memoir *Present at the Creation*.

Of what American policy should be at that moment as the British flag was being lowered, certainly Acheson had the clearest vision. He was the ultimate Europe Firster. Because of that he was also the principal target for those who in different ways were unhappy with that course, either because they loathed the New Deal, or disliked the British, or were deeply isolationist, or were Asia (and China) Firsters. He was very much a man of a ruling elite, who had no doubts about his own right to chart a course (or that it was the right one). But the vision that was so clear to him and men like him had not yet been accepted by a broad spectrum in the country, the millions of Americans who hoped for an old-fashioned normalcy. That made for a great many contradictions in the American outlook toward the rest of the world. The foreign policy of the United States in the years right after the war, Dean Acheson once noted, "could be summed up in three sentences: 1. Bring the boys home; 2. Don't be Santa Claus; 3. Don't be pushed around."

He worked, from the start, in a political combat zone. Acheson had become secretary of state on January 21, 1949, the day after Truman's inauguration. Even before he was named secretary he had been a red flag for the Republicans. The confirmation hearings when he was named undersecretary of state had been unusually difficult and cantankerous, almost a trip wire for the escalating confrontation between the administration and the Republican right wing. There had always been a feeling on the part of the China Firsters that Acheson was their sworn enemy and thus MacArthur's too, that Acheson had been out to clip the general's wings—which was largely true. (When MacArthur had announced that he had more troops than he needed, it was Acheson who had taken him on, saying the occupation authorities were not the architects of policy but only "the instruments of it," a statement that had greatly angered MacArthur.) Because of that, there had been a surprising amount of bad feeling during the first confirmation fight. A number of very conservative Republicans had opposed Acheson's nomination as undersecretary because he had, as Senator Kenneth Wherry charged, "blighted the name of MacArthur." Twelve senators voted for Wherry's move to recommit the nomination, but it was quickly defeated and Acheson approved, 69–1. What was at the heart of the resentment, Acheson later said, was Truman's relationship with MacArthur. "If we could have seen into the future," Acheson wrote twenty-four years later, "we would have recognized this skirmish as the beginning of a struggle leading to the relief of MacArthur from his command on April 11, 1951."

In the new, more partisan era, Acheson became the perfect target for the administration's most conservative critics. That he was attacked by his critics as being a figure on the left was ironic and reflected something about the times. "Only in the heat-distorted vision of Cold War America could Acheson be seen other than as what he was: an 'enlightened conservative' to use a barbarous and patronizing phrase," noted I. F. Stone, who wrote from the left. "Who remembered in these days of McCarthy that Acheson, on making his Washington debut at the Treasury, had been denounced by New Dealers as a Wall Street Trojan Horse, a borer-from-within on behalf of the big bankers?"

Acheson possessed, as he was well aware, a formidable intellect, and to go along with it a comparable and equally powerful sense of rectitude, one that on occasion got him in considerable trouble. He was the son of Edward Campion Acheson, an Episcopalian minister who had soldiered early in his career, migrated to Canada, and fought the Indians in Manitoba, before turning to the ministry and coming to the United States. As such the righteousness of the cause, and the willingness to bear arms in its name, were properly blended in Acheson's home. While in Canada, Edward Acheson had married Eleanor Gooderham, the daughter of a successful whiskey distiller and bank president, and in time he found his way to Middletown, Connecticut, as the local minister, eventually becoming the bishop of Connecticut. Dean Gooderham Acheson was born in 1893 into a very traditional, quite conservative home of tried and true Anglophiles. The family was moderately successful, exceptionally well connected, but in no way wealthy. In time, young Dean went off to Groton, then Yale, where he was the most casual of students, and in time Harvard Law School, where for the first time he applied himself intellectually. He became a protégé of the great law professor and future Supreme Court Justice Felix Frankfurter and was, for a time, private secretary to Supreme Court Justice Louis Brandeis. It was Frankfurter, a kind of one-man clearinghouse and skilled networker for New Deal talent, who helped connect Acheson, by then a successful Washington corporate lawyer, to Roosevelt, who appointed him undersecretary of the treasury in 1933. The Frankfurter connection helped, but so did the Groton one, for Roosevelt had gone there as well.

Acheson was superior in education, dress, and attitude if not wealth, and he was unafraid to show it: his manner, self-evidently one of superiority, both intellectual and social, often grated on those he considered lesser mortals. He was not afflicted by self-doubt. Rather, he was the kind of man who believed that doing the right kind of deals with the right people for the right purpose was just fine, indeed noble, and surely above politics, but that comparable deals made by his opposition reflected a lack of honor and character, done as they were in his eyes by men of questionable motives. He had a simply dreadful touch with altogether too many members of Congress, as if the political process itself had tainted them. He tended to talk down to them, much like a schoolteacher who has given one lecture too many to unruly sixth-graders. He treated us, said Walter Judd, a Republican congressman from Minnesota, a former missionary in China, and one of the key figures in the China Lobby, with "a certain condescension, like he was sorry for us hayseeds, that he was casting pearls before swine." To his critics, with his snobbish manner, bespoke British tailoring, and Guards' mustache, he was the very embodiment of everything they resented about Washington, the government, and the New Deal. "I watch his smart-aleck manner, and his British clothes, and that New Dealism . . . and I want to shout, 'Get out, Get out. You stand for everything that has been wrong for America for years,' " said Senator Hugh Butler of Nebraska. The mustache seemed to be something of a sticking point. Acheson's old friend Averell Harriman had told him to shave it off because it stirred up such resentment—"You owe it to Truman," he had said.

Acheson was more than anything else a man of the Atlantic. He had been an early and passionate interventionist at the time of World War II, and he had been for Roosevelt in 1940 when many of his contemporaries felt a third term was essentially undemocratic. Probably no high figure in the government made the transition from Roosevelt to Truman more readily than Acheson; he had become undersecretary of state in 1945, and almost immediately a great favorite of the new president. Acheson sensed from the start, as few others did, Truman's strength, character, determination, and if need be, fearlessness. What Truman essentially wanted in Europe—the kind of stability that the victors had failed to provide after World War I—was exactly what Acheson wanted. It helped, of course, that Truman, so untested in foreign policy, needed Acheson in a way Roosevelt never had; in turn Acheson liked how straightforward Truman was, a relief to him after what he considered Roosevelt's constantly manipulative presence. Acheson had once told John Carter Vincent, one of his top China people at the State Department, "John Carter, that little fellow across the street has more to him than you think." That there might have been more than a little condescension in such a statement, for he was saying in effect that such a *little fellow* might nonetheless be worthy of working with them, did not, of course, strike him. But the surprising personal ease of Truman and Acheson was in many ways admirable, a model for that of a president and secretary of state. "I have a constituency of one," Acheson once said.

If it was the Age of Acheson, then the age reflected his weaknesses as well as his strengths. Thus on the things he understood best—the need to stabilize the European democracies and to create an economically strong world in Europe to withstand potential Soviet expansionism—the United States was eminently successful. On the parts of the world he cared less about and did not know as well—and on the question of what an anticolonial era would mean to the West—American foreign policy would be much less successful. He was a truly conservative man, conservative in the old-fashioned sense of the word. He was also a man who cared very little about the profound challenge to the old order just beginning to take place in the underdeveloped world, a challenge that in different form, and ever growing force, would bedevil his lineal descendants for much of the ensuring thirty years.

One of Acheson's problems dealing with the underdeveloped world was that it did not yet produce men who were easy for him to deal with, men just like himself, the way the British and to a lesser degree the French and now the Germans did. There were no Anthony Edens or Jean Monnets, or Konrad Adenauers; in no way could he possibly have seen Ho Chi Minh as their equal. In 1952, for example, as the French effort in Indochina was beginning to fail because of the military and political skill of the Vietminh, Acheson remained curiously obtuse. The French were desperate by then, and they had tried to prop up as a legitimate indigenous leader a frivolous, aristocratic playboy named Bao Dai. Regrettably for the French cause, he was far more given to enjoying the pleasures of the south of France than walking among his own people in the rice paddies of his own country, and the Vietnamese, engaged in a revolutionary war at the time, had, predictably, little interest in being led by him. At that point, as David McLellan, one of Acheson's biographers, noted, the secretary of state decided that the fault lay with the Vietnamese people themselves. "They seem to have a typically Eastern fatalistic lack of interest in public support," he commented. "So far as we can see, France has already given them more autonomy than they have seen fit to use." Yet what drove the Vietminh was the absolute reverse—nothing less than a passion to rid their country of a colonial power—and the French commanders in the field never spoke of the passive fatalism of their opponents; rather, the word they used was fanaticism.

Some of this was purely generational. Acheson was a man of his time and place, when well-bred young men attended the nation's great universities to be taught the intellectual underpinnings of the colonial age in lectures given by professors who emphasized the superiority of the Anglo-Saxon peoples and the weaknesses of their non-white counterparts. The most basic of lessons was that the world was ruled by those who deserved to rule. Harvard and Yale were not universities where great faculty members taught about the yearning of the colonized to be free. Rather the students there learned of the innate generosity that colonialism offered those whose good fortune it was to be colonized. Pseudoscientific courses often noted that the brains of people in non-white countries were smaller than those from Caucasian ones. In his generation and in that class, someone who believed strongly in the case of the colonized against the colonizers would have been considered far too left, and very soft indeed, and Dean Acheson was neither of these.

He saw himself as a man of realpolitik. To him, in realistic terms, Chiang's China was finished, cooked. When Mao and the Communists appeared to be taking over the mainland, Acheson had at first seemed to accept that Mao and his men were not Soviet puppets, that one day the United States might be able to deal with them. In February 1949, he felt the civil war was over and that any additional aid to Chiang might well "solidify the Chinese people in support of the Chinese Communists and perpetuate the delusion that China's interest lies with the USSR." That was the view favored by most of the old China Hands, and men like George Kennan. But the politics of the era were changing. At virtually the same time, Senator Vandenberg visited the White House and warned against any cessation of China aid. A few days later, fifty-one members of the Congress asked for a review of U.S. China policy. In late February Acheson met with the congressional leadership about China, trying to buy some time and flexibility. He spoke of the dangers of continuing to support Chiang and made his let-the-dust-settle statement. The next day Pat McCarran of Nevada, a Democrat but one of the leaders in the China Lobby, knowing that they had Acheson in a bind, called for a $1.5 *billion* China aid package.

Acheson had arrived in time for as tumultuous a tour as any secretary of state ever endured, perhaps the single most difficult four-year stretch in the country's history in terms of its foreign policy. Even as he was taking office, Chiang's government was collapsing on the mainland, and the Generalissimo himself was fleeing to Taiwan. (Acheson was sworn in on the very day that Chiang left China for his new island home. "We passed, I coming in, Chiang going out," Acheson later noted with mordant humor.) Things got even worse that fall. Within the space of a few weeks the Soviets tested their first atomic weapon and the Chinese Communists took power in Beijing, announcing the creation of their new government, anathema to a vast segment of the American populace. Both of these events not only signaled a changing global security balance but sent psychological shock waves through the American political system. The United States was no longer the only member of the atomic club, and at virtually the same time, China, a beloved country to millions of Americans because of the missionary outreach programs there, the country that was supposed to be our great ally in Asia, had gone Communist.

Nothing changed the existing American outlook on defense like the first

Russian atomic explosion. On September 3, 1949, a long-range American reconnaissance plane, used regularly to test the stratosphere for any evidence of Soviet atomic activity, returned from its mission reporting an unusually high level of radioactivity. A filter on the plane had registered 85 radioactive counts per minute. Normal background activity would have been about 50. A second filter showed 153 counts per minute. Two days later another plane, flying from Guam to Japan, registered a count of more than 1,000. America's nuclear specialists concluded that the Russians had secretly set off an atomic explosion, presumably between August 26 and 29, somewhere in the Asian part of the Soviet Union. The bomb was immediately dubbed Joe One in honor of Joseph Stalin. Because the British pound had just been devalued and Truman feared that the two news items might set off a panic on the world's financial markets, the announcement of the test was held back until September 23. Truman very deliberately spoke of an explosion rather than a bomb, but the impact was immediate and it was politically chilling. When J. Robert Oppenheimer, the father of the American atomic bomb, testified before Congress shortly afterward, Senator Arthur Vandenberg asked quite nervously, "Doctor, what shall we do now?" "Stay strong and hang on to our friends," Oppenheimer answered. But Oppenheimer himself was now a marked man: he might have weathered a constant series of security checks during his brilliant tour as the head of the Manhattan Project, but his ambivalence about what he had created and the human consequences of the Hiroshima and Nagasaki bombs, and his wariness about going ahead with a hydrogen bomb project, soon cost him his own security clearance.

If the testing of Joe One and the departure of Chiang from the mainland had not been bad enough, Acheson had made his own way significantly more difficult in late January 1950, by seeming to reach out and emphasize his friendship and loyalty to Alger Hiss, a former State Department figure who had just been tried for the second time on perjury—though in the background was the more serious question of whether he had been a Soviet spy during World War II. It was a moment of great arrogance on Acheson's part, an utterly gratuitous statement on behalf of a man convicted of a serious crime, and it was devastating politically, not just for him personally, but equally damaging for the administration he served. The Hiss case had held the national spotlight for almost two years by then. It was later said to reflect all the divisions of a generation in which some on the liberal left who lost faith in the capitalist system because of the Depression and the rise of fascism had become Communist Party members, or at least fellow travelers. That was surely a considerable exaggeration: whatever the failures of democracy in that period, most people on the liberal left remained loyal citizens and did not join the Communist Party or work as its agents. If in the beginning many people had seemed to favor Alger Hiss over Whittaker Chambers, his accuser, a former Communist and a senior writer at *Time* magazine, in their two-man confrontation, it was because at first Hiss seemed by far the more attractive figure of the two, and because there was also an incipient dislike of the red-baiting that was beginning to gain momentum in some parts of the country. Hiss, wrote Alistair Cooke, the British journalist who normally covered America with exceptional insight, "was a subject for Henry James; a product of New World courtesy, with a gentle certitude of behavior, a ready warmth, a brighter, naiver grace than the more trenchant, fatigued, confident, or worldlier English prototype."

In the beginning, on paper, Alger Hiss was the better bet, the very model of the candidate for serious membership in the Eastern Establishment, with perfect bearing and posture, if just a bit stiff and austere. He seemed destined for a great career with the Establishment from the start: Harvard Law School, clerkship with Oliver Wendell Holmes arranged by Felix Frankfurter, holder of proper if not critically important government jobs in the New Deal era; and yet almost surely, the evidence gradually implied, he had been a Communist spy starting in the 1930s and continuing during World War II. As Hiss on the surface seemed all graces, Chambers was the opposite—brooding, dark, disheveled, and paranoiac. He was the survivor of a horrendous childhood and young manhood—an alcoholic father had left home for a homosexual lover when he was a boy. He was a man of absolutes, who had been a true believer when in the Party and perhaps an even truer believer when, bitterly disillusioned, he exited it. In his youth, he believed that all the great truths in the world were being preached by the Party; when he was older and disillusioned, he came to believe that all the great lies in the world were preached by the same Party.

As a senior writer at *Time*, he was considered both talented and the most difficult of colleagues. As he had been on a wartime footing because of his Party membership, when he left the Party he still felt that everyone else should be on that same footing and that all *Time* correspondents in the field who did not share his sense of deep foreboding—indeed doom—about the global struggle taking place might as well be fellow travelers with the Communists. He was the perfect writer for a somewhat gloomy magazine that liked to issue periodic warnings about the decline of the West. The essayist Murray Kempton, who covered that era and the Hiss case with distinction, once noted: "There was no one who could do the drum roll of alarm, of Western civilization come to the brink, like Chambers."

Chambers claimed he had known Hiss well when they were both in the Party. Hiss denied it. But soon certain discrepancies and partial truths in Hiss's story became apparent, and these were picked up on by a young congressman from California named Richard Nixon, who was being helped on the side by the FBI director, J. Edgar Hoover. There were, noted the *New York Herald Tribune*'s Homer Bigart, just too many glitches in Hiss's story, just too many things that did not add up. The jury, trying to decide whether Hiss had perjured himself, split eight to four against him. Then on January 22, 1950, a second jury convicted him of perjury. At the time, Acheson had been secretary of state for a year. There had been a Hiss-Acheson link in the past, primarily to Hiss's brother, Donald, and there had been warnings about the Hiss brothers more than a decade earlier from Adolf Berle, then head of security for the State Department. In 1939 Chambers had told Berle that both Alger Hiss and his brother, Donald, were Communists. Alger Hiss had worked at State during the war, as director of the department's Office of Special Political Affairs, which dealt primarily with UN matters; Donald Hiss had been an assistant of Acheson's during the war and a law partner after. When the question of the Hiss brothers had been raised, Berle later noted, Acheson answered that "he had known the family and these two boys since childhood and could vouch for them absolutely." Later, after the war, when Hiss and Chambers had their first showdown, Acheson covertly helped Hiss prepare a public statement to be used before the House Un-American Activities Committee. That was not known at the time. When Acheson was nominated as secretary of state, he subsequently went before an essentially friendly Senate Foreign Relations Committee, which was a little bothered by the Hiss connection. Some members of the committee even suggested and helped draft a statement that Acheson could read that reflected his own anti-Communism. Some of the Republicans on the committee might not have been so friendly had they known he had counseled Hiss earlier on.

On Tuesday January 25, three days after the second jury convicted Hiss, Acheson was scheduled to hold a press conference. What eventually took place was in no way a journalistic ambush. Acheson knew exactly what was coming. That morning he had told his wife, Alice, that he would surely be asked about Hiss, and that he intended to say he would not forsake him. "What else could you say?" she asked. "Don't think this is a light matter," he had answered. "This could be quite a storm and it could get me into trouble." Alice Acheson then asked if he were sure he was doing the right thing. "It is what I have to do," he answered. His staff was already on edge. His personal aide, Lucius Battle, and Paul Nitze, by then his closest professional ally at State, both pleaded with him to turn aside questions about Hiss. Battle in particular feared that Acheson's stubbornness—his own growing personal rage at all the charges coming from the political right—when combined with his not insignificant righteous streak, might lead him into an incautious misstep. Acheson told Battle and Nitze that he would read from the Sermon on the Mount. That did not necessarily augur well. It felt, Battle said years later, as if Acheson were spoiling for a fight. At a staff meeting that morning, James Webb, the undersecretary, asked Acheson what he was going to say and suggested he be cautious. Acheson repeated that it would be the twenty-fifth chapter of the Gospel according to St. Matthew, the thirty-sixth verse. Carlise Hummelsince, another high State official, advised him that the words had different meanings to different people.

The question was posed by Homer Bigart of the *Herald Tribune*: "Mr. Secretary, do you have any comment on Alger Hiss?" Acheson began by answering that the case was still before the courts, and therefore it would be improper to comment on it. There, his colleagues had thought with some relief, he's made it out. But then Acheson took it a step further. "I take it the purpose of your question was to bring something other than that out of me," he said. "I should like to make it clear to you, that whatever the outcome of any appeal which Mr. Hiss and his lawyers may take on this case, I do not intend to turn my back on Alger Hiss." There it was; he would not turn his back on Alger Hiss, now viewed by much of the country not merely as a perjurer, but as a spy. For a political man already under fire asked about someone he did not really care for that much, someone who had just been convicted of perjuring himself on espionage charges, it was the ultimate arrogance. He then went on to tell the reporters to read their Bible, Matthew 25:36, a passage in which Christ calls upon His followers to understand that whoever turns his back on anyone in trouble turns his back on Him: "Naked and ye clothed me; I was sick and ye visited me; I was in prison and ye came unto me."

Even as Acheson made his statement, the Senate was in session, and Karl Mundt, a conservative Republican from South Dakota, was talking about how Hiss and his Harvard accent had brought about the downfall of China (a policy Hiss had no influence over). Just then Joe McCarthy raced onto the Senate floor and interrupted Mundt. "I wonder," he asked, "if the senator is aware of a most fantastic statement the secretary of state has made in the last few minutes." Acheson's close friend, James (Scotty) Reston, the *New York Times* Washington columnist, was stunned by the stupidity of it—all he would have had to say, Reston believed, was that he would not kick a man when he was down. Average Americans would have understood that. It was, the historian Eric Goldman has noted, "a tremendous and totally unnecessary gift to those who were insisting that the foreign policy of the Truman Administration was being shaped by men who were soft on Communism."

His answer might have been brave, but it was amazingly arrogant as well, a political disaster for the Truman administration. Truman himself thought

Hiss guilty. When the second trial was about to begin, Truman had told his favorite Secret Service man, Harry Nicholson, "Dean Acheson tells me Alger Hiss is innocent. After reading the evidence in the papers I think the s.o.b. is guilty and I hope they hang him." Security issues had by then become ever more political, and the debate increasingly partisan, those on the Republican right charging ever more loudly that the Democrats were the party of treason. And now Acheson had taken the most publicized spy case in the nation and connected it to himself and to the heart of the American government. It would have been hard to think of a greater political gift to the Republicans. Typically, Richard Nixon soon gave a speech, saying, "Traitors in the high councils of our own government have made sure that the deck is stacked on the Soviet side of the diplomatic table." Earlier in the political sparring, a reporter had asked Truman if he thought the Hiss case was a red herring. He had answered in the affirmative. Now, wrote Robert Donovan, "even though he himself had not spoken the words he was stuck with them," and because of Acheson's careless answer, "he had a dead cat around his neck also."

For what was to become known as McCarthyism, a powerful new political virus, was about to be born. On February 9, 1950, fifteen days after the Acheson press conference, and some five months before the North Korean invasion, Joseph McCarthy, the junior senator from Wisconsin, who had been looking for an issue and had been advised that Communists in the government might be a hot-button one, rose at a speaking engagement in Wheeling, West Virginia. There he claimed that he had in his hands the names of 205 members of the Communist Party still working in the State Department. Though State had been warned, McCarthy said, nothing had been done. He detailed how many more people now lived under Communism in the last six years, largely because of the fall of China. Then he connected the dots, Hiss to Acheson: "As you know, very recently the Secretary of State proclaimed his loyalty to a man guilty of what has always been considered the most abominable of all crimes— being a traitor to the people who gave him a position of great trust—high treason." The charges of what became McCarthyism pulled together disparate strands that the far right had been using for several years: that China had fallen not because of overwhelming historical forces that we were powerless to reverse, but because of subversion at very high levels in Washington, which could be traced through disloyal (or hopelessly naïve) China Hands in the State Department, often connected to Alger Hiss.

NOTHING REVEALED THE contradictions of the United States as it moved reluctantly from isolationist power to internationalist superpower so much as the almost desperate struggle of Dean Acheson to upgrade the defense budget on a dramatic scale even as he became the chief target of an increasingly angry and alienated right wing. Acheson by early 1950 had already assigned Paul Nitze to produce the key document in the drive, what would eventually be known as NSC 68, and shepherd it through the bureaucracy. The choice was not a surprising one. Nitze's star was in ascent and he was very much an extension of Acheson himself—his thinking closely paralleling that of the secretary.

Nitze was originally a Forrestal man. One of his most important early sponsors had been George Kennan, much taken by Nitze's intelligence, who had wanted to bring him as his deputy onto the Policy Planning staff, the State Department's special think tank, which he headed. Policy Planning was quite influential in those days. It was where the department's best minds could ponder the consequences of events, at a time when the consequences of events were still considered important, and think in long-range terms about issues that would soon enough be of pressing immediacy. But Acheson had vetoed the suggestion, thinking that Nitze, who had (like Forrestal) originally worked for Dillon Read, one of the top Wall Street investment houses, was too much of a Wall Street operator. Acheson eventually changed his mind, and in the summer of 1949, when Kennan again asked for Nitze, Acheson gave his permission. Acheson and Nitze became ever closer both professionally and personally, even as Kennan was falling into disfavor.

Just four years earlier, Kennan had been a superstar at State, with his brilliant early analysis of Soviet intentions, but now as the Cold War deepened, and lines hardened both internationally and in domestic politics, he was becoming marginalized at State, his influence in steady decline. That he was no longer a major player was proof that the debate, such as it was, had changed, that Acheson was no longer interested in hearing his complicated dissents, thoughtful and worthy though they might be, and that the administration, whether it realized it or not, was being pulled along by the force of events, crossing over fail-safe points without even realizing it. As the power of the political right increased and the administration found itself ever more besieged by critics, Kennan's value was depreciating rapidly. In the fall of 1949 he was told to report to one of the department's regional assistant secretaries rather than to Acheson himself. That meant his access to the secretary was being cut off, and everyone in the department would know it and as his access was being cut off, so his power and influence were being cut off as well. A few weeks later he asked Acheson to be relieved of his Policy Planning duties as soon as possible and requested an indefinite leave.

Kennan was officially replaced in January 1950 by Nitze, although Nitze had actually taken over the previous November. Nitze was much harder line on almost all issues than Kennan, influenced by Kennan less and less, with the notable exception of Korea, where both of them would oppose MacArthur's decision to go north of the thirty-eighth parallel in October 1950, believing too much was being risked for too little gain. Otherwise Nitze was in all ways a man much more to Acheson's liking, and in the decades to follow, he seemed to be the truest disciple of what Acheson believed in. On the basic issue of NSC 68—the effective tripling of the defense budget, which Acheson wanted—Nitze supported the secretary, while Kennan was bitterly opposed to it, thinking it reflected a complete misreading of Soviet intentions and would militarize American foreign policy and bring a constant escalation of the arms race between the two powers.

All of this produced an even greater melancholia in Kennan, a man unusually pessimistic in the best of times, and he became eager to leave Washington and go to Princeton, where intellectual achievement was treated as an end in itself and where he could do his own writing. Yet he was also immensely frustrated by the decline in the value placed on his views, and what he felt was the decision of the men above him to choose the wrong political course—to take what he believed was too simplistic a view of their adversary, one that bracketed the entire Communist world into a monolith controlled by Moscow, rather than seeing it as a complicated universe rife with its own formidable divisions, the many fissures that, he was sure, would eventually reveal themselves, all of them based on nationalism. His was the principal voice arguing against the idea of a monolithic Communism in that era, and in his dark view, no one was listening. In his own sardonic self-assessment, Kennan had become by the summer of 1949, "the court jester, expected to enliven discussion, privileged to say shocking things, valued as an intellectual gadfly on the hides of slower colleagues, but not to be taken fully seriously when it came to the final responsible decision of policy."

No one in government who ever dealt with George Frost Kennan thought he was an easy man to work with. He was complicated and difficult, someone who hungered for influence but, on getting it, was uneasy with its accompanying burdens. He was shy and private, more historian than diplomat, almost too nuanced a man to be of service in a place like the State Department, where decisions were normally based on a certain immediacy. He sought a kind of political perfection in a world where decisions were normally made under terrible stress, and thus usually imperfect. Over a distinguished career as one of America's premier public intellectuals, he often seemed to be carrying on a series of complicated arguments not merely with those who were his colleagues and superiors in the national security complex, and those more hawkish than he or whose views he opposed, but also with himself. It was as if the nuances and ambiguities of policy were on occasion too subtle even for him, and every dissenting point he raised had to be offset by a counterpoint. If he felt on occasion more than a little uncomfortable when being listened to, then he was truly unhappy when *not* being listened to. More than any principal public figure of his era, more even than Acheson, he seemed frustrated by the crudeness of policy debate in American democracy and worried that producing a thoughtful, wise foreign policy for so large and unruly a democracy was the most hopeless of tasks, that the culture was simply too raw and too crass, its political representatives too primitive.

Because he eventually became one of the main dissenters on the Vietnam War, as some fifteen years earlier he had been wary about crossing the thirty-eighth parallel in Korea and heading north, there was a sense, even on the part of some who admired him, that he was not only dovish, but soft in simplistic foreign policy terms. But it would be just as easy to make a far more compelling case that he was the ultimate figure of realpolitik, that he did not want to use American force in Vietnam not because he felt any empathy for the indigenous forces challenging American policy on the battlefield in an anticolonial age, but rather because he did not think that they (or their country) were important enough in the great scheme of things to be worth the expenditure of American lives and capital, especially in wars that would almost surely fail.

He was convinced that bad things would happen if we tried to apply our power where it did not seem applicable. Places like Vietnam and China were outside our reach (and concern) as other places, nearer and dearer to us, were outside the reach of the Soviets. In fact, he believed that there was already an involuntary balance of power forming in the world despite the rhetoric of the two great powers—and in the long run it favored the United States. Power to him (as, ironically, to Joseph Stalin) was about industrial capacity, which could on demand be quickly turned into military capacity. The only world that should concern us greatly was that of the industrialized powers—which, of course, was largely northern and white, with Japan virtually the only important nation in Asia. Kennan had been in favor of responding to the original North Korean invasion only because of the importance he gave Japan in the greater scheme of things, and his belief that a unified Communist Korea, one that the Americans had not bothered to defend, might unnerve the Japanese. Two days after the North Korean crossing, he told the British ambassador to Washington that, while Korea was not strategically significant, "the symbolic significance of its preservation was tremendous, especially in Japan." In reality, George Kennan was a very unsentimental man who looked at the world in the most unsentimental of ways.

He was a brooding figure, much given to pessimism about political events and often, for someone so intelligent and wise, surprisingly insensitive to the moods and feelings of others around him. Deciding to marry a young Norwegian woman, he had written his father in what has to be one of the most muted notes of all time when it comes to describing a youthful romantic impulse: "She has the true Scandinavian simplicity and doesn't waste many words. She has the rare capacity for keeping silent gracefully. I have never seen her disposition ruffled by anything resembling a mood, and even I don't make her nervous." Unlike the other senior policy makers of the era, most of whom came from an already privileged American elite, he was the product of a very modest middle-class home in middle America, the son of a tax lawyer in Milwaukee. But in his own way, he was a considerable snob, decidedly uncomfortable with what he considered the great American unwashed who, in his view, might hinder the ability of the elite to make decisions in a democracy.

Even longtime friends like the distinguished Sovietologist Chip Bohlen, a man unusually sensitive to Kennan's moods, did not find him easy to get on with. When Kennan finally left the State Department after twenty-seven years, he was surprised to find that there was no one to say good-bye to. He had made almost no friends, shared few private thoughts, never gone out of his way to show interest in the men with whom he worked. But of his originality as a foreign policy analyst there was no doubt. Because history became his genuine passion, he tended to see the world in terms of deep historical forces that, in his mind, formed a nation's character in ways almost beyond the consciousness of the men who momentarily governed it, as if these historical impulses were more a part of them than they knew, a reflection of a nation's true DNA. To him the Soviets were really the Russians, and their new rulers, only a modern incarnation of the tsars, clothed in more egalitarian rhetoric, naturally reflected the fears, paranoia, and isolation from neighbors that had been so much a part of the country's past. It was important, he believed, to see what was happening after World War II more as a reflection of traditional Russian impulses and *fears* than of the global ambitions of an overly aggressive Marxist state.

Even as a young man in the late 1930s he had described the Russian character as being formed by "the constant fear of foreign invasion, [and] the hysterical suspicion of other nations." Nor could the influence of the Byzantine church be underestimated, "its intolerance, its intriguing and despotic political systems." In 1943, when most of Washington officialdom still harbored a good deal of optimism about the ability of the United States to get along with the Soviets after the war, Kennan had argued precipitously, given the existing attitude of most of his superiors, that there were hard times ahead and that the Soviets, for historical reasons, would be difficult to deal with when the war was over. In the midst of World War II, however, almost no one, save perhaps Averell Harriman, had wanted to listen to him. Harriman, scion of a great railroad family, was a critical figure in the international politics of the 1940s, Roosevelt's special emissary to both Churchill and Stalin. He was not a great intellectual himself, but he was a great *listener* and a superb synthesizer of other men's ideas, and arguably one of the two or three ablest public men of a prolonged era that, in his case, lasted some four decades. Harriman was impressed by Kennan even though he was then a relatively junior figure in the Moscow embassy. In 1946, Kennan sent back to Washington his famous Long Telegram, a stunning analytic cable of eight thousand words, making a compelling case for how difficult it would be to deal with the Soviets, citing their *Russian* antecedents, and their nation's cruel history. He had cabled just the right words at just the right moment, seeming to explain to much of Washington why Moscow was proving so difficult to deal with, and coinciding with Winston Churchill's speech in Fulton, Missouri, in which he claimed that an Iron Curtain had descended over half of Europe. Kennan had called for what would soon be known as Containment in dealing with the Soviets. The piece was published in the prestigious journal *Foreign Affairs,* its author identified only as "Mr. X"—and it caused a sensation first in Washington and then nationally. He was suddenly the diplomat as star. "My reputation was made," he later wrote. "My voice now carried." His theory of Containment became, for a time, the foundation of Washington's policy toward Moscow, and his cable marked the end of a time when very much idealism still existed about the future of the wartime alliance.

His time as a star did not last very long; he was too independent of mind, too cut off from changing political tides. By 1948, because he traced foreign policy tensions back to what he saw as their historical roots, Kennan thought Washington's reaction to the Soviets had already gone too far, that the Red Army, vast as it was, would not invade anyone. Stalin had done it once with Finland in 1939 and had gotten his fingers burned. Kennan also foresaw inevitable tensions in the relationship between the Chinese and the Russians, caused largely by the vast differences in their histories. He was sure that a proud new China, Communist government or not, that had just won its own revolution, would not want to remain a Soviet satellite for very long. On this he was bolstered by State Department experts like John Davies, who saw China much as Kennan had seen Russia. If Stalin was a de facto tsar, with a tsar's fears and ambitions, then Mao would be but the latest in a line of Chinese emperors with an emperor's fears and ambitions. Russian tsars and Chinese emperors, Kennan was absolutely sure, would not get on well together. In 1947, Kennan wrote, "The men of the Kremlin would suddenly discover that this fluid and subtle oriental movement which they thought they held in the palm of their hand had quietly oozed away between their fingers and there was nothing left there but a ceremonial Chinese bow and a polite giggle."

In government it does not pay to be right too soon, especially if you are considered on the more dovish side. Kennan was prophetic, and he would be proven right in a surprisingly short time as the tensions between the two nations escalated in the early 1960s and there were constant skirmishes between the two great Communist powers along the Russian-Chinese border. But in 1949–50, in an administration increasingly under siege, dealing with the shocking news of Joe One and Chiang's departure from the mainland, his ruminations on the coming tensions between Russia and China were not exactly what Acheson wanted to hear. By 1949, David Bruce, another of the bright rising figures at State, noted that his friend Acheson could no longer bear to read Kennan's cables, believing them too long and windy, finally too literary. His timing was not nearly as good as it had been when he had sent the Long Telegram. But nothing told how quickly the Cold War had escalated, and how the domestic attacks against administration policies had increased, than the fact that Kennan had gone from superstar to outsider in just three years. The problem he posed to Acheson was not merely that he was wordy and argumentative; it was that almost everything he said was right, the affirmation of policies, given different political conditions, that Acheson would gladly have followed but no longer could because of the changed politics of the era. Acheson was too proud to admit it, either at the time or later in his memoirs, but there was in Kennan's dissent, in his unwillingness to adjust to changing political forces, something of an unspoken rebuke to the secretary, a man who did not like to be rebuked, or to admit that he had been bent on any of his policies.

It was not just his dissent on the Soviets and China. Among other issues where Acheson and Kennan parted company was the question of whether or not to go ahead with the hydrogen bomb, or the Super as it was known, which was then being pushed by Edward Teller, a former Manhattan Project scientist who had turned bitterly on Robert Oppenheimer. When Truman wanted a special committee to study the issue of the Super, Acheson chose Nitze, a Teller supporter, to head it, which meant that the special committee would almost surely favor going ahead on it. To Nitze the issue of the Super was a pragmatic one—would the bomb work? He had been convinced by Teller that it would. To Kennan, who had grown close to Oppenheimer, a man anguished over what his own weapon had wrought at Hiroshima and Nagasaki, it was not simply a practical or scientific question but a moral one as well. He thought the Super was nothing less than a potential moral catastrophe. What both Oppenheimer and Kennan believed was that, with the decision to develop the H-bomb, a limitless, unwinnable superpower arms race would be launched, that would, in the end, increase global dangers immeasurably while adding no additional degree of security.

When Nitze's committee reported, as expected, that the United States ought to go ahead with the Super, it suggested as well that a major review be undertaken of the total national security picture. Acheson's hand was very much at work here—this was the study he wanted in order to initiate his long-desired overhaul of national security policies. Nitze would lead it. On January 31, 1950, six days after Acheson's remark about Hiss, Truman gave the go-ahead for such a comprehensive review.

Where Kennan thought of Stalin's Russia as primarily defensive in its policies, albeit with a deep-rooted national paranoia, Nitze offered a very different vision. "In the aggregate," he noted at the time, "recent Soviet moves reflect not only a mounting militancy but suggest a boldness that is essentially new—and borders on recklessness." In effect, he was saying that the United States as a great power could not base its policies on Kennan's assumptions about tsarist Russia, no matter how brilliant their author. What if Kennan was wrong? Kennan after all was a diplomat and a historian, not an intelligence man, and if his view of Russia was wrong, then the United States would have premised its entire security position on a presumption of historic truths, and might end up unspeakably vulnerable.

To Acheson and his allies, Nitze's NSC paper would finally begin the process of making America's military strength compatible with its rhetoric and their vision of its postwar role: the United States would continue to talk big, but it would carry more than just a single big stick—the potentially unusable atomic one; now America would have a more flexible military response. To Kennan, on the other hand, what Nitze (and Acheson) were proposing was a militarization of American policy—in effect, the creation of a national security state, which would drain far too much of the nation's financial resources and would inevitably create in its Soviet rival a comparable military defense state. The Soviet atomic bomb, he wrote, did not really change the balance of power: "Insofar as we see ourselves in any heightened trouble at the present moment, that feeling is largely of our own making."

What was taking place, primarily inside the bureaucracy, was a debate of the most serious and far-reaching nature. Acheson and Nitze moved ahead as covertly as possible. The key person they were marginalizing in their effort was Louis Johnson, the defense secretary. The Joint Chiefs were quietly telling Nitze their needs as Acheson made what was in effect an end run around Johnson. Years later, Omar Bradley would note that the conflict between Acheson and Johnson had created "a rare, awkward, and ironic situation in which the three military chiefs [the commandant of the Marine Corps was not yet a chief] and their chairman were more closely aligned with the views of the Secretary of State than with the Secretary of Defense." Acheson—and Nitze—were far more sympathetic to their problems, the Chiefs believed, than Johnson was. The minimum price to get U.S. defense systems up to what was wanted, Nitze thought, was somewhere around $40 to $50 billion annually. Otherwise, he and the other hard-liners believed, the United States would not be able to execute its military and defense policies, and the Soviets might dominate the world.

When Acheson heard the estimated price, what they called the back of the envelope cost, of around $50 billion, he told Nitze, "Paul, don't put that figure in the report. You're right to tell me and I'll tell the president, but don't put any figure in the report." Finally, on March 22, 1950, they met with Johnson and the Joint Chiefs in Nitze's office to go over the draft document. The meeting started out peacefully enough. Johnson asked Acheson if he had read the draft. Acheson had. Johnson, of course, had not. In fact, he had only heard of it that morning. Suddenly, it became clear to him that he had been completely cut out of the play and totally ambushed. Acheson and his man Nitze were obviously in charge, had clearly been in close communication with the Chiefs, and just as clearly intended to give the uniformed military not only many of the things he had been cutting out of their budgets but more than he had ever imagined possible. He was, he realized, completely isolated. As Acheson later wrote, all of a sudden "he lunged forward, with a crash of chair legs on the floor and fist on the table, scaring me out of my shoes."

Acheson and Nitze, he shouted, were trying to keep him in the dark and he would not tolerate it—he would not be subjected to a humiliation like this. "This is a conspiracy being conducted behind my back in order to subvert my policies. I and the Chiefs are leaving now," he said. Soon after, Johnson went to Acheson's office to argue his case one more time and started screaming that he had been insulted. Acheson waved him away, then had others call Truman to tell him what had happened. An hour later, Truman returned the call and told Acheson to proceed with the paper. The president was not yet approving NSC 68—events in Korea would take care of that—but Acheson and Nitze were in charge of the play. Six months later Truman fired Johnson and replaced him with George Marshall. Acheson was convinced that Johnson was unstable at the time.

NSC 68 was a defining document. It confirmed the American response to the harshness of the Cold War, American mistrust of the Soviets matching Soviet mistrust of Americans, which would in turn create a cycle of ever expanding mistrust and ever greater defense spending on both sides. It defined the global conflict in almost purely ideological terms, especially striking in a paper so secret that it would be seen only by top officials: "The Soviet Union, unlike previous aspirants to hegemony, is animated by a fanatical faith, antithetical to our own, and seeks to impose its absolute authority over the rest of the world." At first, Truman had remained noncommittal about NSC 68 and was quite uneasy with the implicit costs involved. Then, the Korean War began and the Cold War escalated into a hot war, and the force of events had their own financial imperatives. The debate over NSC 68 had become academic, the issue overtaken by events. The budget, which NSC 68 suggested would have to triple, now tripled because of the war. Truman himself never had to make a decision on NSC 68. In fact, by the late fall of 1951, when the fiscal 1952 Pentagon budget was being prepared, it had quadrupled from $13 billion in pre–Korean War days to $55 billion. "Korea," Acheson would note years later at a seminar at Princeton, "saved us."

14

HARRY TRUMAN WAS, whatever else, a decisive man. Even some of Roosevelt's people, who in the early days of his presidency had looked down on Truman, this seemingly undistinguished man who had replaced their beloved leader, now understood that. Some Roosevelt insiders had left immediately, believing they could not give their loyalty to him; others came to respect him and understand that their commitment was to the office and not to the man, and that Truman in his own way was an uncommon man. Though Truman would turn out to be the last American president who had not been to college, he had been exceptionally bookish as a child, was unusually well read, and was a serious, if amateur, self-taught historian. Perhaps most important of all, he did not go around doubting himself once he took office. He might not have sought the presidency and it might have come to him in the most unwanted way, but he was going to serve and make his decisions as best he could. He was not, even before he was elected on his own in 1948, going to be governing hat in hand, as if he did not deserve the office and ought more properly to be secreted away in the small office where they still hid vice presidents. The country deserved better than that. Besides, he understood that if he governed like that, as a kind of stand-in for a great man, he would be devoured by his enemies, some of whom were institutional enemies of the presidency, some of whom were ideological enemies, and some of whom were both. He did not intend to be devoured; history judged the devoured too harshly. A lifetime of dealing with ordinary people, in good times and bad—and there had certainly been plenty of those—had convinced him of his skill in reading and judging others, sensing whom he could trust and whom he could not. It had also taught him to get the best people you can, gather the best information possible, ask the best questions you could think of, estimate the likely consequences, then just make the decision and get on with it. He also knew, as he flew back to Washington on the morning after the North Korean attack, that his decisions in the days to come would be on matters of war and peace. Korea would turn out to be in his judgment the most difficult call of his presidency.

In June 1950, he had already served five years as president, and scored two personal triumphs that had immeasurably strengthened his confidence. Though they were in a sense intertwined, the first—his stunning upset victory over Tom Dewey in the 1948 election—had been the more remarkable. Unlikely as it was, his electoral triumph helped clear the way for his other great achievement—his triumph over the still powerful image of Franklin Roosevelt, which finally gave him a presidency of his own (and growing respect from other politicians, the press, and historians, those who make their living judging the presidencies of other men). Escaping the burden of being Roosevelt's successor, and being a man who had come to the office almost by mistake, was a success all too easy to underestimate. He had never, in fact, let the burden of his predecessor's greatness weigh too heavily on him, though he had been a relatively minor figure in the Senate and a virtually invisible one as vice president. By contrast, Lyndon Johnson, the next vice president to succeed to office because the president had died, had been a towering figure in the Senate before replacing John F. Kennedy (who had served for only three years, in contrast to Roosevelt's twelve); yet by contrast he never entirely escaped the emotional and psychological burden of comparisons with his predecessor, or of the way he had at first attained his presidency.

Truman was an easy man to underestimate. He lacked one of the great strengths of the Roosevelt persona: to a nation accustomed to a presidential voice that had been warm, confident, aristocratic, and altogether seductive, Truman's voice was a distinct disappointment, flat and tinny, with little emotional intimacy. His speeches were uninspiring—blunt and oddly without nuance. Some advisers suggested that Truman try to speak more like Roosevelt, and make his speeches more conversational, but he was shrewd enough to know that that was the wrong path, that he could not emulate the great master. All he could do was be himself and hope that the American people would not judge him for what he was not. He was aware that the comparisons with Roosevelt would be unfavorable at first, and they were. In the beginning, he was an easy target for political jokes, and there was often a cruel edge to them. "To err is Truman," said the acid-tongued Martha Taft, wife of Robert Taft, a key Republican senator. "I'm just mild about Harry" went another. A favorite of the moment, wrote the columnist Doris Fleeson, was "I wonder what Truman would do if he were alive." "Poor Harry Truman. And poor people of the United States," wrote Richard Strout, in *The New Republic*.

Truman became president when he was sixty years old. He was a late bloomer of acceptable but not overweening ambition. His people were farmers and he had done his share of farming as a boy, and in 1948 he had delighted Midwest crowds—his support there was one of the keys to his surprise victory—by telling them that he could seed a 160-acre wheat field "without leaving a skip." He had plowed the old-fashioned way, he added—four Missouri mules, not one of these fancy tractors. In his senior year of high school, through no fault of their own, the Trumans' farm had failed and all chance of a college education for Harry had disappeared. He tried for West Point, his one shot at a free education, but was turned down because of his poor eyesight. (He was blind as a mole, he noted later in life.) His one entrepreneurial attempt, to run a haberdashery shop, lasted a mere three years and ended in failure. He spent much of his time trying to prove to his ever dubious mother-in-law, who came from one of Independence's first families, that he was worthy of the hand of her daughter, that Bess Wallace had not married down. Here success eluded him; he proved better at making the case for his intrinsic value to millions of fellow Americans than to Madge Gates Wallace. He arrived in the Senate in 1934, in his fiftieth year, relatively late in life, as the sparklingly honest representative of the unusually corrupt political machine of Boss Tom Pendergast. It was as if his special assignment within the Pendergast organization had always been to bring it some degree of honor and legitimacy. He was a small-town man with small-town virtues. For much of his life, he wore a triple-band gold Mason's ring and a small lapel button that showed he had served in World War I. He was comfortable in the world of small-town lodges, and was a member of the American Legion, the Veterans of Foreign Wars, the Moose, and the Elks.

But a life filled with a curious blend of disappointments and relatively few successes (at least on the scale of most men who attain the presidency) had created its own set of strengths. "I liked what I saw. He was direct, unpretentious, clear thinking and forceful," General Omar Bradley wrote after their first meetings. He was not much given to self-deception and there was little artifice to him. He was hardworking, and always well prepared. He did not waste other people's time, nor did he want them to waste his. In contrast to Roosevelt (who loved to play games with people even when he didn't need to), Truman was comparatively simple and significantly less manipulative. What you saw, by and large, was what you got. George Marshall had always been uneasy with Roosevelt and some of the games he played with his top advisers. There had been one unfortunate moment when the president had tried verbal intimacy with Marshall, a man who thought the more formal the relationship with a politician, the straighter it was likely to be. Roosevelt called him by his first name, the first step in what was clearly to be a process of seduction. He immediately understood his own mistake by the coolness it generated. It was General or General Marshall thereafter, not George. Marshall for that reason clearly preferred Truman. There were fewer political land mines around.

In the Senate Truman had been all too aware of his own limitations. A great many of his colleagues were better educated, wealthier, and more successful; they knew worlds of privilege and sophistication he could only guess at. As one of his high school friends, Charlie Ross, later a star reporter for the *St. Louis Post Dispatch* and eventually his press secretary, said of him, "He came to the Senate, I believe, with a definite inferiority complex. He was a better man than he knew." America, at the time he assumed the presidency, was changing rapidly, becoming infinitely more meritocratic, driven by powerful egalitarian forces let loose by World War II and new political benefits that went with them, like the GI Bill, which allowed anyone who had been in the military to go to college. Truman, by contrast, was a product of a far less egalitarian America, which had existed at the turn of the century, one where talented men and women did not always attain careers that reflected their abilities and their ambition.

He was very much a man of his time and his region. "He had only to open his mouth and his origins were plain," wrote his biographer David McCullough. "It wasn't just that he came from a particular part of the country, but from a specific part of the American experience, an authentic pioneer background and a specific place in the American imagination. His Missouri, as he loved to emphasize, was the Missouri of Mark Twain and Jesse James." If Franklin Roosevelt seemed to step out of the pages of a novel by Edith Wharton, McCullough added, then Harry Truman came from the pages of Sinclair Lewis.

Little was really known of him as a man, even by those who had placed him on the Democratic ticket in 1944. It was not so much that they had wanted him as that they did not like the other vice presidential possibilities, most particularly Henry Wallace, the sitting vice president. As Jonathan Daniels, the Southern editor, noted, they "knew what they wanted, but did not know what they were getting." He was perhaps as true a reflection of the common man as the country produced for the presidency in the modern era. "What a test of democracy if it works!" Roy Roberts, the editor of the *Kansas City Star* and a part of the inner circle of Republican power brokers, shrewdly wrote during the first days of the Truman presidency. For that was exactly what it was, a test of democracy. He was also a very good working politician, with a keen sense of what was on the minds of ordinary people, their needs and their fears, because his own background was so ordinary and because for so long his life had been so much like theirs.

When he was first catapulted into the presidency, he complained frequently to his friends about his dislike for it—the Great White Prison, he called it—and seemed at one point ready to offer his support in the 1948 race to Dwight

Eisenhower, if he committed to the Democratic Party. Only gradually did he change his mind. The presidency cramped his personal lifestyle and separated him from his family—Bess and his daughter, Margaret, always seemed to be back in Independence and he longed to be with them—but he had never been a man to back off hard jobs, and the more he saw of some of the other men who thought they should replace him, the more confident he became that the country was better served with him in the White House. If he needed to justify his policies by running for election in 1948, then he would make that run—it was not that great a sacrifice. There was a certain bantam rooster cockiness to him. He would not back down from a fight, and, in time, the American people sensed that and rewarded him for it.

His small-town roots were not that different from many of the Republicans who now became his most bitter political enemies, but his own personal odyssey more often than not had been much harder than theirs, and so he had grave doubts about some of the small-town verities that they so unquestioningly believed in. In American politics of that period, people still voted their pocketbooks, and the Democrats, because of the New Deal, still had the economic whip hand, even in much of what was considered the heartland. A small town of eight thousand might have one thousand blue collar workers at a plant, almost all of whom were Democrats; only a handful of a town's residents—factory owners, managers, and ancillary local allies like the banker, the lawyer, and the doctor—were people almost sure to vote Republican. Most ordinary Americans were living considerably better than they had in the past. They did not believe the gains they had achieved were, as the Republicans seemed to insinuate, socialistic. Few working people then felt they would prosper under a Republican administration. "The worker's working every day/ drives to work in a new coupe/ Don't let 'em take it away" went a Democratic Party theme song of the period. The cultural issues that would, starting in the mid-1960s, gradually tear at the Democratic coalition of blue collar working people, children of the great immigrant waves from Europe, black people, and the white politicians of the one-party South, were not yet important. Labor was newly unionized, still extremely powerful, and grateful for its recent economic gains.

When he prepared for his own presidential race in 1948, Truman did not believe the economic base of politics had changed that much. He was a fiscal conservative anyway and very careful in those first three years in office to minimize any tax increases. In addition, he had a sixth sense about how to exploit the fault lines in the Republican Party: the difference between what it said were its policies, when it was at a national convention appealing to a national audience, and what its far more conservative leadership in Congress believed. He judged the Republicans in Congress to be a party out of touch with average Americans in the urban and increasingly influential suburban areas of the big states. They had killed any number of liberal items he had proposed—on housing, aid to education, and medical care, and then had gone ahead at their convention and called for their passage. Well, he planned to put an illuminating light on that split personality; so, when nominated in 1948, he promptly announced that he was going to call Congress back into session—to pass the items the Republicans supported in their platform. It was a masterful move and proved a decisive one as well. The Republicans were not pleased to be summoned—"the petulant Ajax of the Ozarks," Senator Styles Bridges called Truman.

When the 1948 campaign first began, the task before him seemed hopeless. Even the big-city bosses were against him. On hearing that Dwight Eisenhower had no interest in the Democratic nomination, Frank Hague, the Jersey City (New Jersey) boss, said, "Truman, Harry Truman. Oh my God." Everything appeared stacked against him: in the eyes of many, both politically and as a human being, he had seemed to shrink in the vast space left by his predecessor, and the Democrats had been in power too long. There were the inevitable scandals. Some of the close friends whom he trusted had predictably eaten too well at the public trough. The scandals, though they did not touch Truman personally, brought back the scent of the Pendergast machine. The liberal wing of his own party, led by Jimmy Roosevelt, the late president's most liberal son, had tried desperately to draft Dwight Eisenhower, even though most of the people who liked Ike had no earthly idea what his politics were, and despite Eisenhower's own clear rejection of a race. No one seemed to want Truman to head the ticket. "We don't want to run a race with a dead Missouri mule," said Governor Ben Laney of Arkansas.

The 1948 election turned out to be crucial in a way that no one understood at the time, and fateful as well because of the bitterness it created in a party that suffered its fifth straight defeat. The Republicans were prohibitive favorites. Truman, said Clare Boothe Luce, the wife of the country's most powerful publisher, at the Republican convention, where they were celebrating the fall victory even before the summer was over, was "a gone goose." Every knowledgeable political expert had conceded the election to the heavily favored Tom Dewey, who was considered admirable, if not likeable. Early in the campaign the Republican high command had even decided that it would be a waste of the party's money to continue polling, because the outcome was such a sure thing. One major pollster, Elmo Roper, announced in early September that he too would stop polling because the election was a foregone conclusion: "Thomas E. Dewey is almost as good as elected. . . . That being true I can think of nothing duller or more intellectually barren than acting like a sports announcer who feels he must pretend that he is witnessing a neck-and-neck race." All of this had a considerable effect on Dewey himself. When another Republican visited Dewey at his Pawling, New York, farm, Dewey showed him the Roper statement and then said, "My job is to prevent anything from rocking the boat." Clearly the principal aim of the campaign was not so much to define what a mid-century Republican victory would mean as to avoid making a mistake. That, of course, was in its own way a terrible mistake, even though the Democratic Party seemed badly fragmented. It had split three ways, and thereby on paper at least seemed unusually vulnerable: the far left going off with Henry Wallace; while the Southern Democrats, or Dixiecrats, as they would be known, followed Strom Thurmond of South Carolina. None of that seemed to bother Truman very much. Certainly, it made things harder, although the symbols of a party unraveling were far more dramatic than the unraveling itself. (At the Jefferson-Jackson Day dinner in Washington in February 1948, Senator Olin Johnston, a Democrat from South Carolina, bought a large table, which because his wife was on the arrangements committee was set up right in front of the podium. Then, because the dinner would not be segregated, the Johnstons kept the table but made sure that no one showed up—a deliberate insult to the sitting president. "We paid $1,100 to keep this table vacant," one of their friends said.)

What did bother Truman as he approached the fall campaign was that the Democratic Party, though it had been in office for sixteen years, had absolutely no money, and no one was willing to serve as its finance committee chairman. It was an additional but hardly needed reminder of how slim the Democratic chances were. On September 1, 1948, with the start of the campaign two weeks away, Truman had summoned eighty Party luminaries—men with clout and access to money—to the White House to talk about their financial problems. Only fifty had showed up. The president had then asked for a volunteer to run the finance committee. No one stepped up. The next day Truman called Louis Johnson and pleaded with him to take the job. Johnson agreed to do it. He was a classic example of a certain Washington type, a wheeler-dealer, a self-made man with an inflated sense of his political abilities and possibilities. Because he saw no limits to his ability, Johnson tended to move aggressively into any power vacuum he found. He intended when Truman's presidency was finished to run for the presidency himself. His political base was his connection with the American Legion, whose senior officer he had been and whose views on foreign policy he tended to reflect. "He was a gambler," said Jean Kearney, who had worked for the Democratic National Committee that summer. He got into the business of raising money for Truman, she added, "in a cold blooded, calculating way—he gambled that Truman might win, and if he raised money for him, it would advance his own standing as a Washington lawyer and national figure."

At that moment Truman's standing was so low as to be off the charts, and the Democrats were without money, seriously burdened by debt. Johnson came in and signed a personal note for $100,000, which allowed the party to get out of debt and for Truman's train, scheduled to leave Union Station for its whistle-stop tour of the country on September 17, to depart on time, and go farther than Pennsylvania, which for a time had seemed likely to be the last stop. Johnson did a remarkable job as finance chairman, raising more than $2 million in two months. When the campaign was over, Truman was deeply in his debt, which was why, when James Forrestal came apart emotionally, Johnson got the Defense portfolio.

The lack of money as they began the 1948 campaign was more important than the party's interior ideological divisions. The Wallace campaign, from the left, actually gave Truman protection against charges that he might be too far left, since no one was attacking him harder than the Communists and their fellow travelers. As for the Dixiecrats, they carried only four Southern states, for a total of thirty-nine electoral votes. Truman's special strength that year was that he never lost faith in himself or in the American people. He campaigned vigorously in blunt and simplistic terms. Economic issues were still primal. Before Truman started on his campaign, Vice President Alben Barkley had told him, "Go out there and mow 'em down." "I'll mow 'em down, Alben," Truman had reportedly answered, "and I'll give 'em hell." Somehow that part—about giving them hell—had gotten out, and the crowds loved it. There was always someone at every stop egging him on, yelling "Give 'em hell, Harry," and he did just that, and the American people responded enthusiastically. If he could not be Roosevelt, then he had found the perfect role, the cocky little underdog, his back to the wall, fighting back against the big boys. He had not exactly sought that image, but the role suited both him and the era perfectly.

Everyone had been sure that he was finished, except the candidate himself. In the 1948 campaign he managed to define himself in the eyes of his fellow citizens in a way he had been incapable of doing in the previous three and a half years. It was one of the last political campaigns to be conducted from trains, a whistle-stop visit to the American people, often in small towns, where Truman felt an easy affinity with the crowds gathered around the caboose. It was a very comfortable incarnation, utterly authentic. "He is good on the back of the train," his shrewd Democratic colleague Sam Rayburn, the speaker of the House, once noted, "because he is one of the folks. He smiles with them and not at them, laughs with them and not at them."

His gritty, earthy campaign was carried out so close to the voters that it took place under the radar screen of the taste-making part of the media and the top people in the Republican Party (and even many in his own party). The Republicans were already overconfident, given the poor Democratic showing in the 1946 midterm elections, and they believed the myth of Truman's incompetence. Dewey helped out by running a disastrous campaign. "The Dewey campaign," said Clarence Buddington Kelland, a Republican national committeeman from Arizona, "was smug, arrogant, and supercilious." For Dewey campaigned as if he were the incumbent, Truman the challenger, and the Democrats a minority party. His speeches were boring and full of truisms. Some aides, like Herbert Brownell, blamed his wife for not wanting him to engage in partisan attacks because she wanted him to seem as presidential as possible, above the base quality of politics. If that were true, it would not have been the first time she had been a decisive force in terms of his image. Other aides had argued for years that he should shave off his trademark mustache—it had been an asset when he was a tough district attorney, but as a presidential candidate it made him look cold and hard. "His face was so small and the mustache was so large," Brownell lamented years later. But Mrs. Dewey liked the mustache, and so it stayed.

Dewey was in fact an exceptionally able man, well prepared for the presidency after six years as governor of New York—he would eventually be elected for three terms—essentially the same political staircase Roosevelt had taken to the nation's highest office. At forty-six he was young and seemingly modern—the first presidential nominee born in the twentieth century. He had started as a Mr. Clean, a prosecutor intent on going after the New York mob, and perhaps, some critics thought, that was the problem. It had been a role that demanded a certain icy briskness, a manner invaluable to a prosecutor in front of a jury, that was not necessarily attractive in a presidential candidate, where an instinctive, tangible humanity is of the essence. He looked, said the acerbic Alice Roosevelt Longworth in a quip that seemed to cling to him, like "the little man on the wedding cake." He was, said one longtime associate, "cold. Cold as an icicle in February." Even on his campaign train, surrounded by other Republican pols, he would excuse himself at a certain point so he could lunch alone. "Smile, Governor," a photographer called to him during the campaign. "I thought I was," he answered.

Nor was his personal style, or lack thereof, his only problem. The terrible fault lines of the Republican Party were another. To the isolationists, he was the living symbol of everything that was wrong with their party. Colonel Robert McCormick's *Chicago Tribune* hated him for his internationalism and for his defeat in the 1944 election, and constantly belittled him. In what turned out to be the most critical decision of the campaign, he held back from taking up the only issue that might have excited them, that of subversion, and refused to make it a central part of his campaign. Indeed, at a key moment in a debate with Harold Stassen during the Oregon primary fight, he had opposed outlawing the Communist Party. It would, he said—and he was a law-and-order man—only serve to drive the Communists underground. Other prominent Republicans, beginning to sense the blood in the water, and knowing they were in trouble on economic issues, pushed him to use the Communists-in-Washington charge. William Loeb, the right-wing New Hampshire publisher, and Senator Styles Bridges, who was Loeb's man in the Senate as well as the Republican national campaign manager, pleaded with Dewey to use the subversion issue against Truman and the Democrats. He listened to them carefully and then, in the words of one of his campaign aides, Hugh Scott, said he would "fleck it lightly." Instead he thought it demeaning to accuse the president of the United States of being soft on Communism. He was not, he told Senator Styles Bridges, going to go around "looking under beds."

His campaign was uniquely bland. Even as Truman was drawing ever larger crowds, Dewey continued making the same curiously antiseptic, passionless speeches. His campaign, wrote the Louisville, Kentucky, *Courier Journal*, could be "boiled down to these historic four sentences: Agriculture is important. Our rivers are full of fish. You cannot have freedom without liberty. The future lies ahead." Still, victory seemed such a sure thing. The media, which in those pre-television days was still the press corps, helped to make Truman's victory a great surprise because its members spent so much time interviewing one another and ignoring what was happening right in front of them. In mid-September, for example, Joseph Alsop, then an important syndicated columnist with a home base on the influential *New York Herald Tribune*, had witnessed two events: Truman's speech at the national plowing contest in Iowa, before an enthusiastic audience of seventy-five thousand—the president was sharp, focused, and very much on the attack—and soon after, a Dewey speech to a disappointingly small crowd of about eight thousand at Drake University, also in Iowa. A reporter who was responding to political nuance out in the field might have sensed something was up, but Alsop did not. "There was something sad about the contrast between the respective campaign debuts here in Iowa," he wrote. "The Truman show was threadbare and visibly unsuccessful—the Dewey show was opulent. It was organized down to the last noise-making device. It exuded confidence. The contest was really too uneven. After it was over one felt a certain sympathy for the obstinately laboring president."

In mid-October, *Newsweek* polled fifty political writers scattered throughout the country. Every single one predicted a Dewey win. The Truman people

knew the article was coming, but the headline, "Fifty Political Experts Predict a
Dewey Victory," was disheartening nonetheless. Only one man did not appear
to be bothered by it, the candidate himself. "Oh those damned fellows; they're
always wrong anyway," he said. "Forget it, boys, and let's get on with the job."
On the eve of the election, the press was still getting it wrong. Alistair Cooke,
of the *Manchester Guardian,* titled his last preelection piece "Harry Truman—
Study of a Failure," and the people who put out the then-influential Kiplinger
newsletter devoted their preelection issue to "What Dewey Will Do."

In the end Truman won relatively handily: 24.1 million votes to Dewey's
21.9 million; he carried twenty-eight states, with 303 electoral votes, to Dewey's
sixteen, with 189 electoral votes, and he would have carried Dewey's home state
of New York if Wallace had not siphoned off votes on the left. It was one of the
great upsets in American political history. The newly reelected president celebrated famously by holding up for photographers a copy of the *Chicago Tribune* with the headline "Dewey Beats Truman." The comedians had a field day.
"The only way a Republican can get in the White House now is to marry Margaret Truman," Groucho Marx said.

For the Republicans, it was the apocalypse. Roosevelt was gone, but the
Democrats, guided by the little haberdasher about whom they had felt such total contempt, had still won. In addition the Democrats had gained nine seats in
the Senate. They had scored a miraculous victory, but there would be a brutal
price to pay, and foreign policy—or more accurately, loyalty and security as
they affected foreign policy—would be where it would come due, the area
where the Republicans found fertile ground.

That Truman was a truly skilled, superior politician, that he had managed
deftly to work most of the traditional Democratic groups while cutting into
the Republican hold on the farm states, did not dawn on many of his opponents for a long time—he had to leave the White House before many of them
realized how talented he really had been. "I don't care how it is explained. It
defies all common sense to send that roughneck ward politician back to the
White House," said Bob Taft, in words that helped explain why Truman had
won. Walter Lippmann, the noted political columnist, thought Truman did
not have the soul or spirit or belief of a true New Dealer, but that he had
shrewdly kept the Roosevelt political alliance together. To the Republican conservatives, the idea that he could triumph, when it was so clearly their turn,
had been unthinkable. (One of the best books written about that election was
in fact titled *Out of the Jaws of Victory.*) Afterward they blamed Dewey and the
liberal wing of their party for having run another me-too race; though it is
likely that, in the climate of that moment, if Truman had run against their favorite, Robert Taft, the gap might have been even wider.

In retrospect it is impossible to underestimate the immense impact on the Republican Party of the Truman victory—that and the desperate need to find a new issue, which it created, and the decision that the issue would be the fall of China or, in a broader sense, subversion in Washington. What might have happened if Dewey had won, whether the essential bipartisanship that had existed for almost a decade might have continued with only minor adjustments, and whether the bitter accusations of treason against senior officials might have been greatly tempered, remains a fascinating question. If Dewey had been president and John Foster Dulles his secretary of state, would the Republican right have gone after them anywhere near as cruelly as they went after Truman and Acheson? Might the nation have escaped the ugly fratricidal charges that became known as the McCarthy period, but which were broader in what they represented than the charges issued by the Wisconsin senator? Might Dewey as commander in chief in the years to come have had far more latitude in dealing with (and if necessary relieving) an obstinate Douglas MacArthur, a Republican hero? Or might MacArthur, aware that he had less political leverage under Dewey than Truman, have operated with more respect for his superiors?

As the Democrats celebrated Truman's victory, few bothered to ponder what the loss of five elections in a row might mean to the minority party, many of whose most important figures now worried that they might be part of a permanent minority party. For the Republicans, the defeat meant no more Mr. Nice Guy. If they were blocked politically by a blue collar American economy and the rise—and political muscularity—of organized labor, then they would no longer fleck the issue of subversion lightly. Loyalty and anti-Communism would be their new themes, the mantra of attack central to their campaigns. To this end they would be helped greatly by forces outside anyone's control, most particularly the implosion of the government of Chiang Kai-shek, which would finally give them their defining issue. Domestic politics were about to grow far more bitter. The charge against the Democrats would be twenty years of treason.

15

ALL OF THIS—the rise of China as a major domestic political issue, the increasingly polarized debate about American foreign policy, and the fact that the Democratic administration, no matter how hard-line in the view of some of its critics on the left, was being accused of being soft—meant the Korean War was never seen in isolation as just a small war in a small country; it was never just about Korea. It was always joined to something infinitely larger—China, a country inspiring the most bitter kind of domestic political debate. As the Truman administration sent troops to Korea, there was always a vast dark unanswered question haunting them, which was the threat of the entry of Chinese Communist troops into the war, something the president and most of the men around him greatly feared, and that the general commanding in the field and some of his supporters seemed on occasion ready to welcome. The president thus was taking the country into a difficult war with his hands tied. He was also, though no one liked to admit it, politically on the defensive, which was why he had no choice over who his commanding general was going to be.

Even within his administration there had been a constant squabble over China from the moment that Louis Johnson had come aboard and had begun to take on Acheson. The two men started arguing over aid to Taiwan as soon as Johnson entered the cabinet. Just four days after the North Koreans had crossed the border, Senator Robert Taft, the Republican leader, gave a very emotional speech on the floor of the Senate, attacking Truman for not seeking congressional approval to go to war. Taft also said that the North Korean invasion showed that the Acheson policies on Asia were seriously flawed and that the administration was soft on Communism, and called for Acheson's resignation. A few hours after Taft's speech, Averell Harriman, who had been summoned back from Europe by Truman to help Acheson, happened to be in Johnson's office. The phone rang and Johnson took a call—from Bob Taft. Johnson thereupon praised the speech lavishly (especially the part about Acheson resigning). "That was something that needed to be said," he told Taft. Harriman was absolutely shocked—it was like being behind the lines, listening in on the leaders of the enemy. He was even more stunned when Johnson suggested that if Harriman played ball with him he would help make him secretary of state. Harriman immediately told Truman what had happened, and it was the beginning of the end for Johnson as secretary of defense.

Johnson, pro-Chiang and hostile to their essential policy, they could handle easily enough. He overvalued himself politically, and the senior uniformed military despised him. But MacArthur, their commander in the field, was quite another matter. He seemed if anything to want a confrontation with the administration. One of the early skirmishes between himself and Truman had taken place even before the Korean War started, in late December 1948, in *Life* magazine, the powerful weekly published by Henry Luce, a China Firster and a major critic of the administration's China policies. "MACARTHUR SAYS FALL OF CHINA IMPERILS U.S.," said the huge headline. MacArthur had sent a sixteen-page cable to the Joint Chiefs, *Life* reported, which "gave our top military men a historic shock." The Soviets, he had reported, were now in a position to seize Japan. "In the face of facts which seem so plain, how could Washington ever have been so complacent about the consequences of a Communist victory in China?" It was a fascinating piece—the administration's leading military man in Asia had lined up with the administration's sworn enemies on the most sensitive political issue of all. It did not augur well for the future.

The next fight took place in late July 1950. There had been some bitter internal squabbling over Taiwan within the administration, with the Joint Chiefs beginning to shift in their opinion on the value of the island—at its nearest about eighty-five miles off the China coast—now that the Korean War had begun. Word had come in from intelligence sources—later it turned out to be completely wrong—that an immense Chinese Communist fleet of some four thousand vessels was being gathered on the mainland, possibly as part of preparations to strike Taiwan. That triggered even greater concern. Acheson was wary of any action that would connect U.S. efforts in Korea to Chiang and might widen the war, and he was still opposed to giving Chiang aid. In his mind any help to Taiwan was also help to Chiang, and would be a fateful American policy move. Truman, however, was beginning to make his own political adjustments. The president suggested a survey team be sent out to gauge the needs for the possible defense of Taiwan. The Chiefs thereupon passed the suggestion on to MacArthur, who decided he would lead the team. At this point the Chiefs became a little nervous and suggested that he might send someone else on this preliminary run—a senior officer, perhaps—since State and Defense were still working out the ground rules for it. Otherwise it might seem more like something of a state visit than an attempt to estimate military needs.

But MacArthur had no intention of waiting and no intention of letting State in as a player. He took off almost immediately, leaving behind in Tokyo the principal representative of State, Bill Sebald, and taking an enormous group of his own senior military people, so large they needed two giant C-54s. On the way over, MacArthur radioed the Pentagon saying that if the Chinese launched their invasion, he intended to use three squadrons of F-80s to repel them. That heightened the tension for everyone back in Washington, most especially Acheson, who believed that the general had already dispatched the three squadrons to Taiwan, thus vastly exceeding his right of command. Acheson was aggravated, but it was also a reminder to the Chiefs, playing their own game in favor of a commitment if not to Chiang, then to Taiwan, that they did not control MacArthur as they might have controlled any other theater commander. It would have been better if Truman himself had ordered MacArthur to delay the trip, Omar Bradley wrote later.

MacArthur landed in Taiwan on July 29, a month and a week into the war. Chiang's people were thrilled. He was greeted as nothing less than a head of state, and both he and Chiang played it for all it was worth. He gallantly kissed Madame Chiang's hand and called Chiang his "old comrade in arms," though they had never met before. Most important, though there was technically no change in policy, the entire trip gave the *appearance* of a change in policy, or at least the emergence of a separate policy. It was a great boon for Chiang's public relations machinery. Chiang said the United States and China were going to make "common cause" against their mutual enemies. "The net effect of the Nationalist propaganda was to give the impression that the United States was, or was going to be, far more closely allied with Chiang militarily in the struggle against communism in the Far East; that we might even arm him for a 'return to the mainland,'" as Omar Bradley wrote.

Truman and Acheson were both predictably furious. It was a sign, the first of many to come, that Douglas MacArthur did not merely carry out policy but was entitled, at least in his own mind, to make it as well, that he always had his own agenda, and that the agenda was not necessarily the same as that of the president. The president was certain that the general had used the trip to encourage the China Lobby and to increase pressure on him from the right. Hearing how angry the president was, as the furor over his trip mounted in the press, MacArthur aggravated him even more by saying that his visit "has been maliciously misrepresented to the public by those who invariably in the past have propagandized a policy of defeatism and appeasement in the Pacific." That was another slap at Acheson.

Just so there would be no mistaking how importantly Washington took what happened, Truman immediately sent a three-man team to Tokyo and

Korea to make sure it did not happen again, and at the same time to find out how the war was going and how much the command was going to need. This was the team that Matt Ridgway was on when he made his evaluation of Walton Walker. But the key figure was Averell Harriman, already Truman's top troubleshooter. His basic assignment was to improve Washington's relations with MacArthur, find out what he needed in terms of men and materiel, and pass on two messages from the president, as Harriman later noted, first that "I'm going to do everything I can to give him what he wants in the way of support; and secondly I want you to tell him that I don't want him to get us in a war with the Chinese Communists." He was also to try to find out whatever it was that MacArthur had promised Chiang, and to warn him to stay clear of him. But even as Harriman was flying to Tokyo, a story came out of the general's headquarters quoting a reliable source that MacArthur intended to tell Harriman that the war in Korea would prove useless unless the United States fought Communism everywhere it showed its head in Asia.

The Harriman-MacArthur talks were a limited success. The president's instructions, Harriman later reported to the president, were ones that MacArthur might go along with, but his lack of enthusiasm was notable. As a soldier, he would obey, Harriman reported, "but without full conviction." Given Harriman's shrewdness in reading people, that was not a good sign. He was in some ways as grand a figure as MacArthur, had been a major player almost as long, and was in no way intimidated by the general. On arrival, when MacArthur had first-named him—"Averell, good to see you"—he had first-named the commander right back; if it was Averell, then it would be Douglas as well.

It was clear to Harriman that MacArthur thought any form of accommodation with Mao and his China was a policy of appeasement, though he did not put it quite that way. That would come later. He also told Harriman he thought the United States was being too tough on Chiang—they should "stop kicking him around." But though he did not value Chiang's troops—there was no disagreement on that—he was essentially on the other side on the general issue of China, one that had begun to haunt Washington politically. "For reasons that are rather difficult to explain," Harriman reported to Truman on his return, "I did not feel that we came to a full agreement on the way we believed things should be handled in Formosa and with the Generalissimo. He accepted the president's position and will act accordingly, but without full conviction. He has the strange idea that we should back anybody who will fight communism, even though he could not give me an argument why the Generalissimo's fighting communists would be a contribution towards the effective dealing with the communists in China."

One final meeting between MacArthur and the team from Washington had taken place on August 8 at what was still a low point in the war. The North Koreans were then pushing toward the Pusan Perimeter. At that meeting, MacArthur, surprisingly upbeat, had unveiled plans for a surprise landing behind North Korean lines at a port called Inchon, located far up the west coast of Korea. It was the old Bluehearts plan that MacArthur had favored in the very early days of the war, now greatly expanded and upgraded. The Inchon landing, which he had scheduled for September 15, had become not so much a preferred battle plan as a MacArthur obsession. Almost from the moment the North Koreans had crossed the border and driven south, he had been thinking about it. There had been a staff meeting early in July, and a number of his people had been told to think in terms of an amphibious landing and make suggestions. Many sites were suggested: one staff officer had selected a port just behind North Korean lines; the next, a spot about ten kilometers north, still in artillery range of American troops. A third officer, a young major named Ed Rowny, was the boldest, suggesting a point about twenty-five kilometers up on the east coast. MacArthur was not impressed. "You're all pusillanimous," he said. Then he went to a blackboard and wrote out *in French*—Rowny remembered it clearly years later because it was the great MacArthur and a great performance, made even better by the unexpected use of the French—"*De Qui Objet?*" What is the object? And then he took a giant grease pencil and circled Inchon, the port for Seoul, well above what anyone else had suggested. "That's where we should land, Inchon—go for the throat." The younger men spoke about the difficulty of the tides and fears that the port's harbor might be mined, but MacArthur waved the objections aside. "Don't take counsel of your fears—it's simply a matter of willpower and courage." Then he told them to work out a plan for a landing at Inchon.

Now, with Harriman and Ridgway, he made his push for the landing. He normally would need four divisions for such an operation, but American forces being so strapped by the postwar demobilization, he would do it with two, the Seventh Infantry and the First Marines. It was, Ridgway thought, a brilliant presentation of a highly original strategy, and he enthusiastically supported it, becoming the first member of the senior Washington national security team to leap on the Inchon bandwagon. Ridgway had also been impressed by MacArthur's concern about the hardships that the upcoming Korean winter held in store for the troops, a winter much worse, he was sure, than anything they had encountered in Germany. The sooner they struck at Inchon, MacArthur said, the better. Once winter arrived, MacArthur had suggested, it would be so bitter and harsh that non-battle casualties might exceed battle ones. The irony of his argument, given the fact that in late November MacArthur would not hesitate to send the

Eighth Army and Tenth Corps north to the Yalu in murderously cold weather, often still clothed in summer-weight uniforms, would not be lost later on either Harriman or Ridgway. MacArthur, they decided, could argue passionately on either side of any question—based on whether it suited his immediate purpose or not.

To Harriman, the originality of the Inchon landing presentation caught the great quandary posed to civilian leaders by MacArthur, a man of two selves—such a talented, imaginative general, yet so difficult for his civilian bosses to deal with, an officer constantly bordering on the insubordinate, with an agenda always at variance with that of his superiors. They all knew that it was like a reflex action with him to hold back critical bits of information. How did you extract the best from a man who constantly seemed to create his own political undertow, simply did not play by the rules used by other senior military men, and was never even close to being straight with you? How could you employ him and yet control him? Could he, with all his talent, actually stay on your team? Harriman and Ridgway's trip had underlined the MacArthur problem perfectly; the mess he had created with Chiang, and the brilliance of the Inchon plan. In a casual remark that highlighted the dilemma MacArthur always posed for his civilian superiors, Harriman told Ridgway it was crucial "for political and personal considerations to be put to one side and our government deal with General MacArthur on the lofty level of the great national asset which he is." But even as their meeting proceeded in a positive vein, troubling signs for the future abounded. If the relationship between Moscow and Beijing, countries aligned as fraternal allies in the Communist constellation, was soon to prove uncommonly difficult, it would certainly be equaled by the thorny relationship between the American commander in Tokyo and his military and political superiors in Washington.

The civilians knew that there was always going to be a next incident with MacArthur. In this case they didn't have to wait very long. It took fewer than three weeks. This time it was a VFW speech. The general had been asked to speak, or at least send a speech along to be read, to the annual meeting of the Veterans of Foreign Wars, like the American Legion not a constituency of the dovish. Again the speech was about Taiwan. Its military value was not to be underestimated, he said. From Taiwan the United States "can dominate with air power every Asiatic port from Vladivostok to Singapore and prevent any hostile movement into the Pacific." It was in an odd way as if he were carrying ammunition for the nation's adversaries by going so public on so delicate a subject. This—that Taiwan was a great military base for the Americans—was exactly the point the Russians, both for themselves and on behalf of the Chinese, were trying to make in the United Nations, and the point that Washington wanted to minimize in order to limit the scope of the Korean War. Then MacArthur went even further—he tweaked the administration one more time—speaking, it seemed, not so much as its most important commanding general in the field, but as one of its leading political critics at home. "Nothing could be more fallacious than the threadbare argument by those who advocate appeasement and defeatism in the Pacific that if we defend Formosa we alienate continental Asia. . . . Those who speak thus do not understand the Orient. They do not grant that it is in the pattern of Oriental psychology to respect and follow aggressive, resolute and dynamic leadership." If it was not an assault on Truman himself, it was most obviously an all-out slap at Acheson.

Truman was once again furious. Though the speech was already public, and had been moved by the wire service, it had not yet been read to the VFW convention. Truman called in his top people and told Louis Johnson, who agreed with MacArthur on the subject, to tell MacArthur to withdraw the speech—and that it was a presidential order. "Do you understand that?" the president asked. "Yes, sir, I do," Johnson answered. "Go and do it, that's all," said the president (angry at Johnson as well, feeling that he was something of a co-conspirator in all this). But Johnson went back to his office and wavered, not liking the idea of telling MacArthur to eat his own speech. He called Acheson and suggested ways of softening Truman's orders—as if what MacArthur had said was simply one man's opinion and every man was entitled to his opinion. Acheson reminded him that it was an order from Truman. All day long phone calls went back and forth among the various principals, except for Truman. Finally in mid-afternoon, Truman telephoned Johnson and dictated the message to MacArthur: "The President of the United States directs that you withdraw your message for the National Encampment of the Veterans of Foreign Wars, because various features with respect to Formosa are in conflict with the policy of the U.S. and its position in the U.N." Finally it was withdrawn—now making MacArthur the angry one. But just as the speech had been made public and then withdrawn, the incident was over, but not over. Later, after MacArthur and Truman had their final clash and the president relieved him, Truman would sometimes mutter that he should have done it so much earlier, back at the time of the VFW speech.

It was the death knell for Louis Johnson, who was ordered by the president to resign some two weeks later. Johnson broke down in tears when Truman repeatedly told him to sign his farewell letter. Johnson was, wrote Truman's biographer, David McCullough, "possibly the worst appointment Truman ever made." "Nutty as a fruitcake," Acheson said of him. He had managed during his brief tour in office to offend almost everyone in the administration, including the president, the secretary of state, most cabinet members, and almost every senior military official whose path he crossed. The senior military men, often squabbling bitterly with one another over postwar roles, were united by a single common feeling in that time—they all hated Louis Johnson. He seemed to them a crude caricature of their worst nightmares of a civilian politician. He regularly denigrated their skills and the need for what they did. With the atomic bomb in mind, he wrote to one senior admiral in December 1949 (using what the writer Robert Heinl called his "characteristic tact"): "Admiral, the Navy is on its way out. . . . There's no reason for having a Navy or Marine Corps. General Bradley tells me amphibious landings are a thing of the past. We'll never have any more amphibious landings. That does away with the Marine Corps. And the Air Force can do anything the Navy can nowadays, so that does away with the Navy." He was hated in senior Army circles because of the pressures he kept applying to make a vastly diminished Army even smaller. By the time he was fired in September 1950, three months into the Korean War, a mordant joke was circulating in the Pentagon: the Joint Chiefs, it went, had informed Johnson that he could finally call off his relentless troop reduction demands—enough men were being killed in Korea every day to bring the Army's strength down to the desired level. He was despised by almost everyone who had to deal with him. "Unwittingly, Truman had replaced one mental case with another," Omar Bradley later wrote in his memoirs, in a reference to Forrestal.

But the fact that it had expedited Johnson's departure, almost guaranteed before the year was out anyway, was the least important part of the VFW-MacArthur contretemps. It had exacerbated the relationship between the president and the general, who had been forced to back down and respect a presidential order, a process that was as unpleasant as it was alien to him, and it was bound to fester. It was also a clear warning to the White House, like the visit to Taiwan, that MacArthur was a dissident, both hierarchically and politically. It showed that he was by no means in agreement with their policies in Asia, including potentially the aims in the war they were fighting, and that he was more than likely to be a serious opponent on an issue that had come to haunt them, that of China. That was no small fault line: the president and his secretary of state wanted, if at all possible, to separate Korea from the larger issue of China, and the general, if he did not actually want to connect the two— and there is considerable evidence that he did, much of it from things he said, that he got down on his knees and prayed every night that China would enter the war—certainly was in no way bothered by the prospect of a Chinese entry.

To replace Johnson, Truman reached out for George Marshall, exhausted by his previous tours of duty, whose health was somewhat shaky, and who was just a few months short of his seventieth birthday. Marshall had been hoping to slip into a semi-gentrified retirement as head of the Red Cross. Truman, sensing Johnson's fate, had already sent out a recon mission to see if Marshall might be willing to serve again. Marshall said he would serve, but only for six months, with Bob Lovett, a much respected figure in the national security world, coming in as his number two and then replacing him. Are you sure you really want me? Marshall had asked the president. The president might want to ponder, he said, "the fact that my appointment may reflect upon you and your Administration. They are still charging me with the downfall of Chiang's government in China. I want to help, not hurt you." Later, noting the conversation in a letter to his wife, Truman had written, "Can you think of anyone else saying that? I can't and he's one of the *great*?"

Even as the Korean War began, the death of one China and the birth of another hung over the administration—it was the issue from which the administration was beginning to hemorrhage. If in 1948 the Republicans had been in search of an issue, in 1949 their prayers were answered. The collapse of Chiang's regime would prove the first important step in what would eventually become a terrible collision between the United States and China on the battlefield itself a mere twenty months later. On November 3, 1948, the day before the presidential election, Chinese Nationalist forces retreated from Shenyang, the largest city in Manchuria, abandoning for the first time a major city (and control of much of the surrounding area) to Mao Zedong's Chinese Communists. The rout was on. Chiang Kai-shek's armies were in the process of a stunning collapse, each new defeat seeming to ensure that the next one would be bigger and come even more quickly. Sometimes entire Nationalist divisions surrendered and immediately became part of Mao's new army. Other divisions simply disappeared, leaving behind for their Communist enemies millions of dollars worth of American military equipment.

From then on, the United States and a new revolutionary China, sometimes seemingly deaf and dumb to each other's political and military impulses, would stumble in an awkward slow-motion dance toward an unwanted military collision. There had been plentiful signs of Chiang's decline over the previous four years, but because of the propaganda put out by so many journalists favorable to the regime, the end of his rule had still come as shattering news to millions of Americans. Beloved China, a country they had been told during World War II was inhabited by industrious, obedient, trustworthy, *good* Asians (as Japan had only so recently been inhabited by wily, sneaky, untrustworthy, *bad* Asians), had suddenly gone Communist. First Russia, an ally during World War II, had turned out to be an enemy; now, perhaps even more shattering, China had become an enemy as well, an ally of the Soviet Union.

For millions of Americans it felt like a betrayal, and a sinister one at that, because when China's immense land mass and population were added to Russia's enormous land mass and population, the world looked infinitely more dangerous. If both countries were colored pink on a giant geopolitical map of the world, which for political reasons they now often were, that map suddenly looked significantly more ominous. Because the emotions China generated among millions of Americans were greater than those generated by any comparable country, because the Democrats had won five elections in a row and the Republicans were looking for a new, hot issue, the political ramifications of the fall of China would prove staggering. The question now rising—an immensely partisan one—was: Who Lost China? Underlying it was the deeper assumption—and great historical misconception—that China had ever been ours; more, ours to lose. The fall of Chiang's China, though few understood it—or wanted to understand it—at the time, was part of the price of a dramatic alteration of the world's power structure that had taken place during six years of total war. World War II had been more than just the catastrophic struggle between two sides, the Allies and the Axis; like World War I, it would have far-reaching global consequences.

THE CHINA THAT existed in the minds of millions of Americans was the most illusory of countries, filled as it was with dutiful, obedient peasants who liked America and loved Americans, who longed for nothing so much as to be like them. It was a country where ordinary peasants allegedly hoped to be more Christian and were eager, despite the considerable obstacles in their way, to rise out of what Americans considered a heathen past. Millions of Americans believed not only that they loved (and understood) China and the Chinese, but that it was their duty to Americanize the Chinese. "With God's help, we will lift Shanghai up and up, ever up until it is just like Kansas City," said Senator Kenneth Wherry of Nebraska, one of the Republicans who would become a particularly bitter critic of the administration for its China policies (and who once referred to French Indochina as Indigo-China).

Long before Chiang went to Taiwan, and established his rather personal China on location, there were two Chinas. There was China in the American public mind, a China as Americans wanted it to be, and the other China, the real China, which was coming apart and was the sad daily reality of those Americans on location. The illusory China was a heroic ally, ruled by the brave, industrious, Christian, pro-American Chiang Kai-shek and his beautiful wife, Mayling, a member of one of China's wealthiest and best connected families, herself Christian and American-educated, and who seemed to have been ordered up directly from Central Casting for a major public relations campaign. The goals of the Generalissimo and his lady, it always seemed, were exactly the same as America's goals, their values the same as ours as well. The reality of course was completely different. In a way, what happened after World War II was the cruelest of jokes: the impact of all those thousands of American missionaries who had so dutifully and faithfully gone to China over a century would be greater on the politics of their own country than it was on China, the country they hoped to change, and whose culture and politics they barely dented. Millions and millions of American children, as John Melby, one of the more talented members of the American embassy in China's wartime capital, Chongqing, later wrote, had faithfully brought their pennies to Sunday school to give to the poor and unwashed of China. Their parents had heard the missionaries, back on home leave, speak at their churches and evoke not just the marvels of China and the Chinese, but the vast challenge always still ahead for those who desired to do the Lord's work.

The China that existed in reality was a feudal country badly fragmented politically and geographically, a country of almost unbearable poverty, ruled more often than not by regional warlords of exceptional cruelty. It was a country of some 500 million people governed, if that was even the word, by a shaky, corrupt national administration, predatory foreign interests, an infinite number of warlords, and a tiny, self-serving oligarchy that also doubled as the government. To the leadership in much of the West, seeking as it did constant commercial benefits, a weak, vulnerable China was the preferred one. As the civil war continued, it reflected a historic attempt on China's part to redefine itself as a nation, one that would be truly whole, and perhaps even strong, and no longer, as it had been for so long, prey to powerful Western nations from afar and to warlords within. It had been torn apart by more than two decades of on-and-off civil war and by the brutality inflicted on its people during the Japanese occupation. It was a China burdened, now that World War II was over, with a sad, badly flawed leadership under Chiang, hardly equal to the Herculean challenges caused by such severe external and internal problems. It was, in historic terms, ripe for the picking.

There had, of course, been plenty of warnings that Chiang was going to fall. Even during World War II, when the main struggle was supposed to be against the Japanese, the battle between the Nationalists under Chiang and the Communists under Mao was a constant sideshow. Report after report coming in from the field during the war, from both civilians and military men, from men ideologically committed to Chiang as well as those appalled by him, had reflected the view that the Communists had better leadership, both political and military, and had far greater political legitimacy. Even as World War II was ending, very few people who had been there and knew what was happening militarily thought Chiang would make it. Some people in the national security team, like James Forrestal, thought Chiang's chances of winning were so slim that the United States had to be careful not to weaken Japan so much that it could not be used as a North Asian bulwark against the Communists. When World War II was finally over, and the civil war started in earnest, the reports from the field became even gloomier. Chiang had predictably turned inward, his base becoming ever more narrow, his policies ever more repressive. Even a figure as sympathetic to Chiang as Major General Claire Chennault, who had led the American Flying Tiger air units fighting in China during the world war and would be a lifelong hard-line supporter of the Generalissimo, had written Roosevelt near the war's end that if there was a civil war, as there was likely to be, "the Yenan regime [the Communists] has an excellent chance of emerging victorious with or without Russian aid."

Probably as good a date as any for the beginning of World War II is July 1937, when Chinese troops clashed with Japanese invaders near Beijing, close to the Chinese-Manchurian border. If nothing else, it surely ended any hope of the rise of a modern, semidemocratic China under Chiang Kai-shek's Nationalist or Guomindang Party, the kind of China many Americans had hoped for, and dreamed of long after it became the most hopeless of causes. What then took place in China, under the dual force of the Japanese invasion and the constant undercurrent of the civil war, was as powerful and complete a transformation of a social, economic, and political order as the modern world had witnessed. It was a cataclysmic event, driven at first by forces from without, but in no way purely an external challenge. It was, at the same time, a challenge of one China, as yet unborn and potentially lethal in its norms and residual hatreds, to another China, at once weak, cruel, and barbaric in its own way: a challenge by one set of violent, autocratic men to another set of autocratic and ruthless men who had ruled so poorly and with such elemental brutality for too long. It was a system of oppression rather than authority that had been imposed with unparalleled harshness and greed upon ordinary Chinese. The few who benefited were rich, powerful, and lived above the laws, which, in any case, were set by force of arms. The many who were poor existed that way in what seemed like hopeless perpetuity. Every unbearable aspect of their daily lives was marked by some kind of injustice, and the absence of elemental dignity. This China was probably dying even before the first Japanese troops marched into Manchuria.

Chiang's own rise reflected the fragmentation of the older order. He was not so much a leader, as he was portrayed by favorable publications in America, as he was a survivor, a man who existed by balancing warring interests off against each other. His nickname among Westerners, as Barbara Tuchman pointed out in her book on the collapse of China, was "Billiken," after a popular weighted doll that could not be knocked over. He had strengthened his political ties in 1927 when he married into the Soong family, China's most influential family in terms of wealth and connections to powerful interests in the West. Mayling Soong, the youngest member of the family, was Christian, Wellesley-educated, and politically ambitious. Earlier, Chiang had tried to marry her older sister, the widow of China's first president, Sun Yat-sen, and had been rejected. To marry Mayling, he had to get rid of two other wives and convert to Christianity, something he readily did. In time, Chiang became known to the Americans as the Generalissimo or the Gimo, and she, not always affectionately, as Missimo. His marriage greatly strengthened his political connections with the United States and with those who longed for that most unrealistic of things, a modern, nationalist Chinese leader who was both Christian and capitalist.

Chiang's great struggle in those years was with the Communists, who had the good fortune to challenge authority but not to have to govern. All they had to do was exploit the country's myriad grievances and miseries. They did that with considerable skill, tuned brilliantly to the grievances of the peasants as Chiang and the warlords connected to him never had been. Chiang's China gradually imploded—despite vast amounts of American military aid and advice, despite all kinds of warnings, journalistic, diplomatic, and military, that he needed to change and reform his government. A series of American political and military advisers who urged him to use his resources more wisely failed dismally. Their interests and his interests were rarely the same—they wanted him to provide a kind of bold American-style leadership, and he wanted to survive for another day; the corrupt military-political structure the Americans wanted him to get rid of was nothing less than the key to his very political survival. If he had one special talent at the end, it was to appear to agree with his Americans advisers—he did not after all want to hurt their feelings—and then pay no attention to them whatsoever, and keep on doing exactly what he had always done.

When the government finally fell in 1949, there was no surprise involved. General Joseph (Vinegar Joe) Stilwell, the principal American military adviser assigned to work with Chiang during World War II, had decided as early as 1942 that Chiang was utterly worthless, unwilling, if not unable, to use his army against the Japanese. Stilwell was hardly alone among Americans in the region in his distaste for Chiang. The Gimo's nickname among many American soldiers serving in China reflected their frustration with him; Chancre Jack, they called him. Stilwell might have done three tours of duty in China and might have spoken the language fluently, but he was hardly the ideal American representative to deal with so weak a regime and so fragile a leader. He was the least diplomatic of men, edgy, outspoken, cantankerous, and blasphemous; he could be, wrote his biographer Barbara Tuchman, who in many ways admired him, "rude or caustic or sometimes coarse or deliberately boorish." He said what he thought, without much reflection, or tact. There was no difference between his private view of the Chinese leader and what he told any and all who listened to him. He had decided early on that Chiang was virtually useless as an instrument of American policy. Once, the young *Time* magazine reporter Teddy White had asked Stilwell for an explanation of the debacle of Chinese troops during a battle, and he answered, "We are allied to an ignorant, illiterate, peasant son of a bitch called Chiang Kai-shek." A more accurate description might have been that the United States was failing because it was trying overnight to create a China that was in America's image, something very unlikely to take place. Any leader the United States chose would end up failing either his own people or America or, as happened in this case, both. The reality failed because the dream was impossible from the start.

Stilwell regularly reported back to Washington that Chiang was hopeless as a military ally, unable or unwilling to take any of the requisite steps to get his army to engage the Japanese. But in Washington, Stilwell's reports did not greatly matter. Even though the then Army chief of staff, George Marshall, Stilwell's personal sponsor, was on his side, Chiang always held a better hand. On his side was the one person who mattered most, Franklin Roosevelt, who feared that if Chiang were pushed too hard, he might make a separate peace with the Japanese, allowing them to move armies bogged down for so long in China to other areas of Asia. As the war dragged on, the attitude of Chiang and the people around him toward their Western allies, most particularly the Americans, lapsed into one of utter and complete cynicism. As Barbara Tuchman later wrote of his policy, "To use barbarians to fight other barbarians was a traditional principle of Chinese statecraft, which now more than ever appeared not only advisable, but justified. Chinese opinion, according to a foreign resident, held that not only was China justified in remaining passive after five years of resistance, 'it was her right to get as much as possible out of her allies while they fought.' The exercise of this right, she noted, became the Government's chief war effort."

Chiang's army was a mighty one—on paper. In reality, it was increasingly a sham. He allegedly commanded three hundred divisions, but Stilwell believed they were, on average, at least 40 percent understrength, filled with invisible or ghost soldiers kept on the rolls so that their commanders could draw and personally pocket their pay. Early in World War II, when China was allegedly fighting for its life, American advisers were simply appalled by the conscription process. A senior American officer on Stilwell's staff, Colonel Dave Barrett, wrote of one engagement, "The troops had only the poorest equipment.

No medical attention. No transport. Many sick. Most recruits were conscripts delivered tied up. Conscription is a scandal. Only the unfortunates without money or influence are grabbed." The numerous, large, incompetent divisions did not exist by happenstance; they were Chiang's way of buying influence in a corrupt, feudal world already collapsing around him. If he had done what the Americans wanted, he understood far better than they, he might quickly have fallen from power.

Long, bitter, and divisive as it was, the Stilwell-Chiang struggle could have only one outcome: in the fall of 1944, Stilwell, the teller of so many unwanted truths, had thus become the most unwelcome of guests, and was recalled. Roosevelt had chosen to go with Chiang, even though he was a hopelessly flawed instrument of American policy. There were two reasons for this: first, it kept China in the war; and second, Roosevelt had his own hopelessly romantic vision of China, and seemed to believed that if we treated Chiang as the great leader of a great nation, brought him as a high-level leader to some of the conferences among the world's leaders, he would in time morph into what the president wanted.

If Chiang had succeeded politically in the two-man game with Stilwell, that did not make the American general any less of a prophet. Everything he had said came true; the ever more ferocious downward spiral of Chiang's government was nothing less than a profound historical process, the collapse of a nation outside the control of any foreigners, no matter how rich and powerful their own country. No wartime military man had been more successful in a variety of exhausting tasks than George Marshall, but sent on a mission to China in late 1945 to mediate the struggle between the Nationalists and the Communists, he was a study in unadulterated failure—and was all too aware of that fact, for he was much too shrewd a figure not to understand that neither side was going to listen to him, and that the forces he was dealing with were irreconcilable. Marshall was sixty-five at the time and had just retired from the Army, physically exhausted and wanting nothing so much as to become a country squire in Leesburg, Virginia. But Harry Truman, badly shaken by events in China and fearing what the China issue might represent domestically if matters did not improve, had called on him: "General, I want you to go to China for me." So it was that just before Christmas, 1945, John Carter Vincent, the head of Far Eastern Affairs at State, saw Marshall off. He then turned to his ten-year-old son as the plane departed: "Son," he said, "there goes the bravest man in the world. He's going to try and unify China."

The trip was such a disaster that Marshall seemed to age visibly in front of his own aides. He seemed, John Melby, who did some of the translating for him, wrote in his diary, very tired, very sad, and most likely quite ill. It was as if he saw the failure that was coming in China and the toxins it would create in the American political system. At one point in May 1946, he ran into Dwight Eisenhower, also in China. At Truman's request, Eisenhower sounded Marshall out about replacing Jimmy Byrnes as secretary of state, an enormous responsibility for a man already worn down by prolonged public service. "Great goodness, Eisenhower, I'd take any job in the world to get out of this one!" Marshall quickly answered. Hearing of the failure of the Marshall mission, Joe Stilwell said, "But what did they expect? George Marshall can't walk on water." To Marshall, China was hopeless. The one thing he wanted to do more than anything else was to prevent American combat troops from being sent there to support Chiang, as some of the Nationalist leaders wanted. As he told Walton Butterworth, who became head of the State Department's Far Eastern Affairs Office in 1947, "Butterworth, we must not get sucked in. I would need 500,000 troops to begin with and it would just be the beginning." Then he paused and added: "And how would I extricate them?"

Yet for all of the sense that those people knowledgeable about China had of the rot that had set in, as World War II ended, outsiders could be forgiven for thinking that Chiang's position still seemed enviable. He retained the support of the new American administration, though its most influential members doubted his viability. He was a recognized world leader; and the portrait most Americans had of him, thanks to the efforts of a brilliant propaganda machine, was of a great and sympathetic Asian leader. In the fall of 1945 his army, and his party, the Guomindang, controlled all of China's major cities, its entire— if devastated—industrial base, and more than three-quarters of its total population, then variously estimated at between 450 and 500 million people. He had more than 2.5 million men officially under arms, and those arms were relatively modern, having been provided by the United States.

The Communists had fewer than half that number of men under arms and ruled over only an impoverished rural area of northwest China. Yet all kinds of foreign and domestic observers, civilian and military alike, believed that Chiang's strength was a complete illusion and that the government was on the verge of collapse. The finances of the country were a joke. It was for a small handful of people a kind of golden trough, so much money flowing into the country to be handled by so very few Chinese. Clearly it was a situation that might not last long, and it was a time to make as much money as you could as quickly as possible. Critics of the government talked openly of key officials storing away bars of gold for their own future security. Marshall had warned Chiang almost on arrival that far too much of the country's budget—between 80 and 90 percent—was going to the military, and that financial collapse would come before military victory. If the Chinese government, he told some of Chiang's ministers, thought the American taxpayers would "step into the vacuum this creates, you can go to hell." As that became more obvious, the government's only response was to print more currency—"printing press money," as it was known.

Yet Chiang had little sense of his own vulnerability. Now, with the Japanese defeated, he still believed he held the whip hand over the Americans, prepared as he was to fight that country's newest enemy, the Communists. Typically, T.V. Soong, probably the most powerful (and richest) man in the government, was openly contemptuous of the Americans. He went around Nanjing telling Chinese colleagues not to worry about them. "I can take care of these boobs," he said. Certainly, the Americans seemed ready to play their part as scripted by Chiang. Even as the Japanese were surrendering, the United States had managed to turn their forces into a kind of temporary constabulary, staying in place, weapons in hand, until Nationalist, not Communist, troops arrived to accept their surrender. Then the Americans helped airlift or ferry as many as five hundred thousand Nationalist troops from southwestern China to key positions around the country. ("Unquestionably the largest troop movement by air in the world's history," boasted General Albert Wedemeyer, who directed it as the senior American military officer in the region in the post-Stilwell era.) In a number of places in northeast China, the United States sent detachments of their own Marines in, perhaps as many as fifty thousand all told, to hold outposts until the Nationalist troops could arrive. As such, with the help of the United States, Chiang's forces were able to accept the surrender of some 1.2 million Japanese soldiers, along with their equipment, much of it desperately coveted by the Communists.

Yet even when the civil war was apparently going well, the truth was very different. No one was more aware of this than the former American chief of staff. In October 1946, near the end of his tour as Truman's special representative, George Marshall repeatedly warned Chiang not to go after the Communists in their bases in the north and northwest. Chiang was spreading himself much too thin and playing into Mao's hands, Marshall argued. In addition, sensing the kind of war the Communists fought, he tried to make one basic point with the Gimo. The Communists might be retreating, but they were not surrendering. The implications were obvious: when the Nationalists were far from their base camps and supply lines, then, and only then, would the Communist forces strike. Chiang, of course, did not listen. He never did. He was pumped up on victories that were not victories, on the departure of Communist forces from projected battlefields, which was part of the larger Communist strategy. Chiang promised Marshall that he would destroy the Communists in eight to ten months, and then, having rejected all of his advice, he asked Marshall, the most distinguished American citizen-soldier of his generation, a man exhausted and desperate for retirement, to stay on as his personal military adviser. Marshall quite emphatically said no—if he could not influence Chiang as the personal representative of the president of the United States, he knew what chance he would have on Chiang's own payroll. ("Chiang's confidence in me may have been unbounded, but it did not restrain him from disregarding my advice," Marshall said years later, somewhat mordantly.)

For all of Chiang's surface strengths, the Communists at that moment could not have been more confident. They might have been pushed back into the caves of impoverished Yenan, but they had been surprisingly successful in their guerrilla strikes against the Japanese, and even more successful in their efforts to forge a deep relationship with China's vast peasant population. Aware of the mounting problems of the Nationalists, they were absolutely confident of their own destiny and their inevitable victory, and sooner rather than later. In America, powerful religious leaders, men of deep faith, were outraged by the possibility of their victory, but in their own very different way the Communists were men of faith, politics and war having been entwined together into what was virtually a religious fervor, a certainty on their part that they were a force of destiny. For Mao and the men around him were designing what seemed at the time a new kind of war, based initially not so much on force of arms as on gaining the support of the people.

CHIANG HAD BARELY waited for the world war to end before launching his offensive against the Communists, who had hoped that he would do exactly that, would come after them and extend his line of communications. American aid continued to pour in. It was as if he were following an agenda that the Communists had scripted for him. "It is all right for United States to arm the Guomindang, because as fast as they get it we will take it away from them," a Communist representative said at the time. All told, the United States sent $2.5 billion in aid to China from the end of World War II to 1949, when Chiang fled to Taiwan. Indeed, so much military aid had been wasted and stolen during the war that some of the Americans who flew the equipment over the Hump—that is, the Himalayas—from India, an unusually dangerous supply mission given that era's aircraft, had a cynical phrase for it all: "Uncle Chump from over the Hump."

On paper, the Communist Army was at first comparatively small and poorly armed, but they had leadership, discipline, and grievance. They had come to their combat skills and their strategy the hard way. First there had been the Long March, the 6,000-mile, 370-day trek from southern China to Yenan that had begun in October 1934 and that, among other things, had seen the rise of Mao Zedong within the Party. Then there had been the long ordeal of struggling to survive against the Japanese during the war years, which had provided them with a form of warfare that perfectly suited their strengths and minimized their weaknesses. They had fought the Japanese with great skill, using mobile, small-unit guerrilla tactics, striking only when they had overwhelming numerical strength and vanishing when the enemy units were larger and stronger. Now, pursued by larger, better-armed Nationalist forces, they made comparable adjustments on what was a changing battlefield, a battlefield they redesigned to suit their purposes, rather than those of their enemy. They would not hold cities, and they would not fight a stationary war; they would operate out of bases that were so distant as to be almost unreachable by conventional forces. In the beginning they would seek more than anything simply

to capture weapons from the Nationalist troops. Sixty years later, when American forces would fight in Iraq against urban guerrillas, there was a new name
for it—an asymmetrical war.

Despite the vulnerability of their positions in 1945, the morale of the Communists was high. It was not long before a sense of a changing military dynamic was obvious to foreign observers. John Melby, one of the younger State
Department officials, noted in his diary as early as December 1945: "One of the
great mysteries to me is why one group of people retains faith, whereas another from much the same origins and experience loses it. Over the years the
Communists have absorbed an incredible amount of punishment, have been
guilty of their own share of atrocities, and yet have retained a kind of integrity,
faith in their destiny, and the will to prevail. By contrast the Guomindang has
gone through astonishing tribulations, has committed its excesses, has survived a major war with unbelievable prestige, and is now throwing everything
away at a frightening rate, because the revolutionary faith is gone and has been
replaced by the smell of corruption and decay."

Almost from the start the Communist tactics succeeded, while those of the
Nationalists failed. In the fall of 1946, as the civil war intensified, Chiang's
American advisers were pessimistic, but being traditional military men, if anything they overestimated the value of American military gear in a war like this
and underestimated how successful yet simple the Communist order of battle
was. They imagined Chiang's forces ultimately mired in another protracted
struggle, eventually leading to an uneasy stalemate, perhaps with a geographic
division of the country, the Communists getting the north and the Nationalists
the south. They did not understand the particular dynamic of a political war
like this, that the forces and the balance would not stay static. Once the dynamic no longer favored the Nationalists—and that happened with surprising
speed—it would favor the Communists at an ever accelerating pace. "No one
anticipated the speed and skill with which the Chinese Communists would be
able to transfer their anti-Japanese guerrilla campaign into campaigns of mobile warfare," wrote John Fairbank and Albert Feuerwerker in their *Cambridge
History of China*.

Actually, one person had. In the days when Chiang's forces were at their
strongest and had attained some early successes, Mao had not lost his faith,
nor his essential belief that his forces were infinitely closer to the average peasant than Chiang's. In the summer of 1946, when there was a brief armistice,
Robert Payne, a distinguished British historian, visited Mao in his redoubt in
Yenan. Near the end of a prolonged interview, Mao, clearly tired, asked if there
were any more questions. "One more," Payne answered. "How long would it
take for the Chinese Communists to conquer China if the armistice breaks

down?" "A year and a half," Mao answered. It was said, Payne noted, slowly and with absolute conviction, and it proved surprisingly accurate. By mid-1948, the war was virtually over and Chiang's forces were in almost complete retreat. But at the time it had seemed like the wildest of boasts.

At first there had been, on the surface at least, some apparent Nationalist victories; some cities and towns were recaptured from the Communists. But whether they were victories or not was always a question—they might have been part of a larger Communist strategy of bait and wait. The Nationalists took cities and then remained stationary; the Communists had to move constantly and were highly mobile. The Communists learned to be nimble, to move quickly at night. They perfected the art of the ambush. They used tactics "of feint and deceit that seemed to place them everywhere and nowhere," as one American historian noted. Often they would feint a frontal assault against a Nationalist unit while keeping their main force at the rear in well-prepared positions, ready to inflict a brutal pounding on the retreating—and terrified—Nationalist troops (a tactic they would employ again with some significant success against the Americans in the early days of the Korean War). They would often strike at night, when the Nationalists were least prepared. Because of their connection with the peasants, and because their men had often infiltrated Chiang's units, they had excellent intelligence. They seemed to know every move the Nationalists were going to make. When the Communists lost men in combat, they were able, because of their superior political skills, to recruit more quite readily from their abundant local peasant base.

By May 1947, Chiang's offensive had ground to a halt. His poorly led forces, spread too thin, their supply lines too extended, were bottled up in cities, their morale dropping almost daily. They had become bogged down and vulnerable before their commanders even realized it. By the end of the summer of 1947, Mao and his people estimated that of his 248 brigades Chiang had committed 218 to his offensive and had already lost over 97 of them, or nearly 800,000 men. Some Americans, even back in the United States, were becoming frustrated with Chiang. "Why, if he is a generalissimo, doesn't he generalize?" asked an angry Senator Tom Connally, the Democrat who was chairman of the Senate Foreign Relations Committee.

The Communists were getting very little aid from the Russians—a source of eventual tension between Mao and Stalin. By contrast, the Nationalists had become ever more dependent on the Americans. That they were turning over American-made weapons to their enemies at what the Americans thought was an alarming rate did not seem to bother them—the solution was to ask for more. In the middle of 1947, Wellington Koo, the very well-connected, extremely supple Nationalist ambassador to Washington, dropped in on George

Marshall, by then secretary of state. The frustrated Marshall, sick of what Chiang's armies were doing in the field, and equally sick of the political problems that men like Koo were causing for the administration in Washington, told Koo that Chiang "was the worst advised military commander in history." That did not stop Koo from asking for more weapons. "He is losing about 40 percent of his supplies to the enemy," Marshall told Koo and added sardonically, "If the percentage should reach 50 percent he will have to decide whether it is wise to continue to supply his troops." Chiang Kai-Shek, Mao would later comment laconically, "was our supply officer." When Weifang and Jinan fell in 1948, David Barr, the last American senior military adviser to Chiang's army, added, "The Communists had more of our equipment than the Nationalists did."

With the Manchurian city of Shenyang about to fall in late October 1948, Colonel Dave Barrett, the assistant military attaché, and John Melby went to the airport in the capital, Nanjing, hoping to hop a plane north to survey the contested areas. But no planes were going north. They had all been commandeered to bring out the Nationalist generals, their girlfriends, and their personal wealth. Barrett turned to Melby: "John, I've seen all I need to see. When the generals begin to evacuate their gold bars and their concubines, the end is at hand." That so obvious and sad a collapse of a regime was taking place was one thing; what made the political situation back in America much more dangerous and explosive was all the extremely influential people who for a variety of political reasons and loyalties refused to tell the truth when they were back in America, or who tempered their reporting to make it seem that America had failed Chiang, rather than that Chiang had failed himself, his people, and his ally. What infuriated John Melby and many of the people trying to report honestly on the fall of Chiang was the duplicity of various American figures, who spoke one way about Chiang and why he was failing when they were in China; then, on return to the United States, feeling the domestic pro-Chiang political pressure, switched their line, refused to find fault with him, and became powerful voices for the China Lobby, placing all blame for his failures on the administration and the State Department's China Hands, who had been warning of Chiang's flaws and a future Communist victory. It was as if there was one truth that you told in China, when you were surrounded by other Americans and Chinese who knew how pathetically Chiang's forces had fought, and another you told back in the States, surrounded by conservative friends who wanted *their* truths reinforced.

The symbol of it, in Melby's view, was the performance of General Albert Wedemeyer. In the summer of 1947, George Marshall, delighted to be out of China, had sent Wedemeyer, an old friend of Chiang's, on a fact-finding mission.

Generally considered an exceptionally able staff officer, Wedemeyer was a fierce anti-Communist, so it was a calculated risk on Marshall's part, reflecting his belief that Wedemeyer's ideology would be subordinated to his sense of reality. The Wedemeyer trip also represented a shrewd hope on Marshall's part that the reactions of someone as conservative and pro-Chiang as Wedemeyer, after confronting the terrible reality on the ground in China, might help lessen right-wing pressure on the administration. In fact, the Wedemeyer visit did work in the short run, but in the long run it backfired. Within a few days of his arrival, Wedemeyer cabled Marshall that the Nationalists were "spiritually insolvent." The people had lost confidence in their leadership. By contrast, he noted, the Communists had "excellent spirit, almost a fanatical fervor." The government, he decided, was "corrupt, reactionary, and inefficient." Later, asked what had gone wrong with Chiang's cause, Wedemeyer said, "Lack of spirit, primarily lack of spirit. It was not lack of equipment. In my opinion they could have defended the Yangtze with broomsticks if they had the will to do it."

On August 22, 1947, just before Wedemeyer's return home, he was scheduled to speak to a meeting of Nationalist ministers. He had been told by his old friend Chiang to be blunt, but the Gimo, playing a dual game, as he often did, had promptly called John Leighton Stuart, the American ambassador, and suggested Wedemeyer should speak carefully and not be too critical of the Chinese Army. Stuart, however, told Wedemeyer that time was running out and there should be no more niceties. As such, Wedemeyer was brutally blunt. The government, he said, had little support among the people; its failures had allowed the Communists to succeed; it was spiritually bankrupt. It was a devastating moment. One top Chinese official openly wept. The next night a farewell dinner had been scheduled at Stuart's residence. But at the last minute, the Gimo canceled, claiming illness. Missimo, however, would come. Wedemeyer did not need that, so he canceled the dinner.

But soon, back in America, the dedicated anti-Communist Wedemeyer reappeared, pushing the China Lobby line that Chiang had been brought down by a lack of aid and by treachery within the American mission. In December 1947, he went before the Senate Appropriations Committee, where the chairman, Styles Bridges, himself an important player in the China Lobby, asked him about Chiang. The Gimo was, Wedemeyer said, "a fine character, and you gentlemen on this committee would admire him and respect him." Was it urgent, Bridges pressed, to send more military supplies to him? Wedemeyer, who while in China had recommended no further commitment of aid, answered in the affirmative. And did Wedemeyer think the United States had kept its promises to Chiang over the years? "No sir, I do not." The reality and politics of China were clearly different from the reality and politics of Washington.

The end in China came surprisingly quickly. On November 5, 1948, three days after Harry Truman's surprise victory in the presidential election, the embassy in Nanjing advised all Americans in China to leave. At virtually the same time, Mao was warned by Anastas Mikoyan, special envoy from the ever cautious Joseph Stalin, not to let his armies cross the Yangtze River into southern China too hastily, lest it provoke the Americans to enter the Chinese civil war. On January 21, 1949, Chiang turned over nominal control of the Nationalist government to proxies and moved with his gold reserves to Taiwan, making himself into, as a State Department bulletin put it, "a refugee on a small island off the coast of China," having thrown away "greater military power than any ruler had ever had in the history of China." On April 21, 1949, Mao's forces crossed the Yangtze River. Three days later, they took Nanjing, the Nationalist capital. The end was now in sight.

Truman, Acheson, and Marshall had been aware since 1947 of what they wanted in China, a systematic disengagement, with as little participation in the ongoing civil war as possible, and of course with as little domestic political blowback as possible. Like the fall of the tsarist regime during World War I, Chiang's collapse was driven by powerful historic forces far beyond the influence of American policy: a country that was already rotting and barely held together, crushed by the additional weight of a cataclysmic world war. There was, however, a significant difference between the collapse of tsarist Russia and that of Nationalist China. There had never been a powerful Russian lobby in America to mobilize American opinion in the years after the collapse of the Romanov family. The Russian Orthodox Church, to the extent that it existed in the United States, was not connected personally to ordinary Americans as the churches of Protestant and Catholic missionaries to China were. Russia had never been considered America's, and thus could not be lost by America, whereas China was America's, and thus had been lost by America.

And so the fall of Chiang left a gaping opening in the American political fabric. On the domestic political front no one was interested in talking about the tragic inevitability of it. What the administration wanted was some time so that Truman might one day be able to deal with the new Chinese leaders and see if they could be at least partially separated from Moscow. Out of that might have come a new policy that could eventually have ended with the recognition of Mao's China, something, it was then mistakenly believed, that Mao and the others in his government badly wanted. It was not to be.

THE COLLAPSE OF Chiang's China quickly became a defining American political issue. Normally the failure of a regime like that would have made only a modest blip in American politics. But this was a different time. After Chiang finally fell in 1949, much was written about how the United States had betrayed him. The reporting on the coming collapse had been spotty and at least partially politicized: Chiang had powerful allies in American journalism, like Harry Luce, and Roy Howard of the Scripps Howard chain, who had effectively censored the news filed by their correspondents.

The issue was perfect for the Republicans. Chiang's failure was an obvious manifestation of the issue of subversion that they had decided to use after Dewey's defeat. The fact that Chiang ended up on Taiwan made it an issue that would never go away. Ironically, those who had correctly warned that Chiang was not going to make it found themselves on the defensive, accused of undercutting him because they were leftists. The State Department's China Hands were quickly scattered and hidden away in places as distant as possible, lest their careers be damaged even more for having reported accurately. The one important military man who might have made the case of Chiang's failures, Joe Stilwell, had died in October 1946. The administration found itself in a particularly difficult bind: its Republican critics were shrewdly connecting Chiang to the issue that was paramount for Truman and Acheson, collective security in Europe. Truman and Acheson would not be able to get what they wanted for the Marshall Plan to rebuild a shattered Western Europe unless they compromised on China, their policies in Europe effectively held hostage to the approval of their enemies on China.

The administration was very quickly losing the propaganda battle, and so the political battle as well. When, in 1949, Acheson authorized the State Department to put together and make public a China White Paper, a definitive documentary history of how Chiang had failed despite vast amounts of American aid, it proved to be a failure on both sides of the Pacific. In the United States, it was regarded as one last kick administered to a faltering regime, and enraged the China Lobby; in China, Mao seized on it as incontestable evidence—produced by the Americans themselves—that America had constantly worked against his China. It was proof positive the Americans were the enemies of China.

So the administration had played the game out, going through the motions of aiding Chiang, knowing nothing good could possibly come of it, only in order *not* to have U.S. fingerprints on the eventual collapse that the Americans were certain was coming. That was true not just of the Democrats, but of some of the Republicans as well. In 1948, when Bourke Hickenlooper, a conservative Iowa senator, went to Arthur Vandenberg, his political leader, to ask him if a $570 million China aid bill would really do any good, Vandenberg answered, as Thomas Christensen has written, "At least the China collapse would not be placed on the shoulders of the American government." What was important, Vandenberg said, was popular opinion, which greatly favored aid even to a dying China—"We are undertaking to resist Communist aggression, and we are ignoring one area completely and letting it completely disintegrate without even a gesture of assistance."

THE END CAME, but the end was not the end, for political reasons. The United States could not disengage as it wanted to, because Chiang's political constituency in America had become far too powerful. Without either side understanding it, the United States and Mao's China had already begun moving almost inexorably toward a military collision.

If the administration was being attacked back home for doing too little, then in Beijing, in the new China, it was being denounced for having given too much to help save Chiang. In the eyes of Mao and his colleagues, America's acts were not innocent. In their view, U.S. fingerprints had been everywhere on the civil war. The Americans had financed Chiang from 1941 to 1949. U.S. planes and naval transports had ferried his troops to the northern reaches of China in 1945 to take the Japanese surrender. Neutral observers did not do that. In American minds, it was a small bit of help, the minimal the United States could really do—but to Mao and his top people it was egregious interference in their country and in their war. To them, America had acted exactly the way a rich capitalist nation was expected to act.

Out of all of this had come an emboldened new force in American politics, the China Lobby. It was a loose alliance of people brought together for very different reasons. It connected powerful, shrewd, and extremely wealthy members of Chiang's own family, often working in Washington or there on special assignment, to influential conservative American political and journalistic allies and friends. It was at once amorphous, and yet all too real, and highly fo-

cused. It was influential, for a variety of reasons, far beyond its numbers. It became in its time the most powerful lobby that had ever operated for a foreign
power in Washington. What it wanted initially was fairly simple: massive aid to
Chiang for as long as possible. In the late 1940s, in the ever more likely event
that the Communists won, it wanted the United States to continue to view
Chiang's regime as China, and to block any recognition on Washington's part
of Mao's regime; it wanted to keep the new China out of the UN; and finally it
wanted to sustain aid to Chiang on Taiwan. What this lobby wanted, now that
Chiang had lost the war, was for the United States to act *as if he had actually
won the war.* What they really hoped for someday was an unlikely cataclysm
that might send Chiang's forces triumphantly back to the mainland under an
American banner; something, say, like a war between the United States and
China.

The people in the China Lobby came together in some cases because of a
genuine love of China as it once had been—at least in their imaginations—
and a belief that somehow Chiang for all his myriad faults was its only possible leader if it was challenged by the Communists. In other cases, the reasons
for supporting the Generalissimo were ignoble and hopelessly selfish, sometimes little more than the fact that working for the Chinese Nationalists often
paid so well. For a good many people, seizing on the issue was a chance to get
even after a prolonged period of Democratic Party hegemony. Some, like Congressman Walter Judd, who had been a medical missionary as a young man, or
like Henry Luce, the son of a missionary, were not merely China Firsters, but
Chiang Firsters, men who believed as an article of faith that the one great truth
of this struggle was that Chiang and China were one and the same. Many of
them had no love for the Europe First policies that had dominated American
foreign policy for so long and were looking to shift America's essential anti-
Communist focus to the Pacific, where they felt our future lay.

For the China Firsters who had grown up in China as the children of missionaries, that country's pull was deep and unrelenting; China was in some
ways as much their home and their native country as the United States was. In
addition, to say that Chiang had failed was to say that their own parents, who
had devoted their lives to bringing Christianity to China, had been failures (as
indeed, in at least the narrow sense of their mission, they *had* failed). In the fall
of 1946, on one of his trips to China, Luce had been engaged by John Melby,
who suggested that his singular commitment to Chiang rather than to China
was a mistake. Luce immediately rejected Melby's suggestion with an exceptionally revealing answer. "You've got to remember," he answered, "that we
were born here. This is all we've ever known. We had made a lifetime commitment to the advancement of Christianity in China. And now you're attacking

us for it. You're asking us to say that all our lives have been wasted; they've been futile. They've been lived for nothing. That's a pretty tough thing to ask of anyone isn't it?" It was, Melby agreed, but it had to be done because the world and China had changed, because the China they knew was dying.

But it was that kind of passion—and nostalgia—that fueled no small amount of the success of the China Lobby. Much of the political activity was initially directed out of the Chinese embassy in Washington and, for a time near the end in 1948, when Madame Chiang came to this country for an extended stay, from her brother-in-law's home in Riverdale, New York. Chiang's two brothers-in-law, T. V. Soong and H. H. Kung (as well as Wellington Koo, the ambassador in Washington), were very good at the game they were playing. T. V. Soong had once warned John Paton Davies, a talented foreign service officer, and one of the ablest of the China Hands, that there was no State Department memo sent from China that he did not have access to within two or three days. These top Nationalists sometimes seemed to understand how Washington worked better than their American counterparts did, and they had allies throughout the government, a number of powerful Republican senators and even a few renegade Democrats, like Pat McCarran of Nevada. Certainly, though, their greatest ally, the most important man to the lobby, the one who brought a group of people who otherwise might be considered on the fringe of politics and gave them and their cause far greater legitimacy, was not a politician at all, but the most important publisher of the era, Henry Luce.

No one was more critical to the pro-Chiang alliance than Luce—he gave it a national voice perceived as coming from the political center rather than the far right, and he worked hard to suppress any views contrary to his own. Since he was the most partisan of men, and a passionate Republican—"my second church" he called the party—liberal Democrats were always going to be on the defensive in his universe. Some of the other China Firsters had little political respectability, but Luce could manage to change the political balance and to cast doubts on centrists whose more realistic views on what was happening in China he abhorred. Few of the others in the China Lobby were his normal political allies; more often than not they were isolationists, and he was quite possibly the leading Republican internationalist of that time, and thus their sworn enemy at the Republican conventions of 1940, 1944, 1948, and in time, 1952. But he went after anyone who might oppose him on China with ferocity, crushing without hesitation whomever got in his way. He savaged careers—political, diplomatic, and journalistic—without much anguish, or worry about normal moral or journalistic ethics. Those who suffered because of what his magazines wrote deserved their fate, he believed, for straying from his truth, disagreeing with him, or getting in his way.

He was the son of missionary parents in China, brilliant, unusually awkward socially, with a great raw intelligence and a restless natural curiosity. At Hotchkiss, his prep school, and then at Yale, he had been a poor boy, out of step with everyone, always a bit too eager, his parents not connected to the parents of his elite classmates. He always wore the wrong clothes, outdated American styles from a very distant era, copied faithfully in heavy fabric by Chinese tailors. "Chink Luce" was his nickname, a most unwanted one. He once told the novelist Pearl Buck how he had hated prep school and college, because he had felt so different and so poor. As a publisher ever more successful, he became steadily more sure of his truths, chief among them his vision of what America could and should be in the twentieth century, the inventor as it were of the rather heady concept of the American Century. He was an odd mixture of parts that did not seem to mesh perfectly: the Calvinist as journalist; and yet when it came to those who opposed his ideas, he was more like a brutal Chinese warlord who took no prisoners. Early in his journalistic career he had not seemed that interested in rekindling his China connection; it had been very painful and he was busy shedding it, becoming more American than the native sons he had failed to charm at school. But in 1932, at the age of thirty-four, already a stunning success as an editor and publisher, he visited China and the connection was renewed. The Soong family, the wealthiest in China (and perhaps soon the world, because of American aid), played to him skillfully; they were far more adroit in manipulating powerful Westerners, saying all the right things and getting what they wanted, than Westerners were in playing them. He decided in those fateful days that all of China might become a nation of people just like this remarkable family: sophisticated, Christian, capitalist, and seemingly grateful—and that the task of bringing China to this wondrous new incarnation and away from its cruel, heathen past was now nothing less than the *mission* of America in the American Century. He had left China after that visit with his greatest cause.

About no subject did he become more obsessive, or more partisan. When Luce and his wife, the writer and politician Clare Boothe Luce, visited the Gimo and Missimo in 1941, he came away writing that he "had made the acquaintance of two people, a man and a woman, who out of all the millions now living, will be remembered for centuries and centuries." More than any other American, Luce romanticized (and popularized) the modernism that Chiang supposedly represented. No other American was as influential in creating the illusion of a China under Chiang that wanted to be like America. If Chiang's government had been only partially as successful and effective and noble as it was portrayed in the pages of Luce's publications, if Chiang had only had a modicum of the talent that Luce attributed to him, there would have been no China crisis, and the Communists would have been easily defeated.

Nothing could dissuade him not merely of the idea that China wanted a destiny shaped by Americans but of the notion that Chiang and his family were the people to lead the way. Any American political figure who dared get in his way would be destroyed; any information that his talented *Time* and *Life* reporters in the field came up with that revealed the systematic failures of Chiang and the steady rise of the Communists was almost surely going to be censored. No amount of evidence about why Chiang had failed could change his mind—instead he turned ever more venomously on those who collected it. For a long time he hoped that the Korean War might be the way to help bring Chiang back to the mainland. "Harry," his sister, Elisabeth Moore, once told Alan Brinkley, his biographer, "was always looking for the opportunity to over-throw the communist regime in China. He knew that the United States could not simply declare war on the communists, but he thought that the wars the communists started could give us the opportunity to go into China. Part of him really wanted the Korean War to become an American war with China, and he talked about Vietnam in the early 1950s in the same way."

Whether he was a true blue China Lobby member was a fascinating question. Certainly on this one most compelling issue there was an instant solidarity, and he was by far the most important member of the China front. But for the most part he and the other China Lobby people were strange bedfellows. "He was," wrote Brinkley, "more an enabler for them than a real member. He was a genuine internationalist and they were for the most part, and on most issues, isolationists." Most of them were deep down more likely to be the constituents of Colonel Robert McCormick, and McCormick, the leading isolationist of an era, was a political enemy, constantly mocked in Luce's pages. For McCormick, Luce was also normally the enemy, the man who had helped secure the Republican nomination for Wendell Willkie, then Tom Dewey (twice), and finally Dwight Eisenhower. What nonetheless bound them in a rather temporary embrace was China.

Luce's hatred of Acheson because of China became almost pathological. In private he would refer to him as "that bastard." When the North Koreans first crossed the thirty-eighth parallel, he felt vindicated, and ordered his editorial writers to produce what John Shaw Billings, the first editor of *Life* and for more than two decades one of the most important editorial figures in the Luce empire, noted was to be a "self-serving-I-told-you-so editorial on the reversal of Truman's policy towards China." From the moment the Korean War started, *Time* had Acheson in its sights, and by January 1951 it wrote of him, "What people thought of Dean Gooderham Acheson ranged from the proposition that he was a fellow traveler, or a wool brained sower of 'seeds of jackassery,' or an abysmally uncomprehending man, or a warmonger who was taking the

U.S. into a world war, to the warm, if not so audible defense that he was a great Secretary of State."

Both *Time* and *Life*, though more sophisticated than most of their competitors, could, when it truly mattered—in time for presidential elections for example—become naked instruments of their publisher's will. Rarely was the political bias of the Luce publications so clear, however, as in their coverage of China. Luce did his part for the China Firsters by, among other things, censoring or suppressing the reporting out of China by a man who was arguably his greatest journalist of that period, Theodore White. It might be that Luce could not turn night into day, but he most assuredly could take White's dispatches in the field describing defeat after defeat and turn them into reports on victory after victory. White by then had become accustomed to having his work completely rewritten. He had once put a sign on his office door saying, "Any resemblance to what is written here and what is printed in *Time* magazine is purely coincidental." Theirs had been a constant battle—both loved China, but White thought of Chiang as a complete failure and believed that China had to find itself and emerge in a new incarnation all its own. In the fall of 1944, when the struggle between Chiang and Stilwell had reached its height and Roosevelt had decided to relieve him, the general had summoned two influential reporters whom he trusted, White and Brooks Atkinson of the *New York Times*, for a prolonged interview on why he was being called back and why China's cause was so hopeless. For both White and Atkinson it was a great journalistic moment: "This ignorant son of a bitch has never wanted to fight the Japanese. . . . Every major blunder of this war is traceable to Chiang." The story was so big that Atkinson had flown out with Stilwell a few days later on the general's plane, to make sure he avoided the censors, and won the Pulitzer Prize for his reporting; White's thirteen-page report was turned absolutely upside down and made, in his words, "so fanciful, so violently pro-Chiang that it could only mislead American opinion—which it was Luce's duty and mine to guard against."

The administration had been on the defensive about China and subversion from almost the moment World War II ended. At home Truman, under pressure from the right, toughened the government's loyalty and security procedures. In foreign affairs, the China Hands were now conveniently blamed for the very events they had warned were about to take place. In retrospect they would be viewed as one of the most brilliant and talented groups of foreign service officers the State Department ever sent to a foreign venue. But starting in the mid-1940s, off they were packed to Liverpool and Dublin and Switzerland and Peru and British Columbia and Norway and New Zealand. Ray Ludden, one of the more talented of them, went in short order from Dublin to

Brussels to Paris to Stockholm—anywhere but Asia. "From 1949 on I was just putting in my time," he once said. "I couldn't get a job as dog-catcher." In time their personal tragedies became their country's tragedy, as the government made itself blind in an area that would become so important—and where it was critically important, because the forces at play were so volatile and revolutionary, to separate what you did not like from what threatened you. None of the China Hands was a real player in October 1950 when American forces crossed the thirty-eighth parallel heading north, and none would be a player when the key Vietnam decisions were made some fifteen years later.

In the beginning, the purge had been aimed at relatively low- and middle-level officials, but by 1948, the China Lobby people were desperate, ready and willing to go after bigger game. And perhaps the best way of understanding that period when the political debate became so bitter and ugly is to consider that the China Lobby leadership next chose to turn its energies against George Catlett Marshall. He had been a friend of China as a young man, had served there as a young officer, and had always retained that sense of friendship, so that when Madame Chiang came to the United States in late 1948 to plead her case both in Washington and with the American public, she had stayed with the Marshalls in Virginia. Marshall had turned away from Chiang reluctantly, not out of personal pique but because it was so obvious that his China was dying and could not be resuscitated and because Marshall placed the interests of the United States above those of Chiang. It was, he understood, the most fateful and difficult of decisions—giving up on an ally and accepting as the victor in the Chinese civil war an alien, hostile leadership likely to make the world a more difficult and dangerous place. That his patriotism was now under attack because of Chiang's collapse told more about the era than about Marshall himself.

In 1945, when World War II had ended, if there was one American who seemed to stand above any partisan issue and to have earned the gratitude of the entire nation it was George Marshall, the most selfless and least ideological of men, "the great one of the age," in Truman's admiring words. He had, by then, been the primary architect of America's amazingly quick mobilization during World War II. He had taken a small, pathetic, understrength, and under-equipped Army that reflected the country's innocence and isolationism in 1941 and shaped it into the mighty force that crossed the English Channel only two and a half years later. Many ordinary Americans agreed with the president that Marshall seemed, at war's end, the greatest living American; some military people, like Matt Ridgway, thought of him as the greatest American to wear the uniform since George Washington. It was a reflection of the vast divide China had created in American politics that, only five years later, as the man who had been the final arbiter of aid to Chiang, even Marshall was vulnerable, not merely his judgments but his very patriotism questioned.

During World War II, *Time* had always been lavish in its praise of Marshall. The case against him then needed an explanation on the part of his enemies, of why he had turned against the Gimo. The answer, first articulated by the ever deft Wellington Koo in the Washington embassy, was simple: Marshall had become bitter and disenchanted because he had failed so dismally in his mission to that country. It was a poor answer containing no small amount of irony, for if there was ever a public servant who separated duty from ego, it was Marshall. Yet even that would not be enough. Luce's *Time* let him know in a March 1947 cover story that he was about to undergo a new kind of scrutiny. Had he continued to favor aid to China, there would have been no limit to the adjectives used to describe him—he would have been portrayed as the most Spartan of men, cool, decisive, knowledgeable, ready to do in a time of peace what he had done so skillfully in a time of war. Instead, *Time* asked a single, ominous question: "Is Marshall big enough for the gigantic task ahead of him?" It was a warning shot: get aboard, or we will take you out. More, there was a vitally important additional coda: if Luce and the China Lobby could damage the reputation or at least neutralize someone as towering as Marshall, then it was open season on everyone.

In mid-May 1947, Luce met with Wellington Koo, and much of their talk was given over to Marshall. By then Koo knew—from his own talks with Marshall a few days earlier—that the secretary of state feared that the Nationalists were already a lost cause. In effect, it was Koo who decided that they had a Marshall problem. Luce was more optimistic, because Marshall had been an ally in so many other battles. He was sure, he told Koo, that Marshall of all people understood the threat of Communism as others in the Truman administration did not. Luce was very firm: Marshall would understand what Luce called "the great inconsistency between his China policy and the present U.S. world policy." Koo said Luce told him, "Either he [Marshall] would change the China policy by bringing it into harmony with U.S. world policy or he would be discredited." "If he did not change it," Koo added, "Mr. Luce told me, *Time* magazine, which he controlled, would point out the inconsistencies. But Luce believed George Marshall would change the policy, that he was too intelligent not to."

When Marshall did not bend to the will of the China Lobby and the needs of the Luce empire, the line became that he himself was not a leftist or a Communist, but that he had shielded others at the State Department who were. Worse yet, he was getting his information—his lessons on China—from the wrong people. Or as Indiana's Senator William Jenner, a sub-McCarthy McCarthy, eventually put it: "General Marshall is not only willing, he is eager to play the role of a front man for traitors. The truth is this is no new role for him, for General George C. Marshall is a living lie." When someone eventually mentioned Jenner's attack to him, Marshall later said, "Jenner? Jenner? I do not believe I know the man."

If discrediting the people who were seen as discrediting Chiang was one part of Luce's attempt to keep his regime viable in American political terms, then the other part was no less shrewdly targeted. The idea again originated with Wellington Koo. The Chinese embassy people were aware not only of their own growing isolation from the Truman administration but of the administration's thin support on the issue that was central to its own vision of an enlightened foreign policy: greater collective security in Europe. Administration officials were uniformly intent on stabilizing the war-damaged European economies through the Marshall Plan, and Greece and Turkey via what became known as the Truman Doctrine, all as a bulwark against possible Soviet expansionism. It was Koo's idea to tie aid to China to all other foreign policy bills. From now on, there would be no aid to Greece and Turkey, no money for European recovery, without a Chinese aid kicker. "Are we men in Europe and mice in Asia?" Senator Styles Bridges of New Hampshire, one of the most forceful, asked during a Senate hearing, and it was a perfect description of the new position of the Asia Firsters. For the Truman administration, increasingly besieged and lacking broad national support for its foreign aid packages, it was a kind of political blackmail.

THE SPECIFIC ISSUE being used against Truman was China, but the assault was far broader than that. Much of the anger that had been collecting came out of the Midwest, from people who were instinctively, indeed passionately, Anglophobic and who had felt during the world war that Americans had been brought in to settle someone else's mess, and that all subsequent U.S. efforts to build up an exhausted postwar Europe were nothing more than America trying to do England's work for it. These Midwestern conservatives did not see the rebuilding of Europe as part of a new self-interest in a world where, because of modern weaponry, the Atlantic Ocean had shrunk. They were, as Thomas Christensen, a Princeton professor, called them, *Asialationists*. It was as if each party had its own ocean. The Pacific, wrote Richard Rovere and Arthur Schlesinger in 1951, had long been the Republican ocean; the Atlantic, the Democratic one. Even Bob Taft, normally wary of any foreign entanglements, seemed to favor the Pacific. "I believe very strongly that the Far East is ultimately even more important to our future peace than is Europe." The Republicans who were challenging the administration on China had little stake in U.S. policies of recent years. The Democrats, as John Spanier, a prominent political scientist, shrewdly pointed out, had never involved any leading Republican congressional figure in their policy making on China. When Chiang's forces began to collapse, Senator Brien McMahon, a Connecticut Democrat and a member of the Senate Foreign Relations Committee, decided to check out whether there had been any Republican senatorial dissent from official policy in the crucial years from 1947 to 1949. He found not a single suggestion for a changed China policy from any member; nor had any Republican ever stood up in the House or Senate and advocated sending American combat troops there to support Chiang. They had had no answer to the questions Senator Tom Connally of Texas, one of Truman's defenders, had asked his Republican colleague Arthur Vandenberg: "Would you send your own sons to fight in the Chinese Civil War?"

That question was one Vandenberg, a critical bipartisan figure of the period, was already wrestling with as his party began to split apart in those days. He was one of the centrist Republicans who was becoming very nervous about the far right's exploitation of the China issue even as Chiang continued to collapse. It might, Vandenberg warned some of his colleagues, become a two-edged blade if the GOP came to power. Thus, in September 1948 Vandenberg, a potential secretary of state if the Republicans won, wrote to Senator Bill Knowland, one of the leading China Firsters, warning him against pushing the China issue too hard, lest the Republicans soon inherit it. "It is easy," he wrote, "to sympathize with Chiang as I always have, and still do. But it is quite another thing to plan resultful aid short of armed American aid and with American combat troops when practically all of our American-trained and American-equipped divisions surrender without firing a shot."

So the loss of China was merely the visible part of the iceberg, the issue that might help them recover control of the country, making it once again their America. Theirs was the America of the turn of the century, an America of sound business practices and old-fashioned virtues, of which they were exemplars. They did not owe money and did not depend on the government to employ them. They were the town leaders in an era when that leadership was almost exclusively white, male, and Protestant, and they were largely professional men, in an age when the middle class was still narrow. They belonged to civic clubs where almost everyone they knew felt much as they did about the drift of the country away from what they considered Americanism. The New Deal—and the forces that it had opened the door to—was the enemy. Or, as Senator Hugh Butler of Nebraska had said before the 1946 election: "If the New Deal is still in control of the Congress after the election, it will owe that control to the Communist Party in this country." These men were instinctively nativist, believing it a strength, not a weakness. They neither liked nor trusted the America that had elected Franklin Roosevelt and Harry Truman, the big-city America of Catholics, Jews, Negroes, and unions. They distrusted anything or anyone that was different; and now it was time to get even. Roosevelt's America was a *them* and worse, a them that had run the country for almost twenty years.

Both Truman and Acheson were aware of the political game being played, and they were contemptuous of the men who were leading this gathering force. "The primitives," Acheson called them. "The animals," Truman said. Truman had known from the start that China was a loser in both domestic political and foreign policy. At a cabinet meeting in March 1947, the president had complained bitterly about their Chinese allies. As he wrote in his diary, "Chiang Kai Shek will not fight it out. [The] Communists will fight it out—they are fanatical. It [more aid] would be pouring money down a rathole under [the] present situation." The president was, in fact, furious at Chiang and his government and had been since the moment he had taken office. In his mind, he had been handed a failed policy and a treacherous, dishonest ally. There had been some quiet governmental investigations of where the aid money was going, and an immense amount of suspicious currency speculation on the part of Chiang's family had been noted. The Nationalists, Truman said, were nothing but "grafters and crooks. I'll bet you that a billion dollars of [the aid] is in New York banks today," he once told David Lilienthal, a New Dealer and public power advocate who had helped create the Tennessee Valley Authority.

What enraged Truman—and rage was the proper word—was the relentless quality of the political pressure applied by the Nationalists without any compensating military performance on their part. It went against everything he believed in—a government that would not fight, but attacked him politically and constantly demanded more weapons, which its troops did not deign to use. There was one particularly revealing meeting Truman had with Ambassador Koo on November 24, 1948, that reflected (in a phrase that would come into currency in a future war) the vast credibility gap the Nationalists now had. Truman was all too aware as he and Koo sat down together that he was dealing not just with the representative of a troubled foreign nation but with a major political enemy; that Koo, for all his considerable charm, was a de facto leader of a large part of the political opposition and that the embassy had been extremely close to Tom Dewey, whom Truman had just defeated.

Koo's timing could not have been worse, and his condescension toward the American president obvious. "I spoke American to him, rather than English, and we got along perfectly in our talk," Koo later noted. It was not an ideal time for the representative of a dying regime to ask for more military aid. Truman did not seem at all receptive. Did Koo know, the president asked, that he had just received information about *thirty-two* Chinese divisions surrendering to the Communists up around Xuzhou? And that they had turned over all of their equipment to the Communists? No, as a matter of fact, Koo did not know about it, he admitted. On the subject of aid, Truman told Koo, he knew the Chinese people had suffered a great deal and he would talk to Marshall, but that was all he would volunteer. What went unsaid was that thirty-two divisions meant that perhaps 250,000 to 300,000 men had gone over, with a comparable amount of equipment, and that this was not an isolated incident. As soon as Koo left the White House, he checked in with a friend, George Yeh, the vice minister for foreign affairs. How was the battle for Xuzhou going? he asked. Not too badly, Yeh replied. But President Truman had just told him that thirty-two divisions had surrendered there. Was that true? Well yes, admitted Yeh. Such was truth, such was reality in the days when the Nationalist armies were unraveling.

In the final months before the Communist takeover, Major General David Barr, the head of the U.S. military assistance group, actually sat in on planning sessions with Chiang's senior staff as if he were a Chinese general (among other things pleading with them to destroy their gear before they retreated so that it would not be captured by the Communists, one of many suggestions that no one ever listened to). The last American ambassador to China, John Leighton Stuart, was not allowed to meet the senior Chinese Communist leadership because that might have incited the domestic critics of U.S. policy.

Still, if Chiang lost China, he had gained, if not all of Washington, enough political support to keep him in power in Taiwan. In 1952, just after Dwight Eisenhower's election to the presidency, there was a grand dinner party given by Wellington Koo, still Chiang's ambassador, attended by a few of the most powerful China Firsters—Henry Luce, Senators William Knowland, Pat McCarran, and Joe McCarthy, as well as Representative Walter Judd. At one point near the end of the evening they all rose as one and toasted Chiang with their favorite battle cry, "Back to the mainland!"

Part Five

The Last Roll of the Dice:
The North Koreans
Push to Pusan

IN KOREA A showdown was coming. In the early days of August 1950, North Korean forces prepared for their final assault against the still under-manned UN units aligned behind the Naktong River. But the In Min Gun offensive had been slowing down noticeably. The UN command had decided that the Naktong River offered the best barrier behind which their troops might be able to catch their breath, even as new forces were arriving in country from the States. Roy Appleman, the Army historian, described the Naktong as forming a huge moat that protected roughly three-quarters of the Pusan Perimeter. The perimeter, it should be noted, was not small, and so the fighting over the next few weeks took the form of hundreds of small battles and on occasion a few larger ones. Appleman described the Pusan Perimeter as a rectangle, running roughly one hundred miles north to south, fifty miles east to west, bordered by the Sea of Japan on the east, the Korean Strait on the south, and by the Naktong itself for much of its western boundary. The river itself was slow and muddy, no more than six feet deep at its deepest point and a quarter- to a half-mile wide. ("About as wide as the Missouri," said Private First Class Charles [Butch] Hammel of the Second Engineers, who had grown up about fifty miles from the Missouri and who helped build a bridge over the Naktong, just in time for the final big North Korean push, so that they, rather than the Americans, got to use it first.) Without the natural protection the Naktong offered, American forces might not have held. For them, it was more than a barrier; it became a place where Walker could concentrate his troops, and for the first time protect his flanks.

Inside the perimeter, things were getting better. Given the state of the roads and rail lines, there was, for the first time, a chance to bring reserve units up and into action quickly and effectively. Thus, plugging the holes in his lines became somewhat easier for Walker. In addition, in mid-July, the first elements of the Second Infantry Division had shipped out from the States for Korea, and at virtually the same time some elements of the First Marine Provisional Brigade arrived as well, a force that eventually became the First Marine Division and that would spearhead the Inchon landing. All of this added up to a change in the balance of forces: the fighting ability on the part of the American units was about to improve dramatically, and time was beginning to run out on the North Koreans. By the end of August, everyone in the American command knew that a major North Korean strike was coming. The North Korean units, preparing to strike from the north and west sides of the Naktong, were still formidable, some thirteen infantry divisions, averaging about seventy-five hundred men per division, plus an armored division of about one thousand men and two armored brigades of five hundred men each. Though it was still a well-trained army, everything that had come so easily to the North Koreans only a few weeks earlier was now becoming harder. The UN Air Force flew, for instance, twice as many missions in support of the UN troops in August as in July, grinding the North Koreans down, depriving them of food and ammo and logistic support and the ability to rest. By late August, when the decisive battles along the Naktong began, the In Min Gun's best days were already behind it, though few on either side realized this. In the words of T. R. Fehrenbach, who commanded an infantry unit there, it was already "bleeding to death." As Yoo Sung Chul, a retired North Korean general, said years later, "The Korean War was planned to last only a few days so we did not plan anything in case things might go wrong. If you fight a war without planning for failures, then you are asking for trouble."

By the time Kim Il Sung threw his thirteen divisions into the final battle of the Naktong on August 31, the force levels of the two sides were surprisingly equal, and elite American units were still arriving in country. For example, the last of the three regiments of the Second Infantry Division to arrive, the Thirty-eighth Regiment, reached Pusan on August 19. That meant, as some one hundred thousand North Koreans prepared for what they hoped would be the final battle and their assault on the port of Pusan, there were almost eighty thousand American troops from the Eighth Army ready to defend the Pusan Perimeter.

The ability of the Eighth Army to hold on in the previous two months represented an immense personal achievement for Johnnie Walker. Disrespected by both Tokyo and Washington, a tanker in tank-resistant terrain, a commander fighting a war with forces demonstrably weaker than those he had led in France and Germany, in those six or seven weeks from the end of July to the middle of September he was nothing less than a remarkable, fearless commander, doing almost everything right. If American military history has shortchanged any of this country's wars in the past century, it is Korea, and if any aspect of that war has been overlooked, it is the series of smaller battles fought along the Naktong in July, August, and September 1950, and if any one commander has not been given the credit he deserves, it is surely Walton Walker in those battles. "He was," his pilot Mike Lynch once said, "the forgotten commander of the forgotten war."

If the Korean War itself never captured the imagination of the American public, the fighting in the Naktong Bulge and along the Pusan Perimeter was vastly overshadowed by larger battles still to come; and yet in that terrible period it is possible that Walton Walker in Korea was a great commander. With his poorly prepared, poorly equipped, and badly undermanned forces, he was managing ever so slowly to put a brake on the advance of a talented, fierce adversary, even as the country he represented slowly began to accept its new responsibilities. When he had ordered his men to stand and die, he meant nothing less, and he included himself in that edict. If necessary, he intended to be the last American standing when the North Koreans made it to Pusan. One day in early September, he and Lynch—his constant companion—were in Taegu, quite an unimportant town to the rest of the planet before this war started, but by then for them a critical junction. If the North Koreans took Taegu, it might open the door for their army to strike at Pusan, a mere forty-five miles south. Walker had turned to Lynch and said, "You and I may finish up standing in the streets of Taegu fighting it out with these guys. My plan is that if they break through, you stay here with me. And then we'll stay here until the last minute."

Walker was tireless and fearless, flying in his tiny reconnaissance plane, sometimes just a few hundred feet above the ground, almost daring enemy machine guns to bring him down. He would lean out the window on occasion, screaming down at his troops through a bullhorn. If he thought they were retreating or panicking, he would yell at them to get back up on the line and fight, goddamn it! They flew so low that Lynch sometimes removed from the skin of the plane the requisite three stars signifying that this was the personal plane of a lieutenant general. As the history of the Korean War gradually unfolded, and as other commanders, most notably Matt Ridgway, came to the fore, Johnnie Walker faded into the background. What tended to be remembered, if anything at all, was that he had been one of the men victimized by the devastating giant Chinese ambush up along the Chongchon River in late November and early December, a folly that seriously damaged Walker's reputation, even though it had essentially taken place without his consent.

It was unfair, because in the Naktong fighting he patched units together with a deft touch, stealing a battalion from one regiment and lending it to another, using the Marines and the Twenty-seventh Wolfhounds as fire brigades to stanch potential North Korean breakthroughs. He used certain key advantages over his enemy well—greater mobility in this particular piece of real estate thanks to access to a simple but valuable rail system, and a simple but effective road system. The

North Koreans were at a deficit here—they could not shift their forces quickly enough to exploit momentary breakthroughs. Much of their failure in this period reflected weak battlefield planning, failure to concentrate their forces properly, and a failure to communicate effectively as well as shift forces quickly as a given battle required. The speed of battle against an army with the technological advantages of the Americans was escalating all the time—more hardware coming into the country made the pace of battle ever faster. Their limitations, the Americans thought, were not just weaknesses in their communications equipment but basic weaknesses in an army that was too hierarchically organized. To some of the men in the Eighth Army command, Walker seemed more like a magician than a commander, so nuanced was his sense of where the North Koreans were going to hit next. A magician he was not, but he was a very good listener: the North Koreans were using extremely primitive radio codes, which they did not change frequently enough, and the Americans had broken them. Often Walker did indeed know in advance exactly where the In Min Gun was planning to strike. That was one valuable source of information. Another was his own eyes. He and Lynch flew over the In Min Gun positions so often and so low that he had a surprisingly good idea of the enemy troop dispositions and how much they changed day to day.

Still, if there was one word to describe his situation, Walker thought that it was "desperate." He was always short of men and constantly fearful of a Communist breakthrough. He began each day by turning to Colonel Eugene Landrum, his chief of staff, and saying, "Landrum, how many reserves have you dug up for me today?" That was what they needed—more men; always, the call was for more men. For the possibility that the North Koreans might punch through to the sea was a very real one. The one place where Walker had significantly underestimated the In Min Gun's capacity was in the area called the Naktong Bulge, where the river briefly bent slightly to the west before it turned east. That created a small bulge that ran about five miles on a north-south line and about four miles on an east-west one. It became in time the scene of some of the heaviest fighting of the entire war. Because the Americans had pounded the North Korean Fourth Division in that area and had received quite good intelligence from prisoners about how badly beaten down the division was, they assumed North Korean assault capabilities were limited there. What they did not realize was that the enemy force in the Bulge now included not merely some elements of the Fourth but also elements of two other divisions, the Second and Ninth.

There, Walker had placed two of the three battalions of the Second Infantry Division's Twenty-third Regiment, the third being on loan to the First Cav. To say that they were stretched hopelessly thin would have been a singular understatement. Master Sergeant Harold Graham was then serving as an acting platoon leader in Charley Company of the First Battalion of the Twenty-third

Regiment of the Second U.S. Infantry Division. He had already been recommended for a battlefield commission and was waiting for the commission to come through, but ended up being so severely wounded on the first night of the major Communist offensive at the Naktong Bulge that his military career would essentially be ended. Graham estimated that the division, understrength, worn down by earlier fighting, and minus a regiment, totaled around nine thousand men, instead of its normal eighteen thousand men. It had to cover a front of almost forty miles, and the First Battalion of the Twenty-third, with perhaps four to five hundred men, was holding down an area of roughly three or four miles. "I'm not sure we were ever thinner on the ground before a major attack," said Joe Stryker, a platoon leader in Charley Company who had been reassigned to the regiment as a communications officer only a few days before and so was one of the few of them to make it through those days (and who would turn himself into an expert on what happened). "It was a trip wire, I guess, but the smallest, thinnest trip wire you ever imagined," he said. Those were astonishing figures, a description not so much of a genuine defensive position but of a giant human sieve. If every soldier in the battalion had his own helicopter, it might have been doable—but realistically, it was a hopeless task. It had been that way, Stryker remembered, from the moment they had first arrived in country. When he had taken up one of his first combat positions near the front, right after their arrival, he had done what you were always supposed to do in combat—scout out the friendly units on each side of you and work out communications with them. In this case he had gotten in his jeep and driven, and driven, and driven—in all about five miles. Finally he spotted two GIs. They were from the neighboring Twenty-fourth Division and seemed thrilled to see him—they cheered him as a symbol of the entire Second Division's arrival in Korea. He barely had the heart to tell them that he was positioned five miles away.

As the men of the Twenty-third Regiment waited for the attack, the sense of isolation was even more profound than usual. Later, Colonel Paul Freeman, the commander of the regiment, reflected that though Walker's intelligence on what the North Koreans were doing generally had proved extraordinarily accurate, at this one moment in this one area, he had missed it altogether. As August was coming to an end, the men in the First Battalion of the Twenty-third Regiment were aware that something big was coming. They had spent only two days on the east bank of the Naktong when the North Koreans made their major strike. The Second Battalion had moved up behind them, first to the village of Miryang, a staging point for the defense of the Naktong, then to a village called Changnyong, even closer to the river. By the evening of the thirty-first, they were picking up so much information about increasing North Korean movements on the other side of the river that word went out all along the line to expect an attack either that night or the next one.

SOMETIMES IT IS the fate of a given unit to get in the way of something so large that it seems to have stepped into history's own path. So it was with Charley Company that night. Greatly outmanned, it faced the last great push of a huge force from the North Korean People's Army. If many of the American units placed along the long, meandering path of the Naktong were thin, then none was thinner and more endangered than the Twenty-third Regiment, and no unit of the Twenty-third was more endangered than the men of Charley Company, whose members, the handful who survived those few days, eventually came to refer to their unit as "the late Company C." Lieutenant Joe Stryker could not, even years later, believe the imbalance between the two forces that first met at the Bulge. Almost certainly, he thought, two divisions of North Koreans, perhaps as many as fifteen to twenty thousand men, poured through the general area held by Charley Company, with perhaps as many as eight to ten thousand North Koreans coming through their precise position. Normally, Stryker noted, a company, which has a strength of about two hundred men, covers a sector of twelve hundred yards. But the First Battalion, of which Charley Company was a part, had a frontage of sixteen thousand yards, which meant that each of its three companies, none of which was at full strength, had to cover about five to six thousand yards. That meant a platoon of at best about seventy men had to cover two thousand yards, and a squad of about twenty to twenty-five men seven hundred yards, or seven football fields.

Stryker's estimates jibed with the memories of Master Sergeant Graham, who was in charge of Charley Company's Second Platoon with a mortar section and a recoilless rifle section, and with that of Master Sergeant Erwin Ehler, who was in charge of Fourth Platoon, which was a heavy weapons platoon. Graham's platoon was in the center of the Charley Company position. To the left of it was Ehler with the Fourth Platoon and to the right of Graham was B Company of their battalion. To the left of Ehler and his platoon was the road to Changnyong, and then troops from the Ninth Infantry Regiment, also part of the Second Division. The gaps in the line were terrible. "We were so far from each other that we didn't know where the hell anyone else was," remembered Ehler, who was badly wounded that night. Graham's Second Platoon had a front of about two thousand yards. On Graham's right was a gap of about two thousand yards, and after that, the position of B Company, also part of the First Battalion, began. "We could," Sergeant Graham later wrote, "cover the gaps [between us] by fire during the day, but it was impossible at night."

That they were pathetically thin on that line no one knew better than

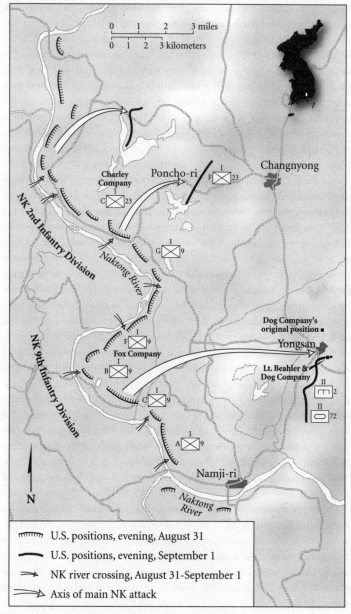

0	1	2	3 miles
0	1	2	3 kilometers

Charley
Company

Poncho-ri

Changnyong

F | I | 23

C | I | 23

NK 2nd Infantry Division

Naktong River

G | I | 9

Dog Company's
original position ■

Yongsan

F | I | 9

Fox Company

Lt. Beahler &
Dog Company

B | I | 9

II | 2

C | I | 9

II | 72

NK 9th Infantry Division

A | I | 9

N

Namji-ri

*Naktong
River*

ᨀᨀᨀ U.S. positions, evening, August 31

▬▬ U.S. positions, evening, September 1

⟶ NK river crossing, August 31–September 1

⟹ Axis of main NK attack

8. THE NAKTONG BULGE, AUGUST 31–SEPTEMBER 1, 1950

Captain Cyril Bartholdi, the Charley Company commander. He was an experienced officer and distantly related to the man who had designed the Statue of Liberty; he had commanded troops in World War II and was very much aware of the vulnerability of his men at this point, that there was no way they would be able to stop the kind of North Korean push everyone was expecting. They were, he understood, part of a fragile little trip wire, there primarily to help warn the rest of the Eighth Army. Their job would be to signal the North Korean attack, slow it down slightly if at all possible, report on its size, and hope that the men back at some distant headquarters might eventually be able to bring enough troops and firepower up to check the attack. The cruelty of their assignment, he understood, might mean that they all were going to die there.

On the afternoon of August 31, the men in the varying units of the Twenty-third Regiment, including Charley Company, had noticed enemy troops assembling on the other side of the Naktong, and in some places even building rafts. The attack was clearly coming soon—in fact, it appeared to be, they thought, virtually under way. The Naktong might be a valuable defensive line, but it was an imperfect one. The North Koreans were known to slip out at night and create what were essentially hidden underwater bridges by putting sandbags on the bottom, invisible to the naked eye because of the muddy quality of the water. Then, when the battle began, their men and their vehicles had a way to cross more easily, and there were fears among some of the Americans, as they waited for the strike, that such a bridge might already be in place.

The first In Min Gun strike was aimed at Baker Company. At 8:30 P.M., Lieutenant William Glasgow of Baker Company reported a bizarre sight, what seemed like countless enemy soldiers holding torches and moving toward the river, the torches spelling out, he reported, the letters V and O. No one ever figured out what the letters meant (if they actually were letters)—perhaps they were primitive directional signals meant to guide different units to the right sector. The North Korean prisoners the Americans eventually took were of little help on this matter. The most that the Americans were eventually able to get from them was that the North Koreans, who were still very confident, expected to reach Pusan in three days.

Then the Communist artillery barrage began. Suddenly, the Americans witnessed a terrifying sight, North Korean troops as far as the eye could see, coming up to the river and crossing it. Within the first fifteen minutes, Charley Company observers estimated that at least thirteen hundred North Korean troops had crossed the Naktong. In the Baker Company sector, it was later estimated, there were four separate crossings of about a battalion each, totaling about a division.

There was a comparable assault on the Charley Company sector. "Like millions of ants crossing the river and coming at us when we first saw them," said Terry McDaniel, a supply sergeant who was there that night. To the Americans, so isolated, so outnumbered, waiting fatefully in their positions, it was a frightening spectacle, a fighting force for which they had great respect, coming at them in such numbers. The initial wave of North Koreans took terrible casualties. "At first they had presented a great target," recalled Rusty Davidson, a company clerk pressed into frontline service because everyone was being pressed into frontline service, "and someone in our platoon had shouted out that it was going to be a turkey shoot, but then there were so many of them, and so few of us, that we soon realized we were the turkeys."

Back at the battalion command post they had expected to be hit, but not this hard or on a battlefield none of them would have chosen. Unfortunately, it was not about choice. If there had been any element of choice, they would have had several other divisions there to share the sector, and Air Force planes overhead to welcome the North Koreans from the air, and a great deal of American artillery already zeroed in on the likely routes. They had too little artillery, and almost no air cover. This was essentially a bare-bones command. The strategy, to the degree that there was one—mostly it was just about instinct—was to try to hold the roads that led out of the east side of the Naktong Bulge toward Pusan, buying time for other American and UN forces to gather. But in any real sense, they were out there on their own. "We were really thin," George Russell, back at Battalion headquarters, remembered, but he laughed even as he used the word. There had to be a better word, he said, and then added, "Thin to the point of being invisible." By midnight Baker Company under Glasgow had pulled back, while Charley Company was completely surrounded and being pounded, so badly isolated and weakened that some North Korean troops had quickly slipped behind it and were already heading for the Battalion Command Post, which they reached early in the morning of September 1. They promptly swung behind it too, cutting it off; it would remain cut off for the next three days.

The moment the report came in about the torchlight assault, Colonel Paul Freeman, the Twenty-third Regiment's commander, told his artillery to start firing. The fire was very accurate—the torches certainly helped—and it momentarily slowed down the In Min Gun, but in the end even accurate artillery fire did not seem to matter much. Back at Battalion they were caught between two conflicting needs—to hold the various company outposts for as long as they could and to get as many men as possible out so they could fight on another day. Realizing that his battalion and regimental positions were also threatened, and that the road to Pusan was the great prize, Freeman had immediately started organizing a blocking force, while signaling the units in the forward positions to hold as long and as best they could. He dipped into his regimental reserve immediately, taking Fox Company, supported by elements of How Company, and placing them under Major Lloyd Jenson, the executive officer of the Second Battalion. Their job was to break through to Lieutenant Colonel Claire Hutchin of the First Battalion if at all possible. Failing that, and they soon failed, they were to try to establish a blocking position on the Naktong to Changnyong road.

Freeman was in a distinctly unenviable position. He had begun the battle against a vastly greater force with only two rather than the normal three battalions under his command. One of these was already completely cut off—losses were clearly going to be devastating—and parts of the other battalion could not break through to it. Because of bad weather the Air Force was no help, and Freeman's artillery was, as ever, short of ammo. Jenson's position, trying to block the main road to Changnyong, immediately became the main defensive position of the regiment, and a battle raged around it for the next two weeks. George Russell, who had fought in cruel, unsparing World War II battles against the Japanese in the Pacific, thought that he had never seen fighting so bitter or relentless and raw. It was the most primitive kind of warfare imaginable. The Americans fought fiercely, fearing they might be pushed off the peninsula, and the North Koreans no less intensely, knowing that if they failed here, this would be their last great strike, and they might be driven north.

Paul Freeman assigned George Company to create a blocking position that finally allowed the First Battalion to pull back on September 3 and regroup at a place they called the Switch (because it was near a former Battalion communications center known as the Switchboard). Thus was the American position significantly stabilized some forty-eight hours after the first attack. By September 3, it became clear that the North Korean Second Division was massed on the main road, and that Freeman was using almost all his troops to block it from heading directly for Pusan. As Freeman later noted, the decisions he made instantaneously in the first few hours of battle were the cruelest he would ever make as a commander. He knew he had to sacrifice certain units to buy time, even as his own regimental headquarters was being overrun on September 1, and he was just barely able to move his headquarters about six hundred yards to the rear.

UP ON THE line near the Naktong, the end was coming very quickly. The North Koreans had rapidly encircled Charley Company and started grinding the men down, squeezing in on them. For the Americans positioned in those tiny outposts on that first night it was like seeing an enemy noose placed around your neck and rather quickly tightened. By midnight there was almost nothing left of Charley Company. Corporal Berry Rhoden led a seven-man re-coilless rifle team on that night. He was all of eighteen, a newly minted squad leader from rural Florida whose previous occupation had been as a local moonshiner. By chance that night he was in a position to watch the destruction of an entire infantry company. Because there had not been enough communications wire to go from Lieutenant Colonel Hutchin's First Battalion CP to Bartholdi's company CP, they had jerry-rigged a communications line to Rhoden's outpost with a separate line to Bartholdi's CP, several hundred yards away. So Rhoden essentially became a makeshift communications relay man and was able to hear the final anguished cries from men in a frontline unit being overrun, and the sad answer from a powerless headquarters that it could do nothing to help. It was heartbreaking, no less so because his own position was about to suffer a similar fate.

He heard Captain Bartholdi plead to Battalion for the right to release his men: "We cannot hold! Repeat we cannot hold! Our only chance is to disband and let every man get out for himself!" Rhoden had relayed Bartholdi's message, wondering if they might somehow be able to send another battalion to the rescue, or perhaps the Air Force could fly some extra missions at the last minute. That was the way, he remembered, it always happened in the movies. But not that night, not on the east side of the Naktong. He and his own men had fought valiantly, but they had started to run out of ammunition after only forty-five minutes of battle, so when Bartholdi spoke those final desperate words, pleading for the right to slip out, he spoke for Rhoden's squad as well. Back had come a voice from Battalion: "Hold your positions at all costs! You cannot disband. Repeat it is imperative to hold your positions at all costs! You must not disband!" Rhoden relayed that message to Captain Bartholdi, and received one last message from him asking for artillery fire or at least illuminating fire. But neither was coming. Then both wires went dead. The North Koreans had obviously cut them. Soon Rhoden heard his end of both dead wires beginning to rustle, and he knew that the North Koreans were pulling on them, trying to locate Rhoden's position. So he cut the wires at his end. Let the sons of bitches pull on a wire that didn't lead anywhere. It was time, he decided, to try to get his squad out of there.

Master Sergeant Graham, the leader of the First Platoon of Charley Company, thought the best thing to do was draw his men into as tight a position as he could and thus maximize their fields of fire. He knew any chance of getting out of there had gone from slim to minuscule. Graham was considered a magnificent NCO by his men. He was a lifer who never married, as if reflecting the old line of so many NCOs: if the Army wanted you to have a wife, it would have issued you one. He was known as the Bull, a generic nickname regularly given to tough (or bull) sergeants. In the past, he had always held back in terms of personal contact with his men. He did not intend to be one of those NCOs who was tough but lovable—for him tough was enough. Years later, he would tell some of them how he had always tried to be a little too tough because he feared emotional attachment, in case he lost them on the battlefield—it would help no one and might limit his freedom to make good decisions. It's bad enough when some of your men are killed—but so much worse when your *friends* are killed. He was, the men under him believed, the kind of sergeant who was at the core of the Army's strength. If anyone could get them out of such a hopeless spot, it was him. Bull Graham was as good a man as they were likely to find. He would set up exceptional fields of fire, never panic, and never think of himself first.

The nature of this fight, Graham quickly realized, was going to be based less on courage than on ammunition: ammo was time. Graham had a seasoned feel for the sounds of battle, and he could tell at a certain point, when Lieutenant Tom Wilson's neighboring platoon outpost went silent, that the North Koreans had overrun it. That meant the pressure on Graham's men was going to increase. It was then that he decided to try to slip his men out. No matter what Battalion headquarters wanted, they could no longer slow down the enemy; they lacked the ammo for it. They were already down to one belt on the machine gun, some of the automatic rifles were completely out, and a number of his men were yelling for more bullets for their M-1s. There wasn't much left but their bayonets. (He had already had his own bayonet either shot or knocked off his rifle; he was never sure which.) Bayonets were not going to do it, not against good soldiers with automatic rifles.

So he gathered his men. He had lost about twelve of them up on that hill. Maybe fifteen, who could tell in the madness of that fight? He never knew how many, because some men were lost and then made it back several days later. When it was all over, the one thing he was proud of was that their position had never been overrun. They moved back toward the Charley Company CP, where they found Captain Bartholdi, Lieutenant Wilson, and maybe seven men from Wilson's platoon, and tried to consolidate their force. Their most desperate need, if they were going to fight their way out, was ammunition. They tried scrounging bullets from dead bodies, but there wasn't very much— it was possible someone had already beaten them to it. By now, at the Company CP, time was running out. They had gathered a quad 50—that is, four 50-caliber machine guns fixed together, mounted on a half-track—and a dual 40, an antiaircraft weapon (twin 40-millimeter guns also mounted on a half-track structure). For a time these were effective against the enemy, but it was only a matter of time. The end was inevitable.

As the enemy fire got heavier, they barely managed to slip some of the wounded out on a supply jeep. Then, just before daylight, the Koreans managed to capture the quad 50 and the dual 40 and turn them against the American position at very close range. That was when they tried to make it out, while bullets and shells kicked up dirt around them. Somehow Graham and some of the remaining men made it to the top of a neighboring hill, only to find that North Koreans were already on a higher, abutting hill firing down on them. That was when Graham got hit for the first time, right in the ass. But somehow they managed to keep going. There weren't many of them in the group now, maybe twenty-five including Captain Bartholdi, Lieutenant Wilson, Sergeant Robert Agnew, Corporal Jessie Wallace, Private First Class David Ormand, and Private First Class Arnold Lobo, the medic. Ormand was already living on borrowed time, some of the others thought. He was the captain's radioman, and earlier his radio had been shot clean off his back. Bartholdi had had to crawl over and pull a badly shaken Ormand out of danger by his legs, then carry him to safety.

Graham remembered them trying to get off their hill, and finally taking cover in a ditch, the captain desperately going through his pockets attempting to find a few last rounds of ammo. That was when Graham was hit again—in the same general area but from a different direction. He was bleeding like a stuck pig, he thought. He lost any feeling in his leg almost immediately. So he took his undershorts off and had Ormand fold them and use them to stanch the bleeding, half-in and half-out of his belt—an instant battlefield bandage, for you made do as best you could in situations like this. The enemy fire was brutal by then. As far as Graham could tell, everybody had been hit. Only a few of them were still able to move. Maybe twenty Americans were now lying dead in the ditch next to him—he could barely tell the difference between the living and the dead anymore. A few of the men who were still functioning asked him what they should do—run, fight, or surrender? Surrendering in another war might have been an acceptable choice, but they had all heard stories—true ones, as it turned out—of American prisoners found with their hands wired behind them, shot through the head, and left in shallow graves. But how could they fight, he thought, when there wasn't a clip of ammo among them?

Graham answered that he was dying and could not tell them what to do. They were on their own. The last he saw of them, they were moving out to surrender. He listened carefully and, hearing no more firing, no telltale sound of bullets, he was relieved that at least they had not been executed immediately. Later, he learned that Wilson and Lobo had been killed; Wallace, Ormand, and Agnew were eventually recaptured by American forces. Graham lay there, bleeding badly, waiting for his death. The gooks got me, he thought. The first two groups of North Koreans who came by left him for dead. The third group discovered he was still alive, stripped him of everything—boots, socks, cigarette lighter, watch, even his much feared little black book with his company shit list, everyone who had pissed him off and the trivial offenses they had committed. No need for that anymore; most of the names belonged to dead men anyway, and he was about to join them. "You officer?" one of the Koreans asked. "No, me GI," he answered. Then what little luck he had seemed to run out. The group had what he called a Smart John in it, an officer who seemed smarter and meaner than the rest of them. He tapped Graham between the eyes with the butt of his rifle, trying to make him get up. Graham tried to signal that he couldn't rise because of his legs. The Korean aimed his bayonet and mocked stabbing Graham in the genitals. Graham shook his head—can't get up, he gestured again. Graham's uniform was soaked in blood below the waist. The officer left him momentarily to check out the other American bodies. Some of the Korean soldiers started teasing Graham—asking in primitive English how old he was and whether he was thirsty. He tried to get a drink from them, but they refused, though they seemed friendlier than the officer. Then the Smart John came back. This is it, Graham thought, my farewell moment. But the Korean, evidently deciding Graham was too far gone to bother with, just grabbed his dog tags and left.

Miraculously, in about twelve hours Graham felt strong enough to begin to crawl off. For the next twelve nights he crawled and limped toward what he thought might be American positions, hiding during the day, moving painfully and slowly and cautiously at night. In the first twenty-four hours, he figured he crawled only about a hundred yards. Eventually, he found a stick and used it as a crutch. He got water where he could find it—even licking the dew off the grass. By the time he made it back to his battalion headquarters, he had a heavy beard and, he swore, his mustache was so long it was curling up at the end. He looked gaunt as hell, having lost some fifty pounds. For a small group of officers sitting there when he crawled in, including Lieutenant Colonel Claire Hutchin, it was as if a ghost had appeared. Major Butch Barberis had just opened a beer. He looked at the apparition, took the beer, and handed it to him. "Best thing I ever tasted," Graham told Barberis. His Korean War was over. Charley Company had, of course, been devastated. Perhaps fifteen to twenty of them made it back to headquarters the next day. A company in a situation like that normally had six officers, but Charley Company had already been down to three, and two of them were killed in the first twenty-four hours.

Captain Bartholdi did not fare as well. He had been with a group of men who were eventually taken prisoner by the North Koreans. They were marched every night for about two weeks, the prisoners bound to one another by wire, making a couple of miles each night. The North Koreans tried to separate the Americans by class and rank, determined to be much harder on the officers, who were, they believed, true representatives of the capitalist class. During the day, while they were waiting, they often did interrogations: Are you from a rich or poor family? they would ask. If you said rich, they would hit you, so soon everyone said poor. Do you like MacArthur? they asked. No, the prisoners answered. Do you like Truman? No, they would answer. Bartholdi had always been known to the men as Captain Bart, and now to protect him they simply called him Bart, but finally after about two weeks of captivity, the North Koreans threatened to kill all the men if their officer did not step forward. Bartholdi did, and they beat him terribly in the next days, and eventually murdered him, placing him in a mass grave along with the bodies of a large number of local Koreans. Most of the other American prisoners were rescued the next day by an American tank unit. Bartholdi was posthumously awarded the Silver Star.

Charley Company had taken the full force of the North Korean attack in those few days and suffered accordingly. Though it was rebuilt, it always seemed to be just a little less lucky than other companies, the casualties it suffered always a little higher. Soon, there were officers in the regiment who would threaten men by saying, "Fuck up here, and you'll be in Charley Company."

SOMEHOW, IN ALL that brutal fighting, they had managed to slow down the North Koreans, who had broken through but failed completely to maximize their success. An entire North Korean division had been waiting in reserve near the Naktong Bulge and, inexplicably, had not been thrown into the battle. Instead, they had paused and regrouped, and that had been just enough time to give Walker's forces a second chance. For there had been Charley Companies all along the Naktong River that night. No one knew better than Walker how little he had in the way of reinforcements and how long it took even the best troops now arriving in country to become accustomed to battle conditions. An elite unit, the Second Division, with an exceptionally proud history, would still not be an elite combat-*tested* unit, not in Korea, until it had served some time on the line. Of the officers now arriving in country as platoon leaders and company commanders, it would be impossible to tell who had the requisite talent and instinct for battle until they were under fire, for that could not be taught, not at West Point or VMI, or in ROTC. Mostly it was about instinct, and that was something only learned in the doing. That sooner or later these new divisions would fight well Walker had no doubt, but it was all about time, and time was the thing he had the least of. He was, Mike Lynch said, like a man with all his fingers in the dike all the time, and there were still never enough fingers.

Later, the military judgment would be that the In Min Gun commanders had failed in that last great assault on the Pusan Perimeter largely because they had used their troops so poorly. If they had concentrated their forces and struck in greater numbers at fewer points, they might have been far more successful. (Of course, if they had done that, they might also have been better targets for American artillery and airpower.) But there would be little satisfaction for Walker in that ex post facto judgment; at the time, he had felt overwhelmed by the relentless nature of the North Korean attacks. September 1, Mike Lynch recalled, had been one of the worst days. They had been flying low over the sector occupied by the Ninth Regiment (of the Second Division) and had seen a company of Americans retreating along a creekbed, even though no enemy force was pressing on them. Worse, in Walker's opinion, they were bypassing perfect defensive positions from which they could slow down the North Koreans. So he told Lynch to take him in as low as he could. Lynch dropped the plane down to three hundred feet, pulled back the flaps, cut the throttle, and glided in just fifty feet above the Americans (hoping, as always, that the engine would start up again). There was the three-star commander of the Eighth Army, leaning so far out the door, he was essentially no longer in the plane, screaming over his bullhorn, "Stop! Go back, you yellow sons of bitches! You are not under attack! Go back, you had great positions!" The troops paid no attention, leaving Walker in a rage. It was one more bugout at a crucial moment, and among troops from a supposedly elite division just in from the States. He told Lynch to fly on to the headquarters of Major General Laurence (Dutch) Keiser, the Second Division commander. Based on his treetop observations and other scattered bits of intelligence, he decided that the Communists had hit the Second Division and driven a hole right in the middle of its sector—about six miles wide and eight miles deep, he later concluded. At that moment, he believed, the Second Division was perilously close to being cut in half.

Like others in the command, he already had serious doubts about Dutch Keiser, fifty-five at the time, a little old for such a demanding command and believed to be an old fifty-five at that. There was a growing feeling that this war had come too late for him. He seemed reluctant to leave his division headquarters, depending far too much on his subordinates to get around. He was in those difficult hours, as Clay Blair rather delicately put it, "operating from his well guarded command post." Sometimes men who are exceptionally brave in one war, when they are young, do not age well as soldiers. So it was with Keiser. He was West Point, class of 1917, had commanded a battalion and won a Silver Star in World War I, where everything had gone right for him and he had been young and brave. But the ensuing thirty-three years had seen a changed officer. He had been away from combat for more than three decades—had not commanded troops in World War II. In the fall of 1948, he had joined the Second Division as the assistant division commander, and in February 1950 had gotten his second star and command of the division, helped along, no one doubted, by his close friendship with his former classmate, Joe Collins, the Army chief of staff. Mike Lynch, who often expressed bluntly what Walker thought privately, believed that Keiser had turned into a coward as he aged, that the demands of this war were simply too much for him. That morning he seemed to be completely overwhelmed by circumstances. Walker's arrival at his headquarters precipitated a brutal scene, one that plays out only in the worst moments of combat, when two men are perched at the abyss, and when there is no more room for failure. Walker was already in a rage when he walked in, and then he saw Keiser's map—a dreamer's map that had nothing to do with the collapsing front he had just flown over. Here was a general, part of whose division was being overrun, and he did not even seem to know it.

"Dutch, where's your division?" was the first thing Walker asked. "Where are your reserves? What are you doing about positioning your reserves? You must hold at Yongsan! If you don't, we could lose Miryang, and if we lose Miryang, we could lose Pusan. You're in the heart of this thing and you don't know what's going on." Keiser, indicating that he was still waiting for his liaison men to return and tell him where different units were, complained that the roads were jammed with troops, which were slowing his men down. Of course, they're jammed with troops, Lynch thought. They're your own damn troops bugging out.

Keiser tried to fill Walker in on where his division was, but nothing he said gibed with what Walker had just seen. "That's not it at all," Walker interrupted him. "I've just flown over your front line." Just then, one of Keiser's liaison officers arrived, apologizing for being late but he had been slowed down by some colonel who was standing at a road junction, ordering everyone to stop retreating. "No son of a bitch who can fight passes this line," the colonel had been saying. "Yes," said Walker, "I know that colonel—that's my assistant G-3."

Then Walker laid down the law: "You get this division under control or I'll take control of it, and I'll run you out of the Armys! I am not going to lose this battle." He explained to Keiser exactly where he wanted his troops to make a stand. Then, as he got up to go, Keiser started to accompany him back to his plane, but Walker shook him off. "You get busy now. I don't need anyone to walk me to my plane." At the plane, instead of getting in, Walker sat down for a moment, obviously trying to pull himself together. Lynch assumed he wanted a moment of quiet until he looked over and saw that Walker was crying. "I can't let this Army be destroyed, but I'm losing the whole Army and I don't know what to do to stop it." He was, Lynch thought, absolutely exhausted. Not beaten, not defeated, not broken, just exhausted, completely wrung out. Lynch wondered how much more the Army could get out of one man in a situation like this before he broke.

Walker needed fresh troops to plug the gaps, but he was losing them to the coming Inchon assault. All too many of the troops coming from the States seemed to be ticketed for the Seventh Division, which would be part of MacArthur's Inchon landing force. In addition, he was about to lose the Marines, who were going to be the main assault force at Inchon. He had been arguing with Tokyo for several days, trying to keep the Fifth Marine Regiment (part of the First Marine Division) under his command. He had reached a tentative agreement that he could have them—but only through September 4, and only if he would do his best not to use them in defense of Pusan. After all, the Inchon landing, scheduled for September 15, was the main event and it was now only two weeks away. MacArthur wanted these troops fresh for so dangerous an assault. As such, they were Walker's more in theory than in reality. But if ever there was a moment when he felt himself perched on the very edge of failure, this was it. After watching the battering part of the Second Division was taking, he called Brigadier General Eddie Craig, the Marine commander, and told him he was going to need the Marines to protect the road to Miryang, and they should start moving up *now*. He also called MacArthur's headquarters and spoke to Major General Doyle Hickey, the assistant chief of staff, who was acting as G-3 (operations officer), with Almond so involved in the Inchon planning. He issued an emotional request for permission to use the Marines— essentially, an ultimatum of the sort MacArthur himself was famous for. "If I lose the Marines," he told Hickey, who was considered by outsiders to be unusually fair-minded, "I will not be responsible for the safety of the front." Those were words that could chill any higher echelon officer. Back came word from Hickey that MacArthur had approved their use in Pusan and that Walker's control of them, if needed, was now extended beyond September 4.

Armies, no matter how great or small, poised between defeat and victory, depend more than anything else on the leadership of junior officers. One of the many junior officers who helped save Walker and the Eighth Army in those first terrible days was a lieutenant from the Second Engineer Battalion of the Second Division named Lee Beahler. With his engineers, he skillfully created a tiny but effective blocking force and, miraculously, stopped the North Koreans at Yongsan just when it seemed like they were going to pour through. By the end of September 1, there had seemed no chance to hold Yongsan. But Beahler and his engineers, in time with other Army units and the Marines joining in, managed to do it. The battle for Yongsan lasted two weeks, and it was continuous and ferocious; to some of the men who fought there, and never forgot it,

Yongsan was both a war within a war, and a war without end. To the GIs and Marines, who heard again and again how important Yongsan was, the village, once taken, was a singular disappointment: two streets, one east-west, one north-south, crisscrossing each other. No more than that. If it had been a town back in the States, as one of the engineers said, the first thing you'd have wanted to do was get the hell out of it. When they finally walked through Yongsan, there was a sense almost of wonderment—that so much blood, Korean and American, had been shed for something that seemed so without value. Men had fought and died for Paris and Rome—more than three hundred thousand Russians had died in the final battle for Berlin—but to fight so long for something that barely existed amazed the Americans, and seemed to emphasize the special madness of this war. But Yongsan *was* important, for the road from there could lead to Miryang, some twelve miles away, and the road from Miryang led to Pusan, and beyond Pusan was a lost war.

Pushed by Walker, Keiser had taken the Second Combat Engineers, who had already seen a good deal of action, almost all of it as infantrymen, and attached them to the already battered Ninth Regiment. Lee Beahler commanded Dog Company of the Engineers. The odyssey that had taken him back to Korea in July 1950 had not been an entirely happy one. He had served in the Army in World War II, then gone back to the Texas College of Mines. There, somewhat to his surprise, he found that he missed the camaraderie and sense of purpose he had found in the Army, and so in 1946 he decided to go back in. There, in the mysterious ways that the Army operated, he had been offered a chance to go overseas and had, he thought, been given a choice of possible destinations. He had expressed a great preference for Europe, but had of course been sent to Korea, a country he quickly came to dislike, in no small part because of its pervasive smell—that of human waste turned into instant fertilizer, a fragrance that bothered many other Americans as well. Nor had he found the Korean people, angry over their years under a colonial reign and unsure of what the Americans represented in terms of their future, particularly sympathetic. Other Americans told him how much more pleasant Japan was and how friendly the Japanese, now defeated and eager to imitate their conquerors, had become. There was surely an injustice in this: the people who had inflicted the cruelest colonial horrors on another nation turned out to be, once the war was over, a great deal more likeable than their victims in the eyes of most Americans.

Nothing during his two-year tour of Korea had given him pleasure, and when his time was up he was thrilled to be going home. But then, in June 1950, newly married, his wife pregnant, he got orders to return to Korea as a combat engineer in a war that did not have a good feel to it. He was heartsick about going back, and the condition of the American units, his own included, made him feel far worse once he got there. Just as they were shipping out, his superiors had opened the doors to the stockades back at Fort Lewis, with a onetime fight-in-Korea-or-be-tried-at-home offer, and he had ended up taking in some men charged with serious crimes. Still, his company as it moved up to Yongsan was at about two-thirds strength, only 150 men in place. (There was one moment, during the brutal fighting at Yongsan, when a young private, grimy and exhausted, who had distinguished himself during a North Korean attack, thanked Beahler for getting him out of the stockade. Such is the complex journey of modern warriors, Beahler had thought.)

The Ninth Regiment, which was supposed to be holding Yongsan, was in terrible shape at that moment. Some of its men, under orders from higher headquarters, had launched an ill-advised probing attack against the North Koreans just as the greatly superior Communist force was starting to cross the Naktong. The assignment, Operation Manchu—the Ninth was known as the Manchu regiment—called for them to cross the river and harass the Communists, and had apparently come down from Keiser's headquarters. Later, many of the people in the division thought it nothing less than a demented order from an officer trying to be aggressive for aggression's sake—under pressure from above. After all, early intelligence reports had already confirmed the considerable size of the North Korean force. The vulnerability of the Americans maximized—for there was nothing more difficult than a river crossing—they had been caught completely off guard when the North Koreans crossed first. Instead of being hit while holding strong defensive positions, many of the frontline troops of the Ninth had been caught in the open, and those elements of the Ninth up along the Naktong were already small and scattered—like the elements of the Twenty-third.

Lee Beahler had been wary of Operation Manchu from the start. He knew from World War II how difficult any river crossing was. The entire business had only confirmed something he had suspected almost since he arrived in country: that he was working with superiors who in all too many instances did not know as much as they were supposed to about combat. When the assault was first discussed, he had asked the regimental commander, Colonel John G. Hill, if his men had been trained in river crossings. Hill had replied that they didn't need special training. Beahler insisted that they did; that he knew because he had been involved when the Thirty-sixth Division had tried to cross the Rapido in Italy, one of the great disasters of the war, the Rapido being fast and high, and the Germans well dug in on the other side. Hill had brushed away Beahler's objections. He had no idea how difficult it was, all the men in the boat made so vulnerable, especially if they had not practiced a comparable assault. He seemed to think, Beahler decided, that crossing a river was like calling a taxi. Hearing Hill reject his warnings, which were primarily about the safety of the men, Beahler's respect for him fell away. He wondered then, and not for the first time, about some of the commanders whose job it was to know so much, but who knew so little and never listened to those who might know more. So the North Koreans had caught the Ninth exposed, on the water itself or at the river's edge. A number of Hill's regimental staff, including his S-3, were killed almost immediately, as was Keiser's aide, Tom Lombardo, a famed West Point football player. Fifty-four years later, Lee Beahler could say of that moment when he first saw the torches of the North Korean troops coming down to the river and preparing to cross, "That's when I began to get a very shaky feeling about what was going to happen, how brutal it was going to be for our forces—and I've still got that shaky feeling, still have it today when I think back to those days." Beahler immediately sent most of his own men back to Battalion headquarters to keep them from being overrun at the riverbank. That night and the next morning, terror was in the air.

On that second day, Beahler was a reluctant witness as the top echelon of a large American unit experienced something akin to a nervous breakdown. Beahler did not know of the angry exchange that had taken place between Walton Walker and Dutch Keiser, but on the morning of September 2 he did watch the relief of Hill, the regimental commander. Brigadier General Sladen Bradley, the assistant division commander, who was out in the field far more than Keiser, showed up at regimental headquarters to find out what was going on. Bradley was clearly enraged by the lack of control he found around him. "Colonel, where's your First Battalion?" he asked. Hill answered that he did not know, that he had not heard from it since midnight.

"Well, Colonel Hill, where's your Second Battalion?"

Hill had not heard from it either. Then Bradley gave him a cold, hard look, one that Beahler remembered all too well. "Colonel, apparently this situation is out of control, and I am assuming command of this regiment." A few minutes later Bradley turned to Beahler and informed him that his company of engineers was now going to fight as infantry and assigned it to move up to Yongsan immediately. It would be the job of the Second Engineers to hold Yongsan for twenty-four hours, he said, until the Marines could arrive and take over. In the process, Beahler would learn that he had a new battalion commander, Major Charley Fry, because the old one, Lieutenant Colonel Joe McEachern, had, like Colonel Hill, not appreciated how fragile the situation was. During World War II, McEachern had apparently worked as an engineer on the Pan American Highway and therefore had no combat command background. He still thought he was there to build roads, not to shoot at North Korean Communists. He had made the mistake of arguing with Bradley over a change in his orders, when Bradley had told him that his men were to stand and die if need be to stop the North Korean advance. "But, sir, these men are specialists," McEachern had protested, "they're not infantrymen. You have to understand that they're technicians."

"Colonel, do you not understand me? Am I not making myself clear? I said stand and die and I meant stand and die, and they will fight as infantrymen." Bradley had answered, and lest there were any other officers who did not understand how critical the situation was and had their own private doubts, he relieved McEachern on the spot, replacing him with the battalion executive officer. "Major Fry, do you understand the order?" Bradley asked him. "Yes, sir," Fry replied instantly. General Bradley then sent the newly relieved Colonel Hill to help Beahler set up his defense at Yongsan. There, Beahler decided, Hill was still not a great asset. Recently defrocked as a regimental commander Hill might be, but he was still a colonel and an infantryman, and Beahler was a first lieutenant and an engineer, which made the relationship chancy. But Beahler was the more experienced combat officer; his unit had led the landing at Salerno in Italy, which meant he had been in some of the bloodiest fighting of World War II. The Italian campaign had been a hard one, and not all those battles had ended up in American glory and victory. Some were defeats, and in defeat, he believed, you often gained the most wisdom; Beahler had learned that one of the keys to successful leadership is knowing an enemy's strengths as well as his weaknesses. That wisdom had, in the few short weeks they had served together in Korea, helped earn him the respect of his men. "Why are some officers better than others?" one of his squad leaders, Sergeant Gino Piazza, once wondered. "Well, they have a feel for it, they anticipate well and they respond well. They see danger points before they happen, and they're good with the men. You have a feeling that what they do is not just about themselves and getting promotions and medals but about the men in their command as well. On that scale, he was one of the best. One of the very best. We were very lucky to have him."

Colonel Hill had immediately wanted to set up a defensive line right smack in the flat paddy land fronting Yongsan. Beahler was all too aware of his own limitations—he might be a good engineering officer, but he was hardly an expert in infantry warfare. Nonetheless, he knew immediately that Hill's plan was a prescription for a disaster, which might cost him his entire company. He did not know who had taught John Hill about infantry tactics, but fighting from an open stretch of rice paddy, with no natural contours to help your individual defensive positions, was madness. What made it even worse was the fact that there would be no flanking American units on his right or left, against an enemy whose favorite tactic was first to flank and then to encircle a defensive position. "If you wanted to pick the perfect place for the North Koreans to mow us down, this was it," Sergeant Piazza said.

Beahler protested vigorously to Hill. He wanted to take his men up a hill behind the little village on the other, or south side of the road to Pusan, backing it rather than fronting it, an infinitely superior place for a defense against a numerically superior enemy. Holding Yongsan meant nothing, control of five or six little huts—it was the *road* leading out of it that was at stake here, and the hill blocked the road out of Yongsan. As he confronted Colonel Hill, Beahler's thoughts went back to Custer at the Little Big Horn. Had anyone protested to Custer about the sheer madness of what he was doing? Had the ordinary soldiers known that their commander was crazed and putting them all at risk? Had anyone in the command understood how the vainglory of their commander undermined their chances of surviving? At that moment, Beahler did not know what was going on around him or what the larger strategy was. The one thing he knew was that he was not going to place his men out in any open paddy, naked to North Korean artillery and mortars and tanks, and the In Min Gun's superior numbers. But there was Hill, a full colonel, telling him he was to fight in the flat land. Only if the North Koreans hit hard enough could he break off and pull back up the hill, he was told. That's absolutely demented, Beahler thought. The North Koreans almost always struck at night, and disengagement from a superior enemy in the midst of battle, even in daylight, is an especially hard military move. To do it at night would be much worse.

The lives of all the men were at stake. What good would it do if Beahler lived to testify at a court-martial that he had opposed the decision that cost him his company? He decided there was no more time to waste arguing. He was on his own; the responsibility was his. Besides, Colonel Hill had just given him his excuse. "Sergeant Nations!" he yelled to his master sergeant, Kenneth Nations. "We've just been hit! Take the company up on the hill!" Colonel Hill said nothing.

A little later General Bradley himself showed up. "What outfit is this?" he asked.

"Dog Company, Second Engineers," Nations answered.

"I thought you were supposed to be out in front of the village," Bradley said.

"No, sir, the company commander said to take them up on the hill—it's a much, much better position as you can see for yourself, General."

"All right, Sergeant, carry on," Bradley replied.

So it was that they had taken the natural protection offered by the hill and fashioned what was in effect a soft horseshoe defense facing the road. When the men finished digging their foxholes, Sergeant Nations came by, took one look, and told them to dig deeper. "We grumbled a lot then, but a little later I would have kissed his ass for making us do it," Butch Hammel, a private first class in Beahler's company, remembered. Across the road was Able Company from the Second Engineer Battalion, which, during the day, had been joined by some stragglers from other companies, but remained, like Dog Company, still badly understrength.

IT WAS A very foggy night, and long before they saw the North Koreans, they heard their whistles and their voices, every command somehow amplified in the darkness, the language seeming harsh and staccato, and then they heard the terrifying rumble of enemy tanks. Just before the battle started, Lieutenant Beahler came over and warned them not to fire until they actually saw the Koreans; otherwise they might be firing on their own men. The First Platoon, the one closest to Yongsan, was hit first. The men in Hammel's platoon could hear the fighting long before they had anyone to open up on. At one point the fog lifted; suddenly they could see the part of the hill where the First Platoon was engaged, and they were able to open up, catching the North Koreans by surprise. Then the battle shifted to Hammel's positions. If there was one great truth to combat like this, Hammel believed, it was the constancy of fear—any man who says that he's not scared in combat is a liar. Every soldier in a situation like that faced a terrible choice. You want nothing more than to live another day, nothing more than to bug out, but you also don't want to be seen by your buddies as a coward. Only the dishonor of running, of letting your buddies down, keeps you from trying to slip away—because of that, he thought, and only because of that, do you stay where you are and keep fighting. All that other stuff they taught you, about fighting for your country and against the Communists, disappeared in the first moments of battle.

Hammel remembered one of his sergeants being hit in the neck that night. It was not that bad a wound, but the sergeant panicked and started running right behind their positions. Someone in the next foxhole started shooting at him, and they had to scream at their buddies, "Friendly! Friendly!" The sergeant was lucky; he lived. They were all pretty lucky, Hammel thought, because they managed to hold off the North Koreans. Well, not all of them were lucky—twelve of them died and eighteen were wounded. Maybe three hours of pure, close, raw combat, he thought, and the price had been very high. But Lieutenant Beahler had placed the men perfectly, and never once during the entire battle had he taken cover himself. The lieutenant just moved calmly from position to position, making sure the men were okay and that they had enough ammo. "I never saw a braver man in my life; I never saw a man so cool under fire," Hammel said more than fifty years later.

When they first took their places on the hill that night, some Korean bearers had helped them settle in, and Gino Piazza was furious about that. He was twenty-three at the time, and if he had not done well in school, he was shrewd about some things—in particular that you could not get something for nothing in a war zone. He did not trust the Koreans in situations like this when no one had really vouched for them. As far as he was concerned, American soldiers should carry their own damned gear up the hill. There were too many instances he knew of where the In Min Gun had infiltrated its men behind American lines, disguising them as civilians. It would be all too easy to turn them into bearers who might slip back across the lines with the exact coordinates of the American positions. Piazza had gotten into a shouting match with one of the junior officers, telling him to keep the goddamn Koreans away, and the officer saying it was all right, these were good guys, friendlies. Friendlies, my ass, Piazza thought. You know nothing about them, *nothing!* If one of them smiles at you and says two words in English, and does your lifting for you, you think he's a good guy. *Goddamn American innocents who go through life only wanting someone to do the heavy lifting for them*. Piazza had chased some of them out, but the next day, despite the worst fog cover Piazza had seen in Korea, the enemy had been able to lob mortar shells with remarkable precision onto their position. A furious Piazza was convinced that those nice helpful Korean bearers had been spotters for the enemy, damned talented ones, and five of the men in his twelve-man squad were now dead.

The battle itself had been hard on his platoon, and Piazza had fought in a rage, as if wanting to avenge any of his men who had been killed by the North Korean mortars. There had been a young man named Ronnie Taylor, barely eighteen, an enlistee from Oakland, Mississippi, whom Piazza felt it was his sacred duty to protect because he was so young, and here he was with a gaping wound in his chest, pleading with Piazza, "Don't let me die! Don't let me die! You've got to get me out of here!" Piazza had assured him they were trying, but he knew that no one was going to make it off the hill during that fight, and so Piazza had fired and fired while cradling Taylor in his arms, listening to his last gasps of life. In his own words, he snapped at that point, grabbed his M-1 and charged down at some advancing North Koreans, screaming out the name of one of the men in his squad who had died with each burst of fire. How men—himself included—reacted to combat like this, how some were overwhelmed by it and some could handle it, fascinated him. One of his men had received what to Piazza's eye seemed like a rather minor wound, only a flesh wound really, but he had unraveled and kept insisting, "I'm going to die"—and he did. Such was the strange psychology of war, Piazza thought. The soldier had talked himself into dying.

It was fortunate that they were on the high ground where Beahler had placed them, because at least two battalions of the Communist troops made three separate assaults starting in very early and continuing into the morning. "They came, and they came, and they kept coming. We laid down a lot of fire on them. It rained down on them," said Corporal Jesse Haskins. "We kept killing them and I began to wonder if we could kill them fast enough. There seemed to be so many of them and they just kept coming, nothing stopped them, there were always more of them and it was as if we might as well not have been there, that what we did just didn't matter." If the engineers had not been perfectly positioned, Haskins was sure, they all would have died.

There was one moment, with ammo running short, when they thought they were going to be overrun. But a kid from another platoon rushed over with a whole box of grenades, the perfect weapon just to roll down the hill. The Americans, without mortars or artillery, had used their bazookas as rockets and relied on their heavy machine guns, as well as their quad 50, which would turn out to be one of the most effective weapons of the war. It was essentially an antiaircraft weapon, capable of truly lethal firepower, and it would be used in this war to neutralize the superior manpower of the enemy; not just to kill, which it did handily, but to create fear. The meat chopper, the GIs called it. Later, when the battle was over, the hillside littered with North Koreans, Beahler thought the quad 50 had turned the battle in his favor. They had been lucky to have it, because they had gotten nothing in the way of artillery fire from headquarters. At one point Beahler had asked for artillery support, and a single shell had come in, far off the mark. Beahler had tried to telephone in some corrections, but word came back that the artillery men were just too green and didn't yet know the fire-direction system.

Among those in Dog Company who had reason to be grateful for Beahler's experience was a young company clerk named Vaughn West, who had been pressed into service that night as a combat infantryman. West had dug his first foxhole, and been reasonably pleased, for the digging had been hard on such a rocky hill. Then a sergeant told him to dig a lot deeper. (After that night, he never had to be told to dig deeper again.) Clerk though he was, he was the best shot in the company and had once won a weekend pass at the rifle range. On occasion, at an officer's club, Beahler would hustle a little competition by casually suggesting his men were such good shots that even his company clerk could outshoot the best rifleman of any other company. Then West would be produced, and he almost always won the bet for Beahler. What stayed in West's memory were the terrible cries in the night. There had been one young enlisted man on a slightly higher part of the ridge who had been hit in the face. In the middle of the battle, West heard him screaming, and then, in the momentary illumination of some tracers, he saw him, his face shot off, crawling and yelling out for his mother. West had known immediately that there was no way to save him.

THEIR CASUALTIES WERE high, but they could easily have been worse. Someone later told Vaughn West that when Beahler saw the list of names, he wept, and later someone back at Battalion, filled with a dumb macho spirit, made a condescending remark about what kind of company commander broke down and cried, but West thought when you lost that many men in battle, maybe you should cry. The men of Dog Company, Second Engineers, had come off the hill late that morning, gotten the briefest of rests, and then been ordered right back up for the second night in a row. Beahler was not happy about it, but orders were orders. His men were exhausted. No one had slept for days—or at least it felt like that. But if the hill was so important the first night, it was probably just as important the second night, or so Beahler figured, and the word was already out that the Marines were on their way. Nonetheless when they headed back, they were dragging a bit. Just then, a Marine tank drove up with four Marines aboard looking very fresh. By contrast the engineers looked, Piazza remembered, like very old men with no taste for battle, which was just what the Marines expected of Army doggies anyway. A young Marine lieutenant, obviously displeased by the sloppy way the engineers were moving up, shouted, "Pick it up, goddamn it! Pick it up! Start looking like soldiers!" As if to shame them, the lieutenant continued, "Do you know who held this hill and stopped the North Koreans this morning? It was the *engineers!*" Piazza looked at him hard and said, "Who the fuck do you think we are? We're the guys who did it." And then they straightened up a bit, picked up the pace, and went on up the hill.

Fortunately for them, the North Koreans did not strike that second night, and in time, with the Marines and other units leading the counterattack, they were driven back. Colonel Hill, however, remained furious with Beahler for disregarding his orders and tried to have him court-martialed. Instead, he was given the Distinguished Service Cross, the Army's second-highest medal. Hearing that Hill still wanted to press charges, General Bradley told him to drop the idea; court-martialing a man who had saved most of his company and won the DSC would only make a fool of Hill. Beahler himself never took much pride in his medal, in part because they had awarded Sladen Bradley a DSC for that night, and his citation said that he had taken a badly disorganized Engineer unit, pulled it together, and sent its men up the hill. Medal givers, Beahler decided, often spoke with forked tongues.

About five days after that battle a mosquito bite gave Lee Beahler Japanese

B encephalitis. He was shipped to a hospital in Japan, where his weight dropped to ninety pounds. He was still recuperating there about three months later when the Second Engineers were hit at a place in the far north of Korea called Kunuri. The news of what had happened at Kunuri was exceptionally bitter for the lieutenant; so many friends had been killed or were missing. That mosquito bite, he realized, had quite possibly saved his life.

ON THE SECOND day of the North Korean offensive along the Naktong, Paul Freeman had summoned his senior officers to a meeting at the Second Battalion's command post. Major George Russell, the operations officer for the First Battalion, remembered that they met in what was essentially a culvert that went under the road, water up to their knees because the rain that day had been the heaviest anyone could remember. Colonel Freeman had been both impassioned and exhausted. They were all exhausted. No one had slept in days. Freeman talked about how difficult it was, with no air support and with Asian hordes descending on them. Asian hordes, Russell had thought, and he started laughing. Everyone was always talking about Asian hordes. "What's so funny?" an irritated Freeman asked. "It can't be that bad," Russell said. But it was that bad, he thought later, it really was just that bad.

Exhaustion was inevitable. By September 3, Freeman and his understrength regiment had been fighting a multidivision attack for three days and nights—and they had been tired well before the attack started. They had been on the line constantly since they had arrived in country in early August. For Freeman, who had missed a chance to command in combat during World War II and had always hoped for a second chance, days like this turned out to be more of an opportunity than he had ever needed. In 1949, Paul Freeman had been worried about his career and the increasing likelihood that his superiors were in the process of defining him as a staff officer rather than a combat officer. Then the war broke out. Up to that moment he had been a planning expert, greatly admired by his superiors in Washington, but in the years immediately after the world war his career had seemed stymied. There were few openings in a rapidly downsizing army for regimental commanders, the command he wanted, and the few that existed seemed ticketed for officers who had already commanded a regiment.

Paul Freeman was forty-three years old when the Korean War began and in genuine jeopardy of being pushed aside by other officers who had made greater names in combat during World War II. He was thoughtful, intelligent, and careful, but in no way charismatic. He was not tall or physically powerful or fierce in manner, as some men favored for leadership appeared to be. Rather he was an unusually handsome man, becoming even more so as he aged and his considerable mane of hair turned completely white. If he was to gain the respect and affection of his troops, it would have to be hard-won. Style and self-created dramatics were not going to do it for him. "He was an absolutely outstanding officer, and his greatest strength," his younger colleague Captain Hal Moore (who would later distinguish himself as a commander at the Battle of the Ia Drang Valley in the Vietnam era and end up a three-star) said, "was his intelligence, his respect for other people, especially the people under his command, and how careful he was. The men who served under him understood that he was always going to be careful and judicious in the risks he took with their lives. That is no small thing. He was a very good listener, paid attention to everything around him, and wasted no one's time or energy. If you were a younger officer coming to command in Vietnam you might go back to the battles where he had commanded in Korea and you would find that he had done everything right."

Freeman was an Army brat, his father having been an early graduate of the Army Medical School, back in 1904, and then a regimental surgeon. In 1907, when Paul Freeman was born, the senior Freeman was stationed in the Philippines, a doctor who, when he went out with cavalry units, simply stuffed the tools of his trade into his saddlebags. The young Paul Freeman grew up on Army posts in Asia and the United States, came to love the Army life, and never really considered another career. He wanted to go to West Point, but had not done particularly well in high school. Nor were the Freemans, after all those years overseas, well connected politically, and so a congressional appointment seemed unlikely. Still, he went to a cram school, worked hard, but just missed a presidential appointment—twelve men passed out of two hundred; he was the thirteenth. His father was then stationed at Governor's Island in New York harbor. He and his father started calling New York congressmen who might have vacancies, and finally came up with one representing a district filled with new immigrants, mainly Yiddish-speaking Jews from the shtetls of Eastern Europe, most of whom had a historic fear of the military, since in the old country its representatives tended to show up in their small villages only, it seemed, to round them up for pogroms. There was no great rush on the part of their children to head for West Point and join what might well be the New World's Cossacks. A congressional appointment came with surprising ease.

Freeman was an undistinguished student at West Point; he was in the bottom half of his class and in no way a gifted athlete. He graduated in 1929, a difficult time to break into the Army. The country was between wars; Wall Street was about to crash. Promotions, always slow, became slower than ever; it took five years and four months for Freeman to go from second to first lieutenant. Army families, unless there was inherited wealth—and daughters of prosperous families were always of interest to handsome young cadets—lived on the financial edge and became brilliant at penny-pinching. When Franklin Roosevelt became president in 1933, one of his first and easiest targets for reducing expenses was military pay, and he instituted a 10 percent cut across the board, which meant that the newly married Paul and Mary Anne Fishburn Freeman had their monthly paycheck cut from $125.00 to $112.50, while the two-and-a-half-month paid leave normally granted to officers immediately became one month without pay. But these were shared hardships; everyone else their age in the military was living through the same thing, and it only served, as so many things do in the military, to tighten the communal bonds.

Paul Freeman, West Point scores notwithstanding, was bright and impressed his superiors from the start, including his future division commander in Korea, the young Laurence Keiser, who was his tactical officer at the academy and became his first company commander when Freeman joined the Ninth Regiment of the Second Infantry Division at Fort Sam Houston in Texas right after graduation. Freeman had tried at first for the newly formed Army Air Force (which only became a separate branch of the service after World War II). To modern young officers it beckoned as the hot new branch of the future. But Freeman failed the eye exam—his right eye fell just short of 20/20. That had raised the most serious career question for a bright young man looking to distinguish himself in a time of peace: what should he try next? He thereupon volunteered for duty in China in the Fifteenth Infantry Regiment, a fabled unit in those semicolonial years when the great Western powers could still, in effect, divide up China territorially and post their troops there. It was a unit in which many prominent American officers, including George Marshall and Joseph Stilwell, had also served. Freeman was drawn by a young man's sense of adventure and by childhood memories of his parents in the Philippines discussing their magical days visiting an exotic China. He arrived in China in September 1933, when the first incidents in what would become a tragic world war were just taking place. An aggressive Japan was in the process of taking over China's five northern provinces—Manchuria—and turning them into Manchukuo, a Japanese protectorate. It was the start of a fascinating new part of Freeman's education, watching a once-great country, more colonized and feudal than most Americans realized, pressured from both outside and inside, eventually collapse from within. Though he became a Chinese language student (and was still fluent enough to interrogate Chinese prisoners during the Korean War), Freeman was very aware that he never really knew China. He was there, he later reflected, in the last days of empire, and the only Chinese he had known were a handful of very wealthy ones who belonged to the same clubs and enjoyed the same sports—polo and horse racing—as Westerners.

Some of the clubs did not even allow Chinese members. He understood that he had no feel for the difficult lives of the great mass of people.

Freeman spent most of World War II becoming an Asia Hand. His very pregnant wife had been sent home in the fall of 1940 as tensions mounted and the Japanese Army seemed poised to strike deeper into Asia. (He did not meet his daughter, Sewell, until she was three and a half years old.) After Pearl Harbor, he worked coordinating activities among various parts of the hydra-headed monster that was the China-Burma-India Theater: a headquarters filled with fault lines, Americans and Brits who did not care for each other, and two key American officers, Joe Stilwell and Claire Chennault, who cared for each other even less, along with representatives of different geographic venues trying to push the importance of their specific locales. He was appalled by the success of the Nationalist Chinese propaganda machinery, which implied, as he later said, that "every Chinese was baring his breast and fighting desperately against the Japanese. This wasn't true at all. . . . Once we got into the war they decided they didn't have to fight at all anymore." He also was able to watch Chiang's victory over Stilwell from a ringside seat—"He [Stilwell] knew too much about China for his own good," Freeman later noted.

In time, he was sent back to Washington, where he became one of Marshall's top aides planning for the Pacific, a great vantage point, he later noted, from which to watch Douglas MacArthur argue with the top Navy people on the dangers of splitting a command in battle. MacArthur spoke brilliantly against it—an irony that did not escape Freeman, whose men would eventually be victimized when MacArthur did the unthinkable and split his command in Korea. Desperate to get out of Washington and finally get a combat command, in November 1944, quite late in the war, Freeman was finally sent to the Philippines as chief of staff of the Seventy-seventh Division, only to be ordered back to Washington in late 1944 to work on plans for the invasion of Japan.

If Paul Freeman had been a skillful and valued planner during the war, he had nonetheless logged almost no combat time, and in the years right after the war, his career seemed to be floundering. In those days the Army used a reviewing system called the Case Board to evaluate each officer's worth during World War II and his chances for assignment and promotion in the future. On the scale used, combat leadership brought a maximum number of points, while running a PX on a domestic Army post perhaps the least. By Case Board standards, Freeman had done poorly. "A pretty undistinguished officer," he had thought, coldly sizing up his own standing as if he were a member of the board. In 1949, ever more concerned about the direction of his career, he visited a colleague who was a military career manager, who explained Freeman's dilemma in perfect Catch-22 terms. Freeman was a bird colonel with several years of experience who needed to command a regiment and attend the National War College. Here, however, was the Catch-22: because of the demobilization, there were few regimental slots available, and division commanders wanted to fill them with officers who had wartime experience commanding, naturally enough, regiments. As for the War College, that too was blocked, because only officers who had served with distinction as regimental commanders could attend. So it appeared likely that Freeman would end his military career as an Army attaché in Chile.

But Freeman was not without powerful friends; he had, after all, spent much of the war working at a relatively high level for George Marshall. A year later, when he visited his career counselor, things had quite magically turned around. "Well, lucky you," the counselor, Pic Dillard, noted somewhat sardonically at their second meeting. For Freeman had been assigned both the command of a regiment and a ticket to attend the War College. Since he owned a house in Washington and the War College was located there, he preferred to go to school first, but the Army had its own special sense of order, and so Freeman was told to pack up and take over his regiment. The financial resources of a regular Army officer were always thin, so he sold the house—the deal being completed on June 25, 1950—before heading for Fort Lewis to assume command of Second Division's Twenty-third Regiment. Freeman had barely joined his unit before it boarded troopships for Korea. Under his command, the Twenty-third (like the division itself) was to participate in and eventually to excel in some of the fiercest fighting of the war.

From the start, in no small part because of his knowledge of China and what had been happening since 1945, Freeman privately viewed the war itself with considerable melancholia—the exact word he used in his letters to his wife. He expressly cautioned her to tell no one else what he was thinking. ("For God's sake don't go putting this out—it's just for you and close friends.") He feared that otherwise his doubts and anxieties, private though they were, might represent an unacceptable attitude for a commander. He told her just how difficult the fighting was and how depressed he was. In his wariness of what American forces were engaged in, he was not that different from many of the officers then taking command in Korea. The realities of the war seemed to dilute much of America's natural military strengths. In his letters there is an early glimmering of what would later be labeled the Never Again Club, those military men who served in Korea and left with a deep-seated belief that American ground forces should never again fight on the mainland of Asia, in part because of the terrible logistical difficulties, but even more because of the inevitable deficit in manpower. These were, it should be noted, his views *before* the Chinese even entered the war, and he worried constantly in his letters that sooner or later they were going to come in. He was haunted by a sense that the proportions in this war were in some way all wrong, what the other side might be able to invest compared to what the United States could safely afford to invest—in a war that was self-evidently peripheral to American national security interests.

Korea was, he wrote on August 9, soon after he arrived, "one of the toughest spots our forces have ever been committed to and we have [come with] far too little and too late. None of us can understand the optimistic and complacent accounts put out by headquarters. The enemy hasn't shown any signs of weakening." The terrain and weather were terrible. "As for me in my job as regimental commander, I'm the model of optimism and enthusiasm. I intend to do my best as a professional soldier." Two and a half weeks later, just before the final North Korean push on the Pusan Perimeter began, he wrote, "We have dug ourselves into the hillside like a bunch of moles. The flies and mosquitoes are terrific and the dead we can't get to bury are beginning to stink. We never even get our shoes off here. Water is scarce and our food has to come up from ten miles back."

Everyone, he wrote home, was always exhausted. There was no time off, no place to rest or sleep, no place to eat. The Americans chose to do their fighting in the daytime; the North Koreans, who had no airpower, at night. That meant the Americans never really got the night off. Even in the rare peaceful moments they had to be on alert, wondering when the next attack might come. Those who slept a little too soundly, it was believed, might never wake up. In the Naktong battle, even though the Americans had stopped the main North Korean thrust in the first forty-eight hours and gradually strengthened their defensive positions, the fighting never abated, not even by September 16, which was the jumping-off day in the Naktong area for the big American counter-assault, coordinated with MacArthur's Inchon landing the day before.

Probably on September 8 the In Min Gun came closest to smashing through the Twenty-third's lines, attacking regimental headquarters from the rear and almost breaking through just at the point where Fox Company, which was in charge of the regiment's defense, was thinnest. It was a terrible night, rain pouring down, one that favored the North Koreans. First Lieutenant Ralph Robinson, nominally the battalion adjutant but just promoted to company commander because Fox had in the previous week lost all its officers, reacted brilliantly. Although the North Koreans had already deeply penetrated his company's position, Robinson managed to slip right through their position under heavy fire in the drenching rain, reach Able Company, detach its reserve platoon, and lead it back. He used Able Company to patch up the collapsing defense and drove the North Koreans off. It was an astonishing accomplishment, his superiors later decided.

After the battles for the Naktong were over, regimental aides estimated that between September 2 and September 15, at least seventeen major Communist attacks took place, all aimed at the heart of the Twenty-third's position. In one letter Freeman wrote his wife after ten days of the Naktong fighting, he noted, "It's poured for the last three days. We've had no air support. (In fact damn little when the weather is good.) Our artillery planes can't go up and we are blind. We're just sitting here, taking it. We have already repulsed thirteen attacks in force—ten of them at night. The nights are the worst. The gooks just pour in all over, and we continue to slaughter them. The rest of the time we're continually under fire. He can bring his stuff across the River at will. We are all disgusted with our Air Force. Our losses are terrific. I have left less than 40 per cent of what I had on the 31st of August when this particular battle started. Almost all of my company officers have been lost. . . . We are bitter about the whole thing. We fight desperately for all we're worth; not only because we realize our course is right, but also because we're fighting for our survival. But it all seems so useless and stupid. To 'liberate' South Korea we're destroying it and its people in the course of war more than we are the North Koreans. All Koreans hate us. Everyone here is an enemy. We can't trust anyone."

He concluded: "Then too I'm more and more convinced that we've been sucked into a beautiful trap where we're having to take on all the fanatical hordes of Asia. It seems our whole regular Army has been committed and chewed up. I see no way of getting out of this thing or any end to it. We can't impose a military defeat on these Oriental fanatics. They just keep coming. Life is cheap. They aren't dependent on supplies or communications as we are. I feel more and more that we have made a supreme error in committing our forces in this bottomless pit." These were the words of an Army commander who had not had a decent night's sleep in weeks. Even the paper he was writing on, he noted, was soggy from the rain.

In the end, he believed the battle along the Naktong had been worth it, for all the hardships and losses they suffered. They had also been incredibly lucky. The North Koreans had had little sense of just how fragile the American positions were. They had had no airplane spotters to tell them how few forces initially stood between them and Pusan. American losses, though, had been terrible. The First and Second Battalions of the Twenty-third alone, according to regimental logs, had suffered over 50 percent killed and wounded. The commanders of every rifle company in the first two battalions had been lost during this two-week period. In some companies, the official report noted, they had been replaced three to five times. Paul Freeman never really forgot those awful days on the Naktong or the grim choices he had been forced to make, sacrificing some young men so others might live. Some seventeen years later, as a four-star making his last tour of Fort Benning before retiring, he discovered that Sergeant Berry Rhoden, formerly from Charley Company, by then a grizzled master sergeant, was still stationed there. Freeman had always remained close to the men who had served with him in the Twenty-third in Korea, and he had sought out Rhoden a number of times, just to talk. Now, on this final ceremonial day, he asked Rhoden to accompany him on his tour. There was another general with them that day, a two-star, and Rhoden enjoyed the byplay between them, four-star to two-star, rarified stuff for an NCO to witness. At one point, Freeman turned to his colleague. "I'd like to introduce you to a member of your command, Sergeant Berry Rhoden. He's an old comrade of mine. Berry is a survivor of a terrible moment when I made the hardest decision I ever had to make as an Army officer. I had to sacrifice his entire company for the good of my regiment and all the other units in the Pusan Perimeter. I had to buy time for the other units to form into a blocking force. And they bought the time we needed. It was a terrible, terrible moment and a brutal decision. It was the hardest decision I ever made. Almost no one from his unit survived. You take good care of him, hear." It was one more reminder to Rhoden that none of them had been able to forget that moment.

THE STAND BY the Second Engineers and the arrival of the Marines to help block the routes to Miryang did not end the Naktong-Pusan fighting. It only abated with Inchon—and even then, despite the threat of being completely cut off, some North Korean units fought on, with the rare tenacity that reminded veterans of the island struggles with the Japanese near the end of World War II. Isolated pockets of resistance, where the North Koreans were entrenched in well-concealed hill or mountain positions, held out for days. "We hit Hill 610 so hard," Lee Beahler said of some of the fighting "that after the battle it should have become Hill 609."

Walton Walker was one of the first to sense the change in the Naktong fighting. During the worst of it in early September he had worried constantly about whether the moment had come to abandon the Naktong defense completely and move back to what was known at headquarters as the Davidson Line, a position drawn up about three weeks earlier at the request of General MacArthur just in case the Eighth Army could not hold. It was smaller, tighter, and easier to defend than the Naktong Line, and much closer to Pusan itself. On the night of September 4, Walker had Gene Landrum, his chief of staff, prepare orders for all units to fall back to the Davidson Line. The next day, he asked Mike Lynch to fly him over the front lines, and wherever they went, the troops, recognizing the three stars recently repainted on the plane, waved. Walker was impressed; the morale of his men was on the upswing, and based on that sense he decided they would try to hold at the Naktong.

The North Koreans had not collapsed. But the great offensive had failed, and they were now the overextended force, caught in strategically vulnerable positions, their supply lines too long, their elite troops badly beaten down by two very hard months of fighting an adversary who had gradually gained the advantage in hardware, armor, artillery, and airpower and was gathering strength by the day, rushing men and materiel to the front. The dream of a three-week race to Pusan had died as completely as that of two hundred thousand Communists in the south rising up to join the battle. The Communists had rolled the dice in that winner-take-all moment on August 31 and had come up short. Ever so slowly, they were being turned, without anyone quite realizing it at first, into an army on the defensive. Suddenly, they were the ones fighting just to hold on.

Lieutenant Jack Murphy was soon a beneficiary of that change. Murphy was a talented recent graduate of West Point, class of 1950, who had found himself on his way to Korea only a few weeks after graduation, his honeymoon cut in half, and he had taken over a platoon in the Ninth Regiment of the Second Infantry Division. He had been involved in very heavy fighting from the moment he arrived, just in time for the big North Korean push along the Naktong. Within twenty-four hours of his arrival at the front, he had been engaged in bitter fighting for which he had received the Silver Star, and his platoon sergeant, Loren Kaufman, the best soldier he ever met, won the Congressional Medal of Honor.

The Naktong fighting, thought Murphy, had been the most bitter kind of combat, a violent death to the loser kind of tug-of-war. For the fighting men, each day was a triumph—or a disaster—because it seemed like it could always go either way: exhausted men in both armies stumbled into one another in small firefights that often ended with bayonets as the arbiters of victory. The victories were anything but clear or grand. Surviving for another day was everything. The problem with taking one small hill was that, sooner or later, some officer somewhere up the ranks was going to find another small hill for you to take. The new hill would be one no one had ever cared about except that it overlooked some narrow dirt road that no one had ever cared about either, which would lead the Communists, if it were not guarded and controlled, to a small port city called Pusan, which no one outside Korea had even heard of until June 25, 1950, and which most Americans still did not care about—unless, of course, the Communists entered the city.

The Naktong fighting was comprised of a thousand little battles, many of them fought with unsurpassed savagery, so many miniature Battles of the Bulge, in George Russell's words, containing all the principal elements of that famous battle, everything but the size and scope and place in history. But if these battles lacked sufficient scope to be worthy of a great historian, they offered sufficient history to last the rest of a man's life and haunt him accordingly, frozen permanently and cruelly in memory.

Murphy had been on the line for some two weeks when he was switched from a platoon in George Company to the command of Fox Company, which had lost all its officers. It was not a move he had been eager to make. He had come to like his men, *his guys,* in that difficult two-week stretch. The relationships, starting from nothing and building each day with each new battle, had become incredibly intense; it was as if they had all been born in the same week in the same hospital in the same small town, had known one another all their lives, and had never made any other friends. But Murphy had no choice—his superiors wanted him to take Fox, and Fox he would take. In some way he sensed that something big was coming up on the UN side. No one at his grade level, fighting out there in the field, knew anything about Inchon, soon to be launched, but there was certainly talk about something big about to happen. Around September 13 or 14, he was never sure which, Murphy was moved back up to the Naktong and ordered to take a huge hill about two miles from the river, where the North Koreans appeared to be very well emplaced. Whenever the Americans got near the hill's base, a rain of mortar fire came down. Fox Company had lost its company commander early in the fighting there, and that was why Murphy, at the age of twenty-four, became a company commander. It was not an assault he was looking forward to—the hill seemed to be filled with natural craggy points where the North Koreans could take cover and fire away.

Murphy tensed just as the assault began, sure that the enemy mortars would tear his company apart. But they moved forward across a partly open field and nothing happened. What should have been a violent battlefield remained silent. He wondered if the North Koreans were waiting for his men to get even closer before they opened up. But there was no resistance even as his men started their ascent. When they finally reached the top unscathed, Murphy could look down in one direction, the one from which he had come, and see how terribly vulnerable he and his men had been, and then look in the other direction and see the reason for the silence: the North Koreans beginning to pull out, turning their heavy guns in the other direction and hauling them away. To Murphy, expecting the worst battle of his young career, a climb up a steep hill under fire from heavy weapons, it seemed like a small miracle, nothing less than the gift of life. Just then he got a call from his superiors telling him to return to the command post because something had happened. That something, he soon found out, was Inchon.

When the In Min Gun broke, they did so poorly, like a conventional army. They were not nearly as experienced in this sort of situation as the Vietminh fighting the French in Indochina, who were long accustomed to dealing with the superior airpower and general firepower of their Western enemy. The Vietminh, as Murphy understood it, were expert at disappearing from battlefields they no longer liked, and would have split immediately into very small units at the Naktong and slipped into the hills, moving mostly at night. But the In Min Gun stuck to the roads at first and for a day or two the Air Force had a free-fire zone. When Fox Company began moving up, Murphy had never seen anything like it—blackened bodies and blackened vehicles all along the route.

Part
Six

━━━━━

MacArthur Turns the Tide:
The Inchon Landing

19

INCHON WAS TO be Douglas MacArthur's last great success, and his alone. It was a brilliant, daring gamble. It surely saved thousands of American lives just as he had predicted. He had fought for it almost alone against the doubts of the principal Navy planners and very much against the wishes of the Joint Chiefs. Inchon was Douglas MacArthur at his best: audacious, original, unpredictable, thinking outside the conventional mode, and of course, it would turn out, very lucky as well. It was why two presidents, who had grave personal and professional reservations about him, had held on to him nonetheless. "There was one day in MacArthur's life when he was a military genius: September 15, 1950," wrote his biographer Geoffrey Perret. "In the life of every great Commander there is one battle that stands out above all the rest, the supreme test of generalship that places him among the other military immortals. For MacArthur that battle was Inchon."

He had understood Inchon's value from the start, that it was the best way to employ his superior technology when his troops were still badly understrength and threatened with being driven off the peninsula. From the beginning, he was determined to avoid a strategy in which American forces were ground up in traditional infantry tactics in harsh terrain by a numerically superior enemy. He eventually carried the day, and in the end it was everything he had promised it would be, although he was so enamored of capturing Seoul—so great a public relations triumph—that he and the officers under him did not throw out a good net to block the retreating North Korean troops, and he partially diminished the value of his own strike. If there was one serious flaw in his plan, it was the totality of his success, which gave him, if anything, more leverage over Washington and the Chiefs. Because he had stood for it against everyone else, on all other issues afterward it was hard to stand up to him. He had been right on Inchon and those who doubted him had been wrong, his supporters now argued when doubters subsequently grew nervous as he pushed his troops ever closer to the Yalu. He had rolled the dice once against great odds, and it made it harder to stop him as he pushed forward toward an even greater roll.

Douglas MacArthur had made the mistake of underestimating the abilities of the North Korean forces in the first days of the war. (He had spoken of what would happen if he could put only one division, the First Cav, into Korea— "Why heavens you'd see those fellows scuddle up to the Manchurian border so quick, you would see no more of them.") But he soon came to realize that he was fighting a ferocious, resilient, well-led, and courageous force, "as capable and tough," he told Averell Harriman in an early meeting in Tokyo, as any soldiers he had ever encountered. That assessment immediately affected his sense of strategy. Therefore, well before the American troops were pressured into the Pusan Perimeter (in danger of being "like beef cattle in the slaughterhouse," MacArthur later said), he was already focused on an amphibious landing that could bring superior American technology to bear in a way that might actually turn the war around with a single, decisive stroke.

The lessons of World War I were always with him. The British, French, and German generals, he believed, had betrayed their men again and again by sending them forward in hopeless charges against the very heart of enemy machine gun and artillery emplacements. It was a war of lion-hearted soldiers, it was always believed, commanded by donkey-brained generals. When it was all over and the awful casualties were assessed, it was almost impossible to tell who had been the victor and who the loser in the set piece battles on the Western Front. Part of MacArthur's belief that Europe was a decadent place, less important than Asia in the American future, was rooted in what he had observed in World War I. The generals on the winning side had been so careless with their men as to make him believe they were representatives of a bygone era. World War I had taught him the dangers of frontal challenges. In his deft campaign in the Pacific, vast island-hopping distances accomplished with minimal casualties, he struck more often than not at islands that were not Japanese strongpoints, a strategy premised on what he had learned in the first war. It was part of his immense complexity as a man that he could sound, in his often overripe Kiplingesque sentences, like a bloodthirsty warrior who loved the thrill of battle almost as an end in itself, but when an actual battle was being planned, could be surprisingly cautious when it came to the lives of his men.

He had used American air and sea power to strike where the Japanese least expected it, isolating and stranding their forward people and strongest positions, rather than contesting them, and he intended to do exactly that again in Korea. As early as July 4, he was already thinking of landing behind In Min Gun lines. He had little sense of how poorly trained, equipped, and led the first wave of American troops he had dispatched to Korea were. In no way were they ready for a complex amphibious operation. At first, the operation was to be called Operation Bluehearts, and it was to take place on July 22. But that was a hopeless schedule. So Operation Bluehearts was junked, but the idea of an amphibious landing was not. On July 10, when Lieutenant General Lem Shepherd, the Marine commander in the Pacific, visited Tokyo, MacArthur had wistfully said that he wished he had a Marine division on hand, and if he did, he'd land them behind North Korean lines. His hand went to the map of Korea. "I'd land them here . . . at Inchon." At that point Shepherd had suggested that MacArthur ask for a Marine division—it would, after all, serve both their interests. MacArthur needed troops, and the Marines badly needed roles and missions. The pressure to cut back the defense budgets had made the Marines' institutional future shaky, and they seemed momentarily to be without adequate political sponsorship. Both the Army and the Air Force appeared eager to usurp the Marines' traditional roles. MacArthur was all too aware of the vulnerability of the Marines: he had been sure Shepherd would jump at his suggestion, and he had. The Marines could, Shepherd promised MacArthur, have a division ready for him by September 1.

The more MacArthur thought about an amphibious landing, the more he fixed on Inchon. One hundred and fifty miles northwest of Pusan, it was on the west coast, well behind the North Korean lines. It was the principal port for Seoul, some twenty miles away, depending on how direct the route was, and even closer to Kimpo, the country's main airfield. Inchon was also potentially a disaster looking for a place to happen. Any amphibious landing was fraught with danger, but Inchon seemed like it might be far worse than any other site. "We drew up a list of every natural and geographic handicap—and Inchon had all of them," said Lieutenant Commander Arlie Capps, one of the staff members on the team of Admiral James Doyle, the Navy's top amphibious planner. Almost everyone agreed that Inchon had the look of a place created by some evil genius who hated the Navy. It had no beaches, only seawalls and piers. The small Wolmi-do (Moon Tip) Island, presumed to be well garrisoned, sat smack in the middle of the harbor, effectively guarding the port and splitting the landing zone in two. The currents inside were notoriously fast and tricky—and none of these factors was the worst of Inchon's perils; the real danger was the tides. Other than the Bay of Fundy, these might be the highest in the world, reaching peaks of thirty-two feet. At low tide, as Robert Heinl wrote in his thoughtful account of the campaign, *Victory at High Tide,* anyone trying to land would have to walk across at least a thousand yards, and at other points up to forty-five hundred yards, of a mud flat, with the gooey consistency of "solidifying chocolate fudge." It was not so much a beach as it was a potential killing field. If someone had thought to mine the harbor, and some harbors in Korea had already been mined with the help of the Soviets, it would be an unmitigated disaster. "If ever there was an ideal place for mines, it was Inchon," said Admiral Arthur Struble, the senior Navy officer in the Pacific. Worse yet, the window of opportunity during which the operation could take place was unbelievably narrow. There were only two days in the near future when the tides would be high enough to permit landing craft access to Inchon's seawalls and piers: September 15, when the tides would be 31.2 feet high, and October 11, when the height of the tides would again reach 30 feet. There was an additional problem—the morning high tide on September 15 came at 6:59, just forty-five minutes after sunrise; the second high tide was at 7:19 P.M., thirty-seven minutes after sunset. Neither was ideal for something as complicated as an amphibious landing. The October date held no attraction: MacArthur was in no mood to wait an additional month with his troops penned up in the Pusan Perimeter, while giving the Communists more time to mine Inchon. The morning of September 15, it would have to be. For MacArthur, it was all or nothing.

Almost everyone else was appalled, most especially the Navy people assigned to plan and execute the landing. Back in Washington the Joint Chiefs were wary, and MacArthur was very much aware of that. Technically they were his superiors, but he saw them as small-bore bureaucrats, men who had gained their power by accommodating themselves to politicians whom he despised. He knew that if he wanted success at Inchon, he had two battles on his hands and the first was with them. He had always expected the Joint Chiefs to oppose the landing. Some of this was his paranoia, but some was reality. He disliked and disrespected Omar Bradley, the chairman, whom he looked on as a pal of Eisenhower (a demerit there), a protégé of Marshall's (another demerit), and a man who had fought, in his view, without great skill or daring in Europe (a third demerit) with far greater forces than MacArthur had ever been given in the Pacific (a fourth demerit) and had now become close to Truman (the ultimate demerit).

If their relationship was terrible, then most of the enmity, as usual, was on MacArthur's side. Each man had collected a good deal of baggage over the years. MacArthur was sure Bradley hated him because he had vetoed a major command for Bradley during the planning for the invasion of Japan. There was no evidence of that, but there was a good deal of evidence that Bradley, like other senior figures in the postwar national security world, was uncomfortable with so senior a figure being effectively outside his reach. MacArthur believed (with good reason) that in 1949 Bradley had been a co-conspirator in a plot sponsored by Dean Acheson to limit his power in Japan by splitting his job. MacArthur got wind of it and was furious. Later, Admiral James Doyle, who did most of the planning for the Inchon landing, mentioned to MacArthur Bradley's lack of warmth when the two had met in Tokyo. "Bradley is a farmer," MacArthur told Doyle.

The Chiefs were wary, in no small part because of the risk itself, so dangerous an undertaking involving so large a share of America's available troops.
(MacArthur himself spoke of Inchon being a five thousand to one shot.) But
some of their wariness stemmed from intra-service rivalries. For a variety
of reasons, some noble, some less so, almost everyone was against the plan.
Among the exceptions were Averell Harriman and Matt Ridgway, and in time
Truman himself, who gave his trust in the end to the man in the field. Inchon's
lead planner, Admiral Doyle, had significant doubts of his own; and like many
other men he had to deal with Ned Almond, who became MacArthur's lead
man on Inchon, and Doyle quickly came to dislike him for his peremptory,
bullying style and his tendency to isolate MacArthur from things he needed to
hear. If they were going ahead, Doyle believed, then MacArthur must know all
the terrible risks involved, and he told Almond this. "The General is not interested in the details," Almond replied, but an irritated Doyle was not to be
brushed aside. "He *must* be made aware of the details," the admiral insisted. In
time he won his case, and made sure that MacArthur knew those details, for in
the details were the dangers.

It was as if Almond had tried to separate Doyle from doing his job, because
MacArthur was always the great MacArthur, a man above mundane details.
Those lesser details—whether or not a plan would work—could be dealt with
by lesser commanders who were lesser men. That grandeur was implicit in the
way MacArthur dealt with everything and everyone. Now he prepared for one
of the great performances of his life—convincing the Navy and other doubters
to go along with Inchon. A great performance was needed before the representatives of the Navy and the Joint Chiefs, and a great performance he would
give.

He was still the most theatrical of men. In World War I he had worn riding
breeches, a turtleneck sweater, and a four-foot scarf—"the fighting dude," his
men called him. He did not merely seek the limelight, he had an addiction to
it. He was aware of camera positioning, always making sure that his famous
jaw jutted at just the right angle for photographs. Indeed, as he grew older, not
only did his staff censor all news photos, ensuring that nothing insufficiently
heroic went out, but they tried to impose certain ground rules for camera an-
gles. Not only was he to be shot, if at all possible, from the right side, but one
Stars and Stripes photographer had been under orders to shoot the general
while kneeling himself, in order to make him look more majestic. He always
wore his battered old campaign hat. It was his trademark, and no photographer was ever to be allowed to show that he was partially bald, and working on
what would be known eventually as a major comb-over. He needed to wear
glasses in his office but did not like to be seen wearing them, and so they too

were not to be photographed. That everything was a performance had always been true. "I had never met so vivid, so captivating, so magnetic a man," William Allen White, the famed editor from Emporia, Kansas, wrote after meeting him during World War I; MacArthur, he added, "was all that Barrymore and John Drew could hope to be." Bob Eichelberger, his senior Army commander in World War II, dealing with the censorship of wartime, had coded his letters for his wife. In them, MacArthur was always Sarah—as in Sarah Bernhardt, the great actress of that era. "Do you know General MacArthur?" Dwight Eisenhower was once asked by a woman. "Not only have I met him, ma'am," Eisenhower answered, "I studied dramatics under him for five years in Washington and four in the Philippines."

Mystique—indeed a certain mystery and distance from mortals—was power, MacArthur believed, and he worked carefully on it. No outsider was to have too much access to him; certainly not until he was ready to perform. What he wanted to project to the larger public was the most calculated of self-portraits. Each word describing him was, if at all possible, to be carefully chosen. When, during World War II, a profile of him was written that described him as being aloof, he tried to have the censors change the word to austere. No intimacy with subordinates was permitted. He was to be above other generals. Dwight Eisenhower, on becoming his top aide in the Philippines in the 1930s, was startled to discover that MacArthur would sometimes refer to himself in the third person, saying things like: "So MacArthur went over to the senator . . ." In these years, he saw himself—and portrayed himself—as the man who embodied the nation's living history, *history's man*. It was an honor to be received by him, and if you came, it was to admire him as an icon, a living monument. There were daily rituals and they were to be observed; for example, at lunches in Tokyo held regularly for visiting VIPs, Mrs. MacArthur would greet guests who had, of course, arrived ahead of MacArthur, and then as he finally entered she would say quite reverentially, "Why, here comes the general now." He would then greet her, in the words of one witness, "as if he hadn't seen her for years."

This then was the brilliant, highly original, temperamental commander who dominated the most important of briefings on Inchon on August 23, almost two months after the first North Korean strike. It took place at MacArthur's headquarters in Tokyo. Joe Collins, the Army chief of staff, Forrest Sherman, the chief of naval operations, and Lieutenant General Idwal Edward, the Air Force operations deputy, flew out from Washington. Hoyt Vandenberg, the Air Force chief of staff, did not attend. It was believed by some sensitive to divisions in the services that he did not want to legitimize an operation that essentially belonged to the Navy and the Marines. The Marines, whose job it would be to lead the landing if Inchon were approved, were not invited to the meeting, their own questions and doubts never to be raised, which became something of a sore point. During the meeting Admiral Doyle and his men briefed the assembled brass in painstaking detail for almost an hour and a half. Nine different members of Doyle's staff got up and spoke about every technical and military aspect of the landing. Then Doyle himself got up. "General," he said, "I have not been asked, and I have not volunteered my opinion about this landing. If I were asked, however, the best I can say is that Inchon is not impossible." With that he sat down.

Joe Collins again suggested that they consider Kunsan or Posung-Myon, south of Inchon, both of them less risky landing sites. His cautiousness did not surprise MacArthur—it was what he expected. Then MacArthur spoke. He had prepared for this moment over and over in his mind. He knew the reservations of every man in the room, and his principal target was Sherman, the Navy chief, who had as yet not signaled what he felt. Without Sherman's approval, without the cooperation of the Navy, there would be no Inchon. Joe Collins might have strong reservations, but the Army brass in Washington would not lightly overrule an Army commander in the field. MacArthur was at his best that day; he took a room full of senior officers who were essentially against him and made them believers. As he started, he later wrote, he heard the voice of his father saying, "Doug, councils of war breed timidity and defeatism." He was not, he said, interested in a safer landing farther south. There was no great benefit in that. "The amphibious landing is the most powerful tool we have. To employ it properly, we must strike hard and deep!" The difficulties presented by Inchon were very real but not insurmountable. He was sure they could do it. All of the arguments he had heard against making the landing, he said, were in reality arguments for its success. There was a very real chance that the enemy would be completely unprepared. "The enemy commander will reason that no one would be so brash as to make such an attempt." MacArthur said he himself would be like James Wolfe at Quebec in 1759. Because the banks of the St. Lawrence River to the south of Quebec were so steep, the Marquis de Montcalm, defending the city, had placed almost all his troops on the city's north side. Wolfe and a small force had, however, come up from the south, scaled the heights, and caught Montcalm's troops completely by surprise. It was a great victory, one that virtually ended the Anglo-French colonial wars in North America. "Like Montcalm, the North Koreans would regard an Inchon landing as impossible. Like Wolfe, I could take them by surprise."

He had great faith in the Navy, he said, instantly wiping the slate clean from what been a historic, indeed marathon, clash of wills throughout the Pacific campaign. If anything, he insisted, "I might have more faith in the Navy than the Navy has in itself." The Navy—and this was said as if Sherman were the only man in the room—"has never let me down in the past and it will not let me down this time." Kunsan, he commented, knowing that it was the favored landing place of both Joe Collins and Johnnie Walker, "would be an attempted envelopment that would not envelop." It might bring a relatively easy linkup with the Eighth Army—but it would only place more troops in a larger Pusan Perimeter, where he believed they were singularly vulnerable. "Who will take responsibility for such a tragedy? Certainly I will not." He would, he swore, take complete responsibility for the Inchon operation if it failed. ("I wouldn't have taken that promise too seriously," Bill McCaffrey, one of Almond's staff members, later noted. "After all,he had said the Chinese would not come in, and when they did, and it turned out he was very wrong, and we were hit terribly hard, he accepted no responsibility at all, and he blamed everyone except himself.") If he was wrong about the landing, MacArthur told his audience, he would be there on the spot commanding. "If we find that we can't make it, we will withdraw." At that point Doyle dissented: "No, General, we don't know how to do that," he said. "Once we start ashore, we'll keep going."

Then he put his sights directly on Sherman and spoke of his affection for the Navy. Long ago, in the darkest moments of another war, he said, the Navy had come to Corregidor and carried him out to safety so he could continue to direct Allied forces against the Japanese. Then, step by step, the Navy had carried him to victory during the Pacific War. "Now in the sunset of my career, is the Navy telling me that it will not take me to Inchon and that it is going to let me down?" In the back row of a room so filled with brass was a young Army officer named Fred Ladd, an aide to Ned Almond. He smiled to himself when MacArthur made the last pitch—he's got them now, Ladd thought. No senior military man will be able to resist such a great personal challenge. Admiral Sherman then spoke for the first time. "General, the Navy will take you in." MacArthur had won. "Spoken like a true Farragut," he replied, knowing he had moved his man. (As he said that, Admiral Doyle, furious with the way his serious objections were being pushed aside, said to himself, "Spoken like a John Wayne.") Then, theatrical as ever, MacArthur lowered his voice, making them strain to catch his words: "I can almost hear the ticking of the second hand of destiny. We must act now or we will die. . . . Inchon will succeed. And it will save a hundred thousand lives." He had carried the day, and he knew it. "Thank you," Sherman said. "A great voice in a great cause."

"If MacArthur had gone on the stage, you would never have heard of John Barrymore," Admiral Doyle later said. Sherman was aboard, although the next day, slightly removed from the power of MacArthur's presentation and his one-

on-one challenge, he felt his doubts renewed. "I wish I had that man's optimism," he told one friend. Collins was still uneasy too, but uneasy or not, the
Chiefs were aboard, and five days later they wired their approval to MacArthur.
(Why, Mike Lynch later asked Walker, had MacArthur triumphed over the
doubts of the Joint Chiefs? "MacArthur has everyone thinking of Korea as an
island, and Seoul the final objective. Once it's taken the war would be over,"
Walker answered prophetically.) Nonetheless, on August 28, the Joint Chiefs
back in Washington were still nervous—so much of their limited resources to
be invested into a plan that had so many things that could go wrong—and they
sent one last message to MacArthur, suggesting Kunsan. The general dealt with
the message in classic MacArthurian style. He never acknowledged that he had
received it or that it existed. He just went right ahead, although in ever greater
secrecy, making sure that the exact plans for Inchon did not reach Washington
until the operation was already under way. He did this very deliberately, holding
back on telling Washington what he was doing until it would be too late to stop
him. What he did was, in the words of Clay Blair, "an astonishing course of deceit and deception." He waited and waited, and then on September 8 he sent
several immense volumes that contained his final plans back to Washington in
the care of a young staff officer, Lieutenant Colonel Lynn Smith, telling Smith
not to get there too quickly. Smith followed orders: The JCS expected a senior
officer but instead got a light colonel at virtually the last minute. Smith was immediately ushered into a room with the Joint Chiefs and began his briefing.
"This is D-day isn't it, Colonel?" Joe Collins asked. Smith said it was. Collins
asked when the assault would begin. "The landing at Wolmi-do will begin in six
hours and twenty minutes—17:30 your time," he answered. "Thank you," said
Joe Collins, "you'd best get on with your briefing." In the long run, what
MacArthur did at that moment damaged him with the Chiefs. He was not playing games with civilian authorities, which (within certain limits) was permissi-
ble, but with his peers, men with four stars, who felt that they were as
responsible as he for the lives of the young men in his command and the success
of the operation. That, within the culture of the military, was unforgivable.
Eight months later, when Truman fired MacArthur, it was, as Joseph Goulden
pointed out, one of the principal reasons that the president had the Chiefs'
unanimous support. It was their way of paying MacArthur back for blindsiding
them on the Inchon planning.

NORMALLY IN AN amphibious landing the element of surprise is crucial, but
strangely in this case it seemed to be missing. Everyone in Tokyo appeared to
know what was coming and where and when it was going to take place. In the
Tokyo Press Club, a great center of rumors about the war, it was already labeled

Operation Common Knowledge. The question of who would command at Inchon had been answered almost as soon as approval came from Washington.
Most senior officers in Washington and some in Tokyo had expected the
command—that of a corps—to go to Lieutenant General Lem Shepherd, the
experienced Marine commander. MacArthur in all ways owed Shepherd a
great deal for his support in getting him the Marine division in the first place,
and Shepherd as a Marine lived by amphibious landings. Everyone, it turned
out, was in for a surprise. The commander would be Major General Ned Almond, who would go forth from then on wearing two hats. When Joe Collins,
the Army chief of staff, first heard the news, he was stunned and furious: he
half rose out of his chair and exclaimed "*What?*" according to John Chiles, an
Almond staff member. Collins did not like Almond, and he did not like the
idea that MacArthur had not only carved out the Inchon command, separating it from Eighth Army, but had given it to Almond, his own man, without
even conferring with the Chiefs. (Among some officers in both Korea and
Washington, it was known thereafter as Operation Three-star, because it
was viewed, among other things, as a blatant attempt to get Almond his third
star.)

MacArthur was effectively minimizing not just Johnnie Walker, the Chiefs
belatedly realized, he was minimizing *them.* No other general would have
dared do something like that, especially without consulting them; it was a classic example of MacArthur being MacArthur, and acting outside the reach and
approval of his superiors, delighting in sticking his finger in their eyes. It was
also a very political move, for it placed much of the Korean command in the
hands of someone whose loyalty was completely to him, and was outside the
reach of the Chiefs. Shepherd might be a fine officer, an old-fashioned man
with old-fashioned loyalties, but that was the problem; he would have been
loyal to MacArthur, but he would have been loyal to the Joint Chiefs and the
Marines as well. That made him in MacArthur's view a man of divided loyalties, and that was unacceptable in this case.

Nobody in the Pentagon was happy with the move, and the Marines viewed
it as a disaster. They were already wary of Almond because he had blocked
both Shepherd, the Marine theater commander, and Major General O. P.
Smith, the Marine First Division commander, who was ticketed to command
the landing from the critical late August planning meeting. In addition, there
was a private fury among some Marines about the way that Almond had
treated Smith, a much revered officer, at their first meeting. Smith had thought
he was going to be briefed by MacArthur himself, but when he arrived at the
Dai Ichi, he found that he was there primarily to see Almond, and then was
kept waiting for an hour and a half. Clearly it was to be Smith's first lesson in

understanding the real command structure. Worse, Almond then greatly irritated the veteran Marine officer by calling him "son," a singularly patronizing
term, especially for a fifty-six-year-old Marine general, who had seen more
combat than Almond had and was only ten months younger than he was.
When Smith tried to make the case for how difficult amphibious landings
could be, Almond blew him off—that stuff, Almond answered, was all "purely
mechanical." Besides, as Smith noted in his diary, Almond said there was no
organized enemy in the area anyway. A supercilious man, Smith thought to
himself, though much of his rage about Almond he decided to keep to himself,
fearing the more he articulated it, the more it might divide the fighting men,
Marines and Army, in the command. Some of the other officers just under
Smith were in a rage. The mildest condemnation came from Colonel Alpha
Bowser, Smith's G-3, who called Almond "mercurial and flighty."

Inchon represented a great gamble: the enemy would have to be completely
asleep for it to work, because the entrance to the port was so narrow. But great
generals, MacArthur believed, take great gambles. Just before his own D-day
he summoned some of the Tokyo reporters assigned to the war and invited
them to come along on the assault, traveling aboard the *Mount McKinley,* his
headquarters ship. (Their dateline of course would then have his imprint on it,
"From MacArthur's headquarters . . .") Just before the ship left Sasebo harbor
for Inchon, there was another briefing, done jointly with Admiral Doyle.
MacArthur was in an expansive mood. He intended to cut the North Korean
supply lines. Nine times out of ten in the history of war, he said, an army was
defeated because its supply lines were cut. One reporter asked whether he
feared a Chinese intervention. The idea did not seem to bother him at all, and
his answer was much like the one he would give Harry Truman at Wake Island
a month later: he was aware of the vast difference in demographics, he said; if
"we commit 150 million Americans, they could still put in four Asiatics for
every American." He therefore would not challenge them in an area of their
strength. But he nonetheless had a plan for the use of airpower to neutralize
them, to play to our strengths and away from theirs and to nullify their massive numbers. "If the Chinese do intervene, our air [force] will turn the Yalu
River into the bloodiest stream in all history." Whether he or those around him
who had done his planning understood how the Chinese fought and how their
strategy at least partially limited the effectiveness of airpower was another
thing. When the Chinese finally attacked, they caught MacArthur by surprise;
his airpower was of little immediate effectiveness, and there was almost no
Chinese blood in the Yalu, which they had long ago crossed, undetected.

20

AT INCHON, MACARTHUR was lucky, in no small part because Kim Il Sung was not the most nimble of adversaries. For whatever reason, Kim had refused to pick up on the possibility of an amphibious landing taking place behind his lines. The Chinese, on the other hand, were very much aware of a massive American buildup in Japan in the weeks before Inchon. Because Japan in the late 1940s and early 1950s was a sieve for espionage, because security at Japanese ports was marginal, and because many Japanese dockworkers were dedicated Communists, the Chinese knew that much of the equipment being brought in was the kind to be used for an amphibious landing. By early August, Mao Zedong was very concerned about what he was hearing about the North Korean offensive. The quick victory promised by Kim in the South had not materialized. The Americans, Mao knew, were stiffening their resistance in Pusan in late August and early September, but they were also keeping what appeared to be two divisions of their best troops in Japan. Amphibious landings were being practiced. Clearly something was up. Mao had spent much of his lifetime fighting adversaries who had not only superior forces but superior weaponry, and so military intelligence had always been critical to his success—the Chinese had learned to avoid their enemies where they were strongest, strike only where they were weakest, and once in battle they always had to be ready to break off contact in order to fight another day. Mao took what was happening—and what he sensed was about to happen—with the utmost seriousness.

So in early August, well before the landing itself, he assigned Lei Yingfu, one of the ablest men on his general staff, and Zhou Enlai's military secretary, to figure out what the Americans were up to and where they might strike next. It was the purest of military intelligence missions. Certain things were clear to the Chinese military intelligence people. In addition to some of the American units there practicing amphibious landings, Japan's harbors were swarming with American and allied ships of all sizes from all over the world. In addition, the American commander, MacArthur, had waged his Pacific campaign using amphibious landings again and again. Lei studied all the available intelligence and decided the Americans were preparing a major trap for the North Koreans, that they were going to land by surprise far behind the In Min Gun's lines. He believed they not only intended to break out from the Pusan Perimeter, but with the amphibious landing they hoped to capture much of the North Korean Army at the same time. Lei studied his maps, tried to think like an American, and decided that the amphibious assault would come at one of six ports, and that MacArthur, given the aggressive nature of his personality, would most likely choose Inchon. On August 23, a week before the final Communist push along the Naktong began (and the day by chance of MacArthur's dramatic appeal to the Chiefs in the Dai Ichi war room), Lei took the results of his study to Zhou Enlai, who was greatly impressed and immediately passed them on to Mao. Summoned by Mao, Lei gave a formidable briefing and offered a three-page memo on MacArthur and his tactics, his mind-set, and his personality quirks. Mao then told Zhou Enlai to pass the estimates on to Kim Il Sung. Some of Kim's Russian advisers were making similar suggestions, but none of this seemed to move Kim. This was hardly surprising. After all, he had risen to power not by battlefield brilliance, but by managing to survive in a cruel political era, and then by being essentially ideologically obedient. Kim held power largely through the largesse of the Red Army. He had not learned anywhere near as many lessons on his way to power as Mao or Ho.

Mao was sure, based on his predictions, that China's role in the war was about to change. By mid-August he believed that the North Koreans had reached the essential high-water mark of their success in the South. On August 19 and 23 he met with Pavel Yudin, a senior Soviet adviser. At these meetings he told Yudin that if the United States continued to send more troops to Korea, the In Min Gun would not be able to hold and would need direct assistance from China. In August and in early September, Mao met with Lee Sang Cho, a North Korean representative in China. In these meetings, he indulged himself slightly—a little chance to pay the Koreans back for the condescending way they had treated him at the start of the war—by going over some of the North Korean military mistakes: their failure, in essence, to seek more of his advice. They had not prepared enough in the way of reserve forces, even as they were striking on so broad a front. They had put too much effort into conquering territory rather than destroying their enemies. Then he mentioned the current vulnerability of places like Kimpo Airfield and suggested that the North Koreans consider retreating and strengthening their defenses at places that were especially vulnerable. He even pointed to the map and specifically mentioned Inchon as the most likely target. But Kim, surprisingly to the Chinese, made no moves, not even to mine Inchon harbor.

The Chinese understood what was happening at the front; the North Korean leadership did not. One of the problems in a totalitarian system like that of North Korea was that bad news tended *not* to filter back with much accuracy from the front to higher commands. That could be true of democratic societies as well, but it was all the more true of deeply hierarchical ones like North Korea. Instead the news was sanitized step by step as it moved upward. Thus, on September 4, when Mao's emissary, Zhai Junwu, told Kim that the war was locked in a stalemate in the Pusan area, the Korean leader did not believe him. His great offensive was just starting, he told the Chinese representative, and would soon break the deadlock. When Zhai mentioned the possibility of a United Nations strike behind North Korean lines, Kim answered, "We estimate that presently a U.S. counterattack is not possible; they do not possess sufficient troop support and therefore a landing to our rear ports would be difficult." Stunned by his response, Zhai returned to Beijing on September 10, five days before the Inchon landing, and then went back to Pyongyang again. He brought with him Zhou's pleas that Kim make a strategic withdrawal. "I have never considered retreat," Kim replied. Zhou was annoyed by the response, and on September 18, three days after the Inchon landing had taken place virtually unopposed, he met a senior Soviet representative to suggest once again that the North Koreans pull back, regroup their units farther north, and play on Western fears that the Chinese or the Russians would enter the war.

THE LANDING ITSELF—thirteen thousand men hit the seawalls and piers—and then the race for Seoul that followed, went not merely as MacArthur had planned, but as he had dreamed. The conditions proved better than expected, the initial resistance comparatively light; Doyle's planning had been skillful and detailed, and the gods of battle favored them in one additional fateful way: they provided a careless enemy commander in Kim. The port of Inchon stuck out slightly into the bay like a truncated thumb. About ten miles east of it was Kimpo Airfield, and another five or six miles east of that, depending on the route taken, was Seoul itself. Two Marine regiments, the First and Seventh, were to take Inchon, followed by Kimpo, and then move east across the Han River and take Seoul itself. Soon there was to be a linkup with Walker's Eighth Army, which would by then have presumably broken out of its positions on the Naktong and be driving north with ever greater speed.

Initially, Marine losses were relatively light: no one killed in the assault on Wolmi-do Island, which opened up the harbor, and only twenty Americans dead at the end of the first day. Gradually, though, as the UN forces moved toward Seoul, the North Korean resistance stiffened. As that happened, tensions between Almond, the Tenth Corps commander, and O. P. Smith, the commander of the First Marine Division, which was part of his corps, grew more bitter. Almond began demanding immediate results, which Smith, trying to complete the increasingly deadly mission without unnecessarily sacrificing the lives of his men, thought unrealistic. Smith (and most of the other senior Marines) came to believe that Almond was an unrealistic commander, a man who listened only to the voice of the man above him and was careless with his orders, insensitive to the lives of the men in his command, and far, far too concerned with public relations. The seeds of such a split had long been there. From the start, top Marine officers had felt that Almond, who had never been part of an amphibious landing in his life, minimized the dangers and difficulties, was improperly respectful of their needs, and did not listen to anyone he outranked. Nor could two officers have been more different. Almond was almost self-consciously audacious; Smith, the least charismatic of Marine commanders, was low-key and professorial. (Indeed, his nickname, which no one dared use to his face, was the Professor.) Some of the tension reflected the very different nature of leadership in the Army and the Marines. The Army was big, and relationships between commanders and their men were often impersonal; the Marines were a small service, the relationship between officers and men more intimate, indeed intense. If anything, O. P. Smith was even more careful than the average Marine officer. He had been the assistant division commander of the First Marines in October 1944, when they landed on the island of Peleliu. That had been one of the cruelest and costliest battles of the war in the Pacific. There had been a major intelligence miscalculation, and the Marines, upon landing, had found their numbers matched by some nine thousand extremely well-dug-in Japanese. It was the kind of experience that tempered a man forever.

If the officers' relationship had begun poorly, it disintegrated once combat began. Indeed the feud, in the words of Marine historian Edwin Simmons, eventually became "the stuff of legends." Simmons, who fought at Inchon and the Chosin Reservoir as a young Marine officer, thought that no small amount of the tension came from the way World War II had been fought in two very different theaters. The Army men who fought the Germans in Europe had been able to bring in vastly superior firepower, and often, when a German unit cracked, large numbers of them surrendered and the rest retreated quickly, allowing the Allies to race ahead and make major gains. The men in the Pacific, Marines and Army, on the other hand, fought a far more grinding war, and when the Japanese gave way, they did it ever so slowly, the Allied advances often seeming to be measured in yards, while relatively few Japanese surrendered.

Smith had warned Almond that the ease of the Inchon landing was deceptive, that they had overwhelmed small detachments of rear-echelon troops, but

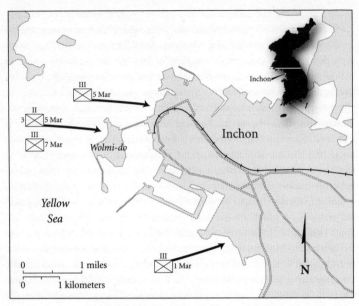

9. THE INCHON LANDINGS, SEPTEMBER 15, 1950

that taking Seoul might be a very different thing. There was, he said, based on some preliminary recons, evidence of a well-defended city protected by thousands of elite North Korean troops. Smith was accurate in his projections. Originally MacArthur's G-2 had estimated about six to seven thousand enemy troops in the Inchon-Seoul area, but as the UN forces struck at Inchon, Kim Il Sung had rushed some twenty thousand additional troops, one full division and three separate regiments, to the Seoul area. There were in the end upward of thirty-five to forty thousand troops defending the Southern capital, some of them relatively green, but they fought hard. The road to Seoul, Smith later noted laconically, was "one of those routine operations that read easier in newspapers than on the ground." The Americans had little superiority in numbers. Their advantage lay in hardware and firepower. The North Koreans had the advantage of fighting defensively. In an urban situation, when street fighting was required, that was no small asset. That meant that the fighting would be difficult and costly, much of it block by block, and that, because of American dependence on heavy weaponry, much of the city was sure to be turned into rubble. But as the offensive slowed, as each hundred yards of ground became dearer, the pressure grew on Smith, and Almond became more aggressive, reflecting pressure from MacArthur. Almond was dissatisfied with the pace

Smith was setting, and he became—in a process to be repeated in several other battles still to come—the de facto division commander, flying around in his small spotter plane, giving orders directly to Smith's regimental, battalion, and even company commanders, without going through Division. He was sure that he was a brilliant tactical officer, and he flew over the battlefield, radioing instructions to whatever unit he spotted below him. Smith protested angrily about Almond's intrusion into his command. "If you give your orders to me, I'll see that they are carried out," he told Almond at one point, but it made no difference. Almond continued to direct Smith's men. Almond's code name was Fitzgerald, and finally Smith issued orders to Colonel Alpha Bowser, his G-3, that he was not to accept any more orders during battle from Fitzgerald without confirmation from Division.

What made the tensions between the two men worse was Smith's belief that the pressure was falsely driven, that it reflected not the need for a quicker battlefield victory as a means of cutting off the North Korean Army but instead a diversion, reflecting an obsession with public relations, the constant need from MacArthur's headquarters for glory. Here the commands in Tokyo and Washington were badly split: Smith, Walker, and the Joint Chiefs, watching distantly from Washington, believed the wise course was to bypass Seoul itself, cut it off, and quickly move east to meet up with Walker's forces, who were driving north. That, they hoped, would mean not just a major victory but the chance to bag much of the North Korean Army. To them MacArthur's and Almond's obsession with Seoul defeated the very purpose of the landing, because it might let much of the North Korean Army slip through. But they knew that MacArthur wanted the capture of Seoul on or before the very symbolic date of September 25, three months after the North Koreans had first crossed the thirty-eighth parallel. MacArthur had originally wanted September 20 as the date for Seoul's liberation, but Almond had talked him out of that. To Smith, Almond was risking his Marines unnecessarily for a couple of extra lines in newspapers back home because that was what his commander wanted. He was not impressed. To him it was a gimmick, nothing more.

MEANWHILE, AT MACARTHUR'S headquarters there was growing frustration with Johnnie Walker and the Eighth Army, which was having some early problems breaking out of its positions on the Naktong. Their frustrations were nothing compared to those felt by Walker. When Walker received his first briefing on Inchon on September 17, and he learned how lightly defended it had been, he became furious. "They expended more ammunition to kill a handful of green troops at Wolmi-do and Inchon than I've been given to defeat ninety percent of the North Korean Army," Walker told a friend after the briefing. He was aware that in a number of places his men were having trouble breaking out of their positions along the Naktong. The river, he believed, had served his troops as a great defensive barrier against the advancing North Koreans, but as it had protected his men from the In Min Gun, now it was slowing them down in their pursuit of the North Koreans. What angered him was the pressure on him from his superiors, and his lack of equipment, especially bridging equipment. First choice on all of it had gone to Tenth Corps, to help cross the Han River, where all the bridges had been blown. What enraged Walker was that these were essentially decisions made by the chief of staff's office, that is, Almond's headquarters, a reflection, he felt, that the dice were loaded against him.

MacArthur and his staff took none of this into account. At a staff meeting held aboard the *Mount McKinley* on September 19, with much of the senior Navy and Marine command present as well ("virtually a public meeting," Clay Blair noted), MacArthur had spoken quite openly and in a very personal way about his frustrations with Walker, and about replacing him with someone more forceful. For Walker, it proved one insult too many. He called Doyle Hickey, the acting chief of staff, and tried to explain that there was a reason why his troops were moving slowly. "We have been bastard children lately," he told Hickey "and as far as our engineering equipment is concerned, we are in pretty bad shape." Then he added: "I don't want you to think that I am dragging my heels, but I have a river across my whole front and the two bridges I have, don't make much."

Even as MacArthur was complaining about Walker, the Marines too were beginning to slow down as they faced far stronger resistance than Tokyo had expected. Almond wanted a de facto guarantee from Smith that the Marines would make the Seoul deadline. "I told [Almond] that I couldn't guarantee anything. That was up to the enemy. We'd do the best we could and go as fast as we could," Smith later said. It was not the answer Almond wanted. If Smith had been an Army officer, it is quite likely that he would have been relieved right then and there. Almond soon came up with his own battle plan designed to speed things up, but one that, in Smith's view, would dangerously fragment the American forces into too many smaller units, rather than maximizing their superior firepower. One aspect of the Almond plan made Smith particularly nervous—in it there was a likelihood that American troops might hit a given part of the city from opposite directions and end up, in the chaos of battle, shooting at one another. He rejected Almond's plan almost out of hand—the work, he believed, of an absolute amateur. It was a most serious dissent—a division commander rejecting a corps commander's plan—and in the process he came perilously close to insubordination.

Some Marines did reach the outskirts of the capital on September 25, and so Almond was able to issue his communiqué saying the city had been taken. That seemed far from the truth to the men still fighting there. "If the city has been liberated," an Associated Press reporter said the next day in his dispatch, "the remaining North Koreans did not know it." Hard fighting in fact went on until September 28. The Americans won in the end because of their awesome firepower, but they had devastated the city in the process. Of the capture of Seoul, the British reporter Reginald Thompson wrote that it was "an appalling inferno of din and destruction with the tearing noise of dive bombers blasting right ahead, and the livid flashes of the tank guns, the harsh fierce crackle of blazing wooden buildings, telegraph and high tension poles collapsing in an utter chaos of wires. . . . Few people have suffered so terrible a liberation."

The damage the harsh, unrelenting battle did to the relationship between Almond and the Marines would have serious consequences. Almond had delivered Seoul to MacArthur on time. He had shown, Clay Blair wrote, some of the same qualities he had displayed in World War II. He was "demanding, arrogant and impatient," had a tendency to fragment his units, as well as to send units forward without sufficient reserves or very much concern about who, if anyone, was on their flanks. He was, Blair wrote later, "courageous to the point of recklessness, and expected everyone else to be. But this attitude was interpreted by many subordinate officers as a callous indifference to casualties and the welfare of his men." He also "placed greater emphasis on the quick capture of real estate (Seoul) for psychological or publicity reasons than he did on the creation of a strong line (the anvil) to stop the leakage of the NKPA northward." Of the varying criticisms made of him after the initial success at Inchon, that was the most serious one. Because of that, too many of the enemy managed to slip through what should have been a trap. "The public relations brigade," Johnnie Walker privately called Tenth Corps in disgust. Yet if it was not the complete tactical success it might have been, Inchon remained in many ways a spectacular victory and a signature personal triumph for MacArthur, the high-water mark of his career. It broke the spirit of the North Korean military and opened all of South Korea to his forces.

Because Inchon was such a success, it changed the nature of MacArthur's command. First of all there were some scores to settle. Those who had been for Inchon would be rewarded, and those who had questioned it now had to pay the price for their lack of faith. Just after Seoul was liberated, Walker's pilot, Mike Lynch, watched in disbelief as MacArthur descended from his plane at the newly liberated Kimpo Airfield, walked right past Walton Walker, the three-star who had valiantly held his forces together in Pusan ("after some of

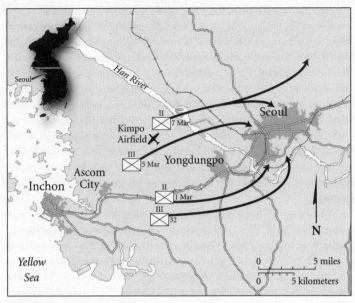

Han River

Seoul

II 7 Mar

Kimpo
Airfield ✗

III 5 Mar   Yongdungpo

Ascom
City

Inchon

II 1 Mar

III 32

Seoul

N

Yellow
Sea

0   5 miles

0   5 kilometers

10. The Drive to Seoul, September 16–28, 1950

the most vicious goddamn battles ever fought against all odds"), snubbing him completely, only to greet Almond warmly. "Ned, my boy," he said. The snub was clear punishment for Walker's having lined up too long with Joe Collins and the other Chiefs on Inchon, but there was worse to come, an act that had grave consequences for all United Nations forces. Walker had assumed that, after Inchon, Tenth Corps, out on loan, would be returned to him and folded back into the Eighth Army. Now he discovered that would not happen. Almond was going to keep his battlefield command of Tenth Corps as well as his chief of staff job. MacArthur was planning to split his command as they headed north.

While the original decision to give Tenth Corps to Almond had bothered a great many senior people both in Tokyo and Washington, it had been viewed at first as a temporary move, befitting the unusual circumstances of the moment. After all, Walker had been overwhelmed simply holding on at Pusan, and MacArthur's headquarters was hardly rich in talent. But now Almond would remain permanently in charge of Tenth Corps, a separate unit that would not report to Walker at all. If anything, Walker would now have to compete with Almond's force in the race north—and an additional amphibious landing was now being planned for Tenth Corps, this time at Wonsan, north of the thirty-eighth parallel on the east coast. In the great early flush of so significant a victory, MacArthur was seizing even greater command control. At the same time, in a fateful way, things began to go wrong. Instead of supplies pouring into the newly captured Inchon for the moment of the kill, Inchon was being used to take men and supplies *out*. Instead of racing east from Seoul to create a giant pincers to trap the retreating North Koreans, MacArthur's forces used this critical period to ready Tenth Corps ever so slowly and awkwardly for the next landing, this time embarking at Pusan and heading for Wonsan. There were the North Korean troops, trying to flee north pursued by Walker's troops, and yet the Seventh Division, part of Tenth Corps, had road priority—as they headed south for Pusan and their next seaborne assault. So, on the narrow main supply route, any convoy moving north had to give way before the Seventh heading south, violating a basic Army canon: never lose contact with your enemy.

Wonsan was, in fact, a disaster in the making from the very start. The Navy was appalled by the idea. Admiral Turner Joy, who was in charge, wanted no part of it, fearing, rightly, that Wonsan harbor would be filled with mines. He tried to see MacArthur in Tokyo to protest, but was never allowed in. The amphibious assault on Wonsan was to prove in all ways a joke. It could have been accomplished far more quickly and easily if one of Walker's Army units had simply driven north in conventional mode. Instead, everything went wrong. The planners were behind schedule, and delay followed delay. Friendly troops reached Wonsan by land first. Ignominiously enough, ROK troops from the Third and Capital Divisions got there on October 10, virtually unopposed. The next day, Walker flew into the port city along with Major General Earl Partridge, the theater Air Force commander. Finding the airport open, Partridge started using cargo craft to ferry supplies in for the South Koreans. Finally, on *October 19,* the troopships carrying the Marines arrived off Wonsan harbor. But Admiral Joy had been right, this time the Communists had deposited some two hundred mines in the harbor, and the Navy had only twelve minesweepers on hand. So the Marines had to stay in their ships while the minesweepers slowly cleared the harbor. Soon, in that prolonged wait, many of the Marines got seasick. Then a wave of dysentery hit. On one giant transport ship, 750 Marines were laid low with it. The Marines, aware that South Korean troops had already taken the town, called their landing "Operation Yo-Yo." The final insult for such proud troops came when Bob Hope, the famed comedian who often entertained soldiers in combat areas, arrived in Wonsan and gave a USO show intended for the Marines, who were still waiting in the harbor in their ships. There on an improvised stage at the Wonsan hangar, he joked that this was the first time he had beaten the Marines ashore. "It's wonderful seeing you all," he told the relatively small audience of maintenance crews, South Koreans, and some brass from the armada. "We'll invite you to all our landings." Only on October 25, two weeks after the arrival of the ROKs, did the Marines come ashore.

But the real danger—and almost everyone in Tokyo and Washington knew it—was not the landing at Wonsan but the splitting of the command. Of all the unspoken rules in the doctrine of the American Army, this was perhaps the most sacrosanct. It was something that you just did not do. When American military men thought of split commands, they thought immediately of the annihilation of George Armstrong Custer's forces at the Little Big Horn. In the future, along with Custer, they would think of Douglas MacArthur and Ned Almond, and the eventual tragedy up along the Chongchon and Yalu rivers. For here was Douglas MacArthur sending his troops into dangerous, hostile, unspeakably difficult terrain (with the weather, as he had once noted, starting to turn against them), and he was, in effect, doubling the vulnerability of each part of his force. It reflected many of the lesser qualities of Douglas MacArthur, but more than anything else it reflected his disrespect for his next potential enemy, the Chinese. That enemy had already studied him carefully, but he had not deigned to return the favor, and the men under his command would suffer bitterly for his carelessness.

Nor was this some small technical matter that slipped by. When MacArthur first allowed Almond to wear two hats, no one could quite believe what he was doing. In the words of Jack Murphy, then a young lieutenant, but later a serious student of the war, it represented "perhaps the greatest conflict of interest at a high level in the American army that I know of."

Those doubts hung over many in the command structure as the Americans moved north. After all, a great many men had wandered into various headquarters and seen maps with the Chinese forces waiting just above the Yalu marked on them. In the midst of the Naktong fighting, Murphy had been called back to Eighth Army headquarters. He had looked at a giant map and his eyes had been drawn to three little rectangles in red, up along the Yalu. Then someone told him that each rectangle represented a Chinese Communist unit. Murphy thought that meant there were three Chinese divisions up there, which he decided was a goodly number of Chinese, until he learned that each mark represented not a division, or a corps, or an army (three divisions to a corps, and three corps to an army, and three armies to an army group), but a Chinese *army group* or, as his friends in the intelligence shop informed him, quite likely a total of *twenty-seven* divisions, by a rough estimate, between 250,000 and 300,000 troops. However scary the Naktong fighting had been, just one look at that map, he thought, was scarier still.

Why MacArthur split his command and then pushed its separate wings so confidently toward a region that screamed out for maximum caution, no one ever entirely understood. Nothing he later said or did adequately explained the decision; nor did anything written either by his own staff members or by journalists sympathetic to him. To Matt Ridgway, since the decision made no sense militarily, there had to be another explanation, especially since MacArthur did not do things casually and because his moves were always political as well as military. It was a sign, Ridgway suggested some forty years later, that MacArthur, post-Inchon, aware of how much more leverage he now had, was in effect creating a separate command in a separate army, ever more outside the reach of Washington and the Joint Chiefs, and of Johnnie Walker. He was going to decrease the role and independence of the Eighth Army commander they had assigned to him, Walker, and create his own system over which he had even more control. Almond was the instrument—a pawn really—of that, Ridgway believed, of taking power from the Chiefs and Washington, and they began to understand what he was doing too slowly and too late. Splitting the command gave him far more—and Washington far less—leverage over the Army in the field. Almond would do whatever he wanted without even being asked. If there were orders MacArthur wanted followed with blind loyalty, Almond would follow them. Walker was another matter, for Walker was not MacArthur's man. The Inchon campaign had revealed flashes of independence on his part. Splitting the command, Ridgway believed, was deliberately designed to diminish Walker's independence and thus to limit Washington's influence on the Korean peninsula. It meant that Walker was no longer the sole Army commander under MacArthur, and that his wings had been significantly clipped; he was now one of two commanders, in effect only a glorified corps commander who still had to go through Almond, in his role as chief of staff, on any number of issues. In addition, because he had been forced into a competition with Almond in a race to the Yalu, he would have a far harder time questioning orders pushing him farther north; he might well be on the defensive with his superior, explaining why his troops had not moved as quickly as those of Almond. In political terms, Ridgway thought, in terms of controlling turf and keeping significantly more power in Tokyo, it was a masterful if dangerous move and a decisive victory in the battle that MacArthur was always waging—the one against Washington. The Chiefs, Ridgway believed, woke up to its full implications much too late.

B Y THE FALL of 1950, Chiang Kai-shek's dream of returning to the mainland was already hopeless, especially since no one on either side of the aisle in Congress, not even the most rabid Chiang supporters, wanted to take responsibility for sending American boys, quite possibly millions of them, to fight in China. Yet the dream of such a return was still very good politics, offering an endless free shot at the White House for its enemies. Their allies in the Chinese Nationalist embassy in Washington encouraged them, although if the top officials in the embassy had news and intelligence that might spell trouble for the United States, they did not always tell their American friends.

In the weeks before the Chinese entered the war, there were massive Communist troop movements toward the Chinese-Korean border. Senior Nationalist officials on Taiwan as well as in the Washington embassy had extremely good intelligence about these movements and, even more important, a rather sure sense about what the Communist government intended to do next. They *knew* how a Chinese government would respond to the crumbling situation in Korea, with American and South Korean armies racing for their border; because it was just how they would have responded themselves. But in fact their intelligence was based on more than instinct. Some of their former colleagues during the civil war who had been dragooned into the Communist Army after their divisions had surrendered were still able to pass on by radio what they had learned of the plans of their Communist commanders. Thus, senior Chinese Nationalist officials had very good intelligence—from former Nationalist officers now in the Communist armies and from sympathetic workers in the Chinese rail system as well as other parts of the old governmental structure. They had a powerful sense of the collision about to take place, from the day the United Nations forces crossed the thirty-eighth parallel, and every bit of intelligence they received subsequently confirmed it. (We know this, in part, because some of their cables on this matter were eventually made public by a dissenter within the Washington embassy.) A Chinese entrance into the Korean War promised a conflict they badly wanted—any hope of a return to the mainland was premised by then on war with the new China. It was their only possible hope for a ticket back. So they were in no rush to alert their American allies about what was going to happen and thus allow them to avoid the consequences of such an encounter. Because the people in the Washington embassy were, by and large, more sophisticated on American matters than their counterparts back on Taiwan, they were at pains to tell those in Taiwan to keep cool and not to share this information with the Americans.

The importance of the Nationalist embassy in Washington cannot be underestimated, in no small part because of the sheer talent of its people, and in part because there was such an important faction of the American political right that wanted to amplify the views of the Nationalists. By 1948, to the degree that the government of Nationalist China existed at all, it did so more in Washington than in China, and its constituents were American politicians and journalists, not the ordinary people of China. It was in Washington that its smartest representatives, men like T. V. Soong and Wellington Koo, operated with great skill. In May 1949, Eric Sevareid of CBS, who had covered China during World War II, reported that "the Nationalist government has all but disintegrated. Its real headquarters, if it has any, is here in Washington where its lobbyists and American supporters are desperately busy trying to scare up another big American aid program for China."

The forces driving the collision between the United States and China were more powerful than people on either side of the Pacific realized—and Taiwan had become, almost unbeknownst to the Americans, the great sticking point from the moment Chiang took up residence there. Even as Mao took power, America had already begun to separate itself from any ability to deal with him. The United States held back its recognition of his government, even as the principal U.S. allies, including the British, began to move toward it, thereby in many ways isolating America rather than the Chinese, while inevitably pushing them ever more firmly into Stalin's arms. In addition, hanging on to Chiang meant defending and protecting him, which meant in the end defending and protecting the island of Taiwan. On its own, in the years before the denouement on the mainland, the Joint Chiefs had seen that island as being in no way critical to America's national security. In March 1949, no less a figure than Douglas MacArthur had said, "There is no earthly military reason why we should need Formosa as a base," a statement deliberately made public by the State Department (which did not exactly endear Dean Acheson to the Pacific commander). Strategic policies can change, of course. Taiwan now certainly had a higher value than before. But the reversal of that policy, the decision to defend Chiang and Taiwan, would have severe consequences. It might be viewed as a relatively minor adjustment by the administration to greatly different Asian needs, but it did not look that way to Mao and his followers. To them, it was a major affront. It kept them from making their country whole. The United States had, in effect, stepped between them and the completion of their revolution, at the very moment when the Americans were cutting off all conceivable channels of communications to them. That meant there was less wiggle room for both sides by the week. In Washington, the Truman administration was reacting by instinct and making what its officials thought was a minor geopolitical adjustment; to the victors on the mainland, what Washington was doing was making the liberation of all China impossible. In their eyes it was nothing less than the act of an implacable sworn enemy.

From the moment Chiang left the mainland, few things concerned the Chinese embassy and the China Lobby more than keeping the United States from recognizing Communist China. They succeeded so well that the recognition of China became an enduring domestic issue, one the Democrats feared even to touch for more than two decades. It would take President Richard Nixon, who as a young politician rode the idea that the Democrats were weak in dealing with the Communists to political power, and thus was himself relatively immune from red-baiting, to break the ice in February 1972 with a visit to China, one that no Democratic politician even then could have taken without quite possibly being red-baited by, among others, Richard Nixon. In the meantime, Americans were left to consider a curious question: Which country was China? Was it that vast nation of 500, and then 600 and soon 700, million people, or that small island off its coast with some 8 million people, 6 million of them Taiwanese and an estimated 2 million new arrivals from the mainland? It was, for a long time, an answer Americans could not get right.

The policy questions were the gravest imaginable: Were Taiwan and Chiang that important, if the very act of continuing the embrace of them might help inaugurate a new and more dangerous chapter in our relationship with a very important nation just coming of age in a new and largely unwelcome incarnation in Asia? Did we really owe anything more to a fallen leader who had systematically failed his own people, treated American military, political, and economic advice with contempt, and served as the major source of weapons for his sworn opponents? Was it worth taking the risk of driving this formidable nation, obviously an ascending power and a potentially dangerous one, and surely one day a great power, into the arms of a sworn enemy? Was it worth reinforcing Mao Zedong in his belief that the United States was but the newest imperial power with designs on his country? Were we willing to do exactly what Mao in some way wanted, playing to his paranoia about the United States and helping to harden his attitudes and policies against us? Those were the real questions of the moment, and the answers to all of them were almost all surely no. But they were also national security questions that were muffled at the time, outweighed as they were by domestic political forces and emotions. Our policy in the end was to continue to support a government that had already died.

No one sensed the future collision more clearly than John Melby, the young China Hand who had been so wise about so many other things as he witnessed the breakdown of Nationalist China. Melby was a fascinating figure; in 1945 he had been sent to China from the American embassy in Moscow at the specific suggestion of Averell Harriman, then the ambassador to the Soviet Union, to keep an eye on what the Russians were up to in that country. Melby soon became one of the embassy's most despairing and impassioned anti-Chiang voices. He understood immediately that the popularity and success of the Communists had nothing to do with the Russians, that it was the Communists' ability to respond to indigenous grievance and to the country's latent nationalism that made them so formidable. That any relationship between the United States and Mao's China would be extremely difficult he never doubted, but neither did he doubt that it was worth a serious try. In June 1948, a year before the final collapse of Chiang's regime, he had written prophetically in his diary, "All the power of the United States will not stem the tides of Asia, but all the wisdom of which we are capable might conceivably make those tides a little more friendly to us than they are now."

The decision in the days immediately following North Korea's strike south, to move the Seventh Fleet into the Taiwan Straits, had been a fateful one, much more than the United States had realized. Mao knew he could not best the American military forces on sea and in the air, so when he finally chose to take on the United States, it would be in Korea, so much more accessible to a vast land-based army. His military could cross the Yalu on foot as they could not swim the Taiwan Straits. If the United States had drawn its line in those straits, Korea was by far the more convenient place for Mao to draw his.

Part
Seven

---

*Crossing the Parallel
and Heading North*

O N T H E   A M E R I C A N side, the decision to cross the thirty-eighth parallel
and head north was in a way a decision that made itself. It was a decision
that the senior *civilian* officials thought they would control when they finally
faced it, but that in the end would control them. When the North Koreans invaded, Truman, Acheson, and Acheson's people at State had simply not given
much thought to what would happen if the tide of war turned and North Korea's forces unraveled. Their first two months as a de facto war cabinet had
been given over to sheer survival. Few minds were concentrated on the then almost abstract problem of what should be done if the way north were suddenly
open. Now, post-Inchon, that question had suddenly become paramount.
Suddenly the appetite for a larger victory had been whetted. The men who had
so carefully controlled the decisions at Blair House back in late June had less
control as an ever greater victory seemed possible. The crucial differences
between senior civilian and military officials and MacArthur about overall
agenda and in attitudes toward China, largely suppressed when the In Min
Gun threatened to take over the entire country, now began to surface. Because
the Communists had started the war by crossing what the Americans considered a border, because so many Americans had already died in Korea, and because the commander in the field had always wanted to go north, the decision
was essentially foreordained. The more successful the United States was in the
South, the harder it was to set limits going north.

Anyone who tried to limit an offensive into the North would be labeled an
appeaser. In fact, Bill Knowland of California, one of the China Lobby's most
powerful spokesmen in the Senate, was already using the A-word. The cumulative force of several years of intensified Cold War rhetoric, words that summoned up a world divided between white and black in moral terms,
contributed to the mandate to go north, even as the issues at stake tended to
demand that people think in terms of gray. It was ever harder to be satisfied
with a truncated, partial success, with the old, always unsatisfactory status
quo. Part of the dynamic was military. It would have been hard to justify

stopping at the thirty-eighth parallel and simply waiting for the other side to rebuild its forces and strike again. The more logical move militarily, and one that the Joint Chiefs eventually fell in behind, was to go a limited distance above the thirty-eighth, build up American airpower significantly, find the right piece of terrain that could be readily defended by artillery, dig in, make any additional assault unacceptable, and then work for a cease-fire. But that would have meant accepting a concept of limited victory in a limited war, and negotiating with people Americans otherwise refused to talk to. Nor was it just MacArthur who wanted to go farther north; if the other senior commanders often had their difficulties with him, then on this issue, they tended for a time at least to be unified—it is virtually a genetic condition among military men that when they have a chance for a breakthrough, they want to push ahead.

The decision to go north prompted a debate that was never really a debate; the forces pushing to cross the thirty-eighth were simply too strong. The most critical domestic change had taken place at the State Department, especially in the slow but systematic erosion of the influence of George Kennan. By the time they faced the decision to cross the thirty-eighth parallel, he was not a major player anymore. He had believed that the risk of either the Soviets or the Chinese coming in was far too great if we tried to unite all of Korea. Paul Nitze, much influenced by Kennan on this single issue, agreed. Kennan was sure that we were heading toward a major crisis, that Washington did not have control of MacArthur, and that something terrible was going to happen. It was his personal policy nightmare: he felt the United States was overreaching militarily for something that did not matter and that would not improve our geopolitical position at all—and doing so at a fearful risk. But he was on the outside looking in by now.

Kennan was hardly alone in being sidelined. Acheson had been making his own political accommodations and battening down the hatches in the Far East section almost since he had taken over at State. Most of the China Hands, or people in charge of them, had been moved out—though Acheson did not like to admit it. He was too proud to let anyone know he was backing down on any issue for political reasons. He was exhausted by the political forces working against him on this issue, of trying to make the rather abstract case that Communism in China and Communism in Russia might be different. (About that time he revealed his frustration in a telling conversation with Clement Attlee, the British prime minister. He had been, he told Attlee, "probably more bloodied . . . than anyone else" in trying to distinguish between Soviet and Chinese intentions, and he thought it was no longer possible to act on the basis of a future split between the two Communist nations.)

As Acheson moved some of the China Hands out, more conservative men were moving in. The team at State, especially on Asia, was being changed very quickly. Dean Rusk, a quiet, centrist-conservative figure, a man of the bureaucracy itself, had become the administration's key man on Asia. Rusk was the opposite of Kennan, who brought great knowledge about Russia and China to the table but was quite insensitive to the ever more pressing realities of domestic American politics. Rusk was acutely tuned to the latter and had much less feel for (and interest in) the former. He was exactly what Acheson wanted at a moment when concessions were needed. Rusk had volunteered to take a demotion from deputy undersecretary of state to assistant secretary for Far Eastern affairs. "You get the Purple Heart and the Congressional Medal of Honor for this," Acheson had told him at the time.

Rusk was to prove the most conventional of men in terms of his feelings about China. Later, during the Vietnam era, he became known as a notorious hard-liner on Asian Communism. But even in the summer of 1950, Rusk was already beginning to emerge as a hard-liner in the department, with views that would cause him no contemporary political problems; he believed the rise of Mao represented a historic change, "a shift in the balance of power in favor of Soviet Russia and to the disfavor of the United States." Rusk, unlike Kennan, saw the Communist world as a monolithic entity. He had been one of the first senior people who argued for bringing John Foster Dulles into the State Department, and when that happened, he and Dulles quickly became allies over the importance of defending Taiwan. On May 18, 1950, Dulles had prepared a draft policy paper suggesting that Taiwan was as good a place as any to draw the line; twelve days later Rusk took the same position. They both painted the island as an attractive redoubt to defend because the United States could wield its long-range air and sea power effectively there, and the Soviets (and Chinese) could not bring their land forces effectively to bear.

Dulles's reentry into the department was a controversial one, itself reflecting the fact that Truman and Acheson were seriously on the defensive against mounting Republican opposition. Dulles had been the shadow cabinet Republican secretary of state and Dewey's chief foreign policy adviser, a man viewed as connected to the political forces of Eastern internationalism. Dewey's 1948 defeat had been a bitter disappointment for him. He had then been appointed to a vacant Senate seat in New York, insisting that he would not run for election; then he decided to run for the seat anyway and, in a special election, lost to Herbert Lehman, the popular former governor, by nearly two hundred thousand votes out of nearly 5 million cast. With that, Dulles, wanting to get back into the world of public policy (and greater public visibility) and knowing there were more presidential elections still to come, started making overtures to the Democrats about some kind of role at State. He would, he told administration officials, help restrain some of the men on the Republican right like Senators Styles Bridges and Robert Taft, but only "if Truman allowed [him] to plan some early affirmative action against 'the Communist menace.'" Not everyone wanted Dulles there—he was known for both his grandiosity and righteousness—but Acheson, hardly one of his admirers, gradually decided that tactically it was a smart move. When Acheson first mentioned it to Truman, the president exploded. Dulles had said too many harsh things about his domestic policies during the 1948 campaign. But Acheson, pushed on Dulles's behalf by Arthur Vandenberg, the leading Republican internationalist, bided his time, then raised the idea with Truman again, and Dulles was finally assigned the Japanese Peace Treaty to work on. John Allison was assigned to work with him. Allison had served in Japan as a young foreign service officer, had briefly been interned in Japan after Pearl Harbor, and had become head of the *Northern* Asia office—a fortunate post, for it meant that he had not been caught in the political crossfire over China.

There was an immediate impact to Dulles's arrival in high-level meetings. In George Kennan's view, Dulles should have been present only at meetings directly pertaining to the Japanese Peace Treaty. His presence, a surprisingly dominating one in certain circumstances, Kennan believed, was a reflection of changing domestic politics, and tilted the debate to a harder line, one reflecting the growing pressure from the right, and bringing that pressure right into the room. By early July, Kennan had already begun to feel that events were slipping out of this administration's control. On July 10, the Americans had received word from the Indians, who had come up with a peace proposal for Korea, that the Chinese seemed to be interested in it. Under it, the hostilities would stop, both sides would go back to the thirty-eighth parallel, and Communist China would become a member of the United Nations. The Chinese seemed amenable, but the Soviets, not surprisingly, were clearly unhappy. To Kennan, the proposal made eminent sense. He thought Chinese membership in the UN of very little national security importance, since the Soviets were already there and had the veto; more, the proposal had the additional benefit of potentially splitting the Chinese from the Russians. He was, he said, quickly shouted down at the meeting, principally by Dulles—for the proposal would, Dulles and his other critics claimed, reward aggression. Dulles had said that it would "look to our public as if we had been tricked into giving up something for nothing." To Kennan, the political reasons for spurning the Indian proposal were all too obvious, and on July 17, he had written in his diary, "I hope that some day history will record this as an instance of the damage done to the conduct of our foreign policy by the irresponsible and bigoted influence of the China Lobby and its friends in Congress."

By July 1950, Rusk, Dulles, and Allison had formed something of a departmental trinity, and all three of them began to argue for crossing the thirty-eighth parallel, at a moment when almost no one else in the bureaucracy was even thinking about the subject. In a memoir of his years in the Foreign Service (*Ambassador from the Prairie: or, Allison in Wonderland*), Allison denied playing any role in influencing the decision to cross the parallel. In that he was all too modest. For during that important period he wrote very tough, indeed quite emotional, position papers, clearly acting as a point man for both Dulles and Rusk. They would then follow up with seconding papers. Their memos often seemed to be aimed at discrediting the more dovish papers coming out of State's Policy Planning, where even under Paul Nitze most of the senior people were nervous about Russian and Chinese intentions. As early as July 1, on returning from Tokyo, Allison had told Rusk in a paper that American forces should not only eventually cross the thirty-eighth but "continue right up to the Manchurian and Siberian border, and having done so, call for a U.N.-supervised election for all Korea." This was, of course, at a time when not being driven off the peninsula rather than conquering it seemed the most basic issue. On July 13, Allison wrote another impassioned memo to Rusk, this one occasioned by an American military official who had rather casually told reporters that American forces eventually wanted to get to the thirty-eighth and stop there. That infuriated Allison. "If I were a South Korean soldier and had heard of the announcement by the American Army spokesman I would be strongly tempted to lay down my arms and go back to the farm." A day later, Foster Dulles followed Allison with an even stronger statement to Nitze. The thirty-eighth parallel "was never intended to be and never ought to be a political line," he insisted. Honoring it now, he noted, would provide "asylum to the aggressor [and was] bound to perpetuate friction and the ever present danger of a new war." If it could be obliterated, all the better, "in the interest of 'peace and security' in the area," Dulles wrote.

Rusk was an important figure at this point, both player and litmus test, the first real hard-liner at that level in Asian affairs under a Democratic administration, and an important figure in tilting the way State, and thus Acheson, saw events now unfolding. The old China Hands might have been more nervous about anything that could tempt the Chinese to come in, but they were gone, and Rusk had few doubts about driving north. Later, after the Chinese struck American forces in the far north of Korea, Rusk told his senior colleagues that the attack "should not be on our conscience, since these events are merely the result of well laid plans and were not provoked by our actions." That was, noted the historian Rosemary Foot, "a fantastic piece of rationalization, designed presumably to bring some comfort to the administration in a time of despair."

That all of this was somehow organized, and that the more hawkish people like Rusk wanted to dominate the play at Policy Planning, seemed clear in retrospect. But Kennan and the people in Policy Planning close to him thought that going north was a tragic mistake. Fighting in Korea at all, he believed, was in pure, rational terms a mistake, because of the varying logistical difficulties, and thus unsound; but given other pressures, among them stabilizing Japan, finally worth doing—a necessary mistake, if you will. But as UN forces went farther north, in his words, the dangers of adversaries lurking there, Chinese or Russian, would grow, and "the more unsound it would become from a military standpoint" because of the way the country spread out like a mushroom and because of the increased logistical problems for our forces and the other side's ability to mass its forces. The idea of advancing above the neck in the North appalled him. But the play was going the other way. On July 15, in a memo to Rusk, Allison entered his "most emphatic disagreement" to a paper by Herbert Feis, a Kennan ally at Policy Planning, who had suggested there was a clear danger of Soviet or Chinese entry into the war if the United States went north of the parallel. The thirty-eighth parallel had always been an arbitrary line, Allison wrote. Only the obvious intransigence of the Soviets had sustained it; the United States, Allison argued, should adapt "a determination that the aggressors should not go unpunished and vigorous, courageous United States leadership to that end should have a salutary effect upon other areas of tension in the world. Notice would be served on the aggressor elsewhere, who is the same as the covert aggressor in Korea, that he cannot embark on acts of aggression with the assurance that he takes only a limited risk—that of being driven back only to the line from which the attacked commenced." Those were very strong words. A week later, the draft of a Policy Planning paper written by George Butler, yet another Kennan ally, again pointed out the risk of the Russians or the Chinese entering the war. The Communists, Butler noted, were unlikely to permit a pro-Western proxy state to exist so near the Russian and Chinese border. That paper provoked the most emotional and militant Allison memo yet, this one on July 24, to Nitze. First, Allison spoke of the shame that would follow if the United States stopped at the thirty-eighth parallel, the loss of American stature in the eyes of the Korean people if we accepted the prewar status as a postwar division. If that happened, "the people of Korea would lose all faith in the courage, intelligence, and morality of the United States. And I for one would not blame them."

Then it really got ugly. Allison used the most explosive and emotional word of that era, the one that had hovered over all National Security discussions since World War II, the A-word. Trying to nail the Kennan wing at Policy Planning, he said that "the [Butler] paper assumes we can buy more time by a policy of appeasement—for that is what this paper recommends—a timid, half hearted policy designed not to provoke the Soviets to war. We should recognize that there is grave danger of conflict with the USSR and the Chinese Communists whatever we do from now on—but I fail to see what advantage we gain by a compromise with clear moral principles and a shirking of our duty to make clear once and for all that aggression does not pay—that he who violates the decent opinions of mankind must take the consequences and that he who takes the sword will perish by the sword." That was strong stuff. That it could ignite an even larger war did not seem to worry Allison. "That this may mean war on a global scale is true—the American people should be told and told why and what it will mean to them. When all legal and moral right is on our side why should we hesitate?" Red meat was on the table. What Allison was saying was perfectly synchronized within the bureaucracy to match what the critical voices from the right were saying. What it showed was that as the domestic political situation had changed, some of the administration's critics were now inside the tent. Gradually, as it became clear which way the secretary of state wanted the play to go, opposition within Policy Planning softened. A few days after Allison's very emotional memo, Policy Planning offered up a milder one that endorsed the idea of a unified, independent Korea. Everyone was getting in line.

These exchanges were still taking place well below the highest level of policy makers. The war itself was going too badly at that moment for them to turn their minds to the issue. Right after the North Korean invasion, Acheson had seemed to speak of the issue in quite vague terms. The United States wanted to restore the South to its previous borders, he said. But by July, he had begun using a different phrase: The troops could not be expected "to march up to a surveyor's line and stop." Throughout July and August, there was an agreement not to talk about it publicly. If either Truman or Acheson was asked about what was going to happen when our troops reached the thirty-eighth parallel, they ducked the question. But Congress, better attuned to the emotions of the American people and with less direct responsibility for events, was more hawkish. Several congressmen were ready on a moment's notice to talk about appeasement, almost taunting the administration. The decision *not* to cross the parallel had already been made, some of them now suggested. "The Hiss Survivors association down at the State Department who wear upon their breast the cross of Yalta are waiting for Congress to go home before they lift the curtain on the next act in the tragedy of Red appeasement," said Representative Hugh Scott of Pennsylvania, almost a week after the Inchon landing. Not crossing, Bill Knowland agreed, would be an obvious case of appeasement.

Everyone, it seemed, including the American public, wanted a larger victory. A Gallup poll taken in mid-October showed that 64 percent of Americans wanted to pursue the North Koreans above the parallel. Polls on such matters, as Vietnam later proved, were notoriously tricky; all sorts of people were for a more aggressive policy as long as they did not have to deal with the consequences. Whether 64 percent of the American people—had they been asked—wanted a shooting war with China was obviously another question entirely. If Acheson had tried to stop the drive north or even slow it down, he would have been caught up in a major fight at the highest levels of the bureaucracy and he would have been fighting at a great disadvantage, on turf that nominally belonged to the military. For the Joint Chiefs too wanted to go ahead, or at least go ahead for a while, in effect until MacArthur's forces ran into Chinese or Russians divisions. For the senior military men it was, in the beginning at least, when they first crossed the line, like giving in to an irresistible impulse: when you had victory in your grasp, you pushed forward, or at least pushed forward until your troops encountered a different, larger, and more dangerous enemy. For them, the moment was particularly sweet in Korea because it had been preceded by considerable humiliations, and this therefore was more than a victory, it was a redemption. Let the politicians come up with their caveats, the soldiers would take care of the battlefield. That was what soldiers did; they advanced. Much later Omar Bradley would take a second look at George Butler's Policy Planning memo warning of Russian or Chinese intervention and say, "Read in retrospect—some thirty years later—this paper is full of good sense." One of the problems with the paper, limiting its influence, Bradley noted, with a sharp jab at his civilian colleagues, was that "Dean Acheson and his chief far eastern advisers, Dean Rusk and John Allison, had adopted a hawkish stance on crossing the 38th parallel."

But at the time it was a different matter. The victories were tangible; the reasons that the military should slow down and respect an army that had not yet showed up on the battlefield were abstract. Maybe as they got nearer the Chinese border, some of the senior military men felt, they could take another look. For the president the political choices were terrible. He knew the Chinese were poised at the border, yet the North Korean enemy was not merely defeated, it was fleeing the battlefield. The failure to pursue on the part of an administration already accused of being soft in Asia would bring severe political repercussions. Instead of unleashing Chiang, the new war cry would be an even more strident and politically resonant one: unleash Douglas MacArthur. A midterm election was only a month away. Twenty-five years after the events, John Snyder, who was the secretary of the treasury in those days, wrote a letter to James Webb, who had been the undersecretary of state, a very influential number two man. "My recollection," Snyder said, "is that President Truman had little choice when he made the decision to proceed northward beyond the

38th parallel. This decision was, in a way, a ratification of actions that were already being taken."

The orders given to MacArthur by Washington were, in fact, surprisingly ambiguous. He was to cross the thirty-eighth parallel, but avoid any act that would engage the United States and the UN in a larger war with either the Soviets or the Chinese. He was to break off contact if his troops met up with either Russian or Chinese forces. When he got near the Chinese border, he was to use only South Korean troops; nor were his troops to go anywhere near the Korean provinces that abutted the Chinese or Russian borders. It was, of course, only a piece of paper, and not a very good piece of paper at that. Charles Burton Marshall, one of the top Policy Planning people who helped draft it, said later, "I was full of awareness that we were kidding ourselves with the neatness of the phrasing." Years after, Acheson would write in his memoirs that if they had only seen into MacArthur's mind as he crossed the parallel, they would all have been a good deal more cautious. But that was disingenuous on his part. They already knew that MacArthur operated like a sovereign, to use Acheson's own word, and that he feasted on ambiguous orders. They also had a strong sense that his goals in Korea were grander than their own. But they were being carried along by the tidal force of events and of the general's formidable post-Inchon status, combined with a changing political climate in which their domestic enemies were becoming more powerful all the time. MacArthur was not merely the leader of the military opposition, but a putative political one as well. That they were more afraid of him than they wanted to admit was always the great secret of the Korean War. They were afraid of him in defeat and they were even more afraid of him in victory.

When, on September 27, they finally made the official decision to go ahead and cross the parallel, Acheson's young aide, Lucius Battle, brought the orders over from the Pentagon for Acheson to sign. Filled with the confidence of the young, Battle suggested that the orders were far too vague for someone like MacArthur. Acheson simply exploded—Battle later noted that he had never seen him that angry before—"How old are you Battle, for God's sake?" Thirty-two, Battle answered. "And are you willing to take on the entire Joint Chiefs of Staff?" Then Acheson signed the orders. It had been a rare moment, Battle felt, when the secretary revealed just how much he was a prisoner of events. Years later, Averell Harriman would sum it all up this way: "It would have taken a superhuman effort to say no. Psychologically it was almost impossible to not go ahead and complete the job." Like some of the other senior civilians, Harriman had understood that Inchon had been a dual victory for MacArthur, not only against the North Koreans but against his enemies in Washington as well. "There is no stopping MacArthur now," Acheson told Harriman immediately

after Inchon. "Inchon was," said Frank Gibney, then a young combat correspondent from *Time,* "the most expensive victory we ever won because it led
to the complete deification of MacArthur and the terrible, terrible defeats that
happened next." "The sorcerer of Inchon," Acheson later called him.

Nothing in those days seemed to stand in MacArthur's way. So what if they
had rushed the announcement of Seoul's recapture, even as fighting was still
going on in the streets? When MacArthur finally handed back control of his
capital to Syngman Rhee, Rhee said, "We admire you. We love you as the savior
of our race." He was the victor and the prophet. There was one more totem
now for MacArthur: a united, non-Communist Korea. That was his ultimate
goal. Nor did he see any great threat to his forces. He was sure control of all
Korea was within his grasp. Joseph Alsop, the hawkish columnist, was with
him right after Inchon and felt MacArthur was on a kind of high, brushing
aside any suggestion that the Chinese might enter the war. "As a matter of fact,
Alsop," MacArthur had told him, "if you stay on here, you will just be wasting
your valuable time." As Matt Ridgway would later write, "Complete victory
seemed now in view—a golden apple that would handsomely symbolize the
crowning effort of a brilliant military career. Once in reach of this prize,
MacArthur would not allow himself to be delayed or admonished. Instead he
plunged northward in pursuit of a vanishing enemy, and changed his plans
from week to week to accelerate this advance without regard to dark hints of
possible disaster." If after Inchon, said Ridgway, MacArthur had suggested that
a battalion get to a position by walking on water, "There might have been
someone ready to give it a try."

That did not mean everyone was really aboard. There was soon a mounting
uneasiness in Washington, first among the civilians and then among the military as well, as MacArthur began to stretch his orders, and as the march northward was accompanied first by threats from the Chinese that they were going
to enter the war in time, and then by the appearance of Chinese soldiers. People in Washington worried as well about MacArthur's own physical and emotional energies to run a full-scale war like this. There were constant reports
feeding back to Washington that he lacked the vigor for command, which
would explain why he never spent much time in country (an essential requisite
for a serious commander). Some officers in the Pentagon had heard from their
contemporaries in the field how distanced he was from Korea itself. They worried as well about his mental processes, and they were bothered above all by
the way he split his command and by the chaotic nature of the amphibious
landing at Wonsan.

There might be days when he looked wonderful, but others when he
looked tired and seemed out of it. His staff, these reports said, was doing a lot

of propping up to make him seem more vital than he was. In most photos he still looked like a significantly younger man, but sometimes another reality crept in, at moments when he could not control the atmosphere and the performance somehow faltered. Reginald Thompson, a British journalist, remembered seeing MacArthur at the ceremonies celebrating the liberation of Seoul, when he had been forced by protocol to take his hat off momentarily, and he had looked "curiously human, old and even pitiable without his hat." Still, so far it had all worked. "Had Napoleon Bonaparte examined MacArthur's career up to the eve of the Korean War," wrote his sympathetic biographer Clayton James, "he undoubtedly would have concluded that he passed the first and foremost test of a commander: he was lucky." After Inchon, that luck finally ran out.

I T W O U L D B E a time of signals sent but not received. Warnings about the Chinese coming in were not picked up in part because no one really wanted to, in part because the people who might have understood what the Chinese were saying had been squeezed out of positions of influence, and in part because in one critical instance the Chinese picked the wrong messenger. The man the Chinese chose as their conduit to the West was K. M. Panikkar, the Indian ambassador to Beijing. Panikkar was an experienced diplomat and a considerable intellectual presence, but he was also unlike the kind of diplomat with which Washington was used to dealing. The Truman administration viewed him as unacceptably far to the left, his messages reflecting his political prejudices, not reality (at least as Washington preferred it to be with *its* particular set of prejudices). Panikkar was a serious writer, the author of several books, including *Asia and Western Dominance,* which had been praised by the noted British historian B. H. Liddell Hart. But he was something relatively new in the diplomatic world, a representative of a newly independent Asian country that had just gained that independence from its colonial master. This was the prism through which he saw developments in Asia, a prism quite different from that of his more conventional colleagues. Unlike Mao's China, India was democratic, but it was non-white, and extremely sensitive to any hint of postcolonial intrusion from the West. Panikkar was not preoccupied first and foremost with the Cold War in the way diplomats from European countries were; instead, he cared about what he felt was the larger struggle taking place, between the colonizers and colonized, between the First and Third Worlds. To most traditional Western diplomats, the Cold War was the transcending historical issue of the era, the drive among non-white people to end colonialism a sideshow; to men like Panikkar, on the other hand, the great historical moment was the coming end of colonialism, and the Cold War was the sideshow. Panikkar saw Mao's victory on the Chinese mainland as part of a larger global anticolonial revolt, a view radically different from that of Washington.

Panikkar had arrived in China in April 1948 in time to witness the final months of Chiang's regime and had been appalled by the corruption. Thanks to unchecked inflation, you needed a suitcase filled with Chinese dollars just to do ordinary shopping, he noted. He had a certain sympathy for Chiang, whom he saw as a man with a medieval mind, in his words "a great man born a century too late," but little fondness for Madame Chiang, "a person conscious of her own superiority . . . [who] has also developed the deportment of a queen." Though Chiang's China was totally dependent on the United States for aid, Panikkar was amused by the attitude of "patronizing condescension" Chiang's top officials displayed to the Americans. To the leaders of the Guomindang, "America was no more than a great barbarian for whose dollars and equipment she [China] had immediate need, but for whose culture she had no great admiration."

Panikkar was the very prototype of an Indian intellectual of his time, educated in India and at Oxford; he had originally been a journalist and in time became a serious historian. He was a close friend of Jawaharlal Nehru's, India's first prime minister, with powerful connections forged during the independence struggles. Neither he nor Nehru were that much at ease with Mao's harsher vision. Mao saw Nehru as too compromised a figure to be a genuine revolutionary, and Nehru in turn was bothered by what he came to consider Mao's callousness about life. He himself was not, Panikkar eventually wrote in his memoir, sympathetic to Communism, for he hated the lack of respect it gave the individual in society. But he felt he understood the forces driving the Chinese revolution, and he disliked the forces he saw trying to stop it. In late July 1950, when Panikkar first talked with Prime Minister Zhou Enlai about Korea, the prime minister assured him that China had no intention of entering the Korean War. But in late August, and again after Inchon, the tone in Beijing began to change, and a variety of Chinese officials began to offer Panikkar a series of increasingly ominous warnings. In their eyes, post-Inchon, the perceived threat from America was changing, so their position of disengagement was changing. Panikkar might not have been the messenger Washington would have chosen, but the world was changing, and as it changed, so did its messengers.

Washington mistrusted Panikkar, and thought him a leftist. As early as September 23, a week after Inchon, Panikkar was told by Nieh Yenrong, the acting Chinese chief of staff, that China would not sit idly by and let the Americans come to their border. Did he know the implications of what he was saying? Panikkar had asked. "We all know what we are in for, but at all costs American aggression has to be stopped. The Americans can bomb us, they can destroy our industries, but they cannot defeat us on land," Nieh had answered. With their military power, Panikkar suggested, the Americans could set China back half a century. "We have calculated all that," Nieh answered. "They may even drop atomic bombs on us. What then? They may kill a few million people. Without sacrifice a nation's independence cannot be upheld." But the problem for the Americans, Nieh added, was that most Chinese people lived on farms. So, he said, "what can atomic bombs do there?" In this, Nieh was giving Panikkar a surprisingly accurate view of what Mao himself was then thinking. At the same time, talking with different Western military attachés in Beijing, Panikkar was hearing reports of trains loaded with soldiers heading north. His reporting, despite Western doubts, proved to be all too accurate.

But the real warning came at midnight on October 2. Panikkar had been asleep for an hour and a half when he was awakened and told that the head of Asian affairs at the Chinese foreign ministry was downstairs. Downstairs he went, only to be summoned for a meeting with Zhou Enlai himself. He asked for ten minutes to get ready, wondering whether he was going to be arrested and deported. At 12:20 in the morning, an unusual hour to set off for so critical a meeting, Panikkar left his home. When he came face-to-face with the prime minister, he found Zhou very somber. The meeting was all business, and the message was brief and blunt. If the Americans crossed the thirty-eighth parallel, he told Panikkar, China would be forced to intervene. Panikkar asked Zhou if he already had news of such a crossing. The prime minister indicated that he had, although he did not know exactly where it had occurred. If the crossing had been made by South Korean troops, Zhou said, that did not matter. It was only American troops he cared about. With that, the meeting was over. Panikkar got home at 12:30 A.M. and immediately filed a complete report on what had happened for his superiors in New Delhi, who in turn informed the rest of the diplomatic world. On October 8, he heard a radio report that the UN had authorized MacArthur to go north. That night Panikkar wrote in his diary: "So America has knowingly elected for war, with Britain following. It is indeed a tragic decision for the Americans and the British are well aware that a military settlement of the Korean issue will be resisted by the Chinese and that the armies now concentrated on the Yalu will intervene decisively in the fight. Probably that is what the Americans, at least some of them want. They probably feel that this is an opportunity to have a showdown with China. In any case, MacArthur's dream has come true. I only hope it does not turn out to be a nightmare."

Edmund Clubb, an old China Hand and a very conservative man personally, was the director of the State Department's Office of Chinese Affairs. He thought that Zhou's statement to Panikkar, which came to him through the British, should be taken very seriously, that it was not a bluff. But there was a general feeling among his superiors that Clubb had been too alarmist in the past and there was no great need to listen to him at this moment. The administration did make one attempt to talk with the Chinese. It tried to arrange a low-key connection between Loy Henderson, the American ambassador to India, and the Chinese ambassador there, but the Chinese wanted no part of it and rejected the initiatives.

Panikkar it would have to be. Certainly the British eventually took his warnings quite seriously, but in general Western diplomats were wary of him. The American ambassador to The Hague cabled Washington to pass on the low opinion the Dutch—another former colonial power now reluctantly in retreat from Indonesia, its colony—had for Panikkar. He had, the Dutch reported, strongly advised Indian Prime Minister Nehru to oppose the original UN declaration branding the North Koreans as the aggressors in the war. The CIA believed that Panikkar was an innocent instrument being used by the Chinese, but that the Chinese were not serious in their threats. Acheson was unimpressed. To him, Panikkar was a mouthpiece for Beijing and not a serious diplomat. Such warnings were the "mere vaporings of a panicky Panikkar." To Acheson, the idea that the Chinese would actually want to fight the Americans and the United Nations seemed unlikely in the extreme. It would be "sheer madness" for them to enter the war when their real problem was that long border with the Soviets, and when they badly wanted to be installed in the Chinese seat at the United Nations Security Council. Few people of that era had a more powerful, logical mind than Dean Acheson, whose skills were those of a great lawyer. He was sure he knew what was good for the Chinese, and at that moment in their history, he was sure, a war with the Americans made no sense at all. Of his many skills, none was the ability to think like a Chinese revolutionary.

In late September, after the In Min Gun started a panicky retreat north, the Chinese began to edge ever closer to intervention. What they would do next—entering the war, taking terrible casualties, but stalemating the Americans and the United Nations in the process—they did for their own reasons, not out of any great love for the North Koreans. Their respect for the Koreans and Kim at that moment was in fact quite marginal. They felt the Koreans had gotten their country too easily: the Chinese, after all, had won their great victory by fighting a numerically and technologically superior foe for decades. In addition, Mao and the others were still irritated by the arrogance and brashness of Kim Il Sung.

The Chinese leaders had been appalled by Kim's lack of response to their warnings about a possible amphibious landing at Inchon. Any Chinese commander who had disregarded such powerful, hard intelligence would have been relieved of command. In early August, as Chinese Army forces began to build up north of the Yalu, the Chinese sent one of their senior corps commanders, Deng Hua, to visit with his Korean military counterparts. Deng crossed the Yalu, got to the border town of Andong, and discovered that that was as far as he could go. The Koreans were not going to let him anywhere near the battle zone.

The Chinese decided to send their troops to Korea because Mao believed it was good for the new China and necessary for the future of the revolution, both domestically and internationally. He also feared what a failure to intervene would mean—that his China, for all its rhetoric, was not that different from the old China, a powerless giant when facing what was in their eyes the armies of Western oppressors. Therefore, almost from the moment it became clear that Kim's offensive was doomed, Mao had begun the planning that would end with the use of Chinese troops in Korea. In early July, a time when Kim's armies were still gaining singular successes on the battlefield, Mao had nonetheless ordered the creation of what became the Northeast Border Defense Army, the NEBDA, to be positioned along the Korean border. It was to include more than three armies from the Fourth Field Army, which had some of China's best troops. Eventually the force numbered thirty-six divisions, or roughly (with support units) some seven hundred thousand troops. Seven artillery divisions and some antiaircraft units were eventually attached.

Mao had felt that there was a certain inevitability in China being pulled into the war, and he wanted to be as realistic as possible in gauging the price China would pay. On August 31, Zhou Enlai chaired a meeting on force levels where the senior people spoke not only of what they would need, but what it might cost in terms of potential casualties in the first year of a war with the Americans. The answer, they decided, was around 60,000 deaths and 140,000 wounded.

The Chinese decisions in the weeks following Inchon were essentially those of one man, Mao Zedong. He was the classic example of the revolutionary as true believer. Starting out with so little, he had been unusually successful during those long years of the civil war—and most of his judgments, however bloody and difficult, had turned out right. He was sure he understood the ordinary Chinese—the peasants—better than anyone else. He believed in China's right to be a great nation again; that the source of its strength was his revolution; and that the revolution had succeeded because it had evoked the purity of the Chinese peasantry and so turned historic political suffering into military strength. His men had been better soldiers than their well-armed Nationalist opponents because of their beliefs. As the principal architect of the new China, in his mind he now charged himself with keeping the revolution true to itself. That kind of belief in a single strand of history and in yourself as its principal figure—in effect serving as history's man—is powerful stuff; it has both its strengths and its weaknesses.

What Mao knew—about China's peasants and their suffering, and the cruelty of the old order—he knew brilliantly; what he didn't know, he didn't know at all and often was unable to learn. That kind of success has the capacity to produce a terrible kind of megalomania. Epic revolutions probably demand someone with a supreme, invincible sense of self, a belief in the price that other men have to pay for the good of their vision; it was what allowed men like Mao and Stalin to rationalize great suffering for the good of the cause. But in such men there were no boundaries, no restraints, and what began as an all-consuming vision became almost inevitably a great nightmare as well; in time, monstrous crimes would be inflicted not on China's foreign enemies, or even its domestic dissidents, but on its own loyal citizens, including many of the men who had served Mao so loyally in those years of civil war and then in Korea. But to understand Mao's action at this critical juncture it is important to think of him always not just as the architect of a revolution but as its guardian as well, someone who believed that his enemies—of whom there were many, domestic and foreign—were always out to destroy his revolution and that he had to move against them before they moved against him.

ON SEPTEMBER 7, a week before Inchon, Zhai Chengwen, the Chinese political counselor in Pyongyang, was recalled by the foreign ministry. There he was asked by Zhou: if the Chinese decided to send troops to Korea, what kind of difficulties would they encounter? Zhai answered that the problems would be primarily logistical in nature. Above all they would have to solve the problem of transportation from different parts of China to the Yalu bases, and then from these bases to the battlefields. When he left Beijing, Zhai believed that the leadership had already made up its mind to intervene. He was right, but it wasn't really the leadership, it was Mao. Much of September was deeded over to two main tasks: getting troops to Manchuria and bringing the rest of the leadership over to Mao's view on the need to enter the war. If there was opposition, it was primarily in the Army, and even there, because the Army was always subservient to the political needs of the party, it was somewhat muffled. Lin Biao was the senior field general, and the man most Chinese and foreigners alike expected to command Chinese forces if they entered the war. Indeed for a long time during the war, because of the intense secrecy the Chinese Communists adhered to, and because UN intelligence was seriously flawed, senior Americans believed that they were fighting against forces commanded by Lin. But Lin had his own reservations. The idea that his men would be exposed to the kind of firepower possessed by the Americans was very disturbing to him. At one point, Lin asked Zhai whether the North Koreans had the strength and the will to fight a prolonged guerrilla war against their enemies, a question that indicated his wariness of a frontal Chinese assault on American forces. His doubts were shared by others in the military and, more quietly, some in the politburo. How much more intense his opposition would have been had he known that the troops would not get promised air cover from the Soviets can only be imagined. Again and again in the three-month period from early July to late September, Mao and others spoke to Lin about commanding the Chinese troops who might fight in Korea. Each time the subject came up, Lin talked about the problems of his own personal health. That was interpreted by many to mean that he had no desire to be a part of an intervention about which he had grave reservations.

In early September, Mao gave a speech to an important party meeting that reflected his decision to intervene. The United States, he believed, would turn out to be weaker than anyone expected. It would be waging an unjust war of aggression, and this would work against the morale of its troops and their battlefield performance. America, he said, had formidable divisions politically and economically at home; it was isolated from other nations and so vulnerable to world opinion. Yes, it could produce a great deal of steel and armaments, but that would not be enough. Its supply lines were far too extended, from Berlin to Korea, reflecting the fact that its geopolitical perimeter was stretched over two vast oceans. He saw America very much through his own political bias. America's young men had fought poorly in the early days in Korea, he believed, not because the world's atomic superpower had let its non-nuclear weaponry slip, but because these were working-class kids fighting for capitalist aims in which they did not believe, and thus less pure of heart and motivation than the soldiers of China. The level of their fighting ability in the early days of the Korean War, he said, was below that of "Germany and Japan during World War II." He did not fear the American's atomic bomb; if they used it, he said, "I will respond with my hand grenade."

His decision that China should enter the war was hardly an easy one. He slept poorly. He would often sit by himself well into the early morning hours, smoking endless cigarettes, just staring at maps of Korea and China, as if waiting for some kind of ultimate truth to emerge. But the fateful decision was always clear. China *had* to enter the war. Taiwan was crucial in all his reckoning. To Mao and others in the Chinese leadership, Taiwan was part of China. Now MacArthur was referring to it as an unsinkable aircraft carrier, which made it de facto American property. To Mao that meant a legitimate part of Chinese territory was seen by his sworn enemy as a weapon aimed against his country. For him that meant the last battle of the Chinese civil war had not yet been fought—something few Americans in power understood. Yet an amphibious landing against a well-defended island—protected by the awesome Seventh Fleet—was almost inconceivable for so primitive an Army. Already one amphibious assault against an offshore island had gone badly, because of the Communists' lack of air and sea power; it had taken place near the end of the civil war and had proved one of the Communists' worst defeats of that war. Mao was pushing the Russians for airplanes and instructors to build up his Air Force as quickly as possible, but for the moment he could not move against Taiwan.

That made Korea all the more attractive. There the confrontation logistically favored the Chinese. Even though they had bases in Japan, American troops pushing north would be strung out, extremely difficult to resupply, and very vulnerable because of the nature of the terrain and weather. The Chinese would have a vast advantage in manpower; Mao could easily put in play an Army four times as large as that of the Americans, and he was sure that his troops would fight bravely and with great discipline. He did not take the ROKs seriously as a fighting force. Against the Americans he hoped to avoid direct confrontation when the enemy was looking for a fight; he preferred to strike when U.S. troops were at their most exposed and vulnerable. He believed that a confrontation with the United States was inevitable, and as such he wanted to pick the location. In addition, Mao's own political calculations were critical in his decision-making. If he defeated the Americans in Korea, and he was sure he would, it would greatly strengthen his political control over all of China after so long and difficult a civil war. Many people in the Chinese politburo thought this was precisely the wrong time to enter a war, because the nation was exhausted and still divided, its finances dreadful, its economy in ruins. War against a rich, powerful country like the United States might only aid China's domestic enemies. Therefore any ambitious expedition like this should be delayed. Certainly, this was what Western intelligence officials, including the top people at the Central Intelligence Agency, thought the Chinese *should* think; it was how *they* would think if they had been Chinese.

Here Mao's domination of the politburo was crucial. The other members were seemingly peers, but he was first among nonequals. He was the embodiment of the new Chinese leadership, and they knew it and deferred to him. He was the one, they believed, who had the greatest insight into the truths of both war and politics; he had the ability to see one step ahead, or as Chen Jian, a gifted young historian at the University of Virginia, once said, he was like a great chess player competing with others who only manage to see what he sees a move or two too late. More than ever, after this decision, he became the great leader, the one the others in the politburo saw as a visionary and trusted because they believed he knew the population better than they did. As he pondered what exactly to do about Korea, he slowly came to see the war as a potential asset, a way to show the *Chinese people* that China was indeed a new revolutionary power on a global stage, which would be a way of extending the party's control domestically. And in this he would eventually prove right. Despite the terrible costs, financially and in human resources, the decision to enter the Korean War would, to the surprise of Western analysts, make Mao exactly the great visionary leader he imagined himself to be, who towered above everyone else. He intended to prove to ordinary Chinese that the Americans had always been their enemies and that there was no middle ground. The Chinese people who were closest to the Americans and to other foreigners were the wealthiest people in the country, and thus his domestic opponents; a war with the Americans, he believed, would help isolate them. The war was, in addition to everything else, a way of bonding the Chinese people to him. It would help him politicize the population. Later he would joke that there were only one and a half people who were in favor of going in—the half person, he said condescendingly, was Zhou Enlai.

There were other reasons to go ahead. Entering the war was proof that the new China could no longer be abused and exploited by foreign powers. Selling this idea to a vast percentage of the Chinese people, Mao was sure, would not be that hard; he had a highly nuanced feel for how much they hated the exploitation of their country by foreigners in the past. His propaganda wars had, in fact, already begun. The State Department had published its China White Paper in August 1949. The white paper was designed to relieve pressure at home, to show that the administration had done all that it could to help what was a self-destructive Nationalist government, and that the collapse was Chiang's own fault. But it was too long and too complicated for ordinary citizens to read, and it only angered the critics, who regarded it as kicking Chiang when he was down. Almost as soon as it was issued, Styles Bridges, Bill Knowland, Pat McCarran, and Kenneth Wherry issued a statement calling it "a 1,054 page whitewash of a do-nothing policy." In China, Mao understood immediately its unique propaganda value. To him the case that Acheson and the paper's authors were making—of how much the United States had done for Chiang—was exactly the one he wanted to make too. It was a gift from heaven, absolute documentary evidence of how insidiously the Americans had manipulated and exploited the government of Chiang only for the good of the United States. The Americans, his line went, were never your friends—and he launched a ferocious nationwide propaganda campaign that stunned Washington, a harbinger of the fact that China's new leaders were in no rush to become friends with the Western colossus. Mao wrote five articles himself attacking the white paper and personally orchestrated the national campaign against it, becoming for a moment a kind of Chinese Madison Avenue man.

Mao was confident—far too confident, it would turn out—that his soldiers would prevail over the superior technology of the Americans. There was no sham to this, no touch of cynicism. This is not just what he said, but what he truly *believed,* and he never altered this view of the coming confrontation with the Americans, although by mid-October a debate would be raging with great intensity in the politburo on this question. That was when it became clear that Stalin was going to renege on his promise to provide air cover for China's troops. In September, the Chinese had played a prolonged game of high-stakes poker with the Russians over just how much help the Russians were going to offer. Stalin was proving nervous about getting into a larger confrontation with the Americans. He had been surprised by the rapid American response to Kim's invasion, and it had made him even more cautious than usual. The Russians, like the Chinese, had warned Kim about the possibility of a landing at Inchon. The idea of an American-sponsored military base right up on the Manchurian border was one more nightmare for Stalin, though it looked increasingly likely that that was the way the war might end.

Now, as the In Min Gun collapsed, Kim Il Sung began to increase the pressure on Stalin to save his army and his country, even though the Russians had told the Koreans from the start that they would not offer combat troops. But perhaps, Stalin told them, the Chinese might. On September 21, a week after Inchon, Stalin's personal representative to Pyongyang, General Matvei Zakharov, urged Kim to ask for Chinese aid. The North Korean leadership was uneasy with the dependency on the Chinese that this might create, yet all the battlefield news was bad, and there was clearly no acceptable alternative. A week later the North Korean politburo finally held an emergency session at which it unanimously decided that if Seoul fell there would be no way of stopping the UN forces from crossing the parallel, and the North Koreans would need help. Kim then went to see Terenti Shtykov, the Soviet ambassador, and asked him to bring the subject of Russian troops up with Stalin. Shtykov refused to let him ask the question, and in his words a "confused, lost, hopeless and desperate" Kim and his foreign minister, Pak Hon Yong, then sent a letter to Stalin on their own. On October 1, Stalin answered that their best hope was to convince the Chinese to intervene. That night, Kim spoke to the Chinese ambassador and asked for Chinese troops. He also wanted to know whether, if the worst happened, the Chinese would allow the Koreans to set up a government in exile in their northeast.

A very delicate game was being played out between all three Communist

11. UN BREAKOUT AND INVASION OF NORTH KOREA

governments. The North Koreans, who had once snubbed the Chinese, now desperately needed their help. The Chinese, thanks to Mao's political beliefs, had decided to enter the war but did not want to tip their hand yet, because they wanted to maximize their leverage with the Russians, most particularly on the issue of air cover. In late September, the Soviets apparently agreed to supply air cover for the Chinese troops. So the forces that would lead to a terrible collision between the United States and China were now fully in motion. On September 30, two weeks after Inchon, the South Korean Second Division crossed the thirty-eighth parallel, and a week later, on October 7, troops of the American First Cavalry Division crossed it as well, on their way to the capture of Pyongyang, and right after that, involuntarily, their first unhappy meeting, in early November, with the Chinese at Unsan.

24

I F T H E R E   W A S an especially cruel irony in what happened next, it was that the very same doubts the State Department's China Hands had reflected in their reporting (which had so angered the China Lobby)—not just their certainty that Chiang was failing, but their doubts about Mao's long-term loyalty to the Russians—turned out to be shared by none other than Joseph Stalin. Stalin, the most important player on the Communist side from the fall of Chiang to the start of the Korean War, the man who skillfully manipulated the needs and fears of his two Communist allies, did not in fact trust Mao. He preferred a unified Communist Korea, one that was grateful to him, and utterly dependent upon him, to a divided one. He also wanted as strong a Korean counterforce as he could muster to the Japanese—a nation the Russians had historically feared and that he was sure the Americans would now seek to rearm. Because he distrusted Mao, he was also eager to maximize the tensions between China and the United States, and a war in which they found themselves on opposite sides worked to his advantage.

In 1949, Joseph Stalin was the dominant figure in the entire Communist world. He had controlled Russia for more than a quarter of a century. Of the leading architects of the Russian Revolution, he was the last one standing. Others might have been more brilliant, more charismatic, better speakers, more original strategists, but he was the greatest apparatchik of them all, the man who seemed to understand best the single enduring truth of that particular revolution: that when it came to the consolidation of power—sustaining it, and making sure that no one did to you what you had just done to your enemies—ideas did not matter much, but police power did. In the world as Stalin knew it, you were either the hunter or the hunted.

He survived and succeeded because he was the one with the fewest illusions (and perhaps the greatest paranoia), the man who understood best when stage one of the revolution was over and stage two—the consolidation of power—had begun. He was the one who broke the system down to its most elemental truth: there were enemies everywhere, and you removed them not only before they struck at you, but before they even grasped that they were your enemy. It was his greatest strength, the sheer darkness of his soul, that he understood this more quickly than others, and pursued it more cold-bloodedly, with fewer restraints.

There was a certain inevitability to the darkness that existed between the two superpowers in the years immediately after World War II—two essentially isolationist countries propelled involuntarily to great power status, with vastly differing political and economic systems, each with its own historical strain of paranoia and each now living in a nuclear world. But no small additional part of the tension was the fact that the Soviet leader was Stalin, and he made everything in the Cold War seem infinitely more dangerous and more threatening, so marginal was his innate humanity, and so cruel a man was he. What he ran was a terror machine. It did not matter if you had committed a crime; a suitable crime could always be found for you. It did not matter if you were a completely loyal Communist and a completely faithful Stalinist, a true believer in the cult of his personality. Someone was always listening, ready to betray you, if only to save himself. It was government run by fear and, finally, madness. In the late 1930s, with a Slavophobic Hitler on the rise, Stalin had purged and virtually destroyed the officer corps and leadership of the Red Army, getting rid of 3 of 5 marshals, 15 of 16 army commanders, 60 of 67 corps commanders, 136 of 199 division commanders. Essentially he stripped his country's defenses and prepared the way for the German invasion to come in 1941. His crimes against his own people were so great as to be essentially beyond measurement. How many people had actually died? Was it a few million, 10 million, perhaps even 40 million? "He was one of those rare terrible dogmatists capable of destroying nine tenths of the human race to 'make happy' the one tenth," wrote Milovan Djilas, the former Communist vice president of Yugoslavia, and heir apparent to Tito, who broke with the Communists, spent time in prison, and eventually wrote one of the most penetrating early insider portraits of Stalin. Djilas saw him as the greatest criminal of all time: "Every crime was possible to Stalin for there was not one he had not committed. Whatever standards we use to take his measure . . . to him will fall the glory the greatest criminal in history. For in him were joined the criminal senselessness of a Caligula with the refinement of a Borgia and the brutality of a Tsar Ivan the Terrible."

The relationship between Stalin and Mao, going back to the early days of China's civil war, had been one of almost total distrust and abiding mutual suspicion. These two men would eventually be considered among the leading mass murderers produced by a brutal system in an unusually violent age. That they disliked and distrusted each other was not surprising. Of Stalin, it could be said that he was the ultimate example of how dark the human spirit could become. Of Mao, it could be said that his leadership of a weak political faction in the 1920s, destined, it seemed, to be destroyed by far more powerful enemies, his bringing it to power, was one of the most remarkable political accomplishments of the twentieth century. But the skills of his leadership in ascent were in time exceeded by the harshness, cruelty, and finally, increasing madness he displayed during his years in power. "Revolution is not a dinner party," he once said. He would in time give ample evidence of that and of the personal corruption as well as the derangement that came with total power.

Each leader thought of himself as a Communist, but each was very much a nationalist as well. There might be, on the occasions they got together, talk of fraternal Communism and how it bonded two great nations and the world's masses, but the truth was that each looked at the other and saw a potential enemy. From Mao's perspective, the Soviets had almost always seemed an insular, conservative force, favoring only what helped Russia, with little interest in aiding potential fraternal allies who did not yet hold power. As early as the 1920s, when he was struggling unsuccessfully against Chiang's forces, Mao believed that the Soviets favored Chiang Kai-shek, and then, as he gradually came to power, Mao had hated their special sponsorship of Gao Gang, a member of the Chinese politburo and regional leader of Manchuria. The Chinese Communists had, he liked to say, repeatedly asked the Russians for arms during the civil war and gotten, in Mao's phrase, "not even a fart." To Mao, the Soviets might be Communists, but they were first and foremost *Russians*. Stalin had liked Chiang, Mao believed, because he was weak, and thus sure to preside over a weak China. To Stalin, Mao might be a Communist, but a most unlikely one, lacking a connection with the proletariat, of which China had little; he was too much like a peasant himself. In the end Stalin simply did not trust the Chinese Communists; they were, he said during World War II, too much like radishes: red on the outside, white on the inside.

Each of them carried a long list of grievances against the other. It was symbolic of their relationship that whatever one partner wanted was invariably inconvenient for the other at that moment, although more often than not in those years the needier partner was Mao. The fact that the Soviets were not giving the Chinese much in the way of aid during World War II was known in America at the time, because Communist officials in Yenan complained quite openly about the lack of help to Western visitors, diplomats, journalists, and members of the Dixie Mission, the American military intelligence operatives from the Office of Strategic Services who had been sent to work with the Chinese Communists, and to push them to do more against the Japanese. (The members of the Mission generally admired the Communists for their military abilities and were privately contemptuous of Chiang's forces.) Since the end of the Cold War, a great many secret documents—studies ordered up by Leonid Brezhnev, the Soviet first secretary during the worst years of the Sino-Soviet split—have become public, and they reflect even greater early tensions in the Mao-Stalin relationship than expected and, on the surface at least, seemingly greater opportunities for American foreign policy, had the United States not been so locked into Chiang.

Was it inevitable at that moment in the history of the two nations, the United States and China, that the chances for peace would be missed? Perhaps Truman's Washington and Mao's Beijing, with greater wisdom and just a little geopolitical luck, might have stumbled into an uncomfortable, uneasy accord in that period, buying some time until the nerve ends were less sensitive. Perhaps the cruelest irony of all was that the main consensus American foreign policy conclusion at the time was that the Communist world was monolithic. If anything, the miscalculations of both sides at this moment helped make the Communist world seem more monolithic than it really was. If there was a sad epitaph for that period it was that to some degree the Americans and the Chinese had both ended up for a time playing Stalin's game.

The tensions between Stalin and Mao and their two countries, always considerable, had grown ever larger as Mao came closer and closer to taking power. Stalin was never in any rush to risk Soviet resources, Soviet interests, or Russian blood in the cause of the larger Communist family. He trusted only what he conquered with his Army and controlled once he had put his secret police in place. The idea of a vast Communist state on his border, flowering in a historically alien country, under a regime that had come to power without his help and owed him nothing, did not thrill him. Thus Mao was a potential rival even before there was a real rivalry. Stalin had long kept Mao at arm's length; he had first invited him to Moscow in July 1947, not by chance at the moment when Chiang's armies were still on the offensive and Mao seemed, to outsiders at least, at the low point of his fortunes. Mao quickly declined to go, believing that if he went, Stalin would try to extract unwanted concessions from him.

Then in late 1947, as the tide steadily began to turn in favor of the Communists, Stalin began to back Mao more openly, but gave him virtually nothing in the way of aid. By January 1948, Stalin confided to Milovan Djilas that he had been wrong earlier in pushing Mao to work out an accord with Chiang. The Americans, Stalin added, were preoccupied with Europe, and while they would never let the Greek Communists win in their then ongoing civil war, Asia was a secondary sphere for them. The Americans would be unlikely to invest their military forces on the Asian mainland, he said. In May 1948, Mao, sure victory was at hand, sent word that he finally wanted to come to Moscow and meet with Stalin. What he desired was recognition from the Soviet bloc at the moment when Chiang finally collapsed. Stalin instead replied that "the revolutionary war in China is in its decisive phase, and that Chairman Mao, as its military leader, would do better not to leave his post." Hopefully, he added, "Chairman Mao will reconsider his intentions." As Goncharov, Lewis, and Xue wrote, "To Mao, Stalin's ever-so-polite letter was a rebuke. As Communist military commander, he could be presumed to know much better than Stalin if this was a good time for a journey to Moscow, and he needed no instructions on the matter."

In late 1948, Mao pushed for a meeting in Moscow on several occasions, and each time Stalin held back. Instead in January 1949, Stalin sent Anastas Mikoyan, one of his most trusted aides, to China, but only under a cloak of absolute secrecy. Stalin still feared what might happen in case the Americans lashed out in the final days. What Mao sensed of Stalin, right down to the final warning that he should go slowly as his forces crossed the Yangtze, was more than anything else his timidity.

Mao was all too aware in those years that Stalin was suspicious of him. Privately he would joke—if that is the word—that he did not enjoy Stalin's trust, and that he was considered a rightist and opportunist by Moscow. Still, he needed Stalin's approval and wanted to be received with some form of honor in the Soviet capital. In April 1949, Mao again passed the word to Lieutenant General Ivan Kovalev, Stalin's personal representative in China, that he wanted to visit. This time, though Stalin again turned him down, the response from Moscow was much warmer and there was praise for him as the leader of a great Communist revolution. Kovalev later noted that Mao seemed quite relieved by the warmer tone of the answer. According to Kovalev, Mao raised his hands and shouted out, "Long live Comrade Stalin! Long live Comrade Stalin! Long live Comrade Stalin!" Finally, in December 1949, he got the coveted Moscow invitation, but only as one of many leaders in the Communist world and not to celebrate his victory in China, extraordinary though it was, but to commemorate Stalin's enduring rule on the occasion of his seventieth birthday.

Part of the problem was that Mao was hardly what the Soviet leadership wanted. He was too proud of his accomplishments and of being Chinese, too independent-minded, seeming to believe that, by leading this great revolution, he was already a major figure, not a supplicant. His very victory had demanded independence, but that same independence made Moscow nervous. If he came to Moscow, would he be sufficiently grateful? The Russians were not even sure he was by their reckoning a real Communist. He was, Foreign Minister V. M. Molotov reported back to Stalin after one meeting, clever, but a peasant: "Of course he is far from being Marxist—he confessed to me that he had never read *Das Kapital*." Reading the translation of Mao's theoretical views, Stalin had been appalled: "What kind of Marxism is this! This is feudalism!" Privately Stalin believed that Mao might harbor what he termed "rightist tendencies" that might one day lead him to be soft on the Americans.

As Mao came closer to taking power, a good deal of jockeying continued between the leaderships of the two countries. The Soviets were trying to find out what Mao felt about Tito, the Yugoslav leader who was about to be drummed out of the Communist family for his perceived dissidence and independence. The Soviets feared there were parallels between Tito, who had already broken with Moscow, and Mao. Moscow, in fact, always suspected Mao of being a closet Titoist, and in time he would indeed become the greatest Titoist of them all. But whatever Mao's reservations about Stalin, the Chinese badly needed some form of international recognition, someone to legitimize them on the world stage, and there was no one else to turn to. Though Stalin privately continued to hold back on other aspects of friendship, on October 2, 1949, the day after the founding of the People's Republic of China, the Soviets became the first nation to recognize the new Communist regime.

IF THERE WERE historic forces working against a true alliance, the relationship was made much more difficult by Stalin's megalomania and by the fact that both men ruled nations where there was no opposition party, and where sycophancy was something of an art form. By 1949, Stalin was already the Great Stalin, and the beneficiary, as it were, of a relentless, all-encompassing cult of personality, while Mao was a relative ingenue in the creation of such a cult: the Soviet cult of personality had already been in effect for at least twenty years. According to the historian Walter Laquer, it had started in December 1929, at the time of Stalin's fiftieth birthday. Leonid Leonov, a prominent Russian writer of the time, typically wrote of the great man that "the day would come when all mankind would revere him and history would recognize him as the starting point of time, not Jesus Christ."

But Mao would soon rival him in the art of totalitarian self-glorification. He might at the beginning have had his doubts about the cult of personality, but he soon came to understand the greatest truth of self-glorification: like so many other dictators, he discovered that what was good for the leader was good for the revolution as well. Besides, as he emerged ever more clearly as China's sole leader, he came to see himself as nothing less than a modern Chinese emperor. His favorite among his imperial predecessors, according to his doctor, Li Zhisui, was Emperor Zhou, a mythical tyrant supposedly much despised by most Chinese because of his appalling cruelty, a man who liked to mutilate and then display the bodies of potential rivals as a warning to other enemies. About his own special role in history and about his own greatness Mao was absolutely sure. It was something he spoke of constantly. "He was the greatest leader, the greatest emperor of them all—the man who had unified the country and would then transform it, the man who was restoring China to its original greatness," as Dr. Li wrote.

In some ways he would prove to be very much like Stalin. The more he schemed against those around him, the more he came to believe that they were already scheming against him. He gradually got rid of all potential rivals, no matter their loyalty to him, to the Party, or to the revolution. As the cult grew, as the ordinary peasants of China came to revere Mao ever more, he became ever more distanced from them in lifestyle. No head of a capitalist society could have lived with more privilege or with more of his country's resources diverted to him. Each province chief built a villa for him—he was always on the move, fearing he would become too much of a target for his enemies if he stayed in one place too long. No head of state in a free society could have lived as a comparable sexual predator, relentlessly devouring young peasant women, who were eager to serve their leader and thus their nation in whatever way he suggested. "Women were served to order, like food," as Andrew Nathan, a Columbia University scholar, wrote in the introduction to Li Zhisui's book. In time, his cult of personality grew to even more gothic proportions that Stalin's. His swim in the Yangtze River, as Laquer wrote, was treated as a turning point in history. "He was," Laquer wrote, "not only the greatest Marxist of all time, he was the greatest genius who ever lived. He had never been mistaken, everything he said was the truth, every sentence he uttered was worth 10,000 sentences [of everyone else]." One Chinese poem summed it all up: "Father is close/ Mother is close/ But neither is as close as Chairman Mao."

His days as a supplicant had been difficult for Mao, and he came to hate Stalin for the way the Soviet leader had treated him. Mao was not a man to take second-class treatment lightly, or to forgive or forget, though when he finally evened the score, it was with Stalin's successor, Nikita Khrushchev. He once held a summit meeting with Khrushchev in his swimming pool, forcing the Soviet leader, who did not swim, to wear a life preserver during the session. It had been his way, he told his doctor, "of sticking a needle up his ass."

IN DECEMBER 1949, Mao finally made his trip to Moscow. Harrison Salisbury, of the *New York Times*, who won the Pulitzer Prize for his reporting from Moscow in those days, remembered the shroud of silence that Stalin had already placed in the preceding months over the news of Mao's coming victory. There was virtually no mention of it in the controlled press; "a snippet on the back page of Pravda, or a few paragraphs inside Izvestia. The word 'China' hardly appeared." Now, with Mao on his way to Moscow, there was more open evidence of the cold Soviet shoulder. Stalin's seventieth birthday was self-evidently a great moment of celebration in the Communist world and an occasion not to be shared with any other event or person. On December 6, Mao set out by train for the Soviet capital. The war was barely over and he was fearful of attacks by Nationalist dissidents. He traveled in an armored car, with sentries posted every hundred meters along the tracks. In Shenyang, the largest city in the northeast, Mao disembarked and checked to see if there were posters of him. There were very few, it turned out, and a great many of Stalin—the work of Gao Gang, whom Mao saw as a pro-Soviet dissident. Mao was furious and ordered that the car carrying gifts for Stalin from Gao be uncoupled from the tram and the gifts returned to him.

Mao's arrival in Moscow on December 16 was an edgy one. He was treated not as the leader of a great revolution bringing into the Communist orbit one of the world's great nations but rather, as the historian Adam Ulam has written, "as if he were, say, the head of the Bulgarian party." V. M. Molotov and Nikolai Bulganin, both senior politburo members, came to the station to meet him. Mao had laid out a handsome luncheon buffet. He asked the two Soviet leaders to have a drink with him. They refused—based on protocol, Molotov said. They also refused to sit and share the food. Then Mao asked them to accompany him to the residence where he was scheduled to stay. Again they refused. There was no major celebration or festive party for him. It was as if Mao was now to learn his place in Stalin's constellation, the real Communist universe; if he was a fraternal brother, then he should know that there would always be one Communist brother who was so much bigger than all the others. One of Khrushchev's aides told his boss that someone named "Matsadoon" was in town. "Who?" the perplexed Khrushchev asked. "You know that Chinaman," the aide answered. That was how they saw him: that Chinaman. And that was how they treated him. The main reception for the Chinese delegation was held not in the Main Hall of the Kremlin but in the old Metropole Hotel, "the usual place for entertaining visiting minor capitalist dignitaries," in Ulam's words.

Things did not get better after the first reception. For days on end Mao was isolated, waiting for Stalin to arrange meetings. No one else could meet with him until Stalin had, and Stalin was taking his time. When Mao first arrived in Moscow, he announced that China looked forward to a partnership with Russia, but he emphasized as well that he wanted to be treated as an equal. Instead he was being taught a lesson each day. He had become, in Ulam's words, "as much captive as guest." As such, he shouted at the walls, convinced that Stalin had bugged the house: "I am here to do more than eat and shit." He hated Russian food. At one point Kovalev, his contact man, dropped by to visit him. Mao pointed outside at Moscow and said, "Bad, bad!" What did he mean by that? Kovalev asked. Mao said he was angry at the Kremlin. Kovalev insisted he had no right to criticize "the Boss," and that he, Kovalev, would now have to make a report.

When Stalin finally met Mao, they proved to have a remarkable mutual instinct for misunderstanding. "Why didn't you seize Shanghai?" Stalin asked, for the Chinese had taken their time before entering the city. "Why should we have?" Mao answered. "If we'd captured the city, we would have had to take on the responsibility for feeding the six million inhabitants." Stalin, already fearing that Mao favored peasants over workers, was appalled. Here was proof of it, workers in a city left to suffer.

The trip to Moscow was in all ways a disaster, and Mao would have a long memory for the way he had been treated. In economic and military aid, he got very little from his negotiations on that first trip—a paltry $300 million in Soviet arms over five years, or $60 million a year. To make matters worse, there were also some Chinese territorial concessions that had to be thrown in. The lack of Russian generosity staggered the Chinese. "Like taking meat from the mouth of a tiger," Mao would say years later. For Mao, very much aware of the scale of his great triumph at home and what it meant in terms of history, the treatment by the Soviets had essentially been a humiliation, but one he had been forced to accept without complaint. "It is no wonder that Mao conceived, if he had not nurtured it before, an abiding hatred of the Soviet Union," Adam Ulam wrote.

ON SEPTEMBER 30, 1950, Kim Il Sung, somewhat humbled by events in the South, and warned off by the Russians when he asked for troops, attended a reception at the Chinese embassy in Pyongyang celebrating the first anniversary of the creation of the Chinese People's Republic. There he asked Beijing's representatives to send the Thirteenth Chinese Army Corps to fight in Korea. The next day, along with Pak Hon Yong, ostensibly the South Korean Communist leader, he sent a letter to Mao asking for troops. To expedite the process, Pak flew to Beijing with the letter, which pointed out that the North would have won the war except for the action of the United States. Now their situation, he said, was "most grave." "It is difficult for us to cope with the crisis with our own strength," the letter said and ended with an urgent request for Chinese troops.

On October 2, Mao began to meet with the Standing Committee of the Politburo, an elite part of the whole. Even the delay of a day, he warned, could be crucial to the future. The issue, he said, was not whether they would send troops, but when, and who would be the commander. Lin Biao, commander of the vaunted Fourth Field Army, who knew the general terrain quite well, was the logical choice. But Lin was ticketed for medical treatment in the Soviet Union, both as an end in itself and as a cover for *not* commanding the troops. So Mao decided on Peng Dehuai. Like Lin, he was an old and trusted comrade in arms. He and Mao had served together since 1928. Mao felt that Peng was exactly the right man because he would share Mao's views politically, and would, despite any private doubts he harbored, accept the post when asked, whatever the terrible dangers in store for his men.

Mao was, some of the men around him thought, almost emotionally immune to the loss of life in a war like this. It was simply the price that had to be paid. China had millions of people, and was on its way to greatness; it could sacrifice far more of them than other countries. He could even accept the possible American use of a nuclear weapon. He once shocked Nehru by saying that the atomic bomb was a "paper tiger." "The atomic bomb is nothing to be afraid of," he told the Indian leader. "China has millions of people. They cannot be bombed out of existence. If someone else can drop an atomic bomb, I can too. The death of ten or twenty million people is nothing to be afraid of." If his political vision demanded a war, then the next great question was: When should China enter the war? When would the forces still gathering along the Manchurian border be ready? The men at the October 2 meeting, led by Mao, chose October 15, two weeks away. By chance, it was also the date being selected by Truman and MacArthur for their first meeting, to be held on Wake Island.

After the October 2 meeting, Mao sent a long cable to Stalin telling the Soviet leader of the Chinese decision. The Chinese troops would be known as volunteers. That was a choice on his part to prevent an all-out war with the Americans. China, he told Stalin, would send twelve divisions at first. He hoped to have a numerical advantage of 4 to 1 in manpower on the battlefield, just enough to neutralize the American superiority in firepower. In addition, he hoped for a 1.5 or even 2 to 1 advantage in mortars, since they would have no heavy artillery. In the beginning, the Chinese troops would utilize a predominantly defensive strategy as they learned how to fight this new enemy. He told Stalin he did not envision a long war; nor did he think the Americans would try to invade mainland China. Mao also officially requested the already promised Soviet air cover for his troops.

At the same time, Mao continued to explain his plans to politburo members, listening to their dissent and gradually bringing his colleagues aboard. On October 4, the full politburo met. There, he asked those present to talk about the disadvantages that went with intervention. A number of members had a great many reservations. They believed their country was exhausted economically and could ill afford another war. They spoke as well of the vulnerability of their troops to the superior weaponry of the Americans. Mao listened and did not try to dissuade them. "All you have said is not without ground," he finally concluded. "But when other people are in a crisis, how can we stand aside with our arms folded? This will make me feel sad." They decided to meet again the next day. For the second part of the politburo meeting, Mao had flown Peng in from his post on the Manchurian border. On the morning of October 5, Mao met with Peng and Deng Xiaoping, another old and trusted comrade, also a veteran of the Long March, a member of the Central Committee, and commander of the Communist forces at one of the final battles of the war, when Chongqing was captured on December 1, 1949. At that private meeting Mao spoke of the deepening crisis in Korea. Time was now a critical factor, Mao said. The Americans were advancing rapidly, virtually without opposition. It was vitally important to act before they reached the Yalu. He was aware, he said, of the dangers and risks involved. He was really speaking only to Peng, a hardened battlefield veteran who was admired by everyone as a soldier's soldier, a man of the army rather than of politics. Typically, after Mao had summoned him from the Manchurian border and put him in one of Beijing's best hotels, Peng had been uncomfortable with the softness of the bed. So he simply slept on the floor. That was what he was used to—the hardships of war. The joke among his peers was that his only marriage was to the revolution.

Peng was Mao's man, the peasant as general. On political matters he had always deferred to Mao, "first as an older brother, then as a teacher, and last, as a leader." "Old Peng," Mao called him. "Old Mao" was the term of endearment Peng, virtually alone among the leadership, could use with the chairman. Sometimes on military matters, when Mao seemed to be a little too theoretical, Peng might even privately refer to him as "the schoolteacher." But he was by no means a lackey of Mao's, and he eventually paid dearly for his independence: a few years after the Korean War was over, Peng stood up to Mao and challenged him on several political issues, and he ended up his years as an enemy of Mao, and thus an enemy of the people, imprisoned, humiliated, and systematically beaten to death. Even in the mid-1950s, he was sufficiently confident of his own role, and independent enough as a man, to talk to Mao's doctor about what he thought were problems with the chairman's teeth. The chairman, it turned out, never visited his dentist, never brushed his teeth, and drank endless cups of tea, thus giving his teeth a greenish pallor. "The Chairman's teeth look like they are coated with green paint," Peng said, but improving the dental work of Mao was by then something of a lost cause.

Peng was a peasant himself, produced by a much harder childhood than that of Mao. He was a man with a shrewd, pragmatic sense of tactics for a newly created army that was almost always going to be outgunned and outnumbered if it fought as a traditional force. On his own back in 1934 he had challenged the destructive strategy of the Party's military leader, a rigid Prussian named Otto Braun, sent to China by Moscow. In Peng's view, Braun's tactics were hopelessly conventional and poorly suited for the Communists' fragile military situation. His victory over Braun in the struggle to define tactics was probably the first great triumph of the Long March. It was the Long March that bonded Peng and Mao: it had been the supreme test, more than six thousand miles both fleeing and fighting against, in no particular order, Chiang's troops, local warlords, backbreaking terrain, appallingly harsh weather conditions, and abiding, pervasive hunger. Of the eighty thousand who had begun the trip in southeast China, perhaps eight thousand finished it a year and three days later, in the distant, barren, impoverished north. In one of the final battles of the Long March, at a place called Wuqi, after more than twenty days of hard fighting, five regiments of Nationalist horse cavalry, about four or five thousand men, had attacked. Mao ordered Peng to defeat their pursuers and not to let them enter the base camp. That he had done, and in return, Mao had written him a poem: "High mountains, dangerous passes, deep ravines,/ The enemy cavalry sweep the length and breadth at will;/ Who dares stop them, astride a horse, gun at the ready?/ Only our general, Peng Dehuai." (Peng said that he later changed the last line to "only our heroic Red Army," and returned it to Mao.)

To understand Peng and why he fought so well was to understand the ordinary Chinese soldiers as well, the grievances that had driven these men, and thus to understand the success of the Communist Army. His beliefs were simple and formed by the harshest kind of life: he believed that the rich were cruel, that the poor were not just poor but utterly defenseless against them; that there was an elemental brutality to every minute of daily Chinese life; and that the struggle to change it was worth dying for. He had been born in 1898 into a peasant home of crippling poverty. His mother had died when he was a small boy. His father was unable to work because he was so sick. The family of eight lived off what was about one acre of fallow, hilly land. Peng himself had to drop out of school at a very early age because he was needed to help the family earn money. He was always aware of the basic injustice, and the sheer cruelty, of life—the youngest of his four brothers had died of starvation at the age of six months. As a boy Peng had been sent out with his grandmother to beg for food, a role he hated and refused to do a second time. Instead he went out into the forest and cut wood, which he sold for paltry sums. Years later he would speak with great bitterness of his seventy-year-old grandmother preparing to beg once again, going out into the falling snow and biting wind, needing a stick to support herself and accompanied by two of his brothers, one of them under four years old. When his grandmother came back with some rice, as Peng later recounted, he refused to eat the food she had gotten by begging.

As a boy he did all kinds of menial things for tiny sums of money—he chopped wood, caught fish, and carried coal. By the age of ten or twelve—he was not exactly sure which—he was working as a cowherd for a rich peasant. At about thirteen, he became, in his own words, a child laborer in a coal mine, turning a large wheel that helped drain water from the mine. He also hauled coal for a few pennies a day, backbreaking work for a young boy, an experience made all the meaner by the fact that the mine went bankrupt and he lost a year of pay. His back, he later said, remained a little crooked for the rest of his life from that work. Returning home with half the promised money in his pocket, barefoot because he could not afford straw sandals, the skin of his feet badly cracked, he was met by his father. "You are very dirty and pale," his father had told him. "You don't look like a human being anymore. You've worked two long years for that son of a bitch for nothing." Then his father had wept.

His teenage years had been even harder. There had been a great local drought, and as he recalled, the landlords and merchants had hoarded the grain and rice in order to drive prices up. Peng took part in peasant protests against the increases, and he was forced to flee his village before he was arrested. Finally, just before his eighteenth birthday, in March 1916, he became a soldier in the Hunan Provincial Army. As a private he made six Chinese dollars a month and was able to send home three of them, just enough to allow his family a frail, subsistence living. It was his introduction to the military—he would serve for the rest of his life, first in the regular army, surviving during its struggles with the warlords, and in time with Chiang Kai-shek as its leader. All the while he became steadily more politicized—especially when the soldiers, as so often happened in Chiang's army, were not paid. At first he had believed that Chiang was a true revolutionary and intended to create a new, more just China; as that faith faded, he gradually turned to the Communists. He and others like him, he later wrote of that time, had "enlisted to make revolution; to overthrow warlords, corrupt officials, local despots, and evil gentry and to bring about a cut in land rent and interest. But now there is neither revolution nor pay while talk of a cut in land rent and interest is heard no more. Yet we are ordered to 'suppress Communists' and to crack down on peasant associations. Who orders us to do such things? Chiang Kai-Shek! A soldier earns 6.50 dollars a month. Paying $3.30 for mess he has only $3.20 left—and this is withheld from us. What a miserable lot we have! We can't even afford to wear straw or smoke coarse tobacco, let alone provide for our parents, wives, children." As he rose in rank, he was proud of helping to turn his troops against a particularly exploitive landlord. He was arrested for that, but managed, with the help of some troops, to escape.

His entire life had been nothing less than a radicalizing experience. In mid-February 1928, he was finally initiated into the Party. Unlettered he might be, but he was quick to understand the kind of warfare the Communist forces had to follow until their strength grew. By 1934, his thinking closely paralleled that of Mao, and as such he, along with Mao, became one of the original architects of a military strategy that called for the Communists to fight a nimble guerrilla war, never to challenge the Nationalists frontally, but to be able to move quickly and strike lethally when their enemies were most vulnerable.

WHEN MAO HAD asked Peng if he would be willing to command the Chinese forces in Korea, there was a certain formality to the request. Mao then asked Peng to speak in favor of intervention at the politburo that afternoon, which he did. Peng had already spent a good deal of time pondering a battlefield in Korea that would match Chinese troops against Americans with their awesome firepower. There was a serious danger to all of China, he told the politburo members; if American troops reached the Yalu, they might strike across it and invade China. It was necessary to use Chinese forces to stop them. That was China's obligation. With that, the mood of the meeting turned in favor of intervention. Peng had given Mao the critical element he needed, the agreement of the man who would lead the troops in battle. What Mao believed, it now seemed, the others believed as well—that Korea was not an isolated problem, but a focal point of larger tensions between the Communist and capitalist worlds; that the troops were not just being sent to save Korea, but to help promote a larger world revolution, especially in Asia; and that China did not want the Americans to have a massive staging area on its border. Finally, no matter what superior technology the Americans had, China, with its superior manpower and greater moral strength, would triumph. What was always in the air at these meetings—not always mentioned but very much there—was the issue of Taiwan. In effect, in the Chinese minds, their country was already at war with America, because the United States had decided to intervene there; if China was too weak to strike at Taiwan, then the American Army coming into range of Chinese ground forces in Northern Korea was the obvious alternative.

On October 8, Mao notified Kim Il Sung that the Chinese would indeed dispatch troops to help him. On the same day, an order was issued to send Chinese troops to Korea: "In order to assist the Korean people's war of liberation, repel the invasion launched by the American imperialists and their running dogs, and to defend the interests of the Korean people, the Chinese people, and of all Eastern countries, it has been ordered that the Northeast Border Defense Army be turned into the Chinese People's Volunteers and the Chinese People's Volunteers move immediately into the territory of Korea to assist the Korean comrades in their struggle against the invaders and to strive for a glorious victory." The date for the invasion was still to be October 15.

Peng immediately returned to his border headquarters and started surveying his needs. He believed from his intelligence that there were four hundred thousand UN troops in country, including the equivalent of ten combat divisions in the front lines, or roughly 130,000 men. Peng then decided he needed more combat troops if he was going to use overwhelming force as the key instrument of victory. Instead of crossing the border with two armies and two artillery divisions, he now planned to begin with four armies and three artillery divisions, which meant he also needed at least seven hundred more trucks and six hundred more drivers.

Soviet air cover was central to Chinese military plans. But the details of Russian military help were surprisingly foggy, especially with D-day so near. On October 9, Peng had attended a meeting of the commanders of the different armies that would serve in his force, and they had questioned him closely on the subject. Their questions were tough and specific, but neither he, nor Gao Gang, the political operative who was working with him, had been able to answer them. In the middle of the meeting they had cabled Mao, asking, "How many bombers can the Command send to Korea after our troops are engaged in operations there? When will [the Air Force] be dispatched, and who will be in charge?" Certainly, those questions were on the minds not just of division and regimental commanders, but of every company commander and platoon leader in the Chinese Army as well. They were, in fact, questions that the Chinese leaders still were trying to get the answers to themselves.

The Chinese troops were in place, poised to cross the border, but still there was no hard word from the Russians. And then the Russians reneged. At virtually the same time that Peng's commanders were demanding answers from him, his civilian peers were pressing the Russians for answers to the same questions. On October 8, Zhou Enlai and Mao's principal interpreter, Shi Zhe, flew to Moscow to discuss the terms of Russian assistance. They arrived there on October 10 with a few other Chinese colleagues, including Lin Biao. Once in the Soviet Union, they immediately flew on to Stalin's home on the Black Sea. There they conferred with the top Soviet leadership: Stalin, Georgi Malenkov, Lavrenti Beria, Lazar Kaganovich, Nikolai Bulganin, and Anastas Mikoyan, as well as Molotov.

Now the stakes in the big-time poker game that had been going on for several weeks were raised again. What ensued was a very complicated byplay among tough, cynical men. Neither side trusted what the other side was saying. When, for example, the Chinese told Stalin that they did not really want to send troops to this war, that their country was exhausted from its civil war, Stalin knew that the reverse was true, that the Chinese had already assured Kim Il Sung they would come to his aid. Stalin began the meeting by saying how perilous the Korean situation was. What, he asked, did his Chinese comrades think? Zhou, who knew better than anyone the degree of commitment Mao had made and intended to sustain, replied that it would be much better for China if it did not have to intervene. The civil war, he said, had been very costly, and China was still recovering.

But if the North Koreans did not get aid quickly, Stalin responded, they could not survive for more than a week. The Chinese should ponder what it might do to China's national security if the Americans controlled North Korea (as if the Chinese had not been thinking about this for months). The Soviets, he then informed his guests, would not and could not send troops, in no small part because they did not want a direct confrontation with the Americans. The Chinese, he suggested, could and should go ahead. The Russians would give them a great deal of materiel left over from World War II and would provide air protection over China's northeast territory and coastal regions, including all Chinese forces on the northern side of the Yalu. That was hardly what the Chinese had hoped to hear, since the fighting was going to take place on the *southern* side of the river. As for sending his Air Force south of the Yalu, Stalin said the Russians would need more time to prepare for an air war against the Americans. The marathon meeting, which went from 7 P.M. to 5 A.M., was not a great success. The Chinese long remembered that the Soviets had reneged on their promise at the most critical moment. The limits of comradeship had been discovered rather early in the game.

So the positions were marked out. Stalin had the stronger hand. He knew the Chinese intended to intervene, more for reasons of their own than for any love of the Koreans, and he knew they were dependent upon him for air and naval technology if they were ever to assault Taiwan. Mao was furious with the Soviet pullback. On October 12, three days before Chinese troops were to cross the Yalu, Mao sent a cable to Peng telling him to put the previous war orders aside for the moment. All troops were to stay in their current positions. He and the rest of the leadership would now have to reconsider. Without the expected air cover, a difficult decision, but one that he felt sure his army could handle, had just become infinitely harder, the casualties likely to be far greater.

Peng too was angry about the Russian decision—it was his men who were now at risk. He reportedly threatened to resign as commander. But none of this greatly affected Mao's thinking. It is quite possible that he was always suspicious of the Soviets and never thought they would do their part. Certainly his decisions had always been based on what was good as he saw it, for *China,* not for the Soviets or the Koreans. Mao was going to send troops in the end because not to do it would show that the new China, his China, was powerless around its borders. So again, Russian air cover or no, he spoke forcefully before his colleagues for intervention. They would be getting a great deal of Russian military gear, and the Russians, he added, would at least protect China's territorial sovereignty. He asked Peng not to resign as commander. Even without Soviet air cover, he believed, they could still fight the Americans successfully. Their superior moral spirit would be the deciding factor. When the meeting was over, the Chinese had decided—again—to intervene. They would attack the South Korean troops first, Mao told Zhou in a cable. "In short, we believe that we should enter the war and that we must enter the war. Entering the war can be most rewarding, failing to do so may cause great harm." Zhou was to continue negotiating with the Russians, he said, to try to maximize the amount of aid they would get. Chinese troops would set up essentially defensive positions in the mountainous areas of the extreme north. October 19 was set as the new D-day to cross the Yalu.

On October 16, Peng met with his division commanders to go over plans and to bolster morale. What he told them was this: if they did not fight the Americans here, they might have to do it on Chinese soil. But he had come back to them without Soviet air cover, and he still faced considerable uneasiness among his subordinate commanders. A number of senior officers in the field had sent him a cable expressing their reservations about fighting the Americans without air protection. "The enemy," the cable said, "could concentrate large numbers of planes, artillery and tanks to wage heavy attacks against us without any worries." The terrain would make it difficult to create defensive positions "in the chilly weather and out of frozen soil. If the enemy started an all-out offensive it would be less than possible for us to hold our ground." The commanders wanted at least to wait until spring. They said they spoke for the majority of battle commanders.

Because of that dissent, Peng flew to Beijing on October 18. Mao listened to his report about the uneasiness of so many senior commanders, but saw no possibility of changing the course of events—or altering the time schedule. The decisions were now finalized. The troops would begin their crossing on the night of the nineteenth. They would cross after dusk and stop moving just before dawn broke each morning. In order to gain experience, only two or three divisions would cross the first night. Peng flew back to Andong and told his subordinate commanders that any additional challenges to the decision would be viewed as insubordination. The way for the collision of the two countries, the United States and China, was now set. On the night of October 19, the crossing began. It went smoothly, although not all the troops were entirely enthusiastic. "The gate of hell," some of those who had once served with the Nationalists called the bridge they took over the Yalu.

There was one other matter to be settled, and that was who would command the troops. Mao had decided on Peng. But Kim Il Sung thought the Chinese would let *him* command their troops. He obviously needed to be reeducated: there was no possibility that a Korean leader, one that the Chinese regarded with complete contempt, was going to be put in charge of Chinese troops. Peng himself was contemptuous of the way that the North Koreans had gone about the business of fighting the South. "Adventurism is all one can see! Military control has been extremely childish. On the nineteenth Pyongyang issued an order to defend to the death. As a result 30,000 defenders could not escape [from advancing UN troops]," he had written in one report. For a time, the Chinese held back on letting Kim know that he was no longer in charge of the war. It was essentially a Chinese command now.

O N OCTOBER 15, five and a half years into his presidency, Harry Truman finally met Douglas MacArthur. By that time, MacArthur's troops were racing toward the Yalu, and Chinese troops were four days from crossing the river heading south. Truman had wanted to meet with MacArthur from the moment he assumed the presidency. Twice the general had turned down what were in effect presidential commands to return to Washington. Now, post-Inchon, it was a good time to get together, the White House believed. For there were politics to the meeting too: the off-year election was coming up in early November; Inchon had been a great success; and Truman and the people around him, after taking so much heat during the early days of the war, were not above trying to share some of the glory that now surrounded MacArthur.

Truman, a man of elemental common sense, had always felt that he did well with people when he sat down and talked with them. Truman believed that he could read other people quite skillfully when they were face-to-face, and they could see that he played it straight, that he did not waste other people's time and on serious issues meant what he said. He had connected with generals like Eisenhower and Bradley, but not MacArthur. Mostly what he sensed about his commander was his grandiosity. Two days before the meeting, while on the way to Wake, he wrote a note to his cousin Nellie Noland, saying, "Have to talk to God's right hand man tomorrow."

In the end what drove the meeting from the White House side was politics. George Elsey, a close personal assistant and sometime speechwriter, whose idea the meeting was, and who pushed hard for it, had first suggested it to Truman in late September, right after Seoul was retaken, during a cruise down the Potomac. There was a precedent for it. Late in World War II, Roosevelt had gone to Honolulu to adjudicate issues that had arisen between Admiral Chester Nimitz and MacArthur. Truman at first was unsure about the trip, and finally went along, his special counsel, Charles Murphy, said, because his staff pressured him to go. No one, of course, spoke openly of the politics of it—but it was always there. Some White House people, most particularly Matt Connelly, the president's appointments secretary, thought it a mistake, and told the president so. Why? Truman asked him. "When does the king go to the prince?" Connelly answered. Dean Acheson, who believed MacArthur was always a hostile force, thought a trip mixing politics and policy a particularly bad decision. He had, he later said, "a vast distaste for the whole idea," and wanted no part of it. When Truman asked him to go, he demurred: "While General MacArthur had many of the attributes of a foreign sovereign, I said, and was quite as difficult as any, it did not seem wise to recognize him as one." Of the Joint Chiefs, only Bradley went. General Marshall, by then secretary of defense, did not choose to go, in part because his own relationship with MacArthur was very poor, and because he did not like mixing politics with national security.

At first Honolulu seemed the most logical venue, but MacArthur insisted that it was dangerous for him to be away from his headquarters for long, so Wake Island was chosen instead, some 4,700 miles from Washington and 1,900 from Tokyo. (One of the real reasons MacArthur did not want to go that far was that he did not like to fly at night.) Nor had MacArthur even wanted to go the shorter distance to Wake. On the way out from Tokyo, the general was in a foul mood, grumbling constantly to John Muccio, the American ambassador to Korea, about being forced to make the trip. What a waste of time, he said, being summoned all this distance primarily for political reasons. Didn't they know "that he was still fighting a war"? A diva like MacArthur wanted no Washington political diva, especially one from the other party, to share his applause. To fly so far to meet the president violated his unofficial sense of hierarchy: people were to come to him.

Still, the meeting did take place on October 15, 1950, with MacArthur almost openly resentful. The encounter spawned many stories, some not true—in particular one that MacArthur deliberately tried to delay his own plane's arrival so that Truman would land first and thus have to wait for the general. Others were true—that the general did not salute the president of the United States. Among those surprised by that quite deliberate sign of disrespect was Vernon Walters, a young officer who was then considered a gifted translator and eventually emerged as a figure close to a number of Republican politicians, including Richard Nixon. It was the second sign that MacArthur did not believe anyone from Washington outranked him, Walters thought. The first had come when he had not bothered to greet Secretary of the Army Frank Pace. "In my book," Walters later wrote, "the Secretary of the Army was the boss of all American soldiers regardless of rank." But to Walters the real snub was the failure of MacArthur to salute the president. That was a very serious breach of protocol. Truman, Walters noticed, took no note of it. That was the good thing about being president; if you decided to see something, then it had happened, and if you chose not to, then it had not.

It was no surprise that the meeting began in an atmosphere of mutual suspicion. But it was also true that, on the surface at least—and it was almost all surface—it went very well. It was taking place, after all, at the best moment in the war so far. But there was a serious issue on the agenda, especially in the minds of the Washington team: the nature of Chinese intentions. Mounting rumblings from Beijing about China entering the war—and not just via K. M. Panikkar—had certainly left Washington anxious. How seriously should they be taken? the president and the men around him wondered. The first words from Truman, Vernon Walters later remembered, were: "All of our intelligence indicates that the Chinese are about to intervene."

The White House had the whip hand in terms of controlling news coverage of the meeting. Truman brought the elite of the White House press corps, but MacArthur was not allowed to bring his favorite Tokyo journalists, especially the wire service reporters from the Associated Press, the United Press, and the International News Service—derisively dubbed "the Palace Guard" by other Tokyo journalists, who often thought their stories could have been written by members of MacArthur's staff, or the general himself. The fact that they were left behind in Japan only added to MacArthur's irritation; the control of images was for once beyond his control. It did not enhance his mood.

The site itself could hardly have been more primitive. Nonetheless, the two men seemed to get on reasonably well, or perhaps more accurately, both were on their best behavior. At their first meeting, MacArthur asked if he could smoke his pipe and Truman answered that he could, adding that he had probably had more smoke blown in his face than any man alive. There were actually two meetings at Wake: a private one between Truman and MacArthur, where they talked about Chinese intentions, and a longer one attended by everyone, where the major issue was once again China—and how quickly the war might be over.

There is an excellent transcript of the main meeting. Vernice Anderson, an experienced secretary who worked for Phillip Jessup, a State Department official, was seated just outside the room where the second meeting was taking place, and because the door was left open, she decided to take notes. As a result, there is a complete stenographic record of the conversation. This became quite important a few months later, when the war turned infinitely more bitter, and when MacArthur showed little desire to accept any responsibility for his miscalculations over the Chinese entry.

Victory, MacArthur had assured Truman, "was won in Korea." After a brief discussion of the postwar future of a unified Korea, Truman asked MacArthur

the critical question—what were the chances of Chinese or Soviet intervention? "Very little," MacArthur answered. "Had they intervened in the first or
second month, it would have been decisive. We are no longer fearful of their
intervention. We no longer stand hat in hand. The Chinese have 300,000 men
in Manchuria." Of these, he said, about 100,000 to 125,000 were situated along
the Yalu, and only 50,000 or 60,000 could have gotten across it. "They have no
air force. Now that we have bases for our Air Force in Korea, if the Chinese
tried to get down to Pyongyang it would be the greatest slaughter in the history of mankind."

As for the threats coming from Beijing, Dean Rusk remembered,
MacArthur was quite dismissive. He did not, he said, "fully understand why
they [the Chinese] had gone out on such a limb, and that they now must be
embarrassed by it."

Then MacArthur spoke about the coming landing of Tenth Corps at Wonsan and the fact that Pyongyang would fall in a week and that North Korean
resistance would effectively be ended by Thanksgiving. He hoped to be able to
withdraw the Eighth Army by Christmas. Omar Bradley asked if there was a
possibility one of the divisions fighting in Korea could be released for duty in
Europe. Yes, the general answered, and suggested the Second Infantry Division, which would have thrilled members of that unit who had fought so hard
in the Pusan Perimeter. The paperwork was soon started for moving the Second Division out of Korea.

Neither Truman nor any of his senior staff pushed MacArthur very hard
on the details. That was, regrettably, true on the most sensitive of subjects, the
instructions they had set out for him concerning the area around the border
and what they were going to do if there were signs of a Chinese—or Russian—
presence. The news was so good that no one wanted to know more. It was as if
what they did not say and did not know would not hurt them. So what would
happen if the Chinese *did* enter the war and somehow managed to elude
MacArthur's Air Force was never discussed. Each of the principals, in the name
of good manners and good politics, dodged the harder questions. MacArthur
could be charming when he wanted to, and though he had grumbled all the
way from Tokyo to Wake about their exploiting him for political reasons, he
was on his best and most supplicating behavior, telling the president that no
commander in history had ever received more support from a president.

Truman, for his part, was no less evasive in dealing with the hard, dangerous questions ahead, especially those posed by the possible entry of the Chinese into the war. No one reminded MacArthur of the embargo against
sending UN troops to provinces abutting Manchuria. All of that was deliberate. At one point, when the meeting seemed to be going far too quickly, Dean

Rusk tried to slow it down a bit, fearing that the skeptical press corps would seize on the brevity and write that this confirmed that it was all about public relations. He passed a note to the president suggesting that they go a bit more slowly. Back came the answer, "No, I want to get out of here before we get in trouble." At the end, before they parted, Truman pinned a Distinguished Service Medal on the general (his fifth), this one "for valor and for courageous devotion to duty and superlative diplomatic skill." On the way to the airfield, MacArthur asked Truman if he was going to run for reelection. Truman responded by asking MacArthur if *he* had any political plans. None, the general answered: "If you have any general running against you, his name will be Eisenhower, not MacArthur." Eisenhower, Truman said, did not know the first thing about politics: "His administration would make Grant's look like a model of perfection."

The meeting in the end had been false in almost every sense. A potentially great threat to UN forces had been minimized, how to deal with it barely discussed. MacArthur had been more right about the meeting than anyone realized: it had been about sharing the Inchon glory in the last weeks before an off-year election. As the two groups prepared to depart Wake, optimistic statements were issued. "I've never had a more satisfactory conference since I've been president," Truman told reporters later that day. A communiqué was drafted and initialed by both men, as one reporter on the scene noted, "as if they were the heads of different governments." The general, John Gunther noted, seemed restless and in a hurry to get away. He took out his pocket watch, looked at it, rubbed it carefully, and put it back in his pocket. He refused to talk to reporters. "All comments," he said, "would have to come from the publicity man of the president," edgy words, as Gunther noted, with a slight stinger in them, for presidents have press secretaries, not publicity men. "Each man," Acheson wrote later, "was to think an understanding had been established, but each would have a different idea of what it was."

One of the problems was that each side had a very different view of whether Chinese entry into the war was a good or bad thing. A few weeks later, when it had all gone sour, Matt Ridgway, who had monitored the unraveling of events with a mounting pessimism from Washington, remembered a moment when he and Harriman had visited with MacArthur back in early August 1950. The subject of Taiwan had come up and MacArthur had suddenly become quite passionate.

If the Chinese were foolish enough to launch an attack against the island, he himself would rush down there, take command personally, and "deliver such a crushing defeat that it would be one of the decisive battles of the world—a disaster so great it would rock Asia, and perhaps turn back Communism." Then he had paused and commented that he doubted they would be that foolish, before adding, "I pray nightly that they will. I would get down on my knees." Not many other American soldiers, Ridgway thought, were praying for a war on the Asian mainland with a nation that had a population of some 600 million. At first, Ridgway had thought it was merely MacArthurian grandiosity, the voice of an old man aching for an even larger place in history. Later, trying to understand MacArthur's drive north, Ridgway wrote, "Whether this vision of himself as the swordsman who would slay the Communist dragon was what prompted his eventual reckless drive to the borders of Manchuria no one of course can now divine. But I suspect that it did add luster to his dream of victory."

Of the two forces that would soon meet on the battlefield, only the Chinese now knew what was going to happen next. The Americans, political and military, remained blissfully, almost consciously, ignorant. Events in Korea were never to be so positive again. Truman would soon find MacArthur as hostile and suspicious as ever. MacArthur, for his part, would eventually write that the Wake meeting convinced him of "a curious and sinister change" that had taken place in Washington, reflecting a diminished administration will to fight Communism. As for Truman himself, in a 1954 interview with Jim Lucas of Scripps Howard, MacArthur said, "The little bastard [Truman] honestly believes he's a patriot."

THAT AMERICA'S WAR aims were not clearly defined, and that there were significant differences in the attitudes in Washington and Tokyo, had been obvious from the very start. As early as July 13, when Joe Collins and Hoyt Vandenberg visited him in Tokyo, MacArthur had spoken quite openly about how his first mission was to destroy the North Korean forces, but that he then intended "to compose and unite Korea." "It might be necessary to occupy all of Korea," he added, "although this was speculative at the time." Now that was his goal: the fact that the men from Washington had wanted to bask in his glory convinced MacArthur that he was more powerful than ever, which in turn made him more difficult than ever to restrain.

Of the American military miscalculations of the twentieth century, Douglas MacArthur's decision to send his troops all the way to the Yalu stands alone. (Vietnam was a *political* miscalculation and the chief architects of it were civilians.) All sorts of red flags were there for him, flags that he chose not to see. So it was that his troops, their command split, their communications often dangerously weak, the weather worsening by the day, pushed north, while the Chinese watched and patiently waited for them on the high hills, already preparing to block the narrow arteries of retreat or escape. The same general who had argued for Inchon because of the vulnerability of the North

Korean supply lines now allowed his own supply lines to grow dangerously long in territory over which he had no control. The same general who had wanted to land at Inchon because it might end the war quickly and spare his troops from fighting in the cruel Korean winter was now ready to send them farther north just as the Manchurian winter arrived. "One of the things I found hardest to understand—and to forgive as a commander," Matt Ridgway said nearly forty years later, "was how completely oblivious the Tokyo command was to the conditions under which our men would have to fight."

OF THE MANY professional sins of which Douglas MacArthur was guilty in that moment, including hubris and vanity, none was greater than his complete underestimation of his enemy. The China he thought he knew—despite all his time in Asia, he had spent almost no time there—was part of a nineteenth-century world. As Bruce Cumings, a historian of the Korean War, noted, Asians in MacArthur's mind were "obedient, dutiful, childlike, and quick to follow resolute leadership." In the late 1940s, that was certainly true of Japan, because the Japanese, having disastrously lost the war, were looking for lessons from the victors. But much of the rest of the region was caught up in nascent revolution. What had happened in the Chinese civil war as much as anything else reflected those changes, something MacArthur never chose to understand. Part of that was his very nature, and what had become the nature of his mystique. He did not ask questions; that would imply there was something he did not know. Instead he was oracular, the man that others came to hear. Major General Dave Barr, the head of the last American military advisory mission in China, a witness to the rise of Mao and very knowledgeable about the tactics of the Chinese Communists, was a division commander in Korea when the Chinese entered the war. He knew more than most American officers about why the Communists had won in China, but MacArthur was not about to let him brief other regimental and division commanders.

The China that existed in MacArthur's mind was one that had not been touched by revolution. He seemed not to care how and why Mao had come to power and seemed to have little interest in the forces that the revolution had unleashed. He showed astonishingly little curiosity about who his enemy was and why they had been so successful in the past. Despite all the information available before the Chinese struck, despite all they got from captured prisoners, Charles Willoughby's intelligence shop knew so little about the enemy command that in late December, a month after the big Chinese attack, MacArthur still thought that Lin Biao, not Peng Dehuai, was the Chinese commander. MacArthur seemed to believe that the Communists' victory in the civil war had little larger meaning. As a military force the Communists were "grossly overrated," he had told congressional representatives in September 1949, a month before Mao proclaimed his government. The way to beat them, he had said at the time, was to hit them "where they are weakest, namely in the air and on the sea." All you had to do, he added, was place "500 fighter planes, under the command of some old war horse similar to General Chennault." He had used his airpower skillfully in his campaign in the Pacific against the Japanese, as a kind of long-distance artillery, and he seemed to believe that he would be able to use it much the same way against the Chinese. That belief in the supremacy of American airpower above all else would prove a military miscalculation that would soon haunt, if not MacArthur himself, certainly the men who fought underneath him. It was as if he believed the Chinese would march right up to American lines in daylight in traditional battle formation, daring the Americans to wipe them out from the air. He had been blinded by his success with airpower in World War II, Joe Collins later wrote, but that had been against fixed, immobile Japanese targets, not against the Chinese as they would appear in this war. There was, regrettably, Collins believed, almost no firsthand sense of the battlefield at his headquarters.

MacArthur had his own mantra about the forces at play. He prided himself on his understanding of what he called Oriental psychology, or in a phrase he used again and again, "the mind of the Oriental." He knew, he would say, that the Asiatic respected powerful men who were strong and unshakable in their vision. One of the great myths of the Korean War, said Mike Lynch, who, after Johnnie Walker was gone, became Matt Ridgway's pilot and watched many of the key players from very close up, "was Douglas MacArthur's claimed knowledge of the Oriental mind. We may have known the rich businessman in Manila, and the cowardly and corrupt Chinese leaders in Chiang Kai-shek's Army, and the condescending Japanese in Tokyo. But we knew nothing about the battle hardened North Koreans, or the dedicated Chinese who had whipped Chiang. It was a classic failure to apply the most basic tenet for military commanders: know your enemy."

MacArthur did not in fact know that much about Asia. He had not been on the Asian mainland since 1905; he paid little attention to events he did not like. To the degree that he knew any Asian country well, it was the Philippines, a nation as different from most other Asian countries as New York is from Texas. There, he had been in fact something of a national hero and was exceptionally well connected with the upper class, and quite well rewarded for his role. In fact he and some of the key members of his staff had received immense payments in early 1942 from the Philippine leader Manuel Quezon, to guarantee their role as influential friends of Manila in the future. Even before he departed the islands for Australia, in one of the most puzzling financial arrangements of the war, Quezon had transferred $640,000 in U.S. dollars to MacArthur and a few staff members. "Seldom, if ever, have American military officers received such evidence of high esteem," Carol Morris Petillo, who wrote of the deal, dryly noted. Of that sum, $500,000 went to MacArthur himself (probably the equivalent of $10 million in contemporary dollars, tax free); Richard Sutherland, his much despised chief of staff, got $75,000; Sutherland's deputy Richard Marshall, $45,000; and Sid Huff, another MacArthur aide, $20,000. The War Department knew of it, which meant George Marshall and surely Roosevelt were aware of the transaction, but no one tried to stop it. Not long after that Quezon made a comparable offer to Eisenhower, by then an important officer in Washington, supposedly for his service in the islands from 1935 to 1939. Eisenhower wisely and graciously turned Quezon down and entered a memo for his official file explaining what had happened.

Like many a general before him, MacArthur believed one war would be much the same as the next—even if it was against an entirely different enemy—so he failed to grasp the differences between the two great Asian armies he had fought in two very different wars. In World War II, the Japanese had fielded a traditional army, fighting a conventional war, vulnerable not because of the limits of their individual soldiers' abilities, but because of the limitations of their country's industrial base. As a military force they were indeed vulnerable to traditional power, most particularly airpower. The Chinese, by contrast, were the least industrialized of major nations, understood their vulnerabilities all too well, and adjusted their tactics accordingly. Much of the way they fought reflected the primitive status of their industrial economy. Their ability to shift vast forces without detection—moving some of their divisions up to fifteen miles at night without a single cigarette being smoked, then burrowing into handmade caves during the day—caught MacArthur and his immediate staff completely by surprise.

So as his troops continued their push toward the Yalu, the Chinese were carefully preparing what was, in effect, the largest ambush in the era of modern warfare. What the Chinese now wanted was for MacArthur to move ever farther north, extending his supply lines even more precariously. When Lei Yingfu had given Mao his briefing on MacArthur's likely assault on Inchon back in late August, the Chinese leader peppered him with questions not just about the general's tactics in the past but about his personality as well. He was, Lei answered, "famous for his arrogance and his stubbornness." That intrigued Mao. "Fine! Fine!" he said. "The more arrogant and more stubborn he is the better." "An arrogant enemy," he added, "is easy to defeat."

Now it was MacArthur's staff, so much an extension of his ego, that played a critical role, making sure that whatever he had wanted to happen was happening, and that anything that cast doubt on his preconceptions was minimized.

Clark Lee, a wire service reporter, and Richard Henschel, a combat photographer who had covered MacArthur together throughout World War II, once wrote that the staff was a reflection of the worst in him because it amplified his worst qualities without any of his redeeming ones. "Some of them," they wrote, "acted like men who had personally lifted him down from the cross after he had been crucified by Marshall-Admiral King-Harry Hopkins [the top Washington people of the moment] and they had determined that nothing again should ever hurt him." It had always been this way. There had been a time years earlier when MacArthur was making a point with General Marshall. "My staff—" he had begun, when Marshall interrupted him. "You don't have a staff, General. You have a court." To Joseph Alsop, a nominally sympathetic columnist, the manner of MacArthur's staff in the Tokyo years seemed like nothing so much as what Alsop had read of the court of Louis XIV. The Dai Ichi Building, he wrote, "was proof of the basic rule of armies at war: the farther one gets from the front, the more laggards, toadies and fools one encounters." No one had more toadies and sycophants than MacArthur, and their tone with him "was almost wholly simpering and reverential, and I have always held the view that this sycophancy was what tripped him up in the end."

By the fall of 1950, their universe was a small but volatile one. If he smiled, they smiled; if he frowned, they frowned. If things worked out well, it was because he was a great man; if not, it was because of sworn enemies in Washington. He had by then "surrounded himself," the historian William Stueck wrote in a particularly apt phrase, with men "who would not disturb the dreamworld of self worship in which he chose to live." Never would the weakness of his staff come back to haunt him as in Korea, and rarely would the failure so revolve around one man—his chief of intelligence, or G-2, Charles Willoughby. There was no area of MacArthur's headquarters where the drop-off between the talents required for the job and the prejudices and bombast of the incumbent was as noticeable as with Willoughby, or Sir Charles, or Lord Willoughby, or Baron von Willoughby—or Bonnie Prince Charles, as he was sometimes known by officers not in the Bataan Gang. Dave Barrett, leader of the Dixie Mission, considered him a major distortionist. "The Prince of Pilsn," he called him in private. Willoughby was a name, said Carleton West, a young intelligence officer who had come out of the OSS, that should have been pronounced with a V—Villoughby— so Prussian, authoritarian, and arrogant was he. "Roger," Willoughby once asked Dr. Roger Egeberg, one of the senior staff members, "do you think I have too much of a Prussian accent?" But you could tell, Egeberg added, that he was very proud of it. "My lovable fascist," MacArthur called him on occasion.

Willoughby was not just MacArthur's principal personal intelligence man; when it came to the war in Korea, he was the only intelligence man who mattered. Most commanders wanted as many good sources of information as possible; MacArthur was focused on limiting and controlling the sources of intelligence. His desire was to have no dissenting or even alternative voices on his watch. It was always important to him that his intelligence reports blend seamlessly with what he had intended to do in the first place. What that meant was that the intelligence Willoughby was turning over to MacArthur was deliberately prefabricated. Highly professional intelligence estimates, which reflected a growing Chinese presence, might have prevented him from making what he wanted most: the final drive to the Yalu. Only after Willoughby's great and catastrophic failure on the whereabouts and intentions of China's armies would the CIA finally be allowed into the region.

Willoughby was a Prussian-born man of the far right, "all ideology and almost never any facts," in the words of Frank Wisner, the head of the CIA's Directorate of Plans. He did not always seem completely assimilated: America should, he told Robert Sherrod, who was working for *Time* magazine during World War II, be fighting a different enemy. "This Washington policy makes no sense," he said. "We should give England to the Germans. Our war is over here [in Asia]." His great hero—other than MacArthur—was the Spanish dictator Francisco Franco, a true fascist who had been supported by the Nazis in his drive to power in the 1930s and who then tilted to the Germans during World War II. Even as he was operating as MacArthur's G-2, he was busy working on a biography of Franco. John Gunther had been surprised by the way, during a dinner in the midst of World War II, Willoughby, who had been bitterly caustic about the American military and political leadership in Europe and Washington, suddenly raised his glass to toast "the second greatest military commander in the world, Francisco Franco," a man who was hardly an ally, or for that matter a friend of the United States. Frank Gibney, who covered Willoughby as a young reporter for *Time,* noted that he was "always talking about the two great generals, and your great job at any given moment was to figure out which great general he was talking about, MacArthur or Franco. He'd be saying he had just gotten another marvelous shipment of wine in from The General, so you had to figure out that that was probably Franco, on the assumption that Spain made a good deal more wine than the people at the Dai Ichi."

In no other American headquarters could Willoughby have reached so important a post, and the higher he rose, the more Prussian he became. On occasion, he even wore a monocle, although, as one fellow officer put it, he was more like Erich von Stroheim, the movie director, than Gerd von Rundstedt, the head of the World War II German General Staff. There was something pathetic about Willoughby's manner, Gibney thought, his self-conscious attempt to seem more aristocratic than he was. "He'd be out there at the Tokyo Club, ready to play tennis accompanied by his claque, the colonels from his shop, on some very hot day. He would look over and see you, and say, 'Gibney, good show, good seeing you out there playing today, Gibney—well, they say that only mad dogs and Englishmen go out in the noon day sun, but here I am too.' And the awful thing was that the claque of colonels would all laugh as if he had said something funny, and you suddenly feared for the intelligence coming into the Tokyo command and headed towards Washington."

There was some debate about his origins. His claims that he was descended from an aristocratic German father and an American mother were generally believed to be false, and most people believed he was a self-invented nobleman. Certainly, he did little to clear up any mysteries about his past. In *Who's Who in America* and in the biography he gave to the Army, Willoughby said he was born in Heidelberg, Germany, on March 8, 1892, and was the son of Freiherr (Baron) T. von Tscheppe-Weidenbach and Emma von Tscheppe-Weidenbach (née Emma Willoughby of Baltimore). But the Heidelberg registry for that date records only the birth of Adolf August Weidenbach, sired by August Weidenbach, a rope maker, and Emma Langhauser, a German. According to Frank Kluckhohn of *The Reporter* magazine, a search of German documents showed no grant from anyone in power of the right to have the "von" in Willoughby's name. One of Willoughby's friends from his early days confirmed that both of his parents were German and that the name Willoughby was a rough translation of Weidenbach, which means "willow brook" in German. Kluckhohn questioned Willoughby about this and thereupon was told that he had actually been an orphan, had never known his father, and was sticking with the *Who's Who* version. Apparently he came to America as an eighteen-year-old in 1910 and entered the Army as Adolf Charles Weidenbach. In three years he made sergeant, left the Army, went to Gettysburg College, did some graduate studies at the University of Kansas, and then taught languages at girls' schools in the Midwest. In 1916, he reentered the Army, served on the Mexican border, and eventually went to France but did not see combat. After the war, he served for a time as military attaché in Venezuela, Colombia, and Ecuador, where Ned Almond first ran across him and, according to Bill McCaffrey, came to hate him. Eventually he became a self-styled military historian and intelligence officer. Somehow in the mid-1930s he connected with MacArthur while he was teaching at Fort Leavenworth, Kansas, a place where the Army sent its most promising mid-career officers for extra training, and in 1940 he joined MacArthur in the Philippines, soon becoming the intelligence expert on his staff. From then on, one of his chief jobs was as amplifier of the MacArthur myth, and he worked all through World War II as well as in the Tokyo and Korean years on a monumental study of MacArthur's military career, said to be three thousand pages long, although the book he finally published was of normal length.

If MacArthur's staff was always unified against any challenge from the outside, then within it there were many factions always struggling to gain special favor from the general; Willoughby and Courtney Whitney, another MacArthur favorite, who being a lawyer as well had helped do some legal work for him on the side, were continually battling to be best boy. Whitney had been especially helpful in the Philippine years with his connections to the upper levels of Manila society, but Willoughby had a great ear for what MacArthur wanted to hear and tended to place him atop the pedestal of history. In 1947, he wrote MacArthur: "There is no contemporary figure comparable to yours. . . . Ultimately [people] have been attached to a great leader, to a man and not an idea, to a Malbrough [sic], to a Napoleon, to a Robert E Lee. Underneath it all, these are age old dynastic alliances. . . . A gentleman can serve a grand-seigneur. That will be a good ending to my career . . . and as I scan the world, the grand-seigneurs are leaving the arena, fighting a bitter rear guard action against the underman, the faceless mob driven by Russian knouts."

That Willoughby existed at all was proof to many senior officers in Washington that MacArthur ran an army of his own, largely outside the reach of the chief of staff. To them Willoughby was a leftover from the other side of World War I, "so much the Prussian type that all he needed was a spiked helmet," in the words of Clayton James, MacArthur's biographer. The intensity of his ideological biases made even others on the MacArthur staff uneasy. In the internal staff struggles over the future of Japanese democracy, Willoughby was an unusually passionate player, trying to rid headquarters of the New Deal liberals whom he tended to see as fellow travelers or Communists. He was also a kind of self-appointed journalistic censor, always on the alert for any journalistic transgression against either the occupation or MacArthur personally. "There were several of us who reported on the struggles within the bureaucracy in those days—serious and very interesting stuff for these were battles over which direction the new Japan would take. That meant reporting about the two main forces in the MacArthur headquarters, the reformers, and the traditionalists," said Joseph Fromm of *U.S. News & World Report.* "Willoughby was absolutely convinced that because I was doing a good deal of original reporting on those divisions, reporting what neither he nor MacArthur liked, that I was a Communist. I remember one day he called me for a special one-on-one meeting, and it was a truly crazed scene. All he wanted to do was talk about Lenin and Marx, man to man, like we both knew what the game was, he the anti-Communist and the man of the law and me, in his mind, the Communist, and thus the outlaw, and we would be equals in this sparring, sophisticates about it, men of the world, but in the end his view of Communism would trump mine." Years later, Fromm got hold of his security file through the Freedom of Information Act. What stunned him was the amount of garbage in it about him, all of it collected by Willoughby and his people in the G-2 section, almost all of it ugly, reams and reams of it, much of it incredibly inaccurate, "the kind of thing that could ruin a person's career if it was taken seriously. What it told about the man who was in charge of collecting it, the waste of time involved, and the inability of that headquarters to deal with reality, was staggering."

Like comparable ideologists on both sides of the spectrum, Willoughby was conspiratorial. What had happened on the Chinese mainland was not an epochal event in which the long suppressed forces of history found a modern political means of expression, but the work of plotters. In a letter to the House Un-American Activities Committee in May 1950, a month before the war began, he claimed that "American Communist brains planned the communization of China." These were fellow travelers, he wrote, who had "an inexplicable fanaticism for an alien cause, the Communist 'Jehad' of pan-Slavism for the subjugation of the Western world." As such, he was closely aligned with some of the more extreme people working on issues of subversion back in America. As early as 1947 he had started his own investigations of Americans operating in Japan, investigations that were not, as Bruce Cumings pointed out, unlike those to come three years later from McCarthy. Willoughby was in constant touch with HUAC, and with Alfred Kohlberg, the man generally viewed as the central figure in the China Lobby, as well as the FBI, passing on raw information about people he thought were dangerously left wing, among them people in the State Department who had taken a dim view of Chiang's chances. Some of what he sent in was eventually passed on to McCarthy for use in his investigations of the wartime China Hands. Later in life, after MacArthur was relieved, Willoughby surfaced with major connections to the extreme right wing in the United States, and began writing ever more virulent, racist, and anti-Semitic articles. When Eisenhower was about to get the Republican nomination in 1952, Willoughby told MacArthur that this proved the Republicans were part of a "clever conspiratorial move to perpetuate the vampire hold of the Roosevelt-Truman mechanism."

That was the intellectual prism through which all critical intelligence would pass in Tokyo. The key to the importance of Willoughby was not his own self-evident inadequacies; it was that he represented the deepest kind of psychological weakness in the talented, flawed man he served, the need to have someone who agreed with him at all times and flattered him constantly. Willoughby was despised by a vast number of other military men in the command. "I was always afraid he would be found murdered one day, because if he was, I was sure that they would come and arrest me, because I hated him so much, and had been so outspoken about him," Bill McCaffrey once said. "MacArthur did not *want* the Chinese to enter the war in Korea. Anything MacArthur wanted, Willoughby produced intelligence for. . . . In this case Willoughby falsified the intelligence reports. . . . He should have gone to jail," said Lieutenant Colonel John Chiles, Tenth Corps G-3, or chief of operations, and one of Almond's most trusted deputies.

Never had his role been more important than in late October, as more and more reliable reports flowed in about the arrival of Chinese troops into the extreme northern reaches of Korea. It was at this moment that Willoughby set out to prove that they were either not there, or, if they were, that they existed only in small numbers as volunteers. He did all he could to minimize the overwhelming evidence that the Chinese had been the ones who struck the ROKs and the Eighth Cavalry near Unsan in the late October–early November assault. A good many men who fought there came to believe that his refusal to act quickly on the evidence presented by the first captured Chinese prisoners, his unwillingness to add a serious note of caution to his intelligence briefings, was directly responsible for the devastation inflicted not just on the Cav at Unsan but upon the Eighth Army soon after, for the loss of so many buddies, and in some cases, for their own long tours in Chinese and Korean prisons. To them, what he represented came perilously close to evil, someone who blustered about the dangers of Communism and the Chinese, but then ended up making their work so much easier by setting the UN forces up for that great ambush. He was, thought Bill Train, a bright, young, low-level G-3 staff officer who fought against his certitudes in those critical weeks, "a four flusher—someone who made it seem like he knew what he was doing—but in the end what he produced was absolutely worthless, there was nothing there at all. Nothing. He got everything wrong! *Everything!* What he was doing in those days was fighting against the truth, trying to keep it from going from lower levels to higher ones where it would have to be acted on."

The importance and value of a good, independent intelligence man in wartime can hardly be overemphasized. A great intelligence officer studies the unknown and works in the darkness, trying to see the shape of future events. He covers the sensitive ground where prejudice, or instinctive cultural bias, often meet reality, and he must stand for reality, even if it means standing virtually alone. Great intelligence officers often have the melancholy job of telling their superiors things they don't want to hear. A great intelligence officer tries to make the unknown at least partially knowable; he tries to think like his enemy, and he listens carefully to those with whom he disagrees, simply because he knows that he has to challenge his own value system in order to understand the nature and impulse of the other side.

In all ways, Charles Willoughby not only failed to fit this role, but was the very opposite of it. He was not harmless, some American Colonel Blimp, long retired, boring the other geezers at some second-rate club with the sad lament that nothing was as good as in his youth, the young no longer as brave as when he had been a recruit. He would have been considered, thought Carleton Swift, a thirty-one-year-old intelligence officer, a buffoon if the impact of his acts had not been so deadly serious. Swift, a CIA man (who had come out of OSS), operated with State Department cover as a consul in the U.S. embassy in Seoul and so was beyond Willoughby's reach. "There was an arrogance to Willoughby that was completely different from the uncertainty—the cautiousness—you associate with good intelligence men. It was as if he was always right, had always been right. Certitude after certitude poured out of him. It was as if there was an exclamation point after all of his sentences. If he said something wouldn't happen, then it wouldn't happen—*it couldn't happen*. He would say things like, 'We *know* that they are going to do this, and we *know* they are not going to do that.' Worse, you couldn't challenge him. Because he always made it clear that he spoke for MacArthur and if you challenged him you were challenging MacArthur. And that obviously wasn't allowed. So that made it very hard for intelligence in the field to filter up to higher headquarters on something that he had made up his mind on." Swift had been one of the young OSS officers who had dealt with Ho Chi Minh in Vietnam during World War II, when the United States was still friendly with him, and then he had been in Kunming during the Chinese civil war, and had come away with a healthy respect for the military abilities of the Communists. He still had some good sources in China, and he had been very aware of the massive movement of Chinese troops to the Manchurian border. In dealing with your sources in those days, he believed, it was all about instinct and trust. He knew that the Chinese were gathering along the Yalu in huge numbers, and that their leadership had said they were going to enter the war. Best to take those promises seriously—especially since everything he picked up from his agents indicated that they were going ahead with their plans to enter the war.

Then, in mid- to late October, Swift started receiving reports from his agents about Chinese troops crossing into Korea. These agents were all Chinese or, in the racist vernacular of the moment, "slopies" (for slope-eyes). The reports varied in quality, but there was enough good stuff to make any intelligence officer pay heed. Nor was Swift alone, for he was hearing similar tales from some of his friends in military intelligence, which he later believed reflected their awareness of the Chinese prisoners taken and being interrogated by General Paik and American headquarters in the Unsan region. But Swift knew something else as well. "None of this was going to affect Willoughby. The Chinese were not going to come in. *He knew it. And he was never wrong!*"

IN FACT, WILLOUGHBY was not only stopping the combat-level intelligence machinery from sending its best and most consequential material to the top in Korea, but he was blocking other sources of intelligence as well, and keeping a careful eye on a small, bare-bones CIA operation that in 1950 existed in Tokyo. By prearrangement with the Navy, a small CIA shop had been set up inside the Seventh Fleet, at its base in Yokosuka, and was being run by a man named William Duggan, an old OSS operative who had worked previously in Europe. From late September well into October, Duggan was receiving some exceptional intelligence from his colleagues in Taiwan on what the Chinese Communist Army was up to. Some of the old Nationalist units, now incorporated into the People's Liberation Army, still had their radios. Sometimes they would manage to slip away at night and make contact with Taiwan to describe where they were and what they were up to. The messages all had a theme: we are all heading north to the Manchurian border; the field level officers believe the decision has already been made to cross the Yalu.

Then, suddenly, in late October, the radios went silent, perhaps because they were by then in North Korea and there was greater control over who had the radios. But there was no doubt that the earlier reports represented very real warnings. A young CIA operative on Taiwan named Bob Myers was picking up these reports from some of the Nationalists he was working with and passing them on to his superiors, and he knew that they had reached Duggan in Japan. What he did not learn until later was that Willoughby had found out about this and had threatened to close down Duggan's tiny shop and run him out of Japan unless he stopped trying to notify anyone higher up about the intelligence he had.

Meanwhile, within the Eighth Army a fierce bureaucratic battle over the intelligence was taking place. The unfortunate man caught between Willoughby above him and the growing doubts among intelligence men working on the ground in northern Korea was the Eighth Army's G-2, Clint Tarkenton. "He was a Willoughby man, not a Walton Walker man, and you must not underestimate the importance of that. You must remember the enormous power that Willoughby had in that overall command structure," said Bill Train, who as a young officer in the First Cav's G-3 shop, was convinced that the Chinese had entered the country in force, and that a major tragedy was in the making: "It was MacArthur's command, not a U.S. Army command, and if you crossed Willoughby it was not just a ticket out of there, it was probably a ticket straight out of your career." So Tarkenton followed the line from Tokyo that, as Willoughby had reported in an intelligence estimate on October 28, three days after the capture of the first Chinese prisoner in the Unsan area, "the auspicious time for such intervention has long since passed; it is difficult to believe that such a move, if planned, would have been postponed to a time when remnant NK forces have been reduced to a low point of effectiveness."

Train, however, was quite alarmed about what had happened at Unsan. He had been pulled into some of the intelligence work because the G-2 section was shorthanded. Now, as he paid more and more attention, he saw undeniable evidence of what appeared to be a large-scale Chinese entry into the war. It was not something that you scoffed at, as Willoughby's shop was doing; it was something that sent a chill through you and made you want to come up with even more information. Technically, intelligence was not even Train's area, but how could you do plans as a G-3 if you did not know who or where the enemy was? Even before the Chinese struck at Unsan, he felt himself putting together a jigsaw puzzle in which the newest pieces gave an ever clearer picture. American soldiers moving north were moving into an area filled with ghosts, but gradually those ghosts were beginning to have an outline. Train was no less struck by the way the intelligence people above him were systematically minimizing or openly discounting the same information. At the very least they should have been pushing harder for more information. Instead they were visibly shrinking the numbers on the enemy, and making it clear that they did not want better information. Whenever Train and his boss in G-3, John Dabney, spotted something that seemed to indicate a serious Chinese presence, Willoughby's people minimized it.

What made the struggle so unequal was that Clint Tarkenton was not an ally. He was not quite an opponent either, but he was caught in a squeeze between a dogmatic, authoritarian boss and an intrusive, unwanted reality. "Tarkenton was in an impossible situation," Train said years later. "Willoughby was his boss and he was a bully and he knew his power and he liked using it, and he controlled that shop both in Tokyo and, because Tarkenton was his man, in the Eighth Army G-2 as well, and he could dominate any intelligence estimates he wanted. Tarkenton, no matter what his real thoughts, was very much under his shadow." Later Dabney also said that Tarkenton was unduly influenced by Willoughby. Whatever they came up with in terms of the Chinese presence, Willoughby had an answer. If the ROKs reported killing thirty-six Chinese during a battle, and the bodies were still on the battlefield, then the answer came back that it was all just an Oriental way of saving face, that the ROKs had fought so poorly they had to claim a certain number of dead Chinese as a matter of pride. If Train came up with evidence that seemed to point to the presence of five or six Chinese divisions in a given area, the answer was invariably that these were different, smaller units from different Chinese divisions, now attached to a North Korean unit.

A most dangerous game was being played out, by one part of the Army, safely quartered in Tokyo, at the expense of another part that would have to fight that very dangerous enemy under terrible conditions. For example, on October 30, after the first attack at Unsan, Everett Drumwright in the Seoul embassy, reflecting the G-2 position quite precisely, cabled State that two regiments' worth of Chinese, perhaps three thousand men, were probably engaged in the North. That was his honest attempt to answer what was the burning question of the moment for his superiors. The next day he cabled again, giving a smaller figure of only two thousand Chinese troops. By November 1, after lower-level interrogators showed that there were troops there from several different Chinese *armies,* Tarkenton, following the Willoughby line, said that it was because smaller units from those armies but not the full armies themselves had showed up.

On November 3, as the reality of Unsan gradually set in, Willoughby upped his figures slightly. Yes, the Chinese were there in country, minimally 16,500 of them, at a maximum 34,000. On November 6, Tarkenton placed the total figure of Chinese aligned against both the Eighth Army and Tenth Corps at 27,000. In reality, the number in country was already closer to 250,000, and growing. On November 17, MacArthur told Ambassador Muccio that there were no more than 30,000 Chinese in country, while the next day Tarkenton placed the number at 48,000. On November 24, the day the major UN offensive to go to the Yalu kicked off—instead of sensing how large the Chinese presence was and getting into strong defensive positions—Willoughby placed the minimum number at 40,000, the maximum at 71,000. At the time there were *300,000* Chinese troops waiting patiently for the UN forces to come a little deeper into their trap.

There was even a major split within the G-2 shop. Not only were a number of subordinate intelligence officers working in the field now absolutely sure Willoughby was desperately wrong, but Lieutenant Colonel Bob Fergusson, nominally senior to Tarkenton and originally supposed to be the G-2, shared their doubts. Fergusson, who had arrived in Korea after Tarkenton took over, tried without success to change Tarkenton's mind. Unfortunately, it was not a man he was wrestling with but a system, and Fergusson was the outsider in it. It was, as Train put it, "the saddest thing I was ever associated with because you could almost see it coming, almost know what happened was going to happen, those young men moving into that awful goddamn trap."

For Johnnie Walker, it simply did not feel right, but he was being pulled along by the power of the command above him. At first, he had stonewalled the war correspondents about the possibility of the Chinese being in country. When the first of several prisoners had been taken by the ROKs, Tom Lambert of the Associated Press, one of the best reporters there, along with Hugh Moffett of *Time,* had picked up on the rumor that one or more of the prisoners was Chinese. They had driven some twenty miles to the Korean regimental headquarters, where a Korean officer, who spoke both Chinese and English, was interrogating a prisoner who wore a quilted jacket and a very different uniform from any they had seen. The prisoner was indeed Chinese, and quite open about it—they were all supposed to be volunteers, he said, but he was not a volunteer. The next day, Lambert and Moffett jeeped over to Walker's headquarters, where they found the Eighth Army commander in what seemed to them still an early stage of denial. "Well, he might be Chinese," Walker said, "but remember they have a lot of Mexicans in Los Angeles but you don't call LA a Mexican city." In fact he had been extremely nervous from the moment the first Chinese soldiers were captured. On November 6, right after some of the damage to the Eighth Cav had been assessed, Willoughby had flown into Pyongyang for a meeting, and Walker had turned to him and said, "Charles, we know the Chinese are here; you tell us what they are here for." The response, as Wilson Heefner, Walker's biographer, noted, was not much of an answer at all.

Walker at that moment felt very much on the outside. At the time of the celebration of the liberation of Seoul, he had told his aide Joe Tyner and his pilot, Mike Lynch, that it would be a big day because he was finally going to learn what the plans were for the future. He had returned later that day utterly confused. No one had even bothered to speak to him about the next step. Once they crossed the thirty-eighth parallel, he would have preferred to dig in about a hundred miles north, along the narrow neck of that part of the peninsula, on a line that went roughly from Pyongyang to Wonsan, and leave roughly two-thirds of the country, much of it largely uninhabited wilderness, untouched. That penetration would have been easier to secure, to defend, and to supply, and it would have made any Chinese or North Korean attempt to attack vulnerable to UN airpower. It fell short by about three hundred miles of going all the way to the Yalu. But it was not to be. In truth, Walker was no longer the Eighth Army commander. He was now the commander of about half of it, bypassed on all major decisions, and very much aware that he was in a competition to reach the Yalu before Almond and Tenth Corps.

None of this was by happenstance, Matt Ridgway thought. Washington might be on the defensive, but MacArthur also knew that there were three magic words that might alert it if they came from his headquarters: "massive Chinese intervention." If there was any evidence that a new enemy had entered the war big-time, the military men, including Marshall and the Chiefs, as well as the political people, would rise from their current passivity and set much more strict limits on what had been a generally free hand for him. Therefore the second real battle in the drive north right after Unsan was a political one, over the intelligence figures.

26

In the background there was a parallel force still at work, that of domestic American politics. The attempt by Truman to share some of the Inchon glory by going to Wake Island failed. On November 7, some three days after the Chinese had overrun Unsan, and even as the senior people at the First Cav were beginning to comprehend the full wreckage of the battle, Americans went to the polls to vote in the off-year election. The Democrats, burdened by a war that was already deeply unpopular, did poorly. They lost five Senate seats and twenty-eight House seats.

The election—the first time the country had been able to vote since the war began—heralded the rise of Senator Joe McCarthy, the junior senator from Wisconsin. He had given his first speech on subversion in February of 1950. To many Americans the war itself now seemed to validate his charges, while to others it had merely reconfirmed their exhaustion with the Democrats. The most immediate beneficiary was McCarthy himself. For a period of about three years in the election's wake, he went on a sensational political rampage. He basked in the easy reverberation of his charges, in the eager way the country seemed to respond, and the play—ever so careless—the media gave him for charge after charge, paying, as it did, very little heed to verification. "Reds Run State Department, McCarthy Claims, Senator Charges Reds Coddled": if a senator had said it, then it was news. Verification never interested him; nor, for that matter, did any serious study of just what the Communists were doing in this country. That was too bad because in the long run he did a serious disservice to the study of the postwar Soviet apparatus in America, and whether whatever success it had came from the relatively small number of people who joined up during the Depression years because they had lost their faith in democracy, or from the tiny hard core of men and women who actually spied for the Soviets. Serious interest in either Communism or espionage was not McCarthy's specialty. "Joe couldn't find a Communist in Red Square—he didn't know Karl Marx from Groucho Marx," as George Reedy, who covered him in those days, once said.

He was the great political roughneck of the era, a populist playing on fears generated by a new and uncertain atomic age. He gloried in how in his own mind he had become the very embodiment of Americanism. "If you want to be against McCarthy, boys," he told two reporters at one instant press conference, "you've got to be a Communist or a cocksucker." McCarthy became the perfect hit man for the right. He was extremely valuable to more sedate Republicans, "a pig in a minefield for them," in the words of the writer Murray Kempton. "Only by 'mucking' can we win, and only a mucker can muck," he once said. The estimable Senator Robert Taft once told him not to worry if some of his accusations did not pan out. He should just "keep talking and if one case doesn't work out, [he] should proceed with another."

In the 1950 elections McCarthy scored two important victories. His primary target that year was Senator Millard Tydings, an old-fashioned, quite aristocratic Maryland Democrat whom Roosevelt had earlier tried to purge because he was so conservative. Tydings had been appalled by McCarthy's charges, so reckless and partisan, and in the summer of 1950 he had taken a subcommittee and studied them, investigating the investigator so to speak. The Tydings Committee eventually criticized McCarthy for his behavior and exonerated most of those attacked by him. McCarthy's accusations, it reported, "represented perhaps the most nefarious campaign of half-truths and untruths in the history of the Republic."

By chance Tydings was up for reelection in 1950, and McCarthy went after him. He made repeated trips from Washington into neighboring Maryland and even used a faked photo purporting to show Tydings with Earl Browder, the head of the American Communist Party, working together. Tydings was defeated, by a surprisingly large margin of forty thousand votes—and the real victor was not John Marshall Butler, who ran against him, but McCarthy. His other main target was Scott Lucas of Illinois, the Democratic majority leader. McCarthy's timing could not have been better—the Democratic machine in Chicago, so critical to any statewide victory, was in bad odor for a variety of reasons, Lucas more vulnerable than he realized. McCarthy made eight trips to Illinois during the Senate race and attacked Lucas among other things for his connections with Dean Acheson, a magically negative name in much of the Midwest. Rural Illinois and rural Wisconsin seemed to share many of the same fears, and McCarthy drew large, enthusiastic crowds everywhere he went. Everett McKinley Dirksen, Lucas's opponent, represented, McCarthy told these crowds, "a prayer for America." Lucas lost as well. Suddenly McCarthy had become a major national figure. Because of the nature of the issues, the elections represented a major setback for the Truman administration and its congressional allies. Overnight McCarthy had become the great national intimidator.

"You couldn't imagine the change in his [McCarthy's] status when he returned to Washington," said Senator William Fulbright of Arkansas. "The Republicans looked on him as the new messiah. The Democrats were just scared to death. He was the same old McCarthy, as odious as ever. But oh my, how things had changed."

What happened was important news politically in the United States and had a profound effect on Korea and Tokyo as well. It meant that at this most critical moment in Korean War decision-making, the president was being undercut by a changing tide in domestic politics, something the general at the Dai Ichi was acutely aware of. The politics of this war were always difficult for the president; now they had become more difficult than ever.

On November 8, the day after the off-year elections, the Joint Chiefs, reflecting a growing fear that the Chinese had entered the war (and a complete lack of trust in Willoughby's reporting), cabled MacArthur again suggesting that, in view of what had happened at Unsan, his mission might have to be reexamined. But on November 9, he came back hard at Washington. He did not intend, as they wanted, to draw a line at the narrow neck of the peninsula. He knew the British (and the French) favored that position, as did many of the senior American commanders actually on the ground, including Walker. That was appeasement, he said, and it found its "historic precedence in the action taken at Munich." He was confident that his airpower could stop any larger Chinese passage to the battlefield. (He was unaware that most of the enemy force was already in country and that it was too late for his airpower to block the route for them.) Then he added: "To give up any part of North Korea to the aggression of the Chinese Communists would be the greatest defeat of the free world in recent times. Indeed to yield to so immoral a proposition would bankrupt our leadership and influence in Asia and render intolerable our position both politically and militarily. We would follow closely in the footsteps of the British who by the appeasement of recognition [of Communist China] lost the respect of all the rest of Asia without gaining that of the Chinese segment."

This then was the fateful moment. Unsan and the assault on the Eighth Cavalry should have marked the point at which they all reconsidered their plan, with the Tokyo command, if anything, more nervous than Washington because its men were at risk. It represented the last real chance to reexamine the war before the full Chinese force attacked. In military terms, MacArthur's troops now crossed the fail-safe point; Unsan and the assault upon the Eighth Cavalry Regiment marked not only a critical moment on the battlefield but also a major defeat for Washington in its war with the general. Dean Acheson and General Omar Bradley both eventually wrote of how poorly the president's advisers had served Truman at that moment. They had been intimidated by their commander in the field, despite their own feelings that they were losing control. In effect they allowed him to keep going north, as long as he was successful, but not to get in a war with the Chinese. His last great offensive would proceed as planned.

AT THE HIGHEST levels in the Dai Ichi, as they had prepared for the final push in late October, just before the attack at Unsan, there was a genuine feeling of euphoria. The enemy had virtually deserted the battlefield. On October 23, *Time* magazine ran an extremely flattering cover story on Ned Almond; "Sic 'em Ned," the cover line said, reflecting the fact that the North Koreans were fleeing and the UN forces were seemingly in hot pursuit. Not only was Almond treated as an exceptional military hero, one with an almost magical touch with the ordinary soldiers ("What's your name? Where's your home town? How long have you been in the service?"), but the cover story also offered a chance for Almond to praise MacArthur extravagantly. In the past, Bill McCaffrey, his closest deputy, remembered, the only two military figures Almond had ever had kind words about were George Catlett Marshall and Robert E. Lee, the only men, until he met MacArthur, he had allowed into his personal Hall of Fame. Everyone else was significantly flawed. Now he spoke of MacArthur as the greatest military genius of the twentieth century. Unfortunately he could not rank him, he told *Time,* against the greatest military men of all time, "because it's hard to compare the present day with the time of Napoleon, Caesar, and Hannibal." The name of Napoleon, as they prepared for a campaign that might entail the worst kind of winter weather against what was potentially the most populous nation in the world, was spoken with no irony.

Dealing with Almond in those days was like dealing with a man who had fallen in love, McCaffrey thought. McCaffrey was probably as close to Almond as anyone, had been Almond's top deputy in World War II, and was permitted to argue with him more than any other subordinate officer, almost, McCaffrey remembered, as if he were a favored son. McCaffrey remained extremely pessimistic about venturing farther north. But Almond simply would not listen to any dissent, though the dangers that lay ahead were obvious. There were all those giant maps at the various senior headquarters, and on them were a great many little red flags, each flag representing a Chinese division, seeming to show hundreds of thousands of Chinese troops poised along the Yalu River. McCaffrey had arrived in Tokyo to be Almond's deputy about a week before Inchon. And every time he looked up at the giant map in headquarters, he could see the curving boundary of the Yalu, and along the Yalu were those little red flags, representing countless Chinese divisions, maybe thirty or more. The first time McCaffrey had seen that map, he immediately understood the dangers it reflected: all those Chinese divisions just waiting up there in the mountains, and the UN supply lines stretched so thin. "What if they come in?" he asked Bob Glass, the corps G-2. "Ned Almond says that we don't have to worry," Glass answered. "MacArthur has thought it all through and it's not to their advantage to come in, so they won't come in."

But the dangers, McCaffrey thought, were both obvious and terrifying. The country mushroomed out dramatically as you went farther north, becoming ever more vast and opening into a kind of mountainous wasteland with few decent roads. Some of the mountains were seven to eight thousand feet high. "Every mile further north was like a mile wider on the front, every mile north was a bit colder, and every mile north the roads got worse: every mile north worked against our basic strength, which was as a technology-based army. Every day it got more dangerous," said McCaffrey, who eventually ended up a three-star. There were more and more ominous signs, and just beneath the Bataan Gang, the next level of officers at the Dai Ichi was becoming noticeably nervous. But they could not argue with Almond. When McCaffrey tried to bring it up, he was always immediately lectured for his lack of faith. "You were against Inchon too," Almond would say, and then he would add, "Bill, you keep on underestimating General MacArthur."

In early December, after the Chinese attack, McCaffrey found himself with Swede Larsen, a Joe Collins aide and a longtime pal. "For Christ sakes, Swede, what were you guys in Washington doing? Didn't anyone notice that we were spread out all over North Korea? Didn't anyone happen to notice it?" Larsen answered, "Bill, did you ever stop to think what it would have been like to tell Douglas MacArthur that his strategic ideas are screwy after Inchon? It wasn't going to happen."

SURELY EVEN MACARTHUR had rarely ridden so high. Colonel John Austin, a member of the First Corps staff, had an image of MacArthur visiting their headquarters at that moment, "erect and supremely confident, absolutely at his peak." It was, Austin later said, like watching "walking history." Rarely had any commander seemed so confident. "Gentlemen," he had told the assembled officers, "the war is over. The Chinese are not coming into this war. In less than two weeks, the Eighth Army will close on the Yalu across the entire front. The Third Division will be back in Fort Benning for Christmas dinner." No one questioned him at this moment, Austin told the writer Robert Smith— "it would have been like questioning an announcement from God."

The initial kickoff date for the final offensive north was supposed to be

November 15, but Walton Walker had felt he was being pushed ahead of himself and he managed to delay it by pointing out how limited his supplies were; Shrimp Milburn, the First Corps commander, had only one day of ammo, a day and a half of fuel, and three or four days of rations. By then Walker was absolutely convinced that he had a minimum of three Chinese divisions in his area, and was nervous about every mile north they had taken after reaching Pyongyang. He had, he later confided to a newspaper reporter, moved as slowly and deliberately as he could, as he crossed the Chongchon, advances so slow that he had received sharp messages from his superior. He had also tried to create positions that would be useful in case the Chinese struck and he was driven back. Later he was sure that he saved a considerable amount of his army because of his caution. He was also quite sure, he told a trusted journalist friend, that he was going to be relieved of his command by Tokyo for his slow-walking and his virtual disobedience.

The date was first pushed back to November 20, then to November 24. On that morning, Walker joined MacArthur as the latter visited the different Eighth Army headquarters, but he had none of the optimism of his superior, who, in front of the various wire service reporters accompanying him, made one of several home-before-Christmas statements. The most memorable was at Ninth Corps headquarters, where John Coulter, the corps commander, told him how little resistance his troops were meeting. MacArthur answered: "You can tell them that when they get up to the Yalu, Jack, they can all come home. I want to make good my statement that they will get Christmas dinner at home." Then he flew off, telling his pilot to pass over the Manchurian border and let him survey the area.

When MacArthur flew off, he left Walker behind on the airstrip. It was not a good moment for the Eighth Army commander. His forces were going forward, and he was very unhappy about it—they were cut off from Tenth Corps on the east, they were spread too thin, and the farther north they ventured, the thinner they were. Only a ROK Corps protected their eastern flank. It was a very good time to be nervous. Walker watched MacArthur's plane take off, and then in front of both Tyner and Lynch, he simply said, "Bullshit." It stunned them both, first because Walker never challenged MacArthur, and second because he *never* used profanity. They were about to fly back to Pyongyang when Walker suddenly decided he wanted to visit the nearby Twenty-fourth Division headquarters. There, he sought out Major General John Church, the division commander, and took him aside. His message was for Colonel Dick Stephens, the commander of the Twenty-first Infantry Regiment, a unit that would be leading the division in the drive north: "You tell Dick the first time he smells Chinese chow to pull back immediately."

But the euphoria only grew in Tokyo. When elements of the Seventeenth Regiment of the Seventh Division reached the Yalu on November 21, there was a celebratory moment—a curiously innocent one. All the senior officers, including Almond and the Seventh Division commander, Dave Barr, the old China adviser, got to piss in the river. MacArthur, victory obviously at hand now, sent Almond a radio message. "Heartiest congratulations, Ned," it said, "and tell Dave Barr the Seventh Division hit the jackpot." To the men in the Seventeenth Regiment who were on point, and who spent their first night along the Yalu dealing with temperatures that dipped to thirty below, it was a horror. In the rush to the Yalu, Lightning Joe Collins, the Army chief of staff, later wrote, "MacArthur seemed to march like a Greek hero of old to an unkind and inexorable fate." Or as Matt Ridgway put it, employing the most tragic analogy any American officer could use, "Like Custer at the Little Big Horn [MacArthur] had neither eyes nor ears for information that might deter him from the swift attainment of his objective—the destruction of the North Korean People's Army, and the pacification of the entire peninsula." For Geoffrey Perret, the MacArthur biographer who wrote that the Inchon landing had been the general's greatest stroke of genius, the rest was pure tragedy. "The most fitting conclusion to MacArthur's life would have been to die a soldier's death in the waters off Inchon at the height of his glory, with his legend not simply intact, but magnified beyond even his florid imaginings. There was only one way it could go from here—down."

SO THE MEN of the Dai Ichi had doctored the intelligence in order to permit MacArthur's forces to go where they wanted to go militarily, to the banks of the Yalu. In the process they were setting the most dangerous of precedents for those who would follow them in office. In this first instance it was the military that had played with the intelligence, or more accurately, one rogue wing of the military deliberately manipulating the intelligence it sent to the senior military men and civilians back in Washington. The process was to be repeated twice more in the years to come, both subsequent times with the civilians manipulating the military, with the senior military men reacting poorly in their own defense and thereby placing the men under their command in unacceptable combat situations. (The title of a book by one talented young officer, H. R. McMaster, studying how the senior military had been snookered by the senior civilians' pressures during Vietnam, was *Dereliction of Duty*.) All of this reflected something George Kennan warned about, the degree to which domestic politics had now become a part of national security calculations, and it showed the extent to which the American government had begun to make fateful decisions based on the most limited of truths and the most deeply flawed intelligence in order to do what it wanted to do for political reasons, whether it would work or not. In 1965, the government of Lyndon Johnson manipulated the rationale for sending combat troops to Vietnam, exaggerating the threat posed to America by Hanoi, deliberately diminishing any serious intelligence warning of what the consequences of American intervention in Vietnam would be (and how readily and effectively the North Vietnamese might counter the American expeditionary force), and thereby committing the United States to a hopeless, unwinnable post-colonial war in Vietnam. Then in 2003, the administration of George W. Bush—improperly reading what the end of the Russian empire might mean in the Middle East; completely miscalculating the likely response of the indigenous people; and ignoring the warnings of the most able member of the George H. W. Bush national security team, Brent Scowcroft; and badly wanting for its own reasons to take down the government of Saddam Hussein—manipulated the Congress, the media, the public, and most dangerously of all, itself, with seriously flawed and doctored intelligence, and sent troops into the heart of Iraqi cities with disastrous results.

Part
Eight

The Chinese Strike

CAPTAIN JIM HINTON, the commander of the Thirty-eighth Tank Company, which was part of the Second Division, and which contained twenty-two tanks, had been nervous from the start. The difference between reality as headquarters in Tokyo imagined it and the North Korea he saw as the Second Division moved north stunned him. In the Dai Ichi Building, Korea was a distant, somewhat orderly, generally manageable place, a map that you could pin to the wall, where the distances were not that great and divisions were only a half inch or an inch away from each other; whereas out here, as he led the Second Division toward the Chongchon River, it was more like an unmanageable military hell, hills turning out to be mountains, winds blowing ever harder, temperatures dropping almost by the hour, every day bitterly cold, except that the next day would be even colder, and make you long for the cold of yesterday. Keeping his tanks alive and functioning in this weather was a job in itself. He had a terrible fear that the cold would get his machines, that at the moment they were most desperately needed the engines would simply refuse to start. His unit had what they called a Little Joe, a generator that could keep the tank batteries charged. But its operation made a hell of a lot of noise, noise that seemed to carry forever, and so Hinton did not like to use it if he could help it. He decided instead to have someone start each engine once an hour, just to keep them all charged. God, it was cold! Sometimes, even when the engines started, the tank wouldn't move because the treads were frozen right to the ground. Then, you would have to get another tank to give it a friendly little tank-shove. He wondered if the big boys whose lives were centered around the Dai Ichi Building and who had sent them up here ever imagined anything like that back where the weather was always cool enough in summer and warm enough in winter, controllable, with the lightest flick of a finger. Certainly, their commander knew nothing about the world they had been plunged into. MacArthur—as many of the troops who specialized in ironies knew—had never spent a night in the field in Korea. The men at the Dai Ichi, Hinton thought, were men of maps, fighting a different war in a different place. The maps had their own distortions, and they were almost invariably benign ones to the men looking at them, making their orders look more doable—more rational—than they really were. Nothing in the Army, the men in the field liked to say, moved as quickly as a Dai Ichi grease pencil across a Dai Ichi map. Communication links from headquarters down to the division level might seem reasonably good, especially given that this Army represented the most technologically advanced nation on the planet, but the actual equipment proved relatively primitive and shockingly unreliable to the men who were in the smaller units, so isolated from one another.

It had just been too quiet, Hinton thought as they moved up. There had been a few little firefights, but they were always followed by the silence, and the silence had its own corollary of fear—it was the almost unnatural silence of complete isolation. Hinton, a veteran tanker, had been going up in a small L-19 spotter plane for several days looking for signs of the enemy, but he could never see a thing. Gradually the quiet and the emptiness came to bother him, as it had bothered some of the more experienced men just before the Eighth Cav was hit at Unsan. The most important question the night before the Chinese actually struck in late November, he remembered, was whether it was a boots-on or a boots-off sleeping period. Boots-on, he decided. "We were more and more isolated, more and more cut off every day," Hinton recalled, "and thus more and more vulnerable. Each day that we went out we were more spread out, and further from other units. The isolation was from our own people—not just from other divisions supposedly on our flanks but from the people in our own division, from regiment to regiment, and in the regiment, from battalion to battalion, and company to company. We knew we were at someone else's mercy, that is, we had to *hope* the Chinese were not coming in. It was an eerie feeling—the terrain seemed to be swallowing us up. As a division we seemed to be disappearing into the vast landscape." If the enemy struck, Hinton and many others were aware, it was going to be exceedingly hard to close and form a tight defensive fist. It was an offensive, he later decided, that might well have been planned for the Americans by the Chinese themselves.

LIEUTENANT PAUL O'DOWD was a forward observer with the Fifteenth Field Artillery; most of the time, though, he was moved back and forth to different units, and he had been attached to the Ninth Regiment of the Second Infantry Division. He was one of the few American officers who knew what had happened at Unsan, that the Chinese had whacked an elite American regiment. Now, as the Americans moved north of Pyongyang, O'Dowd was flying regularly in a tiny observation plane looking for signs of the Chinese, trying to answer the question of where they had gone after their first strike at Unsan. One day they had hammered the Americans, and then they had disappeared. O'Dowd liked to pride himself on his eyesight. You needed good vision to be a forward observer; but his pal, Valdez, who flew the spotter plane and was a captain, had even better eyesight, vision like a hawk. Valdez was as idiosyncratic as he was gifted: if they took ground fire and a couple rounds hit the plane, when Valdez got back to base he would check out the plane for bullet holes, and whenever he found one, he would paint a purple heart around it. Later, Valdez could spot the Chinese at a great distance at moments when O'Dowd could see nothing. Yet right after Unsan, day after day passed as they scoured the countryside without a trace of them. Their little plane had no heat, and for better visibility they would sometimes open its door, so they were constantly stone-cold frozen—and still they saw nothing. It was amazing, O'Dowd thought; an entire army had disappeared. Sometimes Valdez would see what looked to him like footprints in the snow, and they would come down really low and there *were* footprints, which seemed to lead to a hut. So they would call in fire on the hut, but when the shells came in there would be no one there. Later they would find out from their intelligence people that the Chinese had white parkas, and on the rare occasion that the Americans flew over Chinese soldiers, they would lie down on their stomachs, not move, and the spotters in the plane would miss the sighting, great eyesight or not. In those days, Colonel Charles (Chin) Sloane, the Ninth Regiment's commander, was very involved in their aerial recon, very much aware of how dangerous it was. When they came in from three or four hours of spotting, he would often have some hot chocolate for them as he anxiously awaited news of the Chinese. Long, cold days, O'Dowd thought, and not a single Chinese soldier to show for it. Yet O'Dowd was absolutely sure they were out there. They had to be. It made men like Sloane very nervous: an army that has just torn one of your best units apart vanishes from the very face of the earth.

It was getting on the nerves of people back at Division headquarters too. John Carley was a young captain in G-3, operations; just five years out of West Point, he had become an officer too late to be part of World War II. Now he was getting his own much smaller war, but it was as much war as any man might want. Though the Second Division had not had any significant encounters with Chinese troops, there was a steady flow of information coming into its G-2 shop about other units meeting up with them. The questions on his mind and that of so many intelligence officers were: Where had they gone to? If they had appeared once in such large numbers so suddenly, might they not do it again? They were moving into what the Koreans called Tiger Country, presumably because tigers had once actually lived there. The mountains surrounding them were enormous. In late November, the cold cracked the windshield on the small observation plane Carley often used for reconnaissance. Worse, sometime in late November, probably around the twentieth, a constant blue haze obscured the landscape and never seemed to lift. Carley was no weather expert, but he had seen a comparable haze as a young man in Richton, Mississippi, when he had gone hunting with friends on cold mornings and they had set fires to keep warm. He later decided that Chinese patrols had been setting massive fires all over the region to limit American air surveillance. He and the other younger officers in the G-2 and G-3 shops were painfully aware of how fragile their supply lines were, and that the division was moving north on a narrow gravel road with sharp curves that twisted and turned. Such roads were perfect sites for ambushes. "You had to know how vulnerable we were," he said years later, "that we were way out on a limb and seemed to be getting further out every day, the limb less able to support us each day."

THE ONE SENIOR officer who seemed to share his anxieties was Lieutenant Colonel Ralph Foster, the Second Division G-2. Foster was a meticulous man, immune to pressures from those above him, and like Carley, his sense of anxiety was mounting daily. It had started in early November, and he had become, by the middle of the month, a kind of Division worrywart. Their maps showed the north side of the Yalu pockmarked with red flags for Chinese divisions, and then the Chinese had struck at Unsan. Dutch Keiser, the division commander, did not share his fears. Malcolm MacDonald, a young captain who worked in Foster's G-2 shop, found his boss increasingly frustrated by his inability to reach Keiser. The men in the intelligence section were aware of the immense pressure on him from higher headquarters to push forward. But to Foster it felt as if someone was out there watching them and waiting for just the right moment to strike. "You could feel the tension in the headquarters," he said. "We sensed something terrible was going to happen, but we couldn't get anyone to act on it."

IN EARLY NOVEMBER, Second Lieutenant Sam Mace, who commanded the Fourth Platoon of the Thirty-eighth Tank Company in the Second Division, the unit under Jim Hinton, took his men, his tanks, and some extra infantrymen on a long recon patrol. By then they had moved well north of Pyongyang. Mace liked to remember it as the day of the music. It had begun in relatively routine fashion. There was a brief firefight with some North Korean soldiers, but the superior firepower of the tanks overcame the Koreans relatively easily. About eight Koreans were captured, all but one wounded. Mace's men bandaged the wounded, tied up the man who wasn't, left them all in a hut, and headed north to complete their original mission. So far it had all been routine enough, but then two things happened that startled Mace and made someone normally cautious and careful even more so. Being cautious, Sam Mace liked to think, was why he was still alive. Jim Hinton, his company commander, thought Mace was a truly great soldier, quite possibly the best soldier he had ever served with. He could do anything, fix anything, and adapt to any circumstance. He was physically remarkable, and never seemed to tire, which was important because you could not turn yourself on and off in combat based on your body's natural preferences. And he was as smart as he was strong. Mace was a lifer, and Hinton had been pushing him for several years to become an officer, but he always held back, fearing, Hinton was sure, having to compete with college graduates, while all he had was a fourth-grade education. He had been seriously wounded in the Naktong fighting, taken to a hospital where seventy-eight pieces of shrapnel were found in his back, so many that the nurses had held a pool betting on what the final count would be. He had been in a fetal position when the shrapnel hit and that, Mace decided, had been his good luck. While Mace was in the hospital, Hinton had just gone ahead with the paperwork to make him an officer, and when Mace came back to the unit, he found himself a lieutenant. He accepted the change in no small part because he was tired of dealing with officers, Hinton exempted, who did not know a goddamn thing about war and still looked down on you because of your rank—and then, of course, there were the benefits that officers got and enlisted men could only dream of. When the Chinese struck his unit on November 25, he had been an officer for thirty-six hours.

Sam Mace felt he had been through it all. As a boy during the Depression he had grown up in West Virginia, the poorest part of a country in a very poor time. His father had been hexed from the start, a West Virginian without an education, but even worse, a man who could not work in the mines, the one place where poor West Virginians could get work, because he was claustrophobic. He was always in search of work, an itinerant man forced to go from small town to small town with his family, taking the poorest-paying jobs available, if in fact anything was available. That was why Sam Mace's schooling had stopped in the fourth grade; they had lived in too many towns too small to have schools. No wonder he had jumped at a chance to try the Army and had enlisted in 1939, at fifteen. In those days, he said, they would take anyone.

Mace had been a tanker in the days when the changeover from horses to tanks was just beginning. Being a soldier was something he had excelled at from the start, but he was also a bit wild in those early days and so his rank fluctuated constantly between sergeant and corporal, depending on his off-duty behavior. Sam Mace liked to say that he was one of the great American authorities on ambushes, because he had been in three spectacular ones: the one up at Kunuri had probably been the granddaddy of them all, but the Battle of the Bulge in World War II was fairly close to being an ambush and, if so, was certainly a finalist, and he had been there, and there was a terrible one still to come at a place the Americans called Massacre Valley, in mid-February 1951. The Battle of the Bulge stayed with him: he had been with an American armored unit that had been fat and happy, about twenty miles northeast of a place called Bastogne, back in December 1944, all of the men around him sure the war was already over, when the Germans struck. He remembered how thick the fog was at the time. He was a corporal then, newly busted down from sergeant, and they were right smack in the way of the German Panzers.

The Americans had started the first day with seventeen tanks in his unit, and they had lost all but two by the end of it. He had managed to make it out when his tank was hit, and had fought as an infantryman for days, in a kind of hell he had never experienced, a constant artillery bombardment, each shell bringing its own terror. The cold had been unbearable, and in Korea he was often reminded of it, because he had thought the German cold was the worst cold in the world, but Korea eventually was worse than the Ardennes, lasting longer and dominating your life as the Ardennes cold never did. In the Ardennes you always believed that the cold would break in a day or so; in Korea you never did. In early November 1950, moving forward on the front edge of the Second Division, the caution Mace had learned in the Ardennes remained with him. He distrusted everything that he could not vouch for personally and was wary of officers who were casual. Everyone around him might think this was a cakewalk, but as far as he was concerned, they were deep in what he considered Indian territory, and there were no cakewalks in war.

After they had bandaged the Korean prisoners, Mace's men climbed a number of hills before coming to a small bridge that went over a dry creek. This was where they were supposed to turn back. His riflemen were spread out nicely over a wide perimeter, but Mace was tense because they made wonderful targets and he had no idea what lay in front of them. Every yard they went forward was another yard into the unknown. As they came upon the bridge, they were in a deep, broad valley filled with what looked to him like a Korean version of juniper trees, vegetation that seemed to have been put on earth only to hide potential enemy soldiers from his eyes. Then the music started. "The strangest music I ever heard," he remembered. He ordered all his tank drivers to cut their engines so he could catch this foreign, almost haunting sound more clearly. "It was so strange. It seemed to be aimed right at me and my men. Like the enemy was watching us and serenading us and mocking us all at the same time. It was if the valley itself was serenading you," he said. "And it seemed to be coming out of nowhere—maybe right out of the trees. It made the hair on the back of my neck stand out." Later, after the Chinese struck the Eighth Army along a wide front and they all learned how the Chinese used music as a means of giving orders, Mace became convinced it was the Chinese commander, somewhere up in the hills above him, telling his troops that, though they had Mace's tanks and his men surrounded and in their sights, the time was not quite right to attack.

When Mace and his men returned to the hut where they had left their prisoners, the one prisoner who had not been wounded suddenly made a break for it. They shot him. They were puzzled by his attempt to break away—after all, they had been good with the prisoners, giving all of them emergency medical care. After they recovered the escapee's body, they checked him for papers, and he had none. That in itself was unusual because most Koreans seemed to carry a lot of letters and to hold on to them. Then underneath his Korean uniform they found another uniform, that of a Chinese soldier, and what they were sure was an officer's blouse. Even before they did the strip search, the Koreans attached to his unit had insisted that he was Chinese. First the music, then the dead man who might well have been a Chinese officer: none of that was comforting, Mace thought. Later that day Mace told the intelligence people that he thought they had killed a Chinese soldier. But no one seemed very interested.

From then on, as he moved north, he was more cautious than ever. At that moment, the Second Division was on the far right of the Eighth Army. East of it were the Taebaek Mountains, and east of them, unavailable if any unit got hit, was Tenth Corps—even though theoretically it was supposed to be able to help if there were a crisis. (Comparably, the commander of the division on the other side of the Taebaeks, serving as part of Tenth Corps, Major General O. P. Smith of the First Marine Division, was equally frustrated because his left flank was so open.)

In late November, the Third Battalion of the Thirty-eighth Regiment, which Mace and his five tanks were supporting, was on the right flank of the Second Division. They were at a village of about fifteen huts called Somin-dong. Mace had placed his tanks as best he could in support of all three companies of the battalion. He was puzzled that they had moved the battalion headquarters up so near the rifle companies, so close, he said, that you could have hit them with a stone. But then, no one was expecting trouble.

In fact, the Chinese had been waiting patiently, aware of every move the UN forces made, which units were positioned where, and above all, which ROK units were supporting them on their flanks. Of the 300,000 men they had moved into North Korea undetected in just one month, an estimated 180,000 were waiting along the western part of the extended front, in the area commanded by

Johnnie Walker where First and Ninth Corps were positioned, and an estimated additional 120,000 were farther to the east, poised and waiting as Ned Almond's Tenth Corps moved north. As the UN forces moved up, encumbered by an enormous amount of machinery, they were very visible targets. But the waiting Communist Army, containing some *thirty Chinese divisions*, had remained essentially invisible; in the apt words of S. L. A. (Slam) Marshall, the military historian, "a phantom which cast no shadow."

IT WAS AS if one vast part of the Army, the part not commanded by Douglas MacArthur, knew that trouble was imminent, as the other part kept moving forward. On Thanksgiving Day, General Al Gruenther visited Dwight Eisenhower, his old boss from Europe, at Eisenhower's residence at Columbia University. Gruenther's oldest son, Dick, class of 1946 at West Point, had a company in the Seventh Division, some of whose men were very far north and headed for the Yalu. On November 17, four days before his senior officers reached the Yalu and pissed in it, Dick Gruenther (who had been sure they were already fighting the Chinese) was severely wounded in the stomach in one of the small battles that preceded the main Chinese offensive. Al Gruenther, Eisenhower's former chief of staff in Europe, had just finished a tour as director of the one-hundred-man JCS staff, which meant that he was aware of all the warning signals that MacArthur was now ignoring.

At first John Eisenhower, Dwight's son, had thought it odd that Gruenther was there for Thanksgiving, because he had a family of his own. But later he decided that Gruenther was there because Eisenhower was still the man you talked to—he had that special status—when something this serious was going wrong at so high a level. John Eisenhower remembered that a cloud hung over that Thanksgiving Day meal, something that he himself did not entirely understand. Gruenther told his father that the American forces were simply too exposed and far too vulnerable. When Gruenther left, Eisenhower turned to his son and said, "I've never been so pessimistic about this war in my life." John Eisenhower was teaching at West Point at the time, and when he left his father's residence to drive back to the academy, he turned on the car radio and heard a report about how MacArthur was promising the war would be over by Christmas. The next day the Chinese hit.

It was on the night of November 25 that the Chinese finally struck. Rarely has so large an army had such an element of surprise against its adversary. The Chinese had precise intelligence on the Americans, and the Americans on the west coast—the Marines on the east were shrewder and better led—were essentially blind to the trap they had walked into. When the Chinese hit, it became clear that what had driven MacArthur's forces was not so much a strategy as a bet—that the Chinese would not come in. The bet had been called, and other men would now have to pay for that terrible arrogance and vainglory. Worse yet, the bet had had a pathetic little bluff built into it, one that very few senior American officers believed in: that the South Korean Army had become an acceptable fighting force, capable of holding its own against the Chinese. The South Korean troops were absolutely terrified of fighting the Chinese, and predictably, almost all their units simply broke and disappeared in the first shock of assault. (In the case of one regiment, as Slam Marshall noted, some five hundred men disappeared with almost all their weapons, but some of the officers did manage to make it back to Seoul, bringing Syngman Rhee a bottle filled with water from the Yalu River.) The American commanders in the field had known the ROKs were not yet ready to fight if the Chinese came in, but to the men of the Dai Ichi, with their own troops spread so thin, the maps looked better if the ROK units were penciled in. Their prompt disappearance from key positions on the flanks of American and other UN units meant that the Chinese had a series of virtually unobstructed routes into the very heart of the UN positions.

Nor had the American command in Tokyo made allowance for or prepared their troops for the manner in which the Chinese might fight—for the lack of frontal attacks, and for the way they would move at night on foot and slip along the flanks of their enemies, looking for soft spots, while taking up positions behind them in order to cut off any retreat. No one had studied how well and quickly they could move, even at night and when there were no roads. They were much less encumbered by heavy weapons, ammunition, and food than the Americans, and that lightness was their strength (and would eventually be their weakness as well). There had been a mistaken belief in the Dai Ichi that somehow the Chinese would turn themselves into easy targets for the American Air Force. The idea that they disappeared during the day had somehow not been fed into the Dai Ichi's calculations. The Chinese, it turned out, understood a good many of their own weaknesses. They did not do a lot of things, but the things they did, they tended to do well. In those early days before the Americans figured out how to fight them, they managed to turn what were seeming American strengths—a dependency on heavy weaponry and thus on the roads, which were always, it seemed, in the valleys—into weaknesses. Yet to anyone who had been paying attention to what had been going on in China in the years right after World War II, there were few surprises in the way they fought.

28

COLONEL PAUL FREEMAN, commander of the Twenty-third Regiment, was sure that his men had been encountering Chinese troops from the moment they moved above Sunchon. By the time the Chinese finally struck, he was absolutely sure that they had been all around him for at least two weeks, watching his men but not making their move. His own recon patrols kept reporting the most unusual kind of contact with the Chinese—a kind of show-and-feint-and-wait. Some ten days before they struck, one of his more experienced company commanders, Captain Sherman Pratt, had taken a company-sized patrol on a recon and headed north toward Kanggye. As they moved about five miles north, they kept seeing figures on the skyline above them, but always in the distance. Pratt and some of his men decided that, by their uniforms, they had to be Chinese. So he halted his patrol, ordered his men not to fire a shot, turned his vehicles around so they could get out quickly, and did not go very much farther north. Eventually, when he got back to headquarters, he reported to both Claire Hutchin, his battalion commander, and Freeman what had happened. The next day Freeman sent another patrol out, and this time the American force pushed beyond the line the Chinese seemed to be offering as a demarcation point, and the Chinese opened fire. Several Americans were wounded, and the patrol had been forced to withdraw, leaving some wounded behind. On the third day, Freeman sent out another patrol, only to find the wounded from the second mission, lying by the road, all bandaged up and wrapped in blankets.

There were other signs of the Chinese presence as Thanksgiving had approached, and Freeman was convinced there were Chinese everywhere watching. So were his intelligence people. But, as he later noted, they "apparently hadn't convinced anyone in Far East Headquarters." Because of his years serving in China during the war, Freeman spoke Chinese, knew how Mao's men fought, and had taken their threat to enter this war seriously. His mood was deeply pessimistic. He felt privately that crossing the thirty-eighth parallel had been a catastrophic mistake, that the American leadership was placing the entire Eighth

Army in jeopardy, and that America's leadership had ended up playing right into the hands of the Russians—fighting an unwinnable war in Asia while the Russians sat on the sidelines. In that sense, ironically, his forebodings were almost exactly the same as those of George Kennan. Freeman's mood, darker by the day as the division and his regiment moved north, showed primarily in his letters to his wife, and in his cautionary words to his own battalion commanders, to be prepared every night for the worst.

His letters home are a fascinating record of a key commander, caught in a terrible moment, convinced that his superiors were making a miscalculation of epic proportions over which he was powerless. On September 25, when almost everyone else was euphoric about how well the breakout from the Naktong line was going, Freeman remained very cautionary. "I am still apprehensive," he said in a letter on that day, "about the Manchurians coming down from the north." Even before the UN forces crossed the thirty-eighth, Freeman was very nervous because the drive north depended not on American strength—which was self-evidently limited—but on Chinese intentions, and the Chinese had said they intended to enter the war.

The answer, as far as he was concerned—the end to any private doubts he had already harbored—had come with Unsan. His letters reflected his darkening mood, and were becoming more and more pessimistic. He was fine physically, he wrote his wife on November 7, except for the brutal North Korean cold, which was bearable. But emotionally he was depleted. "I just can't see any solution for this monstrous predicament in which our forces find themselves. Surely somebody must have an out, and I have hope of some miracle extricating us from this untenable situation. How our leaders could have become involved so naively without any plan or assurances that the Chinese wouldn't intervene is unbelievable to me. From here I just don't see a solution."

On November 11, the Twenty-third Regiment was supposed to move forward to an assembly point and from there to make the final drive to the Yalu. Freeman was convinced that they had been abandoned by rational thought and policy. "It's the most monstrous situation I can imagine for the U.S. It seems we're playing right into Soviet hands and sinking our might into the Asiatic morass. I don't like it a bit, " he wrote. The most pessimistic of his letters was written on November 13, just eleven days before the American offensive started, and twelve days before the Chinese struck. The great miscalculation, he believed, given the limits of forces available and the dangers ahead, had been the decision to cross the thirty-eighth parallel, instead of making some kind of settlement there. "Even in the darkest days on the Naktong, fighting for our very existence, I could always see a ray of hope, a solution. When we returned across the 38th I thought it was utterly fantastic that we should take such a risk for nothing. I feel now that we are in a combination of the Second Crusade, Napoleon's march on Moscow, and Bataan. I see no end to it but WW III, and to sacrifice all our forces here in that event would be a monstrous error. Even if we battle to the Yalu at a great cost and by mastering logistic obstacles almost akin to those in Burma, we would be further out on the limb with no chance of extrication. It's just an impossible mess and I feel lower than mud about it."

The night before the UN forces were to start the big offensive, Freeman and Claire Hutchin went to dinner with Dutch Keiser, the division commander, who was an old friend of Freeman's. Both Freeman and Hutchin spoke of their complete inability to understand what was going on. Everything they knew indicated that the Chinese were in the area and that they might strike. The worst thing that the UN forces could do was go on the offensive. The only explanation for an offensive move in the face of a threat like that, Freeman said, was that General MacArthur had, in his words, "some very, very secret information that these Chinese were not really going to resist, but [were going to] allow us to push them back across the river." Perhaps, he added, that secret information revealed that the Chinese were there but did not want to be there, and wanted the Americans to push them back over the river. That suggestion, he added, laconically, years later, "turned out definitely not to be the case."

Because of his wariness, Freeman kept his regiment as tightly concentrated as he could, and told all his battalion commanders that they were to be well buttoned up at night. On the first night that the Chinese attacked, the Twenty-third held quite well. Its positions were generally strong, and they ended up inflicting heavy casualties on the Chinese and taking about one hundred of them prisoner, the most Freeman remembered that they ever captured during the war. Because he spoke Chinese, he was able to interrogate the prisoners, and found that most of them spoke the same northern dialect. He spent the remainder of that day trying to consolidate his regiment, and that night the Chinese struck again and ended up capturing the CP of the Twenty-third, although the regiment was able to take it back the next day. What struck Freeman about the Chinese prisoners he interrogated was that not many of them seemed to want to be there. A number of them had feared the American fighting machine. It was a fear, Freeman noted, that soon began to disappear, because the American Army performed so poorly in those first few days—in contrast to how it might have performed if it had been dug in and well prepared when the Chinese struck.

CAPTAIN ALAN JONES was the S-2 (the equivalent of a division's G-2) of the Ninth Regiment, which was on the extended eastern front of the Second Division when the Chinese hit. Though resistance had generally been light, in the few days before November 25 there had been an increasing number of skirmishes with some suspected Chinese units. "My map," Jones said, "was very full of red." The tension, he thought, was very real in the intelligence shop, and he suspected it was equally high among the infantrymen who were in effect virtually on point for the entire Eighth Army.

This was not the first time Alan Jones, West Point class of 1943, had been in the path of an overwhelming enemy attack in bitterly cold weather. Like Sam Mace, he had been in the Battle of the Bulge as a young officer with the 106th Division, when the Germans suddenly struck the seemingly victorious Allied forces with their last great offensive of the war. His father, Major General Alan Jones, Sr., the commander of the 106th Division, had been uneasy with the idea of having his son in the same unit, but young Alan had wanted to get away from a unit that seemed destined for noncombat duty and to get into a frontline unit. That he got and more. His father, on the eve of battle, was nervous about how extended his division was. He was right, and the German Panzers raced past the 106th on both sides. A message from higher headquarters telling the men to pull back was delayed by heavy radio traffic, and young Alan Jones's regiment, the 423rd, caught completely by surprise, had fought as best it could before running out of ammo and surrendering. Alan Jones, Jr., was a prisoner of the Germans for some four and a half months, and he vowed that he would never be a prisoner of war again, a vow he repeated with renewed fervor once he landed in Korea and heard the stories of North Korean atrocities against American and ROK POWs.

Jones thought that the Ninth Regiment commander, Colonel Chin Sloane, had positioned his limited forces reasonably well. All three battalions were on the high ground, not too spread out, and under normal conditions they could have supported one another. But there was nothing normal about what happened that night. Their eastern flank, composed of ROKs, collapsed almost immediately, and then they were hit by wave after wave of Chinese troops. It was as if suddenly there was a brand-new war that began with an attack against the First Battalion—more of a probe, Jones later decided. Then the big hit came around midnight. Jones was at Regimental headquarters when they struck, so he heard the reports as they came in from the three battalions, one report after another, not really panicky, but sharp, strident, with the horror in every word: *they're hitting us . . . my God, they're everywhere . . . we're holding, but they're all over the place . . . every time we stop them more come . . . we can no longer hold, there are so many of them . . . this may be the last message you get from us . . .* It was not one voice, but several, and the voices kept changing as different radiomen were hit, but it all added up to the same thing, the sound of an American regiment being torn apart by a vastly greater Chinese force. There was no way in that isolated regimental headquarters to measure what was happening—except to know that it was beyond their comprehension. Colonel Sloane was very good in those first few hours, Jones thought. He never lost his calm, never panicked, and did his best to move what remained of the regiment back toward Division, toward a place they hoped would be safer, a place called Kunuri.

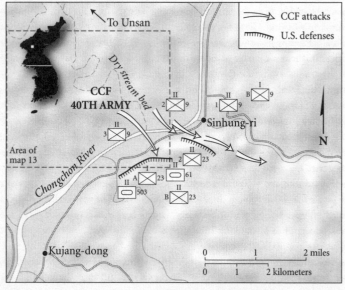

12. CHINESE ATTACK AT CHONGCHON RIVER, ON SECOND
DIVISION, NOVEMBER 25–26, 1950

There are military disasters that are terrible but are at least momentary. Something horrendous happens to a given unit that has been poorly positioned or poorly led, and the individual unit suffers badly, and then with luck that is the end of it, especially given the ability of the American Army to move men around and protect those under attack. But this was a different kind of disaster. It grew worse hour by hour, as if it had a life of its own. In those early hours, a number of companies in the Thirty-eighth and the Ninth Infantry regiments were virtually wiped out. As that happened, unbearable pressure was placed on adjoining units, and on the battalions and regiments they belonged to, making the entire Second Division vulnerable; it was not exactly like toppling dominoes, but it was close enough for that to be a reasonably accurate description of what was beginning to happen.

AT THE VERY tip of the most extended finger that represented the Second Division was the Ninth Regiment, and at its very tip was Love Company of the Third Battalion, and at the most forward edge of Love Company was the Second Platoon, commanded by Lieutenant Gene Takahashi of Cleveland, Ohio. Takahashi—Tak, not Gene, to his men—had, as a Japanese-American, spent part of his World War II boyhood in an internment camp in California. Impressed by the exploits of the famed, highly decorated all-Nisei 442nd Regimental Combat Team in Europe—many of whom had come out of the internment camps—and, like them, eager to prove his devotion to his country, he had in 1945 at seventeen volunteered for the United States Army. The only rule given him by his parents when he asked their permission was that he was to do nothing that might disgrace the Takahashi name. He was an unusual officer in an unusual unit—a Japanese-American commanding a platoon of all-black troops. For though the Army was technically desegregated, there were still some all-black units in the early months of the Korean War. The performance of all-black units at that moment, as the Army was changing so quickly, was often uneven, based on who their officers were, whether they were white, and whether they tried to hardass their troops. Takahashi thought his troops were good men and good soldiers. A few were resistant to direct orders, and tone was always important, but if anything, commanding them made him aware of the nuances involved, a sense on occasion that some orders needed to be explained, and he was sure that this had made him a better officer.

As for the prejudices of that era, Takahashi had been well steeped in them, not just from his time in the internment camp but from an earlier tour in Korea. In 1947, while serving as a young officer with the Sixth Division, he had experienced enough prejudice to last a lifetime. His superior had been a West Point graduate, a captain who hated being in Korea, hated Koreans, and, as a matter of fact, appeared to dislike anyone who looked Asian. The captain took out his frustrations and prejudices by assigning Takahashi every truly crappy job he had. If there was a thankless company task that required a lot of time, was filled with misery, and, even if done well, would bring no credit, Takahashi got it. Someone who was Nisei was still a Jap to the captain, who was clearly out to drive Gene Takahashi from the Army.

Oddly enough, Takahashi decided later, the experience made him a much better officer. He had to plan his time brilliantly. The harder he worked and the better he performed, the angrier it made his superior, who loaded even more work on him. The result, when Takahashi found he couldn't be broken, was a growing self-confidence, a sense that there was no job in the Army, no matter how unpleasant, that he could not do. The uses of adversity, Gene Taka-hashi thought, were not to be underestimated.

Gene Takahashi thought Love Company, by dint of all the hard fighting in the Naktong area, had become a reasonably good, battle-tested unit. It would fight well under normal combat conditions—that is, if the men were well po-sitioned and knew what to expect—but not if it was surprised, and unpre-pared for battle. The men soldiered, he decided, with a far greater index of distrust and a greater wariness of the unknown than the average white soldier. To some degree he believed that reflected the era, when the Army was still partly segregated by race. Many of them—Takahashi understood this all too well himself—had joined the Army to prove something to their country and to escape those very prejudices. To try to prove that those prejudices were unfair and then to encounter them deeply engrained in the Army's command system was, Takahashi thought, very hard on some of the men.

To a degree, the company reflected the personality of the company com-mander, Captain Maxwell Vails, a very decent officer. Vails was a strong, earthy figure, with a good feel for the mood of the men, who in turn liked and re-spected him, which was no small thing. But whether he had any real feel for combat, for what to do when bad things happened (and in this war, bad things were always happening), was another question entirely. It was also an impor-tant one, essentially about what distinguished a great officer from an ordinary or even a good one. There was a private sense on the part of some of the men—and Takahashi agreed—that when their superiors had a dirty assignment, like trying to find out if the North Koreans were secretly dug in on top of a given hill, in effect like pushing a stick into a beehive, it was a little more likely that they would choose Love Company for the probe.

As far as most of the men in Love Company were concerned, by mid-November, the war had largely disappeared. On the day that the great offensive began, they were all still quite upbeat. They crossed the Chongchon River on the first day, at a place near Kujang-dong, leaving most of their supplies behind, including bedding, extra ammo, and grenades. The trucks and jeeps simply could not go any farther, because of the terrain. Perhaps they would catch up a little later. Takahashi later faulted himself for not insisting the men take as many grenades as they could—if he had loaded each man up with grenades, it might have made a difference when the Chinese struck. They did not even have their overcoats with them. They had left these back at the last CP. They did not expect to be gone long. The Chongchon was not very deep, just up to their waists, but it was very cold. Crossing it was not hard, but they made one mistake: they wore their pants, whereas the Chinese, more expert at this—they had learned so much from the Long March—took their pants off for such crossings, which meant that the cold and wet were not embedded in their clothes and did not last as long. The soldiers of Love Company then spent hours of that freezing day soaked and climbing a high mountain about a mile and a half from the river, before setting up for the night. The one thing that put Takahashi on notice was a series of almost perfect foxholes he came across, three feet deep each, and each one a replica of the next, absolutely square, as if done by some expert in landscaping. This was the work of men who knew how to do the little things well. Americans dug their foxholes haphazardly, because they always expected to have superior firepower. The In Min Gun were not much better. These foxholes suggested strongly that a new player was in the game. In the mid-afternoon of November 24, Love Company set up its perimeter just east of the Chongchon.

They were on a relatively high point about three miles north of the tiny village of Kujang-dong, which existed more on maps than in reality—although later, when they all tried to figure out where the Chinese attack had taken place and where so many friends had died, at least it gave them a location on the map. Takahashi, who argued briefly with Captain Vails on the subject, did not like the way the men had been positioned. He thought their perimeter was too much of a straight line and not concentrated on what he was sure were the likely avenues of approach. Lieutenant Dick Raybould, a young forward observer for the Thirty-seventh Field Artillery, whose job it was to support Love Company, agreed. He felt Captain Vails had been too casual in positioning his men. Raybould, who was new to the company, was also surprised when Vails set up his CP on the back side of a hill, a little too sheltered, he felt. Worse, Raybould believed, Vails had assigned different sectors to his three platoon leaders and let them set up for themselves, thus creating a defensive perimeter that did not reflect the hill's contours. They did not have good interlocking fields of fire, and they might, he thought, be vulnerable to flanking movements. Takahashi agreed; he wanted a tighter perimeter, formed in more of a circle to fit the contours, but he had not been able to change Vails's mind.

The fires that they set bothered Raybould too. As far as he was concerned it was like giving your enemy a set of beacons to find you. He saw the men's fires early in the evening and went over to the company command post to complain, only to discover that the biggest fire of all was the one that warmed the company commander, a huge bonfire. A very new lieutenant does not argue with a captain, but later Raybould was sure the fires had served the Chinese well. Takahashi was not so sure the fires were a mistake. As darkness fell, his men were still wearing wet clothes, and he had sent them back, two at a time, to a place he had set up with a small fire, where they could dry their clothes.

They were quite far east, almost the farthest east of any unit of the Eighth Army, except for King Company, which was supposed to be a mile and a half east of them. There were about 170 men in Love Company when it was hit, about forty-five of them in Takahashi's platoon. King Company was probably the same size. Farther east, protecting the eastern flank of the Eighth Army, was a South Korean corps. When Takahashi and the other junior officers had been told at one of their final briefings that the ROKs would handle their right flank, a lot of eyes were raised to the ceiling. To the men who had been doing the fighting over the last three months, it could all too easily mean an instantaneous collapse and then a virtual highway leading directly into their own units. It was one of the many issues that divided the Dai Ichi, where men did the planning, from Korea itself, where men did the fighting.

A lot of things made Takahashi uneasy that night. First off, they could not make contact with King Company. It was supposed to be out there, in the vast, wide-open, unexplored dark space that abutted them, but they had no radio connection and the patrols they had sent out had not made any contact. That of itself was shocking; it meant a large enemy unit could easily slip between them—if King was out there at all. Later, Dick Raybould heard that the Chinese attack came through an area where King had placed an outpost of three men; those men, he was told, seeing how many Chinese there were, had not fired, fearing they would be killed instantly. So no warning shots were heard.

At about 8 P.M., two Asian soldiers rushed into Takahashi's platoon area with their hands up. They seemed in a panic and were shouting a few words of broken English about a huge army headed that way, some of them apparently on horseback. Slam Marshall later wrote that the two men were ROKs, but Takahashi always believed otherwise. They were wearing quilted uniforms of a kind he had never seen before, and there was the language problem: most Koreans spoke a good deal of Japanese, having lived under their colonial regime, and that gave Takahashi relatively easy linguistic access to them; but these men did not speak Japanese. They seemed to be communicating in some kind of international sign language. They were telling Takahashi's men to get out, that they were all going to be killed. It was very disquieting, and later Takahashi decided they were Chinese soldiers trying to panic his men.

Takahashi was sure by then that they were going to be hit, and that it would come from his left, and he shifted his machine guns accordingly. The attack began around 11 P.M. After the first burst of firing, a voice yelled out, asking if they were King Company. It was the Chinese, Takahashi was certain, speaking English. Apparently they had confused the two companies. Then the big attack came. His own men, Takahashi realized from the start, were very badly outnumbered. Later it was believed that at least a Chinese battalion, and quite possibly a regiment, had struck at exactly the point where his Second Platoon was positioned. The Chinese overran their position quickly. What was terrifying was not just the fact that so many Chinese were coming right at them, but that they could hear the sounds of so many others going right past them, and knew therefore that their escape routes were being cut off. Takahashi had a good man on a machine gun to his left, a sergeant named Bly, and he knew it was hopeless when Bly yelled that he couldn't hold his position. "There's too many of them!" he shouted out.

From the moment the battle began, Takahashi never spoke with another officer from Love Company. He knew he was absolutely on his own. If they were

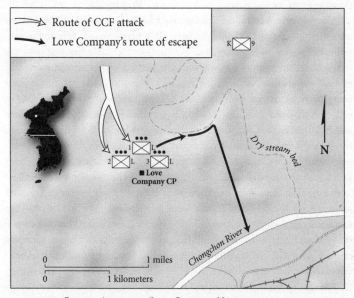

13. CHINESE ASSAULT ON LOVE COMPANY, NOVEMBER 25–26, 1950

going down, he decided, they would go down as a unit. That was where Dick Raybould, who had met Takahashi only the day before, first saw him in action, and he was deeply impressed: here was a brave, steady officer trying to rally his men in a hopeless moment. What impressed Raybould was how cool Takahashi was. Neither of them knew that Captain Vails had already been hit and was probably dead. All Raybould could see was this slim little man trying to rally a doomed unit. "Fall back on me! Fall back on me!" he kept shouting. "Hold together! Rally on me!" It was what a born leader does in the worst of times, Raybould thought. Takahashi's platoon was virtually destroyed, but amazingly enough the few men left from his platoon and some from other platoons were following him, retreating to a higher point on the mountain. Takahashi was aware that he was losing men by the minute, but at least they were making a stand. They had held that position for probably a little under an hour, and then they fell back to higher ground. There his men and the men from the First Platoon made their last stand.

It was as if they had been assigned not so much to a battle but to a fate. To hold the Chinese off any longer, they would have needed a lot of grenades and flares and a lot more ammo. Sergeant First Class Arthur Lee, a platoon sergeant and one of Takahashi's best men, was handling a machine gun just to his left. If Takahashi was going to die taking on what appeared to be the entire Chinese Army, he was glad it was next to Lee. They nodded to each other, the nod seeming to acknowledge that they were both going to die up there, but at least they were going to die like soldiers. They were trying to talk, and to pinpoint the precise place where the Chinese were located, when suddenly the only sound coming from Lee was a gurgle. He had been hit in the throat and was drowning in his own blood. The others fought on, and the Chinese made charge after charge, getting closer to their little knoll all the time, until they finally pushed the Americans off the hill. Almost every man was killed. They had held out against fearsome odds for several hours, but Love Company, which had been a good, solid, competent unit the day before, was gone. Takahashi told the handful of men left to get out as best they could. He tried to lift Lee, but he was already dead. Later, Takahashi and Raybould understood that Love and King companies had been on point not merely for the division, or the corps, but for the entire Eighth Army, and had taken the full brunt of the Chinese attack, that holding the Chinese off for a few hours had been something of a miracle, and it was hardly less of a miracle that anyone made it out of there alive. But that understanding, with the small amount of mercy it offered, came much later.

The final glimpse Raybould had of the fighting on top of that mountain was of Chinese soldiers tackling the last remaining Americans. Raybould tried to take some men with him, but most of them wanted to follow a softer part of the incline that led down the mountain. Raybould was sure that was where the Chinese would be waiting, so he slipped over to a place where the drop was much steeper. The key to surviving, he kept telling himself, was to take his time, not panic, descend slowly, and never give an enemy soldier a silhouette. He eventually met up with some stragglers from King Company and made it back to the Chongchon.

Gene Takahashi was trying to get down the hill when four or five Chinese soldiers surrounded him and took him prisoner. First they took his watch and his cigarettes. He tried to argue for the watch, a graduation present from his mother, but one Chinese soldier put a gun to his head, ending the argument. Then they indicated through sign language that he was to shout out to bring in other prisoners. Takahashi did—shouting in Japanese for others not to come in. Next they took him back to their battalion headquarters. There everyone seemed fascinated by a man with Oriental features wearing an American uniform. He seemed to make them nervous; perhaps he represented a sign that Japan was entering the war. By that time they had also captured Clemmie Simms, the company master sergeant, a strong, highly professional NCO, the very core of a professional Army, who had, Takahashi remembered, only three months to go before retirement.

Later, it would strike Gene Takahashi that he was the rarest of men, someone who had been imprisoned in wartime by two of the greatest nations in the world, the United States and China, though the Chinese imprisonment was quite brief. The Chinese started marching Simms and him away from the battle, probably heading them north. Fearing they might be shot at the foot of the hill, they tried to work out signals for an escape. He started singing a recruit's cadence song, a kind of early rap song, substituting for the usual words instructions on how and when to break away from their captors. At the right moment Simms jumped his man, Takahashi pushed his, and they made their break. As he ran, Takahashi heard gunfire near where Simms had been. He did not see Simms again. Eventually, long after the war was over, Simms's name did show up—on a list of men who had died in a Chinese prison camp in March 1951.

Gene Takahashi was confused and frightened because he was behind Chinese lines—and he was ashamed of himself as well because he had lost so many men and then had been captured. He moved cautiously and carefully, only at night, until he finally bumped into American troops near Kunuri two days later. There he found the rest of his unit, but there was almost nothing left of it.

*   *   *

WHAT BRUCE RITTER remembered from those days was how the sheer terror of the Chinese assault could open up and reveal what was inside a man in a way that no man should ever be opened up. It was like peering inside another man's soul: all the bravado and the veneer were gone, and all the things that most men like to hide from those around them were all too nakedly there for inspection. Some men he fought with behaved with valor and honor in those crucial moments, far beyond what anyone had a right to expect, risking their lives, for instance, to carry off wounded men they had never met before; while a platoon leader who had seemed a perfectly decent officer melted down right in front of him, in a moment of total cowardice.

Ritter was a radio operator with Able Company of the First Battalion of the Thirty-eighth Regiment, which was also part of the Second Division. His was a difficult, exceptionally dangerous job. The North Korean snipers liked to single radiomen out; they had killed three in his unit in a short space of time. The radio had a long antenna, a beacon of sorts for the enemy, invented, it seemed to Ritter, only to signal to their best shots exactly where fire ought to be concentrated. His fellow soldiers always tended to keep their distance from him. Ritter was sure that he was not put on this planet to carry a radio; he was five-ten and weighed 120 pounds at the time. The 300 radio he carried was heavy—it weighed, they liked to say, thirty-eight pounds at the beginning of the day and about sixty by the end. Ritter was twenty-three at the time, having celebrated his birthday a few weeks earlier, during the battle of the Naktong, and still a lowly PFC; promotion had come all too slowly, in part, he suspected, because he was so skinny that he just did not look like much of a soldier. He had done an earlier tour in the country, spoke some of the language, and could be thrown into the breach as a minimalist interpreter. But about the time a company commander discovered how valuable he was, the officer would either be killed or promoted.

On that first day of the offensive, most of the division was back at Kunuri, and he figured his reinforced company, perhaps 230 men, was about twenty-five miles to the north. Their jumping-off place had been a village called Unbong-dong. They were supposed to go about six miles over two days to Hill 1229, more a mountain actually. But they had been taking fire from the middle of the first day and that had slowed them down. They had been short a rifleman, and so Ritter had been turned into a rifleman, not a radio operator, and his chances of living had increased exponentially. About a third of the way to their objective, the incoming fire got so heavy they stopped and took up a position on the back side of Hill 300. The ground was frozen hard and their foxholes were neither deep nor well dug. They began rotating in one-hour shifts—an hour's sleep, if you were lucky, followed by an hour on watch. They were the extreme edge of the division, with the battalion strongpoint about three miles behind them.

When the Chinese struck near midnight—shocking them with the blowing of bugles, the shrillness of whistles, so many enemy soldiers suddenly right in their midst—the company managed to hold for about forty-five minutes before the retreat began. Moving back was hard; it was the worst of conditions—nighttime, with a great many wounded to carry out. Ritter remembered slipping back to another hill and someone trying to set up a perimeter, but there were too many Chinese, and once again they had to pull back. He thought perhaps another forty-five minutes had passed, and their losses were grievous.

They began to straggle back after that to where they hoped the battalion was. By then he was part of a makeshift unit, perhaps twenty or twenty-five men from different companies. Ritter knew no one in his new group, and it was unclear if anyone was in charge. Scenes like this were taking place throughout the Eighth Army that night. In the chaos, stumbling back in the dark, the sounds of the Chinese weapons ever closer, Ritter found himself with an even smaller group, four Americans and two KATUSAs, carrying one wounded soldier on a blanket with no handles and thus no good way to grip it in the terrible cold.

Ritter remembered a great deal about that day and night of horror, but he had witnessed one scene of utter cowardice that was stamped into his brain, the defining memory of that time. Ritter could still remember the wounded man's name—Willard Smith from Anderson, Tennessee. Smith was badly hit, but Ritter was sure he would live, if they could just get him out. Their own retreat was badly slowed down by Smith, but that was what you were supposed to do, carry out your wounded. There was an officer with them, a young lieutenant, but he was not really in charge—no one was. They were all exhausted, perhaps an hour of sleep in over a day, and no food. They had no time to think about how scared they were. They could hear the Chinese in the distance, and the firing seemed to be getting closer.

Finally, around dawn, they reached the bank of the Peang Yong Chon, a tributary of the Chongchon. That was where the young lieutenant broke. "We'll leave him here," he said. "We can send a helicopter for him tomorrow." It was that awful moment, when a man undressed himself in front of the men he was nominally supposed to be leading. The four other American carriers looked at the lieutenant, and they knew he was lying, that there would be no helicopter, not to carry out a dead, frozen body from a place no one would ever find. It was about bugging out and leaving Smith there to die. None of them was thinking straight, they were all exhausted, but they knew that his suggestion was dishonorable, throwing away another's life to save their own. "You're going to leave him to die, aren't you?" Ritter said. The lieutenant never answered. He didn't have to. He was offering them a chance to save themselves.

The hell with it, Ritter thought. You're supposed to do the right thing, even when it all seems hopeless, even if you die doing it. Nothing had ever seemed clearer to him: it was like declaring what kind of man you were. So the four men agreed to carry Smith out, orders or no. The two Koreans came with them. Looking back, many years later, Ritter was surprised by the fact that they had all agreed so readily. He often pondered that. They all assumed they were going to die, and so in some way it was as if the decision carried a judgment with it, perhaps a final one, and you defined your life in the way you responded. With that the lieutenant left Ritter and the three others alone to carry out Smith.

The amazing thing about combat, Ritter came to believe, was how it stripped men down to their essentials. Some men looked strong and tough, and even more important, sounded strong and tough, and then you were in combat and it all changed. Some of them weren't so tough at all, and by contrast, someone who was skinny and mild would turn out to be a very good soldier, strong inside instead of outside. Who could know in advance who the truly brave were? It was a puzzle Ritter never solved, because the answers were always so different.

Burdened by Smith, they retreated slowly. They were as hungry as they were tired. At one point, Ritter slipped off to a tiny village hoping to find some food. A young Korean girl came out of a hut and he asked for some rice. Instead she gave him a hot meal of ground corn, or at least that was what he thought it was. It might have saved them, he decided. They kept being hit by different small Chinese patrols, probably forward units. At the bottom of one hill, they ran into a small group of Chinese who started firing. One of the four bearers, George White, was hit in the foot. Now they had to move even more slowly because of White's wound. The Koreans helped carry Smith, and Ritter dropped back and pulled rearguard duty, armed with the group's only BAR, or Browning Automatic Rifle, a valued weapon because it threw out so much firepower. That was how bad it was, he thought, he was there to hold off the entire Chinese Army with a weapon he had never fired before.

He wondered if any group of soldiers had ever moved so slowly. Finally they went through a long valley and they found a corpsman and got both Smith and White out. For a long time Ritter heard regularly from White, who would always sign off his letters saying, "Thanks for the ride." He tried to contact Willard Smith, and wrote him twice, but he never heard back. The lieutenant who had left them did not fare well. Two days afterward he was captured by the Chinese, and later died in one of their prison camps.

Ritter joined up with men from other fragmented units, and they retreated and fought over two days, finally coming together with survivors of a battered battalion. He knew no one he was with. He remembered at one point that there were some tanks in the middle of a village engaged by Chinese mortars. They were all going to leave the village, and the foot soldiers were told to get on top of the tanks. Ritter climbed on one, remembering that it would feel good because the engine would be running and it would be warm. The Chinese mortar rounds were getting closer and closer, and Ritter was looking out and thinking how good they were with their mortars, when a round landed very close by and he took a piece of shrapnel in the forehead and started bleeding badly. At first, he was blinded by the blood. He had also suffered a concussion, he later decided. Being blinded, he began to panic, sure that he was going to die. Just then he stumbled into a friend, Corporal Seldon Monaghan, who told him, "Well, I see you haven't learned to keep your silly head down, have you?" It was the perfect thing to say, and it calmed him. Monaghan then bandaged him, so that he could see a little, and helped get him back up on a tank, which took him to a MASH unit. He was supposed to go to Pyongyang, but the plane couldn't land and so he flew to a hospital in Japan and missed the heartbreaking retreat from Kunuri. He had used up a lot of good luck in that short span of time, he decided. He also won the Silver Star for helping to bring White out.

ON THE NIGHT that the Chinese hit, Sam Mace, the veteran tanker, had taken his boots off—which was always the big decision in terrain like that: boots on or boots off. He had just taken his jacket off and wrapped his pistol in it, to keep the moisture off the pistol. He had just gotten into his own homemade sleeping bag, a simple bedroll with no quilting—some Army blankets—no feathers, no comfort, no warmth. Just then the first Chinese round landed, a white phosphorous shell. Mace checked his watch: 12:10 in the morning on the twenty-sixth of November. His initial thought was that it was a 4.2 mortar, and he wondered why American troops were firing 4.2 mortars and doing it so carelessly. Then he realized it was the enemy. Mace grabbed his boots and jumped into his tank in his stocking feet. Even in the darkness, he could see people running in the village; then he heard two of his tanks crank up on the other side of town and, along with other battalion vehicles, start south.

The shelling had gone on for about an hour, and he was in the turret, sweeping the hills in front of him with his telescopic sight, paying special attention to a nearby hill where troops from Lieutenant John Barbey's First Platoon, Love Company, were positioned. Then his gunner tapped his knee, and he looked out and saw about fifty men coming down the spine of the hill,

thin and narrow, like a goat trail, so steep that they had to hold on to one another to keep their balance—a human chain. They were already two-thirds of
the way down, when Mace yelled out, "If you're GIs, you better sound off!"
There was no answer, so he told his gunner to wait until they got near the bottom and then put a round of high explosive from his 76mm cannon on them.
At the same time, Mace opened up with his 50-caliber machine gun, and they
wiped the chain out. When it was over, there was a huge pile of enemy bodies
at the bottom of the hill.

Mace then told the gunner to lock his cannon on that pass. Half an hour
later, the gunner kicked him in the leg. "Look, here they come again," he whispered. So they waited until the enemy—they did not yet know they were
Chinese—neared the bottom for the second time, and they opened up again.
The enemy came back a third time, and they wiped them out again. At one
point Mace spotted what looked like a soldier crawling toward his tank, carrying something, perhaps a satchel of explosives, and Mace turned the machine
gun on him and killed him. The next day he wondered why he had not been
alerted by firing from Barbey's position. Later, he learned that the Chinese had
slipped up on the men posted on the hill and bayoneted many of them while
they slept.

When daylight broke, he checked the bodies, and they looked different
from Koreans, bigger and darker, six feet tall on average. Manchurians, someone told him. They all had American weapons, and he had never seen weapons
in better shape; and their packs were equally neat, tied together with a kind of
rope that looked like it was made of a rice plant. He remembered the discipline
with which they had come down the hillside, as if they had practiced it again
and again. He knew the Americans were now fighting a very good, very professional army. The Chinese had knocked out one of his three tanks, and so Mace
collected the men from it, most of them wounded, put them in a jeep, and they
started moving west. For the next two days they were in constant combat with
Chinese forces.

By the end of the second day, Mace had managed to get his two remaining
tanks near the village of Kujang-dong, where he had been told to meet up with
some elements of the Thirty-eighth Regiment gathering there. By then he had
picked up two more tanks. Just before he reached the village, he came upon
around sixty-five very lost-looking American infantrymen, almost numb, he
thought, trying to find their way out, most of them from the Thirty-eighth
Regiment but representing different companies, even different battalions. In a
world that had suddenly lost its coherence and security, safety seemed to exist
only in the tanks. One of their officers, a tanker himself, begged to get inside,
and Mace finally agreed, though he was uneasy about it.

They came into Kujang-dong going very slowly, perhaps two miles an hour. Each tank was carrying about fifteen men. The village was supposed to be in American hands. Normally, Mace did not like to put riflemen on top of a tank, especially at night. It limited his vision and the turret's movement. If you swept the turret and the gun all the way around, you would knock the riflemen off. But normal rules no longer seemed to apply. The village was completely silent when Mace drove in, which of itself was a warning. Suddenly, the entire area exploded on them. They had driven directly into an almost perfect ambush. Every house seemed to have Chinese soldiers with one or two automatic weapons firing away, with Mace's column perfectly zeroed in. It was a monstrous moment, because rule number one for a tanker in combat was that you had to save your tank. Mace told his driver to push it and push it hard—and then he had to move the turret, even though he knew there were people up there. There was no other order he could give, but in giving it he knew that most of the men on top were going to be killed. They were flying now, maybe twelve miles an hour, and there was death all around him. Through his open turret, he could hear the screams of the infantrymen as they were hit, or fell off, some of them to be crushed by the tanks coming after him. In the morning, when he checked out the tops of his tanks, they were covered with a pink, frothy color, as if someone had painted the surface the color of blood, with flesh and even brains mixed in, all of it frozen instantly in the cold. The ambush had lasted perhaps two or three minutes, but it had seemed to last forever, and fifty years later he could still hear the screams of those men and visualize that color on his tanks.

For the next two nights Mace fought constantly with different Chinese units. Finally, on the twenty-ninth, he was ordered back to Kunuri to join up with Division. He was relieved. It would be like heaven, he thought, getting back with your own men with all the protection a massed division could provide. But Kunuri was no heaven; it was all chaos. Just about every semblance of leadership seemed to have vanished. Mace had no time to rest. His tanks had to be resupplied, their guns cleared, and they had to be prepared for what they already sensed was going to be the worst part of all, the retreat from Kunuri. It seemed to him that he had not slept in weeks. He had been at Division headquarters and had seen Colonel George Peploe, the regimental commander of the Thirty-eighth, sleeping on a cot next to him. A regimental commander sleeping in a *Division* headquarters—that brought home better than anything just how broken the American military machine really was. Like everyone else he was hungry, and like everyone else he was very cold. It was twenty below, and in those days they did not even try to calculate windchill. The previous five days had been a kind of hell, and Mace sensed that veteran enlisted men like him out in the units had a far better feeling for what was happening than the men commanding them. Division, it seemed to the men stumbling back, had been hopelessly slow to react from the moment when the Chinese struck.

IN THOSE SMALL units that had been hit so hard, the men believed that the longer they fought, the more time they were buying for their battalions and regiments, and most of all for the division. But were the people at Division and Corps listening? Lieutenant Charley Heath, who was in the regiment's Headquarters Company, always remembered the fury in the voice of Colonel Peploe as he talked with someone at higher headquarters at least two days after the big attack began: *"Yes, goddammit, they had been hit by Chinese, and yes, he damn well knew the difference between a Chinaman and a Korean and did any of them want to leave Division and come down to his headquarters with an interpreter and check on the accuracy of what he was saying because he had some prisoners, because he would damn well like to give them a tour proving they were Chinese, and even if they didn't have an interpreter, he had a hell of a lot of very dead Chinese to prove he was right."* Heath had never seen an angrier officer. "Jesus Christ," Peploe said when he put the phone down. "You'd think those goddamn people at Division would give me credit for knowing a Chinaman when I see one."

SAM MACE'S BELIEF that Division equaled safety turned out to be a great illusion. The worst thing about Division headquarters was the fear in the air. Fear was the terrible secret of the battlefield, Mace believed, and it could afflict the brave as well as the timid. Worse, it was contagious and could destroy a unit before a battle even began. Because of that, commanders were first and foremost in the fear-suppression business; great ones could take the undertow of fear, the knowledge that it was always there, and make it an asset; weaker commanders tended to let it fester. The very same men who will fight bravely under one commander will cut and run under another who projects his own fear. Great commanders are not just men gifted in making wise tactical moves, they are men who give out a sense of confidence, that it can be done, that it is their duty and their *privilege* to fight on that given day. Thus does the strength of any unit ideally feed down, from top to bottom. The commander generates strength in the officers immediately underneath him, and it works all the way down the chain of command.

In Kunuri, it was as if no one was in command. The men who were supposed to be in charge seemed lost and dazed. Dutch Keiser, the division commander, as far as Mace's commander, Jim Hinton, could tell, had been paralyzed by the Chinese attack. Even before that moment, he had been a kind of ghost commander, preferring to let the assistant division commander, Brigadier General Sladen Bradley, be the more visible officer, the one who visited the troops. The degree to which Keiser deferred to Bradley, some officers thought, was a reflection that Keiser himself knew that it was all past him, and that he was too old to be commanding in this war, in this cold, against this enemy. As the division shattered, Keiser had no earthly idea of how to put it back together.

His was the ultimate nightmare for a commander of a large unit: the Chinese were pressing in on him and he was now in danger of losing his entire division. The general belief in the division was that he and the other senior officers had already squandered three days in grasping the extent of the Chinese attack. He and the men above him had been very slow to understand that this was the big one, that as many as twenty Chinese divisions might be operating in the western sector. By November 29, though, everyone in Kunuri knew that the Chinese were drawing closer by the hour, that it was like a noose being tightened around their collective necks, and that the clock favored the Chinese, because there were obviously so many of them, and because they would be able to block the avenues of retreat.

This then was going to be the most important decision of Keiser's career. They had been fighting the Chinese for four and in some cases five days, and the state of their military intelligence was pathetic. They did not seem to know where the Chinese were coming from or how many of them there were. Worse, no one seemed to be sure what the main route out should be.

Jim Hinton agreed with Mace—the confusion at headquarters seemed like a kind of virus. The division had a number of light spotter planes, but as far as Hinton could tell, they had not been up. Mace was shocked when he quickly realized that the entire division was now in jeopardy and that they were on their own. He was sure there was little chance of any relief mission reaching them. There was talk about a British relief column on its way to help them, but he had his doubts. Even in the worst days of the Battle of the Bulge, when he had shivered in the terrible cold at Bastogne and the Germans had pounded away with their heavy artillery, he had believed that someone was on the way. They were so good back then, so damn efficient and powerful, that when things went wrong, they soon went right. But he had no such feeling now. Dutch Keiser was bad enough, but Mace was convinced that the real problem was with the higher headquarters, and that the paralysis worked downward. From then on, for the rest of his life, Mace refused to speak of Douglas MacArthur by name. Instead he simply called him, in letters and articles for veterans' groups, and in conversation, the Big Ego.

If there was a fault line in Korea in those critical hours, it fell between those in the field being punished so harshly and those in Tokyo reluctant to admit that they had blundered into a catastrophic trap. In the field that fault line ran between the senior officers in Division, trying however inadequately to represent the dangers to its men, and Corps, still responding to the hopes and vanities of commanders in Tokyo. Whatever Dutch Keiser's faults—and he was a completely inadequate leader—Corps was worse.

30

A T 4:30 P.M. on the twenty-ninth, with darkness falling, Dutch Keiser radioed to Corps that his situation at Kunuri was perilous. The Chinese
were becoming more audacious all the time, now beginning to fight even in
the daylight. But the people in the command structure just above him, at
Ninth Corps, were even weaker than he was, and may have been even more
culpable for what happened in those critical two days, when they had the last,
best chance to get the division out largely undamaged. The corps commander,
John Coulter, was frozen in place and very slow to respond to the catastrophe
now happening except when it came to moving his own headquarters farther
south, to Pyongyang. Corps was now in danger of losing an entire division,
and Coulter, a weak commander, almost a figurehead and a pawn of Tokyo,
was overwhelmed. His sources of information were poor, he had little sense of
the battlefield as it existed, and he was far too fearful of what were by then
hopelessly outmoded orders from headquarters in Tokyo. More than anything
else he seemed to fear what Tokyo thought. Corps should have been a source of
wisdom and guidance and, if need be, additional troops. If anything, most of
what guidance Corps gave in those vitally important hours proved flat-out
wrong—it was a negative rather than a positive force.

Major General John Coulter, known as Nervous John to much of his staff,
was the most timid of the three corps commanders. That he was not up to the
job was not exactly a secret. When Matt Ridgway took over the command of
the Eighth Army a month later, Coulter was the first corps commander relieved, though the relief was masked as a promotion, for generals were always
to be protected, and a star, his third, was added along with the Distinguished
Service Medal. He was then given a staff job, as Ridgway's liaison officer with
the South Koreans and Syngman Rhee.

He had always been MacArthur's man. He had graduated from the West
Texas Military Academy in San Antonio in 1911, MacArthur's old pre–West
Point school, had served in Mexico with General Jack Pershing before World
War I, then with MacArthur's Forty-second, or Rainbow, Division during the

war, and had been a battalion commander at St. Mihiel. In World War II, he
had commanded the Eighty-fifth Division, which had fought alongside Ned
Almond's Ninety-second Division in Italy. In 1948, MacArthur brought Coulter to the Far East as commander of the U.S. Seventh Division; he then served
as deputy commander of U.S. forces in Korea and commander of First Corps
in Japan. He returned briefly to the United States, but with the North Korean
invasion, MacArthur brought him back to Korea and gave him First Corps
again, officially under Walker, but in effect he was a MacArthur-Almond man
in Walker's upper command structure.

Walker had been unimpressed with the way Coulter had used First Corps
during the Naktong fighting, but it was always difficult to deal with a subordinate you did not like who happened to be a favorite of your superior officer.
Walker dealt with his problem by giving First Corps to Shrimp Milburn at
the time of Inchon. That meant Coulter was essentially in reserve during the
march north—his new command, Ninth Corps, did not even become opera-
tional until September 16 and was then put in charge of mopping-up operations.

In the Army it is the responsibility of a commander to give primary attention to any unit that is endangered. Of all the American units in the Eighth
Army still engaged in the fighting on the western side of the peninsula by
November 30, only the Second Division was in serious trouble. Coulter was the
man who had access to additional forces and had the right to ask *his* superior
commander, Walton Walker, for reinforcements if necessary.

When the Chinese attack had begun, the original attitude back at Corps
had been that this was serious but not apocalyptic. American forces were in
trouble, it was believed, only because the ROKs had folded, thereby momentarily placing some American units in jeopardy. It was, Coulter had said, "a
local problem." By November 27, more than two days into it, the people at Division were becoming frustrated with orders from Corps calling for bite-sized
pullbacks, in effect minor retreats that did not allow regiments or battalions to
break off from the Chinese, regroup, and consolidate at more advantageous
places. They were in effect moving from positions that were vulnerable to
other positions that were no less vulnerable. On the morning of the thirtieth,
Keiser had been engaged in a prolonged debate with Corps for at least three
days. He felt his orders were inadequate, retrograde movements that were
four or five miles at best. He wanted to pull the division farther back and then
regroup. He had argued, for example, with an earlier order to pull back to
Won-ni, which was only a mile and a half north of Kunuri. It was a half-baked
move, Keiser had said, dangerous to execute without granting his division any

real additional security. His division would be just as endangered, just as far out on a limb, once it got to Won-ni.

What that order reflected was the vast distance that by then existed between reality on the battlefield and the illusions that existed in Tokyo. In those first few days, MacArthur's command was still trying to minimize the importance of what had happened—for a full-scale retreat would shatter the last of his great dreams. As Dick Raybould would say many years later of the chaos that hung over his division, "We failed because we were set up to fail." Yet, if anything, at that moment what was happening was obvious, and not only were most of the senior officers in Korea far ahead of Tokyo in their awareness of the scale of the catastrophe, but journalists were as well. On November 28, Homer Bigart of the *New York Herald Tribune,* who was soon to win his second Pulitzer for his Korean War reporting, wrote, "U.N. forces are now paying the initial price for the unsound decision to launch an offensive north of the peninsula's narrow neck. The move was unsound because it was undertaken with forces far too small to secure the long Korean frontier with China and Russia. Even without the open intervention of Red China, the U.N. Army was too weak to justify scattered garrisons along the Yalu River." Bigart added that it might be possible to hold the line at the narrow neck of the peninsula, if the divisions could be moved south quickly enough, "but the overall picture is grim."

Later, Dutch Keiser was blamed for the division's terrible performance on its most tragic day, November 30, but much of the blame belonged to higher headquarters. Still, Keiser was the commander, and commanders have to think for themselves and their troops, and he had taken the advance north, dangerous though it self-evidently was, at face value. From the start he had underestimated the dangers his troops faced, and had scoffed at those who tried to warn him. Right after Unsan, he had given an interview in which he said that the Chinese had not yet committed "their best and most loyal troops to Korea," that those who had appeared were "forced volunteers who do not want to fight" and were not "any more ferocious than the Korean Reds." As for his men, they were "bayonet sharp," ready for any assignment. Those were words he would soon regret.

TO UNDERSTAND WHAT Keiser did not do, and what a great division commander might have done, it is only necessary to know what Major General O. P. Smith, his counterpart with the First Marines in Ned Almond's Tenth Corps, did. Operating in the eastern part of the front, the First Marines were supposed to advance to the Manchurian border near the Chosin Reservoir and then move west and link up with the rest of the troops of the Eighth Army. Smith too had his orders—to push ever faster toward the reservoir and the Yalu—and they came from the relentlessly aggressive, and very abrasive, Almond. "His [Almond's] greatest weakness as a commander in Korea was his conviction that MacArthur could do no wrong," Roy Appleman wrote, rather generously, in his account of the Marine breakout from the Chosin Reservoir. No one had ever faulted Almond for a lack of aggressiveness. "When it paid to be aggressive, Ned was aggressive," said Maury Holden, the G-3 of the Second Division. "When it paid to be cautious, Ned was aggressive." Nothing was going to get in his way.

Here then a great collision was taking place, with Almond, in effect, playing the part of Tokyo's proxy on the ground in the eastern sector, and Smith representing the reality of the battlefield. Even before they collided over the use of the Marines in the Chosin-Yalu area, Smith loathed Almond and was completely distrustful of him. The two men already had a history, of course. Even before Inchon, Almond had postured to Smith, an expert in amphibious landings, about how easy they were, though he had never been part of one. On the day of that landing, Almond had been standing on the deck of the *Mount McKinley,* MacArthur's command ship, with Victor Krulak, a senior Marine officer, watching as the LVTs came out of the mother ship. The LVTs were immense amphibious tractors, essential to getting the troop and equipment ashore. When Krulak in passing told Almond what wonderful machines they were, Almond asked, "Yeah, can those things float?" "I immediately went and told ten people," Krulak noted, "because I didn't want it forgotten. Here was the man commanding the landing force at Inchon asking, 'Can those things float?' "

Even before the final push north began, Almond was, in the words of Martin Russ, who fought in Korea and wrote two exceptional books about it, "at the very top of [the Marines'] always lengthy shitlist." It was a point of pride among the Marines that their officers share as much as they could the hardships of the men in the field, that there not be greater warmth and better food for the brass. To them Almond represented a completely different and very outmoded military culture. His personal trailer was filled with numerous comforts and amenities, most important, heat in a country where everyone else was dreadfully cold. Creature comforts were important to him and he lived in a surprisingly grand style. His trailer even had a bathtub, and there almost always seemed to be hot water. (Smith, offered a trailer with some amenities, turned it down.) In addition Almond had a separate tent with a heater for his toilet. He always ate very well—the best steaks flown in regularly from Tokyo, along with fresh vegetables and the finest wines. The men under his command knew this, of course, and resented it. Nothing travels faster among combat infantrymen in a hellish environment than news of a superior officer's excessive lifestyle. It was, thought one contemporary, like dealing with the last of the World War I generals. There had been a memorable dinner he had given on October 9 to which he had invited Smith and his three regimental commanders. The four Marines had been appalled by the entire performance— they had been served by enlisted men in white uniforms; there were linens on the table with fine china and silver place settings. It was, thought Lewis (Chesty) Puller, one of the regimental commanders and a legendary figure in the Corps, "an unconscionable waste in a war zone." The Marine officers, Puller said, preferred to eat cold rations and use their trucks to haul ammo. There were three thousand men serving the Corps headquarters, Puller estimated—enough to form an additional regiment. To the Marines, good officers simply did not do things like that and retain the respect of their men.

In a way the madness—for that is the right word—behind MacArthur's final offensive showed more clearly on the eastern front than on the west. On the western side the generals might not have been as good as Smith, but Walker himself was wary of it all, reluctant to push his men too hard, and even as he told his generals to go forward, he was warning them of the dangers ahead as well. But Almond was MacArthur's boy, the true loyalist, headstrong and arrogant, determined to make the reality of the Korean battlefield fit the dreams of the commander in the Dai Ichi. That was why the ongoing confrontation between Almond and Smith was so important—it was really a struggle between MacArthur and Smith, with Almond as a self-important, highly impatient middle man, demanding that the men under him follow orders that were essentially conceived in madness, while Smith played the unfortunate role of the subordinate officer, charged with representing the battlefield as it actually was, and protecting the lives of his men if at all possible. Ordered to go north toward the Yalu as fast as he could (the words "barrel through" were sometimes used), Smith systematically tried to undermine his orders. The area in which his division was to operate and dominate the Chinese contained one thousand square miles, filled with rugged mountains, in freezing temperatures. He was absolutely convinced that the Chinese were there in large numbers, and he did not intend to fragment his division in the way that Almond demanded. When the Chinese struck, which he was quite sure they were going to do, he did not want his regiments so poorly dispersed that they were unable to support one another. He tried to impress Almond with the fact that the superior power of the First Marine Division came from using it as a whole, but he felt that, whatever Almond's other skills, listening to subordinates was not one of them. As such, Smith fought his orders as best he could for as long as he could. He slow-walked them when he could and came perilously close to out-and-out insubordination to a superior known for the explosive quality of his temper. Had he been an Army officer and not a Marine, there is no doubt that Almond would have relieved him. In the end, because he was so careful and obstinate, he not only saved the First Marines from total destruction, but saved Almond's command as well.

Major General Oliver Prince Smith was in fact one of the great, quiet heroes of the Korean War. Other Marines thought he should have won the Congressional Medal of Honor for his leadership. Yet, unlike Chesty Puller, his heroics lacked a certain drama, and few outside the Marine Corps knew his name. Smith was highly professional, wary of hubris, almost deliberately noncharismatic, and most important of all, respectful of his adversaries. He looked, as Martin Russ wrote, like someone who might have been "cast in an amateur play as a small town druggist, a man whom older ladies would call nice looking if only he would put on a little weight." His career had been an exceptional one, but it had been slow as well—he had spent seventeen years in grade as a captain. He had been the assistant division commander of the First Marine Division at the battle of Peleliu during the Pacific campaign in September 1944. Peleliu was a small island, not necessarily of great strategic value, that had proved very costly. It was roughly four miles long on a north/south axis and two miles wide on an east/west one, consisting mostly of coral, a place where it was virtually impossible to dig a decent foxhole. It had ended up one of the major disasters—if not *the* major disaster—of the Pacific War, in the view of many Marine officers. "The worst campaign in the history of warfare—far worse than Iwo Jima or the others," said Colonel Harold Deakin, a staff member under Major General William Rupertus, who commanded the First Marine Division there. The Japanese, by then on the defensive, had hunkered down during the prolonged air and artillery assault preceding the landing, and only afterward surfaced to fight with great courage and ferocity. Rupertus shared a good many of Ned Almond's qualities—he was vainglorious, impetuous, contemptuous of the forces arrayed against him. There might be some casualties, he had said before the battle, but "this is going to be a short one, a quickie. Rough but fast. We'll be through in three days. It might take only two." Instead it took a full month of yard-by-yard, cave-by-cave fighting. It had taken, the Marines estimated later, almost sixteen hundred rounds of ammo, both heavy and light, to kill each of the ten thousand Japanese soldiers on the island. So when Smith dealt with Almond, it was as if he had been there once before.

Smith did not intend to be the man who would lose the First Marine Division to the Chinese in some frozen wasteland because he had blindly followed orders he believed bore no relationship to the battlefield. The Marine breakout from the Chosin Reservoir was certainly one of the great moments in the Corps' history—and no small amount of credit for its success was Smith's, more for what he did *not* do than for what he did. When he finally sent his troops forward, he left a number of supply dumps along the way. Those supply dumps, Division operations officer Alpha Bowser later noted, "were ultimately to save the lives of thousands of fighting men, and may have saved the Marine Division as a whole."

The day that the Marines were to kick off their part of the big drive north was November 27, but for almost three weeks Smith had been struggling to thwart a battle plan he completely distrusted. He thought Tokyo a city of fools—first they had split Tenth Corps off from the Eighth Army, and now they were trying to split all of his regiments off from one another, making each part far more vulnerable, and thus playing into Chinese hands. Almond, the Marines decided, loved to break larger forces down into little ones. He favored, albeit on a limited scale, Bowser noted, grand sweeps and broad arrows on his maps—big operations similar to what the Allies had mounted in Europe. The Chinese, Smith had been assured by Tokyo, could not move through these allegedly impenetrable mountainous regions to his west. He didn't think his troops should be operating there in the first place. "The country around Chosin was never intended for military operations," Smith said after the battle was over. "Even Genghis Khan wouldn't tackle it." But Smith had his orders to push forward. He let his subordinate officers know the danger he felt they were in—not that they needed any additional warnings—and that he wanted every unit buttoned up at night in perfect defensive positions, as if that night was the one during which the Chinese would strike. If Smith had his doubts about what they were doing, he also had a certain nervous respect for the MacArthur mystique. When the general decided to push all the way to the Yalu, Smith told one colleague, "Well, he got away with it at Inchon, so he'll probably get away with it here." But, Smith later added, this time he did not.

No one was going to be able to help bail Smith out. By the beginning of November, he had come to believe that the Chinese were probably setting a vast trap for the American forces. On October 29, around the time of Unsan, a ROK unit in Smith's sector had captured sixteen Chinese soldiers. They were from an ammunition platoon, were taller than most Chinese and considerably darker, wore quilted uniforms, and spoke openly of their unit. They were from the 370th Regiment, in the 124th Division, of the Forty-second Army, in the Ninth Army Group. They had crossed into Korea on October 16, they said, and added that there were at least three Chinese divisions—the 124th, 125th, and 126th—from the Forty-second Army in the area. Almond came and met with them, got them to do some close-order drills, and did not seem impressed. They were scruffy-looking and exhausted—they had not eaten in several days. He used, the Marine historian John Hoffman wrote, the phrase "Chinese laundrymen" to describe them, not the first or the last time he would use it. They were not, he told some of the men around him, very intelligent. The Marines were not, as Hoffman wrote, "so sanguine." When Charles Willoughby eventually arrived and checked out the prisoners, he decided that they were part of a relatively small group of Chinese volunteers, perhaps ten thousand men, in effect a token Chinese force, not part of any massive Chinese Army.

Colonel Homer Litzenberg's Seventh Marine Regiment, one of Smith's three regiments, replaced the ROK unit that had captured the Chinese and was almost immediately engaged by a large Chinese force, at least a division and possibly more, at Sudong—the first significant battle between the Marines and the Chinese on the eastern front. It went on from November 2 to 4. "We thought for a while that we were like Custer at the Little Big Horn, and that we were not going to get out—it was very very tough," said Major James Lawrence, who for a time was a battalion executive officer there, and received the Navy Cross for his leadership. It was very hard fighting. The Marines finally fended the Chinese off, but in the process they took heavy casualties—44 dead, 162 wounded, and one man missing in action.

If the ferocity of the battle did not slow down Tokyo or Almond, then it made Smith warier than ever. His job, he believed, was to slow down the journey into that trap if at all possible and, in his phrase, "not go too far out on a limb." Thus did tensions with Almond continue to increase. "Our Marine division was the spearhead of Tenth Corps," as Colonel Bowser, Smith's operations man, noted. "General Almond had already begun to notice that the spearhead was hardly moving at all. We were in fact just poking along—deliberately so. We pulled every trick in the book to slow down our advance, hoping the enemy would show his hand before we got more widely dispersed than we already were. At the same time we were building up our levels of supply at selected dumps along the way."

On November 5, the Marines picked up a lone Chinese soldier sleeping in a hut. Everything he said seemed authentic and in no way hyped up. He was a member of the 126th Division and seemed to be full of information—one of the differences in the Chinese Army was that, as part of the new egalitarian spirit, ordinary privates, through lectures from the political commissars, often knew a great deal about battle orders. The prisoner told the Marines that twenty-four Chinese divisions had crossed the Yalu. On November 7 this was passed on to Almond—and for a brief time Smith thought that this information, along with the news of what had happened at Unsan, had had the effect of sobering Almond up. For the first time he seemed amenable to the idea of Smith concentrating the First Marines. But then the orders came down from Tokyo to speed it up, and Almond pushed Smith to drive ahead faster.

Meanwhile, in the Chinese command post, Peng Dehuai was talking about placing 250,000 Chinese on the western front against 130,000 of Walker's men, or a 1.92 edge in manpower, with 150,000 Chinese against 100,000 UN troops on the eastern front, or a manpower ratio of 1.67. They were by now on the south side of the Yalu, well hidden away in caves. It was almost as if their earlier clashes were a means of taunting the Americans and UN forces, striking at them and disappearing. "To catch a big fish, you must first let the fish taste your bait," General Sung Shih-lun of the Chinese Ninth Army Group, the overall commander of the Chinese forces on the eastern front, told his staff. In mid-November the UN forces were, in the phrase of one senior Chinese officer, "still far from our preselected killing zones."

On November 15 Smith met with Almond, and Almond again pushed harder for speed. The Marines had reached Hagaru, at the south end of the Chosin Reservoir, and now he wanted them to go toward Yudam-ni, fourteen miles away, while another Marine regiment moved east. The third regiment was fifty miles south. The division was still badly fragmented. "We've got to go barreling up that road," Almond said. Smith immediately exclaimed, "No!" but Almond, according to Brigadier General Ed Craig, the assistant division commander, pretended not to hear it. Then Almond flew out. After he did, Smith said, "We're not going anywhere until I get this division together and the airfield [which he wanted midway between the coast and the reservoir in order to airlift the wounded out in case the Chinese struck] built." That day, still bothered by Almond's failure to comprehend the dangers he was sure they faced, and by his insistence on fragmenting the division, Smith did something very unusual—he wrote to the Marine commandant, Clifton Cates, complaining about his orders, citing chapter and verse of the dangers inherent in them, in effect warning that there was a danger of losing the entire division.

The Chinese who had hit Litzenberg had withdrawn north, he wrote Cates, but he had issued no orders to pursue them. His own left flank, he said, was "wide open." The nearest element of the Eighth Army was eighty miles away. His own troops were not able to support one another. "I do not like the prospect of stringing out a Marine Division along a single mountain road for 120 miles from Hamhung to the Manchurian border." He was made extremely nervous by the orders from above. "I have little confidence in the tactical judgment of X Corps or in the realism of their planning. There is a continual splitting up of units and assignments of missions which puts them out on a limb. Time and time again I have tried to tell the Corps Commander that in a

Marine Division he has a powerful instrument, and that it cannot but help lose
its effectiveness when dispersed." Finally, he was obviously worried about the
cold and the mountains. "I believe a winter campaign in the mountains of Korea is too much to ask of an American soldier or Marine, and I doubt the fea-
sibility of supplying troops in this area during the winter or providing for the
evacuation of sick and wounded." Finally in mid-November he got one of the
things he most wanted, a small airstrip near Hagaru. Even that had been hard.
He had done it jointly with Major General Field Harris, who was in charge of
the Marine air operations. One day Almond had asked Harris what he was
looking for, and Harris had answered that it was a small strip so they could
land enough transports to bring in supplies and carry out the casualties.
"What casualties?" Almond had asked Harris—who soon lost his own son up
near the Chosin. "That's the kind of thing you were up against. He wouldn't

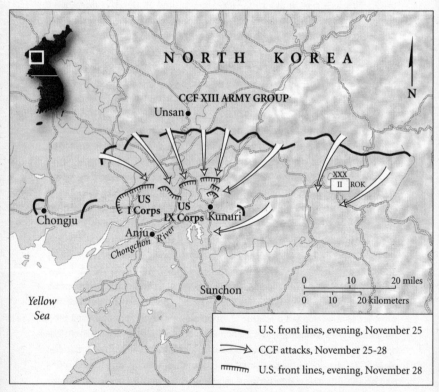

14. THE MAIN CHINESE CAMPAIGN IN THE WEST, NOVEMBER 25–28, 1950

admit there even would be casualties," Harris later told Bemis Frank, a Marine historian. "We took 4500 casualties out of that field."

Smith was now sure that the Chinese were baiting an immense trap for him, and there was one bit of empirical evidence that definitely showed that. That was the Chinese failure to blow the bridge at the Funchilin Pass. The road from Hungnam, the port from which the Marines would eventually disembark, to Yudam-ni, which was their farthest penetration and where they were when the Chinese made their major assault, was seventy-eight miles. On the way north from Hungnam, the road at first was relatively flat. From Sudong, where the Chinese had first struck the Marines on November 2, to Hungnam was about thirty-seven miles. Just north of Sudong and south of Kotori, the road became more and more difficult, elevating at an accelerating rate, twenty-five hundred feet in eight miles, to a terrifying stretch known as the Funchilin Pass, becoming, as Matt Ridgway wrote, "a narrowing, frightening shelf with an impassable cliff on one side and a chasm on the other." At a critical point in the pass the only way to keep going north was over a concrete bridge that covered four gigantic pipes, which pumped water from the Chosin Reservoir to a power plant. The mountain was so steep, and the passageway so narrow, that if the Funchilin Pass bridge were blown, given the hideous nature of the terrain and the overwhelming logistical limitations, it would be the end of the offensive for the American troops, so dependent on motorized equipment. But the Chinese heading north had *not* blown the bridge. To Smith, it was like the dog that hadn't barked. The failure to blow the bridge on the part of so formidable and shrewd an adversary was a sure sign that the Chinese wanted the Americans to cross it—it was virtually an invitation—but it meant nothing to Almond, so disrespectful was he of his adversary. "Smith was sure that they wanted us to come across, and that they were going to blow the bridge after we crossed, thus completely isolating us," said Major (later Major General) James Lawrence, who had been the executive officer at Sudong when the Chinese struck. "It was shrewd of Smith to understand that but it's hard to think of any other capable officer who was paying attention not coming up with much the same scenario. Almond seemed to have so little respect for the Chinese as fighting men that it was as if he didn't care."

By November 26, Smith had essentially won his most important victory. He had consolidated his division to what he considered an acceptable degree. Almond had pushed him to put men just west of the Chosin, at Yudam-ni, and he had two regiments in the general Yudam-ni area, closer to each other than they had been before, but still separated by the reservoir itself. Smith was hardly happy with the entire situation, but it was much better than it had been. When Craig brought the degree of fragmentation that still existed up with him, all he said was "It's what the Army wants."

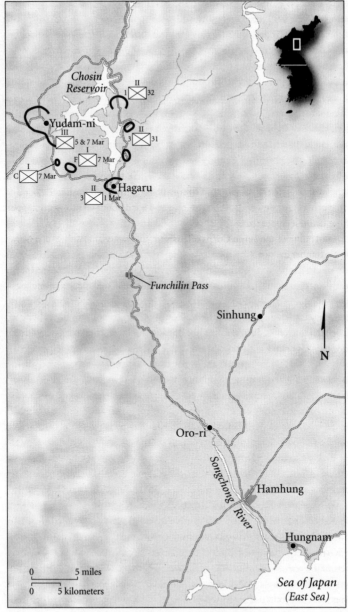

15. The Marine Sector, October–November 27, 1950

To the east of Yudam-ni, where the Seventh Marines were, the reservoir pointed like a very long icicle toward Hagaru, just south of it. Yudam-ni was about fourteen miles west of Hagaru, and the Fifth Marines were on the other side of the icicle. At Hagaru, Smith had posted a battalion from Puller's First Marine Regiment. Another battalion of Puller's troops was posted at Kotori, about eleven miles directly south of Hagaru, on the Main Supply Route, and another battalion at Chinhungni, about another ten miles south. Puller's men were to keep the road open. It might not be ideal, given that their intelligence had now pinpointed at least six Chinese divisions in the area, but with a break or two, it might allow the division to fight like a division. As Colonel Bowser said, "Even so we were now at the end of a long, cold, snow-covered limb. The limb was sixty-five to seventy-five miles long, depending on where you wanted to measure." Smith had, unlike Keiser and some other Army generals, thought long and hard about what would happen if the Chinese appeared.

The timing of the Tenth Corps offensive in the east was important. It began on November 27, *two days after* the massive Chinese assault against the Eighth Army. The Marines had heard some of the early reports, but did not know the scope of the disaster. The essential plan in the east nonetheless was bizarre— the work, said Bill McCaffrey, of madmen. The Marines in Tenth Corps were to drive west to Mupyongni, some perhaps forty or fifty miles away, but each mile likely to be impassable, on roads that might or might not exist. Mupyongni was a village high up on the Chongchon, and thus in the Eighth Army sector; getting there would allegedly link them up with Walker's men. This way they would theoretically encircle any Chinese troops in the area and cut off their escape, and, in the minds of the Dai Ichi architects, cut off all Chinese supply lines as well. Given the thinness of the American forces, and the absolute harshness of the terrain, some mountains reaching seven thousand feet, and the cruelty of the weather, often twenty degrees below, it was pure insanity. The people in the Dai Ichi simply did not understand that those being cut off would be the UN forces themselves, completely isolated in the most unreachable place in the country, that in the unlikely event that the Marines with all their vehicles actually tried to make it through to Mupyongni on what would turn out to be an ox trail really, by then sure to be ice-covered, over mountainous peaks, they would be the perfect target for the Chinese. But for MacArthur this linkup of Tenth Corps and the Eighth Army was a symbol of victory, the crowning moment of a career-crowning campaign, proof that he had conquered the country and the enemy. It mattered nothing to him that even if the Marines managed to get through to Mupyongni, it would have no military value, because they would barely control the land they stood on. No one could talk him out of it. "The plans bore no resemblance to the country. In those days it was like complete insanity in the command," Bill McCaffrey said years later. "From the time we headed to the Yalu it was like being in the nut house with the nuts in charge. You could only understand the totality of the madness if you were up there in the north after the Chinese had entered in full force, and we were being hit and hit again by these immense numbers of troops. And what we were getting from Tokyo was madness—absolute madness. The only real question was whether we could get any of our people out of there, and yet the orders were still to go forward." MacArthur, after Inchon, he added bluntly "was nutty as a fruitcake."

The lead regiment was supposed to be Ray Murray's Fifth Marines, already too isolated for their own good. Of the projected attack west, Murray later said, "It was unbelievable. The more you think about it, the more unreal it becomes. Well, anyhow those were the orders, and that's what we started to do." It was, as Almond's own chief of staff, Nick Ruffner, put it, "an insane plan." It ranked, Clay Blair wrote, "as the most ill-advised and unfortunate operation of the Korean War."

ON BOTH coasts of the peninsula, the recognition of the sheer size and scope of the Chinese offensive was delayed because the Tokyo command remained loath to admit its tragic miscalculation. Johnnie Walker was slow to react, neutralized by conflicting forces and feelings—and by the time he understood the full gravity of the situation, he had little leverage. In the first few days Walker thought there was still time to pull his forces back and establish a line at the narrow neck of Korea, near Pyongyang. By contrast, his opposite number on the east coast, Almond, remained an enthusiast for the attack.

With the great offensive, Ned Almond had gotten his last career command, the one he had so badly wanted, and he had been slow indeed to come to terms with the hopelessness of it, and to tell his superior that it was in effect a failure. As late as November 28, three and a half days into the great Chinese attack, Almond was still refusing to admit the catastrophe it had become and still pushing the Tenth Corps forces to advance. At noon on that day, he choppered up to Smith's headquarters at Hagaru to give one of his patented pep talks. Smith paid as little attention as he could. He was busy consolidating his Marine division, already dangerously close to being entrapped, for what he hoped would be a breakout to the south. To the Marines, there was something almost crazed about Almond then, as if he were commanding an Army still on a great victory march, when in fact it was facing total annihilation. Part of it, they were convinced, was his own subconscious racism, which blinded him to the ability of the enemy. "There was a disrespect for them as soldiers, a belief that they had been fleeing from us because they *should* be fleeing from us not because they might be setting a trap—whereas we who were fighting them and had been fighting them from early November knew how good they were—that's where the phrase 'laundrymen' came from. It was pure racism. It was as if the only person in Tenth Corps who did not know how good they were and how dangerous our position had become was the Tenth Corps commander," said Major Jim Lawrence, a battalion executive officer in those days.

Then Almond flew to the headquarters of Colonel Allan MacLean's Thirty-first Infantry Regiment, part of the Army's Seventh Division, the other critical element of Tenth Corps engaged by the Chinese. Almond had earlier issued orders that had dangerously fragmented the Seventh Division, at the same time creating a gap between the units of the Seventh Division and the Marines. Those orders, as Clay Blair noted, would have tragic consequences. By the time of Almond's visit, Colonel MacLean's regiment was already being hammered badly on the eastern side of the Chosin Reservoir by large numbers of Chinese troops. If there was ever a time to retreat and try to link up with the Marines to the south, this was it. But Almond wanted them to press on. MacLean, who was killed there the next day while trying to lead the Thirty-first Regiment out, was not at the CP but was out with his badly endangered unit, known as Task Force MacLean. But Lieutenant Colonel Don Carlos Faith, a battalion commander in the Thirty-second Regiment, was there. Almond seemed oblivious to the fact that a critical part of his command was being annihilated. Faith, who himself would be killed three days later while leading his badly battered Task Force Faith out of its hopeless position and would receive a posthumous Congressional Medal of Honor for his leadership, tried to explain how desperate their position actually was: they were being hit by two entire Chinese divisions. "That's impossible," Almond said. "There aren't two Chinese divisions in all of North Korea!" The enemy who was attacking them, he said, was nothing more than remnants of Chinese forces fleeing north. "We're still attacking and we're going all the way to the Yalu. Don't let a bunch of goddamn Chinese laundrymen stop you!" He thereupon ordered Faith to retake the high ground he had lost the previous night.

Then—for Almond loved nothing more than on-the-spot medal presentations—he announced that he had three Silver Stars he wanted to give out—one to Faith and two to whomever Faith chose. Faith was appalled, but he thereupon chose a wounded lieutenant and asked him to come and stand at attention to get his medal. Just then the mess sergeant of Headquarters Company, George Stanley, walked by. Faith ordered him over. In front of a few men of Headquarters Company, the pathetic little medal ceremony took place. With that, Almond flew off in his helicopter. A moment later, Faith's operations officer,

Major Wesley Curtis, walked over. "What did the general say?" he asked. "You heard him, remnants fleeing north," said an angry Faith as he ripped the medal off and threw it in the snow. One of his officers heard him say, "What a damned travesty."

When Almond got back to his headquarters later that day, he found a message ordering him to return to Tokyo. Johnnie Walker received the same message. In Tokyo, they quickly went into a somber meeting with MacArthur, who was slowly beginning to comprehend what had happened. "The wine of victory had turned to vinegar," in Clay Blair's words. MacArthur "had been outsmarted and outgeneraled by a 'bunch of Chinese laundrymen' who had no close air support, no tanks and very little artillery, modern communications or logistical infrastructure." His post-Inchon commands, Blair added, had added up to "an arrogant, blind march to disaster." On the afternoon of the twenty-eighth he had sent the Joint Chiefs a message. They now faced, he said, "an entirely new war." "This command," he wrote, "has done everything humanly possible within its capabilities but is now faced with conditions beyond its control and its strength." In that sentence was the first surfacing of what would become known in Washington as MacArthur's Posterity Papers. He was already pulling back from any responsibility for the catastrophe taking place, blaming it instead first on the fates, and then on the civilians in Washington.

ALMOST TO THE end Ned Almond had wanted to drive to Mupyongni. It was, thought Bill McCaffrey, as if he had become a prisoner of not just the orders from Tokyo, but also the myth of MacArthur. Bill McCaffrey had almost lost his own life in the foolishness. Just before the Chinese struck, he had been ordered by Almond to take a small number of men and set up what they called a "jump command post," a small, temporary one, about a couple hundred yards from the Marine headquarters at the Chosin Reservoir. McCaffrey had been ordered by Almond to keep his small CP separate from the Marines, but to use it to pass on Corps orders to the Marines, to push them harder to attack to the west, because Smith now absolutely refused to move—he believed the orders were murderous. McCaffrey would be there as a presence from Corps and a means of goosing the Marines. My job, McCaffrey had thought to himself, is to pass on orders that are crazy to men who know they are crazy, and will surely be killed if they follow them.

Almost as soon as he set up the CP, he was ordered back to Hungnam. As he drove his jeep out of the area, one of the Marines at the last outpost waved him through and yelled out, "Sir, you watch your ass going on from here—there's Chinks all over these mountains." He made it back to Hungnam, got a bite to eat, and, absolutely exhausted, went to bed. Around midnight he was awakened—the lieutenant colonel he had left in charge of the small CP was on the phone, his voice more desperate by the minute: The Chinese were attacking in strength. . . . The CP was about to be overrun. . . . What should they do? McCaffrey told the officer to try to make it to the nearby Marine headquarters, but even as he told him, the radio went dead. None of the men who had manned the small outpost was ever heard of again. I might have been the last man out, McCaffrey later thought.

THE MEETING OF principals took place in Tokyo on the night of November 28, three days after the Chinese struck. It began just before 10 P.M. and lasted almost four hours. MacArthur did most of the talking, and as Blair noted, he was still underestimating the sheer size of the Chinese force by perhaps as many as a hundred thousand men. He seemed to think that only six Chinese divisions, or some 60,000 men, were engaged with Tenth Corps, when by then the more realistic number was twelve divisions, or about 120,000 men, with another eighteen or twenty divisions, and close to 200,000 men, engaged in the west. Walker was considerably more realistic than either Almond or MacArthur. He believed that they had to retreat but with luck should be able to hold a line at the narrow waist of the peninsula, near the North Korean capital. Almond, a prisoner of his earlier miscalculations, still wanted to continue the offensive, but it was far too late for that. It was time to save what remained of both commands—if possible. The word to pull back finally came from headquarters on November 29—very late in the battle, during which each day and each hour that passed had worked for the Chinese and against, in particular, the Second Infantry Division.

If there was one symbolic moment that reflected how disconnected the Dai Ichi headquarters was from the battlefield, it took place at that meeting when Pinky Wright, who was the acting G-3 for MacArthur, suggested, in the midst of this crisis, that the American Army's Third Division, relatively new in country and essentially used as a reserve so far by Almond, set out to cross the Taebaeks and link up with Walker's force. It was a truly astonishing suggestion—a senior in ROTC at an American high school might well have come up with a better idea. That, even Almond noted, simply could not be done—there were no roads going west. Any American unit trying to cross on whatever trails existed would be easy prey for the Chinese.

31

ON THE WESTERN side of the peninsula, the decision to pull back the UN forces brought little relief for the Second Division. Dutch Keiser still had his division up front, in effect offering protection for other American units that were then retreating, but the division itself was in mounting danger. If November 30 was to be the tragic day in which Keiser's division was torn apart, then November 29 was the wasted one, during which he failed, despite numerous appeals, to get his superior at Corps to understand the desperation of his position and begin the breakout, or at least discover what the possibilities were. On the morning of the twenty-ninth, Corps finally gave Keiser permission to go south on the road to Sunchon, about ten miles south of Kunuri. Corps assured Keiser that the road was open. A Turkish brigade, they said, was moving up the road at that moment as a relief column.

John Coulter was greatly enamored of the Turks, even though he knew almost nothing about their fighting abilities. The Turks, striking-looking men, especially with their immense mustaches, simply appeared to him to be fierce warriors, and without much of an initiation process, he had made them his Corps reserve. Now he was throwing them into battle at a critically important moment. They were in general, it turned out, very green troops, led by poorly trained officers, and they suffered from serious language problems in dealing with both the Americans and the Koreans. Early in the fight against the Chinese they had allegedly captured two hundred Chinese soldiers, a wonderful moment at a bad time, which had given everyone a lift—except that the prisoners had turned out to be two hundred fleeing ROKs, who were quite humiliated because they had surrendered to their comrades. Now, sent north to hold a sector to the southeast of the embattled Second Division, the Turks were not exactly the relief force that Keiser needed. The Chinese, already waiting, promptly hammered part of the unit, and many of the troops, reported Paul Freeman of the Twenty-third Regiment, simply fled: "The Turks had been committed, but they had taken a look at the situation and they had no stomach for it and they were running in all directions."

All of this was of little help to Keiser, who had spent the twenty-ninth getting contradictory messages about whether or not the road south was open. At 4:30 P.M. on the twenty-ninth, with darkness falling, he had radioed to Corps that his situation at Kunuri was perilous. In that message, Keiser told Corps that the Turkish brigade that was supposed to reinforce his eastern flank had failed completely, and that his own badly battered Thirty-eighth Regiment, positioned on his east, could no longer hold. What was worse was his fear that his men could not break through on the main road going south to Sunchon, where the Chinese were already gathering, as evidenced by their destruction of the Turkish relief force. Keiser asked for permission to try an alternate route out, rather than the main road, which he feared was blocked by the Chinese. But he could never get any response, other than staff members telling him to stay with his existing orders.

By the morning of the thirtieth, Coulter had had close to four days to understand accurately what the fate of the Second Division might be, even as the Chinese were gathering in ever-stronger units south of it, presumably ready to cut off the road. But he had done very little. Instead he had been busy moving his own headquarters to a safer location on the twenty-ninth and therefore had been difficult for Keiser to reach. It was his staff members—largely powerless—who had been forced to deal with Keiser's increasingly desperate pleas. (Coulter, Paul Freeman bluntly noted later, had simply "fled the battlefield.") His aides had passed on useless bromides indicating, for instance, that the British Middlesex Battalion was on its way north to help, when it was completely stalled out well south of what the Americans would eventually call The Pass, the critical bottleneck on the road out, about five and a half miles south of Kunuri. Perhaps more than anything else, the limited force sent in relief told it all in this sad tale of always too little and always too late. With as many as six Chinese divisions closing in on an American division trapped with marginal escape routes available, and other than untested Turkish troops, Coulter had sent a British battalion.

By the night of the twenty-ninth, Keiser was all too aware that a vast front was collapsing on him. Two of his three regiments, the Ninth and the Thirty-eighth, were no longer really combat-ready. He had three choices. The first would have demanded an exceptional anticipatory sense of what to do if the Chinese struck in force. That choice would be to consolidate the division, in effect circle the wagons, and use the awesome firepower of an American division against the Chinese, resupplying his own men by air, until the enemy was worn down. That would have meant turning the Second Division into an instant airborne division, momentarily isolated behind enemy lines, but still indefinitely resuppliable. That, one of Keiser's artillery commanders, Lieutenant

Colonel John Hector, suggested to a subordinate, Ralph Hockley, a few months later, was the way they should have gone. Eventually, based on some of the lessons learned at Kunuri, that would indeed become a critical part of the future American strategy, and under Matt Ridgway's directions and Paul Freeman's leadership, it was employed with great success at Chipyongni some two and a half months later. But no one had given it a moment's thought before the Chinese struck, and by November 29, events had already outstripped this option.

That left Keiser with two choices: go south to Sunchon as Corps had ordered, or go west, on the only other road out, to Anju. Whether that road was open no one was certain. The road to Anju ironically was mostly an American-made one, having recently been built up from little more than a trail by Hobart Gay, the commander of the First Cav. When the Cav had driven north after Unsan, Gay had become increasingly nervous about the Chinese presence, and at one point earlier in November when the division CP was positioned at Kunuri, he had ordered the engineers to work on the road to Anju to make it capable of servicing an American division, "just because you never know when you might need an extra way out, if they hit again," as he told Lieutenant Jack Murphy, whom he was trying to recruit as an aide. But the Second Division's intelligence remained shockingly bad. On the morning of the twenty-ninth, Keiser had jeeped over to Corps headquarters, still just a few miles west of his headquarters, and flown back in a light spotter plane because the road traffic was so heavy. His visit to Corps had not been a great help. Coulter had not been there. From the plane he had seen the roads choked with people moving south. At first, he had believed these were refugees. If that was true, there was hope that his troops too could get out. Later, he would decide that he might well have seen Chinese troops. Back at Kunuri the pressure was building as the Chinese forces closed in, and he kept getting conflicting reports about which route out might be safer and which he was permitted to use.

On the thirtieth as on the twenty-ninth, Corps continued to withhold permission to go out west, while continuing to feed Keiser illusory reports on the alleged strength of the Chinese on the road south and on the British relief force, code named Nottingham, supposedly fighting its way north. No one mentioned to Keiser that the road was now actually in much worse shape because it was littered with the carcasses of the vehicles that the Turks had been using, clogging up what had been a rather narrow pathway in the first place. Corps thought the Chinese positions were some six miles south of where they actually were. Division thought the same thing. Corps thought the British relief team was making progress, when it had been completely stopped. So did Division. Worse, Division thought on the morning of the thirtieth that the Chinese block was relatively thin and that a strong party could smash through.

"The hope was that [the Chinese] were in a relatively small place far down the road, and that when we got there we could suppress their fire there, drive them off, or just barrel through" was the way Captain Alan Jones, the Ninth Regiment intelligence officer, put it. Neither Corps nor Division knew whether the road west to Anju was open. Henry Becker, the division provost marshal, and thus in charge of its MPs, had erroneously reported that it was blocked. But even if it were open, Keiser was not sure he had permission to go out on it.

NOTHING SHOWED JUST how vulnerable they were and how little time they had left more clearly than the first Chinese attack on Division headquarters on the night of the twenty-ninth. Early that evening the headquarters commandant visited various units clustered around the schoolhouse that served as headquarters, to warn them of a probable attack that night. Captain Malcolm MacDonald, the young assistant G-2, took his telephone and some of his other equipment and moved them outside the schoolhouse to a nearby building foundation. Sure enough, about 8 P.M., the mortars and the machine gun fire began. MacDonald watched, fascinated. He could see the flash of the Chinese weapons about three hundred yards away. One of the first mortar rounds landed on a nearby tent, igniting it and thereby giving the Chinese an exceptionally good look inside the perimeter. There had probably been a company of Chinese involved—undoubtedly just a probe—and it took about an hour to drive them back. But it underlined how dangerous the division's status was, how little buffer there was between them and the enemy, growing stronger by the hour. It was not a comforting thought for MacDonald. You might expect enemy troops to slip up to a regimental headquarters. But to a division headquarters? He had never heard of it before.

At one point during the afternoon of the twenty-ninth, Major General Milburn, the First Corps commander and a close personal friend of Keiser's, had called in to see if he could offer any help. His sector was to the west of Keiser. He had heard about the Sunchon road being cut. How was it going? he asked.

"Bad," Keiser answered. "We're getting hit in my CP."

"Well, come out my way," Milburn said, meaning the road to Anju.

It was a tempting invitation, but it would have to be cleared through the people at Ninth Corps. Earlier on the afternoon of the twenty-ninth, with Corps' approval, the division had sent some of its trains of heavy equipment out by the road to the west, that convoy linking up with men of First Corps moving south. But that was a very different thing from committing the entire division to the road. In the meantime there was a swirl of rumors about what was open and what was closed—and Division headquarters seemed effectively blind.

Very late on the twenty-ninth, after the mortar attack on headquarters, Keiser called Corps one more time suggesting they take the Anju road out, and was turned down. Thus, at about 1 A.M. on November 30, he summoned his top staff and told them that Coulter had just ordered him to attack down the Sunchon road at dawn. Coulter had flown over the road that afternoon and did not think the Chinese block was very strong. He was confident, he had added, that the Second Division should be able to break through. With that, the argument was over. The road south might be narrow, with high banks on both sides, just perfect for an ambush; it might be cluttered with American vehicles, which would slow down traffic, all of it a prescription for a retreat through hell—but they now had their orders.

ON THE MORNING of the thirtieth, the Second Engineers were waiting for their place in the convoy slated to head south. The convoy was moving at a pathetically slow pace. None of the battalion's senior officers was happy with the decision to go south. They all knew, in the way that soldiers always know, that it was very bad on the road, and getting worse; the reports coming back were ever more ominous, and the engineers were well aware that their exceptionally heavy gear would be a prime target. Captain Larry Farnum was acting as both the S-2 and S-3 (intelligence and operations officer—in a division it's G-2 or G-3; in a regiment or battalion it's S-2 or S-3) of the battalion because his superior did not trust the nominal S-3. On his own, because the engineers were so burdened with heavy gear, he had been running recon units, trying to figure out which way out was best, and he was convinced that the road to Anju was still open and the road south effectively closed—that any attempt to push a force as clumsy as a division down it would meet with disastrous results. He knew that a number of attempts to remove the Chinese blocks along the road had already failed. The situation, he believed, was clearly out of control.

On his own, Farnum went to Division headquarters early on the afternoon of the thirtieth and pleaded for the right to go out west. At least, he pleaded, let's send our heavy gear out west. But Colonel Maury Holden, the division G-3, kept saying he had his orders and could not change them. When Farnum pushed him hard, Holden, widely regarded as the ablest officer at Division, resisted him and kept repeating that it was *orders, and orders were orders.*

The problem, Holden told Farnum, was Tokyo. Talking to Corps, he said, was like talking to Tokyo because they were so fearful there. "But because I was such a brash young captain and because so much was riding on it," Farnum recalled, he pushed Holden to try one more time. So Holden, with a shrug of resignation, got on the radio. "You and I know what the answer is going to be," he added. He spoke to Corps briefly and shook his head again. Then he turned to

Farnum and said he had to go, they were closing up headquarters; his jeep was already loaded, and he and the top division officers, surrounded by ack-ack guns and tanks, were heading south. And with that, as headquarters packed up and left, communications between different units of the Second Division, always bad, became even worse.

So it was that the men of the Second Division began their retreat from Kunuri. They were beleaguered before they started, exhausted, many of their units already badly battered. Of the three regiments, the only one not already torn apart in the previous five days was Paul Freeman's Twenty-third. It was assigned to hold the line against the vast Chinese forces gathering north of Kunuri.

By the time Keiser sent out his weakened battalions of the Ninth Regiment to help clear the sides of the road south, the Chinese had moved to within a mile of his headquarters and had fire positions over a full six- or seven-mile stretch of the road. They were already dug in on the high ground and would have been hard to dislodge even by fresh troops with plenty of fire support. The Chinese might not have heavy weapons, just mortars and machine guns, but they were good with those mortars, and their burp guns threw out a lot of fire at close range—it was, by the testimony of a good many American officers, the best basic infantry weapon in Korea. It lacked the accuracy of the M-1 rifle or the carbine, but it provided a lot more firepower a lot more quickly. The burp gun was a formidable weapon in that war: it sounded, said Captain Hal Moore (eventually a three-star general), "like a can of marbles when you shook them, but on full automatic it sprayed a lot of bullets and most of the killing in Korea was done at very close range and it was done quickly—a matter of who responded faster. In situations like that it outclassed and outgunned what we had. A close-in patrol fight was over very quickly and usually we lost because of it."

Keiser had started the day by trying to clear the ridges on both sides of the road, assigning two battalions from the Ninth Regiment to do the job (one for each side of the road). But he overestimated the strength of the now ravaged Ninth—both units, according to Alan Jones, were at less than half strength, at most 300 men in a battalion that should have had at least 800 to 850 men—and quite likely fewer who were truly able-bodied. No one was sure of the numbers, but it was possible that they had started the day with a division of Chinese covering the road, and more arriving as the hours wore on.

The Second Battalion of the Ninth Infantry Regiment, commanded by Major Cesidio (Butch) Barberis, had been hit repeatedly by the Chinese since the twenty-fifth, probably harder than any other infantry battalion in the division. By the end of the first day of the Chinese attack, George Company of the Second Battalion, which normally had around two hundred men, had had seventy-three either killed or wounded, while E Company was down to a handful of men. All of Barberis's men were exhausted—in the first three days of fighting his men had crossed the Chongchon four times. He had received a significant whiskey ration before the Chinese struck, and each time his men made it across the river, he would insist that they change their socks and then he would give them a shot of whiskey right then and there, and a second one for their canteens. By the time Barberis and his men had reached Kunuri, Barberis, though still commanding, had been wounded, and had about 150 of his original 970 men—the number he'd had when he had first crossed the Chongchon—available to fight. That pathetic little unit was now designated to drive a large, well-entrenched Chinese force off one of the ridgelines.

It wasn't going to happen. Long before he reached his assembly point, Barberis looked up and saw movement on the high ground in the distance. He got on the radio and asked who was up on the ridgeline. The ROKs, he was told. He looked through his field glasses and noted two machine guns, as he put it, "looking down my throat." Colonel Sloane, the regimental commander who had sent Barberis to the ridgeline, had been told earlier in the day that there might be two Chinese companies up there. Instead, according to Malcolm MacDonald, the intelligence officer, it was minimally two regiments, around six thousand men. Now Barberis called Sloane and told him, "I'm four thousand yards from my assembly area and I see enemy positions. I think I've got my tit in a wringer." Then the Chinese machine guns opened up. "All hell broke loose," Barberis said. His unit was quickly attacked from the other side of the road as well. He called Sloane, who told him to come back for a conference. Then the Chinese struck with mortars, and Barberis was wounded for the second time. The retreat down the road south had barely begun, and the road was already littered with the dead and with disabled vehicles.

IT WAS DUTCH Keiser himself who told Captain Jim Hinton, the company commander of the Thirty-eighth Tank Company, to take his tanks and lead the way south. Hinton had his tanks lined up at the very head of the column when Keiser walked up to him and said, "We've got a little roadblock down there, about two hundred or four hundred yards deep. Do you think you can get through?" Hinton answered—thinking almost the moment the words were out of his mouth what a smart-ass he was, thirty-five years old and cocky as hell. "Well, General, I've been running roadblocks for five days, so I guess I can run another one." Privately, Hinton had grave doubts about going south. He had done his own recon two or three miles down the Anju road, the one that went out west, that many of the officers wanted to try, and it looked open to him. It was, for a Korean road, not bad, if anything even a little wider than most. The one thing he understood in the midst of all the uncertainty was that the men giving the orders that day had no earthly idea of what they were doing. The roadblock that Keiser had mentioned to him, allegedly about two hundred to four hundred yards long, was in reality several miles long.

Hinton decided to use Sam Mace to lead the convoy—an easy choice, for Mace was his best man. So he ordered Mace to take his five tanks and clear the road south to Sunchon. They started out, Mace up front, and Hinton in a jeep two or three vehicles back, followed by more tanks and then infantry loaded up on big deuce-and-a-half trucks. They had gone several hundred yards when the Chinese opened up from both sides. Hinton was immediately hit in the wrist. His exec officer called in and said that they were sitting ducks out there, and Hinton replied that no one had to tell a sitting duck that it was a sitting duck. So he amended his order to Mace. It was now How Able, or in translatable, basic English, Haul Ass. A roadblock of four hundred yards at most, the hell you say, Hinton thought bitterly. This one looked like it went on forever. They had walked right into one of the largest ambushes in American military history.

Mace thought the exact same thing. He had been told that when he headed south he was to clear the enemy out and then meet up with a British armored unit that was heading north. Well, a small roadblock, he could take care of that. But the road was a skinny one. It was immediately apparent that it could easily be blocked by just one disabled tank or overturned heavy truck. There was a high bank on the eastern side that might have been designed for a prolonged ambush. Mace's five tanks were to lead a convoy interspersed with trucks and with some infantrymen riding on top of the tanks to help control the road and suppress, if need be, Chinese fire from the high ground. From the start, Mace's tanks took heavy fire from the hillside. It was a slow, wildly dangerous start-and-stop process, of letting the infantrymen off the tanks and then firing back to suppress Chinese fire; Mace had a profound sense of foreboding that he and his men had somehow become bit players in a script written by the enemy.

Among the infantrymen was Lieutenant Charley Heath of the Thirty-eighth Regiment. About a quarter mile into the journey, Mace came upon an abandoned M-39 vehicle blocking the road. There had already been other vehicles in their way, and Mace had been able to tank-doze them off to the side. The M-39 was big and its tracks were locked. But Mace was one of those men who seemed to know how to do everything. He yelled out for someone to unlock the tracks, and Charley Heath suddenly appeared, a target for every Chinese soldier on the heights. That's a good man, Mace thought, and he yelled out instructions on how to move the levers to release the tracks. Out of that moment came a lifelong friendship begun in what both thought was a curious place, on that god-awful, narrow road, the Chinese firing away from both sides, men getting killed all around them. Heath felt like bait for the Chinese until finally he got the levers right and the wheels released, and Mace smashed the M-39 to the side. On the way back to his tank, Heath suffered a concussion when an American fighter-bomber dropped a rocket a bit too close, and soon he could barely see because his eyes began to bleed from the effect of the explosion. Still, he had made it to the M-39 and back alive. Lucky Charley, he had thought to himself, at least so far.

A little later, Mace swung his tank around a sharp curve and almost froze. There ahead of him, about three miles away by his reckoning, he could see the section of the road called The Pass. Here, for about five hundred yards, the road had been cut through what appeared to be one large hill. The banks on *both* sides were very sharp and steep—and the passage was exceedingly tight. As he got closer, it seemed as if any enemy soldier on either side could almost reach out and touch the American vehicles. If the Chinese knocked out even one or two of them in The Pass, Mace thought they might be able to stop this already cumbersome American convoy from getting out. As he finally drove his tank into The Pass, he wondered for an instant if it might not be the last thing he would ever do in his life. But to his surprise, the world did not explode.

The Pass was already littered with vehicles—the ruins of the Turkish convoy that had been torn apart the day before—the carcasses of jeeps, weapons carriers, two-and-a-half-ton trucks, a grand trail of useless metal that the Chinese could now use against the Americans. Mace did not know whether he was more scared or angry at that moment, because this wreckage clearly had been there some time and no one had said a thing about it. Where the hell had any aerial recon been? he wondered. Corps had lots of spotter planes. Why hadn't Division known on its own? So he cleared the road as best he could. It was a miserable, dangerous job, but he was lucky, he thought later—though if there were such a thing as real luck, he wouldn't have been in Korea at all—the Chinese had not yet filled in positions on either side of the road, and so the firing was lighter than it would be later in the day. Mace and another tank driver rammed everything in sight out of the way, maybe thirty or forty vehicles. If they hadn't, the disaster that day might have been immeasurably worse. As he finished trying to clear the area, Mace wondered briefly why Keiser had not sent one of his own men along and used Mace's tank as a recon vehicle, or at least had a light spotter plane flying overhead. When they finally pushed through, Mace and his men were the only members of the Second Division who knew just how dangerous the road south was—how many Chinese were already gathered there, with at least forty machine guns, he was sure, as well as countless mortars trained on the road. He knew as well that the British were not going to be of any help—but there was no way to get word back to Keiser's headquarters because his tank radio did not connect with Keiser's. It was the perfect preamble for the disaster still to come.

Mace found an American and British position just to the south of The Pass. Some of the Americans felt that the British had not tried very hard to fight their way through, and the British in turn felt that the Americans were expecting them to work miracles. An American colonel rushed over and told Mace to turn his tanks around and go back, but he answered no way, there was just no room on the road. He had done his best to clear it. Then he watched the convoy dribble through ever more slowly, the noise from the battle becoming louder as ever more Chinese manned The Pass with ever heavier weapons. Some of the Americans who emerged alive after coming through The Pass seemed so badly shaken that to Mace they appeared more like the living dead. What had been for a time a small hell was in the process of becoming a very big hell, he thought.

CAPTAIN ALAN JONES, the Ninth Regiment's S-2, had watched the day turn into a nightmare, almost minute by minute. The intelligence had been hopeless really. Communications between different units and the commanders had gotten worse throughout the day, especially after the senior officers left the CP and headed south. If the Americans named one particularly bad stretch The Pass, they came up with a fitting name for the entire cruel six miles from Kunuri to Sunchon. The Gauntlet, they called it—for they were men who had to run The Gauntlet. The first thing Jones was aware of as he moved through The Gauntlet was that he was witnessing the complete breakdown of order and hierarchy. In the Army, structure was believed to be everything, and this day the structure had simply disappeared. Once it was gone, it was very hard to get back. Altogether too many units had simply disintegrated, and there was less and less command structure all the time.

What he was witnessing was nothing less than the destruction of much of an American division right in front of his eyes, something he would never be able to forget. A vehicle would be hit, and it would block the road for others, and some brave soul would try to move it aside, and all the while the Chinese would be pouring fire down on them. Bodies lay right in the middle of the road—some possibly still alive, for all anyone knew—and the driver of the next truck or jeep would have no choice in that narrow passage but to run right over them. Sometimes a driver might hesitate, and if he did, his vehicle instantly became the next target, and the convoy would be slowed just that much more. The men themselves more often than not seemed numbed by it. Some of them just huddled along the side of the road, and sometimes it was hard for Jones to tell who was dead and who was wounded, and who was simply paralyzed—men whose bodies still functioned but whose spirits were broken.

It was hard to estimate the time of day, but Jones believed he had gotten onto the road about 2 P.M. His orders were simple. Colonel Sloane had told

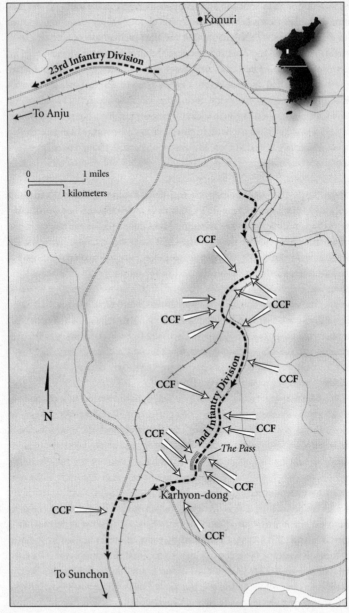

16. THE GAUNTLET, NOVEMBER 30, 1950

him to get through to Sunchon and set up an assembly point for the rest of the regiment. Jones's jeep was hit fairly early on, and his driver was wounded, but he managed to get the driver into another vehicle. When he got back to his own jeep, its engine had been hit and it had stopped running. He managed to push it off the road and began walking. From time to time he was able to gather some men, all from different outfits, around him in a hastily formed mini-unit, and they would return fire in quick little spasms of combat, and then in the confusion the group would disintegrate, and a little farther along another unit would form up around him. The men, beaten, emptied out physically and spiritually, and leaderless, were caught in something that was simply too big for them; a few were able to fight back, but as the command structure was gone, so was much of their will to fight.

The one thing he had decided was that he was going to walk out and fight another day, or he was going to die on that road trying. He was not going to be captured again by anyone. He had gone about four miles down the road on foot when he happened to look up and see a Chinese gunner pointing a machine gun right at him. It was a rare thing, Jones thought, to catch a glimpse of a man who intended to kill you. There was no doubt that he was Chinese, and that he was manning an American 30-caliber machine gun. He was about a hundred yards away, midway on the forward slope of a hill. Jones could see the muzzle flashes even as he dove for a ditch at the side of the road. As he did, he was hit in the foot. Under other circumstances, it might not have seemed like such a terrible wound, but the bullet tore that foot apart and there was a lot of bleeding, and when he tried to put a tourniquet on it, he kept losing consciousness.

Now effectively he had only one foot. He was sure he was going to die. Just then a jeep drove by with Captain Lucian Truscott III, Captain John Carley, and a third officer inside. They saw Jones struggling with his wound—he looked purple, Carley remembered—and they stopped. Truscott carried Jones to the jeep, and the third officer bandaged his foot. Somehow they made it to Sunchon, though Jones had little memory of the rest of the ride. He never learned the name of the officer who had bandaged his foot. He was soon flown to a hospital in Japan. More than fifty years later, Jones was living in a special Army retirement home near Fort Belvoir, when one day he noticed a newcomer and asked if he wanted to join him for lunch. They were both, it turned out, Korean veterans, both former members of the Second Division. In fact both had been caught in The Gauntlet. At a certain point Bill (Hawk) Wood looked at Jones and asked, "Say, you wouldn't be the officer whose foot I bandaged that day on the road to Sunchon, would you?"

MALCOLM MACDONALD, THE young intelligence officer who had been caught in heavy fire when the Chinese raked Division headquarters on the night of the twenty-ninth, started November 30 by checking the headquarters area. There he found the body of a young friend of his, Lieutenant William Fitzpatrick; he had taken a bullet in the head the previous night. MacDonald had seen a good deal of death in those few days, but the death of someone he knew and liked seemed to mark the day from the start. Later that morning, he was standing outside headquarters with a young photo-interpreter, Private John McKitch, when the Chinese snipers began shooting again. McKitch was hit in the upper arm. Just a little less wind and he gets it in the head, MacDonald thought, and a little more wind and I get it in the gut. The fact that the snipers were zeroing in on them was a sure sign that it was time to go. Then the order to get out came down. Each man could bring his weapon, his ammo, a first aid kit, and a canteen of water. They had to leave their duffels and their arctic sleeping bags—the very few who had them—behind. MacDonald went out in the jeep of Lieutenant Colonel Ralph Foster, the division G-2, and it was start-and-stop all the way, under constant fire.

It was a day of tears, MacDonald thought years later. Some men wept and others perhaps should have. At one point, as they were coming up on The Pass, the convoy stopped and MacDonald walked toward the head of the column to find out what the delay was. Along the way, he saw Butch Barberis, commander of the Second Battalion of the Ninth Regiment, standing by the side of the road. Bullets were landing everywhere, but Barberis seemed immune to danger, in no way afraid of the Chinese, but not moving either. He and MacDonald had been friends, young officers of roughly the same age posted together back at Fort Lewis before the war, and MacDonald had always thought of Barberis as perhaps the single most fearless officer he knew. It was just like Barberis to stand there contemptuous of enemy fire, rallying his troops, MacDonald thought. Then he noticed that Barberis was weeping. "Mac," his friend said, "I've lost my whole battalion."

On that retreat, just when you thought you had been through the worst of it, there was something worse ahead, something to haunt you for the rest of your life. As they came to The Pass, the convoy began to pick up speed, and MacDonald, by now leading one subsection of it, drove as quickly as he could, because there was safety in speed, and death at every stop. As he came around a big curve, making what was on that road fairly good time, MacDonald saw a two-and-a-half-ton truck lying on its side, and alongside it a bunch of GIs trying to flag him down, pleading with him or anyone else in the convoy to stop. It was as if the entire scene were taking place in slow motion. He did not have to hear them to know what they were saying, that they believed they were going to die unless he helped them.

It was, thought MacDonald, the worst moment of the worst day of his life. If he stopped, he feared, the Chinese would hammer the convoy and then block the road again. He had his mission—to get a jeep already loaded with wounded out and make room for those other vehicles. So he hardened himself and just kept driving. "I said a prayer for those poor souls there along the road and I asked for their forgiveness," he remembered years later. When he finally reached a small ford at the end of The Pass, one that the Chinese were covering with a devastatingly accurate machine gun, he was sure that he was not going to be able to cross. But then a B-26 came in on a napalm run and took out the machine gun. Finally across, MacDonald had a hard time grasping that he was actually going to live. Of one thing he was sure—none of the men who had been there that day was ever going to be quite the same again.

DUTCH KEISER LEFT his headquarters in the early afternoon. By the time he went out, he was well aware that his division was caught in a trap of monstrous proportions. He and the other senior officers had given up their vans to the wounded. He was not in good shape. He had been fighting a cold for several days and left wrapped in a parka. The journey out did not favor generals much more than it did enlisted men. At one point Maury Holden, the G-3, was kneeling behind a jeep firing into the nearest Chinese position next to Major Bill Harrington, the assistant G-2. Suddenly Harrington fell over on top of him, shot right through the heart.

Even with the constant fire, Keiser and his group moved reasonably well until they neared The Pass. Then the convoy stalled. So Keiser and the others got out of their jeeps, witnessing the same physical and emotional destruction that so many others had seen. For the first time he realized how completely it had already unraveled—the sheer scope of the tragedy. He was shocked by how few of his men were firing back. He moved among them, shouting, "Who's in command here? . . . Can't any of you do anything?" He finally decided to recon The

Pass himself and began to walk it, at one point trying to step over a body in his path. Tired, he did not get his foot high enough and stepped on the body by mistake. Suddenly, the body spoke: "You damned son of a bitch!" The voice stunned Keiser and he found himself apologizing—"My friend, I'm sorry"—before continuing on his way. It was an epitaph for the day. There was death all around him, and he understood that it did not matter how little help he had gotten from Corps. It was all his responsibility. It was the destruction of *his* division and it was intensely personal. Corporal Jake Thorpe, Keiser's bodyguard, who had dedicated his life to protecting him, had been killed that afternoon while manning their jeep's machine gun. At first, they had placed Thorpe's body in the back of the jeep, but eventually, because there were so many wounded lying along the road, they had had to leave it by the roadside in order to make room. That was a hard thing to do, leaving behind the body of a man who had given his life protecting you.

WHEN GENE TAKAHASHI finally made it through The Gauntlet, he was stunned by what had happened to his company, his battalion, and his regiment. He had known it was bad, but it had been so much worse than he had realized. Love Company was down to about a dozen men. As far as he could tell, he was the only officer left—all the others had either been killed, seriously wounded, or were missing in action. When they had an assembly a few days later near Seoul, only 10 men of the original 170 of Love Company were there. Of the 600 men in Takahashi's battalion, only 125 to 150 made it through. As combat units, Love and King companies, which had been on point for the division when the Chinese assault began, no longer existed. The Third Battalion barely existed. And the Ninth Regiment was well under half strength.

AS OTHER UNITS from the Second Division were being torn up on the Sunchon road, Paul Freeman was trying to save his regiment. In the days after the initial Chinese attack, some of his frustration showed over the fact that he had sensed accurately what was coming and his superiors had ignored him. He told Reginald Thompson of the London *Daily Telegraph* how well the Chinese had been fighting despite their limited hardware. "Without air and artillery they're making us look a little silly in this godawful country." On the morning of the thirtieth, his Twenty-third Regiment was the last barrier between the rest of the Second Division and the massive Chinese forces closing in from the north. Its job was to hold the Kunuri perimeter for as long as possible and then follow the Ninth and the Thirty-eighth down the Sunchon road. But Freeman could see that going south was hopeless.

Freeman had been spending a lot of time with his own artillery officers,

Paul O'Dowd, the forward observer for the Fifteenth Field Artillery Battalion, noticed. He was always checking in, asking what they were hearing, and there was a good reason for that, because when all the other forms of communications were breaking down, the artillery generally had the best communications left. The artillery *had* to have good communications; if they didn't, they risked killing their own troops. So they had their own spotter planes, and their reports from the field were very good, or at least very good on the scale of communications that existed by then. They knew from the start that the road south was only for the dead and dying. O'Dowd, who had been studying Freeman, knew immediately what he was up to, and decided that he was a damn smart officer. Other division officers tended to categorize the artillery as a unit to which you gave orders, not one you listened to. Because of what he was hearing, Freeman decided relatively early in the day to go out on the Anju road, the route Shrimp Milburn had offered to Keiser.

By noon on the thirtieth, Freeman's position was already desperate. He knew he had very little time left. He could actually see the masses of Chinese troops who had crossed the Chongchon, and he told Division of his growing vulnerability. What made his circumstances even more difficult was how poor his communications with Division were with Keiser on the move. Soon, he could reach Division only through Chin Sloane's jeep radio, with Sloane, commander of the sister Ninth Regiment, designated to relay messages as best he could to Keiser. Then he lost even that connection. In the early afternoon, Freeman was still trying for permission to go out west. He finally reached Colonel Gerry Epley, the division chief of staff, and Epley told him he could not change his orders. Then the communications got even worse.

Sometime later Freeman reached Sloane and asked if Sladen Bradley, the assistant division commander, could call him—he desperately needed permission to switch his orders. About two-thirty, Bradley called and Freeman made his case to go out west. The decision had to be made immediately—and they had to move before night fell: the Chinese were being held off only by superior American firepower, principally the artillery. With darkness, the enemy would be able to move at will, and Freeman's regiment would be doomed. He wanted to leave by the Anju road about two hours before dark. About 4 P.M. Bradley, who had been unable to reach Keiser, called back and gave him permission to do whatever was best for his regiment. Freeman then asked the commanders of units still remaining in the Kunuri area if they wanted to go out with him. Some chose to, some did not.

It was getting toward dusk, and everyone knew how bad the whole thing was. Paul O'Dowd was with the artillerymen who by then were buttoning up their guns, preparatory for the last move. If they went south, it was going to be a very bad trip, they all knew, because they had two spotter planes flying over the road and the reports on the destruction were shocking. It sounded like a massacre to O'Dowd. But for the moment he had only one job, getting those guns out of there. Lieutenant Colonel John Keith of the Fifteenth Field Artillery Battalion had told him to load up their guns, and he was doing just that, sure that they had fired their last round in the Kunuri region. Just then one of his forward observers, First Lieutenant Patrick McMullan, showed up and started screaming, "Fire mission! Fucking Chinese! Fire mission! Fucking Chinese everywhere! Fire mission!" O'Dowd had never seen McMullan so out of control—he thought maybe he was drunk, for some of the men in other units had been drinking that day. "Fire mission! More fucking Chinese!"

"We're on closed station march orders," O'Dowd told him, which was the exact phrase they used for the moment when they had closed it up and were ready to get out. But gradually O'Dowd got more information: the Chinese were moving in for the kill right out in the open in daylight, seemingly thousands of them. Just then Colonel Freeman walked by and asked O'Dowd what was going on, and O'Dowd explained what McMullan had seen. "Get the goddamn guns into fire positions," Freeman ordered.

There they were, all those Chinese, perhaps five thousand yards away, a vast field of them closing in just as McMullan had said. Freeman told the men that their mission was to delay the Chinese, even if they did not get out in time themselves, even if they did not get out at all. The regiment, Freeman later remembered, unloaded all its weapons and ammo, and the men laid everything out in front of them. This is where they were going to make their last stand, he thought, and quite possibly die. The artillerymen had unloaded the big 105s from the trucks and pointed them in one direction—eighteen howitzers in all, the last guns of Kunuri. It was called a Russian front in the artillery. Paul O'Dowd had fought in two wars, survived the worst of the Naktong fighting, and he had never seen anything like this. Everyone in the unit—cooks, clerk typists—helped take shells off the trucks and carry them to the guns. They fired everything they had in what seemed to O'Dowd about twenty minutes, though it probably took longer. There was a lot of ammo because they had shells that two other artillery units had left behind. They were firing so fast that the guns were overheating and the paint was peeling, just rolling off the guns in giant chunks. The recoil systems on those guns were going to be ruined, O'Dowd decided, but there was no time to worry about that. He was just a little scared that the chambers were so hot the guns might blow.

It was an apocalyptic moment. The noise was deafening, eighteen guns that never stopped. How many rounds went out in that brief span—three, four, five thousand? Who knew? And then, suddenly, it was over. They had fired their last shell. After all that noise, the silence was overwhelming. Then they destroyed the guns with thermite charges, so the Chinese could not use them. They had completely stopped the Chinese attack, and Freeman believed that, even more important, the Chinese had dug into defensive positions, because an artillery barrage like that often signaled the coming of an infantry attack. The last orders Freeman gave were "Get the hell out of here, and don't stop!" The road to Anju was completely open and the Twenty-third ran into very little Chinese resistance.

33

I F THE SECOND DIVISION was the tail end of the Eighth Army now heading south, then the Second Engineers were at the very end of the tail, the last
of the units to go out. Gino Piazza, who had fought so well with Dog Company
of the Second Engineers during the worst of the Naktong fighting, thought
that November 30 was the worst day of his life. For the first time, he was sure
he was going to die. As far as he could tell, many of the officers at more senior
levels had bailed on the men. A number of the officers in the Second Engineers
had gone out in a group. There had been one young second lieutenant, John
Sullivan, whom Piazza particularly liked and who had wanted to stay with the
men because he thought that was what officers were supposed to do, but he
had gotten his orders, and so had said good-bye to Piazza—in tears. All too
many of the officers whose job it was to get the Second Engineers into the
larger convoy had in Piazza's opinion just been goddamned old-fashioned
cowards who did not give a damn about the men. "It was the moment of truth,
the moment when you needed your officers most, and they were trying to separate all the officers from the men and ferry them out by themselves—turning
the retreat into some kind of officer's club for safety!" Piazza said.

Engineers do not move lightly, something infantry commanders often
seemed to forget. For more than a week before the Chinese made their initial
strike, the Engineers' commander, Colonel Alarich Zacherle, had been pushing
Division to make a decision on all their heavy construction gear, the bulldozers and heavy trucks loaded with bridging equipment, which was at the heart
of what engineers did. In any military convoy, Zacherle had tried to remind
them, this would make the Engineers the slowest of the slow and the easiest of
targets, slowing down everyone else. Zacherle wanted permission to send the
heavy stuff back four or five days before the Chinese attacked. They were sure
as hell not going to build anything new this far north. There would never be an
instant airstrip to sit alongside the Yalu River. Each day when Piazza had asked
Zacherle if they had a decision on the heavy equipment, the colonel would
simply shake his head—and there was an implication, Piazza thought, in the

way he answered that Zacherle did not think the men in charge knew what the hell they were doing. And so they were stuck with all that heavy gear now.

The night before the final retreat, Zacherle had visited Gerry Epley, the Division chief of staff, to find out what was going on. Epley had then invited him to go out with some of the Division staff. Zacherle was surprised by the offer. No, he had answered, he would go out with his own men. He thought that was the right way to do it. He was already—at least, so some of his men thought—badly shaken by the damage inflicted on his unit. The Second Engineers had lost up to two hundred of their nine hundred men in the first seventy-two hours of the Chinese attack. Zacherle had always taken his command quite personally and was proud of the fact that he knew—or at least thought he knew—every man in the battalion by name. In most circumstances such an attitude greatly aided morale. But now his affection for and commitment to his men made things harder for him.

So the Engineers were going to have to go out late, and they were going to have to go out burdened with all their heavy equipment, waiting for their place, which would be near the end of that cumbersome main convoy. They were all formed up, Dog Company in the lead, Headquarters Company next, followed by Able, Baker, and Charley companies. As the afternoon moved along, though, there was a growing sense that the situation was hopeless—word kept filtering back to the waiting units that the convoy was being torn up just a mile or two down the road. There they were, Piazza thought, ever so patiently waiting their turn to be part of a growing disaster. Piazza was in the lead jeep. They were told they would get their slot in the convoy around 4 P.M., but the convoy was moving ever more slowly and the time was being pushed back. Soon it was dusk and they hadn't moved; then dusk had gone and it was getting darker. The 503rd Field Artillery passed them with its heavy guns. The Engineers were next. Just then five trucks from one of the artillery units cut in front of them, five big deuce-and-a-halfs. Normally, Piazza hated anyone doing that, but in this case he felt more philosophical—you want it, big guys, he thought, you're welcome to it.

Then his jeep led the Second Engineers into the convoy. Everyone was scared to death. They were in the convoy only thirty minutes, the artillery trucks just ahead of them, when the artillerymen came upon a small cut in the road, hills on both sides, and suddenly, in Piazza's words, all hell broke loose. It was as if the Chinese had been waiting expressly for the artillery and its carriers, all those big guns in those big trucks, moving so slowly, and they struck with their perfectly sighted mortars. The firestorm was overpowering—the artillerymen had driven into the perfect trap within a trap. The trucks simply exploded, one after another. Five had entered the trap; five were now on fire. All those men, surely some Piazza had gone drinking with over the years, blown up just like that, one moment as alive as he was and then gone. If you sat down to dream up the worst possible scenario for your buddies, this would be it. In real life, he thought, you were supposed to wake up and find out that it was only a nightmare, but there was no waking up from this. You could not move forward; you could not move back; and right in front of you, hundreds of men whom less than an hour ago you had lightly cursed for cutting into the line, were dying.

TO GINO PIAZZA, the convoy seemed completely stalled. Then he heard a new set of orders. "Abandon your vehicles and assemble on the side of the road! Abandon your vehicles and assemble on the side of the road!" No one even knew where the orders came from or who had given them. So the men of the Second Engineers began to leave their vehicles and scramble up the hill on their right. Piazza wanted to blow up their trucks, which had a lot of communications gear he did not want the Chinese to capture, but he was told the Air Force would fly over the next day and blow them up for them. For the first time since he had been in Korea, Piazza found himself truly despairing. He sensed that his will to survive, which had helped sustain him during the Naktong fighting, was leaving him. He had never been especially religious, but now he started to pray. His prayers were very specific. He offered prayers for the souls in purgatory. That went back to his childhood in Brooklyn. It was the prayer his mother always offered up when something bad happened. Her explanation was quite simple: If you had lived a good life, then you went to heaven. But if you hadn't, and the chances were that Gino Piazza, given his myriad flaws and imperfections, had not, then the more prayers you offered for the souls in purgatory, the less they suffered—and maybe it would help you as well when you got there.

Strangely enough, it seemed to work, or at least it worked for him at that moment. At the very least it calmed him. He realized that in such chaos no one else was going to save him, so he had to save himself. If the Chinese wanted his ass, he decided, they were going to have to come and get it. There were a lot of men gathering on that hill, hundreds, he thought, maybe even a thousand. No one seemed to be in charge—so he might as well lead. He formed up one group and started for the crest, and his band seemed to grow larger by the minute because no one else seemed to be leading. The Chinese spotted them and raked their area with machine gun fire, which sent some of the men racing downhill again. A few NCOs who were helping Piazza tried to stop them, because when they were on the road they became perfect targets, but it was too late. They had broken when the machine gun opened up. Piazza doubted whether many of them ever made it out.

* * *

WHAT ALARICH ZACHERLE remembered most about the day when the Chinese captured much of his unit was how bad the communications were. No one seemed able to reach anyone else. It wasn't the fault of the radio operators—they stayed at their stations at the expense of their own safety— just poor equipment, and very poor leadership. He was supposed to come out near the end of the convoy, with the Twenty-third Regiment right behind him, and on a number of occasions each unit failed in its attempt to reach the other. Years later, long after Zacherle had returned from his two and a half years in a prison camp, he finally met Paul Freeman, who assured him he had tried to reach him several times to tell him the original plan was being abandoned, that his regiment was going out on the west road, and the Engineers should come with them. It had been a tense moment, because Freeman's unit had made it out relatively unscathed, while so many of Zacherle's men had been killed or captured. "Hell, yes, we would have loved to come out with you," Zacherle told Freeman, and assured him that he bore him no animus. What had happened that day, Zacherle believed, was the fortunes of war.

Back at his spot where the Engineers were waiting, Zacherle knew it was all coming to an end. The road wasn't going to open up; not for heavy equipment, that was for sure. Even before the end, Zacherle gave the order to blow up some of the heavier stuff, the trucks and bulldozers. They used phosphorous grenades to burn the gears. Then, sometime in the very late afternoon, with the Chinese closing in, they burned the unit colors. He and the other officers did not want the Chinese to capture them and flaunt them. They were in a wooden box, and Zacherle ordered an extra dose of gasoline poured on them. Burning the colors, that told it all. Then it was time to start walking out. The Engineers were more vulnerable than other units—they were known as *combat* engineers, and they might be used as infantry, but they had no automatic weapons and no mortars. In any confrontation with the Chinese they would be seriously underarmed.

Bob Nehrling, battalion adjutant for the Second Engineers, knew that it was all over too. They had started the day as part of a blocking force for Division headquarters, and they were a unit, Nehrling decided later, that could be sacrificed. Somebody, somewhere up the chain of command had decided that. Nehrling was with a group of about thirty-five staff officers from Battalion, and Zacherle had told them that they were going to have to get out as best they could. They never had a chance, Nehrling thought. They had barely moved from their waiting point near the road when suddenly there were Chinese everywhere, as surprised to come across them as they were to be surrounded. The Chinese who captured them were headed south, and so for a time they too kept going south, the group of prisoners increasing steadily as stragglers from the Ninth and Thirty-eighth regiments were captured. Pretty soon they had about twenty infantry officers with them as well as engineers. It was the beginning of a terrible time, from which very few of them made it back.

GINO PIAZZA TRUSTED his instincts in no small part because he had nothing else to go on. It was dark by then and no one had a compass. Piazza had a general sense that they needed to head southeast, and he knew the terrain better than most because he had done some recon earlier on, looking for mines in the area. He managed to line up the general direction he wanted by sighting on two stars—it was the most primitive kind of compass sighting—and soon he found an old railroad spur heading that way for them to walk along. His group—maybe five hundred at tops, and two hundred at its smallest—took fire constantly. Piazza, with a carbine and several hundred rounds of ammo, was careful to fire only when he had a target. When it was over, he had very few rounds left, so he knew he had been firing through much of the night.

Some of the officers in his group kept wanting to turn right—as if some tidal pull were affecting them—a direction that would surely bring them back where they had started out, but gradually, in the mysterious way that these things work, Piazza took command of this bedraggled unit. He seemed the only one with the requisite confidence. Eventually, in a clearing, they came across another group whose leader, an officer, wanted to dig in for the night. But Piazza argued with him. They could not dig in, he insisted; they lacked the weaponry to hold the Chinese off, and the Chinese were right on top of them. In the end, they kept going as Piazza wanted. Once, from a high point, they looked down and spotted a tunnel on the tracks below. Some of the men wanted to go down there, as if a tunnel were the perfect hiding place. Piazza told them not to, but a number went anyway. It was exactly where the Chinese would look first, he believed. What looked safe was not safe; what looked hard and unsafe was probably safer. Anyway, safe was somewhere else in the world.

Finally, they spotted the main Kunuri-Sunchon road. Some of the men wanted to go down immediately, because it looked like the easiest way out. The road, Piazza understood, represented the familiar to American troops and they found comfort in the familiar. He had to fight that impulse not just in himself but in the men he was leading. When some soldiers peeled off from the group and made for the road anyway, the Chinese opened up on them immediately. Gradually, Piazza sorted out command functions with other NCOs, so they could have some structure if he was hit. He even found an officer, Lieutenant Wilbur Webster, from the Eighty-second AAA, or Anti-Aircraft Artillery, an antiaircraft unit used thus far as an infantry weapon, and suggested he take over, but Webster said, "No, Sergeant Piazza, you're doing just fine." And so they slowly worked their way along the high ground, resisting the temptation of the easy, and they eventually made it back. Perhaps three hundred men came out with Piazza. He thought the prayers to those in purgatory had made the difference.

PERHAPS NO UNIT in the Second Division was hit as hard as the Second Engineers. When the retreat was over and they assembled near Seoul, it seemed as if each man stood where once an entire platoon or squad might have been. Gino Piazza, who became a kind of ex officio historian of the group, believed that there had been about 900 men in the battalion as it was moving north. There were a total of 266 men in that final formation, he remembered. Perhaps as many as 500 men had been lost in that one day—it was a ghost battalion now. You couldn't be exact on the figures, Piazza believed, because some of the men had been back in rear echelon positions and had not been hit by the Chinese. But it had been a terrible day. The Second Engineers, Piazza later reflected, with untempered bitterness, paid an unusually high price for the stupidity and arrogance of other men.

LATE IN THE afternoon, Paul Freeman started moving his regiment west toward Anju. After it was all over, there was some muted criticism of him, because he had come out a different route and had not protected the rear of the convoy. But most of the men who knew what happened that day thought he had done the right thing—that whatever terrible fate befell the other units in the convoy, Freeman's regiment would not have made any difference, because the assault had not come from the rear, it had come from the retreat itself, from the Chinese already in position firing as the division came into their sights. Freeman, most observers thought, had not only done the right thing but had done an exceptional job in responding to changing battlefield pressures and saving what would have been an otherwise doomed unit.

Night was falling as the Twenty-third went west out of Kunuri. They had no idea at what moment the Chinese might strike and cut the Anju road—only that if it happened, they would be bound to the road and badly outnumbered. By chance, the key bridge on the approach to Anju was still in American hands. A company from the Fifth Regimental Combat Team, a part of First Corps, had been sent there to cover its own corps' retreat. The company commander was a young captain named Hank Emerson, who went on to considerable fame as one of the most audacious commanders during the Vietnam War, when his nickname became The Gunfighter.

At that moment, Emerson's orders—absolutely terrifying, since the Chinese in great numbers were on the move south—were to try to hold that bridge until the late afternoon. He had one company with which to do it. Chinese divisions were headed right at him, and the cold was a brutal enemy all its own. (He still remembered quite precisely more than half a century later that the temperature that day hit twenty-three below.) As Emerson waited, he began to think about something that he would ponder for much of his career: what was it like for a unit of infantrymen who believed that those above them had decided they were more or less expendable as part of a larger need for the rest of a division's survival? Were they some kind of unfortunate offering to the gods of battle? As darkness settled in and the cold only deepened, Emerson's tension grew. Just when he thought he might be able to leave, a small American spotter plane was shot down nearby, an unwanted sign of just how close the Chinese were.

Emerson and his men had been assigned to rescue the downed flyers, when he happened to look up. There, coming from the east, was an immense caravan of American troops heading toward his bridge. There had been no heads-up from his superiors about an American unit coming through. As far as he could tell, communications being what they were, no one from First Corps knew this unit was coming out. It was like a vast lost patrol appearing out of nowhere, the men looking exhausted and bedraggled, but somehow proud and determined as well. Some men, those who could, were walking, others were crowded into trucks and on top of tanks, sometimes on top of one another. The column stretched as far as he could see. Someone passing by told Emerson they were from the Twenty-third Infantry Regiment.

What Emerson remembered best about that day—other than the fact that when he radioed in, he was then ordered by his superiors to give the Twenty-third all his trucks, which meant that his own men eventually came back riding on the outside of his tanks—was that the commander of the Twenty-third came in on the last vehicle, a jeep with a mounted machine gun. Emerson immediately understood the meaning of that—a commander who had made himself one of the most vulnerable members of his outfit should the Chinese catch up with them. The last man out, Emerson thought, that's good; that's what a real commander does. The commander, whose name was Paul Freeman, stopped briefly to talk to him, and was very cool, and very much in command—as if something like this, taking a regiment down a back road to escape three or four Chinese divisions, was something he did every day.

"Son, what outfit is this holding this bridge?" he asked.

He has no more idea who we are than I do who he is, Emerson thought. "Sir, this is Company A of the Fifth Regimental Combat Team."

"Well, son, God bless Company A of the Fifth Regimental Combat team. Thank you for what you're doing here." And then Paul Freeman passed through, and not long after, Company A pulled out as well. The last units whacked by the Chinese from the west side of the peninsula were now headed south for safer positions and with luck—if that was the word—preparing to fight another day.

It had been one of the worst days in the history of the American Army, surely the worst in the history of the Second Infantry Division, at the end of the worst week in the division's history. The numbers were heartbreaking. In those finals days of November, the Ninth Regiment had lost an estimated 1,474 men (including non-battle casualties, which usually meant frostbite); the Thirty-eighth Regiment, 1,178; and the Twenty-third, 545. The Second Engineers had lost some 561 men to battle casualties. An infantry regiment had an authorized strength of about 3,800 men; when it was time to regroup, the Ninth had only about 1,400 men left; the Thirty-eighth, 1,700; and the Twenty-third, 2,200.

LIEUTENANT CHARLEY HEATH had never dared think he would make it out alive. But because he had gone out with the first group of tanks, he was one of the first to arrive, and he had been able to watch the other men from the division as the fortunate ones reached Sunchon. Every story seemed to be worse than the last, as the Chinese presence along The Gauntlet had grown stronger, and he heard stories about so many friends who had died that day. But there was one scene that he always remembered: his regimental commander, Colonel George Peploe, just standing there weeping. There had been moments when Peploe had seemed to those who served under him almost unbearably cocky, but this was a different man; it was as if he had been wounded, but all the wounds were on the inside. He was standing there crying, unable to stop, when one of his battalion commanders, Lieutenant Colonel Jim Skeldon, came over and held him and tried to steady him, more for emotional than physical reasons. But Peploe could not stop weeping, and then Skeldon, in the most tender of acts at the end of the most violent of days, took off his helmet and held it up to shield Peploe from the view of others, so no one else would be able to observe him crying. Though Peploe had lived when so many of his men died, it had clearly been a kind of death for him as well.

34

THE LEADERSHIP AT the top in the Second Division had been terrible. By contrast, because O. P. Smith had anticipated what the Chinese were going to do, the Marines were in much better shape. Their regiments were by no means perfectly connected, and still very vulnerable to being separated, and not nearly as close to their base at the port of Hungnam as Smith would have liked. The forward units near Yudam-ni were still far too exposed, and out on much more of a limb than Smith preferred, but at least they were somewhat better connected because he had stood up to Almond. Still, the vulnerability was unnerving. But at least they were not chasing wildly to the west to link up with the Eighth Army, as his orders had originally demanded. There was very little about their subsequent heroic march back to Hungnam that had to do with luck—most of it was the result of great individual courage and exceptional small-unit leadership—but on two points they were fortunate. First they benefited from the fact that the Chinese struck when they did, instead of waiting an additional day or two, by which time Ray Murray's Fifth Marine Regiment might have been farther west, and thus more cut off from Litzenberg's Seventh Regiment and the rest of the division; and second, that the Chinese had such poor communications and so little ability to adapt to the changing reality of battle. Had their communications been more modern, as Colonel Alpha Bowser later said, the First Marine Division would never have made it back from the Chosin Reservoir.

Their breakout from the Chosin Reservoir is one of the classic moments in their own exceptional history, a masterpiece of leadership on the part of their officers and of simple, relentless, abiding courage on the part of the ordinary fighting men—fighting a vastly larger force in the worst kind of mountainous terrain and unbearable cold that sometimes reached down to minus forty. Of all the battles in the Korean War, it is probably the most celebrated, deservedly so, and the most frequently written about. As the news reached Washington and then the country about the dilemma of the First Marines, seemingly cut off and surrounded by a giant force of Chinese, there was widespread fear that the

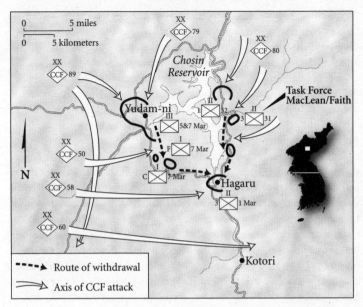

0 5 miles
0 5 kilometers

XX CCF 79
XX CCF 80
XX CCF 89
Chosin Reservoir
Task Force MacLean/Faith
Yudam-ni
III 5&7 Mar
XX CCF 50
F 7 Mar
N
XX CCF 58
C 7 Mar
Hagaru
3 1 Mar
XX CCF 60
Kotori

- - - ▶ Route of withdrawal
⟹ Axis of CCF attack

17. BREAKOUT FROM CHOSIN RESERVOIR, NOVEMBER 27–DECEMBER 9, 1950

division might be lost. Omar Bradley himself was almost certain they were lost. When the First Marines started the breakout, there were six Chinese divisions aligned against them, or roughly sixty thousand soldiers. In the two-week battle in which the Marines fought their way back to Hungnam, Smith believed that they had fought all-out against seven Chinese divisions and parts of three others. An estimated forty thousand Chinese were killed and perhaps another twenty thousand wounded. From November 27 to December 11, when the main battle with the Chinese began, the Marines lost 561 dead, 182 missing, 2,894 wounded, and another 3,600 who suffered from non-battle injuries, mostly frostbite.

The small number of men missing in action compared to the number of men killed and wounded is testimony to the discipline of both the officers and the men. The division's valor in fighting on island after island in the Pacific was well known long before the Korean War started. It had already distinguished itself, during the Naktong fighting, stopping breakthroughs whenever the North Koreans had momentarily penetrated the UN lines, and had performed with excellence after Inchon in the battle for Seoul. But this was its greatest challenge. Whether at that point any other American division could have made it out of what still seemed like an almost complete trap is doubtful.

"It was the strongest division in the world," said one of its public information officers, Captain Michael Capraro. "I thought of it as a Doberman, a dangerous hound straining at the leash, wanting nothing more than to sink its fangs into the master's enemy, preferably one with yellow skin."

Some of the Army division commanders had been worried about the Chinese during the drive north, but most of them had been like Dutch Keiser and not acted on their fears. Smith had. He had, among other things, made clear to every officer in the division what he was to do when the Chinese struck. They would fight from the high ground, moving on paths if need be, but not anchored to the roads, as the Chinese hoped. They would use their artillery as their best weapon, the equalizer. They would move primarily during the day and they would try to button up at night. All of this meant they were prepared emotionally and strategically for the battle ahead, as most of the Army units had not been. The cold was if anything a more determined enemy than the Chinese. It was pervasive and never let up, and as if the natural cold registering on the thermometer up there on the Manchurian heights wasn't bad enough, most of the time they were in a kind of Manchurian wind tunnel where the cold had a constant extra bite to it. The men came to look like Ancient Mariners who had sailed too close to the North Pole, all of them bearded; their beards, filled with ice shavings, told the story. The cold made men want to quit and give up—made it hard to want to fight and live for another day—and yet every day they kept fighting. Years later, when one of the senior NCOs visited Chesty Puller at his home outside of Washington, Puller greeted him and said, "Hey, Sarge, thawed out yet?"

They did not like to think of it as a retreat: it was not as if they had met an enemy moving at them from the North and pulled back to the South. A journalist had asked Smith during the fighting what he thought about the Marines' retreat from Chosin and he had bristled. "Retreat, hell," he had said, "we're simply attacking in another direction." The Chinese had, of course, blown the bridge at the Funchilin Pass after the Marines had crossed over it heading north, just as Smith had anticipated, and it seemed for a time like a death warrant—perhaps they *were* trapped there—but the Air Force had done a brilliant job of dropping the parts of a Treadway bridge in, and miraculously it worked; they were able to air-drop in enough sections, and somehow the engineers managed to put it in place. It allowed the Marines to go across when they returned south, a feat of engineering and ingenuity to match the courage of the men who were fighting. The First Marines had been completely surrounded, and in one of the great dramatic examples of sheer military strength they had fought their way through. At least four Chinese divisions were rendered combat ineffective during the battle.

There were many bleak military moments in the Korean War, but this was not one of them. In 2002, some fifty-one years after the battle, when Ed Simmons, who had fought there, wrote his history of the Chosin breakout he noted that in their 140-year history the Marines had received 294 Congressional Medals of Honor. Forty-two were awarded during the Korean War. Of that number, fourteen were awarded for action during the Chosin breakout, seven of them posthumously. Yet Smith's leadership, his almost prophetic sense of the battle that was to come, never gained the admiration of the man whose corps he had saved. Almond still could not bring himself to praise Smith—for to admit what Smith had done was to admit his own awful miscalculations, and his blindness to the forces that had awaited him. "My general comment is that General Smith, ever since the Inchon landing and the preparation phase, was overly cautious executing any order that he ever received," Almond said years later.

But in the end, for all of the unmatched heroism, it *was* a retreat—they had all gone too far north and they had been hit by a massive force and forced to move back. Smith and the Marines, proud though they were of their withdrawal, knew that. The one person who refused to admit that it had been a catastrophic mistake was MacArthur. The Marines subsequently prepared a history of what had happened and sent it to MacArthur, and he had objected to the use of the word "retreat." "In all my experience I was never more satisfied with an operation than I was with this one," Smith quoted him as saying. Then the Marine general added, "Now what are you going to do with a man like that?"

THE ASSAULT UPON the Second Division in the west had been by contrast an epochal horror, moments of great courage dwarfed by the chaos and confusion and almost complete lack of leadership at the top. All in all what had happened in those days when the Chinese attacked the Army in the west, and in certain sectors of Tenth Corps, constituted, in the words of Dean Acheson (not an entirely disinterested bystander, for he by then seethed with hatred of MacArthur), the greatest defeat suffered by the American military since the battle of Bull Run in the Civil War. The men in the Second Division who made it out that day were always, some other veterans of the war thought, just a little different from most other veterans. Just as so many men who fought in Korea tended to be different when they came home, in the same way, the veterans of that one week, the week of the Chinese attack and the retreat down The Gauntlet, were just that much different from the other Korean veterans. There was very little bluster to them. They did not talk readily about their experiences, even to those who had also served in Korea. They seemed to recoil from those who might praise them or talk of them as heroes. They thought of themselves only as survivors. As their units had been devastated, so too, in different ways, had many of them been damaged. Certainly something had been lost in many of them. One day they had been soldiers with countless buddies, part of an army that had gained the upper hand in a war that most of them hated, sure that a very difficult stretch in their lives had almost ended, and on a triumphant note at that. A week later, so many of their buddies were gone, often to indescribable fates, which all too often they had witnessed. Many of them bore not just the normal burden of the survivor, that uneasiness over why they had lived when someone they valued greatly and perhaps thought of as a better soldier had died, but a secret feeling, expressed to no one else, that over the six or seven days when so many of their friends had been killed or captured there had been some moment, maybe no more than a split second, when they might have been just a tiny bit braver and thus other men might have lived. Making it through had brought with it the immediacy of relief in living one more day, but often as they thought back on what had happened, what they had witnessed and done, there was the endless self-doubt as well.

DUTCH KEISER KNEW from the moment the day was over that there was likely to be a need for a scapegoat, and that he was the most obvious choice. He was, in fact, relieved of his command four days later: an announcement from Tokyo indicated that he had a serious illness. A few days later Keiser called on Slam Marshall, the Army historian who was in Korea doing interviews for what became his book *The River and the Gauntlet,* and told him exactly what had happened. He had received a message from Eighth Army headquarters informing him "that he was ill with pneumonia and must report to a hospital in Tokyo." Keiser knew instantly that they were about to tie the can for the defeat on him. He told Marshall he deeply resented being "the goat for MacArthur's blunder." So he drove down to Seoul to see Lev Allen, the Eighth Army chief of staff.

The conversation, he said, had gone like this:

Allen asked, "What the hell are you doing here? You're ill with pneumonia."

"You can see for yourself I don't have pneumonia, so cut the bunk."

"But are you going to comply with the order?"

"Yes, because it is an order, but I don't want you to kid around with me." Then Keiser started to leave.

Allen ventured one last line: "By the way, General Walker says he will take care of you with a job around his headquarters."

"You tell General Walker to shove his job up his ass," Keiser said.

But that was just the beginning. Dutch Keiser was the easiest of targets. In the field, the entire military leadership was almost completely discredited. Walton Walker might not have liked the idea of the drive north to begin with, but the scope of the defeat underscored his own limitations as a field commander powerless in dealing with his superiors. He was sure that he was going to be relieved of his command, that he too would be a scapegoat. Ned Almond was protected politically in Tokyo as Walker was not, and his forces had been saved from complete destruction—but only because of O. P. Smith's virtual insubordination. After Chesty Puller helped lead his regiment out to Hungnam, a *Time* magazine reporter had asked him what the great lesson of the battle was. "Never serve under Tenth Corps," Puller had immediately answered. A few weeks later, when Matt Ridgway showed up in Korea to take command, he met with Smith, and the one thing Smith asked him was that the Marines never again be placed under Ned Almond's command, a request to which Ridgway readily agreed.

A FEW WEEKS after the breakout from Kunuri on the Anju road, Paul Freeman ran into Keyes Beech, the *Chicago Daily News* reporter. Beech was intrigued by Freeman's role: he had been in China as a young officer and he had seen the Chinese Army up close in those days when it had been something of a joke. Now he was fighting them. What did he think? "These are not the same Chinese," Freeman had answered.

I N T H E D A Y S following the retreat from Kunuri, the great question was not whether it was bad, but how bad it was going to be. How far south would they have to retreat? When Johnnie Walker had met with MacArthur in the late-night session on November 28, he had been confident that if they retreated back to the Pyongyang area and created an east-west arc where the country was narrowest, Pyongyang-Yangdok-Wonsan, they could hold. Later Truman himself would talk about this line and say that that was where they should have drawn a line in the first place. The arc looked relatively narrow, especially compared to the vast wider spaces north of it, as the country mushroomed out. But at the waist it was still 125 miles long—with seven American divisions covering it, which meant a division sector would be about twenty miles. It was still very far north; the roads were terrible, and it would be extremely hard to supply many of the units. The Chinese might well be able to slip around them, thus isolating them. They were in effect now dealing with all the cautionary realities that they had paid so little attention to in the previous six weeks. But as the first Chinese success became apparent, the *myth* of battle, so important to the men engaged, suddenly favored them: there were so many of them, they were such fanatics, fearless in the face of their enemies; they fought brilliantly at night; they could slip up on a UN position and be inside it before the first shot was fired. The fear factor, which had weighed on the Chinese before the battle began, the fear of vastly superior American weaponry, now burdened the UN forces. The most dangerous virus that can infect any army—the fear of its adversary—had now struck the Eighth Army. As they had so recently underestimated Chinese military capacities, they now magnified them. As they had gone so cavalierly north, they were now unprepared to hold any kind of a moderate fallback position. In the west it was not a retreat but a rout, of an army that had become, because of the carelessness at the top, a shambles.

Now, it seemed, no one was in charge. The people in Tokyo, their illusions of total victory completely shattered, were frozen. In a way, it was as if the crisis existed within MacArthur himself: he had always wanted those around him to see him as omniscient; now that he had been defeated on the battlefield by an Asian army and peasant generals, it was as if he had lost faith not just in his own forces but in himself. He had spoken before the Chinese entry into the war of achieving the greatest victory in the history of Christendom, of rivers running red with Chinese blood. Now he spoke in hardly less apocalyptic terms of either widening the war (and using the atomic bomb) or abandoning the Korean peninsula altogether. The last thing he was prepared to do was admit the mistakes he had made, and then try to piece his broken army back together. He was a man who liked to talk about the Asian concept of losing face; now he himself, good Caucasian though he was, had lost face not just before the entire world, but before his own troops, and perhaps most important of all before himself. Later, both Omar Bradley and Matt Ridgway talked of this as a period where his mood swings, always considered a problem by other commanders and senior civilians, were more pronounced than ever.

To no one's surprise MacArthur did not take responsibility for the defeat; if anything he soon spoke as if he had been the principal victim of Washington's policies. Even worse, as a commander he could not bring himself to visit his men or the country where the defeat had taken place, as if to go there would mean having to face those who knew how badly he had failed. He stayed in the protective lee of the Dai Ichi, among his staff, not visiting Korea until *December 11*, two weeks after the Chinese strike. Some of his cables back to Washington in those days smacked of the purest fantasy: he claimed that Tenth Corps, in great jeopardy on the east coast when the Chinese had come in, was not, as everyone in Washington knew, fighting for its very life, but still on an offensive mission and had tied down six to eight Chinese divisions that might otherwise have been hammering the Eighth Army. "When messages like that came in," Ridgway later said, "it was as if the madness were in the room."

There had been a moment just before the Chinese struck when, as his biographer William Manchester wrote, MacArthur had been "a colossus bestriding Korea until the nemesis of his hubris overtook him." And then after the worst had happened, "he could not bear to end his career in checkmate." Suddenly, he looked to outsiders, even those who bore him some measure of goodwill, like an old man hopelessly out of touch. The British general Leslie Mansergh, who visited him in Tokyo then, observed that "he appeared to be much older than his seventy years. Signs of nerves and strain were apparent." He seemed to Mansergh completely disconnected from the battlefield reality: "When he emphasized the combined efforts and successes of all front-line troops in standing shoulder to shoulder, and dying if necessary in their fight against communism, it occurred to me that he could not have been fully in the picture. I cannot believe he would have made these comments in such a way if he had been in full possession of the facts which I would inevitably learn later, facts that some Americans had been less than staunch. It occurred to me then, and was emphasized later, that the war in Korea is reproduced in Tokyo with certain omissions of the more unpalatable facts."

He became, Clayton James, his generally sympathetic biographer, wrote, "depressed and short tempered at GHQ and often spent the nights suffering insomnia and pacing back and forth along the hallway at his home. His moods would swing to extremes—from buoyant optimism about winning the war before Christmas 1950, to alarmist predictions a little later that his troops would be forced to withdraw to Japan unless mightily reinforced." No one around him, James noted of that period, could bring certain subjects up with him, such as his dubious choice of Ned Almond as a corps commander or his decision to split his forces. He was irritable when the press made fun of him for relabeling what had once been a grandiose all-out boys-home-before-Christmas offensive as "a reconnaissance in force," successful, in his words, because it prematurely triggered the Chinese attack.

The mood swings had always been a problem, as the people dealing with him in Washington were very much aware. Omar Bradley wrote of "his brilliant but brittle" mind snapping in this period when he realized that his civilian superiors in Washington were not going to permit an all-out war with China, a larger war in which he would be able to reclaim victory and thus redeem himself. Matt Ridgway described him to one writer as a man capable of being brilliant and completely lucid at one moment and the next minute, during the very same conversation—as if he had suddenly thrown a switch—soaring off into a private world that only he understood (and inhabited), where defeats were not defeats and the victories of his adversaries not really victories. When he described MacArthur's behavior in the weeks after the Chinese entered the war, Dean Acheson would quote Euripides: "Whom the gods destroy they first make mad."

In the days after the Chinese attack and as the extent of the defeat became clear, it often seemed surreal for those reporters dealing with the command, the contrast between reality in Korea and in Tokyo. Joe Fromm, the *U.S. News* reporter who had been on Charles Willoughby's enemies list, long remembered one particular scene in that stretch. About a week after the defeat at Kunuri, there was a press briefing in Tokyo at which Willoughby presided. There he was, the chief of intelligence, at the lectern, as full of certitudes as ever, seemingly unshaken by defeat, and trying to prove that he and his people in G-2 had been right about the Chinese all along, had, in fact, been tracking them from the time they left the south of China and had known exactly what they were planning to do. Indeed, even when MacArthur had made his famous home-by-Christmas pledges, he had known that a great many Chinese had already crossed the Yalu and that there were troops from at least thirty divisions on both sides of the border in easy striking distance of American forces. Well, if that were true, one reporter asked, why had he gone ahead with his major offensive, knowing he was outnumbered three to one? "We couldn't just passively sit by," Willoughby answered. "We had to attack and find out the enemy's profile." The command, it turned out, had not been surprised at all. "I went back to my office," Fromm said years later, "and I thought to myself, Now they say that they always knew, because they're never wrong, and now they say they were never surprised because they can never be surprised, and yet if you checked with the kids who fought there, someone fucked up, because the kids who fought there didn't know about all the Chinese the way MacArthur and Willoughby knew about them. It's madness. Pure madness. Someone is crazy."

Gradually a new line began to emerge from Tokyo. To the degree that things had gone wrong, it was because Washington had hamstrung MacArthur, preventing him from attacking Chinese bases on the other side of the Yalu. He had not waited very long to launch his own defense in friendly journals and with friendly editors. On December 1, ten days before he could bring himself to visit his men in the field, a long article appeared in *U.S. News* in which he attacked the administration for not letting him go in "hot pursuit" of the Chinese by bombing their Manchurian bases. That, he said, placed on him "an enormous [military] handicap, without precedent in history." In Washington it was viewed as another Posterity Paper. Truman was predictably furious. On December 6, he imposed a gag rule on all parties, demanding that any policy statements on Korea by anyone be cleared with State. Of all the rules put in place at this time, it was the one MacArthur paid the least attention to.

Later Bradley ruminated that this was another critical moment when the Joint Chiefs badly failed the president. Washington had been impotent, forced to listen to bad news without being able to do anything to change the nature of the battlefield. To Bradley it seemed that "MacArthur was throwing in the towel without the slightest effort to put up a fight." In Washington, they knew that the Chinese had broken off contact after Walker retreated south of Pyongyang, and showed no taste for pursuit. "Why then," Bradley wondered, "was the Eighth Army running to the rear so hard and fast? Why hadn't MacArthur gone to Korea to steady Walker and rally the troops with his famous rhetoric? It was disgraceful." It was a defeated Army. Walker probably should have been relieved right then and there; his position had been untenable for too long. A new man was obviously needed on the battlefield, either

Matthew Ridgway or Jim Van Fleet, another rising star who had done well in steadying anti-Communist forces in Greece. In addition, MacArthur should have been *ordered* to combine his two forces, Eighth Army and Tenth Corps. In the top echelon at this time, only Dean Rusk, Bradley noted, seemed to be pushing for such serious acts to break the mood of pessimism that had taken hold of the military. (Why, Rusk asked, couldn't we "muster our best effort and spirit to put up our best fight?" The British, he said, had done that time and again early in World War II—why couldn't we?)

It was the bleakest time for the Truman administration. The war, which the president had thought was virtually over, had not only been enlarged, but the commanding general was now surfacing as the administration's most serious adversary, as much a political as a military one, blaming the administration for a lack of support, and in effect for the defeat. The president himself, normally very much in control in press conferences, had slipped badly on November 30, as the Chinese offensive began. He answered a question about what the United States was going to do in Korea by saying they would do whatever was necessary to meet the challenge. "Will that include the atomic bomb?" another reporter asked. Truman could easily have ducked it, but he answered, "That includes every weapon we have." Then another reporter asked, "Does that mean there is active consideration of the use of the atomic bomb?" And Truman responded, "There has always been active consideration of its use." Then he made things even worse by saying it was something the military people would have to decide and adding that the military commander in the field would be "in charge of the use of all these weapons."

That terrified a great many people—American citizens and allies alike—because it implied that MacArthur, the commander in the field, was in charge of whether or not to use atomic weapons. Slowly, awkwardly, the administration pulled back from the president's words. The Joint Chiefs were especially weak in those months. Brave and otherwise independent men often became quite bureaucratic once they were members of the JCS. That reflected one of the great secrets of the military culture—how officers who had been so brave in battle, fearless when it mattered, could be so bland and cautious as they reached what was seemingly a career pinnacle. That had been true in Korea; it would be even truer in Vietnam. There were, it appeared, two very different kinds of courage in many military men—bravery in battle, and independence or bravery within the institution—and they did not often reside side by side.

The Chiefs wanted MacArthur to consolidate his forces, to fold Tenth Corps back into the Eighth Army and create a unified command in which American troops would be protecting the flanks of the main force. They believed that the superior mobility of their own forces, when combined with the limited logistical ability of the Chinese, would allow the UN troops to pull back forty or fifty miles, regroup, and then present a much more formidable defensive line—backed by air and artillery—should the Chinese continue to advance. Except for the difficult talk of extricating the Marines from the area around the Chosin Reservoir, it was doable, they believed, because in most places the Chinese had broken off contact after their initial strike. As early as November 29, the Chiefs had cabled MacArthur suggesting just that. It was—and this was critically important—a suggestion, not an order. But he immediately turned it down, cabling them on December 3, "There is no practicality nor would any accrue thereby to unite the forces of Eighth Army and Tenth Corps." The Joint Chiefs were stunned. They could not understand the military logic behind the cable, except that, implicitly, their suggestion might have been taken as an indictment of his earlier decision to split his forces. The cable was a reminder that even when the general was wrong, he was never wrong.

His cables were now full of the most pessimistic of predictions. Unless he got vastly more troops, his forces would soon be forced to withdraw into beachhead bastions. The Chiefs were unnerved by the rising tone of pessimism—indeed panic—in these cables. Bradley later went through some of them, angrily writing comments in the margins, and added quite bitterly of that period that MacArthur had "treated us as if we were children."

THE ENTRANCE OF the Chinese and the terrible UN defeats in the North did not make America more cautionary. Rather it sharpened the existing political divide, made the China Firsters more hawkish, cast few doubts among the faithful about MacArthur's decisions, and subjected the administration to even more pressure, sending Truman's popularity spiraling still further downward. For those in the China Lobby it was absolute proof that American policy in Asia had failed; to Henry Luce it showed that he had been right on China all along as Acheson had been wrong. Now perhaps, Luce hoped, the administration would be more resolute in Asia. As one of Luce's biographers, Robert Herzstein, wrote, Luce had always seen Korea not "as a police action, or a quagmire, but as one promising front in the war to liberate China." Now the publisher was more aggressive than ever. John Shaw Billings, a senior Luce editor who kept a careful record of Luce's thoughts and feelings, noted in his diary on December 5, even as the rout from Kunuri was still taking place, "Luce wants the Big War, not now perhaps, but sometime." Luce was more convinced than ever that his vision of a major confrontation in Asia was right and that Communism could be rolled back—if the administration did not get in the way. At the same time, as their belief in the eventual and inevitable confrontation between the Communists and the West grew more certain, Luce and some of the senior people around him began to worry about the location of their offices, just in case the Communists dropped an atomic bomb. The Time-Life offices were about two miles from Manhattan's Union Square, considered the city's atomic epicenter. There was serious talk of moving the headquarters several miles farther away to Manhattan's Upper West Side, and some people even talked about moving the headquarters to Chicago. Nor eventually did MacArthur's weak showing before the joint Senate committees affect Luce, who wanted to make him *Time*'s Man of the Year for 1951 but was talked out of it by his editors.

A NUMBER OF the men who were part of decision-making in Washington remembered the weeks that followed the Chinese entry as the darkest period of their governmental service, a moment of paralysis. They were under constant attack, and the man who should have been helping out and leading the resurgence of their military forces had become their leading critic. Every bit of news, it seemed, was bad. There was a horrible vacuum in leadership and no one in Washington seemed to be able to fill it.

Particularly upsetting was the fact that these were not the flawed troops the United States had thrown into Korea back when the war began: these were the best the country had, and yet they had been hammered badly; and now the Americans were fighting the most populous nation in the world, whose underarmed forces suddenly seemed invincible. It was a horrendous equation: the war was much bigger, the enemy more powerful, the domestic political support for it greatly diminished, and becoming slimmer by the day. In general, those who worked in that administration are now regarded as among the ablest men of a generation. The phrase "The Wise Men" has been applied to them in the title of an admiring, best-selling book. But all of them, even as they had sensed during October and November that something terrible was about to happen, had been silent, frozen in place, while MacArthur continued to stretch his orders. They and the civilians who had gone to Wake Island had never asked MacArthur the tough questions when it mattered, in no small part because the political tide was moving away from them. They, who had never trusted him, had acted as if he were some kind of prophet, authorized to speak not merely for his own command but for the Chinese commanders as well. Now, as he unraveled in Tokyo, they once again seemed powerless to do anything about him or the command.

It was not just the Joint Chiefs and the senior political people like Dean Acheson who failed to restrain MacArthur at that juncture, it was also the most respected public official of the era, George Catlett Marshall, who had just moved over after an enviable tour as secretary of state and an all too brief retirement to become secretary of defense. Of the senior group, he was the most knowledgeable and experienced, an icon of icons, more like a father figure than a peer to most of the men serving Truman. He was the quietest and most modest great figure of an era: he never raised his voice, never gave angry commands, never threatened or bullied people. His strength came from his sense of purpose and duty, which were absolute; his almost unique control of his own ego; and his ability to separate what mattered from what did not. Because of his awesome self-discipline and stoic personal qualities it was easy to underestimate Marshall's full value. He was often seen as being primarily skilled as a great management man, and what he did *not* get credit for was his sheer intellectual firepower, something he was quite content to mask. George Kennan might have been a more classic example of a gifted intellectual figure working in a bureaucracy, and Acheson, with his cutting wit and his formidable verbal skills, a more forceful figure in any public debate, but Marshall quietly possessed a rare mind of uncommon intellectual strength, with an exceptional sense of the consequences of deeds. In some ways he was self-taught during that long and difficult career, but he had used every position he ever held, no matter how lowly and disappointing, to understand the forces at play around him. What he had come up with was the rarest of things, and the hardest thing in the world to seek, and that was wisdom. His was the most pragmatic kind of intelligence, never flashy, and he always made clear that a deeply held sense of duty was more important than sheer brilliance; far fewer men talked of Marshall's brilliance than they did of MacArthur's, but in a quiet, reserved way, Marshall tended to get the larger forces of history at play in his era right, as MacArthur often did not. His decline in that period was a grievous loss for the Truman team.

At this critical juncture, as in the days after Unsan, Marshall was surprisingly passive. It was probably his weakest moment in a long and distinguished career. Why he failed puzzled some of the others. Perhaps, thought some of his admirers, his long and unhappy personal relationship with MacArthur, one that went all the way back to World War I, was part of the problem. Perhaps, they thought, Marshall was a little more loath to set limits as he might have for another officer, for fear of becoming the caricature that MacArthur had created of him. But it had to be more than that. Was it the very nature of the job itself as Marshall saw it—that the job of secretary of defense was to support the commander, or the uniformed Chiefs, and not to impose his own will on men in uniform? In effect, did it mean that he was much freer to stand up to MacArthur when he was a senior figure at State than when he was at Defense? Or was he uneasy about usurping the powers of the Joint Chiefs? Had, in effect, his very strength, his modesty, his sense of a proper hierarchy, become a weakness? Certainly that was part of it. But finally it is important not to lose sight of the fact that the George Marshall of 1950 was not the George Marshall of World War II, that the crushing hours and burdens of both the war and the postwar era had taken their toll, that his health was slipping and he was simply not as strong a man physically or intellectually as he had been in that earlier incarnation. What made it worse was his standing among them: they instinctively deferred to him, took their signals from him, and now there were no signals.

MacArthur's mood swings, some of the Washington people thought, were reflected in his estimates of the size of the Chinese forces facing him. Typically, he had gone almost overnight from grave underestimation to significant overestimation. The numbers he and Willoughby liked to use for Chinese troop strength before they struck were piddling, perhaps sixty thousand in country. Now MacArthur told Joe Collins, who had come to visit him, that he faced *five hundred thousand men* on the battlefield and his airpower was hamstrung in dealing with them because of the Manchurian sanctuaries.

The impotence of Washington angered one senior officer, Lieutenant General Matt Ridgway, more than all the others. He had been uneasy with MacArthur's drive north from the moment it began. The dangers were too great, the ordinary infantrymen placed at too much risk. There seemed to be too little thought of the consequences. Now, with the front collapsing on them, the troops still at risk, and no clear strategy at hand, Ridgway was appalled by the failure of MacArthur to rise to the occasion. He was equally appalled by the lack of purpose and command in Washington, the willingness of the men one rank above him to be part of this strange vacuum of leadership.

Of all the senior military men in Washington, Ridgway became the most outspoken as MacArthur seemed to unravel. Ever more bad news kept coming in, and no one in Washington was standing up to take charge. The Joint Chiefs continued to make the most tentative suggestions to MacArthur, who treated their recommendations with complete contempt, while demanding more and more troops—he seemed to want four additional divisions, divisions they simply did not have. The good thing about the success of Inchon, they had all believed just a few weeks earlier, was that they were going to get a division back for Europe. The last thing they wanted, with American military strength stretched so thin elsewhere, was to pour more troops into the Korean theater. "We want to avoid getting sewed up in Korea" was the way George Marshall had once noted it at a meeting. Then he added the crucial kicker: "But how could we get out with honor?"

There were, Ridgway thought, too many meetings where nothing was being decided, where everyone was sitting around waiting for someone else to do something. The other generals, Ridgway wrote, were still "in an almost superstitious awe of this larger than life military figure who had so often been right when everyone else had been wrong." On Sunday, December 3, the senior national security and military men, including the Joint Chiefs, Acheson, and Marshall, all sat through yet another long meeting where, in Ridgway's mind, they were once again unable to issue an order, to correct, in his words, a situation going from "bad to disastrous." Finally, Ridgway asked for permission to speak and then—he wondered later whether he had been too blunt—said that they had all spent too much damn time on debate and it was time to take some action. They owed it to the men in the field, he said, "and to the God to whom we must answer for those men's lives to stop talking and to act." When he finished, no one spoke, although Admiral Arthur Davis, who had replaced Al Gruenther as the director of the JCS staff, handed him a note saying, "proud to know you." Then the meeting broke up. Ridgway started talking to Hoyt Vandenberg, the Air Force chief of staff, whom he had known since he was an instructor and Vandenberg a cadet back at West Point.

"Why don't the Chiefs send orders to MacArthur and tell him what to do?" Ridgway asked his old friend.

Vandenberg shook his head. "What good would that do? He wouldn't obey the orders. What can we do?"

At this point, Ridgway, in his own words, simply exploded. "You can relieve any commander who won't obey orders, can't you?" Ridgway would never forget the look on Vandenberg's face: "His lips parted and he looked at me with an expression both puzzled and amazed. He walked away then without saying a word and I never afterward had occasion to discuss this with him."

IN THE MEANTIME, MacArthur's army was in full-scale retreat. The Big Bugout, some called it. The retreat covered some 120 miles in ten days, even though the Chinese, momentarily at least, had little offensive capacity to press any advantage. That rush south represented the total disintegration of a fighting force, as Max Hastings wrote, "resembling the collapse of the French in 1940 and the British at Singapore in 1942." They were fleeing, one British officer wrote later, "before an unknown threat of Chinese soldiers—as it transpired, ill-armed and on their feet or horses." As the surviving men of the Second Division pulled back, they passed huge bonfires visible from miles away, as vast stores of equipment, supplies that had still been coming into the country when the great offensive started, were destroyed, lest the gear be captured by the Chinese. Some of the men were still in their summer-weight uniforms, and hearing that winter uniforms, which had finally arrived in country,

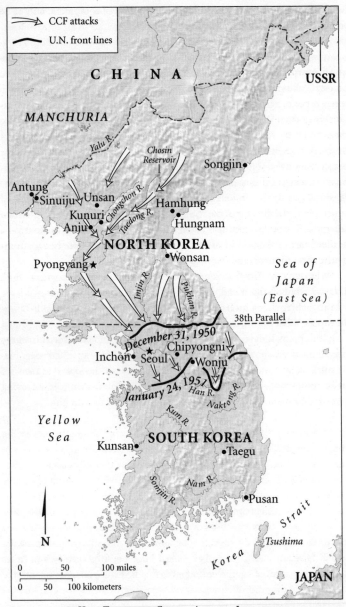

18. HIGH TIDE OF THE CHINESE ADVANCE, JANUARY 1951

wcrc being burned, they tried to get near the stores of equipment, only to be turned away at gunpoint by MPs.

In early December, the remnants of the Second Division gathered at Pyongyang. There, any hope for digging in and drawing a strong defensive line in an arc moving east from the North Korean capital—let alone retreating in an orderly fashion—disappeared. The Pyongyang railroad station was a mob scene. American troops, confused and despairing, hoping to depart by train as quickly as possible, waited in passenger cars first for two days with no locomotive ever becoming available. Meanwhile thousands of frightened, angry Korean refugees poured into the city, hoping to flee south. In their anger they began looting everything in sight. The search for a locomotive seemed interminable. Some of the headquarters people were trying to protect the division's records, but it soon became clear that if they got out at all, the only thing they would get out with was the men themselves, and they started burning Division records and military currency. There was for the men waiting on the train a terrible sense of shame. Finally, early in the afternoon of December 4, a locomotive was produced, and four hours later the train left.

By December 7, they had found a bivouac area at Yongdongpo, near Seoul. They were in bad shape in all ways. "Going through it all was god-awful, the terror when the Chinese hit, the terrifying run through The Pass, but it was during the chaos after we broke contact and moved south, unable to put it all back together, that I was ashamed of my Army, not the men in my unit, or the men in my division, not after the hell they had been in, but of the men who were in charge of us," said Sam Mace. "We'd fight again, I knew, and I knew we could fight well if we were led well, but that was a moment of complete disgrace and of shame."

36

WALTON WALKER ALWAYS drove recklessly. He and his driver regularly pushed their jeep too hard on Korea's terrible, narrow, icy roads. But it had seemed just a minor idiosyncrasy of a man under far too much pressure in a role that had never fit him, until the morning of December 23, 1950. Walker, his driver, his aide, and his bodyguard were all in the jeep speeding on the northbound lane of a road where the vehicles heading south were badly stacked up. Suddenly, a weapons carrier from a South Korean division swung into his lane, and there was no time to avoid an accident. The jeep flipped and all four men were thrown into a ditch. The other three lived. Walker died almost instantly. At the time of his death he was exhausted and beaten down, sure he was about to be relieved. That would have been a singularly inglorious way to end a career. He was completely dispirited: everything he had done to hold his troops together on the Pusan Perimeter would be forgotten, and instead, the disaster up along the Yalu would be his epitaph. He would get his fourth star and, ironically, high praise from Douglas MacArthur as well, but he would get both posthumously.

The man who would relieve him was slightly younger than the men of the Eisenhower-Bradley-Patton generation. Matt Ridgway had been on the rise at the end of World War II, ticketed to lead an airborne corps against Japan just as the war ended—a prized assignment. He had already been the recipient of a *Time* magazine cover story, a significant mark of fame in that era. He was the rare figure, so good at what he did that both Washington and Tokyo, apart on almost everything else, agreed that he was the right man—indeed the only man—to succeed Walker. When he got the news about Walker's death, MacArthur immediately asked for Ridgway. His standing in Washington was, if anything, even higher. If Truman and the JCS had been able to choose their own man at the outbreak of the war, then Ridgway almost surely would have gotten the Tokyo command. He was the best the American Army had. He had become, even before he took command in Korea, the standard against which other officers were measured: Was he as good as Ridgway? Was he a younger Ridgway? He was fierce, purposeful, relentless—the perfect man to take command at a bad time in a bad place in a war that had suddenly gone from bad to worse, and to put back together an Army that was unraveling. He did not varnish things for his superiors; nor did he waste much energy being warm or chummy. Everything about his manner—to superiors, subordinates, and the men who fought under him—implied that they were employed in a serious, deadly business, and no time was ever to be wasted.

"If Ridgway had been there from the start as the Eighth Army commander," said Jack Murphy, the young West Point graduate who won the DSC in his first few days at the Naktong and later became an amateur historian of the war, "there would have been no domination of the Eighth Army by Tokyo, no defeat at Kunuri, no panicking when the Chinese hit, and no surprise that they had entered in such large numbers. You would have had a command on location that knew the terrain and the difficulties that it created. You would not have had a distant command in another country, fighting what was a very different and much more comfortable war, but not really knowing what was going on. You would have had *no* tricks played with the intelligence about the Chinese. You would have had Grade A intelligence, and you would have had a lot better corps, division and regimental commanders, a lot sooner in the game." The GIs admired him, even if they did not love him. They knew that he did not play games, that he had a genuine feel for them and their hardships, that he would be on their side if they had legitimate grievances, and that, most assuredly, had he been their commander from the start, they would not have headed north in summer-weight uniforms (if they had headed north at all). Now he was going to take over the Eighth Army. Ridgway got the news on the night of December 22. He did not tell his wife, Penny, until the next day; then he packed a few things and set off for Tokyo.

If ever an American officer was perfectly suited for a particular moment in American military history it was Matthew Bunker Ridgway when he was summoned to take over the shambles of a dysfunctional Eighth Army. He was the flintiest of men, rather humorless, fiercely aggressive, as unsparing of himself as he was of others. One could not think of him except as a soldier—and not a peacetime soldier either. Though he had none of the grandiosity of MacArthur, he had his own mystique and his own very personal and quite lofty sense of his role in history. He believed that he and the men he commanded were the direct descendants of those who had gone before them, dating back to Valley Forge, and that they owed a great deal to those who had preceded them in uniform. It was as if George Washington and the men who fought at Valley Forge were always looking over their shoulders. Ridgway sometimes talked in an almost mystical way of those who had fought in the Revolution or the Civil War, and of the need for his men to be worthy of the hardships they had suffered.

Though he was fiercely anti-Communist, he was not, like MacArthur, on an ideological crusade. The enemy was the enemy and should be analyzed on the basis of its actual strengths and weaknesses. If ideology made the Chinese or North Koreans better, more committed soldiers, then attention should be paid to that fact. When he first heard that North Korean troops had crossed the thirty-eighth parallel, he immediately wondered whether, in his words, it represented "the beginning of World War III . . . Armageddon, the last great battle between East and West." He immediately told his aides to watch for any unusual Soviet troop movements throughout the world. At the same time, he pushed his superiors, Bradley and Collins, to ask for at least a partial mobilization. "If we take this action and war does not come, we have lost money. If we do not take it and war does come we risk disaster."

Ridgway was in his own way a very serious hawk, but unlike MacArthur, he accepted that this was a limited war, that the civilians running it had pressures on them officers in the field might not grasp, and that the main battlefield might end up being thousands of miles away from Korea, most likely someplace in Central Europe, where the Soviets had placed so many armored divisions. In August 1950, knowing that pressure was even then building to relieve Walton Walker, Joe Collins had asked Ridgway what command he would prefer. Ridgway had immediately answered that, if this country were headed for World War III, he would prefer to fight in Europe. But in August, when it became clearer that Korea was an isolated war, Ridgway's attitude changed. Only the fact that relieving Walker might have caused an even greater crisis of confidence among American forces had prevented him from getting the command earlier.

He was an imposing man, forceful and trim, never an extra pound on him, five-ten but, thanks to the sheer force of his personality, seemingly much bigger. He was a Spartan. He worried that America was in decline because of the country's ever greater materialism; he warned that it was becoming a place where people never walked anymore and that the nation's men were becoming softer every year. His views, ironically, were not all that different from those of the Chinese commanders who launched their successful assault on American troops. He believed a loss of fiber had contributed to the disappointing early performance of America's young men in Korea. They had become too dependent on their machines and their technology. The first thing he intended to do when he took over the command was get them out of the warmth of their jeeps and trucks and make them patrol exactly as their predecessors had done, climbing the hills on foot. If they shared nothing else with their enemy, they would share the cold.

Ridgway bristled with personal purpose: he had an innate sense of how to lead, of what motivated fighting men—and what did not. There were at least three moments in his career when his country had reason to think of him as someone who, by dint of intelligence and character, set himself apart from his peers. The first was when he led the airborne assault on France on D-day in June 1944. The second was in 1954, after elite French forces had been trapped by the Vietminh at Dien Bien Phu and pressures grew on the Americans to come to their aid. At that time, as chief of staff of the Army, he wrote a memo so forceful in assessing the extremely high cost of an American entry into the war in French Indochina (and the potential lack of popularity among the Vietnamese of such a war) that President Dwight Eisenhower, on reading it, put aside any idea of intervention. And the third was when he took over the shattered Eighth Army, in late December 1950, and in two short months reinvigorated it, thereby blunting a powerful Chinese offensive that threatened to drive UN forces into the sea or push the Americans into using atomic weapons.

But there was an earlier, perhaps even more instructive moment that caught his character perfectly, thought the military historian Ken Hamburger. By June 1944, he was already the Great Ridgway and people listened to him. But in September 1943, he had managed to talk his superiors out of what would surely have been an ill-fated and tragic airborne assault on Rome. He had done that at a moment when he had comparatively little status in the upper echelons of the military hierarchy. It was in the middle of the Italian campaign, and the Italian government, officially still part of the Axis along with Germany and Japan, was about to make a separate peace with the Allies. Marshal Pietro Badoglio, the Italian commander, had suggested that an American airborne division make a parachute jump into Rome to link up with the Italian Army, which would then turn its guns on the Germans. Ridgway's division was slated to make the jump, but to him, everything about the plan smelled wrong. He had no way to validate the words of Badoglio—would he do as promised, and even if he did, would it make any difference, given the formidable quality of the German troops in the Italian capital? The risk to his men, Ridgway thought, was unacceptable. So he had begun to fight his way through a rather casual command structure that was all too ready to take Badoglio's word at face value.

Even as D-day for this mission approached, with all his superiors signed on, surprisingly few questions had been asked about Badoglio's ability to pull off his sudden switch. When Ridgway first challenged his superiors, they were initially quite indifferent to his concerns. At the last minute, Ridgway sent one of his deputies, Maxwell Taylor, on a daring mission behind German lines to meet with the Italians and recon the situation. Better, he believed, Taylor's eyes and ears than Badoglio's promises. Taylor reported back that all of Ridgway's doubts were valid: the Italians were in no position to fight as promised, and his airborne division might well be completely destroyed. Then, with his men already in their planes and the engines warming up, the mission was called off. That night Ridgway had shared a bottle of whiskey with a close friend, and then, drained by the closeness of disaster, he began to cry. To do what he had done at that moment, to place his entire career on the line, was, Hamburger thought, the mark of an uncommon soldier, someone whose courage away from the battlefield was the same as that on it.

There was a constancy to his code of honor. He had been assigned to command the Eighteenth Airborne Corps in the final battle for Japan, but then the war had ended quickly. MacArthur had invited him to attend the surrender on the battleship *Missouri*, a great honor, but he refused to accept—only the men who fought in the Pacific, he believed, should attend. Still, there was no false modesty to him—he knew he was good, and that was not by happenstance. Bill Sebald, the American ambassador to Japan, wrote a draft speech that Ridgway was to give on his arrival in Tokyo at the moment in 1951 when he finally replaced MacArthur as the commander of all American forces in the Far East and became as well the de facto governor-general of Japan. In it, Sebald had him saying "with due humility." Ridgway edited the phrase out. "Bill, I'm humble only before my own God, not before the Japanese people or anyone else." Subordinate officers were loath to fail to meet his expectations. He was a man who believed in the basics: infantrymen should get out and patrol; they should know their fields of fire; they should be smart and aggressive; and they should take the battle to the enemy. He was not a man who went around threatening to relieve subordinates. He would simply relieve them.

He was not caught up in the vainglory of war. He never tried to sugarcoat what war was about. When he nicknamed his first major Korean offensive Operation Killer, he received a note from Joe Collins suggesting that such a name might be difficult for the Army's public relations people to deal with. Ridgway was not moved by the objections of PR people on this or any other issue. The name, he had been told, was too bloodthirsty and lacked sex appeal. Later he wrote, "I did not understand why it was objectionable to acknowledge the fact that war was concerned with killing the enemy. . . . I am by nature opposed to any effort to 'sell' war to people as an only mildly unpleasant business that requires very little in the way of blood."

He was aware that he was in charge of the most precious kind of national resource—the lives of young men who were dear to their parents. "All lives on a battlefield are equal," he once said, "and a dead rifleman is as great a loss in the eyes of God as a dead General. The dignity which attaches to the individual is the basis of Western Civilization, and this fact should be remembered by every Commander." That did not mean he did not fight the enemy with full ferocity or take a certain pleasure from a battlefield littered with their dead, for he always knew the alternative, a battlefield littered with American dead. After the battle of Chipyongni, when the Chinese finally broke and the Americans killed thousands of them in flight with air and artillery strikes, one of the company commanders spoke of the battlefield as covered with "fricasseed Chinese." Ridgway liked that phrase and, on occasion, would bring it up with other commanders.

There was a vast unacknowledged difference in his and MacArthur's concepts of leadership, produced not merely by greatly different temperaments but by different visions of leadership in very different eras. So much of MacArthur's own energy went into building the commander up as a great man—as if, for the men in the ranks, fighting under so great a general would in itself make them great as well. Ridgway's concept of leadership was better suited for a more egalitarian era. He intended not to impose his will on his men, but to allow the men under him to find something within themselves that would make them more confident, more purposeful fighting men. It was their confidence in themselves that would make them fight well, he believed, not so much their belief in him. His job was to teach them to find that quality in themselves. Like MacArthur, however, he knew the importance of myth and was skilled at creating his own. "Old Iron Tits" was his nickname, based on the belief that it was two grenades he had pinned to the harness in front of his chest (one was a grenade, the other a medical kit). But the message was clear—Matt Ridgway was always ready to fight.

He had been intimately involved in Korea from the moment the war started; in effect, he was the Joint Chiefs' man on the war. When the bazookas used by American troops had been unable to penetrate the skin of Russian T-34 tanks in the early days of the war, he was the one who personally shepherded the new 3.5 bazooka through its manufacturing and distribution process, with his own men making sure any delays in the system were quickly pinpointed and corrected. He created a kind of pre-FedEx super-supply system that soon negated a critically important North Korean advantage in armor and so helped stop their assault on Pusan. He was not part of any Army cliques, but he was a Marshall man—Ridgway dedicated his book on Korea to Marshall as the greatest American soldier since Washington.

Ridgway arrived in Korea on December 26, 1950. The first thing he remembered was the cold—"It stuck to the bone," he noted. He had already flown to Tokyo and met with MacArthur, who told him, "The Eighth Army is yours, Matt. Do what you think best." That statement in itself signaled the end of one phase of the Korean War—in the past, everything had been run out of Tokyo. Now the command was his. The question was: could he keep his troops from being driven off the peninsula? Because Korea was such a grinding war, with such an unsatisfactory outcome, not many military men emerged from it as heroes. Grim wars that end in stalemates may produce men who are heroes to other soldiers, but not to the public at large. To George Allen, one of the CIA's ablest men, and a man who had briefed Ridgway regularly, he was nothing less than "the most underrated senior U.S. military officer of his immediate postwar generation, superior in most respects to his contemporaries—Mark Clark, Joe Collins, Omar Bradley, Maxwell Taylor, Arthur Radford, Arleigh Burke, the lot." Thus Ridgway was revered in years to come not so much by ordinary Americans, who had largely turned away from the war, but by the men who fought there and knew what he had done. In Korea he was the soldier's soldier. General Omar Bradley, a plainspoken Midwesterner not readily given to superlatives, wrote years later of his performance in Korea, "It is not often in wartime that a single battlefield commander can make a decisive difference. But in Korea, Ridgway would prove to be the exception. His brilliant, driving, uncompromising leadership would turn the battle like no other general's in our military history."

On arrival, Ridgway almost immediately started to tour forward positions. He was appalled by what he found: defeatist attitudes on the part of his commanders, low morale, and almost no military intelligence of any significance. He visited one corps commander who did not even know the name of a nearby river. "My God almighty!" he later said of that particular piece of ignorance. How could there be decent intelligence when all the American units had broken off contact with the enemy and were fleeing south? "What I told the field commanders in essence," he later wrote, "was that their infantry ancestors would roll over in their graves if they could see how road-bound this army was, how often it forgot to seize the high ground along its route, how it failed to seek and maintain contact in its front, how little it knew of the terrain, and how [it] seldom took advantage of it." He was sickened by finding an army broken in spirit, "not in retreat, but in flight," as Harold (Johnny) Johnson, who had been at Unsan, said. Ridgway thought the corps commanders shockingly weak, the division and regimental commanders too old and more often than not out of touch as well as ill-prepared for this war. Before he took the command, he had already spoken to Joe Collins about the need to be tough with the senior people in the field. "You must be ruthless with your general officers. Be ruthless with them because everything depends on their leadership."

Nothing enraged him more than the maps at the various headquarters he visited. Each American unit, it seemed, was surrounded by little red flags, each flag indicating a Chinese division. But many of his units simply had no idea how many Chinese were near them, because they were not sending out patrols. Not to know the location and strength of the enemy was in his eyes as great a sin as a commander could commit. He changed that quickly. He was everywhere in those days. He visited each headquarters, not just Division and Regimental, but sometimes Battalion and Company, arriving in his little plane flown by Mike Lynch, landing where he had no business showing up and often where no airstrip existed. What he wanted was for the most forward units to go out and find the enemy. They were to patrol, patrol, patrol: "Nothing but your love of comfort binds you to the roads," he kept repeating. "Find the enemy and fix him in position. Find them! Fix them! Fight them! Finish them!"

Very quickly he promulgated a new Ridgway rule of mapping. He would look at the local map with a red flag or two on it and ask when the last time was that the unit had had contact with the Chinese. At first the usual answer was four or five days—for most American units were in fact staying as far away from the Chinese as possible. With a gesture of complete contempt, Ridgway would then reach out and take the flags off the map. The new rule was that a red flag could stay on a map only if the unit had made contact in the previous forty-eight hours. The unstated corollary of this rule was equally simple: if the commander of the Eighth Army, a known and feared hard-ass, returned and found the situation unchanged, it would quite likely not just be the little red flags that would disappear, but the unit commander as well.

Because he was Ridgway, he had the kind of leverage with Tokyo that Walton Walker could only have dreamed of. If he wanted an officer for a command who was still serving back in the States or even in Tokyo, that major or lieutenant colonel or brigadier was on his way the next day. Unlike the men back in Washington, he did not fear a showdown with MacArthur if need be. The generals in Washington had been intimidated in the past by MacArthur, but now Ridgway was the man in Korea, and MacArthur, in Tokyo, was effectively the man on the sidelines. Ridgway might as a courtesy keep MacArthur clued in, but there was no question as to who was in command. For the men back in Washington, civilians and military, the change was a great relief. Ridgway might have his needs—a lot more artillery units—but he understood the problems Washington was dealing with, the fact that his command was only part of a larger geographical puzzle. For the first time since the war began, Washington and the command in Korea shared the same vision that this was to be something new, a limited war, and thus spoke the same language.

37

WITH RIDGWAY'S ARRIVAL, MacArthur, his forces defeated by the Chinese along the Chongchon and Yalu rivers, had lost not only his great gamble but in effect his command as well. Blame Washington for the limits imposed on him, he might; call it a victory because his troops had been on a giant recon patrol, he also might; but the senior (and middle level) military men who understood what had really happened in late November and early December knew exactly who the architect of the disaster was. Now he spoke ever more pessimistically of what he needed: four more divisions at least and a full air campaign against the Chinese mainland in order to destroy China's industrial capacity. Almost everything he wanted implied an even larger war, when by contrast the administration, its European allies, and surely the American people wanted less of a war. What Washington hoped for was some kind of stalemate, superior U.S. hardware against superior Chinese demographics. The most immediate question in Washington was: could the United Nations troops hold or would Korea be another Dunkirk?

The collision between the general and the president, which had been in the offing since the very beginning, was now about to take place, and at full force, at a terrible moment. The general wanted to expand the war, and the president, fearful of possible military confrontations elsewhere, wanted to localize and then end it. MacArthur had moved fatefully from being a military man, at least ostensibly carrying out the orders of the president and his military superiors, to becoming a dissenting policy man, armed with the exceptional powers and influence granted by his long service, his uniform, and his formidable political allies in Congress and the media. There was a certain inevitability to this and, in the weeks after the Chinese entrance, a series of escalating incidents. Effectively moved aside as the principal military officer by the arrival of Ridgway, MacArthur now embarked on a course of his own, as openly disobedient as a commander in the field could be in dealing with civilian policies, while pushing solutions viewed by senior officials in Washington, London, and other allied capitals as catastrophic.

That MacArthur was promoting a completely divergent agenda was obvious to Ridgway the moment he arrived in Tokyo. The two men spent an hour and a half together on December 26, 1950, much of the time taken up by a monologue delivered by MacArthur. It was quickly clear what the commander in the Far East wanted. "There isn't any question that MacArthur wanted to go to war," Ridgway would say later, "full war with Communist China. And he could not be convinced by all the contrary arguments. . . . He reluctantly acted in accordance with the policy, but he never did accept it. He wanted to go to war with China." That would become ever clearer in the weeks ahead. As a start, he wanted to use Chiang's troops in a strike against the mainland, telling Ridgway that the way was open because so many of Mao's troops had been shifted to Korea. "China is wide open in the south," he told Ridgway. Ridgway, in his own way distinctly a hawk, momentarily agreed with him, even though southern China being open to invasion was then a genuinely dubious proposition. The Communist Army was, by now, so large that Mao could afford to send a half million men into Korea and yet keep vast numbers of troops in reserve, precisely where Chiang might be expected to strike; and even if the road *were* open, whether Chiang's defeated troops were the ones to go down it was another question entirely. In the past, MacArthur had shown little respect for Chiang's troops, though he had felt the administration had not treated Chiang personally with the proper respect.

If Ridgway was more hawkish in some ways than others in the administration, if he had an even darker, more sinister view of the Communists than many of the staunchly anti-Communist men he was working with, he also knew the limits of the hand he had been dealt. Washington wanted to bring the Chinese to the negotiating table without investing significantly more resources in Korea. ("We are fighting the wrong nation," Acheson told Bradley at the time. "We are fighting the second team, whereas the real enemy is the Soviet Union.") That, Ridgway knew, would be his job, and it would be a bloody one—to make the Chinese pay so high a price that victory would seem as out of reach to them as it already seemed to Washington. He believed he could fulfill that mission. He was certain that American troops, well led, could damn well give a better account of themselves than they had just done up at Kunuri. He did not believe that the Chinese could easily push them off the peninsula as many in both Tokyo and Washington feared. "Ironically," as Clay Blair wrote of Ridgway's success in the weeks to come, "he would greatly undermine MacArthur's position and his own deeply held views about how to deal with the threat posed by world communism. He would in effect become an instrument of what many might call 'appeasement.'"

If there was going to be an unspoken limit on the number of divisions allotted him, then he would compensate with far greater firepower, especially more artillery—which was why he so quickly pressed for more artillery units. He was shocked—given the enormous potential advantage that artillery offered and the limits that the Chinese and North Korean styles of warfare placed on them—that the Americans had not emphasized their advantage in big guns earlier. Now he asked for ten more National Guard and Reserve artillery battalions. The use of artillery as a key factor in the kind of grinding war he was already envisioning was obvious. After all, the United States was rich with weaponry and ammunition but wanted to conserve its manpower; and the Chinese were desperately limited in their ability to bring in heavy guns, which, in any case, would be vulnerable to U.S. airpower. Ridgway intended to even out the demographics in the crudest, cruelest way possible—with long-range guns. The new artillery units were ordered in country as quickly as possible. Like others before them, the men of these units were originally supposed to go to Japan for training, but the pressures of the war being what they were, they debarked in Korea instead.

From the start Ridgway believed the war could be fought as what he called a meat grinder. On January 11, just two weeks after he had arrived in country, he wrote his friend Ham Haislip, the Army's vice chief of staff, "The power is here. The strength and the means we have—short perhaps of Soviet military intervention. My one overriding problem, dominating all others, is to achieve the spiritual awakening of the latent capabilities of this command. If God permits me to do that, we shall achieve more, far more than our people think possible—and perhaps inflict a bloody defeat on the Chinese which even China will long remember, wanton as she is with the sacrifice of lives."

In mid-January, when Joe Collins came through Asia to see MacArthur and Ridgway, he told Ned Almond he would soon be getting his third star. That was like a last tip of the hat, a final courtesy for MacArthur. Collins had come out with another member of the Joint Chiefs, Hoyt Vandenberg of the Air Force. Their first stop had been with MacArthur on January 15. Just a few weeks before, his dark cables might have struck terror in them. Now he was just an old man they had to check in with but whom they no longer feared and whose estimates and projections they no longer trusted.

When Collins and Vandenberg left Tokyo to see Ridgway in Korea, they found him in a significantly more optimistic mood than they expected, sure, as he had written Haislip, that the job was doable and he could do it. His confidence was contagious—and those who did not share it would soon find themselves at other jobs. He was changing the Eighth Army as quickly as he could into an effective fighting force. He understood something that few others realized at the time. The Second, the Twenty-fifth, and the Seventh divisions had taken heavy casualties, but the physical damage to the Eighth Army was less than everyone imagined; the real damage had been psychological or emotional. Those divisions had lost a great deal of equipment, yes, but that could be replaced. The surprise that had resulted from stumbling into a giant Chinese trap and fighting a brand-new enemy in such poorly chosen terrain had magnified the sense of damage, and the resulting defeat had crushed his army's *morale*. That was what had to be rebuilt—the spiritual or psychological side of his force.

Collins cabled Bradley that night with a fairly positive view of the visit. It was, noted J. D. Coleman, who both fought in the war and then became a historian of Korea, the first good news anyone had gotten back at the Pentagon in almost two months. Bradley later called it "a turning point. For the first time we began to think the Chinese could not throw us out of Korea, even with the self-imposed limitations under which we were fighting." When Collins returned to Washington, he briefed Truman on how well Ridgway was doing and how the morale of the Army was improving. He and Vandenberg had found MacArthur to be a querulous old man, dreaming of a war they had no intention of fighting. Ridgway by contrast was unintimidated by those early Chinese victories and the awesome size of their force; he seemed to have his finger on the strength and weakness of every unit and was full of confidence about what his forces could do. That was the way he had commanded in World War II, up front with his lead unit so that he could have as immediate a sense as possible of what was happening and which units might need help—an airborne division, after all, was not a place where you lingered back at your own CP. He was, his talented World War II deputy Jim Gavin, a famed airborne commander in his own right, once said, always drawn to the cutting edge of battle. "He was right up there every minute. Hard as flint and full of intensity, almost grinding his teeth with intensity; so much so that I thought that man's going to have a heart attack before it's over. Sometimes it seemed as though it was a personal thing: Ridgway versus the Wehrmacht. He'd stand in the middle of the road and urinate. I'd say: 'Matt, get the hell out of there. You'll get shot.' No! He was defiant. Even with his penis he was defiant."

As Ridgway began to change the command structure and get rid of some of his division and corps commanders, the great question among many senior officers was what he was going to do about Ned Almond. A number of senior officers in the Eighth Army (and, of course, Marine officers) regarded Almond as a co-conspirator in the disastrous events up north and had hoped that he would be quickly moved aside. But Almond was not going to be relieved. He was aggressive at least, and Ridgway had a serious need for aggressive commanders, but from now on he was going to have to play it straight—there would be no gamesmanship nor end runs around Matt Ridgway. He would for a time be allowed to keep command of a corps—Ridgway was appalled by how weak his other corps commanders were—but he would have to give up his job as chief of staff. Neither Ridgway nor Joe Collins (for somewhat different reasons) wanted the look of a bloodbath at the top, and neither wanted to cross MacArthur unnecessarily. Almond was still MacArthur's boy. If there was to be a major confrontation, let it be over something more important. So Almond remained in place, the officer everyone was watching. He would get his third star—MacArthur had lobbied hard for that—but his wings were going to be partially clipped. Bill McCaffrey had accompanied Almond on the day he met with Ridgway for the first time. It had been a long meeting and hardly a happy one. Almond had gone inside alone with Ridgway, with McCaffrey waiting outside. McCaffrey could tell from Almond's mood afterward that he was badly shaken. He had emerged quite deflated, still a corps commander, but that and nothing more: a man who had just been told in a very tough way the new rules of the headquarters and that he was no longer going to play games with the Eighth Army commander.

The changes in the fighting force began, of course, with the commanders. Major General John Coulter of Ninth Corps, who had performed so badly along the Chongchon, was seemingly promoted, given a third star, and sent off to a staff job in Tokyo; it was part of the code of the Army that when a senior officer failed in combat, great effort should be taken to protect his reputation and any sense of disgrace minimized, in no small part to show that the Army did not make mistakes. Ridgway did not immediately relieve the First Corps commander, Shrimp Milburn, who was an old friend. But there was a widespread belief that Milburn bore some of the responsibility for the disaster at Unsan, so Ridgway moved his own headquarters up to Milburn's, as a means of prodding him to be more aggressive.

There, his presence dominated the scene. Among headquarters officers, he became known as "the man who came to dinner" and "an honor we didn't deserve." In contrast to MacArthur, who never spent the night in Korea and who saw the war primarily in theoretical terms, Ridgway was there all the time. He wanted the fighting men in the field to know that he shared their knowledge and their hardships, and he wanted field commanders to know that he could not be fooled. His presence put everyone to a constant test of excellence. The corps chief of staff later said of that period, "Oh God! He came to *every* briefing *every* morning. . . . He'd go out all day with the troops, then when he came back at night I'd have to brief him again—on *everything,* even minor things like which way the water drained in our sector." Though Milburn was kept on for a time, Ridgway relieved proxies as a means of delivering his message.

Ridgway sat in on an early briefing with the corps G-3 Colonel John Jeter, and promptly made his displeasure with Corps known. During the briefing, Jeter went through a list of fallback positions. Ridgway asked what his attack plans were. Jeter answered that there were no attack plans. The next thing anyone knew, Jeter was gone, and word of it spread throughout the entire Eighth Army. It was probably not fair, relieving Jeter instead of Milburn, but nothing in Korea was fair then. Soon three division commanders were on their way home. They would be praised for what they had done, given medals and honorable new jobs, but the Eighth Army was not going to retreat anymore. Ridgway intended that they move forward whether they liked it or not. With that came a grudging nickname: "Wrongway Ridgway."

The other thing they were going to do was know their enemy—one more sign that the days of grandiose contempt for an Asian enemy, so racist in its origins, were over. More than most senior American commanders of his era, Matt Ridgway had a passion for intelligence. The American Army had always taken its intelligence functions somewhat casually; the men assigned to intelligence duty tended to have been passed over in their careers, not quite good enough for the prized command positions. Often the lower ranks in the Army's intelligence shop were very good, but their superiors were not respected by their peers. Perhaps it was the nature of the modern American Army—it had so much force and materiel that when it finally joined battle, intelligence tended to be treated as a secondary matter, on the assumption that any enemy could simply be outmuscled and ground down.

There were a number of reasons for Ridgway's obsession with intelligence. Some of it was his own superior intellectual abilities; he was simply smarter than most great commanders. Some of it was his innate conservatism, his belief that the better your intelligence, the fewer of your own men's lives you were likely to sacrifice. A great deal of it was his training in the airborne, where you made dangerous drops behind enemy lines with limited firepower and were almost always outnumbered and vulnerable to larger enemy forces. Certainly, his wariness about joining Marshal Badoglio in taking Rome reflected an airborne officer's insistence that his intelligence be the best. George Allen—who as a young CIA field officer in Vietnam briefed Ridgway daily for several weeks as the French war in Indochina was coming to its climax in 1954, later said he had never dealt with a man so acute and demanding, not even Walter Bedell Smith, who had been Dwight Eisenhower's tough guy in Europe and later took over the CIA. Ridgway's sense of the larger picture was so accurate, Allen believed, because of his determination to get the smallest details right. It was Ridgway's subsequent report on what entering the war in Indochina would mean—five hundred thousand to one million men, forty engineering battalions, and significant increases in the draft—that helped keep America out of the war for a time.

Charles Willoughby, one colleague said, would have lasted about an hour on Ridgway's staff. The CIA, blocked from the Korean theater by MacArthur and Willoughby, was soon welcomed back. Starting at Eighth Army headquarters and running through the command, there was going to be a healthy new respect for the enemy. The Chinese had identifiable characteristics on the battlefield. They also had good, tough soldiers. Some units were clearly better than others, some division commanders better than others, and it was vital to know which these were and where they were. Now Ridgway intended to study them. There would be no more windy talk about the mind of the Oriental. The questions would be: How many miles can they move on a given night? How fixed are their orders once a battle begins? How much ammo and food do they carry into each battle—that is, how long can they sustain a given battle? Ridgway was going to separate battlefield realities from theoretical discussions about the nature of Communism. The essential question was: How *exactly* can we tilt the battlefield to our advantage?

Ridgway now intended to play at least as big a role in the selection of the battlefield as his Chinese opposites. For a time, he started his day by getting in a small plane and, with Lynch at the controls, flying as low as they could, looking for the enemy. With that many Chinese coming at his army, there had to be signs of them, evidence that they existed, but he saw almost nothing. That he found nothing did not, as had happened in November after Unsan, create a lack of respect for them—rather it brought greater respect for the way they could move around seemingly invisible. Gradually Ridgway began to put together a portrait of who the Chinese were and how they fought—and so, how he intended to fight them. The Chinese were good, no doubt about that. But they were not supermen, just ordinary human beings from a very poor country with limited resources. Not only did the Chinese operate from a large technological disadvantage, they had significant logistical and communications weaknesses. The bugles and flutes announcing their attacks could be terrifying in the middle of the night, but the truth was that, with only musical instruments, they could not react quickly to sudden changes on the battlefield. If they had a breakthrough, they often lacked the capacity to exploit it immediately. That was a severe limitation; it meant that a great deal of blood might be shed without their getting adequate benefits. In addition, certain logistical limitations were built into any attack they made—the ammunition and food they could carry was finite indeed. The American Army could resupply in a way inconceivable to the Chinese and so could sustain a given battle far longer.

Ridgway spent his first few weeks in country pressing everyone for information about the Chinese fighting machine. By the middle of January, he felt he knew much of what he needed to know. This war, he decided, was no longer going to be primarily about gaining terrain as an end in itself, but about selecting the most advantageous positions available, making a stand, and bleeding enemy forces, inflicting maximum casualties on them. The key operative word would be "pyrrhic." What he now sought was an ongoing confrontation in which every battle resulted in staggering losses for the Chinese. At a certain point, even a country with a demographic pool like China's had to feel the pain from the loss of good troops. He wanted to speed up that moment, to let his adversaries know that there were no more easy victories out there for the picking, no second shot at a big surprise attack. If the war was to be a grinder then the great question was: which side would do the more effective job of grinding up the other?

The first thing Ridgway realized was that it was a disaster to retreat once the Chinese hit. The key to their offensive philosophy was to stab at a unit, create panic, and then, from advantageous positions already set up in its rear, maul it when it retreated. All armies are vulnerable in retreat, but an American unit, because of all its hardware, condemned to the narrow, bending Korean roads, was exceptionally so. What the Chinese had done at Kunuri, Ridgway learned, matched their MO when they fought the Nationalists in their civil war. But no one, it appeared, had been paying much attention. The disaster at Kunuri, he believed, had not been writ so large because the Chinese were such magnificent soldiers or even had such an overwhelming advantage in manpower. Even as far north and as vulnerable as they were, if the American units had been well buttoned down at night, if each unit had had interlocking fields of firepower with reliable flanking units (and had not counted on the ROKs to protect them), the outcome of the battle might have been different. Even at Kunuri, the military had had the capacity to resupply the troops by air until the Chinese were exhausted. Ridgway's long training as an airborne man was critical to the strategy he sought now. He meant to create strong islands of his own, sustain unit integrity with great fields of fire, and then let the enemy attack. It was, he believed, why Colonel John Michaelis, with his Twenty-seventh Regiment Wolfhounds, had been so much more successful than other regimental commanders in the early part of the war. Michaelis was an airborne guy, and he did not mind if his men were cut off as long as unit integrity was preserved. He knew he could always be resupplied by air.

What Ridgway wanted to do was start the Eighth Army moving north again—for reasons of morale as much as anything. In mid-January, he began the process, sending Michaelis's unit toward Suwon. He named this first offensive action Operation Wolfhound in their honor. Michaelis had known Ridgway before Korea, but not well. Still, he had been struck by Ridgway's fierce beetle-eyed glare—that was how he would later describe it—that went right through you. Ridgway had been in Korea only a few days when he called him in.

"Michaelis, what are tanks for?" he asked.

"To kill, sir."

"Take your tanks to Suwon," Ridgway said.

"Fine, sir," Michaelis answered. "It's easy to get them there. Getting them back is going to be more difficult because they [the Chinese] always cut the road behind you."

"Who said anything about coming back?" Ridgway answered. "If you can stay up there twenty-four hours, I'll send the division up. If the division can stay up there twenty-four hours, I'll send the corps up." That, thought Michaelis, was the start of a brand-new phase of the war, the beginning of the turnaround. Without the Chinese leadership realizing it, a very different UN force was coming together in Korea.

Part Nine

Learning to
Fight the Chinese:
Twin Tunnels, Wonju,
and Chipyongni

38

THE CHINESE WERE about to encounter a very different American command structure, and thus a very different American Army, in three battles in mid-February 1951, at Twin Tunnels, Chipyongni, and Wonju. But even before the two forces collided there, significant fissures had been appearing in the Chinese command structure. They had first showed up during the earliest discussions between China's military and political leaders, in September and October 1950, when Mao was pondering the question of intervention. Back then Lin Biao had opposed the coming war, fearing greatly superior American firepower that the Chinese could not possibly match. He argued that the firepower of an American division was roughly ten to twenty times greater than that of its Chinese equivalent. He and some of the other military men made an additional point: there was such a vast gap between U.S. capabilities, given the country's awesome industrial base, and China's limited ability to sustain a modern war, that replenishing equipment alone might prove a crisis in itself.

The fact that Lin had even made the argument—before excusing himself from an unwanted command because of alleged problems with his health—reflected a deep uneasiness among many of the Chinese military men, as well as the almost complete supremacy of the political people. They were all political men, of course, even the military men understood that; their basic doctrine made clear that political realities came first, military ones second. This was how and why they had been so successful in their long, demanding civil war. Their lack of an ability to replenish their weaponry had not been a problem— they had always been able to capture additional weapons from Chiang's forces. Their doctrines had all been based on almost unshakeable political truths in that war, but it had been waged on *Chinese soil*, where their ease in gaining and holding the loyalty of the peasants, long denied elemental dignity and basic economic rights, gave them an unassailable advantage. Whether the same dynamic would work in a foreign land was an open question, even if it was an Asian one with a comparably aggrieved peasant population and where in the

North, at least, the Chinese represented an ostensibly fraternal Communist party. If politics, as Mao believed, had its special truths that they knew better than anyone else, then military men like Peng Dehuai, political though they also were, knew that the battlefield had its truths as well. The political and military truths had dovetailed perfectly during the Chinese civil war, but they would separate in Korea, where Chinese troops in the eyes of most Koreans would be simply another foreign army and where the appearance of Chinese soldiers would have its own colonial implications.

After the battles along the Chongchon, Mao was ever more confident; Marshal Peng on the other hand was aware that much of his success had stemmed from the fact that the Americans had stupidly stumbled into a trap. He was concerned as his troops headed south; he had no air cover, and his logistical limitations were clear to him from the start. In Mao's mind, however, the Americans had behaved as he had predicted, as capitalist pawns pressed reluctantly into an unwanted war. There were times now, as the Chinese moved south and Mao pressed for a more aggressive strategy, that Peng would shake his head, turn to his aide, Major Han Liquin, and complain about Mao becoming drunk with success. In Peng's much more conservative view, there had already been serious signs of the difficulties ahead. Just feeding his vast army was a problem—in much of December they had gotten by subsisting largely on rations that the Americans had left behind, but their troops were now, he felt, half-starved. If they drove even farther south, the problem of feeding, and supplying his army with ammo, would be even worse.

When his forces had caught the Americans utterly ill-prepared at the Chongchon River, even when they had isolated an American unit, they often found it difficult to finish that unit off, especially given the U.S. control of the skies. (That complete control had occasioned a certain droll humor among the crews of American antiaircraft guns. When fighters or bombers flew overhead, the men would identify them as "B-2s." As yet there was no B-2 bomber in the Air Force inventory, so some soldier not yet clued in would ask in surprise, "What's a B-2?" And the answer would invariably come back, "*Be too* bad if they weren't ours.") U.S. firepower was, as advertised, exceptional, and because of the Americans' airpower and the mobility of their ground forces, they had a capacity to come to the rescue of isolated units that the Chinese had never seen before.

Even at Kunuri, far more of the American fighting force had escaped than Chinese planners had imagined possible given the total surprise the Chinese achieved and the incompetence of the senior American command. But it was during what the Chinese called the Fourth Campaign, or Fourth Phase, that their vulnerabilities became fully apparent and tensions between the field commanders and the political men making the decisions broke into the open. The First Campaign had lasted from October 24 to November 5 and focused on the destruction of the ROK forces leading the advance north and then of the Eighth Cav at Unsan; the Second Campaign was the assault along the Chongchon and against the Marines at the Chosin Reservoir in late November and early December. The Third Campaign took place in early January after much debate between Mao and Peng, who wanted to delay it, sensing that his exhausted troops were being pushed too hard for political reasons. It involved a quick push south behind the retreating Americans, during which Seoul, the Southern capital, changed hands for the third time in six months. As the campaign ended, the lead Chinese armies found themselves deep in the South, at the thirty-seventh parallel. The Fourth Campaign, presumably to start in January, would be the big one, the one that Mao hoped would take them perhaps another hundred miles farther south and leave them ready to strike at Pusan.

But as the Americans retreated down the long, thin peninsula, the Chinese began to experience some of the very problems that had frustrated their enemies—most particularly the problem of extended supply lines in a country with primitive roads and rail systems. Because they lacked air and sea power, this was a significantly more serious problem for them. When the Americans had moved north, they had been able to use trucks and trains without fear of being attacked from the air. They could, if necessary, transport badly needed ammo and food by air and sea. Not only did the Chinese have far fewer motorized vehicles to supply a vast army, but the trucks and trains were a perfect target for the ever stronger American air wing. It was Mao's turn now to be distanced from the battlefield, and to see it, as MacArthur had, not as it actually was, but as he wanted it to be in his mind. Mao had misread the easy early victory up north, even as some of his commanders understood why it might not happen so readily again. As the historian Bin Yu noted, Mao now "encouraged by China's initial gains began to pursue goals that were beyond [his] force's capabilities." That placed the burden of dealing with reality squarely on Peng's shoulders.

In a way Peng was an almost perfect counterpart to Ridgway—they could not have been more similar in what drove them and the way they saw and handled their own men. It would not be hard to imagine some switch in ancestry and an American version of Peng commanding the UN forces, and Ridgway, in a Chinese incarnation, the Chinese. Like Ridgway, Peng was a soldier's soldier, unusually popular with his men, because he was sensitive to their needs. The more successful he became, the truer he remained to what he had been. Sometimes when his troops were moving long distances on foot, and other peasants, or coolies as Westerners called them, were serving primarily as bearers, carrying heavy loads strung over poles, he would take the pole from one of them and take a turn himself, which greatly impressed the troops and served to remind everyone—his men and himself—where it had all begun and, perhaps equally important, *why* it had begun. He was a man absolutely without pretension, which endeared him greatly to his troops. During the Long March, out of personal devotion, his men had twice carried him for long distances on a litter after he had been struck down with a severe fever. On one occasion when he was very sick in Sichuan, his men had refused to leave him behind; nursing him and carrying him along was their way of thanking him for the humane way he had always treated them.

He was straightforward and no less blunt than Ridgway. It amused him when some of his former colleagues in what had been in the beginning a peasant army began to take on airs once they defeated the Nationalists. Peng still preferred to bathe in cold water, even when hot water was available, because he had always done so, and because this was what peasants did. In his lifestyle he preferred an almost monastic simplicity, and was uneasy with unwanted creature comforts. He preferred curing illnesses with herbs rather than modern medicines prescribed by doctors, and he always ate very slowly, deliberately so, he said, because he liked to think of the days when they had first started out, always hungry. Now that he had enough food, he intended to savor it.

Peng was a good deal shrewder than some of the other people in the politburo gave him credit for. He had never been fooled by his early success up along the Chongchon. Even before the war began, he had believed that, given the unusual nature of the Korean peninsula, the opposing armies would have a terrible time getting supplies to either end of the country. "Korea," he had told his staff before the war began, "will be a battle of supply." That was why he argued successfully with Mao that when they hit the Americans all-out for the first time, they should do it from positions as far north as possible.

But he also knew in what were for him the heady, good days of November and December how near the bad days might be. In the period after the success of the Second Offensive in late November, he was quite shrewd in sizing up the residual strength of the defeated American forces, and the price his troops had already paid, especially around the Chosin Reservoir. The Marines had fought back with a ferocity that belied Mao's convictions about how the soldiers of a capitalist army would perform. When Peng spoke with his senior people, he

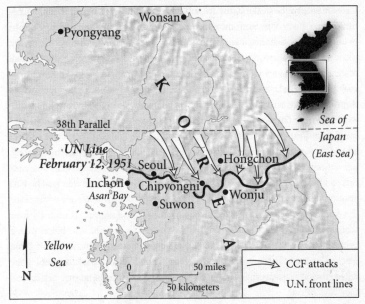

19. THE FIGHT FOR THE CENTRAL CORRIDOR

would on occasion let a certain sarcastic note enter his voice about Mao—
"some self-proclaimed experts on the art of war," or "some military experts," or
"some people who see the conduct of war in dogmatic terms." He was furious
when both the Russians and North Koreans argued strongly in December that
his troops should pursue the Americans more aggressively. The Russians were
not putting *their* men into the field, and as for the North Koreans, he was bail-
ing them out from their own incredible mistakes and poor leadership. He
hated the pressure they put not so much on him, but on Mao, to move more
rashly, the implication being that the Chinese were showing the world that
they were not as good Communists, or as brave as Russians might have been in
the same circumstances.

Peng's constant mantra with his staff was the need for supplies. He had, at
the start, commanded an army of some three hundred thousand men, and it
grew even larger as he prepared for future battles. As he had predicted, the logistics were a nightmare: in December, he had at most three hundred trucks to
ferry supplies to his men, and those trucks had to travel in the dark with their
lights off, making at best a total of twenty to thirty miles a night. Resupply of
both ammunition and food became the great vulnerability of his army. On the

Chinese side much of the logistical support was done not by trucks but by Chinese bearers, who carried food and supplies south to Peng's men, often on foot over enormous distances, and who, that part of the journey done, carried the wounded back north. Under these circumstances, much of his army existed, once it neared the thirty-eighth parallel, on a diet that was just a bit above starvation levels. Foraging was unpromising: as they moved back and forth across the Korean peninsula, both sides destroyed land and crops, something that weighed more harshly on the Chinese forces than on the Americans, who did not have to eat off the land. A cruel, arctic winter ensured that there was no abundant local food source for the Chinese troops; if Mao's soldiers had, to use his famous phrase, been the fish swimming in the ocean of China's peasants not so long before, now they were swimming in more hostile waters. The Korean peasants turned out to be just as dismayed to see them as they were to see the Americans or the ROKs, for almost nothing good happened once the war arrived in your village. As a result, malnutrition was a serious problem. Peng's soldiers had, in the phrase used in those days, to fight their hunger with "one bite [of] parched flour and one bite [of] snow." When their buddies were killed, they often scavenged their bodies for extra bullets and any extra food they could find.

When the Chinese launched their Third Campaign on New Year's Eve 1950, food from China met only a quarter of the army's minimum needs. Because of the American bombing campaign, casualties among truck drivers were higher than among the combat troops. The troops themselves were in a constant state of exhaustion. By February, they had been fighting continuously under difficult conditions and essentially living off the land for more than two months, but UN airpower left little chance to rest, even in safe areas removed from the front lines. The cold was very hard on the Americans and their feet, and American commanders issued warning after warning about care of socks and feet, but it was much worse for the Chinese: their men traveled in high-top sneakers, and that made frostbite a constant problem for them. In time, many Chinese soldiers could not get their swollen feet into their sneakers and so simply wrapped them in rags to go forth to battle.

Thus, even before the Third Campaign began, with his vast army still north of Seoul, and Mao badly wanting them to recapture the Southern capital for its propaganda value, Peng was lobbying to slow the offensive down so his men could rest and regroup. On December 8, 1950, he cabled Mao requesting a pause until the spring; in addition, he wanted to keep the battle area above Seoul. He believed that the American and UN forces had not been that badly damaged in the fighting in the North, and were now increasingly well dug in. It might simply be too costly to assault them and their wall of firepower south of Seoul. To Peng it made little military sense to risk so much for the small political victory that would come with the liberation of Seoul. Mao felt quite differently; so did the Soviets and Kim Il Sung. If originally Mao had seen the decision to enter this war as a way of serving notice on the rest of the world—especially a Communist world so long under the hegemony of the Russians—that this was a new China, now he was slowly becoming a prisoner of his own pride and vanity.

In this way, the exceptional success of the early battles was turning into a burden for Peng. Because the Chinese had done so well, ever more was expected. The Soviets, through their ambassador to Korea, continued to push Peng to race ahead. Given the fact that the Soviets had not even made good on their promise of air cover, Peng was underwhelmed by Russian exhortations. To him they suggested admirable Russian battlefield audacity—paid for with Chinese lives. But Mao wanted much the same thing as the Russians; with the entire world watching, he badly desired the symbolic political victory that would come with the capture of Seoul. Besides, he had become contemptuous of the American forces—the early defeats had convinced him they were even weaker than the Chinese Nationalist armies he had defeated. By then some of America's allies and some senior members of the Truman administration were talking about negotiating a cease-fire at the thirty-eighth parallel, but Mao was dubious. That his enemies wanted a settlement was proof to him that they knew they were losing and wanted to prevent a total defeat. Such a precipitous settlement was a trick on their part. On December 13, he sent Peng a cable pointing out the political dangers of failing to pursue their enemy. If Peng slowed down now, he warned his commander, the rest of the world would become suspicious of Chinese strength.

On December 19, Peng cabled back, warning against "a rise of unrealistic optimism for quicker victory from other parts," a reference to the Soviets and Kim Il Sung and, implicitly perhaps, Mao himself. Instead he proposed a rest period to be followed by the next major campaign. Mao wanted that campaign to start in early January, some six weeks ahead of Peng's preferred schedule. Some adjustment for Peng's needs was made; but, as Bin Yu has written, the final compromise reflected Mao's vision, and because of that, in his words, the "political goals defined by Mao tended to go beyond the CPVF's [the Chinese People's Volunteer Forces] capacities."

What Mao wanted, Mao got. On New Year's Eve, Peng struck, and eventually his troops did reach the thirty-seventh parallel, but the American retreat this time was careful and they took relatively few casualties. Ridgway had been in country only a few days when the offensive began and he was furious with the ROK performance. "It was," he wrote in his history of the Korean War, "a dismaying spectacle. ROK soldiers by truckloads were streaming south without orders, without arms, without leaders in full retreat. Some came on foot or in commandeered vehicles of every sort. They had just one aim—to get as far away from the Chinese as possible. They had thrown their rifles and pistols away and had abandoned all artillery, mortars, machine guns, every crew-served weapon." If he was pleased about anything, it was that unlike what happened during the retreat from Kunuri, the Americans here lost very little equipment.

The one important question was: could they hold a line above Seoul? Ridgway reluctantly decided that they could not ignore the kind of pressure the enemy could apply to the impermanent bridges built by the American engineers across the Han River. He could not risk isolating part of his army on the north side of the Han when the bridges behind them could be so easily destroyed. His choice was a difficult one—especially for a man who always wanted to attack and now more than ever wanted to infuse some positive energy into his men: but they had to give up Seoul and go south. On January 3, he told Ambassador John Muccio to inform President Syngman Rhee that he was going to have to take his government and head south yet one more time, and do it very quickly at that, because the bridges would be closed to all but military personnel by mid-afternoon of that day. On January 4, Seoul was burning again and the bridges over the Han had been blown.

The Third Campaign now seemed like another great success, and inevitably created pressure on Peng for yet more victories, and a belief among some in the Beijing leadership that he was being far too cautious. The idea that the Russians might think the Chinese timid appalled Mao. The balance between the two countries might change significantly in the next decade—as Soviet premier Nikita Khrushchev started a de-Stalinization campaign and the Chinese claimed the mantle of Communist purists—but at that point, China was still the untested junior partner, and the Russians still had the right to judge the Chinese. Thus, it was easy for the Russians to goad Mao. Russian representatives in Beijing kept pressuring Mao to pursue the enemy. So too did Kim Il Sung. He met with Peng at his headquarters and asked him to pursue the Americans more audaciously.

Peng controlled his temper. The Americans were not actually defeated, he said. They had held their army together better than Kim realized. They might simply be trying to lure the Chinese too far south, so that they could strike back with another amphibious landing (a not so subtle reminder of mistakes made in the past). Still, the retaking of Seoul seemed like a significant propaganda victory, and there were huge rallies in China celebrating its recapture. In late January, Mao cabled Peng with his directives for the next campaign. In the process, Mao suggested, Peng's forces would wipe out twenty to thirty thousand enemy soldiers. It was as if the chairman had not heard a word Peng had said in the last few weeks, caught up as he was in his own dreams of glory.

39

BY EARLY FEBRUARY, the Chinese and American armies were stumbling toward a defining confrontation in what was known as the central corridor of Korea. It was a confrontation Ridgway now eagerly sought and about which Peng remained somewhat uneasy, though if the two forces had to meet, he greatly preferred that the central corridor with its mountainous terrain be the principal battleground. If he won, there would be little the UN forces could do to stop him. He intended that his troops could once again move up the mountainsides on foot at night, leaving the Americans once again warm in their vehicles on the roads deep in the valleys. So the Fourth Phase offensive would be launched, with control over the Wonju-Chipyongni area as its goal.

Ridgway's intelligence was gradually improving, but it was still far too fragmentary, given how much was at risk. He had a sense that a major Chinese campaign was coming and that it might be in or at the edge of the central corridor region. But he was not sure exactly where, or how large it would be, and he wanted more precise information. In fact, he wanted far more than that. Ridgway had already moved the Second Division into the general area. It was now part of Tenth Corps, under the command of Ned Almond. The Second Division had in effect replaced the First Marines, whose commander had made it clear that they did not want to serve under Almond again. Ridgway was planning a major attack to the west of Tenth Corps, and he wanted the Second Division to cover his own right flank. That put Paul Freeman's Twenty-third Regiment on the far right flank of all those forces, where it would play a critical role in the fighting to come.

ONE OF THE first things Ridgway had done after arriving in country was to make the Second Division whole again. Dutch Keiser had been relieved by Walton Walker and replaced by Major General Bob McClure. But Ned Almond had despised McClure, and he lasted only thirty-seven days as division commander. In his brief tenure, one of the things McClure fixed on was making all the men in the division grow beards. "He had seen beards on some of the Turkish soldiers and decided it made them look very tough—very warrior-like—and so the Americans should have them as well, and so we had to grow them and most of us hated them," remembered John Carley, then a captain in the division's G-3. Almond was a clean-look kind of general; he wanted uniforms and chins neat, and so the beards and McClure were both soon gone.

Slowly, starting in mid-December, the division, now stationed at Yong-dongpo, was being put back together. Fresh troops and better equipment arrived from the States. A battalion of French troops, mostly from the French Foreign Legion, was assigned to the Twenty-third on December 11, boosting its strength immediately. The First Ranger Company was also added, while the badly torn up Thirty-eighth Regiment received a battalion of Dutch soldiers. On December 15, some two weeks after it had been hammered at Kunuri, the Second Division was again declared combat effective. By late December, it was operating in the Hoengsong-Wonju area, and its top intelligence people were hearing reports that Wonju might be the next big Chinese prize.

Wonju was the southernmost part of what would become a brutally contested piece of central corridor terrain roughly in the shape of a triangle, with the villages of Hoengsong and Chipyongni serving as its second and third points. Of the villages in the area, Wonju was the most important, both as a railhead and road center. Ansil Walker, who fought at Chipyongni, noted that if the Chinese controlled the triangular area, they would gain a formidable base from which to strike at Taegu, about a hundred miles south, and bitterly disputed in the earlier Naktong fighting. It would be like a knife poised at Pusan, he said. That was, in fact, very much the way Marshal Peng saw the coming battle. He had held his last staff meeting on December 27 and had worked hard to improve the mood of his men—some of whom were a bit edgy about fighting the Americans now that they might be better prepared. When they struck this time, Peng said, "the imperialists will run like sheep. Our problem is not Seoul. It is Pusan. Not taking it. Just walking there!" With that, as his aide Major Liquin noted, the mood in the room improved. Then Peng went to the map. "It is there at Wonju," he said, "that the battle will be decided. A breakthrough at Wonju will carry us all the way down to Taegu." He was clearly speaking with greater confidence and more bravado than he felt.

By mid-January, Ridgway's headquarters was receiving reports that enemy soldiers were pouring into the area. At first, Ned Almond, in whose Corps sector most of the fighting took place, and who was not as passionate about intelligence as Ridgway, thought they were North Koreans, but they turned out to be preponderantly Chinese, moving in (as they had in the past) at night and on foot, away from the roads, and so for quite a while failing to trigger any reliable estimates of just how large a force was gathering.

On January 25, Ridgway, by now a month in country, launched his first major offensive, named Operation Thunderbolt. Troops from First Corps and Ninth Corps moved forward cautiously, almost shoulder to shoulder, so that the Chinese could not slip through them or behind them and attack their flanks. Ridgway wanted neither gaps in his line nor any significant section of it given over to the ROKs. Thunderbolt's objective was limited; he wanted his forces to go about twenty miles north and reach the southern bank of the Han River. He wanted to do it cautiously and incrementally—only as the offensive seemed to be working were more units going to be added. Ridgway did not want to start north, find that he had underestimated the number of Chinese in the sector, and thus discover that instead of being on the offensive he was now on the defensive.

Operation Roundup, Almond's part of the operation, run out of Tenth Corps, was scheduled to kick off on February 5. Even before it started, Ridgway was concerned about the growing Chinese presence in the central corridor region, to the east of where most of Thunderbolt would take place. He knew his forces were understrength there, and he wanted to keep both Wonju and Chipyongni from falling into Chinese hands. As a result, on January 28, he started sending units of the Twenty-third to probe the Chipyongni area, starting with a place they came to call Twin Tunnels.

As January came to a close, the scene was set for two epic battles, the first involving the greatly outnumbered Twenty-third Regiment in what became a Communist siege of Chipyongni; the second, a few miles away at Wonju, bringing elements of the Second Division, the Thirty-eighth and Ninth regiments, along with members of the 187th Regimental Combat Team, to fight an estimated four Chinese divisions. Both were bitter battles, and in both it was uncertain who would emerge victorious until, quite literally, the final hours. That was especially true of Wonju, where elements of the Thirty-eighth Regiment were initially hit so hard that the area became known as Massacre Valley. The two battles were connected and yet quite separate; it was the battle of Chipyongni that long resonated with allied commanders in Korea, and quickly became the model for how to fight this new and formidable enemy. Wonju, on the other hand, was a victory in the end, but it reflected the fact that some senior commanders, like Almond, still had the capacity to underestimate the enemy grievously.

IN EARLY JANUARY, Ridgway had assigned the Twenty-third Regiment to the defense of Wonju, thus placing Colonel Paul Freeman and his regiment under the command of Almond for the first time. It was not to be a happy relationship. Freeman's forces were already engaged in early skirmishes around Wonju when, on January 9, he had his first meeting with Almond. A large enemy force was

well dug in on a major hill just south of the village. Two battalions had been ordered into the battle by Division, one of them from the Thirty-eighth Regiment
and commanded by Jim Skeldon. His battalion was on the left side of the main
road, working its way toward the hill, while a battalion of the Twenty-third Regiment worked the right side of the road. When Almond and Freeman had their
first encounter, the battle was not going particularly well. The American force
was probably too small for the job. Almond was a commander who, much more
than most comparable officers, had his favorites, Almond's Boys. When they
served him well, he pushed hard for choice slots for them, guaranteeing him not
merely talent but loyalty. He was very hard on commanders of comparable ability who were not his boys. Freeman was not one of Almond's boys, and it struck
him that his corps commander seemed to take an immediate dislike to him. If
Bob McClure was still the nominal division commander, it quickly became clear
to Freeman that Almond was the real man in charge, the corps commander as
division commander. Freeman had been moving up closer to the battle to check
out exactly what was happening, when he came upon Almond, McClure, Nick
Ruffner (the corps G-3 but soon to replace McClure), and Al Haig, a young Almond aide (and one day to be a major White House player), gathered on a hill
overlooking the part of the battle where Skeldon's troops were engaged. Almond
immediately asked Freeman, "Who's in command here?"

"Colonel Skeldon," Freeman replied. Where is he? Almond wanted to
know. On the next hill, Freeman answered.

"Aren't you in command here?" Almond pressed. No, said Freeman; he
commanded another unit, a little farther back. "What are you doing up here?"
Almond asked. "I came up to see if I could help out," Freeman answered. "Well,
why isn't a stronger force being used to get back to Wonju?" Almond asked.
Freeman replied that they had been told to use only two battalions. That, he
was aware, put the onus completely on McClure. Just then the interrogation
was interrupted by an enemy mortar attack and everyone hit the ground. Freeman was grateful for the interruption.

Finally Almond and his team decided to leave. On the way down the hill
they ran into one of Freeman's sergeants. Almond, as Freeman remembered it,
decided to make small talk, about how cold it was. "It's so cold that the water
froze in my trailer this morning," Almond said—an attempt to buddy up,
Freeman thought, and a poor one at that. "You're goddamned lucky to have a
trailer and a basin of water," the sergeant answered. It was icy and treacherous
moving down the hill, and Almond slipped, going down right on his butt.
Freeman extended a hand to help him up. "If I need your help, I'll ask for it,"
Almond said. A great first meeting, Freeman thought to himself.

At the bottom of the hill it only got worse. There was a soldier chopping wood and doing it poorly. Almond promptly told him he was doing it wrong, and if he was not careful, he might chop his foot off. "I hope to hell I do; maybe they'll send me out of this goddamned place," the soldier replied. Freeman was aware that he had lost even more points. Another soldier was in a foxhole behind a tree. Almond ordered him out, got in, took his rifle, and decided the foxhole commanded a poor field of fire, which it did. He complained bitterly about this to Freeman. From then on, the view of Freeman back at Almond's headquarters was that he was soft and timid, a man who did not push his troops hard enough. He appeared to be an officer marked for relief just as soon as Almond could get around to it.

That was in sharp contrast to the way the men of the Twenty-third saw their commander. But none of this mattered; from then on Freeman was a marked man at Corps headquarters. By contrast Freeman, like all too many subordinate commanders under Almond, found the corps commander to be dangerously overconfident about the superiority of his own tactical views at all times, thinking himself at once a better company commander, battalion commander, and regimental commander than any of the men serving under him. Freeman's view of Almond coincided almost exactly with that of O. P. Smith of the Marines. Unlike other high-ranking officers Freeman had dealt with, Almond was a poor listener; he seemed to feel that there was only one way to go about any assignment: push farther ahead ever more quickly, whatever the shortcomings or the consequences. All of this made Freeman the man on the spot, his regiment virtually on point in its sector as the Chinese prepared to strike. Matt Ridgway wanted a major confrontation with the Chinese, and Paul Freeman found the enemy for him, however involuntarily, when the two great armies finally stumbled into each other in mid-February.

40

IN A WAY, there were two battles of Chipyongni. First came the battle of Twin Tunnels, between the two gathering armies, in which the Chinese nearly overwhelmed the UN forces. That, in turn, triggered the battle of Chipyongni. All of this was part of a larger contest for control of the transportation arteries leading south through the central corridor. Chipyongni itself was about fifty miles east of Seoul, about forty south of the thirty-eighth parallel, and about fifteen miles northwest of Wonju. The Twin Tunnels were "about three miles southeast of Chipyongni," in the words of historian Ken Hamburger, who wrote with exceptional clarity of both battles. There, he noted, the railroad "abruptly turns south to east and tunnels under two ridgelines before turning again to the south and east. The terrain in the tunnels area consists of the two ridgelines generally running north to south and rising to about one hundred meters above the valley floor. The ridgelines curve toward one another in the north where they close into a horseshoe with a single constricted road leading to Chipyongni. As this road leads out of the valley, it crosses the east-west railroad between the two tunnels that give the area its name." The valley floor, Hamburger noted, ran about five hundred meters from east to west, and one thousand meters from north to south. Several high hills of about five hundred meters each surrounded it.

The American command was beginning to look at nearby Chipyongni as critical, because it would help them control the access to Wonju, the larger communications center, where the Americans, like Peng, now believed one of the fateful battles of the central corridor would be fought. In late January, as Ridgway's forces over on the west began their first major operation, the Second Division found itself ordered to protect its flank on the east, and at the same time to move into the Chipyongni area and try to locate the Chinese Forty-second Army. Ridgway's intelligence people believed it was hiding out somewhere in the central corridor but had not yet revealed itself. For it was one of those great contrasts of the first year of the war, the stark difference between the two armies and the way they maneuvered: on the eve of battle, even facing a force that had nine divisions in it, the Americans did not yet know where the Chinese were; by contrast, hiding an American division on Korean soil would have been comparable to hiding a hippopotamus in a pet store.

There were three stages to the Twin Tunnels battle: a recon, and then two battles, each of escalating violence. The Eighth Army's Operation Thunderbolt, Ridgway's main drive and his attempt to reclaim the initiative in the war, kicked off on January 26, and the first recon into the Twin Tunnels area, led by Lieutenant Maurice Fenderson, took place the next day. Fenderson was new to the Twenty-third, having arrived right after the Kunuri fighting, for which he remained eternally grateful. He was assigned to Captain Sherman Pratt's Baker Company, given its first platoon, and as an added welcome assigned to take his men and recon an area to the east where there were some railroads and, he was told, two tunnels. There were scattered reports of some Chinese troops operating in the area. All he had to do was go over there and check it out—nothing much to it, he was told.

It was an eerie assignment. Even the spot his motorized patrol started out from was already deep in enemy territory, far north of the American lines. At every moment he feared a possible ambush. As a kid of seventeen, straight out of high school, Fenderson had served in World War II, as part of the Seventieth Division, mostly trying to keep up with George Patton as his tanks raced across France. That race, its sheer muscularity, stood in stark contrast to the patrol he was now leading. This was about being apart from other American units, and, more than anything else, about the loneliness of war. If bad things happened, you were out there by yourself. His patrol proceeded to the assigned location, perhaps a mile south of the tunnels, very cautiously. There, they spotted soldiers, almost surely Chinese, and a brief firefight ensued. Fenderson was then ordered to return to base, which he did, feeling he had done his job and been lucky as well.

The next day, on Almond's orders, Freeman sent out a larger force to recon the area, setting in motion the next stage of the Twin Tunnels struggle. The men in this task force were to patrol the area, but if at all possible not engage any larger enemy force. Elements of two companies were sent in, the reconstituted Charley Company of the Twenty-third Regiment, commanded by Lieutenant James Mitchell, and a company from the Twenty-first Regiment of the neighboring Twenty-fourth Division, commanded by Lieutenant Harold Mueller. About half the men from Charley Company were brand-new, hardly surprising given all the hits the company had taken in the last few months. Many of them were just out of the repot-depot, where replacement troops arrived, and few were trained combat infantrymen. The two units were to join up at the village of Iho-ri and then head for Twin Tunnels, some fifteen miles away.

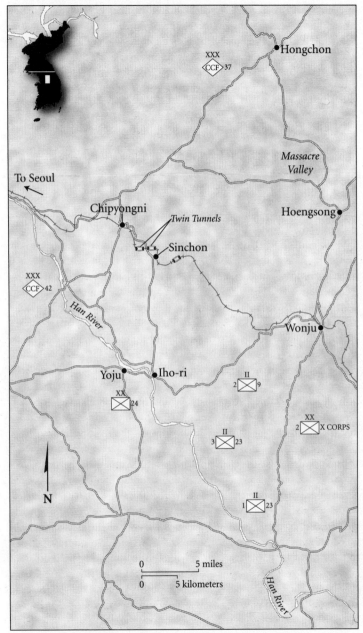

20. **THE TWIN TUNNELS—CHIPYONGNI-WONJU AREA, JANUARY–FEBRUARY 1951**

It was a relatively small combined force—four officers and fifty-six enlisted men. The weaponry was quite heavy for so small a unit: eight BARs, two heavy machine guns and four light ones, a rocket launcher, a 60mm mortar, and both a 57 and a 75 recoilless rifle. In a fight, nearly half the unit would either be firing a heavy weapon or assisting on one. They also had two three-quarter-ton trucks and nine jeeps. A liaison plane flew overhead, a spotter in case Chinese units, unseen from the ground, were moving in on them. The plane enjoyed better communications with their base than did the men on the ground, and the plane's link to the men on the ground was weak. Captain Mel Stai, the assistant battalion operations officer, had also joined the unit. He was supposed to return to Battalion headquarters when the patrol left Iho-ri, but he decided on his own to stay with them to Twin Tunnels. In his jeep was the only radio capable of contacting the spotter plane. It was slow going all day—there was a lot of snow on the icy road, and also heavy fog, all too typical of the Korean winter. The spotter plane was of little value for much of the morning.

They reached the Twin Tunnels area around noon, well behind schedule. Mitchell waited at the south end of the valley that led to the tunnels, until Mueller caught up with him. So far everything had gone reasonably well. Mitchell had kept his jeeps about fifty yards apart in the convoy and the trucks with the heavy weapons farther back so if the jeeps were hit, they could quickly come to their aid. It was at this point, as Ken Hamburger later wrote, that a kind of Murphy's Law took over—and everything that could go wrong began to go wrong. They had stopped just where the main road led north to the tunnels, but a side road shot off east to the nearby village of Sinchon. Because the patrol was late, Captain Stai volunteered as a courtesy to go into Sinchon by himself and look it over, allowing the main body to continue without interruption. He drove partway to the village, left his vehicle at the side of the road, and walked in, taking with him, of course, the only radio compatible with the one in the spotter plane. That was a critical mistake. His jeep was soon destroyed, his driver killed, and Stai was never seen again.

Effective communication between the force on the ground and its eyes and ears in the sky was now gone. Up in the spotter aircraft, Major Millard Engen, the battalion executive officer, had spotted a sizeable force of enemy soldiers moving rapidly toward the Americans from the slope of Hill 453, which dominated the southern approach to the Twin Tunnels area. He immediately tried to radio Lieutenant Mitchell to get out of the valley as quickly as possible, but of course, he could not get through. Soon there was no need to warn them that the Chinese might attack—they were already being hit hard. The spotter plane then turned back to refuel, but not before Engen radioed regimental headquarters that the patrol was in danger of being wiped out.

In fact, even as they entered the open valley, they had been trapped by a considerably larger Chinese force. Private Richard Fockler, who was caught along with the other men in the patrol when the Chinese struck, later remembered that they were just about to have lunch when the first mortar round landed near them. Almost immediately other weapons joined in. The drivers were ordered to turn their vehicles around immediately. But the road was so narrow that it was hard for the jeeps, let alone the trucks, to maneuver. They had just gotten most of the vehicles facing the right way when the lead jeep was hit. The driver, Fockler remembered, panicked and stalled it out, blocking the rest of the convoy. Then a Chinese machine gun began hammering away at them, the tattoo of an automatic weapon on a metal target, followed by the worst noise imaginable, Fockler believed, a kind of terminal sound, that of coolant draining from a radiator. When the Chinese began to fire, there apparently was a brief disagreement between Mitchell and Mueller. In Mueller's view their only chance to avoid total annihilation was to head for the high ground—a hill just off to the east—and dig in. For a brief moment, Mitchell still hoped they might be able to fight their way out by road. Then Mueller yelled to Mitchell: "We're going to have to get to the top of that hill. The Chinese are coming up from the other side. This is our only chance!" The Chinese understood that as well, so both sides started racing for the hill and the high ground. But if they were in a race for the hill, and if time was suddenly the critical factor, then the Americans were going to have to travel light, leaving most of their heavy weapons behind. In the end, they took only a rocket launcher, a light machine gun, and some of the BARs.

The day the patrol was hit happened to be the twenty-first birthday of a young man named Laron Wilson, a driver for Headquarters Company of the Third Battalion of the Twenty-third Infantry Regiment, who had been loaned to Charley Company. The patrol was going to be an easy one, he had been assured, because the recon the previous day had made only the most minimal contact with the enemy. Wilson was just a little uneasy: for all of the assurances, going on a mission always had an element of uncertainty and danger, and he was going to be doing it without knowing anyone else in the unit. When he connected with the men he was to drive from the Twenty-fourth Division—four soldiers, all of them strangers, with a light machine gun—he felt very much alone. He did not even know the other jeep drivers from the Twenty-third, and that added to the loneliness—you were always supposed to know the men you went to war with, because in the end you fought for them as much as for yourself. It was never a lark, anyway, he believed, not up where they were operating, where they might well be completely surrounded by Chinese and not even know it until it was too late. One thing he noticed—rather enviously—was that the men from the Twenty-fourth Division all had the new reversible parkas that were just arriving in country. They were warmer, and one side was white, which offered that much more camouflage in snowy Korea.

Wilson had joined the Army in 1948 right after finishing high school in Salt Lake City. He had always intended to be a soldier. When he was a boy and American troops had marched down Salt Lake City's main drag during World War II, he had unfailingly rushed into the streets to watch. He loved the sight of those mighty convoys heading for a nearby Army base. In high school, he had taken ROTC because he was so sure that the Army would be his career. He had been in the Twenty-third for more than a year. The last night that his unit had spent in the States before shipping out in late July had been his first wedding anniversary. He had been given permission to spend the night with his wife at a nearby hotel. This had greatly irritated his first sergeant who, not married himself, did not believe that any serious soldier should have a wife or anything else not issued by the Army. As he headed into Twin Tunnels, Wilson was still dealing with the idea that he had just become a parent—his first child, Susan, had been born only three weeks earlier. The reality of that was hard to come to terms with because he was so far away, but it had immediately made him feel he had a lot to live for.

He had fought through the Naktong battles and made it out of Kunuri. He had great faith in Colonel Freeman and special confidence in Captain John Metts, commander of his Headquarters Company, as cool a customer as he had dealt with. In those final hours at Kunuri, when everything was falling apart, Wilson had been in the process of disassembling a cooking stove. Just then, with the Chinese getting ever closer and the tension becoming unbearable, Captain Metts appeared. Wilson put together a plate of food and some coffee for him, anything to fight off the numbing cold, and joined him with a coffee of his own. Suddenly, the Chinese started firing away. Two bullet holes promptly appeared on the stovepipe right next to him, and Wilson quickly hit the ground, spilling coffee all over himself. Metts never moved. "Well, that's two more rounds we don't have to worry about" was all he said. Somehow they had managed to slip away on the road west to Anju. Their jeep conked out on the road and they chained it to a tank. Not the most elegant way to leave town, he thought, but it had worked.

The trip that day to Twin Tunnels from Iho-ri had been relatively uneventful until they entered the valley. Then Wilson heard the hateful sound of Chinese horns and bugles. Many years later, he still believed he had the sequence of events right: they had heard the Chinese instruments before they actually saw the enemy, although others disagreed. Suddenly they were caught in the terrible chaos of yet another battlefield where the enemy has seen you before you've seen the enemy—that worst of all possible moments. An American officer was yelling for them to hurry up, move the jeeps so they could get the hell out of there. He thought that was Lieutenant William Penrod, who had ridden at the front of the convoy. But then the same officer clearly realized that the Chinese had set up a blocking force exactly where the Americans had entered the valley, and suddenly he was shouting—it was like orders changing in mid-sentence—for them to get the hell up on the hill. Then he heard Mueller yelling the same thing. All of the officers grasped by now that they were badly outnumbered. Just how badly they were about to find out.

They started up the north side of the hill, where the snow was heaviest and the ground more slippery, as the Chinese went up the south slope. Penrod had told Wilson to carry two cans of ammo, about twenty pounds extra in each arm, he thought. There were a couple of times when, weighed down as he was, he did not think he was going to make it. But Penrod was turning out to be a marvelous officer, pushing the others when the only thing they really wanted to do was quit (even if it meant Chinese captivity and probable death). Down at the bottom of the hill, Wilson noticed, was a small cluster of men, seven or eight of them—Fockler's group, he learned later—all brand-new to the regiment and on their first combat patrol. Penrod was shouting at them, "Come on, goddamn it! Come on!" But they did not move, which surprised Wilson, whose instinct was always to believe that there was safety in numbers.

For the men cut off at the bottom of the hill it was the worst of all possible scenarios: their first taste of combat, and nine of them, all apparently new to the regiment, including Fockler, found themselves separated from the rest of the unit, unsure of which way to go, absolutely terrified, and with no one in command. They headed for a cluster of huts, because it seemed to offer some kind of protection. Later, it was claimed that a small group of them had panicked and refused orders to go up the hill. The much-maligned victims, Fockler would say. That was wrong, he believed. They did not refuse orders—they never heard them. "The truth is we fought like hell," he said, and then many died because of the confusion of war. He did not know much about the others because they were so new—they were linked to one another in the annals of the regiment without knowing one another. There was a kid from North Carolina, just married, about whom Fockler recalled only one thing—he said he had not yet finished paying for the wedding ring. Allan Anderson from Massachusetts, as he remembered. Anderson dropped his weapon by mistake when the fighting began, went back to retrieve it, and was shot and killed. Richard Norman, he remembered because it was his seventeenth birthday. He was hit by a concussion grenade, his wound bandaged by his friend Rudolph Scateni of Chicago, and both of them were killed later in the day. Robert Walsh, from upstate New York, who briefly shared a defensive position with Fockler, was also killed that day. Thomas Miller from California, a BAR man who fought hard and swore he had killed fifteen of the enemy, died as well. The seven, "all killed on one/twenty-nine/fifty-one," Fockler would say half a century later as if repeating a mantra for the worst day of his life. "All killed on one/twenty-nine/fifty-one. . . . All killed on one/twenty-nine/fifty-one. . . ." Other than Fockler, only Miller's partner on the BAR, Guillermo Untalan, who was from Guam and looked Asian—"the Chinese thought he was one of theirs and he slipped away from them"—made it out alive, though he was wounded.

Eventually, Fockler saw where the main body of the unit had gone, and he and a buddy, Private Clement Pietrasiewicz, tried to cross from the tiny village back to the hill. But Fockler was hit in the right leg, and a few minutes later the Chinese captured them both. "It seemed to me like a regiment that surrounded us but it was most likely a squad," he said. Fockler tried to rise up to surrender, and when he did, Pietrasiewicz surrendered too. "I was waiting to see what you did," he told Fockler. Because of his wound, Fockler could not walk on his own, so Pietrasiewicz served as his crutch. As they neared the village, they saw a group of Chinese soldiers and Fockler said, "Hey, Pete, look at all those litter bearers."

"Not for you, Fockler, not for you," Pietrasiewicz answered. It was the last thing his buddy ever said to him. They were separated at the village and Fockler never saw him again. He was sure Pietrasiewicz had been taken to a POW camp, and after the war, when they started publishing lists of repatriated soldiers, he searched them carefully. Eventually he was told by Division record keepers that Pietrasiewicz had never been seen again.

Fockler, now a POW, lay down on the ground. Chinese soldiers wandered by to see if he had a watch they could take, never going for his wallet—a watch had value, he thought, a wallet did not. Then he watched as the Chinese set about destroying the vehicles the Americans had abandoned. They pried the thatched roofing off the local huts, spread it on top of the jeeps and trucks, poured gas on it, and set everything on fire. Then they simply left. No one seemed very interested in Fockler, so he crawled into one of the huts, slipped under a straw mat, and waited either to be killed or rescued.

The next day, he crawled what seemed like miles back to the road—fifty-two years later, as a tourist in South Korea, he checked out the actual distance and discovered it was only a mile and a half. As he was crawling toward what he hoped might be help, an American fighter dove in and strafed him, so he rolled into a ditch and waited there, spending one more night on his own. The next day he began to crawl again, until, finally, an American captain in a jeep spotted him.

WHILE THE MEN who had been separated were being torn apart, the rest of the task force was scrambling up the hill under constant machine gun fire from an adjoining hill where the Communists had already set up positions. Laron Wilson was tiring quickly as he climbed, needing to rest more frequently—and the enemy fire was getting heavier. About two-thirds of the way up, he stopped, sure that he was incapable of taking even one more step. That was when Lieutenant Penrod came down for him, telling him he had to make it, and they *had* to get to the high ground. Not knowing where the energy was coming from, but knowing that if his mind gave in to his body, he was surely dead, he pressed on. When Wilson reached the makeshift perimeter, he was exhausted, his clothes soaked with sweat in that freezing cold, and he was certain of one thing—if the Chinese didn't get him, the sheer cold would, that he was probably going to freeze to death on that hill. But he had made it, a triumph of adrenaline-driven fear over normal physical limitations. Better yet, he had managed to bring the ammo with him, even though at certain moments as he had climbed, he wanted more than anything else to leave it behind. Later he was glad he had brought it up, because that night they ran perilously short early on, and if not for those two extra cans he had carried, they all would have been dead.

About forty of them had made it up the hill, along with one light machine gun, eight BARs, and a bazooka. The semiautomatic, crew-served BAR was one of an infantryman's best friends, much prized by the men who fought in Korea, because it could be used single-shot or as an automatic weapon. Two men handled it, one firing, the other feeding it a clip of twenty rounds; Wilson became a feeder. The BAR man that Wilson worked with was from another unit, and later he could not remember his name (it was Private William Stratton). Wilson wondered, years later, if he had ever known it during those long hours when their lives were so closely bound together. Could they really have fought there, literally body to body, without exchanging names? Had Wilson ever mentioned that this day, possibly the last in his life, was his birthday? The only thing he knew about the BAR man, other than that he had a coveted white parka, which meant he was from the Twenty-first Regiment, was that he had been a hell of a soldier. The Chinese launched assault after assault, their heads popping up as they tried to break into the perimeter, and Stratton just sat there, and waited and waited, and then fired, almost, it seemed, at the last millisecond. They had eight clips to spend, just 160 rounds of ammo to last what might well be their lifetime, and he had wasted nothing. Bless him for that, Wilson thought.

The Chinese kept pouring fire in their direction and finally hit the BAR man's right hand with a round, knocking off a couple of his fingers. But even that did not stop him. Wilson helped him bandage the hand, and he kept on firing. In all the wildness and the desperation of that fight the gunner still managed to boast, in the age-old sardonic language of soldiers, that he now had his million-dollar wound, his war was over, and he wanted the names and phone numbers of everyone else so that he could call their loved ones when he got back to the States. Especially their girlfriends. Later, when the Chinese firing got even worse, he kept going around to the others, a number of them wounded by then, telling them that they were going to make it out, that they had to keep the faith and not give in mentally.

Nothing stopped Stratton. When he could no longer use his right hand, he switched to his left. When more Chinese assaulted their position, he stood and emptied the BAR at them, and was hit a second time—in the chest. Another soldier crawled out and pulled him back to the center of the perimeter. Then a Chinese grenade landed between his legs. He screamed in pain.

"For God's sake shut up!" Lieutenant Mitchell said.

"My legs have just been shot off," the BAR man yelled.

"I know it, but shut up anyway," Mitchell replied. A little while later Stratton was hit for the fourth time and died.

Almost everyone up on their tiny perimeter was hit that night. Penrod and Mueller had gone around telling the men not to cry out when they were wounded and not to moan from their wounds because they did not want to give away the vulnerability of their position and encourage the Chinese. At dusk the men on the hill had gotten a boost when an Army spotter plane marked some of the Chinese positions for American jets that raked the area with rockets, napalm, and machine gun fire. Then the little plane returned and dropped some ammo and medical supplies. Most of it missed the perimeter, but one case of ammo got through. The pilot made pass after pass trying to drop ammo off, coming in so low they could see his face. Wilson added him to his pantheon of heroes, someone who risked his life again and again on behalf of men he had never met, pushed by an exceptional internal code of honor.

Finally the pilot came in low and dropped a yellow streamer that said, "Friendly column approaching from the south. Will be with you shortly." But how shortly was shortly? If it was a long shortly, they would not live to see it. The men knew that when darkness fell, the Chinese would be coming again and then maybe again and that there were always too many of them. That evening, as predicted, they did, with machine guns, grenades, and burp guns. Mitchell eventually moved his men back from the edge of the knob, in part because they had so little ammo that he did not want any wasted on mere sounds—they were only to fire when they actually saw a Chinese head.

Back at headquarters for the Twenty-third, when Colonel Freeman heard that the patrol had been hit by a major Chinese force, he immediately ordered up an air strike. He was told by the spotter plane that at least two battalions of Chinese, perhaps even a regiment, had struck this small patrol. That made it a fight of quite possibly two to three thousand against sixty. Freeman immediately ordered Lieutenant Colonel Jim Edwards, commander of the Second Battalion, positioned about ten miles nearer Twin Tunnels than the rest of the regiment, to put together a relief force. Edwards chose Captain Stanley Tyrrell, commander of Fox Company, one of his best young officers. It took about two hours to mobilize the men and the requisite gear, especially the heavy weapons—a section of 81mm mortars and a section of heavy machine guns. Edwards ordered Tyrrell to play it tough but smart, to try and rescue them that night, but to make sure his own troops were in a solid defensive position first. If need be, he was to button up for the night and attack in the morning. Tyrrell took off with a total of 167 officers and men.

Tyrrell's assault was almost letter perfect—in the words of Paul Freeman, "one of the most brilliant small-unit actions in the Korean campaign." His column arrived in the area about 5:30 P.M. As soon as the men reached the area, the Chinese opened up with two machine guns from Hill 453 across the valley. Tyrrell's driver dove into a ditch. "You'd better get in the ditch, Captain. The Chinks will get you," the driver exclaimed. "To hell with the Chinks," Tyrrell replied.

Tyrrell decided he had to take Hill 453, the tallest in the valley, before he did anything else. Otherwise his men would be cut down. He prepared two platoons to attack the hill from separate flanks, and used his third platoon to lay down a withering mortar barrage and heavy machine gun fire just ahead of the attacking troops—so that a wave of death preceded them up the hill. The intensity of it, unusually deadly fire for so small a force, was too much for the Chinese, who abandoned the hill. There were many moments during the Korean War when the Chinese fought to the last man, but not that day, not on Hill 453.

The two flanks of Tyrrell's relief force came together about 10:30 P.M. Tyrrell immediately set up a strong defensive perimeter on the hill, which would give him good covering fire when he went to relieve the survivors on a nearby hill. Tyrrell originally intended to hold through the night on top of Hill 453 and attack in the morning, but a medic who had been with the holdouts slipped through the Chinese lines and found his way to Tyrrell's position. The besieged men, he said, were in desperate condition, almost out of ammo, three-quarters of them already dead or seriously wounded. With that, Tyrrell decided to continue the attack right through the night.

UP ON THE knob of the hill, during the late afternoon, some of the men had noticed dust being kicked up by what were probably the jeeps and trucks of an American column. But Wilson doubted they would get through in time. The Chinese seemed so close—sometimes only thirty or forty feet away, and there were so many of them and so few Americans that every assault made the defense that much weaker. More men were incapacitated or dying all the time. Some men who had been wounded were now dead, and some who had been able-bodied were wounded and unable to fire back. The living were busy scrounging bullets from the bodies of the dead. Wilson decided that his birthday was a disaster. How could you reach the moment when you were finally a grown-up, and could buy a drink in any state in the Union, and that was the end of it? What bothered Wilson most was that he was never going to see his daughter.

Once, when the Chinese were making a rush to the top, Wilson pulled the pin on his last grenade, but then when the Chinese broke off, ammo being so valuable, he lay down on it to keep it suppressed. Afterward he thought he might even have fallen asleep momentarily in that position. He remembered, in a dreamlike way, the last part of that night before Tyrrell's men arrived, part of it obviously real and part of it very fuzzy. He believed a few Chinese had actually penetrated the perimeter, and that one of them had kicked him hard in the ribs. In his memory the Chinese had reached the top and Lieutenant Penrod had told his men to pretend to be dead, and in time the Chinese had left. But he was unsure how much of what he remembered had any truth— although in the following days his side gave him a lot of pain, as if someone had in fact kicked him there.

He remembered the sound of heavy fighting when the troops from Tyrrell's company first started coming up the hill, and then a silence, such a deathly silence that he feared the relief column had been wiped out. Then around eleven that night, voices speaking English—as yet unseen—were yelling not to fire, because they were GIs. Someone on the knob yelled, "Who won the Rose Bowl game?"—but they were in *Korea,* so who the hell knew the teams in the Rose Bowl, let alone the winner?

It took almost four hours to get all the men—alive, wounded, and dead— off that hill, with Wilson still carrying his live grenade. At one point, he slipped and fell and the grenade got away from him, but he quickly grabbed it, threw it as far as he could, and no one was hurt. Of the sixty men who had started out on the patrol, thirteen were dead, five were missing (and presumed dead), and thirty were wounded, many quite seriously. Only twelve came out unscathed, one of them being Laron Wilson, who lived well beyond his twenty-first birthday. From then on, whenever he had troops in his jeep, he tried to make sure that at least one of them had a BAR. The survivors, grateful for their rescue, later had a banner made up that said, "When in peril, send for Tyrrell."

THE NEXT DAY, Ned Almond ordered the Twenty-third Regiment right back to the area. He wanted action and he wanted it immediately. He wanted the Chinese cleared out and he wanted prisoners. By then, Almond was hardly a welcome figure around regimental headquarters. He was not the division commander, but he always acted as if Nick Ruffner, the nominal division commander, did not exist. He was already regarded by many of the senior officers in the Second Division much as he had been by the First Marines. His style, wrote J. D. Coleman, who served in one of the units that fought under him at Wonju and then wrote an exceptional history of that battle, was "to bully, to meddle, and to constantly interfere with the normal chain of command. He had an enormous ego and he spared no one—officers or soldiers—in his efforts to demonstrate his superiority." By the time of the Twin Tunnels battle, Ruffner, formerly Almond's G-3 at Corps, had become the Second Division commander, and George Stewart the assistant division commander, which was unusual because he was not an Almond man and was not trusted by his superior.

The failure to respect the Chinese at Chosin seemed not to have slowed Almond down or, amazingly enough, made him significantly more respectful of the enemy. To many of the men who admired Ridgway and understood some of the reasons why he had not relieved Almond, there was nonetheless a feeling that allowing Almond to remain as a corps commander had been his one big mistake in those early months. As Ken Hamburger noted, for the men of the Second Division, Almond had gained an unwelcome "reputation as a martinet who often commanded by instilling fear in subordinates."

After Almond gave his order to return to Twin Tunnels, the Twenty-third assembled some six miles short of the area. Paul Freeman was not happy with the order. He thought it impetuous. Over on the west coast Ridgway was moving his forces up in a relatively consistent tightly knit line, trying not to expose any one unit, and always careful about his flanks. But here, Freeman felt, his regiment was being pushed too far ahead of UN lines and well out of range of most of the division's artillery support. As for air support, the weather made it problematical. Sometimes the best lesson learned on the battlefield was that of modesty, but modesty was not yet a virtue in Tenth Corps—audacity for audacity's sake was. As Freeman saw it, Almond's audacity just played into the Chinese hands. What made it worse as far as he was concerned was that the troops being put at risk were Freeman's.

It was, Freeman felt, as if they were being told to charge right into the valley. By contrast, Freeman was already beginning to think that, against the Chinese, the best method was to probe, find the enemy, make sure you were in easy range of your artillery, and dig into good positions on the high ground, and then if at all possible let the enemy come to you. Ridgway, aggressive but cautious, was already devising a comparable strategy. "Lure and destroy," the French would soon call it.

Paul Freeman's unhappiness with the order sending his regiment back into Twin Tunnels, so far out of reach of the Division artillery, was palpable. Brigadier General George Stewart, the assistant division commander, who also feared he was about to be relieved, happened to be with the Twenty-third when the order came down, and he remembered an embittered Freeman saying, "They're going to murder my regiment." Stewart told him he had no choice— you had to accept your orders. But aware that there was an ominous feel to the entire scenario, Stewart decided to accompany the Twenty-third to Twin Tunnels. He too believed that Almond was impetuous and often gave orders that were not well thought out, but he also believed that Freeman, though exceptionally able, was unusually combative with superiors if he thought his men were being put at risk.

So Freeman sent two battalions—the newly attached French unit and his Third Battalion—for what would be the second full stage in the battle of Twin Tunnels. To them he attached a regimental headquarters company, a regimental mortar battery, a tank company, and a medical company. In addition, the Thirty-seventh Field Artillery Battalion and an antiaircraft unit, whose lowered weapons made unusually vicious infantry weapons against both the North Koreans and now the Chinese, were made part of the force. Freeman placed the artillery battalion about three miles south of Twin Tunnels and left many of his other vehicles there; he then turned their drivers into infantrymen, thereby giving his heavy guns an extra ring of protection. No one was going to be wasted, and he could not spare any additional infantrymen to protect the guns.

What Freeman knew was that before he moved into the valley, it was imperative to take and control Hill 453, which commanded the area, and which momentarily was vacant. His troops moved slowly up its slopes, covered with ice and snow, carrying a lot of gear. Perhaps earlier in the war they might have complained about the climb, Freeman later wrote, but no longer. They had learned by then that the hard way was the better way, that those who stayed on the roads were more likely to be ambushed and die. They had learned as well to bring extra ammo even if it meant fewer rations, and to dig deeper foxholes even through what sometimes seemed like rock-solid frozen earth and ice. If that was true under normal conditions, then it was more important than ever when they were twenty miles from any other friendly unit, in a place where, only the day before, a violent ambush had taken place. The enemy, his men knew by then, liked to set traps for lazy, road-bound Americans. For, almost without anyone noticing it, the Second Division and the Twenty-third Regiment—fairly typically of American units in Korea then—were beginning to become part of a skilled, battle-tested army. The defeat at Kunuri masqueraded the fact that this process was already under way. If the Second Division, for example, had arrived in country in pathetic physical condition and not yet really shaken down, the constant fighting up and down hills in the Naktong Bulge had changed that. The physical condition of most of the men had improved dramatically. They were gradually becoming every bit as battle-hardened as the men who had fought in the Battle of the Bulge or on Iwo Jima.

That was one of the great mysteries of combat, the process of going from green, scared soldiers to tough, grizzled, combat-ready (but still scared) veterans. Some men, a small percentage, never made it; they remained green, a burden to themselves and the men around them, in a permanent, hopeless incarnation as soldiers. They were incapable of or unwilling to break out of their civilian selves. Most men, however, whether they liked it or not, went through that transformation. They might regret it when they came home, and it might be a part of their lives they never wanted to revisit, but they did it. This had become their universe, and it was a small and brutal one, cut off from all the things they had been taught growing up. Most important of all, it was a universe without choice. No one entirely understood the odd process—perhaps the most primal on earth—that turned ordinary, peace-loving, law-abiding civilians into very good fighting men; or one of its great sub-mysteries—how quickly it could take place. One day troops were completely raw and casually disrespectful of whatever training they had received. In basic training, the machine gun bullets that whistled overhead were designed *not* to hit you. Then they found themselves on a battlefield in places like the Naktong, in situations that were terrifying, where any mistake might be fatal for them and their friends, and they became tough, experienced soldiers, knowing the elemental rules of survival. Suddenly they could fight almost by pure instinct. "How do you recognize a North Korean or Chinese soldier? What do they look like?" a young replacement soldier named Ben Judd asked an older veteran when he first joined the Twenty-third Regiment, just before Chipyongni. "You'll know 'em when you see 'em," the soldier had answered, with what Judd came to realize was the wisdom of the ages.

Writing in *The Saturday Evening Post* of the very troops who had been so green only a few months earlier but fought so well at Twin Tunnels and then Chipyongni, the veteran correspondent Harold Martin said, "Much of their wisdom is the battle know-how the individual soldier picks up as he survives fight after fight, the simple things the books have always taught, but no soldier ever learns until he has been shot at: to keep off the sky line; to spread out in the attack, instead of bunching up like quail; to dig deep when on the defensive; to treat his communications equipment as tenderly as he would treat his sweetheart; to keep his socks dry and his weapons clean; and to hold his fire until the enemy is close enough to kill."

The same thing had happened to Freeman. He had wrestled at first privately with his own self-doubts and pessimism, doubts shared by some of the other officers who met him: Was he a staffy—that is, a staff man who talked big but was always back at headquarters—or a real commander? Was he a planner or a fighter? Now those doubts had long since been answered. He had commanded the men in the Naktong fighting, depriving the North Koreans of what they had wanted most of all, the road connections that would lead them to Pusan. Then he had brought them out of Kunuri in fine shape, in effect fighting off bad orders that would have taken them down The Gauntlet and surely gotten many of them killed. He had done the hardest thing for any commander, he had won their trust in battle. When he had started, they knew nothing about him as a commander; now there was a growing pride in what they had accomplished, and that pride extended to him. The trust came in part because they believed he was focused as much on taking care of them as he was on pushing his own career. That was a crucial factor. The men always watched for any telltale sign that a commander thought more of his career than of their lives; it was as if any man who had that overweening ambition always gave off a special odor that even the youngest and most naïve private could detect.

So when they had gone into Twin Tunnels, they had done it with a certain combat-produced wariness, for they were effectively behind enemy lines. If, in the days to come, the men of the Twenty-third felt that they were operating on their own, they were right; they were uncommonly exposed, an isolated salient with little additional support to count on. Ned Almond had showed up at the headquarters late on the afternoon of January 31, irritated that Freeman had not yet made contact with the Chinese, irritated as well that Freeman had not simply gone straight into the valley and driven right through on his way to

Chipyongni. It helped confirm his growing view of Freeman as too timid a commander. Others, including General Stewart, who had measured the Chinese and knew how easily they could hide during the day, several divisions right on top of you and not a single soldier detectable, thought it was a lot better to move cautiously than audaciously, better to end the day on the high ridges of Hill 453 than to race too quickly into the valley of Chipyongni, and arrive there too late in the day to gain the high ground. Twin Tunnels itself was an exceptionally difficult place to defend. What was particularly troubling was the fact that the two critical high points in the area were separated and not mutually supportive. Thus the attackers, if they had great numbers—and the Chinese surely would—could in effect isolate each of the high points from the other.

George Stewart sympathized with Freeman and thought he was right tactically to err on the side of caution, but Stewart himself was extremely vulnerable in the chain of command. He had been brought in by the departed Bob McClure, and thus was regarded as the pal of a despised former commander; he also knew that, because of Almond's dominating nature, the division had a serious need for someone outside Almond's control. But he understood as well the need to tiptoe around, that he was always on Almond's turf, and that if anything went wrong, it would be blamed on him and he would be gone. Indeed, he realized, he might be gone even if nothing went wrong.

Now he steeled himself and told Almond that Freeman was right to be wary in a situation like this, and that they were moving up cautiously because of the size of the force encountered just the day before and an awareness that even larger forces were probably in the area. In addition, he said, they had decided to stay on Hill 453 because they had taken up their positions relatively late in the day and they needed to be on the high ground at night. But Almond was still bristling with aggressiveness, and he ordered Stewart to put Chipyongni under fire immediately—it was as if he needed to do *something*, anything, before he left, to put some mark of his own on this action. It was not an order Stewart wanted to obey, but he felt he had no choice, as much to protect Freeman as himself. It was, he later noted, a ridiculous order, but he took a tank and rode over to Chipyongni. There he encountered no enemy fire, and, wary of shooting up Korean huts and schoolhouses for no particular reason, he fired a few rounds over the village's buildings, then returned to Freeman's headquarters.

Freeman was by then furious with Almond and angry with Stewart as well—by firing, Freeman felt, Stewart had signaled to the Chinese that they were back in the Twin Tunnels area and on their way to Chipyongni. Now, Freeman felt, Stewart had sent up a come-and-get-us flare. Stewart privately agreed: the firing on Chipyongni had added nothing to their security, and quite possibly diminished it. Like Freeman, he always wondered whether the subsequent battle of Twin Tunnels would have developed as it did if he had not gone down to Chipyongni and shot those pointless rounds into the air. That afternoon, Captain Sherman Pratt, one of the company commanders, remembered watching Freeman simply explode, as he talked to Lieutenant Colonel Jim Edwards, one of his battalion commanders. "I don't mind the corps commander being around and there's no problem with him telling me what to do. He should as a courtesy go through his division commander, but that's between those two. What I can't accept is his telling me how to do it, especially if I think his way is dangerous to my command and mission." Pratt, a World War II vet, had never seen a senior officer that angry at a superior. "If Almond wants to be a regimental commander, damn it, let him take a reduction to bird colonel and come down and be one," Freeman had added. Then, still in a rage, he drove off in his jeep.

It was very fortunate that Freeman had immediately gone to the high ground and had his men prepare strong defensive positions, because his force, a little more than half a regiment with a very limited reserve, was soon hit by at least a division-sized Chinese force. "Whether the regiment could have held out that night [in the basin] at Chipyongni with only two battalions against the kind of onslaught it suffered at the tunnels is doubtful," Ken Hamburger wrote. If the first stage of the Twin Tunnels battle had been a relatively minor battle with the survivors rescued by Tyrrell, then the second stage of Twin Tunnels was a major confrontation between a medium-sized UN unit and a much larger Chinese force with no intention of pulling back.

Both battalions of the Twenty-third were in relatively good fighting shape, at about 80 percent strength, which meant that Freeman had around fifteen hundred men committed to the battle. Against them were an estimated eight to ten thousand Chinese soldiers. His French unit was newer to the country, but its men were also fine, experienced combat troops, mostly French Foreign Legion veterans. Almost all of them were battle-tested, many already having served in Indochina, and they were led by General Ralph Monclar, one of the more charismatic figures of the Korean War. Monclar was a nom de guerre. His real name was Magrin-Vernery. He was the son of a Hungarian nobleman and a Frenchwoman, and was only sixteen when he enlisted in the French Foreign Legion (having lied about his age). He was already a sergeant when he entered St. Cyr, the French West Point. He graduated in 1914, just in time for the First World War. He had served with distinction then, and again in World War II. (When the Germans overran France, he escaped to England and led a Foreign Legion armored unit in North Africa.) He had been wounded at least thirteen times in his career, walked with a pronounced limp, and used a walking stick, which never seemed to slow him down.

By 1950, he was a three-star general, and when France decided to send a battalion to Korea under the UN flag, he asked for the right to command it, taking a reduction in rank to lieutenant colonel in order not to violate the chain of command. His superiors in Paris thought he was too old for the Korean assignment, but he felt a man was never too old to command in a cause in which he believed, and with that he won his argument. Monclar led with zest and exuberance. He thought the French, some five years into their own colonial war in Indochina, were lucky to be fighting Communism, even if it was in a far-off place like Korea. The American units came to love fighting alongside the French, because they never had to worry about their flanks. If there was one problem, it was that the French were almost too jaunty. They liked to kill with bayonets and tended to boast about it.

There had, fortunately, been enough time for the UN troops to adjust their mortars to cover likely avenues of approach. Some of the French officers, however, were nervous that their men might be too worn out from climbing to the high ground and establishing their positions. It was, of course, very cold. Freeman and Monclar, who normally got on well, squabbled over some fires the French soldiers had lit to keep warm. Freeman was appalled and called Monclar to tell him to extinguish them. Monclar said he would do it—in the morning. "Tell 'em, now!" Freeman insisted.

"But, *mon colonel,* they are such little fires," Monclar protested.

"Big fires or little fires get 'em out, damn it, and do it now! You've already given your position away to every Red within a hundred miles!"

Monclar took one more shot at keeping the fires: "*Mon colonel,* it is as you say without doubt. But if they know where we are, they will attack us. Then we will kill them." Freeman did not answer that one, and soon the French fires went out.

There was some scattered firing during the night, quite possibly Chinese probes. Then about 4:30 A.M. the sounds of bugles and horns were heard, and the Chinese struck in force. At first nothing seemed to favor the UN force. The Chinese had the advantage of very heavy fog cover during the early hours of their attack, which allowed them to come very close to the UN positions before they could be identified; even when the fog finally lifted, the heavy overcast sky that replaced it was nearly impenetrable for air support. Freeman, hearing the first sounds of the Chinese attack, sure that it was a result of the one tank assault on Chipyongni, turned angrily to Stewart: "I told you this was going to happen." Then he added, "What do you want me to do now?" They really didn't have much choice, Stewart responded—it was, after all, a moment that demanded a certain fatalism: "Let's kill as many Chinese as we can," he said.

For the Americans it was a puzzling Chinese attack, coming so late in the

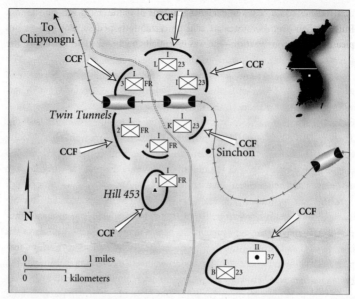

21. Battle of Twin Tunnels, January 31–February 1, 1951

morning, so many hours of darkness missed, and then continuing through the afternoon, long after the enemy normally broke contact. Later, reviewing the battle, Freeman decided that the Chinese had been caught at least partially by surprise by the appearance of such a relatively large American force and had scrambled to deny their enemies the road to Chipyongni. There were a number of signs that the Chinese were not well prepared for their attack, that it was a last-minute decision forced on them by the unexpected American move into the area. One indication was that late kickoff time, and another was the fact that the Chinese clearly lacked adequate ammunition for their heavy weapons.

The fighting was as bitter as any the Twenty-third Regiment encountered. Through much of the battle, there was a sense of what Freeman had feared from the start, the isolation of his men from the rest of the division. Ruffner, the nominal division commander, kept calling Stewart on the half hour, asking if things were really as bad as the reports he was getting. To Stewart the calls clearly reflected a lack of respect for both Freeman and himself, and showed a reluctance of Division and Corps to move instinctively to help a unit under assault. At one point when Ruffner's doubts showed, Stewart told his superior that he was standing in the blood of his radio operator who had just been shot. Then he held the handset of the phone out the window of the hut he was in, so that Ruffner could hear the deafening sounds of battle. Help was on the way, Ruffner then promised. Stewart said he certainly hoped so. But he was not pleased by the conversation—he was essentially being asked, in the midst of a ferocious battle, if he was really telling the truth.

Again and again the Chinese seemed ready to overrun the French and American positions. Freeman had to shift his troops constantly. He was virtually without reserves. Everyone—clerks, drivers, cooks, mechanics—had been committed, and he soon began to worry about running out of ammo—the Twenty-third had not been completely resupplied since some earlier fighting near Wonju. He and Monclar were in constant communication—by 2 P.M. the Chinese were about to overrun one of the French strongpoints. The French company commander there, Major Maurice Barthelemy, had radioed back that he could no longer hold and had received permission to take what remained of his company and pull back. Monclar met with Freeman, and they decided to focus whatever available firepower they had on the hill where the French were embattled—the guns of their two tanks, all their available mortars, and their twin 40mm cannons—in other wars antiaircraft weapons and, in Freeman's words, "the sweetest weapon around for vacuum cleaning a ridge." Meanwhile, the French battalion commander told his Third Company to hold the ground they were on to the last man, no matter how many Chinese attacked. Then he planned a final desperate counterattack. For ten minutes the Americans fired every weapon they could onto the ridge. Then Barthelemy's men charged the Chinese position with bayonets fixed. Terrified by the intensity of the attack, the Chinese finally broke and ran. Stewart, watching from the CP, was impressed. "Magnificent," he said half to himself. Monclar, in turn, standing next to Stewart, was impressed by how cool the American general appeared, calmly smoking his pipe. "What he didn't know," Stewart admitted later, "was that I bit the stems off three pipes that day."

That proved, however, only a momentary respite. Daylight it might be, but a cloudy daylight, and the Chinese, willing to take huge losses on this day, kept the battle going. By mid-afternoon, they once again appeared poised to push what was left of the UN forces off their last strongpoint, on the East Tunnel, where Item Company was positioned. The UN forces, having taken heavy casualties, were absolutely exhausted, low on ammo, and seemed not to have made a dent in the Chinese numbers. It was the low point of the day—all that valor, and they were going to be defeated anyway. The American air liaison officer standing near Stewart asked the general what was going to happen next. In about twenty minutes they would all be dead, Stewart answered. What about air support? Stewart asked him. Several flights were stacked up above them, the liaison officer answered, but they simply could not pierce the heavy cloud cover. Just then they looked up, and a small blue patch of sky appeared right above them. Could they do anything with that? Stewart asked. The liaison officer immediately radioed the planes. "We are directly under the break and we need help!"

With that, the aircraft pounced. It was, the imperiled Americans thought, a kind of miracle. "Like a Hollywood battle," Freeman wrote. In came the flight of Marine Corsairs, World War II prop planes first used at Guadalcanal in February 1943, and perfect for this kind of operation with their six 50-caliber machine guns, eight rockets, and room for five-hundred-pound bombs. What made them ideal for a run like this was their ability to stay over a target longer than the more modern jet fighters could. The Marine pilots circled several times to be sure they had marked the exact demarcation line between Item Company and the Chinese, then they struck. "What beautiful air support!" Freeman later wrote: first, the five-hundred-pound bombs, the daisy cutters, right on top of where the Chinese were bunched up for what would certainly have been their final assault. Then the rockets, "gook goosers" the troops called them, followed by the 50-caliber machine guns. Flight after flight struck, twenty-four in all as Freeman counted them. Finally the Chinese began to run and the battle was over. Of Freeman's force, 225 men had been killed, wounded, or were missing. They found 1,300 Chinese bodies just along their perimeter. The total Chinese losses were placed—it was a rough estimate—at about 3,600 killed and wounded or about half of a division—the 125th Chinese Division, as they discovered from their lone prisoner. (The fighting had been too intense to take more, and he had been badly wounded.) That division was part of the Chinese Forty-second Army. For weeks Matt Ridgway had been looking for the Forty-second Army. Now Paul Freeman had found it for him.

IN THE LATE afternoon, the Air Force air-dropped more ammo and other supplies in, and a relief force, the First Battalion of the Twenty-third, which had marched all the way, finally arrived. Freeman and Monclar remained nervous that the Chinese might strike again that night. But for the time being the Chinese were through. The regiment spent the day consolidating its position and then, on February 3, got its next assignment—to advance on Chipyongni, about four miles away, and occupy that critical village.

42

CHIPYONGNI TURNED OUT to be the battle Matt Ridgway had wanted from the moment he arrived in country. It was one of the decisive battles of the war, because it was where the American forces finally learned to fight the Chinese. For years after, what Paul Freeman did there was studied at the Command and General Staff School at Leavenworth as a textbook case of how to deal with a numerically superior enemy. Turning point though it was, like other battles in Korea it was rarely known outside the world of the men who fought there, or the military men and scholars who studied the history of the war. But at that small village the almost mythical sense of Chinese superiority, perhaps even invincibility, came to an end. By then, a mordant humor had emerged among the soldiers when it came to the Chinese and how many there were likely to be in battle: "How many hordes to a platoon?" went one line; "I was attacked by two hordes yesterday and killed both of them" went another. When Chipyongni was over, there was a new sense, not just among the commanders but among the fighting men themselves, that if they held the right positions with the right fields of fire and had the right leadership, the burden of battle would be on the less heavily armed Chinese. Equally important, when it was over, the Chinese knew it too.

Chipyongni was one of those many small Korean villages that war celebrates as peace does not. It was fairly typical for the country—a mill, a school, and a Buddhist temple. Along the main street ran a small stream. All in all, it was not much, at least by Western standards. By the time the Twenty-third Regiment arrived to take up its positions, the mill had been demolished, the school and the temple destroyed, and most of the villagers were gone. In that way it was also all too typical of the Korean countryside of that moment—competing armies came and went in this war, and every time one of them arrived, there was less of the village left. But to both sides it had a disproportionate strategic importance, because it controlled passage—by rail east and west, by road north and south— through the central part of the country, where there were few other routes of any consequence.

To the surprise of Freeman and his men, they entered Chipyongni without opposition. For whatever reason, the Chinese, who were moving a great many men around in the sector, let the Americans take it unchallenged. Though his defense was eventually cited as a textbook case in the use of limited forces, in the beginning Paul Freeman was not entirely pleased with his situation. He would have greatly preferred, as he told Captain Sherman Pratt, to hold a series of hills around the village that were much higher than those he finally settled on, but given the limited number of men at his disposal, his forces would have been spread too thin if he had. His very first decision was subsequently viewed by experts in infantry tactics as unusual, but in the end brilliant. The most basic rule for an infantry commander, especially one contemplating a defensive stand against an enemy with vastly superior numbers, is to hold the high ground. Nominally the higher hills or mountains in that area would have created an almost impregnable defensive barrier. But to man them would have necessitated a ridgeline defense some twelve miles long, and a perimeter with a four-mile diameter, which would have required a division, not a regiment. A perimeter that large might have been a much easier one for the Chinese to break through at key points, rolling the entire defensive line up as they preferred to do.

So Freeman wisely chose to concentrate his defense on the smaller but closer hills. That gave him a rectangular defensive perimeter only one mile in depth by two miles in length. On almost all sides he held ground high enough to present serious problems for any attacking troops. In a way he was setting up the kind of defense that a good many American commanders had been pondering since they were first hit by the Chinese along the Chongchon. No less important was what he was *not* doing. He was not preventing his heavier guns from supporting one another; he was not making it impossible for one of his reserve units to come quickly to the aid of a troubled position.

He was also, he hoped, exploiting a great weakness of the Chinese, their lack of heavy artillery pieces. The Chinese would hold the distant higher ground, to be sure, but the Americans would have the advantage in long-range artillery. As for machine guns, the Chinese would have plenty of them, but planted on the distant higher ground they would be of little or no value. The Chinese, he had to expect, would have mortars and would surely use them well. But perhaps UN airpower would be able to take some of them out, if the weather broke just right. The other crucial advantage that Freeman had was time. He was the first American commander to have the luxury of time in this new war and some idea of what to do with it. His troops arrived in Chipyongni on February 3; the Chinese attack did not come until the evening of February 13: ten precious days to prepare his positions. Every man in the Twenty-third was aware of the regiment's vulnerability and that their lives depended on how well they dug in (though the Army historian Roy Appleman walked their foxholes in August 1951 and was surprised that they were not deeper). Fields of fire were measured for mortars and artillery pieces, marking precisely all potential avenues of approach. Barbed wire was strung until it ran out. Mines were planted until they had no more of them. A small airstrip was cleared, which would allow them, if need be, to bring in supplies and evacuate the wounded.

For the first time, Freeman believed that he had almost too much ammunition. On that, he learned soon enough, he was wrong. Spotter planes flew overhead every day trying to pick up any Chinese movements in the surrounding hills. Every day, Freeman sent recon patrols out, trying to find out what the Chinese were up to. As the days passed, and they got closer to the Chinese D-day, there was just one hitch. In a battle that was both separate and yet *very* connected, ROK forces attacking north from nearby Wonju, about ten miles to the south and east, had collapsed, and American and Dutch forces fighting with them were now in danger of being overrun and annihilated. The drive of UN forces north of Wonju that had begun on February 5 was by February 14 going very badly. The ROK advance that had initiated the larger battle on Wonju was, a number of senior people in the division, including George Stewart, believed, part of an ill-conceived, almost bizarre Almond plan. He had sent the ROKs north as the lead element, which had amazed everyone. When the Chinese struck the ill-prepared ROKs—and estimates were that there were four Chinese divisions operating in the Wonju area—they had quite predictably destroyed the ROKs, and it had opened up vast avenues for the Chinese into the American and Dutch forces. That greatly endangered the entire Wonju area, and quite possibly Chipyongni as well. Thus even before the battle of Chipyongni began, its defenders were in ever greater jeopardy. Not only did the battle of Wonju have a priority on any call for airpower, but there was now a fear that unless the balance at Wonju was redressed, the Chinese might soon be free to throw even greater forces, perhaps four more divisions, at Freeman.

By February 10, the small patrols that Freeman was sending out had determined that the area was swarming with Chinese and his terrain was shrinking by the hour. That Paul Freeman is now considered one of the three or four most distinguished regimental commanders of the Korean War, his reputation based largely on his performance at Chipyongni, is not without considerable irony. For in the days immediately preceding the battle, he wanted badly to pull back, fearing the immense buildup of Chinese all around his perimeter. By February 12, it was clear to him that his men were soon to be encircled by an overwhelming force. That was bad enough. Worse yet, American forces in two of the Thirty-eighth Regiment's battalions were being cut up just north of Wonju, and it was possible that the rest of Tenth Corps might not be able to hold the town itself. Already two relief forces sent out to reinforce Freeman, one of them the British Commonwealth Brigade, had been hit hard and found themselves unable to break through. To Freeman, his lonely salient facing what seemed to him like all the Chinese ever sent to Korea was "sticking out like a sore thumb."

When he asked for permission to pull back, he was told that Ridgway wanted him to stay put. As the moment when the Chinese would attack grew even closer, all the senior officers of the Twenty-third knew that some kind of argument was going on at a pay level far above theirs. All the other UN units in the area were pulling back—but not the Twenty-third. Their orders on February 12, as recorded by the regimental operations officer, were to stay put: "We are to remain. By order of Scotch." (Scotch was the code name for Ridgway.) On that same day, Major John Dumaine, the regimental operations officer, told Captain Pratt that Freeman wanted to pull back, but he was doubtful they would be able to get out now, partly because of the masses of Chinese moving in around them: "I don't think we could withdraw now if we wanted to. The latest report by Shoemaker [Major Harold Shoemaker, the regimental intelligence officer, who would die at Chipyongni] is that the road south, our only avenue of escape, is already swarming with Chinese and is closed. Even if we got permission to withdraw, we would have to fight another gauntlet to get out. I think we are going to stay and fight it out." That seemed to seal it; a siege was already on and airdrops of supplies already taking place. For those at Chipyongni, their destiny, they now knew, was something they would have to determine themselves. They were on their own.

But Freeman and Ruffner at Division still hoped to get their orders changed. Even Almond agreed, in part because of the growing failure of other units under his command. Almond had flown in to meet with Freeman around noon on February 13, aware that the battle around Wonju was going very badly, which placed Chipyongni in even greater jeopardy. He found Freeman anxious, talking about the possibility of losing his entire regiment in this battle. Freeman asked for permission to withdraw on the morning of the fourteenth. He wanted to retreat to Yoju, about fifteen miles south, even though there was an increasing likelihood that the Chinese had cut the road. His position, he said, was very fragile. He had the approval of Ruffner, the division commander, to move back, and now Almond seemed to agree as well.

Inside the Twenty-third perimeter, word got around very quickly that they were going to pull back. In fact the commander of the RCT (Regimental Combat Team) antiaircraft battery, sure that they were soon to retreat and believing he had too much ammunition to take out with him, asked for permission to fire some of it into the distant hills. Lieutenant Colonel Frank Meszar, the regimental executive officer, told him to wait another day just to be sure. By the time Almond got back to his corps headquarters, Freeman had changed his mind—he no longer felt he could wait an additional day and wanted to go out on the thirteenth. Right after his meeting, Freeman sent a message to Division headquarters: "Almond here about 1½ hours ago, asked my recommendation when I could move back to Yoju. I told him in the morning. I have changed my recommendation to as early as possible this evening. . . . Pass this request to CG Xth Corps and relay answer to me as soon as possible." Now the decision belonged to only one man, the man who had wanted this particular battle in the first place. Ridgway remained immune to additional pleas from inside Chipyongni. What he did promise was that, if Freeman stayed and fought, he would make sure a relief force punched through. If need be, he said, he would send the entire Eighth Army to rescue them.

As an old airborne man, he was convinced that Freeman's troops, well dug in and with a good deal of firepower, could be resupplied with ammunition and other needs by air. This then was the test battle he had been hoping for; imperfect perhaps, but one never got the perfect battle. It pitted, if things worked out, superior U.S. firepower against superior numbers, in a venue more or less chosen by the Chinese rather than by us, and as such ought, Ridgway hoped, to be a litmus test for the rest of the war.

Sometime in the late afternoon of the thirteenth, Sherman Pratt visited Freeman and found him fatalistic. Freeman showed Pratt a map that reflected their complete encirclement by perhaps four divisions of Chinese troops, he said. He told Pratt simply, "If they [the Chinese] want it, they are going to have to come and fight for it. I think we are ready—that we can fight well where we are now." Early on the evening of the thirteenth, Freeman called his commanders together. There had been a lot of talk about pulling back, he said, but it wasn't going to happen. "We'll stay here and fight it out." He wanted every commander to check each foxhole and each field of fire one last time. The attack, he said, might come that night.

He had placed the First Battalion on the northwest sector, the Third Battalion on the northeast and east sectors, the French battalion to the west, and the Second Battalion to the south. He had some fifty-four hundred men under his command, a beefed-up regiment, a regimental combat team. The Chinese, it was believed, had elements of five divisions, a force of perhaps thirty to forty thousand men. Chipyongni was to be not just a battle but a siege. The only way for Freeman's forces to get more ammo and food was by parachute airdrops.

43

EVEN AS THE defenders at Chipyongni were digging in, the battle of Wonju was coming to a climax. The Wonju battle plan, Operation Roundup, had been pure Ned Almond and it had been a curious one, especially at this stage of the war. Almond's assault was part of a larger Ridgway-planned offensive—in effect, the right flank of Operation Thunderbolt. But it was significantly less cautious than that of his commander, even though his assigned terrain was more mountainous and so better tailored for the tactics of the Chinese. Almond once again ignored warnings from his senior intelligence people that the Chinese command had shifted the core of its forces into the area and the Chinese were up to something big. The fiasco along the Chosin, so much of it his responsibility, it was believed, had not created a new, more tempered, and wiser Ned Almond. Now, ten weeks later, given another chance to engage the Chinese, he was still far too aggressive, still careless about his incoming intelligence, still given to sending out units that could readily be isolated by the Chinese and thus destroyed, still underestimating the professionalism and the tactics of his enemy. All of this ended up, as Clay Blair wrote, "evoking memories of Almond's operations in northeast Korea." "Almond's Folly," Jim Hinton, who had made it out of Kunuri successfully but who was seriously wounded in the coming battle, called it. What Hinton remembered was the fury of Colonel Robert Coughlin, the new commander of the Thirty-eighth Regiment. Almond had effectively taken over command of his regiment, Coughlin told Hinton, breaking it up into smaller units, separating the battalions from one another, isolating them, and making each battalion that much more vulnerable. That was in contrast to the force moving north on the western front, where the different units were quite tightly bound to one another. If the Chinese struck, it would be hard for these weakened units to defend themselves. As far as Coughlin could tell, it was the exact opposite of what they were supposed to have learned from the first go-round with the Chinese.

For those Americans who admire the military, the remarkable presence of a great military force within a working democracy, Almond's role in this war remains, more than half a century after he left the battlefield, singularly disturbing. Almond was old school, but it was a dubious old school. In the ultimate democratic institution where men were supposed to be judged only on their battlefield performance, and their willingness to die if need be, he refused to judge them on merit and instead preferred to hang on to his prejudices. To the end he held on to the racism of his early years. In 1971, six years into the combat phase of Vietnam, when he was long retired, he was still saying as forcefully as he could that integration weakened combat units.

His racism had always been a critical part of the problem. His prejudices did not necessarily set him apart from other senior officers in the Army at that moment, but there was an intensity—a passion—to them that disturbed younger officers around him, not to mention the black soldiers and officers who were the victims of his racism. He thought of blacks, some of whose first victories as full American citizens were about to take place in this war, as an inferior species. If they served at all, it should be in some servile way, what was called "ash and trash." Harry Truman and now Matt Ridgway were trying to desegregate the Army, and Ned Almond in his own way was trying to resegregate it, trying as best he could to create separate black units.

In mid-January 1951, during an early battle around Wonju, a black captain named Forest Walker successfully led a bayonet and hand grenade charge against some well-dug-in North Koreans. His battalion commander, Butch Barberis, greatly admired and by then a lieutenant colonel, whose word was never doubted by his peers, told Ridgway about Walker's valor a day later, and Ridgway, visibly impressed, ordered the Silver Star for him. Eventually Almond found out about the medal, stopped it, and had Walker relieved of his company command. When one of his favorite officers from World War II, Bill McCaffrey, finally got a regiment in Korea, a command expedited by his connection to Almond, the general was furious with his old friend for integrating it. McCaffrey had placed three black soldiers in every squad. "You didn't," Almond said.

"Yes, sir, I did," McCaffrey replied.

"You of all people should have known better than that," Almond shot back—a reference to their days together with the Ninety-second.

"But, General, it's working," McCaffrey insisted.

Almond just shook his head. To him, it was like a betrayal by a member of his family.

What was important about Almond's prejudice, loathsome as it was in itself, was that—in addition to being extremely painful for the black soldiers serving under him—there were serious professional consequences to it. For there were men who fought under him and studied him, who believed that his racism did not stop there. As J. D. Coleman noted, Almond saw the Chinese in much the same way. One of the reasons he pushed his troops forward so recklessly in the Chosin Reservoir fighting was that he did not take the Chinese seriously as an opponent. He believed that even if they showed up on the battlefield, they would flee from American forces, because they were a lesser people. That was what was so important about the laundrymen phrase; he saw this talented enemy not as they had become on the battlefield. Instead, they were still, in his eyes, the kind of people who should be back in America, doing the laundry of white people.

Coleman, who had fought with the 187th Regimental Combat Team under Almond, believed his lack of interest in the way the Chinese fought, his failure to learn from earlier battles against them, was but one more reflection of what he called Almond's "incipient racism." In the weeks that followed the battles in the north that had gone so badly, none of his commanders was ever summoned to discuss what had been learned so far about the Chinese. "Post-Korea we did a lot of studies on their tactics," Coleman said years later, "but at the time we did very little—there was no attempt to put together as quickly as we could in those first few weeks what we had learned about them, their tactics, their strengths, weaknesses, logistical limitations, how they tried to panic you and then set up an ambush south of you. There was a lot to learn and we didn't learn it. It was as if we didn't need to—they were not seen as a foe worthy of study. And it cost us badly at Hongchon and Hoengsong and Wonju [all part of the greater battle for Wonju]. I've always put it off to a kind of innate, unconscious American racism. Almond failed to learn quickly enough from the first defeat and I think it was because his prejudices blocked out his intelligence." As late as mid-February, Almond seemed to think all he had to do was hit the Chinese a little harder, Coleman believed. "His racism tainted every decision he made in battle," Coleman said.

Operation Roundup was the name that Almond gave to his battle plan for the Wonju area. It looked like a perfect Fort Leavenworth plan. There was even a certain grandeur to it. It was large scale and involved much coordination between different units. If it had been done at Leavenworth, a theoretical battle in a theoretical country (preferably a much flatter and warmer one) against a theoretical enemy (that made its approaches down major roads, easily identifiable from the air), it might have been impressive. There were lots of arrows driving ever so relentlessly on critical enemy positions, an envelopment here, another there, all ending wondrously in a double encirclement of the village of Hongchon, which lay about twenty-four miles north of Wonju, by then in American hands. Naturally, the success of this assault was based on perfect coordination between the participating units and the willingness of the Chinese to let the Americans do pretty much what they wanted to do, rather than smuggling four or five divisions of their own into the area and thus knocking the arrows askew.

To anyone with a sense of what it was actually like to fight in Korea, the flaws of Almond's plan were painfully obvious. Wonju was an extremely large, dangerous area, one that threatened to swallow up his somewhat limited UN forces. The weather was erratic, with great banks of clouds coming over each day, limiting any ability to make good use of American air superiority; and finally, Almond's forces were once again far too dependent on the professional skills of the South Korean forces. In this battle, Almond had done something that other officers found absolutely inexplicable: he had placed some American units *under* the command of ROK officers, which meant if things unraveled, which they were quite likely to do, the Americans would not have complete control over their own forces. Of the many strange things that Ned Almond did during this war, this was probably the most bizarre. The assumption of other officers was that Almond, who did not respect the ROK performance any more than most Americans, meant this as a confidence builder, as George Stewart noted, to show the ROKs he had more confidence in them than he really did, in hopes that they would therefore fight better. As for the South Koreans, they were in no way happy with the plan and thought in their own way that it was racist. General Paik Sun Yup, the best of the ROK commanders, in his memoir of the war, suggested that Almond was planning to use the Koreans as cannon fodder meant to absorb the heaviest punishment in the initial Chinese attack.

So Operation Roundup started with two ROK divisions, the Fifth and the Eighth, in the lead, participating with elements of two of the Second Division's regiments, the Thirty-eighth and the Ninth, as well as the 187th Regimental Combat Team, an airborne unit. On the other side, yet to show their hand, were four Chinese divisions from the 100,000 to 140,000 Chinese troops now in the central corridor region immediately above Wonju, readying themselves, with many more obviously available. At first, all seemed to go well for the UN forces, in no small part because the Chinese wanted them to go well—the more they succeeded in the first stage of the drive, the more isolated they were going to be when the Chinese struck. So the Chinese and the North Koreans pulled back, letting the American and South Korean forces push ever deeper into alien terrain. As J. D. Coleman noted, "The movements of the ROK and American units could not have been more favorable for the Chinese if General Peng had personally been in the X Corps Command Post and drawn them up himself." By February 10, the UN/ROK position was, in Coleman's words, like "an indefensible balloon inflated into enemy territory." On February 11, at

10 P.M., three Chinese divisions suddenly hit the ROK Eighth Division and it simply vanished, some seventy-five hundred men and officers gone like that, although three thousand men would eventually show up back at UN command posts.

The Chinese attack did not come as a complete surprise to Ridgway's headquarters, which was increasingly uneasy over intelligence reports indicating the gathering of an enormous Chinese force in the greater Wonju area. In fact, the intelligence coming from Ridgway's G-2 shop was surprisingly accurate. Lieutenant Colonel Robert Fergusson, the Eighth Army deputy G-2, who back in November had had a much more realistic sense of the Chinese threat to the Eighth Army than had his superiors, turned out to be quite prescient about what was going to happen. Only on the likely date of the Chinese attack was he off—by four days. Ridgway took the G-2's report seriously: on the eve of the start of the battle, his foot was already on the brake, and he was telling his forces not to move farther north. But Almond's foot was not—despite warnings from his own G-2, Lieutenant Colonel James Polk. Polk would later note that although he had issued serious warnings about the number of Chinese in the area, he had not paid enough attention to the word of one very important prisoner, a former Chinese Nationalist doctor who had given stunningly accurate estimates of the Chinese force about to attack—they simply had not believed that a doctor who was only a captain would know so much. Although Almond's Corps headquarters received an order from Ridgway to hold its positions on February 11, no comparable message went out from Corps to subordinate units for hours—and when it finally did, it was two hours *after* the Chinese struck.

It was a disaster in the making, a curious repeat of what had happened in late November when the main Chinese attack had come. As the ROK units collapsed, a number of units in Tenth Corps, especially the First and the Third battalions of the Thirty-eighth Regiment, were immediately cut off. What made the problem worse was Almond's bizarre command structure and the fact that so many of his subordinate commanders were so fearful of him and were slow to make their own decisions. Lieutenant Colonel John Keith, commander of the Fifteenth Field Artillery Battalion, which had been assigned to support ROK troops, immediately found himself in danger of being cut off. He called headquarters about 1:30 A.M. on February 12, knowing everything was collapsing on him, and asked Brigadier General Loyal Haynes, the division artillery commander, for permission to pull back. Haynes, a timid officer, was unable to give him an answer; he had to clear it with Ruffner or Corps. By the time the approval came through from Almond himself an hour and a half later, it was too late; the Chinese troops had completely cut Keith off, with all his unit's heavy gear and giant trucks. The ROKs whom Keith was supposed to protect (and who in turn in a situation like this were supposed to help protect him) were long gone. Keith's only road out was narrow and mountainous, and controlled by the Chinese. He soon joined up with a battalion of the Thirty-eighth Regiment, also under heavy attack and just as badly cut off. Together they tried the road, but as Clay Blair noted, the Chinese troops "had created a gauntlet, not unlike that which the 38th Infantry had run below Kunuri." In the end, on the way south to Hoengsong, the Fifteenth Field Artillery Battalion lost five howitzers, four 155s, and one 105.

Just before dawn on February 12, what was left of the badly banged up First Battalion and Keith's artillerymen reached the Third Battalion of the Thirty-eighth, just north of Hoengsong. But here too the Chinese were pressing in and the American perimeter was fast shrinking. Just south of them the Chinese had yet again cut the road. At Corps everyone was aware of one order above all others from Ridgway—they were not to lose any more artillery pieces. If the Chinese overran Keith and his men and took more heavy guns, the ramifications for Corps were going to be very serious. Keith was ordered to continue south to Hoengsong where, it was hoped, he and the units with him would be able to create a strong defensive position. So the artillerymen moved out, accompanied by the remaining troops from the First Battalion. But after going about a half mile south, they were hit so hard by the Chinese that no one could move, and they were pinned down for some four hours. Finally Corps ordered the Third Battalion to leave its perimeter, join up with the other two units, and help drive through the Chinese blockade. At the same time, Corps ordered an armored infantry relief column from the 187th Regimental Combat Team to fight its way north and link up with them. It too was hit hard by the Chinese, but eventually broke through. It was dark now and the Chinese still controlled the road. Yet there was some hope that the larger combined force by now led by the 187th could break out again and make it south. Then one of the lead trucks in the convoy, which was towing a 105 howitzer, flipped over, blocking the road. That was the worst possible news for the men trying to get out.

From the start the Chinese believed they could control the road simply by disabling the larger Americans vehicles just as they had below Kunuri. They concentrated their fire on the driver compartments of the big trucks. Their fire was so heavy and so well concentrated that there was no possibility of clearing the road. Most of the big guns would have to be left behind. Fourteen 105s and five 155s were abandoned, along with 120 trucks, some of them carrying wounded. It was in all ways a disaster. Colonel Keith was first listed as missing in action and then as probably having died in a prison camp. Fortunately, the Dutch battalion fighting hard at Hoengsong managed to hold; and the varying forces of the

Thirty-eighth along with some of the artillery men managed to retreat through Hoengsong and back to Wonju. The losses had been devastating: the two battalions along with the Dutch battalion suffered more than two thousand casualties. There were about ten thousand ROK casualties as well. Ridgway, hearing the news, was furious, and soon showed up at Tenth Corps headquarters and gave Almond a ferocious blistering. It was, said Lieutenant Colonel Jack Chiles, who was an Almond deputy at the time, the worst ass-chewing he had ever heard. Ridgway did not yet know of the full casualties in the battle, but he knew how many artillery pieces they had lost, and that in his book was sinful, the loss of big guns to the enemy. There was a great deal of talk about reckless misuse of artillery, and a great deal of emphasis, Chiles said, "*that this will never happen again!*" But for whatever reason—fear of upsetting MacArthur, the incompetence of his other corps commanders—Ridgway did not relieve Almond.

The knowledge that the equivalent of an entire battalion had been lost was brutal enough, but a month later, during another American offensive, some Marines went through the same valley and discovered that the battlefield was littered with American bodies, those of the men of the Thirty-eighth Regiment who had been killed trying to get back to Wonju. Salvage and recovery troops were sent in and recovered more than 250 American and a large number of Dutch bodies, including that of their battalion commander, Marinus den Ouden. Most of the men had multiple bullet wounds—a sign that they had fought to the last and had eventually been overrun. After the war was over and a more careful accounting was done, the regiment's death toll for the three days of battle was placed at 468. Of that total 255 died on the battlefield and another 213 in captivity. Keith's Fifteenth Field Artillery Battalion lost 83 men killed that night, and another 128 in Communist prison camps. "Massacre Valley," the Marines called the area. One Marine posted a sign that reflected, among other things, the bitterness over the nomenclature chosen for the war: "MASSACRE VALLEY/SCENE OF HARRY TRUMAN'S POLICE ACTION/ NICE GOING HARRY."

THE COMMUNIST SUCCESSES in the central sector were mounting. Three days into what had started as an American offensive, the Chinese were now moving in on two of the prizes they had sought from the start, Wonju and Chipyongni. As the Chinese seemed ready to take Wonju, fears for Chipyongni grew. So far almost everything the Americans had done in Wonju had gone wrong, and the Communist victories had seemed like a continuation of what had happened around the Chongchon. Then, with both Wonju and Chipyongni at stake, the Americans caught a major break, the kind that can turn defeat into victory.

On the morning of February 14, a small artillery spotter plane was flying over the Som River, which cut its way through the mountains northwest of Wonju. One of the observers, Lieutenant Lee Hartell of the Fifteenth Field Artillery Battalion, happened to look out. There, along the sandy beach of the river, was an unusually heavy tree line, or so he thought at first, a lot more trees than one usually saw in that area. He decided to look again. This time he noticed that the tree line was moving. It was not a tree line, he suddenly understood, but a vast Chinese force, seemingly well camouflaged, and so confident that they were moving en masse in daylight as they almost never did, and did not even freeze as they were supposed to when a plane came over. With victory so close and time so precious, they now had too little respect for their enemies and had simply ignored the spotter plane. Hartell and his stunned pilot placed the force at as many as two divisions, perhaps fourteen thousand men moving four abreast, almost surely on their way to the final battle for Wonju. Hartell radioed in his find and called for artillery fire. The battle was soon to be memorialized by the Americans as the Wonju Shoot.

The first round was a white phosphorous marker, and with that, the Wonju Shoot began, as the Americans poured in a brutal barrage of artillery fire on the Chinese. The Americans had massive artillery ready to fire on the Chinese force—some 130 big guns, thirty 155s and one hundred 105s—and a commander, Brigadier General George Stewart, who, though not an artillery officer, knew how to exploit a stunning break like this. If there was one senior officer in the entire corps who stepped forward and acted professionally in the midst of the larger battle of Wonju and Hongchon and Hoengsong, it was Stewart. Among the men of the Second Division he was considered the most rational, professional, thoughtful, and perhaps most important of all, independent senior officer.

Stewart had become the assistant division commander almost by chance. He was someone who had always thought he would be an infantry officer, had graduated from West Point in 1923, but had not managed to get an infantry command. When World War II started, he was too old for a junior command and did not have enough going for him to get a more senior one. Instead he had been given one of those vital assignments no one really wants, but which need to be done and done well. He was made chief of transportation for the Allied forces, first in North Africa, then in Italy, next in the Southwest Pacific, and he was in charge of transportation for the invasion of Japan when the war ended. He had performed brilliantly at his various tasks, an irreplaceable man in two theaters of war. But his abilities worked against his career ambitions. He was too badly needed elsewhere to get the infantry commands he always wanted. He had ended the war as a brigadier general, had been bumped down to colonel during the demobe, and then promoted back to brigadier in January 1947. He was, thought Ken Hamburger, the soldier, historian, and teacher, "one of those special men the Army produces, talented and brave and thoughtful, all in all an exceptional officer, but not quite ruthless enough to be a great general. The great generals, men like Ridgway, though they are not reckless, know when the moment arrives when you have to risk the lives of your men in the call of duty." Stewart in 1950 was still doing logistics and had overseen the logistics of the Inchon landing, still longing for that infantry command that was always just out of reach.

In early December, as the Chinese drove south, Stewart was told that—lest the Chinese overrun it—his logistics command would move south to Pusan. He wanted no part of the move. His son, George Stewart, Jr., a 1945 graduate of West Point, was a lieutenant in the 187th Regimental Combat Team. The idea that he would be operating from a safe slot in a safe haven while his son was in harm's way the elder Stewart found singularly offensive. He visited the Eighth Army chief of staff, Lev Allen, and asked for a different assignment. Allen told him to get on with his assignment and get to Pusan. But on his way out of Allen's office Stewart ran into Bob McClure, who had just been given command of the Second Division. On a whim, he asked McClure whether he needed a good assistant division commander. Because the then-ADC, Sladen Bradley, was in the hospital, Stewart was given the job, at first on a temporary basis, eventually permanently. His position in the hierarchy was vulnerable, more so after McClure, his sponsor, was so quickly relieved. Stewart had limited authority, more adviser than commander; he was to give no commands on his own. Everything he did had to be cleared with Ruffner, who had replaced McClure, and that meant, in effect, with Almond, who wanted him gone.

Earlier, with Wonju about to be assaulted by Chinese forces, the size of which they were just beginning to comprehend at Corps, Almond had put Stewart in charge of the town's defense, and he did it in a distinctly Almondesque fashion. He ordered Stewart to Wonju late on the day of February 13, the day before Hartell spotted the two divisions, and left behind for him quite specific instructions on how to fight the battle: "General Almond directs that you take command of all the troops in the vicinity of Wonju, defend and hold that important road junction at all costs. The General believes that the Chinese will attack on your right, BUT THE DECISION IS YOURS. The General believes you should place the one intact BN of the 38th on the line, BUT THE DECISION IS YOURS." Then, having passed on the orders, the G-3, as Stewart noted, immediately departed the endangered post.

The instructions, Stewart decided, were completely worthless. He had studied the terrain and, with the limited intelligence he had, decided the attack would come from the left—in this he was correct—and so he held in reserve the one good battalion of the Thirty-eighth that remained. Though he was an infantry officer and not an artillery man, he was exceptionally knowledgeable about the uses of artillery because of some cross training he had done in the 1930s. Now, with a relatively small defensive force under his command and perhaps as many as four divisions on the attack, he knew he was going to need all the expertise in big guns that he could muster, and he was shrewd enough not to count on any help from Loyal Haynes, the division artillery commander, whom he, like many other men, considered an exceptionally weak officer. Upon arrival, even before the battle started, he ordered Haynes to have his men prepare data so that they could fire on critical points of approach upon command; he wanted map overlays prepared that could allow his artillery to hit different points simply by using a preselected number. In effect, he wanted to be able to call in massive fire instantaneously without any calculation in the middle of battle. No time was to be wasted.

Thus, when Hartell first spotted the Chinese, Stewart and his guns were ready. Catching a giant Chinese force in the open with so many artillery tubes at his disposal, he intended to maximize his advantage. On several occasions that day Haynes tried to slow Stewart down, but he was ignored. With Lieutenant Hartell still able to fly over the scene and call in adjustments, the artillery men very systematically poured shell after shell on the Chinese. And yet the Chinese kept coming. Nothing, it seemed, could stop them, not even this merciless hail of fire. For this was one of their great weaknesses at that point in the war: once a battle was initiated, they had little ability to make adjustments. So the artillery shoot went on for more than three hours. At one point Haynes asked Stewart to stop because they were running low on ammo—but Stewart, knowing this was a chance he might never have again, waved him off. "Keep firing until the last shell is used," he said. He then ordered up an immediate ammo resupply from Japan. It was, as J. D. Coleman pointed out, in its logistics a stunning symbol of a most unlikely American advantage. Additional artillery shells could arrive for the Wonju garrison in hours—whereas for the Chinese it often took several days or more to get more ammunition to a battle. A little later Haynes called Stewart to insist that they had to slow down because his guns were overheating. Again Stewart paid no attention. "Keep firing until the gun barrels melt," he ordered.

It was the turning point in the battle. An estimated five thousand Chinese were killed and thousands more wounded. Though there was more hard fighting to come, Wonju had been saved. The Chinese losses in the central corridor were monstrous, possibly as high as twenty thousand killed and wounded. At the command level there was no doubt that Stewart was the hero of the battle, though Almond, he eventually noted, seemed quite unappreciative. Late in the afternoon, when the artillery shoot was over, Brigadier General William Bowen, the commander of the 187th RCT, arrived at Wonju CP headquarters, and Stewart was ordered rather peremptorily to return to Division headquarters. ("Corps felt my presence was no longer necessary," he dryly noted.) Almond awarded Bowen a Silver Star for his part in the battle but awarded nothing to Stewart. Honoring him, after all, would mean that Stewart had correctly reversed Almond's own erroneous instructions on how to fight, and more important, that he was a worthy ADC and would henceforth have to be taken seriously in the division hierarchy.

Though the Chinese offensive had been blunted at Wonju, Chipyongni still stood exposed.

44

L IEUTENANT PAUL MCGEE of Belmont, North Carolina, had finally gotten his first real taste of combat when George Company of the Second Battalion of the Twenty-third Infantry Regiment relieved a French company on the top of the ridge at Twin Tunnels. McGee commanded George Company's Third Platoon. It had taken long enough—he had tried to join the Marines on December 8, 1941, when he was seventeen, but had been rejected by the Corps because he was color-blind. His subsequent service in World War II had somehow disappointed him. Only when he and his men climbed the hill at Twin Tunnels to relieve the French was McGee struck by how brutal war truly was, and how callous it seemed to make the men who did the fighting. George Company had arrived after the fight was over, just in time to survey the carnage of a terribly hard-fought battle. McGee could understand much of the battle just by letting his eyes follow the trail of Chinese bodies, hundreds of them it seemed, representing the early waves of the enemy's assault, corpses that were now frozen, fixed permanently in the final moments of their lives. It was as if he had discovered a giant, open-faced Chinese burial ground. As he and his men climbed the hill, it only got worse: French soldiers were coming down, carrying their dead on a path so narrow they had no choice but to descend single file, two-man teams hauling out the dead, using the most primitive kinds of slings, the body being dragged on the ground on a rope between two men.

What struck McGee was how casual the living seemed about what they were doing, how immune to death they were. The French soldiers were talking—laughing, sometimes—as if nothing had happened; and yet the bodies they were carrying had been their buddies just the day before. There was no sign of mourning. He wondered if the French were different from American soldiers, or whether this was part of the secret ritual of survival, known only to other combat troops who had made it through their own small hells, because if you thought about it too much, you could no longer function. McGee pondered that again at the top of the ridge, where the French position had been.

The word was that the French tended to dig deeper foxholes than the Americans, but because of the rocks and the ice, their holes were not very impressive, in some places just a couple of inches deep, and everywhere on the ground was blood; in some cases, brains spilled out. For the first time McGee wondered what he had gotten himself into.

Well, he had done it all by himself. He had chosen this place, had volunteered to go to Korea, and worse had pushed to be with the frontline troops, thereby violating the most basic law of the Army, which was never to volunteer for anything. Truth be told, he had not merely volunteered, but had systematically pressured the Army to give him his own rifle platoon. He had forced the Army to pluck him from the job it greatly preferred for him—as an instructor back at Fort Benning, Georgia, training other young men to go to Korea—and to send him all the way here instead. Now, ten days after that first jarring view of the carnage of battle at Twin Tunnels, he was at Chipyongni, waiting patiently in his foxhole on the south side of the perimeter, guarding the sector that would turn out to be the most vulnerable part of Paul Freeman's regimental defense.

McGee was a country boy from rural North Carolina, and he had wanted to serve his country for a long time. After the Marines turned him down, he had joined the Army and waited patiently in England to cross the Channel for his chance at battle. He was not in on D-day or anything else that mattered in the subsequent weeks. He envied those who, to his way of thinking, were luckier. Instead his unit, the Sixty-sixth, or Black Panther Division, was held in reserve. Then, during the Battle of the Bulge, it had been chosen to go in with the Third Army and reinforce the embattled troops near Bastogne, and McGee had been pleased. But during the Channel crossing, a German U-boat hit a transport carrying one of the division's other regiments, and 802 men went down with the ship. Because of that, they had pulled McGee's division and regiment back and finally sent it to another area, near St. Nazarre, where its job was to keep German units guarding sub bases bottled up. That had seemed more like police work than combat, and when the war was over, McGee wondered if he would ever get his chance. He was too young to realize that, for those eager enough, there was always going to be enough war to go around.

McGee had returned to North Carolina, and stayed out of the service for about a year and a half before joining the reserves. He and his older brother Tom, with whom he was very close, were running a small grocery store and filling station in the Belmont area, and there was one Army recruiting sergeant whom they liked and who had them marked down as possible enlistees. The McGee filling station and store was not a stunning financial success. People were moving from the country to the city and suburbs, and the store was already beginning to run on credit. So the sergeant kept coming by and selling them the virtues of the Army in a time of peace—the chance to see the world, without the likelihood of ever having to fight for their country. Finally the McGee brothers, Paul and Tom, agreed to re-up if they could choose their area, pick their unit, and serve together. The sergeant said that would be just fine. They picked the Far East because they had already been to Europe, and Asia sounded much more exotic. They got what they wanted—Japan and the Seventh Infantry Division, Paul in Able Company, Tom in Baker Company of the Seventeenth Regiment. Paul McGee was surprised by how much he liked the Japanese people, who were friendly, and Japanese women, who were even friendlier in those days, because when he had been fighting in Europe he had not hated the Germans, but for some reason he did not understand at the time he *had* hated the Japanese.

Japan had turned out to be good duty. The only thing that had bothered McGee was the terrible shape the Army was in. He remembered one cold, rainy day when he was giving a training lesson on how to set up a combat outpost. General Walton Walker came by, complimented him on the job he was doing, and told the assembled GIs to pay attention to this fine young soldier who knew something about warfare, because sooner or later they were going to be in a war. Then Walker asked McGee if he wanted to be an officer. That was an interesting question because McGee was already an officer in the Army reserve, but as an active soldier he was only a sergeant with two rockers. He had been wary of becoming a regular Army officer because in his mind they were mostly West Point men, or college graduates anyway, and he did not think that a country boy with a shaky tenth-grade education would stack up well against them. Then Walker asked if McGee would be interested in Officer Candidate School (OCS), and that seemed like a better idea. He said yes, but only if his brother Tom could come along. Walker thought it could be done. So both McGees filled out their papers, but it turned out you had to be at least a sergeant for OCS, and Tom McGee was a mere corporal. So only Paul McGee ended up at OCS after all.

When the Korean War started, Paul, back in the States, could not wait to get over there. He immediately volunteered to go, but the Army, ever the contrarian force, held him at Fort Benning, while his brother, with the Seventh Division, was cut off near the Chosin Reservoir in late November. That made him want to go more than ever; he was sure Tom needed him, even after he was one of the lucky ones who made it back from the Chosin. In time the Army decided that it *did* need Paul in Korea, and that he *was* an officer, not an enlisted man, and since platoon leaders were in great demand, they shipped him out. He was assigned to the Second Division and managed to con people into putting him in the Twenty-third Regiment because it was closest to Tom's Seventeenth Regiment in the Seventh Division, which was also part of Tenth Corps. He had gotten up to the Twenty-third Regiment in January and was immediately sent to the Second Battalion. The people at Battalion were so happy to see him that they offered him the heavy-weapons platoon, filled as it was with mortars and machine guns. Instead he asked for a rifle platoon in George Company because that was the unit nearest to his brother's regiment.

The people at the Second Battalion headquarters thought he was a lunatic. "McGee, you're crazier than hell," one of the officers said. "We're losing platoon leaders in our rifle companies every day. But the heavy weapons platoon— that's another thing. That's the best deal we've got. You're surrounded by all that firepower, and they're about three or four hundred feet back from the front line where the other troops are." No, McGee replied, he knew all that, but he wanted to be up on the line, wanted to command nothing but men who really wanted to fight under him, and he wanted to be as close as he could to the Seventeenth Regiment. That first night he got word to his brother, and Tom drove right over in a jeep to see him. "What the hell are you doing here?" Tom McGee asked. "I came out here to get you out of this goddamn place," Paul McGee said. "Boy," answered Tom, "you're really going to be sorry. People are getting killed here every day—you should have stayed back home." So it was that Paul McGee had taken command of the Third Platoon of George Company, whose perimeter at Chipyongni was approximately five hundred yards long—the equivalent of five football fields.

Waiting up there on the line, he knew the time was coming close when the Chinese were going to hit. He had been on several patrols, and enemy activity had increased dramatically every day, while the range of the patrols had shortened accordingly. He had also heard through the rumor mill that any attempt to withdraw from the village had been rejected. That guaranteed that they were going to stay and fight. He was finally going to get his chance. On February 13, the word was that the Chinese were likely to come that night.

George Company's position was hardly ideal. It jutted farther out than the rest of the defensive positions and lacked the elevation of most of the other UN defensive points. It faced Hill 397, and they knew there were Chinese there. In fact, it was as if there were a ridge that emerged from the George Company position and virtually connected it with Hill 397, almost, as Ken Hamburger noted, like a finger extending from their position to the Chinese position. That gave the Chinese a natural approach to McGee's platoon. As he waited for the battle to start, Paul McGee had no idea that his sector would prove to be the most bitterly contested in the entire battle, or that his battalion commander, Lieutenant Colonel Jim Edwards, would in his after-action reports name this small part of the larger perimeter McGee Hill.

McGee had a total of forty-six men in his platoon. They seemed like good men, but he had no way of really knowing, because he had never fought with them before. He had made sure their foxholes were adequately deep—four feet at least. His own was just fine, four feet wide, six feet long, and about six feet deep, with a firing step that allowed him to duck when he wanted to, and fire back when he was ready. But, regrettably he thought, theirs was an oddly barren hill. There was no way to create any kind of cover around their foxholes— no logs, no debris of any sort. That made it possible for attacking troops to lob grenades in. Worse yet, although a good deal of barbed wire had gone up around the greater Twenty-third perimeter, they had run out of it before reaching George Company. There had been just enough to place a double apron in front of George's First Platoon, but none in front of McGee's position. At that moment, whatever Division and Corps could spare, whether it was airpower or barbed wire, went to Wonju.

If McGee was unhappy about this critical shortfall, he accepted it as well. That was the deal and soldiers were meant to accept the deal. If it had been a perfect battle in a perfect world, they would have had enough of everything, not just barbed wire, but logs to protect the foxholes, and enough mines, and a hell of a lot better communications. But it was not a perfect battle in a perfect world—it was going to be a difficult battle in a godforsaken place—most battles were. Some of the regiment's engineers came and helped create two fougasse bombs, taking fifty-five-gallon drums, filling them with a mixture of napalm and oil, in addition to what they hoped was a reliable ignition system, all in a lethal homemade mine, which they then buried. It was a potentially devastating weapon; each fougasse might take a lot of Chinese with it, but as a one-time weapon it was no substitute for barbed wire. As it happened, neither fougasse went off—perhaps the engineers had not done the ignition system right, McGee thought. They also created some other homemade mines, taking some hand grenades, pulling their pins, but keeping the ignition suppressed inside a ration can and running lines to them so that when the lines were jerked, the grenades would explode.

The Chinese hit first, as expected, on the night of the thirteenth. McGee heard the bugles around 10 P.M. Then they started coming—and just kept coming and coming. Some people had said they would come in human waves, but that was not quite right, unless you thought of a very small wave, and then a slightly bigger one each time, as if the attack was first a squad, then a platoon, then a company. They were clearly looking for the American positions and marking them, wasting if need be a good many lives in the process. The first night, McGee thought, went quite well. He had ordered his men not to fire on

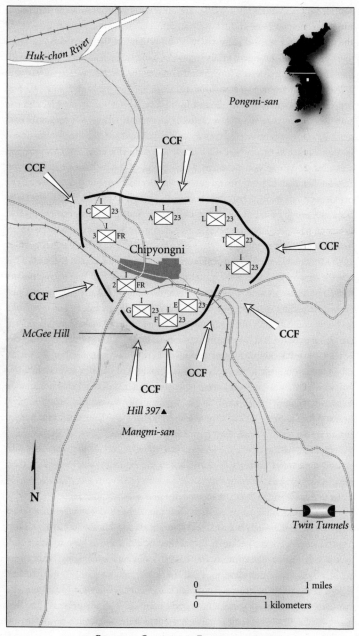

Huk-chon River

Pongmi-san

CCF

CCF

C ⊠ I 23
3 ⊠ I FR
A ⊠ I 23
L ⊠ I 23
I ⊠ 23
K ⊠ I 23

Chipyongni

CCF

2 ⊠ I FR

CCF

G ⊠ I 23
E ⊠ I 23
F ⊠ I 23

McGee Hill

CCF

CCF

CCF

Hill 397 ▲

Mangmi-san

N

Twin Tunnels

0   1 miles
0   1 kilometers

22. Battle of Chipyongni, February 13–14, 1951

sound, but only when they actually saw the enemy, in order to conserve ammunition. When dawn came, there were stacks of Chinese bodies sprawled around the position, but no one had penetrated it, and McGee had lost no men.

The Chinese had, however, discovered a blind or dead spot right in the center of his position. It was a dry creek bed, about four feet deep, almost like a giant ditch, that seemed to come directly from Hill 397 and empty out right on top of the George Company position. It was quite literally a natural channel into the George Company sector and allowed the Chinese very good cover right up to the foot of McGee's small hill. The Chinese could hardly have done better, if months earlier, knowing that there might be a battle here, they had carved the channel out themselves. McGee knew it was a dangerous avenue into his position, but there was not much he could do about it. With dawn just arriving on the morning of the fourteenth, he noticed some Chinese soldiers near the mouth of the creek bed, and told Bill Kluttz, his platoon sergeant, to fire his rocket launcher at the spot. Kluttz hit a tree, which gave him an air burst illuminating about forty Chinese soldiers, who rose up out of the cover of the trees and started running back across the flat land right in front of the American position; the Americans opened up with their machine guns and caught most of them in the open field. Now they knew for sure that the Chinese were going to keep on using the creek bed for protection.

COLONEL PAUL FREEMAN thought the first night of the battle had gone reasonably well. All positions had held and his casualties were surprisingly low. He knew he did not entirely control the course of the battle—the Chinese would do that, depending on how many men they were willing to feed into the fight. He worried, though, about his supply of ammunition. There were so many attackers that, no matter how much his men had, it probably was not going to be enough. The Air Force was trying to air-drop more, but most of it was falling outside the perimeter. Still, morale was high, which was a critically important factor in any siege. It was almost as if his men were eager to be here, and anxious to be given a chance to make up for Kunuri.

Freeman kept busy during the night moving around the perimeter, checking in with his different subordinate commanders. If there was a place of vulnerability, it was to the south and southwest, where George Company and the French battalion were potential targets. But he had already spoken to Jim Edwards, the commander of the Second Battalion, which included George Company, about moving reserve units up to reinforce those positions. Then, at daybreak of the fourteenth, a Chinese 120mm mortar round landed right next to Freeman's tent. The regiment's intelligence officer, Major Harold Shoemaker, was grievously wounded and died a few hours later; several other officers, in-

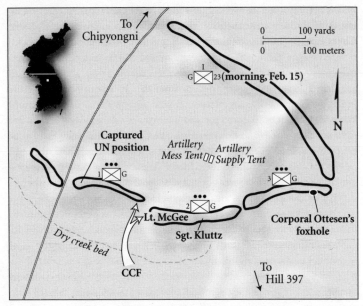

23. McGee Hill, February 13–15, 1951

cluding Freeman, were wounded less severely. He took a small slice of shrapnel in his left calf, which did not seem serious: Freeman had been lying down on his cot when it happened, and had just reversed his position so that his feet were where his head had been. He and Lieutenant Colonel Frank Meszar, his good friend and the regimental executive officer, later joked about what might have happened if he had not reversed his position on the cot. It was, they decided, the kind of luck you needed in battle. While the wound itself did not seem that bad, there might have been a break in the lower leg that would have to be dealt with later. Captain Robert Hall, the regimental surgeon, quickly dressed the wound, gave Freeman two aspirin, and told him to get in touch if he had any problems.

Freeman continued to visit forward positions, often virtually alone, with a limp. But the wound was what Ned Almond had been waiting for, and using it as his excuse, he moved immediately to relieve Freeman of his command in the middle of a battle. He had wanted to put one of his own boys in charge of the Twenty-third for some time. A few days earlier, he had made his first try. Irritated because he thought Freeman was not forcing his men to use dry socks to prevent trench foot and frostbite, he sent Lieutenant Colonel John Chiles, his operations officer, to Ruffner to tell him to relieve Freeman. That was the last thing Ruffner wanted to do with a serious battle looming. He looked at Chiles and replied, "Do you know what? My radio just went out of whack. I have no way in the world of reaching Paul Freeman." That provided only a brief stay of execution.

The senior officers in the Twenty-third were furious that Almond would use a marginal wound as an excuse to change commanders in the middle of a battle that was going well, and was about to increase in intensity. To substitute for a much admired officer someone no one knew and who would always be considered part of a coup was appalling, they thought. Dr. Hall had received a call from Colonel Gerry Epley, division chief of staff, almost as soon as word of the wound had reached higher headquarters.

"How serious is the wound?" Epley asked.

"It's not that serious," Hall answered. "Maybe under normal conditions you might evacuate him for treatment. But these aren't normal conditions."

"What do you mean by that?"

"Well, this is a tough place and this is a very tough battle and he's the one man holding the regiment together. We're surrounded, we're going to be short of ammo. The men can see that some of the ammo drops are falling short, but they absolutely believe in Freeman, and they believe that he'll get them out of here. The Twenty-third Regiment believes in itself because he's led them before. Without him I think it's a different regiment. Evacuating him would be unnecessary, unwanted, and undesirable."

Hall instantly knew he had been too candid. Epley's voice changed. He was furious, Hall realized: how dare a surgeon tell him what to do on a military matter. "Don't you dare to presume to tell me about tactical matters! We don't need any of that from you. I asked you for a medical judgment. I just want to know how deep the wound is. That's all the answer I need from you."

But Hall thought he would give it one more shot. He was not, after all, a kid, and he had no time for the politics of Division or Corps headquarters now. He had been a combat surgeon in World War II, had fought in the Battle of the Bulge, and had gone into civilian practice for a time. When Korea began, he had asked to go back on active duty and volunteered specifically for the Second Division after it had been hit at Kunuri, because he had lost some close friends up there. In all of this he had been motivated by old-fashioned loyalties. Now, he felt, those same loyalties gave him the right to speak candidly. Besides, who knew more about the mood of the regiment than a doctor, whom soldiers often told things they would never tell other officers. This regiment, he insisted to Epley, more than most, believes in its commander, and takes much of its strength and identity from his presence and leadership. It would be extremely dangerous for regimental morale if he were pulled out. Epley signed off angrily, and Hall knew they were going to pull Freeman anyway.

Freeman was enraged. This was his battle and his regiment, and he did not want to leave. There was nothing worse in terms of unofficial Army codes than to be relieved of command in the middle of a battle. "I brought them in," he told headquarters during one call, "and I'll bring them out." He tried talking Ruffner out of it, but in a fight between Almond and Freeman, Ruffner was powerless. Freeman finally turned the matter over to George Stewart, the one man at Division whom he trusted. Freeman told Stewart he was not going to give up his command or be evacuated. Being relieved like this was the worst disgrace that could befall a commander, a career ender. Stewart, who knew Freeman was at least partially right, listened sympathetically. No one, he said, was going to question his performance. It was not going to damage his career, but if he did not leave as ordered there could be far more serious consequences. Finally, Freeman realized he had no choice. In the military, after all, you could not challenge orders.

But later that day, when Chiles flew in, Freeman managed not to be at the little airstrip to go out on the same plane. It would be used to take out wounded men, but not the outgoing regimental commander. Chinese mortar fire was falling on the strip as the plane landed, and the pilot needed to get out quickly. For the moment, the Twenty-third had two regimental commanders. "I told Chiles to find a shelter and stay out of my way until my departure," Freeman said years later. Chiles was shrewd enough to stay in the background and let Freeman run the show through the night of the fourteenth and well into the late morning of the fifteenth. Even when Chiles officially took command at midday on the fifteenth, he let the regimental exec, Frank Meszar, who knew the relative value of all the subordinate commanders, continue in Freeman's role.

45

MATT RIDGWAY HAD given Paul Freeman his word that if the Chinese attacked in full force, he would send help, and he intended to make good on his word. He was prepared to send the British Commonwealth Brigade, and the Fifth Cavalry Regiment under the command of Colonel Marcel Crombez. The Fifth Cav was a part of the First Cavalry Division. But help was not going to arrive any too quickly. The Commonwealth Brigade had a better, more direct route to Chipyongni, but it had run into an enormous Chinese blocking force and quickly found itself embattled and stalled, hardly in a position to rescue another trapped force. So Crombez was ordered by Major General Bryant Moore, the neighboring Ninth Corps commander, to get to Chipyongni in a hurry. In a case like this unit titles are often confusing: the First Cav itself was not a cavalry division, it was what the Army calls straight leg, that is, regular infantrymen; but the Fifth Cavalry Regiment, a part of the First Cav, was armored, and had been held in reserve at that time by Ninth Corps, at a base near Yoju. When he first started out on the rescue at Chipyongni, Colonel Crombez's force had twenty-three tanks, three infantry battalions, two battalions of field artillery, and a company of combat engineers. It was a not inconsiderable force. Crombez would have plenty of firepower. In addition, if things went badly, there was always the possibility of dispatching air cover to protect him.

Crombez first heard about the mission on the morning of February 14, when General Moore called to say that it looked like he might be used in the relief of Freeman's force. At 4 P.M., Moore called back, telling him he would have to move out that night to relieve Freeman's regiment—"and I know you'll do it." An hour later, Charles Palmer, newly promoted to two stars and made the commander of the First Cav, arrived at Crombez's CP and confirmed the order. Crombez was something of a controversial figure—a man who dressed with dash, wearing a cavalryman's yellow scarf (as if he were fighting the Indians back in the Wild West), having an oversized eagle painted on his helmet, and pinning a grenade on his harness much as Ridgway did. He also carried with him a blue poker chip that he would flip up and down while talking with his men, telling them they had to know when to play their blue chip—the implication being that a great combat commander had a sixth sense about battle and always knew when to strike. Some in his unit thought, however, that he did not fight with equal dash. He had, until then, seemed the possessor of a self-invented mystique, one not actually forged on the battlefield. Some of the men under him thought he sought glory too intensely, wanted a star too badly, and did not seem adequately committed to them. "Brave, yes. Professional, no," Clay Blair quoted a fellow West Pointer saying.

By the time he had his force ready to move, much later on the fourteenth, it was already dark, not the ideal time to push forward on roads where the Chinese might already be dug in. That first night Crombez made it to Yoju, about ten miles south of Chipyongni. There his units waited while the engineers built a bypass around a blown-out bridge over the Han River. Having finally managed to clear the Han on the evening of the fourteenth, his tanks were slowed by another blown bridge over a creek near Koksuri, about five miles from Chipyongni, and never really got moving until the morning of the fifteenth. Paul Freeman, monitoring Crombez's progress by radio, knew that no relief party was going to make it through on the fourteenth. Meanwhile the heaviest fighting yet at Chipyongni was taking place on the night of the fourteenth and into the morning of the fifteenth. Freeman, aware that the relief mission was moving more slowly than expected, then requested all the air strikes he could get, but almost nothing came—because the Air Force was so committed to the fighting at Wonju. What he did get was a light spotter plane—the Firefly, the men called it—that dropped flares; a wonderful addition to the battlefield, Freeman later said, because it turned "night into day." His men, he knew, were going to have to hold out a second night before help arrived.

IN THE ANNALS of the Korean War few incidents are as controversial as that of Marcel Crombez's final dash to the rescue at Chipyongni. Yes, he got there, and he got there in time, and yes, what he did was what Matt Ridgway had ordered him to do. But there was an unnecessary recklessness to it, which resulted in unnecessary losses among the infantrymen who accompanied him that many involved felt reflected an almost cavalier disregard for their lives. That he had put the mission above the proper care and treatment of his own men angered those infantrymen who survived, and left a bitter aftertaste in the accounts of historians who believed the same results could have been achieved with far fewer casualties, and who in addition wondered, when it was over, about the personal courage of the rescue commander himself. It raised one of the great questions of command in wartime: Does elemental success in

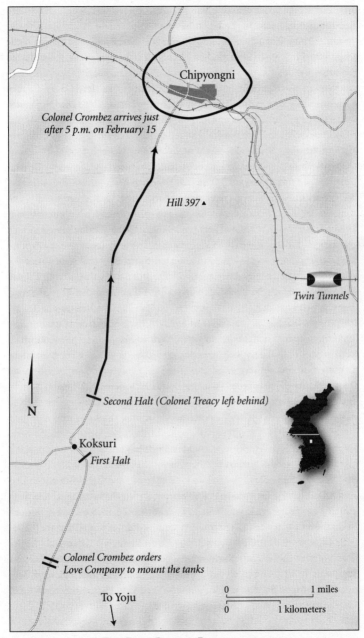

Chipyongni

Colonel Crombez arrives just
after 5 p.m. on February 15

Hill 397 ▲

Twin Tunnels

N

Second Halt (Colonel Treacy left behind)

Koksuri

First Halt

Colonel Crombez orders
Love Company to mount the tanks

To Yoju

| 0 | | 1 miles |
| 0 | | 1 kilometers |

24. TASK FORCE CROMBEZ, FEBRUARY 14–15, 1951

a crucial battle excuse all other failures and lapses? And if you succeed, are there are other issues you should answer to?

On the morning of the fifteenth, Crombez ran into heavy Chinese resistance just south of Koksuri. He had placed his infantrymen on either side of the road, but his progress remained slow. At that moment it was not clear whether his tanks would be able to push through in time. Around noon Crombez received a message from the CP of the Twenty-third (by then under Chiles) saying, "Reach us as soon as possible, in any event, reach us."

The importance of his mission had repeatedly been made clear to Crombez from the start by his superiors. He was visited by General Moore, the Tenth Corps commander, who told him to be there by evening, and then by General C. D. (known to his peers as Charley Dog, to match Army terminology) Palmer, his rather crusty division commander, and then by Nick Ruffner, the division commander of the besieged unit. All three of them pleaded with him to hurry. "I'll do it personally," Crombez promised. Finally, General Palmer landed in his chopper to talk to Crombez, check how things were going, and ask when he might reach Chipyongni—one more unneeded reminder that time was of the essence. "I'll get there and before dark," Crombez had assured him. Palmer then lent his chopper to Crombez, who scanned the area and saw that the road was still open but that the hills were full of Chinese. The decision to defend Chipyongni was Ridgway's, and it was vital to his larger strategy for the war. Thus the pressure on Crombez to get through was immense, each visit or call a reminder of how badly Ridgway wanted this one; it was as if the heat falling on Crombez was a direct extension of the heat coming down level by level from Ridgway to the officers—nothing but brass—immediately below him.

From the moment the battle began, Ridgway seemed to believe that the tide of the war depended on its outcome, that the sooner the Americans and their UN allies showed they could handle the numerical superiority of the Chinese, the more quickly other victories would come. What was at stake was not just a specific small piece of terrain, but the very psyche of his army. If Freeman, and now Chiles, could hold, it would be a symbol to all the other fighting men that they had entered a new phase of the war, one in which the Chinese had been stripped of the immense psychological advantage they had gained at Kunuri. In the months to follow, Ridgway was determined to keep adjusting the battlefield odds, to make things better for the men under his command—better food, warmer clothes, better armaments, better commanders—and to wage a campaign by artillery and air that would turn the lives of the Chinese soldiers into pure misery. But first and foremost he needed to change the mind-set of his own men.

At a certain point, Crombez called Chiles and said he did not think he could get there with his full train of infantrymen and supply trucks and ambulances. "Come on, trains or no trains," Chiles replied. Then Crombez made a fateful decision, one that would forever after cling to his reputation as a kind of permanent asterisk. He decided to turn his charge to Chipyongni into an armored assault. He would get rid of most of the non-armored part of his column, narrowing it down from three battalions to a much smaller, more streamlined force. He would take his tanks and the engineers—he needed the engineers to remove land mines, for the Chinese used their sappers skillfully. In addition, he would place a company of infantry on top of the tanks, and, less burdened, go all out. What bothered the men who made the rest of the assault, and the historians who wrote about it afterward, was the decision to put the infantrymen on top of the tanks.

To mount on the tanks he chose Love Company, with its 160 men, led by Captain John Barrett. Lieutenant Colonel Edgar Treacy, who had begun the rescue mission as the infantry battalion commander, was appalled by the idea. It violated every aspect of Army doctrine—if the Chinese continued to hit the convoy, the infantrymen riding on the tanks would be sitting ducks for the Chinese machine guns and mortars. Both Treacy and Barrett protested the order—the casualties would be horrendous, they said. Not only were the men on the tanks likely to be exceptionally vulnerable to Chinese fire, but when Patton tanks heated up, they could set a man's clothes on fire. In addition, the sweep of one of the tanks' big guns could knock men off at any time. What most men—certainly military historians who wrote about it—believed was that the tanks should have been buttoned up, with perhaps some infantrymen and engineers riding inside protected vehicles that followed behind the tanks. Then they could have gone hell for leather to Chipyongni. At the very least, if the infantrymen got off, there had to be some very dependable means of communication between their commander and the commander of the tanks.

What made the battlefield confrontation between Crombez and Treacy particularly difficult and caused subsequent events to be touched by exceptional bitterness and anger was the fact that there already appeared to be unusually bad feeling between the two of them. Both were West Point men, but theirs had been very different West Points and very different careers after graduation. Crombez had been born in Belgium, had enlisted in the Army in 1919, and had made it to West Point, graduating in 1925. He had always retained a rather heavy accent, and had been seen by his classmates as a heavy-handed striver, too crudely ambitious in terms of the academy's culture. What had attached itself to Crombez early on was the back-channel word that he wanted it all too much and yet did not have the right stuff. At the start of World War II, he was sixteen years out of the academy and was, in terms of command possibilities, a little too old for the lower ranking commands and not good enough for the more senior ones. He had done stateside training for most of the war. By war's end, he had made colonel. Like almost everyone else in the postwar military, his personal position shrank and he became a light colonel.

After the war, he finally got a command, being placed in charge of two separate regiments of the Seventh Infantry Division in Korea. He was, in the vernacular of the Army, something of a hard-ass, a petty one at that, it was believed, someone who seized on small things and made them too important. Before the Korean War started, he seemed disproportionately interested, for example, in keeping the troops stationed near Kaesong away from the hookers in town. Troops being troops, they were going to find a way to connect, even if it meant slipping the women into the barracks, as they sometimes did, disguised as ROK soldiers. Crombez once showed up at a company headquarters and threw a fit because in the little stand where the soldiers could buy some basic needs, the different candy bars for sale were not lined up properly. Still he had managed to hang on and, in 1949, was promoted once again to colonel, this time permanently. When the war started, he was given command of the Fifth Cav. His position, however, was in jeopardy, for Ridgway was eager to replace most of the regimental commanders with younger men. As the oldest of them, Crombez was a prime candidate to be sent somewhere else and thus fall short of getting his star. It was an unenviable situation, one likely to make an already aggressive officer even more so.

By contrast, Lieutenant Colonel Edgar Treacy was as close as you could get to being Crombez's mirror opposite, a gifted younger commander of virtually the same rank who had graduated from West Point ten years later. He was a kind of golden boy, with admirable connections within the Army's hierarchy, and yet beloved by the men in his battalion. Whether the bad feelings began because the younger man's career seemed so effortless, blessed as he was with personal grace and the support of powerful superiors, or because Treacy, as some men believed, had sat on the board that recommended that Crombez be reduced to lieutenant colonel at the end of World War II, no one was sure. But the tension had been apparent since the early days of the Naktong fighting, when Treacy was a battalion commander under Crombez.

It had flared into the open during the difficult fighting that had taken place in mid-September. They were in the Taegu area, engaged in a vicious seesaw struggle to take Hill 174, when Crombez ordered Treacy's Love Company up it three times. The third time, Treacy finally objected to what he felt was a suicidal assault. The North Koreans, extremely well dug in, drove them back again, inflicting heavy casualties. Then Crombez ordered Treacy's Item Company up the same hill, and Treacy objected. "The enemy knows that we'll be coming. . . . The gooks will be ready for [us]. Item Company is the only company of good strength in the regiment and probably Eighth Army and if they get chewed up that will be the last strong company gone to hell." But Crombez insisted. So once again up they went, eventually taking the hill at a high price, only to be driven off by a ferocious Korean counterattack. Once more Crombez ordered Item to take the hill. This time Captain Norman Allen, the company commander, refused the order. "Colonel," he told Treacy, his immediate superior, "I never thought I would ever have to do this, least of all to you, but you can report to Regiment that Captain Allen of Item Company refuses the order!" Treacy had turned to him, quite weary, Allen remembered, and said, "That's all right, Norm. I understand. I refuse the order too!"

Then Allen had asked Treacy what he had been doing on Hill 174 himself the day before—a battalion commander going forward on an extremely dangerous assault that he was in no way supposed to be part of. Treacy pointed out that four days earlier the battalion had had almost 900 men. Now they were down to 292. "If I had been ordered to take Hill 174 again, I was going to refuse the order, and I wanted to insure that there would be no basis for a charge of personal cowardice!" he told Allen. He did refuse the next order, and Allen learned later that Crombez had called him yellow in front of the other battalion commanders. What tore at Treacy was the unnecessary loss of men in useless assaults in this particular stretch of fighting. At night, some of the other officers had noticed that he seemed to be mumbling to himself just before he went to sleep. At first they thought he was saying his prayers. One officer asked if Treacy were reciting Hail Marys. No, the answer came back, he was reciting the name of each man in his battalion who had died and asking God's forgiveness for his own responsibility in his death.

NOW, ON THE road to Chipyongni, Treacy found himself in a very difficult position—asking a superior, who was under almost unbearable pressure and who clearly bore him some animus, *not* to put his infantrymen on top of the tanks. Crombez was unmoved by his protest. He made only one concession. If the Chinese hit them hard, he would stop his tanks while the infantrymen got off, and he would use his considerable suppressive firepower on the enemy. Then there would be a signal for the men to reboard before they moved on. Treacy responded by demanding the right to accompany his men. He could not ask them to do what he himself was not willing to do. But Crombez denied that request, ordering Treacy to take command of the rest of the convoy and to move forward to Chipyongni only after the road was cleared. So it was that the 160 men of Love Company boarded the tanks.

Barrett, the company commander, and the tank company commander, Captain Johnny Hiers, worked out signals. If the tanks were going to move on, Hiers was to radio Barrett, giving the infantrymen time to remount. But the poor quality of their radios, plus the overwhelming noise of the tanks and the chaos of battle, offered little guarantee of success. Treacy was sure something terrible was about to happen. He told Barrett to leave behind one man from each squad in case Love Company needed to be reorganized after the mission. That would give them a kind of ghost structure to rebuild around. In addition, he asked every man in the unit to write home and put any personal effects in the letters.

Thus did the rescue convoy set off, each tank spaced about fifty yards from the next. The newer Patton tanks were in the lead; the older Shermans, with less mobile big guns, followed. Crombez was, as the historian J. D. Coleman notes with considerable irony, in the *fifth* tank, with the hatch *closed*. The combat engineers would ride on top of the first four tanks, the troops from Love Company on the others, ten men to a tank, with the last four empty. Captain Barrett rode on the sixth tank. Colonel Treacy argued for and won the right for a two-and-a-half-ton truck to follow the column to pick up any wounded men. Just as the convoy was moving out, Treacy jumped aboard the sixth tank and rode with Barrett.

The first time the tanks stopped and the infantry got off, the fighting went reasonably well. It was a relatively light engagement. Crombez seemed delighted by the way his tanks and the infantrymen were hammering the Chinese. "We're killing hundreds of them!" he said over the intercom. But even before that battle ended, the tanks under Crombez's orders suddenly roared off, seemingly with no warning to the infantrymen. About thirty infantrymen, some of them wounded, were left behind. As the tanks were pulling out, Captain Barrett, who had barely made it back onto a tank, yelled out to the others, "Stay by the road! We'll come back for you." It was exactly what Treacy had feared, especially because there was not that much pressure from the Chinese. Barrett later told Clay Blair that, after they reboarded, Treacy insisted he would bring formal charges against Crombez when it was all over. Then it got even worse. About a mile out of Koksuri, as Martin Blumenson, the military historian, has written, they were hit much harder. The Chinese were in strong positions on the ridges on both sides of the road, firing down at them. Some of the infantrymen dismounted, moving out about fifty yards on either side of the tanks. Suddenly, again without any warning, the tanks took off. Among those wounded and left behind were Colonel Treacy and a corporal named Carroll Everist. Treacy was hit relatively lightly, a flesh wound near his mouth, Everist more seriously, in the knee. Treacy dressed Everist's wound, and then gave him his medical kit. He seemed more worried about the state of the other men who had been stranded than about himself, Everist remembered. Soon Chinese soldiers arrived and took a group of seven of them prisoner. The small battle had turned into a mini-disaster for the exposed infantrymen. This time even more men had been left behind. As Ken Hamburger points out, in the course of the rush to Chipyongni exactly how many infantrymen were actually left behind remains in dispute—at least seventy, perhaps one hundred.

When the Chinese first captured them, Everist was too seriously wounded to walk, so Treacy carried him several miles on his back. Soon, the Chinese decided that Everist slowed them down too much and left him behind to die. Eventually, after the battle was over, he stumbled and crawled his way back to American lines. Treacy was taken to a North Korean prison camp. He survived his wounds, but his health soon began to fail. Captain Barrett, who followed what happened to his battalion commander very carefully, later talked with a number of POWs when they were sent home in 1953 and was told that Treacy died about three months after his capture. His health failed in part—so Barrett was told—because he gave what little food he had to other prisoners. "I put him in for the Congressional Medal of Honor," Barrett told Clay Blair, "but Crombez killed it." Crombez also put a note in Treacy's file saying he had disobeyed orders—an appalling, essentially posthumous (and thus unanswerable) assault on another officer.

Back on the southern perimeter of Chipyongni, the second night of battle was going poorly for Paul McGee's platoon. The Chinese had found, if not a superhighway, at least an access route into the American position, where the two pieces of terrain, one Chinese-held, the other American, seemed to feed into each other. For the second night of battle McGee would have liked more men, but every man—except those in the reserve units—was being used. He would have to make do with what he had.

The Chinese could get closer to the American positions in front of George Company than anywhere else, and they pushed that advantage hard. There were many, many more of them on that second night, and they began their attack far earlier, at dusk, adding a new and unnerving touch: just before the assault one of their buglers had blown Taps, the American ceremonial tribute to the dead. Then they struck, maybe, McGee thought, a regiment-sized force hitting his tiny sector. They quickly overran two foxholes belonging to the neighboring First Platoon, on McGee's right. That meant his men were soon taking lethal machine gun fire from the First Platoon area, fire that cut right across his own positions. He called his company commander, Lieutenant Thomas Heath, who called down to the First Platoon commander, who in turn assured Heath that the platoon was still in position and had not lost any foxholes. Unbeknownst to both Heath and McGee, the master sergeant commanding that platoon had set up his CP in a small hut on the *back* side of the hill and had not ventured out to check on his forward positions.

Told by his superior that the First Platoon was still holding at all points, McGee was not at all reassured. Each burst of machine gun fire from his right increased his doubts. This time when he called Heath, he was more specific: "There's a machine gun up on our right in the First Platoon section and it's kicking the shit out of us, and it sure as hell ain't one of ours." So Heath made another call to the First Platoon leader and the same answer came back. "McGee," he was told, "we're still up there." Later, McGee thought that when one of your platoon sergeants said he was being hammered by flanking fire

from a friendly position, someone had to verify it. Someone had to be responsible. That breakthrough on his right cost him dearly. Because of it, his men
had been terribly exposed and he had lost more men by being flanked than by
frontal attack. He was more than a little bitter—losing so many more men
than necessary because of another platoon leader's carelessness.

Knowing they had discovered a weak point in the American lines, the Chinese pushed harder, using the most primitive kind of explosives. One fought
them, McGee thought, tried to kill them, and yet admired their bravery. A soldier would crawl forward pushing a pole with a stick of dynamite at its end. If
he went down, another would take over, until they were right on top of an
American foxhole, and then the dynamite would detonate. The human cost
was terrible. McGee and his men kept firing, ever so carefully, determined not
to waste ammo, killing pole carrier after pole carrier, amazed that there was always one more man to pick up the pole.

The Chinese wounded one of McGee's squad leaders, Corporal James
Mougeot, by throwing a grenade in his foxhole, and Mougeot had come out of
the hole shouting, "Lieutenant McGee, I'm hit, I'm hit!" When he made it to
McGee's foxhole, McGee tried to calm him down. "I'm not hit bad," Mougeot
finally said, and prepared to go back to his position. Just then McGee noticed
a couple of Chinese soldiers only about twenty yards below his platoon's forward position. One of them kept calling out McGee's name, learned, he assumed, from Mougeot's calls. "Who's that?" he asked the BAR man next to
him. "It's a Chink," the BAR man replied. So McGee rolled a grenade down the
hill toward the Chinese soldier, who, wounded, tried to roll down the slope toward his lines, but McGee took the BAR and killed him.

Slowly, however, the battle began to turn in favor of the Chinese. One of the
keys to holding McGee's increasingly vulnerable position was a machine gun
right in its center, being fired by Corporal Eugene Ottesen and his men. With a
superb field of fire, Ottesen was able to cover a spur on a hill that the Chinese
had to cross in order to reach them. So the Chinese had gone after his machine
gun from the start, and sometime that night they had hit the first of his men
firing it. That was when Ottesen himself took over. As long as Ottesen could
fire, McGee was in a reasonably solid position. But the Chinese threw wave after wave of men at the position. Ottesen never panicked, even though he knew
he was a marked man. He kept firing—short, tight bursts—undoubtedly, like
McGee, sure that he was going to die there. McGee marveled at Ottesen's bravery in such a terrible moment—true courage, he thought, from some secret
storage place that few men had.

Sometime around two in the morning, Chinese soldiers managed to lob
grenades into Ottesen's foxhole and suddenly the gun went silent. McGee

yelled over to Sergeant Kluttz asking what happened to the machine gun, and
Kluttz shouted back that the Chinese had knocked it out. Ottesen was dead,
his body never recovered. (He was eventually listed as MIA.) Now McGee's
left flank was open, and the Chinese were pouring through. McGee ordered
Corporal Raymond Bennett, a squad leader whose men had not been especially hard hit yet, to try to retake Ottesen's position. Bennett himself was
quickly hit—by a hand grenade that blew off part of his hand, then by a bullet in the shoulder, and finally a piece of shrapnel in his head. But some of his
men managed to dig in and block the opening where Ottesen's gun had been.

McGee's overall position was now desperate. There were too many holes in
it, and too few men to hold back the Chinese. He had a good many wounded
men and had called back to Company for litter teams, but there were no litter
teams available either, and ammo was also turning out to be a problem. Sometime early on that second morning they became aware that they were running
short, that they could not keep up with their rate of firing. There was always
another attack. It seemed at that moment like a battle without end in a war that
also seemed without end. The war was not limited, but the ammo was. The Air
Force had tried to resupply, air-dropping boxes of ammunition with para-
chutes. But they had been forced to come in very low because the perimeter
was so tiny and they did not want the parachuted ammo to fall behind Chinese
lines. As a result, many of the crates had been damaged when they hit the
rocky, frozen ground. That meant McGee's BAR kept jamming because damaged shells sometimes stayed in the chamber. McGee had a small pocketknife,
which he used, again and again, to pry the bad casings out, but the gun continued to jam, and finally, in his frustration, he had dropped his knife and
couldn't find it.

Private First Class Cletis Inmon, his runner, who was in the foxhole with
him, trying to help out, handed McGee his own mess knife, but it was too big
for the chamber. So McGee reluctantly gave up on the BAR and went back to
his carbine, a weapon that very few fighting men liked. He thought the carbine
was fine, especially for a battle like this—the M-1 had more range, but here the
killing was taking place almost face-to-face, sometimes at ranges as close as
twenty to thirty yards. But then his carbine started acting up on him too. The
cold weather had gotten to it; the oil in the weapon had frozen, and he could
not get the bolt to go all the way home. Even as it jammed, he saw a Chinese
soldier moving in on him, and so he slammed the bolt home as hard as he
could and shot him.

The Chinese now held positions on their right, where the First Platoon was
being overrun, and sometime that morning, the Second Platoon on their left
pulled back without telling him. That meant that McGee's Third Platoon was

in a salient jutting out and almost completely surrounded. By the early morning, McGee had a sense—it was instinct more than anything else—that the handful of men in his platoon still alive and firing were the key to the survival of the entire Twenty-third Regiment, and that the longer they could hold out, the better the chance the regiment had of surviving. If the Chinese pushed through here and took their position, they might be able to sweep through on the soft flank of all the other regimental positions. His thinking, which his superiors later came to agree with, was based not merely on the intensity of the fighting or the fragmentary reports he had received on the relative stability of the line elsewhere, but on his sense that the regiment's defense was at its thinnest exactly where George Company was. Every once in a while another of his guns would stop—now a BAR in front of him suddenly went silent—and he would realize the battle was steadily turning against them, and that if the Chinese took his position it would be like a giant arrow aimed at the very heart of the regiment. By 2 A.M. he figured there were still several hours to go until daylight, and he knew they could not hold out much longer.

Battles like this, even when the smallest units are engaged, are never static, and the fight on what came to be called McGee Hill had a rhythm of its own. Thus, each lost foxhole was a new Chinese position, allowing ever more Chinese to come up the hill and making the other foxholes ever more vulnerable for the Americans and easier for the Chinese to attack. Cletis Inmon, McGee's runner, thought he had never seen so many Chinese as that night—even though it was dark, you could see them fairly clearly, because they were so close. It was, he decided, like an endless line of soldiers that started someplace back in the middle of China, maybe a thousand miles away, whatever the distance was, marching all the way to Korea, one long line emptying out right in that little creek bed in front of them. Until that night Cletis Inmon thought he was one of the luckiest men in the United States Army. He was a country boy from Garrett, Kentucky, and had signed up to fight in Korea because a sixteen-year-old from his high school had been killed there and somehow he felt he owed it to him to go there and pay them back. He had done his basic training at Fort Knox and arrived in Korea just in time for a big Thanksgiving dinner, and then headed north on a truck to join George Company and the Twenty-third Regiment up near the Chongchon, a river they had never studied back in Kentucky. They were well north when they came upon an American lieutenant blocking the road who said they couldn't go any farther because the Twenty-third was cut off and no one could get through to them. Inmon, who was religious and did not drink or swear, thought that God's hand was on him because, had he arrived a few days earlier, he would have been up there himself when the Chinese first came in, and he was sure he would have been killed.

The other thing that confirmed God's blessing was landing in a unit with men like McGee and Kluttz, who knew all the little tricks of combat and were skilled at breaking a new man in. It was a curious thing, what you remembered about it all a half century later, but he recalled Kluttz telling him before the battle of Chipyongni just how to deal with the Chinese, who, he said, were very good soldiers. They were very canny, he said. They would sneak up very near your foxhole and then lie low and listen to the sound of the clip in your M-1. There was a little click the M-1 made when a clip was finished, and as soon as they heard that click, they would charge while you were changing clips. That meant you had to be able to snap the next clip in very quickly. McGee had told Inmon that he picked him as a runner because he was sure that Inmon would not let him down. Someone else might think being a runner was unusually dangerous duty, but Inmon considered it good duty because you didn't have to lug a radio around all day and make yourself the perfect target for the enemy. He had started the second night, with three other men in a foxhole right next to McGee. There was, he remembered, a Filipino; another guy brand-new to the outfit, his first day in battle; and a third man about whom he could remember almost nothing. All three were killed that night. Inmon never remembered the name of the new guy—all he could recall was that he had showed up in a brand-new uniform, and it had stayed new, no wrinkles, none of the usual grime, except the next day it was covered with bloodstains.

Inmon had been handling a BAR that night, and eventually he moved into McGee's foxhole as the battle wore on. Sometime that night, probably around 1 A.M., his luck ran out. He heard a whistling sound and then he was hit and he grabbed his face. He had been hit by shrapnel, and blood was pouring out. He completely lost control, so much so that he was ashamed later. "I'm hit! I'm hit! Get me off the hill, McGee! Get me off the hill!" he screamed.

"Quiet down, Inmon," McGee said. "You quiet down. Don't you be yelling—they'll hear you. You lie down now! We'll get you off." McGee called over to the next foxhole, to Kluttz, to send the medic over, and somehow the medic got to Inmon's foxhole. The shrapnel was over his left eye, and he could now see only through his right eye. But they cleaned him up a little and his nerves began to steady. McGee asked him if he could see well enough to fire his M-1. Inmon said no. "Can you load the magazine for my carbine?" McGee asked. Inmon found he could still do that, and he loaded while McGee kept firing. A little later, when the fighting died down momentarily, McGee asked the medic if he thought he could get Inmon out. The medic said yes, and he half-carried, half-dragged Inmon down the hill to the aid station. Inmon was amazed: he knew that McGee still needed him, and that he could still be useful as a loader. One of his last thoughts before he passed out from the drugs at the aid station was that McGee had been willing to die up there alone, but one of his last acts had been to try to save Inmon's life.

McGee had sent his other runner, Private First Class John Martin, back to tell Lieutenant Heath that they were in a desperate situation, that they needed more of everything, especially men and ammo, and if at all possible litter bearers. Heath then asked his artillery unit to loan him some men, and Lieutenant Arthur Rochnowski assembled fifteen of them. Martin led them back up the hill, but when they reached the crest, the Chinese had opened up and a mortar round immediately killed one man, wounded another, and panicked the rest of them, and they raced down the hill again. Heath gathered up some of the panicky artillerymen, but as they reached the ridge the Chinese were there, and they fled again. Heath was screaming at them as they scattered, "Goddamn it, get back up on that hill! You'll die down here anyway. You might as well go up on the hill and die there." Martin, however, rallied a few men, picked up some ammo, and went back up the hill.

Up on the hill McGee knew it was pretty much over; he was going to die there. It was down to Kluttz and him fighting side by side with a couple of other men nearby. He was oddly fatalistic about it. He felt no self-pity at all. He had volunteered, had wanted this battle and this war, and he had gotten all of it. If he felt bad, it was for his mother and father, who would take it hard. He and Kluttz were in the same foxhole by then, McGee firing a BAR, which he had taken from a man two foxholes over, and Kluttz with a machine gun taken from a wounded gunner. Kluttz was a damn good man who was not going to break, not even here at the end. "Kluttz," McGee yelled out, "I believe they've got us."

"Well, let's get us as many of the sons of bitches as we can first," Kluttz replied, and they opened up with both weapons.

Then Kluttz's machine gun jammed and that seemed to be that. "Kluttz, let's try and get out," McGee shouted, and then threw the last of his grenades. Sometime early on the morning of February 15, probably about 3 A.M., their ammo almost completely gone, McGee, Kluttz, and two other men managed to slip out. Of the forty-six men in McGee's platoon, only four were able to walk out on their own power. Everyone else was killed, wounded, or missing in action. Paul McGee received a Silver Star for his bravery and leadership, as did Bill Kluttz.

IN THE VERY early morning of the fifteenth, among his last commands, Paul Freeman had tried to send some reserve units, including the Ranger Company, to stiffen the George Company position. If they had been unable to drive the Chinese off the hill, they had somehow managed to neutralize them, and as dawn approached, the chances of the Chinese exploiting their position began to shrink. By mid-morning, George Stewart and some of Freeman's pals at his own regimental headquarters were telling him that he simply had to leave as Almond had ordered or events might take a very ugly turn for him. So far, they reminded him, he had done everything right, but there was a time when you had to accept the fact that you were in a command structure. Besides, his colleagues argued, the battle was essentially done. Crombez had apparently broken out of the last of the traps set for him by the Chinese and would almost surely be there before nightfall. Lieutenant Colonel Jim Edwards, commander of the Second Battalion, whose forces were still bitterly engaged near McGee Hill, told Freeman that the Chinese had been driven off. It was something of a white lie, Edwards noted later, but otherwise, Freeman might have refused to leave and surely would have been court-martialed by Almond. With that, Freeman flew out for treatment at a MASH unit at Chungju. There, he was met by Ridgway, who congratulated him, told him he had done just fine, and awarded him the DSC. After talking with Ridgway, Freeman believed he would go to the States briefly for R & R, and then return to Korea. He had, after all, spent eight straight months of constant fighting in the line and needed a bit of a break. He was now confident that, like Mike Michaelis, against whom he always measured himself, he would get his star. But Paul Freeman did not return to Korea. Instead, much to his chagrin, he was assigned to make public appearances to explain the war to civic clubs—he was uncommonly good-looking and spoke well. Whether his return was blocked by Almond he never knew. He went on to a full career and eventually received four stars.

THE CHINESE HAD finally taken the ridge of McGee Hill, but it had cost them dearly: McGee was told later that when the battle was over they found the bodies of more than eight hundred enemy soldiers immediately in front of his position. The surprising thing was that when the Chinese had finally gained it, albeit with the hours of darkness disappearing, and having expended such a terrible amount of human resource, they hesitated and so failed to maximize their success. It was a failure not caused by lack of bravery—they had been absolutely fearless against an enemy with the terrifying capacity to create areas that were nothing less than killing zones. Not only did the Americans have the capacity to hammer a given target with endless artillery rounds, but they had now added to it a new weapon that the Chinese quickly came to fear, a jellied death that American planes could spread from the air and that had the capacity to burn out entire units in fiery communal deaths. It was called napalm.

With their troops finally atop the high ground, the Chinese failed to exploit their breakthrough. Their troops fought tenaciously once there, beating back repeated American attempts to drive them off. But in front of them that morning lay a far greater victory, had they been ready. They could have rained fire down on the Americans below. It was a fateful moment, and they simply stayed on McGee Hill. They certainly had enough troops available in that sector, and they might have been able to move more men over from other sectors in the west and east. But they never did. Perhaps the breakthrough had come too late in the day and they were simply not ready for it. It reflected at the very least a failure in communications, but possibly a failure of imagination as well.

One of the great weaknesses of the Chinese at that point in the war, the Americans were beginning to discover from prisoner interrogation, was the rigidity of their command structure. It worked top-down with little flexibility and little room for individual initiative at lower levels. It produced brave, rugged, incredibly dutiful foot soldiers who often served under middle-level commanders who, in the midst of battle, had neither the authority nor the communications ability to make critical decisions as the battlefield changed. Wonju had been a classic example of that, of their inability to adjust in mid-battle. That was in stark contrast to the American Army, where the initiative of good NCOs was valued and the ability to adjust to a battle as it unfolded was becoming a major asset.

There were other limitations the Americans began to discover about this fierce new enemy. The Chinese could fight with great intensity for two or, at most, three days, but limits in ammo, food, medical support, and sheer physical endurance—as well as the intensity of the American airpower—affected their ability to exploit any advantages or breakthroughs, and magnified any breakdowns or defeats. By the third day of a given battle they began to run out of everything and needed to break off contact. Chipyongni and Wonju were the great primers for all of this. At different moments, both battles had seemed as if they might come out a different way.

Matt Ridgway had not only gotten the battle he wanted at Chipyongni. Equally important, he was learning priceless lessons about an enemy he badly needed to understand. He had already received a number of early lessons in the strengths of the Chinese; now, for the first time, he was learning their weaknesses.

THE SOUND OF a column of tanks on the approach is not a gentle one, and most of the men besieged at Chipyongni heard their rescuers long before the relief column arrived. There had been one last desperate attempt on the part of the Chinese to stop the tank column. About a mile south of Chipyongni, there was a cut in the hills, where the road narrowed, with high ground on both sides, a perfect place for an ambush. The cut went on for about 150 yards and the Chinese were dug in about fifty feet above the road waiting with their mortars and bazookas to hit the tanks. The lead tank, struck by a bazooka round, made it through, as did the second and third. A bazooka round penetrated the fourth tank's skin and ignited ammunition inside. Some of the crew, including Captain John Hiers, were immediately killed. The driver was badly burned, but in a great show of valor, he gunned the engine and somehow managed to drive the tank through the cut so that the road remained unblocked for the rest of the column.

Crombez's tanks arrived at Chipyongni a little after 5 P.M. Just as his column was approaching, three American tanks inside the perimeter ventured out to fire at the Chinese behind their lines, and there was a tense moment as the two tank forces eyed each other warily, the rescuers and the rescued, neither quite sure who was who, before the defenders understood that the Cav had arrived and the siege was broken. At almost the same moment, the Air Force started hitting the surrounding hills with napalm. Suddenly the Chinese began to break and abandon their positions. For a brief time it was a free-fire zone, as thousands of the enemy were caught moving through open territory, and the American commanders poured artillery, tank fire, and napalm down on them. To the Americans watching from the hills surrounding the village it was, as one American soldier said, like "kicking an anthill" and suddenly seeing, rather than ants, thousands and thousands of Chinese emerge from a place where you thought none existed, and only then becoming truly terrified, as if realizing finally just how many Chinese had actually surrounded them.

Nothing reflected the complexity—and the moral ambiguity—of war more clearly than Crombez and his mission. To the men trapped inside Chipyongni, exhausted, low on ammunition, fearing they could not hold out another night, Crombez's tankers were nothing less than saviors, who like the storied cavalrymen of a thousand western movies, had arrived just in the nick of time. To the men of Treacy's battalion, it was another matter entirely. Captain Barrett was in a rage. Love Company had been torn apart, and so many men, he believed, had died so needlessly.

To the men of the Twenty-third, Captain Barrett at that moment did not seem like a hero or a rescuer so much as a madman, an officer completely out of control, running around with his pistol out, screaming about Crombez and his goddamn blue chip and how he had gotten all of Barrett's men killed. Barrett kept shouting that he was going to kill Crombez. He was in so violent a rage, his desire to kill Crombez so genuine, that the medical team of the Twenty-third eventually had to give him a shot to sedate him. A French soldier, Corporal Serge Bererd, remembered the men of Love Company being so exhausted, and in such a state of shock from the assault, that they could not respond when he tried to talk to them. "They were just too tired to kill [Crombez]," Bererd said. Men like Bererd, who had endured the siege and felt grateful to be rescued, were puzzled by the violent attitude of Crombez's infantry—they were not men celebrating the success of an extremely dangerous mission, but mourning what in their minds was a defeat.

THE DAY AFTER the battle was over, Sergeant Ed Hendricks, who had arrived with the Fifth Cav, saw a terrifying sight—twenty to thirty trucks, all giant deuce-and-a-halfs, lined up to take the American dead out. But the men doing the loading couldn't lay the bodies down the way they normally might have, flattened out. The dead had been frozen as they had died, arms and legs sticking out in every direction, some frozen in firing positions. Their bodies had to be stacked awkwardly atop one another, the loaders using the space as best they could. Fitting them in, Hendricks remembered, was like doing a giant jigsaw puzzle. It was the worst thing he had ever seen.

That same morning, when Crombez asked the men of Love Company which of them wanted to return to their base along with his tanks, none volunteered. Many of the Love Company infantrymen who had been left behind when Crombez had driven ahead eventually found their way back. Total casualties for the unit were thirteen killed, nineteen missing and likely captured, thus thirty-two likely dead, and more than fifty wounded. Crombez wrote in his after-action report that his force suffered only ten men killed in action. He also noted that Colonel Treacy had disobeyed orders by joining the attack column. That, as Ken Hamburger noted, was shocking of itself, extremely close to an official reprimand for a man missing in action and most likely dead. Captains Barrett and Norman Allen went among the officers and men taking signatures and statements recommending Treacy for the Medal of Honor. Their recommendations never left the Fifth Cav. When the papers were brought to Crombez, he threw them on the floor and ground his boot on them. "Medal of Honor, no, goddamn it, no. If he ever returns to military control, I will court-martial him." Crombez, however, quickly put himself up for an important medal, dictating his own recommendation for the Distinguished Service Cross. The recommendation wound its way up through the Army command until it reached the chief of staff of the Eighth Army, Brigadier General Henry Hodes, who turned it down, saying, "No son of a bitch earns a DSC inspiring his troops buttoned up in a tank. I know. I am an old tanker." But Crombez apparently made a personal appeal to Ridgway, who told Hodes that yes, the medal was questionable, but to give him the DSC anyway—after all, he had promised Freeman that if his men fought and held at Chipyongni against those terrible odds, he would send the entire Eighth Army in to relieve them if need be, and Crombez had done just that. So Crombez got the DSC, and eventually one star, and retired as a brigadier five years later. In his book on the Korean War, Ridgway never mentioned his name. To experienced Ridgway-ologists, that was a sure sign of the commander's own ambivalence and distaste about what had happened.

47

STILL, EVEN IF the defense had been imperfect it had been a major victory at a site that the Chinese, not the UN, had chosen, and Ridgway had gotten what he had wanted. Taking and holding terrain, so important in other wars, was less important here. Inflicting unbearable losses on the Chinese was now perceived to be the key to winning, or at least proving to the Chinese that *they* could not win. If Douglas MacArthur had once been lulled by preconceptions, it was now Mao's turn to be the prisoner of his own mind-set. As MacArthur had failed to factor in the effect of a political revolution in a country he had known almost nothing about, so Mao now failed to factor in the effects of the vast American technological superiority, and the ability of American troops when commanded by a great general. As Mao had once said of MacArthur, arrogant, egotistical men were easy to defeat.

Peng Dehuai, warier than Mao of an all-out confrontation with the Americans, had been more realistic about future confrontations back in January. The question following Chipyongni and Wonju was whether he would finally be listened to. There had already been considerable tension between the two men in the months preceding Chipyongni. But the defeats and the casualties had come as a shock. "Chipyongni," said Chen Jian, the Chinese historian, "changed everything. Up until then the Chinese thought they were doing very well and they thought they knew how to fight the Americans—that they had the secret. They were sure they were going to win the war and do it very quickly. They had all the momentum starting with the victories up along the Chongchon river." The defeats at Chipyongni and Wonju were devastating to Peng. He had used frontline Chinese troops, the best he had from his best divisions. And in the end they had suffered grievous casualties and his men had been forced to flee the battlefield. While the Chinese were always secretive about casualties, the Americans estimated that they might have killed as many as five thousand soldiers at Chipyongni alone. To Peng it was obvious that this was a new and very dangerous foe with—because of its airpower—a very long and a very quick reach.

Peng, who hated to fly—if he could not walk to a destination, he greatly preferred trains—flew to Beijing on February 20 to see Mao. There is a difference of opinion among historians as to whether he went on his own or was summoned there. It is at least possible that the initiative was Peng's, that he felt he had to explain in person the nature of the changed battlefield they now faced. When he reached Mao's house in mid-morning, the chairman, very much a night person, was asleep.

Mao's bodyguard tried to block Peng. "You can't go in there—he's still sleeping."

"You cannot stop me," Peng answered. "My men are dying on the battlefield. I can't wait for him to wake up." So Peng barged in and woke Mao and told him that they had an entirely new war on their hands. There would be no rush to Pusan, no great American retreat south. They now had to prepare for a long war, and they were going to rotate some of their troops because the kind of combat they were engaged in was exhausting to the men. That morning they agreed upon some rotation of troops, even though part of Mao, clearly dreaming different dreams from Peng and other commanders on the battlefield, still believed that the entire Korean peninsula might yet be his.

CHIPYONGNI AND WONJU were huge victories for the United Nations, a major turning point in the war. What was particularly encouraging to Ridgway was the fact that he had not chosen these particular battlefields; the Chinese had selected them, on terrain far more favorable to them than existed near either coast. Though there had been mistakes and some United Nations units had suffered disproportionately, Ridgway had gotten a kind of textbook example of what UN forces might do if even partially prepared for an attack in decent defensive positions. It was a warning to the Chinese leadership of what the future might hold. Even when some of Ridgway's units had been momentarily isolated, he had, in at least one critical showdown, been able to send a relief column in time. Ridgway was sure that his intelligence would get better and that his airpower would now be able to limit the ability of Chinese forces to gather and strike, as well as their ability to resupply and feed their troops. In that he was correct. He thought it would only be a matter of time before the Chinese realized that they, like their UN adversaries, had run into a certain kind of wall.

Part
Ten

*The General
and the President*

48

IN WASHINGTON, THERE was a profound sense of relief, for the fact that they would no longer have to think the unthinkable and be forced off the peninsula in some terrible Dunkirk-like humiliation, as MacArthur's cables had only recently seemed to imply. But the improved battlefield did not end the tensions between Tokyo and Washington. If anything, the Far East commander now became even more difficult in his dealings with Washington, more openly critical of the Truman administration's strategy for the war, more openly condescending about Ridgway's successes (except when taking credit for them), and finally more openly political, as if he were not merely a commander under the authority of the president but wore the hat of military consultant on hire to the Republican leadership in Congress as well. Where he had only recently dissented from Truman and the Joint Chiefs in doomsday terms, claiming that the sheer size of the Chinese Army meant the United States lacked the ability to stay on the peninsula without major additional forces or the use of nuclear weapons, his argument was now quite different. He was frustrated, he told sympathetic editors and politicians on the right, because we had lost our will to win in Korea, even though by his terms winning translated into nothing less than all-out war with China on the Asian mainland.

Now, his reputation damaged by the first great Chinese offensive and the retreat of his troops, with his military peers in Washington paying less and less attention to him, and with Ridgway stalemating the Chinese forces in a way he had said could not be achieved, MacArthur seemed to be spoiling for a fight with Washington. The fight was more political than military. This was to be about a wider war, or perhaps even a total war, with an adversary that the senior civilians (as well as their military advisers) considered an ancillary enemy: China, not Russia, had already showed in its struggles against the Japanese that it had the capacity to absorb endless numbers of invading troops even as the invaders might think they were winning.

There were, it should be noted, no political benefits from Ridgway's successes for the Democratic administration. An embattled administration remained no less embattled, an unpopular war no less unpopular. What the Ridgway strategy seemed to promise was more of the same, more of what had made the war unpopular in the first place. The longer it went on, it now appeared, the greater the political price to be paid. The domestic issue that the Republicans had seized on, subversion, seemed to some people to be validated by the fact that we were now fighting the Chinese Communists in Korea. If, in terms of his relationship with the Joint Chiefs and the president, MacArthur was on the defensive, he still had reason to believe that the people who were for him back in America, whose political agenda and geopolitical vision he seemingly embodied, were on the ascent. It was a situation guaranteed to bring out the worst in him. Cut off, and essentially bypassed by Washington, he was spoiling for a fight.

The president—and in terms of the public's exhaustion with the Democrats, there was no easy separation from the Roosevelt administration, which had preceded him—had probably governed for too long in too hard a time, where there were too many forces outside his control. The news that the Russians had the atomic bomb, the fall of Chiang, the Hiss case headlines, and the Korean War itself had placed the administration in an ever more unpalatable position. With the Chinese engaged in Korea, the war seemed darker than ever, without an acceptable solution in sight. What made this so hard to swallow for Truman and the men around him was the fact that the military situation had gotten much worse because of the miscalculations of MacArthur, who was now lining up against them politically and showed no interest in accepting any of the blame.

All of this made the final collision between the president and the general inevitable, for there were no restraints now on the general's side. By late January 1951 there were signs that he was committed ever more publicly to pushing for a larger war. He had flown to Suwon on January 28. Ridgway had greeted him on arrival, and the journalists gathered around them had overheard MacArthur say, as he stepped off the plane, "This is exactly where I came in seven months ago to start this crusade. The stake we fight for now, however, is more than Korea—it is a free Asia." The word "crusade" as well as the reference to a "free Asia" were immediately picked up by British journalists and published in London, greatly upsetting the British government, which sensed, accurately enough, that the commander in Tokyo wanted a larger war, quite possibly an all-out war with China.

MacArthur did not see what was now taking shape in Korea as most other senior military men, and certainly the Joint Chiefs, did. No command interested him save his own. He had no interest in the threat the Soviets might pose in Europe. Always aware that the Soviets could easily make countermoves if the United States escalated the war in Korea, Truman feared crises in, among

other places, Berlin, Indochina, Yugoslavia, and especially Iran. A minor incident would be created, the president liked to say, and the Russians would use it
as an excuse for an intervention. As for bombing China's cities, Truman and
his people thought the general was overlooking what would happen *after* the
bombs dropped. Then the first calls would go out for the UN to bomb the Soviet port of Vladivostok and the Trans-Siberian Railroad, because of all the
materiel the Russians would send in by train. Truman doubted very much that
MacArthur considered the way this would escalate the war, ultimately placing
Japanese cities at risk from *Russian* countermoves.

When Joe Collins and other members of the Joint Chiefs tried to make
their case to MacArthur, he simply turned a deaf ear. As Max Hastings, the
British military historian, wrote, "It will never be certain how far MacArthur's
affronted personal hubris influenced his attitude to the Chinese, how far he
became instilled with a yearning for crude revenge upon the people who had
brought all his hopes and triumphs in Korea to nothing. [But] it did seem
probable that he did not consider it beyond his own powers to reinstate
Chiang Kai-shek's Nationalist regime in Beijing." If Hastings was not entirely
sure what drove MacArthur in those last months in Tokyo, Omar Bradley had
few doubts. As he later put it, in words unusually harsh for one general to write
about another, "MacArthur's reaction arose, I feel certain, at least in part from
the fact that his legendary military pride had been hurt. The Red Chinese had
made a fool of the infallible 'military genius.' By then it must have been clear to
him that his failure to send X Corps in pursuit of the North Korean Army after
Inchon and to split his forces and send X Corps to Wonsan was an error of
grave magnitude. . . . Furthermore, the Chinese had made a mockery of his intelligence estimates, of his vainglorious boasts that his all-out air assault including bombing the Korean ends of the Yalu bridges would make northwest
Korea a desert, and his assertion that our men would advance to the Yalu and
'be home by Christmas.' The only possible means left to MacArthur to regain
his lost pride and military reputation was now to inflict an overwhelming defeat on those Red Chinese generals who had made a fool of him. In order to do
this he was perfectly willing to propel us into an all-out war with Red China
and possibly with the Soviet Union, igniting World War III, and a nuclear
holocaust."

If anything, Ridgway's almost immediate successes at Chipyongni and
other places with the same force levels MacArthur had so recently deemed
wholly inadequate made things worse. What others viewed as a limited victory
was, in effect, a second great defeat for MacArthur's pride. Equally wounding
was the fact that, because of his battlefield successes and his blunt, candid
style, Ridgway was developing a very admiring press corps. The limelight,

which MacArthur so craved, was, late in his career, going over to a subordinate, something he had never permitted before. Reporters liked Ridgway; he was professional and straight, a general obsessed by his mission, who spoke to them in an honest, blunt way, not unlike Joseph Stilwell had. His obsession seemed to be with the war itself, and not how he looked in their dispatches. He was generous in crediting subordinate officers. There was a tone in the new coverage that MacArthur especially hated, an implicit sense that the good Ridgway was replacing the bad MacArthur, someone in touch replacing someone hopelessly out of it.

Soon a new pattern emerged: Ridgway would plan a major offensive, and just as it was about to kick off, MacArthur and his top people would suddenly fly in from Tokyo, go to the relevant headquarters, where the general would immediately hold a press conference—as if to steal back Ridgway's increasingly admiring press corps—and claim credit for the planning. When Ridgway's Operation Killer was about to kick off, MacArthur flew to Suwon and announced that it was he who had ordered the attack. Ridgway later wrote angrily that neither MacArthur nor his staff had had any part in the planning of the operation: "It is not so much that my own vanity took an unexpected roughing up by this announcement as that I was given a rather unwelcome reminder of a MacArthur that I had known but had almost forgotten," a general all too eager to keep his "public image always glowing."

As Walter Millis wrote, the one person not ready to deal with the improved military situation was the general himself: "MacArthur had provided for every contingency save one—the contingency of 'success.'" Soon MacArthur escalated his assault on the Truman administration in a constant series of barbed remarks to journalists and political figures and in his cables back to Washington. As early as December, after Truman put out his directive demanding that all statements on Korea be cleared through the State Department, MacArthur quite deliberately violated it. His complaints against the administration were of a kind: the limits imposed upon his command, unique, he seemed to think, in the history of warfare; the lack of an adequate number of troops to get the job done; the sanctuaries offered his enemies, with no mention of the sanctuaries the Americans had—most notably the industrial and port facilities of Tokyo and Yokohama, exceptionally tempting targets that the enemy did not touch. It was all part of the odd set of quid pro quos now being established as the great powers struggled to figure out what in this ever more dangerous world they could actually do and what they dared not do. At the heart of MacArthur's messages lay the most politically charged aspect of all, what he began to describe as a failure of will on the part of an administration unwilling to seek a real victory. In the rhetoric of the time, failure of will sounded perilously close to appeasement.

His line was relatively simple: a stalemate in Korea was a defeat, while only a wider war with China would bring genuine victory, and in the past America had always sought total victory.

The Republicans back in the United States had been charging the administration with appeasement and the loss of China—now here America was fighting the Chinese, and the country's most famous general was all but accusing the same administration of appeasing the enemy. His new dissent was perfectly tailored toward his political constituency, the more militant anti-Communist part of the American right wing. They wanted, it seemed, to win China back without the loss of a single American boy on Chinese soil. More, these calls had a certain popular resonance now that the United States was stalemated in Korea. Some voters were angry and frustrated; they wanted something different even if they were not sure what it was; it need only cost very little in human terms—that is, in terms of American casualties.

If the United States did not defeat Communism in Asia, MacArthur suggested in letters to his close friends in the press corps and in Washington, the failure would cost them dearly in Europe. One could save Europe from Communism only by saving Asia from Communism first. He was eager to do it, and the forces, he assured them, were there—for there were those troops of Chiang's ready to march. He was willing to inflict on the Chinese, and on Communism, a terrible defeat, if only Washington would free his hand, he lamented. There was no small irony in this because MacArthur had been one of the most influential people in bringing the Russians (and thus the Communists) into Korea in the first place. That had been some six years earlier at the end of a different war against a different enemy, and he was then the man charged with commanding the Allied force about to invade the Japanese home islands. He was hardly alone in wanting the Russians to enter the Pacific War. Most senior military men felt the same way. The few who knew about the Manhattan Project were hardly sure it would work or become so decisive a military instrument. That he wanted the Russians to enter the war in order to alleviate the pressure on the Allied forces was the most natural impulse for any general. But now, it was as if the second Douglas MacArthur, the MacArthur of the Cold War, had never even been introduced to the first Douglas MacArthur, the commander during World War II, who had once wanted Soviet help.

Now, the Cold War deepening, he implied that he had *always* opposed Russia coming into the war. Unfortunately for him, there were any number of witnesses who knew better. One of them was Colonel Paul Freeman, who, having held a brief combat command in the Philippines in late 1944, was about to fly back to Washington, where he was once again to work for

George Marshall. Before leaving the Philippines, however, Freeman was suddenly summoned for a command performance by MacArthur. It was a fascinating meeting that lasted for almost two hours. Freeman understood that he was to be a messenger to Washington, an instrument to express the general's views. The first part of the meeting was devoted to MacArthur's traditional resentment of Washington. Freeman listened and finally dissented as best he could to a great figure. General Marshall, he said, had frequently supported MacArthur as much as possible in terms of forces and supplies and had taken MacArthur's side in his desire to liberate the Philippines when the top Navy people wanted to bypass them and go directly for Taiwan. That was not exactly what MacArthur wanted to hear, but sheer personal honor dictated that it be said.

The second part of their meeting proved far more interesting. MacArthur knew that the invasion planning was at a serious stage, and as the putative commander, he wanted to get his own feelings in: "I will not consider going into any part of the Japanese islands unless the Japanese armies in Manchuria are contained by the Russians." That would be strong stuff for them back in Washington, Freeman knew, a general with MacArthur's rather considerable political following insisting that it would be a no-go in Japan unless the Russians entered the war. When the meeting was over, MacArthur's aide Bonnie Fellers immediately had MacArthur's views typed up and cleared so that Freeman could bring them back to Washington.

There was nothing unusual about what he wanted. Most senior military men believed that, based on their experiences fighting the Japanese on various Pacific islands, the mainland battle would be a cruel struggle, house by house, cave by cave, with terrible casualties borne by both sides. That Douglas MacArthur, even in 1944 the American commander with the closest ties to the American right wing, wanted the Russians in was important. But what made these views even more important was the fact that, twelve years later, in 1956, when MacArthur had more than ever become the darling of the right wing, those views had become an embarrassment. He was, after all, a man who had always believed that the truth was whatever he said it was at that moment, and in the early 1950s he had started giving interviews claiming that, had he been in charge of the decision-making in those final days of World War II, he would never have brought the Russians into the war.

That was the MacArthur that all too many other high officials in the Pentagon had dealt with too often in the past, the MacArthur who redid history to suit his immediate needs. Now the Republican administration of Dwight Eisenhower decided to strike back. When that happened, Paul Freeman got a private tip from friends in Washington warning him that the original papers he had brought back from the Pacific were about to be released and that he should keep his head down because it was going to get very ugly for a few days. The exchange was a reflection of the internal struggle between the two Douglas MacArthurs: the pragmatic military man who wanted all the help he could get before a difficult invasion, and the general who had become a politician and who needed to bend old facts to fit them into a new political reality in which he had never been wrong.

But in the first months of 1951, more frustrated than ever, MacArthur moved toward a historic showdown with the president of the United States. At first it was quite a one-sided affair—the general nicked Washington and then nicked it again, and only when administration officials refused to respond did his challenges become more serious and frontal. In a way, the people in Washington had been setting themselves up for something like this for almost a decade. In their minds, dealing with MacArthur had always been like making a deal with the devil. They had few illusions about him, or how little loyalty he was likely to show to their policies at critical moments. But Washington had usually gotten what it wanted when it needed it, not just the talent, but the myth of the talent, especially vital back early in World War II. But the longer the men in Washington had delayed confronting MacArthur because the price seemed so large, the more the price had gone up because the myth, which Washington had helped create, kept growing, fed quite consciously by the general himself.

For more than a decade, two presidents and their top advisers had allowed MacArthur to lionize himself at their expense. When, in the years following World War II, they had less need for his talent, they nonetheless delayed any confrontation out of fear of him—exactly because he had already attained too much stature. (Although Truman had often complained about Roosevelt's deification of the general, and spoke privately of how Roosevelt should have let the Japanese capture MacArthur at Bataan, he too had feared taking him on and let the cult continue.) Each year not only had the price gone up, but the timing had become less favorable for them, as the political forces aligned with the general became more powerful. Now, very late in the game, when they indeed had no choice but to pay that price, it had become exorbitant. For an elaborate process of self-deification had been taking place for a very long time, mostly at government expense. Now the piper had to be paid.

But whatever chance MacArthur might have had of bringing some of the Joint Chiefs with him had disappeared with Ridgway's successes. Admiral Forrest Sherman, the naval chief and probably the most hawkish figure of the Chiefs, who had momentarily seemed like an ally when there was so much talk of being driven off the peninsula, was now slipping away. As that happened, MacArthur turned his fire ever more precisely on administration officials and the president himself. They were the ones blocking his will, stealing his final victory from him, the men, in William Manchester's words, "thwarting his last crusade."

What began now was, if not a deliberate campaign to force the president to fire him, then surely the next closest thing. If he could not have his way in Korea, he was going to do all he could to bring down those who stood in his way. Specifically, he now set about systematically violating Truman's December 6 directive. The gag rule was a joke, he said. He was, he told one luncheon guest, "an old man of seventy-one" and therefore had nothing to lose by ignoring it. If they fired him, so be it. Clay Blair, who wrote more meticulously than any other historian about this stage of the war, put the number of violations of the gag order at six, some major, some minor. "To MacArthur watchers," he wrote, "a pattern seemed to be emerging. MacArthur would fly to Korea, visit the battlefront, then issue a communiqué containing criticism of the Administration's war policies. But again, no one in Washington felt inclined to rebut or reprimand him. Officially MacArthur was ignored." Among other things he had taken a quick slap at Truman in speaking of the war as a "theoretical military stalemate." Reporters quickly turned that into a more down-to-earth phrase, "die for a tie": in other words, good men were still going to have to die for a stalemate in Korea.

The last thing the people in Washington wanted, now that they seemed able to contain the Chinese armies, was an additional war with their own theater commander. But a war it would be. On March 7, for instance, MacArthur started out a press conference in Korea by tweaking President Truman, with references to what he called the serious, indeed abnormal inhibitions placed on him, the lack of additional forces given him and other restraints imposed from Washington. Then, at a moment when Washington was just beginning to contemplate trying to move Beijing to the peace table, he mocked the Chinese for their failures and their own limitations—virtually taunting a proud enemy that had just defeated him. That in itself greatly angered the president because MacArthur had just made it a great deal harder to negotiate with China.

In a military sense, MacArthur was also becoming increasingly critical of Ridgway's strategy. All that Ridgway had gained, he now said publicly and with contempt, was "an accordion war"—a war where the UN forces might move up twenty or thirty miles during an offensive, only to move back when the Chinese attacked again in force. If no one in Washington thought such a war was ideal, they were convinced that it was punishing the Chinese infinitely more than their own forces, perhaps on a casualty ratio of ten or fifteen to one, and that the alternatives were much worse. Yet it was an insulting phrase, and Ridgway smoldered when he heard it. Here was his superior speaking so condescendingly about what he and, perhaps even more important, the men fighting under him had seen as a considerable success. It was an assault on their morale, if nothing else, from someone who was supposed to be on their side. Five days after the MacArthur press conference, Ridgway held his own. For UN troops to reach the thirty-eighth parallel, he said, would be a "tremendous victory." Then he added—as clear a dissent from the views of MacArthur as he had yet uttered—"We didn't set out to conquer China. We set out to stop Communism: we have demonstrated the superiority on the battlefield of our men. If China fails to throw us into the sea, that is a defeat for her of incalculable proportions. If China fails to drive us from Korea, she will have failed monumentally." Years later, MacArthur paid Ridgway back. Although he had been MacArthur's own choice to succeed Walker, in an interview with Jim Lucas, a star writer for the Scripps Howard chain, which was always favorable to him, he ranked Ridgway "at the bottom of the list" of his field commanders.

There was, of course, more to come. MacArthur wrote Hugh Baillie, the head of United Press International, and one of his chief journalistic admirers, that with a force of the size needed to hold the line at the thirty-eighth parallel, as Washington now wanted to limit the war, he could also drive the Chinese back across the Yalu. Most assuredly Matt Ridgway did not agree. That was his fourth violation of the gag rule. Two far more important assaults on the administration were still ahead. On March 20, MacArthur received a top secret cable from Washington notifying him that the administration felt it was the right time for a major peace initiative. With the new successes that Ridgway had enjoyed on the battlefield, there was a chance of talking, and eventually stabilizing the lines at the thirty-eighth parallel and ending this grim, mutually hopeless war. It was an embryonic feeler at best, and there was an awareness that Mao might not yet be ready to move forward, but at least it was a beginning.

The important thing was that Washington was ready to talk. Truman intended to make a major speech in the near future suggesting that both sides go to the negotiating table and end up somewhere back near where the war started. To MacArthur that kind of stalemate was nothing less than a defeat. Informed of what Washington intended to do, he set out quite deliberately to sabotage it. On March 24, as he was paying another of his visits to Korea, his office released a communiqué again taunting the Chinese military leadership.

"Of even greater significance than our tactical success," his communiqué said, "has been the clear revelation that this new enemy, Red China, of such exaggerated and vaunted military power, lacks the industrial capacity to provide adequately many critical items essential to the conduct of modern war." He then enumerated some of what he saw as China's weaknesses: the Chinese enemy "lacks manufacturing bases and those raw materials needed to produce, maintain and operate even moderate air and sea power, and he cannot provide the essentials for successful ground operations, such as tanks, heavy artillery and other refinements science has introduced into the conduct of military campaigns." He then mentioned China's inability to control the sea and air. When these limitations were "coupled with the inferiority of ground fire power, as in the enemy's case, the resulting disparity is such that it cannot be overcome by bravery, however fanatical, or the most gross indifference to human loss."

It was a remarkable, singularly insulting document, a simultaneous assault on two capitols, Beijing *and* Washington. With its publication, whatever chance there was of a first step toward a peace process was lost for the time being. It was, in Blair's words, "the most flagrant and challenging" violation of the Truman directive yet. His communiqué reached Washington about ten o'clock on the night of March 23. Dean Acheson, Bob Lovett (by then the number two man at Defense), and Dean Rusk were together at Acheson's house and they were all livid. "A major act of sabotage," Acheson called it. Truman gave no inkling of his own personal decision on what the next step should be, but Acheson, probably the counselor best attuned to him, later wrote that his state of mind "combined disbelief with controlled fury." His daughter, Margaret, later quoted him as saying, "I couldn't send a message to the Chinese after that. He [MacArthur] prevented a cease fire proposition right there. I wanted to kick him into the North China Sea right there."

The communiqué had taken the struggle between the president and the general to a new level. It went to the question of who the commander in chief was. The next day, Truman met with his top people, and the idea of a peace proposal was dropped. With that, the central issue became not so much whether to fire MacArthur, but when. Lovett, usually so low-key, wanted to do it then and there. Marshall fretted about the anger such an act might create on the Hill, and its effect on the defense appropriations bill. Acheson was nervous about its broader political ramifications. There was also the question of the Joint Chiefs—would they come along without a dissenting voice? Getting senior military men to turn on one of their own was always a sensitive business. If just one chief failed to go along with them, MacArthur's position would be greatly enhanced. But there was also no doubt that Truman had made his decision and was merely waiting for the right moment.

That came soon enough. MacArthur had received, at roughly the same time, a letter from the Republican leader in the House, Joe Martin, a passionate backer of Chiang and a China Lobby member, soliciting his views about Asia, and in particular the use of Chiang's troops in opening a second front against the Chinese. This was something Martin greatly favored. "Your admirers are legion and the respect you command is enormous," Martin wrote. MacArthur, he added, could answer confidentially or publicly. To most military men this might seem like a trap set by a tricky politician to catch an innocent, unworldly general: to MacArthur it was nothing less than a golden opportunity.

When MacArthur answered Martin on March 20, he set no restrictions on how Martin could use his words. His views, he said, were "to meet force with maximum counterforce, as we have never failed to do in the past. Your view with respect to the utilization of the Chinese forces on Formosa is in conflict with neither logic, nor this tradition." Then he added, a now familiar litany of explanation and complaint: "that we fight Europe's war with arms while the diplomats there fight it with words; that if we lose the war to Communism in Asia the fall of Europe is inevitable, win it and Europe would most probably avoid war and yet preserve freedom. As you pointed out, we must win. There is no substitute for victory."

49

JUST AS MACARTHUR wanted, Joe Martin took the bait and read the MacArthur letter on the floor of the House on April 5. Nothing could have been more political or more potentially injurious to so embattled a government (or, for that matter, more terrifying to its allies).

There was one additional thing that strongly affected Truman and the men immediately around him in those days that was not part of the public record, but helped generate the feeling that MacArthur was a rogue general. As Joseph Goulden wrote in his authoritative book on the Korean War, the National Security Administration, the supersecret institution that was in charge of listening covertly to the rest of the world when it thought it was communicating privately, was picking up intercepts from its listening station at Atsugi Air Base near Tokyo. Mostly that station was used for listening in on the Chinese, but sometimes it listened in on friendly countries as well. In the late winter of 1950–51, the people there picked up a series of intercepts from both the Spanish and Portuguese embassies in Tokyo. Those were embassies with which MacArthur had closer ties than Washington because of Charles Willoughby's affinity for their respective dictators, Francisco Franco and Antonio Salazar. In these messages the Spanish and Portuguese diplomats told their home offices that MacArthur had assured them he could turn Korea into a larger war with the Chinese. Paul Nitze of Policy Planning and his deputy Charles Burton Marshall eventually saw the messages, as did the president. According to Goulden, when Truman read them he slapped his desk in anger. "This is outright *treachery*," he exclaimed.

The day after Martin revealed the general's letter, Truman wrote in his diary: "MacArthur shoots another political bomb through Joe Martin, leader of the Republican minority in the House. This looks like the last straw. Rank insubordination." Then he listed for his own purposes some of MacArthur's previous actions. He ended the diary note, "I've come to the conclusion that our Big General in the Far East must be recalled." He was still careful at the meetings with his own top people, however, to withhold word on his own decision.

He and the men around him were, they knew all too well, in a lose-lose situation. There was no upside now. A president who dismissed a famed and honored general in the middle of a highly unpopular war could not but suffer in the short term. The immediate political impact would undoubtedly favor the general. History was another thing. Truman was confident that the historians would come along and rescue him, perhaps after he left office, although they might take their own sweet time getting there. He was a shrewd enough politician to know that he would pay dearly in the coin of his administration's present value. That said, he did not waver. MacArthur's behavior, he believed, cut to the very core of a democratic society, to civilian control of the military. As for the general's vision of the war, he later wrote, once again summoning history, it reminded him of Napoleon saying, after he had advanced all the way to Moscow in his ill-fated invasion of Russia, "I beat them in every battle, but it does not get me anywhere."

All of that made the choice surprisingly easy. Truman also believed that there was a curious historical precedent for what was happening. If MacArthur saw himself as someone descended lineally from Washington and Lincoln, Harry Truman saw him less flatteringly, as the modern reincarnation of George McClellan. McClellan was the general who, in Truman's view, not only served Lincoln poorly in the field, but had treated him with open contempt, often deliberately keeping him waiting before their scheduled meetings. McClellan openly referred to Lincoln as "the original gorilla."

McClellan's ego was enormous, greatly exceeding his talents. He had seen himself as nothing less than the savior of the country. If, he said, "the people call upon me to save the country—I *must* save it & cannot respect anything that is in the way." There were countless letters to him from ordinary citizens, he liked to claim, urging him to run for the presidency or to become the dictator of America. He greatly preferred the idea of dictator, and he was willing, he sometimes added, to make that sacrifice. He hungered to run against Lincoln, which he finally did, unsuccessfully, in 1864, gaining 21 electoral votes to Lincoln's 212. "A great egoist," Truman later said of McClellan. "A glorified Napoleon. He even had his picture taken with his hand in his overcoat, like Napoleon."

In the winter of 1950–51, Truman assigned Ken Hechler, a thirty-six-year-old White House staffer, to research the Lincoln-McClellan relationship in the Library of Congress stacks. The parallels, he discovered, were startling, though McClellan, in contrast to MacArthur, was an overly cautious general. He was, Hechler wrote, "so supremely self confident that he could not take orders well; he dabbled in politics; he thought his commander-in-chief Lincoln was crude, ignorant, and uncouth; and he expressed too freely his opposition to emancipating the slaves."

McClellan's constant statements on politics, in effect unsolicited political advice—not unlike those of MacArthur—became a steady irritant to Lincoln. Hechler's memo detailed the lengthy correspondence between the president and the general, culminating, after a year of increasingly contentious messages, in Lincoln's decision to relieve him of command of the Army of the Potomac in November 1862. Hechler handed his research in to the president, only to discover, to his surprise, that Truman knew almost all of it anyway and already took some comfort from it. After all, nearly ninety years later, Lincoln was the most honored of presidential names and McClellan among the least valued of military ones. The president understood that history in this case was going to be his ally, that he was not the first president to have trouble with a general with a superiority complex.

Nonetheless, Truman moved cautiously. Martin spoke on a Thursday. That Friday, April 6, Truman met with Marshall, Acheson, Bradley, and Harriman and, without giving away his own inclinations, asked them what he should do. Marshall was still cautious. Acheson wanted to fire him, but warned, "You will have the biggest fight of your Administration." Harriman pointed out that Truman had been struggling with the MacArthur conundrum since August 1950. Truman then asked them all to meet again later the same day. He asked Marshall to review all the messages that had gone back and forth from Washington to MacArthur, to check out whether he had actually been insubordinate. Bradley was assigned to check out the feelings of the Joint Chiefs, so critical in any forthcoming political battle. When they met later that day, Marshall suggested not firing MacArthur but bringing him home for consultations. Acheson and Harriman were strongly opposed to that—they envisioned the political circus that would take place. Because Joe Collins was out of reach, it was decided to wait until Bradley could talk to him. They all met again on Saturday, slowly, surely focusing on the inevitable.

When that meeting was over, Marshall and Bradley went back to Marshall's office. Both were soon to retire. Marshall had already taken a great deal of abuse from the right wing, while Bradley, who had not been in the China line of fire, was still unscathed as a grand figure of World War II. If they relieved MacArthur, Bradley knew, he and a military career of sterling quality would no longer be immune to the ugly virus of the ongoing political struggle. In addition, both men feared that firing MacArthur might politicize the Joint Chiefs. They tried drafting a letter that would, in effect, tell MacArthur to shut up, but it was a little late in the game for that. There were no half measures left. The general had forced their hand.

That Sunday, Bradley met with the Joint Chiefs. They were still trying to figure out some way to avoid a vote on MacArthur's relief, so odious a decision for senior military men dealing with the most senior military man of all. There was some talk about separating MacArthur from the Korean command, leaving him only with the defense of Japan, but they knew he would never accept such a solution. In the end they all signed on to relieving him. With that the Chiefs met with Marshall. It was a grim and sobering meeting. Firing MacArthur was like tearing pages out of your most prized history book. Marshall went to each of them and asked if he would concur in the decision should Truman fire MacArthur. Each did, as did Bradley, though he was not a voting chief.

On Monday, April 9, Truman met with his senior people again and for the first time revealed his own position—that MacArthur had to go. Ridgway would replace him and Jim Van Fleet, who had risen to prominence during the Greek civil war, would take command of the Eighth Army in Korea. This, he told them, was about elemental constitutional processes, not about politics. Nothing revealed his attitude as clearly as a mild rebuke he gave to one of his speechwriters working on a statement just before he announced the decision. There had been an argument between Charlie Murphy, a senior White House figure, and Ted Tannenwald, a junior member of the staff and a Harriman man, over the announcement. Tannenwald wanted to include the fact that the decision had been made with the unanimous agreement of the Joint Chiefs and the president's most senior civilian cabinet members, especially Marshall, whose name still held real authority for many Americans.

At their final meeting on the statement, the president went around the room in what was a speak-now-or-forever-hold-your-tongue moment. Tannenwald again suggested that the president add the fact that he was doing this at the unanimous suggestion of the Joint Chiefs and his senior officials. But Truman quickly cut him off. It might have been as fine a moment as he enjoyed as president, a reflection of his rare ability to understand what the office truly was about and to rise to its needs. "Not tonight, son," he told Tannenwald. "There'll be plenty of time for that later. But tonight I'm taking this decision on my own responsibility as President of the United States and I want no one to think I'm trying to share it with anyone else. That will [all] come out in 48 or 72 hours, but as of tonight this is my decision and my decision alone."

So it was done and the president prepared to address the nation. At the last moment, Averell Harriman noticed that the statement did not mention that Ridgway was replacing MacArthur, so they wrote it in by hand, ushering in, in addition, a more modern era. (The first thing Ridgway did when he took MacArthur's job was to move a telephone into MacArthur's old office, thus connecting the commander with the outside world.) The reason he had made the decision, the president said, was irreconcilable differences over policy. Then he added: "General MacArthur's place in history as one of our greatest commanders is fully reestablished. The Nation owes him a debt of gratitude for the distinguished and exceptional service which he has rendered his country in posts of great responsibility. For that reason I repeat my regret at the necessity for the action I feel compelled to take in his case." He was sure, he told staffers, that MacArthur had wanted this confrontation: "I can show just how the dirty so and so double crossed us. I'm sure MacArthur wanted to be fired. He's going to be regarded as a worse double crosser than McClellan." Everyone, he added, "seems to think I don't have courage enough to do it. We'll let them think so and then we'll announce it." Later, privately, he spoke of MacArthur in much blunter terms: "The difficulty was that he wanted to be the Pro-consul, the Emperor of the Far East. He forgot that he was just a general in the army under his commander in chief, the President of the United States."

MacArthur knew the firing was coming. The day before he had seen Ned Almond. "I may not see you anymore, so good-bye, Ned," he had said. Almond was puzzled and asked what MacArthur meant. He answered: "I have become politically involved and may be relieved by the president." That was absurd, Almond insisted.

The firing itself, despite Truman's largely generous words, was badly botched. Frank Pace, the secretary of the Army, was supposed to tell MacArthur personally, but in Washington, the *Chicago Tribune,* ever hostile to the president, was on to the story, and the White House feared that MacArthur might resign before he could be fired, attacking Truman in the process and placing the White House on the defensive. Because of that, the White House decided to rush the announcement. The news was given out at a rare 1 A.M. briefing on April 11, Washington time, and it reached Tokyo by radio before the general had been officially notified, making the White House look infinitely more callous and MacArthur far more the victim. Even as he was being fired, his aides suggested, he remained the great MacArthur. Though the general himself did not meet with the press at first, Major General Courtney Whitney, one of his top aides, did. "I have just left him," Whitney told reporters at the time. "He received the word of the president's dismissal from command magnificently. He never turned a hair. His soldierly qualities were never more pronounced—this has been his finest hour."

THE ASSAULT ON Truman was immediate. "Seldom has a more unpopular man fired a more popular one," wrote *Time* magazine, whose publisher, not unlike the general himself, was not that hostile to the idea of a larger war with China. MacArthur, *Time* added, was "the personification of the big man with the many admirers who look to a great man for leadership. . . . Truman was almost a professional little man." The immediate reaction in the country was similarly partisan and exceptionally violent. Richard Nixon, who was a considerable political beneficiary of Chiang's collapse in China and the tensions generated with the Chinese during the Korean War, called for MacArthur's immediate reinstatement. Senator William Jenner of Indiana, who had already accused George Marshall of treason, now said, "I charge that this country today is in the hands of a secret inner coterie which is directed by agents of the Soviet Union. Our only choice is to impeach President Truman." MacArthur was quickly cast (much as he intended) as both hero and martyr; and the president who stood for civilian control over the military in firing him, as the villain. After a long and often distinguished career, MacArthur's lesser side had finally caught up with him; he had become, in the end, too much like his father. He was, as Max Hastings summed up, "too remote, too old, too inflexible, too deeply imprisoned by a world view that was obsolete to be a fit commander in such a war as Korea."

Truman and his advisers had expected a serious explosion, but it was much worse than any of them had imagined. Huge crowds turned out for MacArthur everywhere. It began in Tokyo, where, as he departed, some 250,000 Japanese, many of them weeping, most of them waving small Japanese and American flags, lined the streets. Giant crowds gathered in Hawaii, where he landed after midnight, and an even larger one met him in San Francisco, again after midnight—a crowd so immense and so emotional that the security people could not hold them back. When he eventually came to New York for a ticker-tape parade, it was said that 7 million people turned out, twice as many as Dwight Eisenhower had drawn on returning victorious from World War II.

The reaction continued to be deeply emotional. "It is doubtful that there has ever been in this country so violent and spontaneous a discharge of political passion as that provoked by the president's dismissal of the general," wrote Arthur Schlesinger and Richard Rovere in their book on the confrontation. "Certainly there has been nothing to match it since the Civil War."

It was a political and geopolitical confrontation of the utmost gravity and presented the country with the ultimate kind of constitutional crisis. George Reedy, later a press officer for an enterprising young senator from Texas named Lyndon Johnson, but then a young reporter for United Press, later recalled that it was the only time in his life when he thought the government of the United States was truly in danger. He had felt, he said, watching MacArthur go up Pennsylvania Avenue on his triumphal arrival in Washington, that if the general had said, " 'Come on, let's take it,' the adoring crowd that thronged the streets would have gone with him." It was as if the country were about to explode with long suppressed rage from all the frustrations of this new, unsatisfying postwar incarnation. The struggle seemed to cut across every fault line in the country. There were fights in bars between strangers and fights on commuter trains between old friends. When Dean Acheson got into a taxi in Washington right after the firing, the cabdriver looked at him and asked, "Aren't you Dean Acheson?" "Yes, I am," the secretary of state answered. "Would you like me to get out?"

In a way that few understood at the time, it was a kind of giant antiwar rally, not just anti–Korean War, but probably anti–Cold War as well, a reflection of a kind of national frustration with a conflict that was so unsatisfying and distant and gray and brought so little in the way of victories and seemed so strangely beyond the reach of our absolute weapons. It was about the frustration of living side by side with an unwanted enemy who was real and powerful in an age that, because of the sheer terror of weaponry, seemed to preclude any concept of total victory. It bridged eras in a way. It was the last hurrah for a great hero of World War II, combined with a powerful, visceral protest by a nation that did not enjoy its new superpower status. It was produced by almost equal parts of love and anger. It was very powerful stuff.

It was also very political—not the acclaim of the crowds, the millions of Americans who rallied to MacArthur's cause, which they saw as something simpler than it was, but the challenge of the Republican right. Herbert Hoover, filled with distaste for the country's political direction after his own unfortunate presidency, his own political wounds still uncommonly raw, spoke for the forces long beaten down who now felt they were on the ascent. After meeting with MacArthur upon his return from Tokyo, Hoover talked of "the reincarnation of St. Paul into the persona of a great General of the Army who had come out of the East."

At first, the general had it all his way. He was in complete control of this drama, and his villains were, for the moment, compelled to play their roles much as he scripted them. It all culminated in a single powerful, if somewhat overly sentimental speech he gave before a joint session of Congress. There, he had made his case, and seemingly made it effectively. There was, he said, as he had said in letters to so many of his admirers, *no substitute for victory.* In this entire matter, he claimed, the Joint Chiefs were in agreement with him, as were almost all military leaders he knew. Those who did not see what he saw, those who did not want to use all of America's force in Korea, were guilty of appeasement. The A-word was in play several times, and there was no doubt who his target was. The people who would "appease Red China" were, he said, "blind to history's clear lesson, for history teaches with unmistakable emphasis that appeasement but begets new and bloodier war." Those who thought we lacked the forces to hold the Communists in both Europe and Asia were wrong. Considering that particular view, he swore he "could think of no greater expression of defeatism." He had wanted reinforcements, but could not get them from Washington. He had wanted to use the six hundred thousand Nationalist soldiers on Taiwan, but was not granted them. "Why, my own soldiers asked me," he said, suggesting endless nonexistent conversations with ordinary soldiers in their foxholes, "surrender military advantages to an enemy in the field?" He could not, he insisted, answer them. That day, even before his final summation, the applause was tumultuous; the Democrats, already on the defensive, sat silently in their seats.

Then came the great peroration, rich and powerful, full of nostalgia and bathos, but virtually irresistible and perfect for the emotions of the occasion: "I am closing my fifty-two years of military service. When I joined the Army even before the turn of the century, it was the fulfillment of all my boyish hopes and dreams. The world has turned over many times since I took the oath on the plains of West Point, and the hopes and dreams have long since vanished. But I still remember the refrain of one of the most popular barracks ballads of that day, which proclaimed most profoundly that—'Old soldiers never die; they just fade away.' And like the old soldier of that ballad I now close my military career and just fade away—an old soldier who tried to do his duty as God gave him the light to see that duty. Good-bye." These were the seemingly modest words of one of the nation's most immodest men, who had absolutely no intention of fading away. The spontaneous response was overwhelming. "We saw a great hunk of God in the flesh and we heard the voice of God," said Congressman Dewey Short of Missouri. Truman was, predictably, blunter: "It was nothing but a damn bunch of bullshit." Acheson thought that there was a certain relief to having it all over. It reminded him, he said, of the father who lived just outside an Army post with his very beautiful daughter and spent all his time worrying about her virginity. Finally, one day she showed up pregnant. "Thank God that's over," he had said.

For so many Americans, rarely had their nation's policies seemed so errant, and rarely had one figure—a famed, bemedaled *general*—spoken so confidently of what seemed like an easier course, one that would quickly settle a war with so much less American bloodshed. All of this set the stage for an epic moment in a democracy, though not many people saw it that way at the time. To them the epic moment was MacArthur's speech with its high-octane emotions; what followed, the analysis of the choices at stake, and the consequences of those choices, debated as they were in Senate hearings, lacked the same glamour but were far more important. At first it did not seem like an entirely fair fight: one side had title to all of those passions; the other side was forced to make an unpopular case for an unpopular war that, in effect, no one wanted to hear—that it was a victory merely to limit a localized war, that victory now was simple human survival.

For any serious student of what was soon to come, there were important warnings that MacArthur's next appearance in Washington would not be so pleasant or heroic. When Truman and MacArthur had met on Wake Island six months earlier, Vernice Anderson had by chance (or not, as later claimed by the general's angry partisans) sat outside the open door to the main meeting and kept that stenographic record of the talks, including MacArthur's cavalier assurance that the Chinese would not enter the war. That she had kept a record was not exactly a secret. When the Truman team returned to Washington, her notes were typed up and sent to various participants, including MacArthur, for approval. On November 13, 1950, just before the main Chinese attack but after the Unsan and Sudong ones, Stewart Alsop had mentioned in one of his regular columns for the *New York Herald Tribune* MacArthur's assurances that the Chinese would not enter the war.

None of this had created much of a stir. After the main Chinese entry, a conservative magazine had asked MacArthur directly whether or not he had said that the Chinese would not enter the war, and he had denied it—it was, he insisted, "entirely without foundation." There were a few stories printed, based on limited leaks by an irritated administration, that indicated that MacArthur had indeed given those assurances. But when, after his firing, the assault on Truman grew ever more violent, the White House decided to answer back by releasing the transcript. Tony Leviero, the *New York Times* White House correspondent, was already sniffing around the story. When he spoke with George Elsey, a senior White House aide, about the Wake meeting, Elsey immediately went to Truman. Leviero was considered straight and reasonably friendly by the White House.

If there was to be a leak, Elsey suggested, then here was the right man with the right paper for the job. "Okay—you can give it to Tony," the president said, and with that Leviero and the *Times* got the full transcript. The paper published it on April 21, and the next year Leviero won the Pulitzer Prize. The MacArthur people were furious; it was a smear, General Courtney Whitney said. If it was not nearly enough to cripple the growing assault on the White House, then anyone knowledgeable about how things like this played in Washington now had reason to wonder just how well the general and his record would fare in Senate hearings scheduled to begin on the Hill.

The showdown finally came in the Senate hearings. The Republican right was sure the momentum was going its way. Its leaders in the Senate had no doubt that MacArthur, forceful and charismatic as ever, had all the answers (which were their answers) and spoke for real Americans. What was it MacArthur had said at San Francisco's City Hall in front of half a million adoring citizens? "I have just been asked if I intended to enter politics. My reply was 'No.' I have no political aspirations whatever. I do not intend to run for any political office. I hope my name will never be used in a political way. The only politics I have is contained in a simple phrase known to all of you—'God Bless America.'" That, as Joseph Goulden noted, was the general's own coy way of signaling that he might indeed be available for a political run, for one last try.

Given the power of the emotions now in play, none of the top Democrats was eager to lead the hearings and get in the way of so powerful a force. So it fell to Richard Russell, the Georgia Democrat and senior senator on the Armed Services Committee—a truly conservative man in the old-fashioned sense of the word, with unparalleled respect among his peers in the Senate and, because of the nature of the one-party South, completely immune to the political pressures of the moment—to head the committee. He was a towering figure of the Senate, probably closer personally and ideologically to conservative Republican senators than to liberal Democratic ones, though he could never run successfully for national office because of the issue of race; he was an all-out segregationist. In other circumstances, a figure holding such a gavel in such crucial hearings, as Robert Caro noted in his book *Master of the Senate,* might have had a chance to become an instant national figure and a household name. But to take the gavel now was a dubious honor. It was not a role Russell sought, but it was a role, however odious, he felt obliged to accept. The MacArthur committee would be a joint one, combining the Armed Services and Foreign Relations committees. The Democrats would technically have an advantage because they were the majority party and because some of the Republicans, like Leverett Saltonstall and Henry Cabot Lodge of Massachusetts, were Eastern internationalists, but the emotions of the moment, to which all senators were finely attuned, greatly favored MacArthur.

WHAT THE REPUBLICANS hoped for was a great national platform for the general. He would be the great patriot who had been wronged and betrayed by wimpy politicians, and here in the national spotlight he could slay his—and, more important, *their*—opponents with that great voice and that all-encompassing knowledge of the world. He would dismantle on their behalf not just Truman, Acheson, and Marshall, but their policies over the previous decade. What the Republican right wanted was nothing less than for these Senate hearings to launch the 1952 presidential election campaign. There was, however, a serious problem for MacArthur. The passions his return had triggered had not actually represented an endorsement of his policies, most especially not of a wider war in Asia. Instead, the emotional welcome for him and support for his policies were two very different things—especially as those policies were placed under increasingly serious scrutiny, and the consequences of following them became clearer.

What then do you do in a democracy when passions outpace the realities of the moment? Richard Russell pondered that question, and eventually decided that slowing the process down to focus on substance might limit the passions. He wanted, to the degree that he was able, to marginalize the headline-hunting. So it was that the most critical thing Russell did was to disarm the emotions of the hearings. The hearings, he decided, would be full; they would be as thoughtful and judicious as he could make them and they would not be covered live—they would be covered instead almost live. Reporters would not be allowed in the hearing room, nor would the cameras of that new media form, television, be allowed in—even though, with its audience beginning to grow, as many as 30 million Americans might have watched every day. There would be a record, and it would be given out to reporters almost as soon as someone had testified. But they were going to be talking about issues of national security even as the war went on, and Russell was in no rush to have a discussion of the most secret aspects of American foreign policy made available to the country's enemies. Thus, the stenographic record of the hearings would be edited immediately by censors from the Defense and State departments.

Four votes on whether or not the hearings should be closed were brought by the Republicans, and four times Russell won, albeit narrowly. So on May 3, 1951, the hearings began, and as they did, so did the demythologizing of Douglas MacArthur. He could not, as he had so often done at the Dai Ichi in Tokyo, dominate this political situation and deliver his carefully rehearsed monologues without challenge. The Dai Ichi was not a democratic setting; this was.

During the Senate hearings, he did indeed use phrases like "history teaches us" and "history shows," as if there were just one simple lesson to be passed on and he was history's designated voice. For the first time, though, great hero or not, he had to bow to democratic procedures, facing tough questions from men every bit as partisan and egocentric as he.

As the first witness, he answered questions for three days, and it was in no way a virtuoso performance. He was forced to deal with a rather more complicated record than he might have wanted. These men felt they could challenge his thoughts and his facts. Nor were his answers necessarily what the Republican right wanted. Each day his case seemed a bit weaker, he himself a bit smaller, and his opponents, indeed his punching bags, like Acheson and Marshall, a bit more thoughtful and better grounded in the issues.

One of the great problems with Douglas MacArthur, something that had bedeviled those who had dealt with him for years, was that he did not always tell the truth. He used the truth when it suited him and his cause, and readily departed from it when it got in his way. The truth posed a great dilemma for a man who always had to be right, and yet, for all his grandeur, he was mortal like everyone else, and was often wrong, on occasion very wrong. Because he was surrounded by so many sycophants and no one ever challenged him, his own distortions eventually became crystallized as truths. Challenges to his version quickly became seen as the distortions of sworn enemies. When he had spoken before the Congress upon his return, he had lied shamelessly about one critical point. He had claimed that the Joint Chiefs supported his positions. Perhaps he had convinced himself that they did; for there had been a brief moment after the Chinese came in and before Ridgway was just arriving that some of them had pondered some of his proposals. But when Ridgway turned the war around, he had lost them again. Perhaps, in his own mind, he who had gloried in mocking and belittling them now truly believed that they had indeed supported him. Perhaps he believed that the old codes were more powerful than the truth, that, in the end, if it came down to a collision between the military and civilian politicians, then like it or not, all military men would be bound by a kind of institutional loyalty to back him up. Though he had not necessarily been loyal to them in the past, they, men of less grandeur, would nonetheless be loyal to him now.

He was wrong. He had treated the Chiefs with contempt from the beginning. He had made countless end runs around them, had been systematically disrespectful of their views, and had spoken of them privately with great contempt—and the Army being one of the world's most gossipy places, they knew just what he had said about them in private. He had snookered them again and again. Placing Almond in charge of Tenth Corps had symbolized his contempt for them. To have claimed their support at this moment was a grievous political mistake.

But it was more than just the Chiefs. He had very little support in the Pentagon itself, though some senior officers certainly remembered the greatness of the younger MacArthur. When he began his own testimony before the Russell committee, George Marshall spoke eloquently of how hard it was for him to challenge what MacArthur had said because of MacArthur's distinguished career. But there were many younger officers with shorter memories, not nearly so conflicted, who were furious over his disregard of orders, his failure to accept responsibility when the Chinese came in, his systematic challenge to civilian control of the military. It was often their contemporaries and friends who had been killed or wounded at places like Kunuri and the Chosin, and the bitterness they felt was not softened by any memories of the earlier MacArthur. This then was the reckoning. He was disliked, on occasion hated, among many younger officers in much of the building. Far more knowledgeable on the record than young Senate staffers, these younger Pentagon officers now gleefully guided members of the Senate and their staffs toward the glitches in MacArthur's case.

Day by day he was diminished. When Senators like Brien McMahon, a Democrat from Connecticut, began to question him about larger command responsibilities—dealing with the Russians, for example—he quickly began to back down. This time he did not give a soaring lecture about stopping the Communists in Asia in order to save Europe (even if the ungrateful Europeans themselves did not understand the importance of being saved by fighting a larger war with the Chinese). Asked about the Russians in Europe, he answered only that it was not his responsibility, for he was merely a theater commander. But wasn't that the crux of the problem? McMahon and others asked. Truman administration officials had always argued from the position of men dealing with global responsibilities, who had to be aware of potential challenges in places far beyond Korea, and adversaries more dangerous than the Chinese. MacArthur had made it very clear, McMahon pointed out, that if the administration followed his policies calling for a wider war against the Chinese, the Russians would not enter the war. He was surely entitled to those beliefs, the senator said, but what if he was wrong? Hadn't MacArthur also believed, McMahon suggested, that Red China would not enter the war? Was that not right? "I doubted [their entry]," MacArthur admitted. It was a damaging admission that did not enhance his reputation as an expert on what the Soviets would do if the United States was entrapped in an ever larger war with the Chinese.

Did the general, McMahon asked, think that American and Allied forces would be able to withstand a Russian attack in Western Europe? "Senator," MacArthur answered, "I have asked you several times not to involve me in anything except my own area. My concepts on global defense are not what I am here to testify on. I don't pretend to be the authority now on those things." It went downhill from there. MacArthur soon found himself on the defensive, even when it came to his own suggestions about driving the Chinese from North Korea. Questioned closely on this by Senator Lyndon Johnson, the general, who had mocked Ridgway's strategy as an accordion war, was unable to speak with any confidence about whether or not the Chinese might strike again if driven above the Yalu. Might they not wait there for another such moment, creating a vaster, more dangerous, perhaps even more permanent accordion war? He did not think, he testified, that they would then enter Korea again. It was not the most satisfying of answers. When his third day of testimony was over, though Russell had been extremely gracious—almost reverential with him—he had, in Joseph Goulden's words, "labeled himself a commander with parochial interests and knowledge. No longer could he posture as the master world strategist whose view from the Dai Ichi sanctuary was superior to that of diplomats and other militarists."

He was followed by George Marshall, then the Joint Chiefs, and finally Acheson, all of whom made the administration's case with considerable skill. Marshall was especially strong. He shared none of MacArthur's confidence that a wider war against the Chinese would not bring in the Soviets. There were far too many places where they might easily strike back at the United States and where, because of the logistics, the Americans, rather than the Soviets, were vulnerable. In addition, what MacArthur wanted America to do would sever the United States from its most important allies, while shattering every alliance the Americans had built and upon which so much of U.S. security was now based. Marshall emphasized that the great division here between the general and Washington was not, as so many hoped, a deep ideological struggle, but instead something far more mundane, a split between a theater commander with limited responsibilities whose orders from men with broader responsibilities were "not those he would have written for himself."

That kind of disagreement was not so unusual, Marshall said. All theater commanders felt the same way and wanted an outsized share of available resources. What made MacArthur's disagreement exceptional was the public way he had expressed his displeasure and disagreement with the president's policies. One after another the Joint Chiefs expressed the depth of their disagreement with MacArthur's positions, and displayed for all to note that they were not his allies in this conflict. They detailed how the unwritten rules of the war, about which the American right wing and MacArthur himself were so critical—the use of sanctuaries was mutual—had actually favored the UN rather than the Chinese, because Japan was so vulnerable to attack and because the Russians had not attacked what they saw as our Japanese sanctuaries. Perhaps the key moment came when Bradley said that to follow MacArthur's plan would involve the United States "in the wrong war at the wrong place at the wrong time, and with the wrong enemy."

Though the Republican right had fought against censoring the hearings, in the end they were lucky to get that decision, because the excised parts of the record included a devastating critique of one of their great beliefs—about the value of Chiang's troops in this war. The critics of the administration were for a wider war, but not at the risk of using large numbers of American troops. That meant the question of whether to use Chiang's army was critical. MacArthur claimed in the hearings that they represented "half a million first class fighting men." They were, in terms of ability, "exactly the same as these Red troops I am fighting." Not everyone agreed; if they had been as good, most Americans who had served as advisers in China believed, they would not have lost in the first place. His view of them, it turned out, was a judgment based on that brief ceremonial visit to Taiwan in August 1950. Almost no one in the Pentagon agreed professionally with that judgment. These troops were in fact regarded as a disaster waiting for another place to happen. A thirty-seven-man mission sent to Taiwan by the Pentagon at virtually the same time, which had spent a good deal of time on the ground, Marshall testified, had found that the "condition of training and equipment . . . was so low that they could not be depended upon to defend" the island, let alone invade the mainland. Instead of preventing them from recapturing their homeland, we were protecting them from being overrun in their island redoubt.

As for giving them more equipment, their record for losing their equipment during the civil war was unparalleled and made the Joint Chiefs reluctant to give them any more. Bradley was particularly blunt. He said the Nationalist troops might defect to the Communists at the first opportunity. Moreover, he added, if a Communist force was actually able to land on Formosa, it might win the island over thanks to defections. Joe Collins added: "We were highly skeptical that we could get anything more out of these Chinese than we were getting out of the South Koreans, because these were the same people that were run off China in the first place." The testimony about the Chinese Nationalist troops reflected what most military men felt in private. It just was not the sort of thing one said publicly about the soldiers of an ally. But because it was censored, the myth of Chiang's troops, that extraordinary army of more than half a million men—America getting something for nothing—was allowed to continue.

The hearings represented a great education for Americans about the complexity of the world they now inhabited. Many who had thought Washington did not have a larger policy for dealing with the Communist world began to understand the containment policy that had been put in place. None of this painful process of education was what the Republicans who had pushed for the hearings, smelling blood in the waters, wanted. After six days of Omar Bradley's testimony, with the other Joint Chiefs still to follow, Senator Bourke Hickenlooper, the conservative Iowa Republican, suggested to Russell that the hearings were taking too much time and that there was really no need to hear the other three chiefs testify. That was a sign that the great Republican hope—that they could use the hearings to reveal a vast gap between the Truman people and the uniformed military—was dying. Hickenlooper's proposal was rejected fourteen to eleven. The hearings were going to run their course, and every day they lasted, MacArthur shrank further on the political landscape.

FOR THE TRUMAN administration the MacArthur hearings were a significant victory. The historical record—if not the political center of the country—had been reclaimed. A longtime adversary had been partially defanged, albeit a little late. Given the political damage already done by the fall of China, by the entrance of Chinese forces into the war, and the firing of MacArthur, Truman might be the winner in the long run but not in the short term, given the emotions triggered by the conflict. He might have title to the Constitution, and that would help him one day with historians, but the Republicans still had title to the flag, and that was more important in the political equation.

If some of its policies had been exonerated, the administration itself had ended up being severely, perhaps terminally, wounded by all these events, most particularly the entrance of the Chinese into the war. The defeat along the Yalu, Dean Acheson wrote to Harry Truman five years later, "destroyed the Truman Administration." There was not a lot for the administration to celebrate when the hearings were over. Not all of the damage came from the war, the fall of Chiang, and MacArthur's frontal challenge, but it was the most visible part. It was time for the Democrats to go. They had been in power too long, twenty years; they had made too many enemies, and the body politic, inevitably, had changed and shifted during that period and had different needs than it had had back in the hard and painful days of 1932.

Part
Eleven

—————

The Consequences

E VEN THE SHREWDEST of men do not always know when their most
dramatic moment is over and it is time to leave the stage; for the self-
absorbed that is far more likely to be true. So it was for Douglas MacArthur. "If
he had retired the day after Inchon, every town in America would have had
a school named after him," said Bill McCaffrey, then a mid-level officer on the
Tokyo staff, "but the longer he stayed, and the more he said, the more he damaged himself." In the end, he simply did not grasp the politics of it all—what
the cheering had been about (and perhaps more important, what it had *not*
been about) when he first returned home. He thought it had all been about
him, not understanding that he was merely a trigger device for something
larger. For a time he still chased his dream, giving speeches all over the country. The crowds dwindled, and as they did, his voice inevitably became more
strident. Many of his most passionate followers drifted elsewhere in search of
another candidate. The game plan for the conservative right had never really
centered around him. His real job had been to damage their enemies. If the
lightning struck, they would have gone with him, but their real candidate had
always been Bob Taft, whose father had taken down MacArthur's father some
fifty years earlier in the Philippines, and with whom MacArthur had the most
uneasy of political alliances.

That was still true as 1952 approached. Taft, infinitely more isolationist
than MacArthur, was the candidate of the conservative Republicans. At their
convention that year, MacArthur gave the keynote speech, but the handsome
and charismatic old soldier, the man who had stood so confidently before
the Congress a little more than a year earlier, had disappeared. In his place
was a civilian—indeed a politician—who seemed not only more partisan,
but much older, appearing in what was one of the most alien and uncomfortable roles of his life, that is, speaking on behalf of another man. He was not, it
became clear early on in his speech, very comfortable with his own words. The
delegates in the arena soon became restless and began to abandon their seats.
Millions of other Americans, sitting in their homes, watched as he emptied the

floor. He knew that he had somehow failed, and the next day did not take calls.

If there was a deeper irony embedded in this final chapter of his life, it lay in the effect his actions had on two of his adversaries. The first was Truman. If the president was momentarily wounded, he nonetheless won his larger bet, for he had believed in the restorative quality of history and he was proven right. The polls might have shown him at a political nadir when he left office, but his stock constantly rose in the years to come, until he was viewed as one of the most admirable of all American presidents, as well as a figure seriously underestimated in his time. No small part of that growing respect came from his willingness to stand up to MacArthur. In an odd way, MacArthur, who so looked down on Truman as a little man, had enhanced Truman's reputation for courage and integrity, and made him a bigger man.

So much of that painful confrontation, Truman believed, was easy because it was about a basic belief in the Constitution and civilian control of the military. Years later, Vernon Walters, the translator for several presidents, who had witnessed the moment at Wake Island when MacArthur had failed to salute, visited Truman in Independence, Missouri, and asked the former president if he could raise an indiscreet question. So Walters began to ask about that moment. Before he could finish, Truman interrupted: "Did I notice that MacArthur did not salute the President of the United States? You're goddamned right I noticed." Then, noted Walters, Truman's voice softened a bit. "I was sorry because I knew it meant that I was going to have trouble with him, and I did. I fired him and I should have done it long before I did. Right or wrong, he just did not understand how the United States is run."

The other unlikely beneficiary of the MacArthur challenge was Dwight Eisenhower. If there was going to be a general called to political office in 1952, it would be Eisenhower, not MacArthur. Eisenhower's political ascent seemed to underscore the degree to which MacArthur had been overtaken by the political and social changes of the previous forty years. Eisenhower was very much a man of the twentieth century; while MacArthur always seemed a man of the previous one, and his rhetoric—he wrote and spoke, Eisenhower once said, "in purple splendor"—was that of a time when there were still moral absolutes. Eisenhower was by far the more egalitarian man, a better listener and a far better compromiser. He was a general, but unlike MacArthur he never looked or sounded like a man on horseback; he seemed as natural in civvies as in uniform. The least strident of men, Eisenhower was, the country decided, the right man to lead them into a gray, uncertain nuclear age, one in which there were not going to be total victories: he was thoughtful, strong, but not too militaristic, fair-minded and pragmatic, a man who could deal with the

Russians either way, hard or soft. Moreover, Eisenhower himself was worried by the assault upon the administration from forces that were in his view essentially isolationist. The increasing likelihood that, under a Taft presidency, the country might turn away from its international responsibilities ensured that the general, rather grudgingly, made himself available for the nomination.

52

CHIPYONGNI HAD SIGNALED the beginning of a new stage in the war, one that lasted two more years without granting either side any turn-of-the-tide victory. The commanders of both armies were largely without illusions—though some illusions might still remain among the political figures above them. But from then on it became a grinding war. I want you, Ridgway told a group of Marine officers about that time, "to bleed Red China white." It became a war of cruel, costly battles, of few breakthroughs, and of strategies designed to inflict maximum punishment on the other side without essentially changing the battle lines. In the end, there would be no great victory for anyone, only some kind of mutually unsatisfactory compromise.

Each side had managed to neutralize the forces of the other, but both seemed somehow powerless to stop the war itself. The Chinese launched a major offensive in the spring of 1951, costly to them, and of only marginal success. They threw some three hundred thousand men into the line. Some of the most intense fighting of the war ensued, with insignificant benefits at the cost of horrific Chinese casualties. For the Western command, however, it was a reminder of just how good the Chinese troops really were and how many of them there were, which dampened any great desire to plan offenses to punch north of the thirty-eighth again and head for the Yalu. The commanders in the field did not always agree—the Eighth Army commander Jim Van Fleet was for a time very restless with the limits placed on him and thought, once he had stopped the Chinese offensive in May 1951, that it was his turn to drive north. But Washington had been through all that once before, and the results had been horrendous, and it had no intention of investing more American and other lives in trying it a second time.

But no one knew how to end it. The war had settled into unbearable, unwinnable battles; it had reached the point where there were no more victories, only death. Both sides wanted to get out, but neither seemed to have the political skills to do so, and the figure of Joseph Stalin, not unhappy to see two potential rivals caught in so unhappy a war, slowed down any chance of getting out easily. Both the United States and China were also slowed by their policy of nonrecognition—the only place they recognized each other was on the battlefield, at gunpoint. Nonetheless peace talks, or at least armistice talks, began in mid-July 1951 at Kaesong, the ancient Korean capital just below the thirty-eighth parallel, and went forward at a speed somewhat slower than a snail's pace. Eventually moved to Panmunjom in the no-man's-land of the thirty-eighth parallel, the talks were slowed by great ideological hostility and distrust, and by the fact that neither of the ancillary powers, the two Koreas, wanted to admit the existence of the other. What also turned out to be a major deterrent to progress was the issue of repatriation. There were a large number of Chinese prisoners who did not want to go back to the mainland. One estimate suggested that there were some twenty thousand Chinese soldiers being held prisoner, and only about six thousand wanted to be repatriated. That made a difficult process even harder.

BEFORE THERE COULD be peace in Korea, the American political process had to come to terms with the idea of a stalemate in a limited war. The Democrats, unhappily cast as the war's architects, were badly limited in their ability to do that. But a Republican president, especially a centrist Republican one, might be able to bring home the kind of imperfect settlement that a Democrat could not. Thus the great political battle of 1952 was not waged in the general election, but rather at the Republican Party's convention in Chicago, between the moderates and the conservatives. The anger there was visceral; it was as if all the long-simmering bitterness over foreign policy—and the parallel powerlessness among the right-wing members—surfaced at that convention. Everyone there believed that thanks to the war, they were now going to have the best chance to win in more than two decades—an even better chance than in 1948. And in the view of the right-wing isolationists there was Dwight Eisenhower, previously not even a declared Republican, arriving at *their* convention ready to steal *their* nomination. Who even knew if Eisenhower, who had worked so easily with Roosevelt and Truman, was *really* a Republican? "I Like Ike," said the Eisenhower buttons. "But What Does Ike Like?" countered the Taft buttons. The tensions on the convention floor and on the Chicago streets were far more bitter than normal. John Wayne, the actor, who had been, at thirty-four, an acceptable age to fight in World War II (Jimmy Stewart, a year older, had an exceptional war record) but had decided to do the war in celluloid because his career was just beginning to take off, was a particularly vocal Taft delegate. The star of many war films, Wayne at one point jumped out of his cab and yelled at an old mess sergeant who was running an Eisenhower sound truck, "Why don't you get a red flag?"

Taft himself seemed to think he could use the Korean War and the firing of MacArthur as central issues. Just before the convention, he announced that if elected he would name MacArthur "deputy commander in chief of the armed forces," whatever that actually meant. Senator Everett Dirksen was Taft's man, the key floor leader for the Midwestern wing, ready to fight to the last to stop the Eisenhower intruders. The leader of the Eisenhower forces was the twice-defeated Tom Dewey. At one point Dirksen stood at the podium and pointed down at Dewey, the archenemy of his own people, now the leader of the Eisenhower surge, and said: "Reexamine your hearts before you take this action. We followed you before and you took us down the road to defeat." Then, his finger still pointed at Dewey as if it were a weapon, Dirksen added, "And don't take us down that road again." It was the highest drama of the convention.

But to many ordinary delegates at the convention, hungering for a presidential victory, the promise of Eisenhower with his immense charm was more seductive than that of Taft's greater ideological purity. And Eisenhower it would be, both at the convention and in the general election. There was even a chemical formula for his campaign, worn on pins by his supporters, K_1C_2, or, translated into politics: the Korean War, corruption in government, and Communists in government. During the campaign he had uttered one single sentence that had virtually guaranteed his election. "I will go to Korea," he had said. Translated from the codes of politics to the public at large, that meant, "I will end the war." He won the election handily, by 6.6 million votes. He went to Korea, met with both General Mark Clark, who had the old MacArthur job, and Jim Van Fleet, who had the Walton Walker job, both of them more hawkish than Eisenhower and both irritated by the limits imposed on them—they were not allowed major offensives and were to focus on minimizing casualties. They were both filled with plans on how to intensify the pressure on the Chinese. Eisenhower barely listened. He wanted out.

Eisenhower was probably the perfect centrist candidate for that moment as America went through the torturous, grudging process of becoming an international power. He was thoughtful, careful, and experienced, the least jingoistic of military men. He was what the country wanted and probably needed just then, a tempered and tempering figure in an edgy and surely dangerous time. His sense of internationalism was impeccable and hard-won. He had led the largest invasion force in the history of mankind. He was, in personal terms, the anti-MacArthur, generous with subordinates, quick to give them credit, brilliant at suppressing his own ego, and capable of fending off the considerable ego of others.

His election also spelled the end for a certain kind of overt McCarthyism and, finally, for the senator himself. McCarthy had never quite understood the boundaries and limitations under which he operated, that he was useful when he attacked a *Democratic* president, not a Republican one. He did not understand that his role changed once Eisenhower had been elected, and so he continued on, reckless as ever, until in 1954 the Republican center began to move against him, resulting in his eventual censure. If McCarthy himself was censured in 1954, that did not mean that McCarthyism itself was dead—the willingness of prominent politicians in one party to attack their political opponents, not because of a valid disagreement over policy but on grounds of loyalty, accusing those they opposed of treason, and of aiding and abetting the Communists, continued; and some of the issues that had burdened Truman and Acheson still smoldered just under the surface. Much to his surprise, Eisenhower, new at the political game, quickly found that on some key issues he had more support and greater sympathy from the Democrats in Congress than from his own party. "Republican Senators," Eisenhower wrote in his diary a few weeks after becoming president, "are having a hard time getting through their heads that they now belong to a team that includes rather than opposes the White House."

WHAT THE ELECTION of Eisenhower also did was ease the way for a future settlement in Korea. Then in March 1953, both the United States and China caught a break. Joseph Stalin, the man covertly pushing the Chinese to be more obstinate, died, opening the way to finding a solution. Both sides were now freer to get a settlement than they might have been only a few months earlier, the Americans because Eisenhower could bring home the same kind of disappointing settlement that Truman might have been pilloried for, and the Chinese because Mao no longer had Stalin looking over his shoulder.

A routine letter to the Chinese from Mark Clark, the United Nations commander, suggesting an exchange of sick and wounded prisoners, drew an immediate and positive response. In late April 1953, the exchange, known to the Americans as Operation Little Switch, took place. The way was now open for further progress. But it was still a difficult task. Syngman Rhee, furious about the inconclusive nature of the potential solution, the fact that he would, like Kim Il Sung, after all that bloodshed and sacrifice, once again rule only half a country, tried to undermine the talks. First he announced in May that he would not be a party to any settlement and that the South would fight on alone—a threat that was palpably embarrassing to the Americans but also palpably empty. What he got in return was an offer of a bilateral security from the United States. Then, in mid-June, as both sides seemed to be moving ever more quickly toward a settlement, Rhee moved again to undermine the talks.

He pulled his guards from the prison camps in the South, allowing some twenty-seven thousand North Koreans, who might have been forced into repatriation, to escape and slip back into South Korean society, thereby enraging Pyongyang. But even that did not stop the process. The two larger powers wanted out.

The war went on grimly and meanly as the peace talks continued; the battles became an especially cruel way for each side to show to the other that if it was not exactly winning, then nevertheless it could stay there forever. By mid-1952, the war had begun to resemble more than anything else the worst of the First World War: trench warfare, days and nights of living under constant artillery barrages, men caught in the wrong place at the wrong time with almost all meaning subtracted from the fighting and dying. By then both sides had created seemingly unassailable extensive defensive lines. It was as if the Chinese, who had been so cavalier with their manpower in the earlier months of the war, had morphed their troops into a different kind of Army in the previous two years, skilled at this different kind of warfare. Given UN air and artillery supremacy, they had gradually adjusted their style of fighting. They had created quite exceptional tunnels, triumphs of raw, primitive engineering (and eventually to be copied and perhaps exceeded by the North Vietnamese, first in their assault on the French at Dien Bien Phu in 1954, and then in time in their war with the Americans). In Korea these tunnels went from Chinese positions relatively removed from the point of assault to the very mouth of an attack point. They allowed the Chinese relative immunity from UN firepower until the very last moment of an attack. In addition, the Chinese had their artillery pieces, usually ones captured during their civil war, hidden away, virtually invisible to detection even from the air. They were positioned on the *back* side of the mountains, often in caves laboriously carved out of the mountains themselves. A given artillery piece would be slipped out periodically, would fire about twenty rounds of frighteningly accurate fire at the American positions, and then be wheeled back into the cave. "By the time our counterfire guys could fix its location, their gun was safe and its crew was safely back in the cave too, sucking down their rice," said Hal Moore, who had commanded a rifle company in those days. Their defensive positions were exceptional, "very tough to crack—they were hard-core, heavy duty, professional diggers," Moore said. "Their lines were built around deep caves, catacombs with large underground rooms sometimes twelve or fifteen miles behind the front lines. Because of that our artillery, bombers, and close air support had little or no effect on them."

Their troops were much admired by the American commanders in the field for their discipline and tenacity. The Americans were rotating their frontline people more and more quickly because it was such an unpopular war, but the

Chinese were more often than not keeping the same units and the same troops engaged on the line for extended periods, and the American commanders in the field marveled at how well they seemed to be able to move at night without exposing themselves. As the war had continued, it had obviously become a kind of two-track struggle: the peace talks at Panmunjom, slow and agonizingly difficult, and the fighting itself, just enough input to let the other side know that neither side, Western nor Eastern, was going to lose military face.

So it was with the battle of Pork Chop Hill in the spring of 1953. Pork Chop Hill, or Hill 255, was almost a symbol of the sheer emptiness of the last stages of the war, so much to be invested for so little gain. It was a bitter and bloody battle that took place in several stages, and it involved a small number of American infantry units, positioned at the extreme outer point of the UN lines, struggling for one of the most distant outposts on the UN exterior line. It had no great strategic benefit, and it was only of value because it had been deemed of value and because whichever side held it, the other side wanted it. The battle was more accurately a series of battles, for Pork Chop Hill had been going on for more than a year, culminating in the final battles of the Korean War in July 1953. The closer the people talking at Panmunjom came to some kind of a settlement, the more the value of Pork Chop seemed to go up, and the bloodier the fighting for it became. In late March of 1953, the Chinese attacked the hill and were driven off, but in the process took a neighboring outpost on a higher hill, Old Baldy, making Pork Chop that much more exposed. Major General Art Trudeau, the commander of the Seventh Division, wanted to take Old Baldy back, but Lieutenant General Maxwell Taylor, the new commander of the Eighth Army, refused permission for fear of additional prohibitive casualties. Taylor himself was under orders to clear any assault larger than two battalions with his superiors in Washington. That order in itself reflected Washington's desire for less not more war at this point.

In mid-April 1953, just as they were moving ahead on Little Switch and Panmunjom, the Chinese struck again, some twenty-three hundred of them, attacking the tiny garrison at Pork Chop. What ensued was a furious artillery battle. Slam Marshall, who wrote of that battle as he did of the fighting up near Kunuri, said that during the first day of the artillery barrage, the nine artillery battalions of the Second and Seventh divisions fired 37,655 rounds, and on the second day alone an additional 77,349 rounds. "Never at Verdun were guns worked at any rate such as this. The battle of Kwajalein, our most intense shoot during World War II, was still a lesser thing when measured in terms of artillery expenditure per hour, weight of metal against yards of earth and the grand output of the guns," he wrote. "For this at least the operation deserves a place in history. It set the all time mark for artillery effort."

The American troops managed to hold. In July 1953, the Chinese tried once again. The battle went on ferociously for two days, with both sides in a virtual stalemate on the crest of the hill. King Company, commanded by Lieutenant Joe Clemons, took the hardest hit. Clemons had gone up there with 135 men in his command and came back with 14. The fighting went back and forth over five days, from July 6 to July 11. On the morning of July 11, Maxwell Taylor drove up to Trudeau's headquarters and told him that Pork Chop was not worth the investment of any more American lives, that the battle was over. The remaining American forces slipped off the hill, unbeknownst to the Chinese. When someone asked Major General Mike West, the commander of the British Commonwealth Division, what he would have done to get Pork Chop back, he answered, "Nothing. It was only an outpost." Sixteen days later, on July 27, a truce began in Korea.

A difficult, draining, cruel war had ended under terms that no one was very happy with.

53

P ERHAPS ALL WARS are in some way or another the product of miscalculations. But Korea was a place where almost every key decision on both sides turned on a miscalculation. First, the Americans took Korea off their defensive perimeter, which in turn encouraged the varying Communist participants to act. Then, the Soviets gave a green light to Kim Il Sung to invade the South, convinced the Americans would not come in. When the Americans entered the war, they greatly underestimated the skills of the North Korean troops they were going to face, and vastly overestimated how well prepared the first American troops to go into battle were. Later, the Americans decided to drive north of the thirty-eighth parallel, paying no attention to Chinese warnings.

After that, in the single greatest American miscalculation of the war, MacArthur decided to go all the way to the Yalu because he was sure the Chinese would not come in, and so made his troops infinitely more vulnerable. Finally, Mao believed that the political purity and revolutionary spirit of his men greatly outweighed America's superior weaponry (and its corrupt capitalist soul) and so, after an initial great triumph in the far North, had pushed his troops too far south, taking horrendous losses in the process. For a time it seemed like the only person who got what he wanted was Stalin, who, fearing Titoism on Mao's part, and a possible Chinese connection to the Americans, was not unhappy when the Chinese decided to fight the Americans. But even he, so cold-blooded and calculating, miscalculated several times. He originally thought that the Americans would not enter the war, and then they did. If he was not at first unhappy with the idea of them fighting the Chinese (with the Russians sitting on the sidelines), then the long-range consequence for the Soviets would prove complicated indeed. The Chinese would remain bitter about what he did *not* do for them in those vital early months, and those feelings of resentment contributed to the Sino-Soviet split a few years later. But perhaps even more important, the Chinese entrance into the war had a profound and long-lasting effect on how Americans looked on the issue of national security.

It gave the ultimate push forward to the vision embodied in NSC 68. It greatly increased the Pentagon's influence and helped convert the country toward far more of a national security state than it had previously been, so increasing the forces driving that dynamic that in ten years Dwight Eisenhower, in his farewell speech as president, would warn of a "military-industrial complex." It would help define the Communist world, in American eyes, for years—and quite incorrectly—as a monolith, and so diminish the political influence of men like George Kennan, who placed greater emphasis on nationalism and age-old historical imperatives. It would poison American politics, where the great fear would become—for domestic political reasons rather than for geopolitical ones—losing a country to the Communists. Because of that, American policy toward Asia became deeply flawed, and this would profoundly affect American policy toward a country barely on the American radar screen at the time, Vietnam.

Certainly Kim Il Sung miscalculated, not just that the Americans would not send their troops to defend South Korea but the myth of his own popularity and that of his revolution, convinced as he was that two hundred thousand Southern peasants would rise up as one when his troops moved south. He not only failed to make his country whole but encouraged the Americans to upgrade the importance of South Korea, not only defending it militarily but financing its growth in the postwar era into an infinitely more viable society than his North. Fifty years after the end of the war, there were still American troops garrisoned there, and the South had become something of an economic beacon to underdeveloped nations, its economy infinitely more vital than that of the Soviet Union itself in the late 1980s. Comparably the North remained a sad, grim backwater, as xenophobic as it was totalitarian and economically destitute.

FOR MANY AMERICANS, except perhaps a high percentage of those who had actually fought there, Korea became something of a black hole in terms of history. In the year following the cease-fire, it became a war they wanted to know less rather than more about. In China the reverse was true. For the Chinese it was a proud and successful undertaking, a rich part of an old nation's new history. To them it represented not just a victory, but more important, a kind of emancipation for the new China from the old China, which had so long been subjugated by powerful Western nations. The new China had barely been born, and yet it had stalemated not merely America, the most powerful nation in the world, the recent conquerors of both Japan and Germany, but the entire UN as well, or by their more ideological scorekeeping, all the imperialist nations of the world and their lackeys and running dogs. In that sense it had been a victory of almost immeasurable proportions, and it had been, in their minds, theirs and theirs virtually alone. The Russians had committed some hardware, but had held back at the critical moment on manpower, men who had talked big and then had cheered from the sidelines. The North Koreans had been boastful, far too confident of their own abilities, and then had failed miserably at crucial moments, and it was the Chinese who had saved them. It was not out of character and hardly a surprise in the eyes of the Chinese that the North Koreans, in their historic accounts of the war, largely withheld credit from the Chinese. They were not, the feeling went, very good about being saved. If the Chinese at that moment had lacked the military hardware to chase the Americans off Taiwan, then they had instead used their abundant manpower, their ingenuity, and the courage of their ordinary soldiers to stalemate the Westerners on land. Afterward, the rest of the world had been forced to treat China as a rising world power.

More than that of anyone else it was Mao's personal victory. He had pushed to go ahead when almost everyone else had wavered and had feared that their brand-new China, already financially and militarily exhausted by the sheer struggle of taking power after the civil war, might fail. Mao was the one who had seen the political benefits, both international and domestic, of making a stand in Korea. If the consequences had turned out to be far bloodier than he had imagined, if the Americans with their superior weaponry had eventually fought better than he had expected and inflicted greater damage on his armies, then he could accept that; he had a tolerance for gore as part of the price of revolution, and he headed a nation that might not be rich in material things, but was very rich in manpower, in the numbers of men it could sacrifice on the battlefield on its way to greatness. That was something he had always believed in when most of the others around him hesitated. It was not that he knew the demographics better than the others in the leadership group; it was that he was willing to make the calculations more cold-bloodedly than they did.

What had been at stake in the Korean War, and it was to hang over subsequent wars in Asia, was the ability to bear a cost in human life, the ability of an Asian nation to match the technological superiority of the West with the ability to pay the cost in manpower. During Korea and soon enough in Vietnam, American military commanders and theorists alike would talk about the fact that life in Asia was cheaper than it was in the West, and they would see their job as one in which they used vastly superior military technology to attain a more favorable battlefield balance, even as their Asian adversaries were determined to prove to them that in the end that was not doable, that there would always be a price and it would always be too high for an American undertaking so distant, and so geopolitically peripheral.

Because the Chinese viewed Korea as a great success, Mao became more than ever the dominant figure in Chinese politics. He had shrewdly understood the domestic political benefits of having his country at war with the Americans. As he had predicted, the war had been a defining moment between the old China and the new one, and it had helped isolate those supporters of the old China—those Chinese who had been connected to Westerners—and turned them into enemies of the state. Many were destroyed—either murdered or ruined economically—in the purges that accompanied and then followed the war. From then on there was no alternative political force to check Mao; he had been the great, all-powerful Mao before the war began, and now, more than ever, his greatness was assured in the eyes of his peers on the Central Committee, who were no longer, of course, his peers. Before the war he had been the dominant figure of the Central Committee, a man without equals; afterward he was the equivalent of a new kind of Chinese leader, a people's emperor. He stood alone. No one had more houses, more privileges, more young women thrown at him, eager to pay him homage, more people to taste his food lest he be poisoned at one of his different residences. No one could have been contradicted less frequently. The cult of personality, which he had once been so critical of, soon came to please him, and in China his cult matched that of Stalin.

There was in all this a scenario not just for political miscalculation but for something darker, for potential madness with so much power vested in one man, a man to whom so much damage had been done earlier in his life. That was always a critical element of what happened next: Mao as a young man, not unlike Stalin, had been hunted too long and too relentlessly, as it were, by so many enemies; the deepest, most unwavering kind of paranoia grew out of that past and was the most natural part of his emotional and political makeup. At the same time he had become the principal architect of an entirely new political economic-social system. He existed and operated in a nation without any personal limits on him and yet where everyone could be an enemy. Both his power and his paranoia were without limits. He who had been for so long the ultimate outsider now lived a life of imperial grandiosity. He no longer needed to listen to others; if the others differed from him on issues, it was because they did not hold China's welfare as close to their hearts as he did, and were perhaps enemies of his and of China as well—the two he judged to be the same.

He was sure that he was right on all issues—his words as they escaped his mouth were worthy of being codified as laws. China, he had decided, *his* China, was ready to rush into modernity—the Great Leap Forward, it was

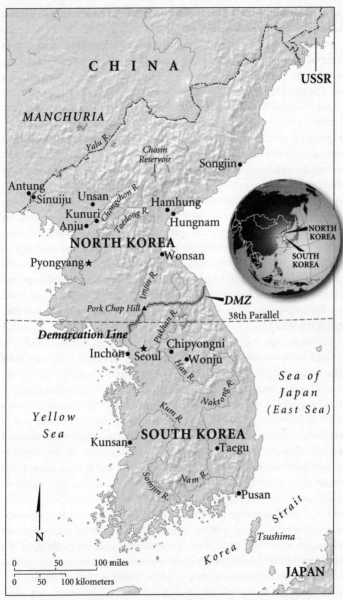

25. THE KOREAN PENINSULA AFTER THE CEASE-FIRE, JULY 27, 1953

called, and the burden of turning a poor agricultural society into a modern industrial state virtually overnight fell on the peasants. If he had once been uniquely sensitive to their needs, more tuned to them as a political force than anyone else in the leadership, he now seemed prepared to put the entire burden of modernization, brutal though it would be, on them for his larger purpose. His new China would, if need be, be built on their backs. It was their job to make his dreams, no matter how unlikely, come true. The Great Leap Forward was probably the first example of a turn toward madness: as it went on, the peasants suffered more and more, under growing pressure to produce more agriculturally than ever before, even as there were conflicting pressures for them to convert to a kind of primitive industrial base, as if there were to be a small foundry in every Chinese backyard. The Great Leap Forward was always more vision than reality. Figures on agricultural production were severely doctored to make the program look like a success. Almost everyone in the bureaucracy knew that it was largely a failure—the phrase that the distinguished Yale historian Jonathan Spence used was "catastrophic hardship"—but for a long time no one dared challenge Mao. The genuine independence of the rest of the Central Committee seemed in decline; the power and authority of Mao in a constant ascent. His will had become the national will; his truths were everyone's truths. He was never wrong. If he said that night was day, then night had become day.

Because his hold over the government was so complete, because his need to dominate every decision was so total, he forced anyone who was a potential critic or dissenter, no matter how essentially loyal, into the most dangerous role. Those who challenged him were not merely wrong, they could become, if the issue were serious enough, enemies of the people. Those who thought they were his friends and peers and old colleagues were, it turned out, badly mistaken; they were his friends and allies only as long as they agreed with him on all issues all the time. No one suffered more than one of his oldest allies, Marshal Peng. He was a simple man who had always known his limits and thus his place, a true Communist, a man who always deferred to Mao on politics. But Peng was also a proud man, every bit as confident of his sense of the peasants' welfare. Peng became a dissenter almost involuntarily—almost, it seemed, as if Mao wanted a break with him, wanted to turn on him and make him an enemy. By 1959, the early results of the Great Leap Forward were in and China was in the midst of a terrible famine. Yet ever higher agricultural yields were being reported. Almost every senior official understood this—that the chairman's Great Leap was buttressed by lies and falsified statistics, but no one dared take him on.

Finally Peng did. He was by then the minister of defense; as the Sino-Soviet split had become more serious, it was believed that he felt that it had gone too far. That in itself might have been a problem. But there had been no break with Mao. Peng's very simplicity, his lack of political instincts, his hard-won old-soldier truths were what involuntarily turned him into a rebel. In 1959, he returned to his boyhood region around Hunan and spoke with the local peasants, who were quite candid with him about their plight, and he discovered that there was a vast Potemkin Village arising in China, that the truth as envisioned by the country's highest officials and reported to them, and the truth as borne on the shoulders of its ordinary people, were completely different. Then, in the summer of 1959, six years after the end of the war, thinking he was a good member of the Party, almost surely not understanding the full consequences of what he was doing, thinking he would have some political allies because he had such powerful truths on his side, Peng went to a conference of the Party leadership at Lushan and there wrote a cautionary private letter to Mao about what he felt were some of the problems. The letter was filled with the obligatory references to all the successes they had gained, but it did contain a surprising number of cautionary warnings. Mao immediately reprinted it and made it available to everyone at the conference, changing the nature of the letter, and thereby casting Peng as an enemy of the government. With that, Peng had apparently played into Mao's hands—he asked for his letter back, but did not get it. Mao turned the letter into a frontal political challenge. Though almost everyone at the meeting agreed with him and knew the larger truth of what he had written, no one supported him publicly. As Jonathan Spence noted, "Mao . . . [treated] . . . Peng's well intentioned and confidential comments as tantamount to treason, but then when Mao circulated copies of the letter to the other senior members of the Communist Party, none of them came to Peng's support, even though most of them knew that the Marshal's analysis was correct. It was the ultimate act of political corruption. It meant that the Central Committee by then reflected the whims of Mao, no matter how mad, more than it did the needs and realities of China. Historians," Spence added, "now see this period as a turning point in the collapse of moral courage at the heart of the Party apparatus." In the next seven years, Spence noted, "more than 20 million Chinese died of famine." The madness had been not just legitimized, but institutionalized.

With that, the chairman called on Marshal Lin Biao, a longtime rival of Peng's, and asked him to appear at the conference and attack Peng. It was over for Peng—he was no longer defense minister; he was soon under house arrest; and as the Cultural Revolution eventually took place, starting in 1966, he became a familiar target, placed on stages in show-and-abuse theaters, where he was repeatedly attacked physically and verbally, humiliated as part of a vast national theater where he was supposed to confess his crimes. He was eventually beaten to death, a bitter payback for so many years of bravery and loyalty. One of the principal charges against him made by the Red Guards was that he had "opposed Chairman Mao all his life." When the Red Guards attacked and beat him, crushing his ribs and his lungs, often knocking him unconscious, he never bent. "I fear nothing," he would shout at his investigators. "You can shoot me. Your days are numbered. The more you interrogate, the firmer I'll become." By the time he died from his beatings, he had been interrogated 130 times. As Mao destroyed Peng, he destroyed much of what had been the best and most idealistic part of the Chinese revolution, turning his government in the process into one where only his own monomania could flourish.

BY THE BEGINNING of the twenty-first century, no society seemed more different from the South than North Korea. To the degree that there were successes in North Korea, they had been the very early ones, because it was from the start a completely totalitarian structure, imposed always from the top down, all done with a ruthless efficiency, enforced by a brutal security system imported from Moscow. That was a specialty of the Russians in those years: they might not do agriculture and housing or industrial development well, but they did state security extremely well; they were masters at creating authoritarian societies. Thus in the years immediately after World War II, while the Americans and the government in the South had struggled, often ineptly, displaying incompetence and inefficiency rather than skill and mastery—the Americans being new at the old game of having client states—the Russians in the North had seemed singularly efficient: it was what they did best. What to do in Korea after the war was something Washington had thought very little about, and the government they had installed in the South was corrupt and often inept. By contrast, despite a lack of deeply rooted legitimacy or any great popularity, the North Koreans displayed from the start a sense of purpose and an ability to control their population that was unnervingly efficient. If the Russians had begun the process, then Kim Il Sung continued it; others might mock him, but to the surprise of some of his early handlers, he turned out in time to be a shrewd student of modern totalitarianism, expert in the suppression of other men and their ideas and thoughts.

He was also an almost perfect reflection of a certain kind of Korean paranoia, of what the past, the war, and his country's colonial status had done to his generation and his country, made all the worse by his adaptation of the Soviet system. It was as if all possibilities for his people—political, economic, and social—were frozen by it. That paranoia would play as important a role in his own stewardship of the nation as any ideology—perhaps it was his true ideology, even though he would become one of Communism's sole surviving true believers. That he was so deft a survivor and player in the international Communist world surprised others: as tensions mounted between the Russians and the Chinese in the late 1950s and early 1960s, Kim seemed able to promise his hand and his favors alternately to both sides, playing them off against each other while limiting their hold on him (and his own dependence on either).

But those early successes were the rare ones, and they were always imposed downward from the top; the North was a land without debate and discussion, or finally, choice. It was a place where you learned how to salute and to obey; a world without any mechanism for change. As a society, North Korea was like a living organism that simply could not breathe and was always on a respirator; as it could not breathe, it could not grow. For societies to grow, they have to be able to develop both in the right way and sometimes in the wrong way, for there is no perfect journey—you learn as much from your mistakes as from your successes. But in the North there was no criticism, no wrong step; every step, because it had been taken by Kim Il Sung, was always the right one. As such the North soon became a model for a new kind of highly personalized, airless, Asian totalitarianism, a land without oxygen, even more totalitarian than Mao's China because China was so large that it was harder to control. In time, North Korea became one of the most xenophobic places in the world. As South Korea often seemed to bumble—veering back and forth from totalitarianism to what sometimes seemed like tiny increments of democracy, North Korea never stumbled—and that was its great sin. It remained frozen in a terrible monomania, a land with only one man whose thoughts could be acted on.

No political rivals were allowed to develop. Kim was the equal of Stalin in the art of purging his rivals. The only word that mattered was that of Kim Il Sung, and he was always right, which meant any alternative view of politics, economics, and agriculture was wrong. In the 1980s and 1990s, as both Russia and China began in different ways and in different degrees to adjust to moderating forces, Pyongyang grew ever more distant from them, unable to change and unable to adjust—because any change might mean a fall from power for Kim. As other Communist societies, once exceedingly fraternal to North Korea, began to change and were ventilated by new forces, North Korea if anything became more didactic and more rigid, more a prisoner of one-man rule than ever; the more other Communist nations changed, the more distrusting and self-isolating the North became, and the more convinced its leader was that he was alone and could trust no one.

It was as if he alone had fought every battle, won every victory in the struggle for North Korea's independence. The Chinese were furious when they visited the museum dedicated to the Korean War in Pyongyang and found what a tiny role they had played in saving their sister state; they were barely worthy of mention. At the same time, as a means of proving to his own population (and quite possibly himself) that his way was right and that the citizens of North Korea, despite famine and constant police procedures and an abysmal standard of living, were blessed in their good fortune, the cult of personality grew more profound, leading him past his former tutors, Stalin and Mao. A giant sixty-six-foot bronze statue of him stood in the center of the ninety-two-room Museum of the Revolution. The city also had an Arch of Triumph, even grander than the one in Paris; it celebrated Kim's return from Japan in 1945. It was a city—and a country—literally never absented by a likeness of him.

He was always referred to as the Great Leader. He had five great palaces, which no one else dared live in or use. All traffic stopped when he drove down one of Pyongyang's thoroughfares. His photo, and, in time, lest there be any mistake about the succession, that of his son, hung everywhere. Ordinary people somehow managed in their everyday dress to carry a photo of him on their jackets or tunics or dresses. By the later 1980s, according to Don Oberdorfer, who wrote about the two Koreas, there were at least thirty-four thousand monuments to Kim Il Sung in the North, not including park benches where he had once however briefly sat and which were thereafter covered with glass. Once asked by a Soviet official about what appeared to be the cult of personality in his nation, he had answered that it was simply part of the history of the land: "You don't know our country. Our country is used to paying respect to elders—like China and Japan, we live by Confucian culture."

His people starved, and the production from his factories was considered pathetic. He was from the start something of an international outlaw, trying to arrange the assassination of rivals in Seoul and kidnapping people from the South he felt could be helpful to his state. He seemed, as he aged, to have two main dreams, first to develop an atomic weapon of his own, and second, to name his son, Kim Jong Il, as his successor. Nothing reflected the growing change between his country and that of the South more than the ability to look at photos taken from above the two Koreas at night by satellite—the land below the thirty-eighth parallel alive with lights and commerce of all kinds, the land above the parallel blacked out, a kind of self-inflicted wasteland.

Kim had in the end created a nation in his own image, one without vitality and hope, taking an existing totalitarian system and, by dint of adding his skills and fears, strangling it. North Korea became more isolated all the time, outside the reach of even its former allies like China and Russia, and still hoping to create an atomic weapon so that then at least it could be a viable outlaw state.

OF THE SUCCESSES that America was responsible for in the post–World War II/Cold War era, what happened in South Korea was probably the most impressive and dramatic—ranking even above the success of the Marshall Plan, which had delivered financial aid, materiel, and technical assistance to European societies that had in the past been fully developed powerful societies but had been badly damaged physically by the war. Korea, by contrast, had little in the way of a democratic past and little in the way of a middle-class life or an industrial base. What was created there after the war was politically, economically, and in many ways socially strikingly new. Powerful, more advanced neighbors had systematically colonized and exploited Korea's people. Their talents had long been dormant. Certainly there had been foreign witnesses in the past, most of them missionaries, who had understood the vast potential of the Korean people, their hunger for a better life, their innate talents, their surpassing work ethic—right up there with that of the Japanese—their Confucian respect for education, and the way they had maximized what limited opportunities were available to them. But the peninsula's history—that is, its geography—had too often been bleak. There had always been a more powerful regional player, a nation on a power ascent of its own, eager to dominate Korea and to suppress its people. In the period immediately after World War II, the South had appeared to be headed for more of the same, with the Americans now a player, poorly prepared for an old colonial game, bumbling and fumbling, curiously ignorant of modern Korean history, quick to get many things wrong and to underestimate the possibilities of the future for Korea. The Americans hardly seemed an improvement on great powers who had been there in the past, other than that they seemed to know less about Korea's history than so many of their predecessors and existed at a far greater geographical distance, which might have been a plus. They helped impose on the South Syngman Rhee, a genuine patriot, but a man whose idea of a democratic society was one where he and his closest allies could do what they wanted, and everyone else should be watched.

But whatever else, the Americans were willing (because of their broad anti-Communism) to have their sons die on Korean soil, and they were not there as conquerors or, in the classic sense, imperialists. In time, as the Cold War became less intense, they were willing to adjust to some of the more democratic impulses taking place in the society, impulses often imported back from the United States by Koreans who had gone to America to study and had been affected by the freedoms they discovered there; many who had gone to study engineering had learned about both engineering and democracy.

So it was under the American aegis in the midst of the Cold War, which had so immediately followed a hot war, that South Korea was allowed to modernize, first militarily and then technologically and industrially, but not politically; that was not part of the original package. But then, in some thirty years,

in retrospect an amazingly quick turnaround, there was a startling democratization of the society, a surprising by-product of the other aspects of modernization. What happened in South Korea was an odd mix of revolution with
evolution, all taking place at an unusual rate of speed. It had begun with the
need, self-evident during the Korean War, for a better South Korean Army, and
that had to begin with better, more professional Korean officers. Too many of
the existing ones at the start of the war were hacks who held their positions out
of loyalty and willingness to play their part in the massive national corruption.
In 1952, under pressure from the Americans, a new military academy was in-
augurated, based to an uncommon degree on West Point. Many of the early
faculty members were American officers. The curriculum, like the one at West
Point, was tilted heavily toward engineering. Many of the country's most talented young students were sent there—and it became an instant source of
meritocratic talent, a place where a generation of talented young Koreans
could get a badly needed education and prove their worth, and break through
some of the social restraints of the past.

It was an early harbinger of a new, potentially more modern society. It was
probably the first step in creating what became in effect a new class in Korea, that
of modern, purposeful, increasingly well-educated young men who wanted to
bring a new definition of modernity to their country. The consequences of the
military school and its then critical role in the nation were greater than any of
its founders realized they might be: in effect the more the Army—and the
country—modernized technologically and economically, the more the old ways
were going to be seen as archaic and corrupt, and the less control that Rhee and
the men who eventually replaced him had over the country. And in some ways
the association of these students with their American teachers was fateful. The
American officers represented something new. Their body movement and language reflected two quite contradictory things—respect for the military hierarchy and yet a high degree of personal freedom within that same hierarchy.

It was the first critical step in the modernization of an educational, social,
and then economic, and finally political, order. As the military system was
modernized, so too were other colleges and universities; as the nation gained
in stature and talent and confidence, it began to want to be a player economically on the international scene, and that same engineering talent was put at
play there, a kind of state-guided, state-propelled capitalism. In some ways
it was not unlike a smaller Japan, although the victories in Korea were far
greater, because there had been an earlier precedent for some of Japan's economic successes, but little for those of Korea.

What happened in South Korea in the 1960s and 1970s was a fascinating human and societal story, a great lesson in the uses of adversity. The people who

ran the country, Rhee and the men around him, did so for some thirty years in a narrow and dictatorial manner, but even as they did and as they suppressed a series of student protests, the currents within the country for a better life were becoming more powerful. Economic success gradually begat an increasing social optimism and confidence, and in time a growing restlessness on the part of the population, manifest first among its students. That change was taking place in home after home, even as Rhee and the government thought they could do business as usual and that all the power in the society existed at the top. It was a case of a nation, surely not the first and surely not the last, changing in its expectations and aspirations without the hierarchy at the top understanding the new forces. When Rhee finally fell from power in April 1960, the chief of staff of the ROK Army said, "Personally, I respect Dr. Rhee. But history has turned him down, has scorned him and lost its trust in him. I, who saw the march of events, am sick inside about it."

In the background to all of this there was the leavening influence of the United States; in those early years the American government at the highest level, still deeply engaged in the Cold War, might have constantly tilted toward an authoritarian definition of Korean leadership, but there were other influences of America as well; many of the young Koreans had studied in the United States and discovered that you could be a loyal citizen and a free person at the same time, that loyalty to the state often had a built-in complexity to it that allowed you to disagree with the government's actions while still loving your country. So it was that South Korea, in small steps that few people understood at the time, and that no one planned or expected, stumbling toward a freer society, began the process in the late 1970s of serious democratization. More young Koreans were feeling more confident about their own abilities and lives and wanted greater increments of freedom to go with the greater increments of prosperity. The kind of talent and ambition that some of the early missionaries had spotted in another century—the capacity for hard work, the immense discipline, the desire for more education—were manifesting themselves on a national scale, and this had its own dynamic. Once the people of the South sensed the possibility of a better life, it was hard to slow them down.

The government tried for a time to suppress those forces, but it was overtaken by the very successes it had authored—the more successful the economy, the more confident ordinary Korean citizens felt about themselves, and the more they wanted to share, both economically and politically, in the fruits of their success. The government faced a crisis that it never really understood—in a sense a vast nationwide protest driven by rising expectations. At first the pressure for political liberalization came primarily from the universities and the students, but in time the labor unions joined up and ordinary citizens of the middle class followed them. "Korea by 1987 had irrevocably changed," said Gaston Sigur, who was assistant secretary of state for East Asia and the Pacific in the late 1980s. "The middle class had become a power. And it could no longer be disregarded. The government wasn't dealing with a handful of left-wing students. They may have been out in front, but it was plain that you had strong middle class support for the demonstrations." In a stunningly short time, South Korea had morphed itself into a dynamic, highly productive, extremely successful democracy. "I cannot think of another country, at least in recent history, that went so swiftly from an authoritarian system to a democracy on its own," a member of the party of Roh Tae Woo, a truly democratically elected president of Korea, once told Frank Gibney. In the South the great success had come because the top of the political hierarchy had been forced, no matter how reluctantly, to pay attention to the needs and aspirations of the bottom and middle of the society.

FOR THE AMERICANS and others who had fought there, who had more often than not felt the lack of recognition in their own country, and who had not particularly liked the country when they were there, the success of South Korea as a nation brought a sense of belated validation to their sacrifice, and the sacrifice of others who had not come home, and granted them a legitimacy and honor that they had not always felt.

So many of them had for so long kept it inside themselves. No one wanted to hear about the war when they had first come home, and so they never talked about it, not to their families or to their oldest friends. Or when they did, no one understood—or, worse, wanted to understand. Their children more often than not would grow up knowing only that their fathers had served in the war, but almost nothing else—which units they had been with and what battles they had fought in. They would complain about their fathers, that they were never willing to talk about the war.

It was all bottled up. What they had done and why they had done it were still important to them—they were proud of having gone, and proud also of how well they had done under dreadful conditions. They mourned those who had not come back, but they shared it only with one another. More than half a century later, this was still the defining experience in so many of their lives, and a number of them had become, in their own way, amateur historians. Late in life they wrote their own memoirs, sometimes privately published or simply Xeroxed and stapled together, done often somewhat belatedly at the urging of their children and grandchildren. A surprising number of them had, in effect, their own history rooms, with small libraries devoted to the Korean War, and with large maps of the country showing selected battle areas pinned to the walls. But the rooms, like so many of the experiences and the memories, were effectively closed off to outsiders. No one, save the others who had gone, had offered the proper respect for what they had done and why they did it back when it had mattered. It was as if a critical part of the experience, the validity of it as judged and valued by others, had been stolen from them.

They shared, then, this one great bond—that they could talk to one another and that those who had been there would always understand. They kept in touch by phone and letter, and then late in life by the magic of the Internet, a wonderful means as well of locating old buddies who had been lost in the shuffle of time. Their alumni associations were important, and they took their division and regimental newsletters seriously, as well as their annual conventions. Friendships were sustained, and sometimes new ones flowered between men who had been in adjoining units but had not known each other in Korea itself. At the reunions they gathered in small groups, often men who had been at a particular battle, summoning their pasts through the haze of half a century of memories. In the words of Dick Raybould, an artillery forward observer in the Ninth Regiment of the Second Division, "You go to the reunions and you find yourself trying to remember what you've spent the last fifty years trying to forget."

Gradually some of them began to go back to visit South Korea. At first it was something of a trickle, and then more of them went and came back and talked about it, and they went on organized tours with other veterans. They visited places where they had fought during the Naktong battles, and certain special battlefields, like Chipyongni. They did not visit the area around and above Kunuri and The Gauntlet, where the terrible defeat had first been inflicted on them, because that was the other side of the parallel and could not be visited. But they, many of whom had hated the country when they first served there, were impressed, first by the success of the country itself, its remarkable modernization, but also by the sense of gratitude that they felt on the part of the local people—far greater than anything bestowed on them in their native land. And they took pride in one additional thing: that if it had not been a victory in the classic sense, in some way what they had done had worked, because it was the crossing of an existing border in the Cold War; and because they had made their stand, it had not happened again.

Epilogue

AN IMMENSE AMOUNT of damage had been done to the Democratic Party by those years. There was a legacy from all this, a price still to be paid, and it was paid, first by the Democratic Party, and then in time by the country. There were many forces that had worked against the Truman administration at the end. It wasn't just the Korean War and the fall of China, it was something larger that was in the air, a mounting sense of fatigue with the Democrats, an exhaustion from a very difficult, grinding era, both international and domestic, with which they had tangled for too long. The Democrats by 1952 had, whatever their successes both economic and political, served for seven very hard postwar years, years in which both the administration and the nation were forced into a new kind of war that produced anxieties rather than victories. The Communists appeared likely to stand as an enemy in perpetuity. Americans, not surprisingly, wanted a change by 1952. But the lessons of that era were nonetheless haunting, and it was like a virus that got into the bloodstream of the Democratic Party, placing it perpetually on the defensive. For the Republicans had found their issue—they were in their rhetoric always tougher on the Communists. They sold their party as the one that would more eagerly stand up to Khrushchev or his successors. National security had changed: there was a genuine Communist threat out there, but measuring it accurately became more difficult because it was now so deeply entwined with domestic American politics. The Democrats were, in the decades that followed the 1950s, haunted by China as an issue, seemingly unable to answer the charges against them as they were put forth in the raw crucible of the political arena, unable to explain the complexity of what had happened so far away. China became their Achilles' heel. The larger question that arose from those years after the Korean War was soon ignored: whether or not America could separate serious and genuine national security concerns from the increasing power of simplistic anti-Communist rhetoric expressed in domestic political campaigns. Was the country wise enough to identify what was a real national security threat and what was not? And that quandary, because of the vulnerability of the Democratic Party, helped lead America into Vietnam. The successes of the Democrats in stabilizing Europe after World War II were largely ignored; they had, after all, seemingly failed on China.

In the years that followed the 1952 campaign, the Cold War deepened exponentially as a political issue, even as the outer limits in terms of real power alignments were largely settled. More, it was no longer just a struggle with the Soviets over Europe, a theater where the Russians were clearly the imperial power, imposing their will by force and inflicting their cruel little police states on unhappy satellite nations and where the United States was often identified with indigenous nationalism, a deep national longing for some form of Christian, democratic capitalism. Now the battlefield was perceived as spreading to the Third World. There indigenous forces were in the process of rising up against what had often been Western colonial or neocolonial regimes, often turning to the Communists for aid and weapons. The countries where these challenges were taking place were rarely in pure geopolitical terms terribly important or powerful, nothing that could shift the global balance; they were the kind of countries whose overall value George Kennan would have scoffed at in terms of realpolitik, and where he would have been sure there would be an inevitable conflict between Moscow and some local Communist government. The British, and in time the French, were learning that there was no upside to trying to sustain colonial relationships in this new era, and were pulling back, but now, somewhat to the surprise of its allies, America began to step in under the banner of anti-Communism.

Gradually even the Democratic Party made its adjustments to the changing political dynamic. By 1960 most of the contradictions of the era were reflected almost perfectly in Jack Kennedy, probably the party's most attractive young candidate. Kennedy was an intellectually superior, quite skeptical, uncommonly modern political figure. There was a certain iciness at his political core that suited him well in this new political age, framed as it was by nuclear weapons, and therefore one that demanded ice instead of fire in a leader. He seemed to embody little in the way of genuine political passion—other than to be a rational man, as if being a rational man would always be enough. This meant that Kennedy, more than any other Democrat of that era, came to represent the conflicting forces of the New Deal Democratic Party as it evolved into the era of the Cold War Democratic Party, a young man who at least on the surface took a harder line than the candidate who had preceded him, Adlai Stevenson. No longer would a Democratic candidate dare be accused of being soft on Communism. "Isn't he marvelous!" the ever hawkish columnist Joseph Alsop once said about Kennedy during the 1960 campaign, "a Stevenson with balls." In the 1960 election Kennedy and the Democrats, if anything, took a harder line on the subject of Fidel Castro, who had come to power in Cuba during the Eisenhower years, than did Kennedy's opponent, Richard Nixon. For Cuba by then had become the litmus test for a presidential macho index. (In the 1960 campaign Lyndon Johnson, the Democratic vice presidential candidate, had gone through the American South telling people at each stop that he would know how to deal with Castro: "First I'd wash him. Then I'd shave him. And then I'd spank him.") In that same campaign, Kennedy also accused the Republicans of creating a missile gap with the Soviets—thus showing that perhaps it was the *Republicans* who were soft on Communism, and at the same time, however involuntarily, feeding the nation's nuclear anxieties. His charge turned out to be true; there was a missile gap—the United States had two thousand and the Russians had only sixty-seven—but it kept the Republicans just a bit more on the defensive, and Khrushchev, delighted to look more powerful than he was, never corrected Kennedy.

Kennedy might have thought privately that our China policy, our insistence that Taiwan was China, was a quaint kind of irrationality, a sentiment he was willing to express with some of his more liberal aides, but he was not about to take any political risk to change it, at least not in his first term. He could be stunningly candid about these things in private, for personal candor was part of his charm and added considerably to his reputation as a realist. But Kennedy's candor was always a *private*, rather than a public thing. Because of that, those exposed to his private side liked him even more, and saw him not as being timid, but instead as being realistic. After the election, he told those liberal advisers to whom he had earlier seemed to promise a new policy on China that he could not talk about China for the present. Perhaps in the second term . . . So much, it was clear, was going to have to wait for the second term.

Instead his administration was embattled—indeed on the defensive— from the start. The margin of victory over Nixon was paper thin, barely a hundred thousand votes. Then the administration, hoisted on its own petard, went along with a bizarre CIA plan to support Cuban rebels who wanted to take the country back from Castro by landing them on Cuban beaches. The Bay of Pigs plan, run by the CIA not the military, with Kennedy cutting back some of the air cover, failed miserably and predictably. In political terms, Kennedy was seriously wounded by its failure, more on the defensive now than before. At a meeting with Khrushchev in Vienna two months later, the Soviet leader, mistaking the Bay of Pigs escapade for a sign of Kennedy's larger weaknesses, decided to bully him. The only place where the West and the Communists were fighting with real bullets was Vietnam, and as a means of showing Khrushchev that he was made of sterner stuff, Kennedy decided to up the ante there.

There was, however, a great unanswered issue about Vietnam—if the Democrats could not deal with China, which their party had been accused of losing, how could they avoid the same pitfalls in Vietnam? The question went unanswered because it went unasked. In the administration no one even discussed China. That Vietnam might now become their China and they would be blamed for losing it to the Communists was a far more immediate question for them. So a line was to be drawn there. Their policy on China was one of essential silence. Yet China and Vietnam were two parts of the same issue. Of the two countries, China was the done deal—a policy that was deceased—the other, Vietnam, was a work in progress, or perhaps more properly, a tragedy in the making. They were tied to each other by the same political forces: one could not deal with the real challenge of the Communist-nationalist forces in Vietnam, because one could not deal with the issue of why those same forces had won in China. The people who did not want the Americans to lose Vietnam, another Asian country that had never been theirs, were largely the same people who had already frozen U.S. China policy. The new administration, so filled with confidence about changing what it considered outmoded Dulles policies, decided to lay off the most outmoded one of all and continue the fight to keep Communist China out of the UN. On China, Kennedy was, said the prominent China expert Allen Whiting, who served in that administration, "a profile in caution."

Typically, at his home in Hyannis Port in the summer of 1961, Kennedy met with Adlai Stevenson, by then his UN ambassador; Harlan Cleveland, the assistant secretary of state for international organizations; and Arthur Schlesinger, his aide and historian. When they got to the subject of China, and the president's desire to keep Mao's China out of the UN for the foreseeable future, Kennedy, sensing the moment had arrived to strengthen everyone's resolve just a bit, immediately called out to his wife, "Jackie, we need the Bloody Marys now." He wanted, he told a dubious Stevenson, to buy at least one more year before dealing with China. That year soon stretched on.

At a meeting a few weeks later, with Stevenson, Schlesinger, McGeorge Bundy, his chief national security aide, and Ted Sorensen, his top domestic adviser and principal speechwriter, the subject of China came up again. Stevenson, Kennedy said, was in a terrible position, one of keeping the real China out of the UN. "You have the hardest thing in the world to sell. It really doesn't make any sense—the idea that Taiwan represents China. But, if we lose this fight, if Red China comes into the UN our first year in town, your first year and mine, they'll run us both out. We have to lick them this year. We'll take our chances next year. It will be an election year; but we can delay the admission of Red China until after the election. So far as this year is concerned you have to

do everything you can to keep them out. Whatever is required is okay by me."
Stevenson asked if the blockage was to be for one year or more permanently.
At least for a year, Kennedy answered. He himself was going to make clear to
Chiang Kai-shek that he could not make the issue of China at the UN a domestic political issue. And then he offered a curiously innocent description of
how he was going to get a group of China Firsters—Harry Luce, Walter Judd,
and Roy Howard—and bring them around on the issue. Anyone listening to
him at that point, knowing how passionate these other men were on the subject of Chiang, and how little connection they felt to Kennedy's own election,
might have wondered if his normally cool, realistic appraisal of political forces
had completely deserted him. Changing their position on Chiang was not
something those men were likely to do because of a friendly presidential
phone call. John Kennedy at that point was the most rational of men, carrying
on the most irrational of policies.

In the late fall of 1961, Kennedy decided to up the ante in the ongoing but
still relatively low-key guerrilla war in Vietnam. At the time there were only six
hundred American advisers in South Vietnam. His was the most dangerous of
moves geopolitically even if at first it was a limited commitment of advisory
and support troops, totaling perhaps some seventeen thousand additional
Americans by early 1963. The Kennedy escalation meant that even if the commitment was in the beginning relatively small, nonetheless the flag had been
planted ever more deeply and planted in a country and a war where the United
States did not by itself control the dynamic and where the forces gathering
against the American proxy were driven by a deep historic dynamic. It was
America, because it was great and mighty and rich, believing it was in control
of events but following a path over which it would have less and less control; in
effect it was following the French path. "The Americans are walking in the
same footsteps as the French," said the journalist-historian Bernard Fall, who
was eventually killed there, "but dreaming different dreams."

The Kennedy commitment in Vietnam was more than anything else driven
by domestic politics. As he could not deal with China in his first term, he could
not afford to lose another country—one where there was an actual shooting
war taking place. Saving South Vietnam from Communism, though it became
the rallying banner for an ever increased American presence, was always peripheral. It was much more about a Democratic administration not wanting to
be driven out of Washington. Nothing reflected the change caused in American domestic politics by the Cold War more than the increasing escalation of
the Vietnam War. The wartime America that had been against any colonial
presence was frailer, that vision replaced by the new anti-Communism. Dean
Acheson, now a Democratic foreign policy elder statesman, a traditionalist

and a man of Europe anyway, and now badly wounded in the struggle over the fall of China, had become in this new era, on this derivative issue, one of the leading hard-liners. Some of his old colleagues from the Truman days were shocked by his hawkishness. George Elsey, one of Truman's top White House aides, would say years later, "The one thing I can't forgive about Dean is how he switched sides on Vietnam—he who should have known so much why it wouldn't work became all too much like the right wingers who had criticized him all those years." Acheson became ever more hostile to what he considered the soft-liners in the administration, men like Stevenson, Chester Bowles, and Kennan. It was almost as if he made a practice of taunting his old colleague Kennan in that period, as the political distance between them seemed to widen. When Kennan was named ambassador to Yugoslavia by Kennedy, Acheson told friends in an uncommonly cruel remark, "Tito is going to have a field day playing with poor George's marshmallow mind."

In addition, the Kennedy administration had done something extremely dangerous when it increased the larger mission to Vietnam; it corrupted the truth to suit its political needs for short-term political profit—in effect buying time to get through to the 1964 election. Because in the process it planted the flag ever more deeply, it needed ever greater results, for appearances were everything, and it needed them faster. But those results were not forthcoming, because the policy never worked. Never. Therefore, to compensate for the failure to produce the desired results in the field, the Kennedy administration soon created something quite extraordinary—a giant lying machine, one based in Washington, with its major affiliate in Saigon, a machine that not only systematically rejected all pessimistic reports from the field, and punished those who tried to tell the truth, but created its own illusion of victories and successes, victories and successes that never existed. It was a great exercise in self-deception: what the great lying machine did in that period was delay the arrival of the truth in Washington by some three years, and of course it also began the process of diminishing the credibility of the government of the United States. What was lost in those three years was the ability to make wiser judgments about whether the commitment worked. In November 1963 John Kennedy was assassinated.

There would be no second term during which he could think about crossing the fail-safe point of sending combat troops. As his predecessors had left him with an immense burden in the existing policy on China, now he left his successor a policy that was an immense trap in Vietnam. Kennedy had always retained his mordant sense of humor. One day when he came out of an NSC meeting in which they had discussed some disastrous problem handed down to them by previous administrations, he said, "Oh well, think of what we'll pass on to the poor fellow who comes after me."

The poor fellow who followed, whom no one had ever thought of as a poor fellow, most especially those who had been run over by him in the past, or at the very least had their shoulders massaged and ended up voting on the side of an issue that they had not intended to vote on, was Lyndon Johnson, and the gift the Kennedy administration passed on was Vietnam, where by the fall of 1963 the Viet Cong had virtually won the war. The United States had spent three years making Vietnam seem more important in terms of geopolitics than the Washington authorities privately believed it was. By the time Johnson arrived, part of the rationale for the Americans doing what they were doing there was that they were already doing it, and not to continue to do it, in the cancerous way that these things feed on themselves, would weaken the United States elsewhere. Each cynical speech by some American official over the previous three years about how well the Americans were doing and how important Vietnam was became the rationale for the investment of more American bodies in a war that could not be won.

LYNDON JOHNSON WAS, by contrast, a very different president from Kennedy, and whereas Kennedy had (privately) made distinctions between hard Communism in Europe and Communist-nationalism in the Third World, Johnson made few comparable distinctions in the Communist world, and he left less room for serious doubt among the men surrounding him. The rest of the world was for him a much more distant place than it had been to Kennedy. If Johnson came out of the 1964 election with a landslide, he intended to use his accumulated power as quickly as he could on domestic issues, not, as Kennedy would have, on foreign ones. Foreign policy had never interested him greatly unless it impinged directly on domestic policy. As Philip Geyelin, one of the best of the Washington foreign policy analysts, wrote prophetically in 1965, as he measured the approaching collision of Johnson and the world, "The point is that Lyndon Johnson never was really interested [in the world] except as a practical need to be arose."

Lyndon Johnson knew nothing of the subtle strength of this small but fierce country, still fourth-rate to him, how it had managed to hold off mighty China in the past and defeat mighty France so recently. Yet in Vietnam history was fate. The men and women on the other side were the same people who had driven the French out, the heroes of the revolution, a revolution the United States chose not to see as a revolution; comparably, most of the top people in the South Vietnamese Army, fighting as it were on the pro-Western side, had also fought alongside the French during a revolutionary war. The other side's leaders were skilled, brave, and had their form of political-military tactics, very similar to those of Mao and his compatriots, down pat. No one who had

fought them would ever underestimate either their ability or their patience—
only powerful men in Washington who had no experience in this new kind of
war would mock them for their lack of traditional battlefield organization. In
the early war games that the top Americans had played back in Washington—
a group on one side playing for Hanoi, their rivals playing for America, each
making countermoves against the other—it always turned out that Hanoi had
more options than the United States did, and could keep coming without paying an exorbitant price. In time they stopped playing the war games because
they always ended so badly.

In 1964, as Johnson edged closer to the final decision on the war, there were
three factors that tended to make him hawkish. The first was the nature of the
man himself, his own image of himself, the need to stand tall, not to back off
when he was challenged, and to personalize all confrontations and to see them as
a test of manhood. Pierre Salinger's job, Johnson told the principal Kennedy
press officer when he first became president, was to sell Johnson as a big Texan
who was both tall and tough in the saddle. Of a rebel leader in the Dominican
Republic Johnson had told McGeorge Bundy, "Tell that son of a bitch that unlike
the young man who came before me I am not afraid to use what's on my hip."

The second factor was an innate, almost unconscious American racism, the
kind that had bedeviled so many officers in the field at the beginning of the
Korean War, the notion that because Asians were smaller and from a lesser
part of the world with lesser industrial and technological accomplishments,
they were a lesser people and could not stand up to American technology and
American troops. Certainly miscalculations of that kind had been costly in
Korea, at the very beginning of the war, when everyone had underestimated
the ability of the North Korean troops, and even more later on, when
MacArthur had miscalculated what the Chinese would do and how well they
would fight. Vietnam, when Johnson spoke about it at NSC meetings, was often "a raggedy ass little fourth rate country." On occasion, like Ned Almond, he
used the word "laundrymen" to describe the combatants.

Sometimes too, as he came close to the final decision on whether to send
combat troops to Vietnam, Johnson's racism showed in the way he spoke of
the Vietnamese as being like Mexicans, the kind of lesser people you had to
show some strength to before they got the message and gave you the respect
you deserved. The Vietnamese, he would say, were not going to push Lyndon
Johnson around, because he knew something about people like this, because
back home he had dealt with people just like them, the Mexicans. Now, Mexicans were all right if you let them know who was boss, but "if you didn't watch
they'll come right into your yard and take it over if you let them. And the next
day they'll be right there on your porch, barefoot and weighing one hundred

and thirty pounds, and they'll take that too. But if you say to 'em right at the start, 'Hold on, just wait a minute,' they'll know they're dealing with someone who'll stand up. And after that you can get along fine."

And finally, and probably most important of all, there was the politics of it, because he was *always* a political man. That was what mattered most, and this time he got the politics wrong—he went to the politics of the past, not the future as it might have been if he had kept us out. Beneficiary of a landslide victory over a seemingly much harder line candidate, Barry Goldwater (in part because he had said he would not send American boys to do what Asian boys should do for themselves), Johnson misread the politics of his own victory. His sense of the war's politics and the price of losing Saigon led him back to the fall of China and to the ferocious political forces that had been unleashed domestically. Johnson was immensely sensitive to those forces, because they had been unusually important in the two places he knew best: Washington, where he had seen senators who opposed Joe McCarthy destroyed, and Texas, where the local McCarthyism had been unusually virulent and very well financed by oil interests. It was in Texas, where, as Johnson made the mutation from liberal New Deal congressman to U.S. senator, he had gradually become politically closer and quite dependent upon some of the same powerful right-wing figures, the men of oil who had backed McCarthy.

China weighed heavily on him as he made his ultimate Vietnam decisions. He talked about it all the time. In private he would often go on about how China had destroyed the Democratic Party back in the early 1950s, and how the country might be engulfed in a resurgence of McCarthyism if Vietnam went under. Truman and Acheson had lost China, he would say, and it was like a mantra, and when they lost China they lost the Congress, because the Republicans in the Congress had finally found their issue. When he was alone in private moments with close friends and assistants like Bill Moyers and George Reedy, it would all pour out, his fear of losing what he prized most, the Great Society, which would be his signature accomplishment as president, losing it because he had been weak on Vietnam.

He had been there the last time it happened, he would say. Hell, he would add, Truman and Acheson had even been accused of appeasement, could you believe that? "You boys are young," he told Moyers and some of the other young men, "and you don't understand the connection of the Congress to Asia. They won't give me the Great Society and Civil Rights if Ho is running through the streets of Saigon." The Congress, he said, did not care about that kind of legislation. "They'll push Vietnam up my ass all the time. Vietnam, Vietnam, Vietnam. Right up my ass." He was, Moyers thought, far more than

Kennedy, caught in the recent past. He did not see the country as changing, especially as Kennedy had in the final few weeks of his life, which gave Kennedy a sense that peace might now be an issue. Oddly enough Johnson did not think the American people wanted the war, but he did not know how to get around the political system in Washington, which he thought did. He did not see the possibility that easing tensions in the Cold War at that moment might have new political benefits, or that the country might be changing, and a new generation, less a prisoner of the worst of the Cold War tensions, emerging.

What he did not see and could not see, in no small part because in the end there was a large part of him that was a bully, was that on the eve of battle with the forces of North Vietnam in 1965, America's military and political strengths were on the surface, in some ways self-evidently awesome, while its weaknesses for a war like this were hidden away. Those weaknesses were basic; America's inability to adjust to a distant war that was more political than military, its innate impatience, and the inability of its troops to become *Vietnamese* were far greater than any policy maker realized. Comparably the Vietnamese weaknesses were on the surface, and were self-evidently considerable—their lack of a great deal of modern military hardware—but their strengths were formidable, just beneath the surface. Those strengths were in their own way for this kind of war far greater than America's, because in the end it was their country.

SERGEANT PAUL MCGEE got out of the Army in June 1952, a little more than a year after he had held off the Chinese at McGee Hill on the south side of Chipyongni. McGee had wanted to stay in, because he liked the Army, and felt that he was a good and perhaps even a skillful soldier, but he was forced to take a hardship discharge to help out his family back in North Carolina. His father had started a small machine shop where he repaired parts for the machines used in the cotton mills, but then his father's health had slipped badly, and Paul was needed at home. When he had fought in Korea he had never had any doubts that he was doing the right thing. He had volunteered for it, and even during the worst of the battle of Chipyongni he did not doubt the decisions that had brought him there. The ensuing half century did not change his mind. It had not been a popular war, he thought, and most of the country seemed to have forgotten about it long ago. But it mattered to him and some of his friends who had also fought there, and he thought that they had done the right thing, and it had been worth it for all the hardship and the loss of life. He thought the fact that the Communists had not tried anything like Korea again showed that America had been right in fighting there. He had missed being in the Army when he came back to Belmont, and on occasion in those years after Korea, the Army seemed to miss him; sometimes it sent recruiters down to see how he was getting along, and to see if he had any second thoughts about coming back in. When they were trying to start the Special Forces at nearby Fort Bragg in the late 1950s, someone had looked at his records and decided he would make an ideal Green Beret, and they had put a good deal of pressure on him, but his family obligations outweighed his personal feelings that it was exactly the right kind of job for him. If he had gone back in he might have gotten a third war, he thought, the one in Vietnam, and he wondered if he would have made it back from Vietnam.

He did not know anyone who had gone to Korea who felt differently about that war. He was on occasion filled with sadness when he thought of the men he had known there who had not made it back. Sergeant Bill Kluttz, his buddy from that battle, had died recently, and they had stayed close to the end. McGee did not go to many of the veterans reunions anymore because the men were all getting older and fewer, and fewer of them were able to attend, and it made him sadder when he showed up and the ranks had thinned. He was still in touch with Cletis Inmon, who had been his runner up on McGee Hill, and they talked about once a month. They were able to communicate in those phone calls without actually saying things—he knew what Inmon was thinking when they were on the phone together, without many words passing between them—they had been there, had shared those dangers, and that set them apart from almost everyone else for the rest of their lives. They did not need words to bind them together; their deeds were the requisite bond. All in all, he thought, he was glad he had gone and fought there. It was a job to do, nothing more, nothing less, and when you thought about it, there had not been a lot of choice.

Author's Note

IN A WAY, the roots of this book go back to a series of long conversations I had in 1963 with Lieutenant Colonel Fred Ladd. He was the senior adviser to the ARVN (or South Vietnamese) Ninth Division, based in Bac Lieu, in the middle of the Mekong Delta, and was one of my favorite officers. We stayed friends until his untimely death in 1987 at the age of 67. Fred Ladd was a general's son, a West Point graduate, a thoughtful, brave man of great honor. Once when his Vietnamese counterpart, the division commander, had given a very rosy-eyed portrait of how well the division was doing to a group of senior American officers, Fred had taken the American commander in Vietnam, General Paul Harkins, aside to tell him that things were not going nearly that well. For that bit of honesty he was sharply rebuked by Harkins for casting aspersions on a fine Vietnamese officer's words. In a way, Vietnam became a great roadblock in Fred's career, and he could never reconcile himself to reporting optimistically about a war that was being lost.

Vietnam was, of course, the obsessive subject matter at hand, but as we got to know each other we talked more and more about the Korean War, where he had also served, with gathering interest on my part. It was only thirteen years since the Chinese had entered that war, and Fred spoke often of the tragic quality of a war, almost over, that had suddenly become infinitely larger and more violent as they came across the Yalu and caught most of the American units by surprise. He had been a general's aide at the time, ironically to Major General Ned Almond, who is a prominent figure in this book. He spoke cautiously about Almond in those sessions, a discretion that was a compromise, I suspect, between high personal loyalty and considerable professional reservations. What I do remember from our talks was the terrible ordeal of the troops, some of the men only a year or two older than I was (I was sixteen when the Korean War started), caught in that freezing cold by this massive attack, surely the largest ambush in American military history. During those sessions in Bac Lieu and when Fred stayed with me at my house in Saigon, we went over the subject of those days again and again. What I did not realize at the time was that he was the teacher and I was the student, and the subject was not just Vietnam; it now included Korea as well.

The images of that moment, when the Chinese struck, stayed with me. As when I had returned from Vietnam and I had needed to find out what had happened there and why, and thereupon had written *The Best and the Brightest*, I remained haunted by the images I had created in my own mind of those weeks in November and December 1950, and I was determined to write about it one day. Now, forty-four years after I first heard Fred Ladd's stories, here is the book.

A book like this does not have a simple, preordained linear life. A writer begins with a certainty that the subject is important, but the book has an orbital drive of its own—it takes you on its own journey, and you learn along the way. It became not just the story of the Chinese entering the war and what happened in those critical weeks. On the way there was a great deal of political history to be learned, all of which formed the background on both sides. And there were other battles to be studied—people kept telling me about the brutal fighting in the early Pusan Perimeter days, and so I had to learn about that. And then one day someone mentioned the Battle of Chipyongni to me—the battle where the American commanders first learned how to fight the Chinese.

When I began *The Best and the Brightest* in 1969 it was a much easier book for me. Vietnam had been a central, dominating part of my life for seven years by that time. Thus I knew to an uncommon degree the overall map of it, the players, and the essential chronology. That was not true for me with Korea. So I spent much of the first two years not merely reading the existing bibliography and interviewing people but getting a feel for what had happened. I had very good teachers—most of them combat infantrymen who had survived it all. I am grateful for the kindnesses and courtesies extended to me by so many men and so many families in the homes I visited. To those whom I visited and interviewed, but whose stories did not make the book, I offer my regrets but my thanks, because all the interviews helped shape my sense of the war. I found many of the senior officials in the Korean Veterans' groups, especially those of the Second Infantry Division, to be exceptionally helpful in guiding me toward veterans of those battles in which I was especially interested, or which they felt I had to master.

One of the great pleasures of what I do comes from the constant sense of surprise of the reporting—how many people turn out during the interviews to give more than you expected and thus enhance the entire experience. That forms something I particularly prize in what has been a fifty-two-year journalistic career: a respect for the nobility of ordinary people.

One story will suffice along this line. When I was working on the book a number of people had suggested that I interview a man named Paul McGee who lived on the outskirts of Charlotte, North Carolina. I called him. The first call, the introductory one, was not a great success. He did not seem very enthusiastic about seeing me. But we made a date to get together on a Saturday, which was to be my getaway day after a week on the road. That had been a particularly hard week—five interviews in five days in five different North Carolina towns. On the morning of my scheduled visit with McGee it snowed heavily in Charlotte—a truly miserable day. My plane back to New York was scheduled for 3 P.M. I was staying at an airport motel. The temptation to bag the McGee interview and take an earlier flight was overwhelming; then I thought again, why not see him? I had come all this way and this was what I get paid to do. So I went out and found his home and for four hours it all poured out, what had happened in those three days at Chipyongni when he was a young platoon leader. It was if he had been waiting for me to come by for fifty-five years, and he remembered everything as if it had been yesterday. He was modest, thoughtful, and had total recall. The story of how his platoon had held out for so long came out in exceptional detail, along with the names and phone numbers of a few men who had made it out with him and who could confirm all the details. It was a thrilling morning for me, nothing less than a reminder of why I do what I do.

Acknowledgments

BECAUSE OF THE nature of this book, events that took place more than fifty years ago, my interviewing was different this time than for most of my books: fewer total interviews, but a great deal more time spent trying to decide which battles mattered and only then finding the varying surviving veterans. That meant I spent more time trying to figure out which veterans to interview; and when I did find what I thought were the right people, going back repeatedly to them. Here is the list of interviewees (I am not using military rank because in many cases the rank kept changing): George Allen, Jack Baird, Lucius Battle, Lee Beahler, Bin Yu, Martin Blumenson, Ben Boyd, Alan Brinkley, Josiah Bunting III, John Carley, Herschel Chapman, Chen Jian, Joe Christopher, Joe Clemons, J. D. Coleman, John Cook, Bruce Cumings, Bob Curtis, Rusty Davidson, James Ditton, Erwin Ehler, John S. D. Eisenhower, George Elsey, Hank Emerson, Larry Farnum, Maurice Fenderson, Leonard Ferrell, Al Fern, Thomas Fergusson, Bill Fiedler, Richard Fockler, Barbara Thompson Foltz, Dorothy Bartholdi Frank, Lynn Freeman, Joe Fromm, Les Gelb, Alex Gibney, Frank Gibney, Andy Goodpaster, Joe Goulden, Steve Gray, Lu Gregg, Dick Gruenther, David Hackworth, Alexander Haig, Dr. Robert Hall, Ken Hamburger, Butch Hammel, John Hart, Jesse Haskins, Charles Hayward, Charley Heath, Virginia Heath, Ken Hechler, Wilson Heefner, Jim Hinton, Carolyn Hockley, Ralph Hockley, Cletis Inmon, Raymond Jennings, George Johnson, Alan Jones, Arthur Junot, Robert Kies, Walter Killilae, Bob Kingston, Bill Latham, Jim Lawrence, John Lewis, James Lilley, Malcolm MacDonald, Sam Mace, Charley Main, Al Makkay, Joe Marez, Brad Martin, John Martin, Filmore McAbee, Bill McCaffrey, David McCullough, Terry McDaniel, Paul McGee, Glenn McGuyer, Anne Sewell Freeman McLeod, Roy McLeod, Tom Mellen, Herbert Miller, Allan Millett, Jack Murphy, Bob Myers, Bob Nehrling, Clemmons Nelson, Paul O'Dowd, Phil Peterson, Gino Piazza, Sherman Pratt, Hewlett Rainier, Dick Raybould, Andrew Reyna, Berry Rhoden, Bill Richardson, Bruce Ritter, Arden Rowley, Ed Rowny, George Russell, Walter Russell, Perry Sager, Arthur Schlesinger, Jr., Bob Shaffer, Edwin Simmons, Jack

Singlaub, Bill Steinberg, Joe Stryker, Carleton Swift, Gene Takahashi, Billie Tinkle, Bill Train, Layton (Joe) Tyner, Lester Urban, Sam Walker, Kathryn Weathersby, Bill West, Vaughn West, Allen Whiting, Laron Wilson, Frank Wisner, Jr., Harris Wofford, Hawk Wood, John Yates, and Alarich Zacherle.

In addition, there are a number of interviews I did for earlier books, which connect directly in this one, including the aforementioned long talks with Fred Ladd, and interviews and talks with Homer Bigart, the legendary *Herald Tribune* and *New York Times* reporter, a close friend and my predecessor in Vietnam, Walton Butterworth, Averell Harriman, Townsend Hoopes, Murray Kempton (another close friend), Bill Moyers, George Reedy, James Reston (my original sponsor at the *New York Times*), Arthur Schlesinger, Jr., John Carter Vincent, and Theodore White, another good friend. In addition, when I wrote *The Best and the Brightest,* I became friendly with General Matthew Ridgway. He quite liked the book (in no small part because he was one of its rare heroes) and we stayed in touch. Late in his life, around, I think, 1988, we had a series of telephone calls, and during one of them he began talking about doing another book about the Korean War. He was clearly dissatisfied with parts of his earlier book, perhaps goaded by Dean Acheson, who had in a somewhat friendly way in a letter suggested that Ridgway had pulled his punches in describing his view of MacArthur's behavior in those days. I think he was also stung by MacArthur's own subsequent criticism of Ridgway's conduct of the war. At this point his voice changed somewhat, and he became edgier and sharper of tone. He also started free-associating over the phone about the reasons he believed MacArthur had gone so far north, and in particular, why he had split the command—to diminish, Ridgway said, the influence and independence of General Walker and particularly the Joint Chiefs, to make Walker compete with Almond, who was completely under MacArthur's control. It was really aimed at the Joint Chiefs, he said; and as his forces moved north it shifted ultimate power and control of the mission to Tokyo from Washington and Korea itself. He was also very critical—almost bitter in tone, I thought—about how completely removed the Tokyo command was from the reality of the battlefield, and the failure of Tokyo to understand what it was subjecting American soldiers to. As he continued to talk I took rough if imperfect notes and later consolidated them. There was the suggestion in that conversation that perhaps he would do another book and might want to do it with me. When a few weeks later I called back to see where his thinking was, he had pulled back from the idea of a book. He was, he said, in his early nineties (he was born in 1895), and it was more work than he wanted. But some of that conversation is reflected in this book.

*   *   *

I AM INDEBTED to a great many people for their help with this book, starting with the men of the Second Infantry Division, especially the officers of their Korean War alumni association, and particularly Chuck Hayward, Charley Heath, and Ralph Hockley. From the First Cav, Joe Christopher was exceptionally helpful in connecting me with men who fought and survived Unsan. Edwin Simmons went out of his way to assist me with access to the First Marines and helping me find men like Jim Lawrence, who were unusually knowledgeable about O. P. Smith.

I want to thank others who helped me: Tom Engelhart, who edited the book, which given its complexity was never an easy process; Ben Skinner, a talented young writer in his own right, who did additional research for me on the American decision to cross the thirty-eighth parallel and head north; and my neighbor Linda Drogin, who volunteered on this book as in the past to do some vital checking for me. I would also like to thank my friend Joe Goulden, who not only wrote one of the best and most penetrating books on the Korean War but was a source of constant assistance and encouragement to me. I want to mention the scholars of the Cold War International History Project of the Woodrow Wilson Center in Washington, and in particular Kathryn Weathersby, for their help in this book—the Center is a remarkable source of new information on areas long closed off to Westerners.

I was welcomed and treated with uncommon kindness at a number of libraries. From the U.S. Army Military History Institute at Carlisle, Pennsylvania, Dr. Richard Sommers, chief of patron services, as well as Michael Monahan, Richard Baker, Randy Hackenburg, and Pamela Cheney; from the Marines, known properly as the History Division of the Marine Corps University, Dr. Fred Allison, Danny Crawford, and Richard Camp; at the Douglas MacArthur Archives in Norfolk, Virginia, James Zobel was exceptionally helpful; at the Harry Truman Library, Michael Devine, the director, Liz Safly, Amy Williams, and Randy Sowell; at the Lyndon Johnson Library, Betty Sue Flowers; from the Franklin Roosevelt Library, Alycia Vivona, Robert Clark, the supervisory archivist, Karen Anson, Matt Hanson, Virginia Lewick, and Mark Renovitch; and from the New York Public Library, Wayne Furman, David Smith, and my friend Jean Strouse. At the Council on Foreign Relations, Lee Gusts was generous and helpful. As ever, the entire staff of the New York Society Library was helpful and helped create what is an oasis for me and other writers in the city.

At Hyperion Bob Miller and Will Schwalbe had faith in this book and its value from the start and stayed with me, even though, like most books, it came in somewhat behind schedule. Others at Hyperion for whose support I am grateful are Ellen Archer, Jane Comins, Claire McKean, Fritz Metsch, Emily

Gould, Brendan Duffy, Beth Gebhard, Katie Wainwright, Charlie Davidson, Vincent Stanley, Rick Willett, Chisomo Kalinga, Sarah Rucker, Maha Khalil, and Jill Sansone, and from HarperCollins, my old friend of more than thirty years, Jane Becker Friedman. I am grateful for the help of my friends and lawyer-agents, Marty Garbus and Bob Solomon. My friend Carolyn Parqueth once again transcribed most of the interviews. Charles Roos is my computer expert and he saved me from crisis after crisis—on those terrible days when my manuscript seemed to have departed my computer.

No one who sets off to do a book like this is ever the first; someone has always been there before, and we in this business are always aware of those who went before us and our debt to them, especially when the events took place more than fifty years ago. So it should be noted that among the books listed in the Bibliography, certain books were truly essential, most notably Clay Blair's encyclopedic *The Forgotten War*, the most important primer for anyone dealing with Korea; William Manchester's *American Caesar*; the books of Roy Appleman; S. L. A. Marshall's *The River and the Gauntlet*; Joe Goulden's *Korea*; Max Hastings' *The Korean War*; and Martin Russ's *Breakout*. *Uncertain Partners*, the book by John Lewis, Sergei Goncharov, and Xue Litai about the relationship between Stalin, Mao, and Kim, is a groundbreaking work, its value greatly enhanced by my own long conversation with Professor Lewis. My friend Les Gelb, until recently the head of the Council on Foreign Relations, was as ever a wise consultant and a thoughtful ally.

My two friends Lieutenant General Hal Moore (who commanded a company in Korea) and Joe Galloway, who together wrote what I consider the best book on combat in Vietnam, *We Were Soldiers Once . . . and Young*, were not only constantly supportive but gave me valuable guidance. In addition my friend Scott Moyers, who has been uncommonly helpful in my work for more than a decade, kept an eye on me and helped me out when I was struggling with the manuscript. I want to acknowledge my immense admiration for the esteemed photographer David Douglas Duncan, who came out of Chosin with the First Marines and is revered by them for that alone. With his remarkable photographs he has been able to remind us of what all those men went through in those days; I am proud that he was willing to let me use one of his photographs for the jacket of the book—it's a badge of honor.

Afterword

by RUSSELL BAKER

David Halberstam had put the finishing touches on *The Coldest Winter* in the spring of 2007, just five days before his death in a car accident in California. He had essentially finished the book months earlier, but with a book there is finishing, and then a little more finishing, and then a final finishing, and after months of revising, checking and rechecking, slashing, inserting, and wrestling with endless pages of manuscript and printed proofs, he stopped by his publisher's office on an April Wednesday and dropped off his final corrections. This was the book as he wanted it to be, and he was happy with it. It is the book now at hand.

He had worked at it off and on for ten years—his first formal proposal for what came to be called "the Korea book" was drawn up in 1997—but the idea sprang from a 1962 conversation in Vietnam with an American soldier who had fought in Korea. In a sense *The Coldest Winter* is a companion book to *The Best and the Brightest*, which dealt with America's failure in Vietnam. The Korean War had ended in stalemate while he was still in high school. He was in his twenties when he started covering Vietnam for the *New York Times*, and by that time the Korean War did not mean much to him, or to many other Americans except the soldiers who had fought it. Americans neither celebrate nor long remember their stalemates. Halberstam sensed that this forgetting masked some turning point in the history of America's political development after World War II. How had we gotten from Korean stalemate to Vietnamese disaster? He set out to understand, then re-create, a time of extraordinary political bitterness that Americans had put out of mind.

Finally, on a Wednesday in April, he finished this monumental task and by the following Monday, not being a man to relax after completing a big job, he was in California to do some work on his next book. This one was to be about professional football. It would be the twenty-second book he had written over nearly fifty years. His first, published in 1961, was *The Noblest Roman*, a novel about small-town corruption in the Deep South. His only other novel, *One Very Hot Day*, had a Vietnam setting, but he was a man prone to a kind of

667

moral outrage not readily accommodated in fiction. As a reporter in Vietnam he had discovered that the plain, astonishing, outrageous, absolute implausibility of the real world made it far more fascinating than whatever world any but the greatest fiction writer could possibly imagine. He spent the rest of his life trying to be the best of all possible journalists.

Halberstam thought journalism a high, sometimes even a noble calling, and was sometimes cruelly dismissive of those who belittled it and especially of those who betrayed it. One of his earliest books, *The Making of a Quagmire*, dealing with the Vietnam War, put an antique word back into common use while introducing the country to the then astounding possibility of American fallibility.

With *The Best and the Brightest*, his sixth book, he returned to the subject of Vietnam and established himself as a singular force in what was being called "the new journalism." This involved the use of fictional techniques to interest readers in complex matters that many might otherwise find forbiddingly tedious. The aim was to create the sense of a storyteller weaving a tale. The writer was expected to remain faithful to the facts but not to encumber the story with constant explanations of how the facts were obtained. *The Best and the Brightest* was a masterful illustration of the technique and, though traditionalists once fumed about its unorthodox journalistic method, it is now regarded as an essential classic of Vietnam War literature.

After that the books came in profusion: big books like *The Powers That Be*, *The Reckoning*, *The Fifties*, *War in a Time of Peace*; books about the world of sports like *The Amateurs*, *Summer of '49*, *Playing for Keeps*, and *The Teammates*; books both short and long, written simply because he thought they ought to be written: *The Children*, for example, celebrating a group of young Southern blacks who had been in the vanguard of the civil rights struggle in the 1960s; and *Firehouse*, a tribute to his neighborhood fire fighters. (On September 11, thirteen of them left the firehouse for the World Trade Center; twelve did not return.)

This next book, the football book that had brought him to California, demanded a great deal of interviewing. There was nothing unusual about that. Interviewing was the bedrock of his work. His books were filled with the sound of people talking, and getting the sound right required endless interviewing and patient listening. *The Coldest Winter*, for example, opens with the voices of American soldiers happily discussing their apparent triumph over the North Korean Army while several hundred thousand Chinese soldiers are silently closing the trap that will annihilate them.

The Teammates begins with Dominic DiMaggio's wife, Emily, objecting to her husband's plan to visit his dying teammate, Ted Williams: "I just don't want you driving to Florida alone," she says in the book's third sentence. In *Ho*, his character study of Ho Chi Minh, a French army officer on page one starts talking in a Vietnamese bar about the defeat at Dienbienphu: "It was all for nothing . . . I let my men die for nothing."

Halberstam once said that after finishing Harvard he deliberately sought work on small-town Southern newspapers so he could learn how to talk to ordinary people, a skill not much cherished in the Ivy League, but indispensable to success in journalism. Getting people to talk was vital to his distinctive way of writing history, because he believed in the individual human as history's agent. It is doubtful that he was ever much interested in a Tolstoyan view of man at the mercy of history's tides, and for good reason. Take that road and journalism becomes absurd; Halberstam was a journalist, heart and soul.

He needed to understand the connection between the human and the event. He was constantly trying to understand why a nation with such high aspirations, led by the most excellent people, so often ended up in one quagmire or another. His work assumed a vital human agency behind historical developments. Belief in the importance of these human forces led naturally to the study of people, and they appear in astonishing variety in his books: powerful men like the Kennedys, Douglas MacArthur, Ho Chi Minh, Lyndon Johnson; great athletes like Michael Jordan and Ted Williams; important policy shapers like Robert McNamara, Brent Scowcroft, and Madeleine Albright; but also a young man rowing a single scull in hopes of making an Olympic team that almost no one else cares about, and a bunch of black kids risking their lives for the right to vote and eat an ice-cream sundae sitting down, and those thirteen firemen headed for the World Trade Center.

To bring them to life on the page he had to hear people talking. So he interviewed and interviewed. For his twenty-second book, the one about football, he was on his way to interview a Hall of Fame football player named Y. A. Tittle. The crash occurred on his way to the interview.

Notes

For further details about the sources listed in these notes, please refer to the Bibliography, which begins on page 697.

INTRODUCTION

PAGE

1 *"nastiest little war"*: Hastings, Max, *The Korean War*, p. 329.
1 *"If the best minds"*: Goulden, Joseph, *Korea*, p. 3.
1 *"sour war"*: Ibid., p. xv.
2 *"a police action"*; Paige, Glenn, *The Korean Decision*, p. 243.
3 *"[was] another mountain"*: author interview with George Russell.
4 *put their losses at roughly 1.5 million*: Hastings, Max, *The Korean War*, p. 329.

CHAPTER 1

PAGE

9 *so raw it made you gag*: author interview with Phil Peterson.
10 *"we did it, buddy"*: author interview with Bill Richardson.
10 *"the thirteenth platoon leader"*: author interview with Ben Boyd.
11 *"Kim Buck Tooth?"*: Breuer, William, *Shadow Warriors*, p. 106.
13 *"they were going to be overrun"*: author interviews with Barbara Thompson Foltz, John S. D. Eisenhower.
13 *"On to the Yalu"*: Paik, Sun Yup, *From Pusan to Panmunjom*, p. 85.
14 *"No, I'm Chinese"*: Ibid., pp. 87–88.
15 *"diplomatic blackmail"*: Spurr, Russell, *Enter the Dragon*, p. 161.
16 *"We're all going home and we're going home soon"*: author interview with Ralph Hockley.
17 *"damn near annihilated that very first night"*: author interview with Pappy Miller.
19 *"He was the best"*: author interview with Lester Urban.
20 *his advice had been ignored*: Blair, Clay, *The Forgotten War*, p. 381; Harold Johnson oral history, U.S. Army War College Library.
20 *"To say it was careless"*: author interview with Hewlett (Reb) Rainer.
21 *thought he was crazy at the time*: author interview with Bill Richardson.
22 *particularly enticing target*: author interview with Fillmore McAbee.
23 *little curiosity about either*: author interview with William West.
23 *"than battle-tested officers"*: Ibid.

24 *"strangest sight I have ever seen"*: Appleman, Roy, *South to the Naktong, North to the Yalu*, p. 690.

25 *encircled on three sides*: Ibid., p. 691.

26 *"twenty thousand laundrymen"*: author interview with Ben Boyd.

30 *"Walsh is dead!"*: author interview with Bill Richardson.

31 *"gooks all around us"*: author interview with Robert Kies.

33 *"Well, He is, He is"*: author interview with Bill Richardson.

34 *"We have to act on our own"*: author interview with Phil Peterson.

35 *without knowing they were Chinese*: author interview with Ray Davis.

40 *Do you ever forgive yourself for some of the things you do in life?*: author interview with Bill Richardson.

41 *as an adviser in Vietnam*: author interview with Robert Kies.

42 *"Custer at the Little Big Horn"*: Rovere, Richard, and Schlesinger, Arthur M., Jr., *The General and the President*, p. 136.

43 *"something from the wreckage"*: Blair, Clay, *The Forgotten War*, p. 391.

43 *"SOME OF WHICH WERE CHINESE"*: Ridgway, Matthew B., *The Korean War*, p. 59.

44 *The drive north would continue*: Ibid., p. 60.

44 *"The most elementary caution"*: Acheson, Dean, *Present at the Creation*, p. 466.

CHAPTER 2

47 *"with the point of a bayonet"*: Goncharov, Sergei, Lewis, John, and Xue Litai, *Uncertain Partners*, p. 138.

48 *"strike the Southerners in the teeth"*: Ibid., p. 135.

48 *"Dean really blew it on that one"*: author interview with Averell Harriman for *The Best and the Brightest*.

49 *still much feared regionally*: Goncharov et al., *Uncertain Partners*, pp. 136–137.

49 *"from any direct involvement"*: Ibid., p. 140.

49 *"I am ready to help in this matter"*: Weathersby, Kathryn, Cold War International History Project, Numbers 6–7, Winter 1995–96.

50 *quietly taken out and executed*: Goncharov et al., *Uncertain Partners*, p. 144.

50 *met three times with Stalin*: Shen Zhihua, Cold War International History Project, Winter 2003, Spring 2004.

50 *"You have to ask Mao for all the help"*: Goncharov et al., *Uncertain Partners*, pp. 144–145.

51 *he had answered "arrogantly"*: Chen, Jian, *China's Road to the Korean War*, p. 112.

51 *the Chinese would send troops*: Shen Zhihua, Cold War International History Project.

53 *the north-south rail lines*: author interview with Jack Singlaub.

54 *"out of the question"*: Kennan, George F., *Memoirs 1925–1950*, p. 484.

55 *"are hitting all along the front"*: Goulden, Joseph, *Korea*, p. 44.

55 *"FIFTY MILES NORTHWEST SEOUL"*: Paige, Glenn D., *The Korean Decision*, p. 88.

56 *"it was a very amusing picture"*: Myers, Robert, *Korea in the Cross Currents*, p. 83.

56 *"the great design of human freedom"*: Allison, John, *Ambassador from the Plains*, p. 130.

56 *specifically written for Dulles*: Paige, Glenn D., *The Korean Decision*, p. 74.

57 *"one arm tied behind my back"*: Allison, John, *Ambassador from the Plains*, p. 129.

58 *"I don't know what G-2 in Tokyo"*: Ibid., p. 131.

58 *"what was happening in his own backyard"*: Ibid., p. 135.

58 *"such a dejected, completely forlorn"*: Ibid., pp. 136–137.

59 *"symbolic sacrifice alongside his men"*: Hastings, Max, *The Korean War*, p. 65.

CHAPTER 3

PAGE

60 *the greater MacArthur's role in the creation would be*: author interview with Alex Gibney.

61 *"Let them help themselves"*: Leary, William (editor), *MacArthur and the American Century*, p. 255.

61 *"as we would California"*: Cumings, Bruce, *The Origins of the Korean War, Vol. II*, p. 233.

62 *"looked like hell"*: Tuchman, Barbara, *Stilwell and the American Experience in China*, p. 522.

62 *"swift betterment to their condition"*: Myers, Robert, *Korea in the Cross Currents*, p. 8.

63 *"the same breed of cat as the Japanese"*: Blair, Clay, *The Forgotten War*, p. 38.

64 *"crushed in the battle of the whales"*: Oliver, Robert T., *Syngman Rhee: The Man Behind the Myth*, p. 9.

64 *"either elucidation or explanation"*: Myers, Robert, *Korea in the Cross Currents*, p. 28.

65 *"The Japs interest me and I like them"*: Zimmerman, Warren, *First Great Triumph*, p. 465.

65 *"peoples of the civilized world"*: Ibid., p. 465.

65 *"the Japanese imperial wolf"*: Myers, Robert, *Korea in the Cross Currents*, p. 27.

66 *"utterly unable to do for themselves"*: Goulden, Joseph, *Korea*, p. 7.

66 *"future redeemer of Korean independence"*: Oliver, Robert T., *Syngman Rhee: The Man Behind the Myth*, p. 111.

67 *Koreans held on to no such hopes*: Myers, Robert T., *Korea in the Cross Currents*, pp. 36–37.

67 *parts of the Japanese power structure*: Ibid., p. 37.

69 *"who have suffered for their faith"*: Hoopes, Townsend, *The Devil and John Foster Dulles*, p. 78.

69 *"much less comfortable with movements"*: Hastings, Max, *The Korean War*, p. 33.

69 *"corrupt, and wildly unpredictable"*: Blair, Clay, *The Forgotten War*, p. 44.

CHAPTER 4

PAGE

79 *as he was then known in Pyongyang*: Spurr, Russell, *Enter the Dragon*, p. 132.

79 *"worn the people out"*: Scalapino, Robert, and Chong-sik Lee, *Communism in Korea*, p. 314.

80 *"more power and autonomy"*: Martin, Bradley K., *Under the Loving Care of the Fatherly Leader*, p. 49.

80 *"the most among thirty million Koreans"*: Armstrong, Charles, *The North Korean Revolution*, p. 228.

80 *"Great Sun of democratic new Korea"*: Ibid., p. 228.

CHAPTER 5

PAGE

83 *"kickbacks were commonplace"*: Blair, Clay, *The Forgotten War*, p. 51.

84 *"the same disaster that befell China"*: Goulden, Joseph, *Korea*, p. 34.

84 *"was simply inexplicable"*: Blair, Clay, *The Forgotten War*, p. 57.

CHAPTER 6

PAGE

89   *"most probably to world war"*: Allison, John, *Ambassador from the Plains*, p. 131.

91   *"meet them on that basis"*: Truman's writings, the Harry S. Truman Library.

91   *"which is of great deterrent importance"*: Cumings, Bruce, *The Origins of the Korean War, Vol. II*, p. 48 and p. 780.

91   *"as near like Tom Pendergast"*: McCullough, David, *Truman*, p. 451.

91   *"liked the little son of a bitch"*: Ferrell, Robert (editor), *Off the Record*, p. 349.

91   *"an innocent idealist"*: Ibid., p. 452.

92   *Truman was worthless*: Ibid., p. 452.

93   *"if we don't put up a fight now"*: papers of George Elsey, June 26, 1950, the Harry S. Truman Library.

93   *"to let them have it!"*: Donovan, Robert, *The Tumultous Years*, p. 197.

94   *"No one believed that the North Koreans were as strong as they turned out to be"*: Ibid., p. 199.

95   *"I'll handle the political affairs!"* Paige, Glenn D., *The Korean Decision*, p. 141.

95   *"Haven't been so upset since"*: letter from Harry Truman to Bess Truman, June 26, 1950, the Harry S. Truman Library.

95   *"profitless and discreditable"*: Isaacson, Walter, and Thomas, Evan, *The Wise Men*, p. 512.

98   *arranged a dinner*: Wellington Koo oral history, Columbia University Library.

98   *wanted to concentrate on Korea*: McFarland, Keith D., and Roll, David L., *Louis Johnson and the Arming of America*, pp. 260, 279–280.

99   *"block headed undertaker"*: Isaacson, Walter, and Thomas, Evan, *The Wise Men*, p. 494.

99   *"those bandits in Korea suppressed"*: George Elsey memo, June 30, 1950, the Harry S. Truman Library.

99   *"but we can't be sure they'll be"*: Frank Pace oral history at the Harry S. Truman Library.

100   *"such a sense of relief and unity"*: Goldman, Eric, *The Crucial Decade*, p. 157.

100   *"get Herbert Hoover off the can"*: D. Clayton James interview with John Chiles, the MacArthur Memorial Library, Norfolk, Virginia.

CHAPTER 7

PAGE

102   *"an 'untouchable'"*: Soffer, Jonathan, *General Matthew B. Ridgway*, p. 114; Blair, Clay, *The Forgotten War*, p. 79.

102   *"usually chose to ignore it"*: Eisenhower, Dwight D., *At Ease*, p. 213.

102   *"made for lesser men"*: Hastings, Max, *The Korean War*, p. 65.

104   *" 'the greatest man in history' "*: Swanberg, W. A., *Luce and His Empire*, p. 311.

104   *"a general too long"*: author interview with John Hart.

105   *"hostile and suspicious foreign government"*: Kennan, George F., *Memoirs 1925–1950*, p. 382.

108   *not actually gain that medal for another twenty-seven*: Manchester, William, *American Caesar*, p. 15.

109   *"within two thousand miles"*: Dower, John, *War without Mercy*, p. 152.

109   *"It means an imperial policy"*: Karnow, Stanley, *In Our Image*, p. 96.

110   *used to identify Asians*: Dower, John, *War without Mercy*, p. 151.

110   *"for whom Christ died"*: Karnow, Stanley, *In Our Image*, pp. 127–128.

111 *"The ball has begun"*: Ibid., p. 140.

111 *"is a dead one"*: Dower, John, *War without Mercy*, p. 152.

111 *"If old Dewey had just sailed away"*: Karnow, Stanley, *In Our Image*, p. 106.

112 *"any less than I do"*: Zimmerman, Warren, *First Great Triumph*, p. 390.

112 *"like an Asian potentate"*: Ibid., p. 391.

113 *"a comparatively short period"*: James, D. Clayton, *The Years of MacArthur, Vol. I*, p. 39.

114 *"like Robert E. Lee"*: Manchester, William, *American Caesar*, p. 41.

114 *"everything he wanted to be"*: James, D. Clayton, *The Years of MacArthur, Vol. I*, p. 347.

CHAPTER 8

PAGE

116 *"great bad man"*: *Infantry* magazine, Spring 2002.

117 *"of social discipline then"*: Manchester, William, *American Caesar*, p. 26.

117 *"How am I doing, Dad?"* James, D. Clayton, *The Years of MacArthur, Vol. III*, p. 183.

119 *"selecting him as one of your Generals,"* Manchester, William, *American Caesar*, p. 93.

119 *"knows him quite well"*: James, D. Clayton, *The Years of MacArthur, Vol. I*, pp. 169–171.

119 *his armies at twenty-six*: Manchester, William, *American Caesar*, p. 134.

CHAPTER 9

PAGE

121 *their pilots must be white*: Manchester, William, *American Caesar*, pp. 170–171.

121 *bottle up the Japanese fleet*: Ibid., p. 186.

122 *"it isn't the same"*: Ibid., p. 281.

122 *"They're my allies!"*: Ibid., p. 337.

122 *"since Darius the Great"*: Gunther, John, *The Riddle of MacArthur*, pp. 41–42.

123 *"and send you home"*: Manchester, William, *American Caesar*, p. 322.

125 *"blackmail and assault"*: Ibid., pp. 149–150.

125 *"Yes, my friend, of course"*: Perret, Geoffrey, *Old Soldiers Never Die*, p. 157.

125 *"I told that dumb son"*: D'Este, Carlo, *Eisenhower*, p. 222.

126 *"Incipient revolution is in"*: Eisenhower, Dwight D., *At Ease*, pp. 216–217.

126 *"would have been threatened"*: Manchester, William, *American Caesar*, p. 152.

127 *"the other is Douglas MacArthur"*: James, D. Clayton, *The Years of MacArthur, Vol. I*, p. 411.

127 *"our worst politician"*: MacArthur, Douglas, *Reminiscences*, p. 96.

128 *"a lie would serve him just as well"*: Manchester, William, *American Caesar*, p. 240.

128 *it went out as he directed*: Rovere, Richard, and Schlesinger, Arthur M., Jr., *The General and the President*, p. 22.

128 *"a symbol of our nation"*: Lee, Clark, and Henschel, Richard, *Douglas MacArthur*, p. 87.

129 *" 'can risk being first rate' "*: Gunther, John, *The Riddle of MacArthur*, p. 23.

129 *" 'Communists and British imperialists' "*: Ibid., p. 42.

130 *"obvious from the evidence"*: Ferrell, Robert (editor), *The Eisenhower Diaries*, p. 22.

130 *"of every true patriot"*: Rovere, Richard, and Schlesinger, Arthur M., Jr., *The General and the President*, pp. 23–24; Manchester, William, *American Caesar*, pp. 362–363.

131 *a MacArthur run*: James, D. Clayton, *The Years of MacArthur, Vol. III*, p. 195.

131 *"such skunks as"*: Ibid., p. 200.

131 *"whooping it up for MacArthur"*: Manchester, William, *American Caesar*, p. 357.

132 *"to which I might be called"*: Gunther, John, *The Riddle of MacArthur*, p. 61.

132 *"is as low as a rug"*: Manchester, William, *American Caesar*, p. 524.

133 *"Custers, Pattons, and MacArthurs"*: Ferrell, Robert (editor), *Off the Record*, p. 47.

133 *"Doug didn't bother me"*: Ibid., p. 60.

134 *only to MacArthur were they sent out*: author interview with Bill McCaffrey.

134 *"tired of fooling around"*: Ayers, Eben, *Truman in the White House*, edited by Robert H. Ferrell, p. 81.

134 *first with the War Department*: James, D. Clayton, *The Years of MacArthur, Vol. III*, p. 19.

134 *"cannot spare the time"*: Ibid., pp. 22–23.

135 *"like to pin a medal"*: Ibid., p. 22.

135 *"Wait a minute"*: Ibid., p. 19.

136 *"up to heroic stature"*: Ayers, Eben A., *Truman in the White House*, edited by Robert H. Ferrell, p. 360.

136 *"you can find all the answers"*: James, D. Clayton, *The Years of MacArthur, Vol. III*, p. 60.; Rovere, Richard, and Schlesinger, Arthur M., Jr., *The General and the President*, p. 92.

136 *"whipped them just the same"*: James, D. Clayton, *The Years of MacArthur, Vol. III*, p. 109.

136 *"wasn't so bad"*: Leary, William (editor), *MacArthur and the American Century*, p. 243.

136 *for selling out to State*: Bradley, Omar, *A General's Life*, p. 526.

CHAPTER 10

PAGE

138 *they visited the latrine*: author interview with Colonel Jim Hinton.

138 *for spare parts*: author interview with Sam Mace.

140 *"physically unprepared for war"*: Toland, John, interview with Keyes Beech for *Mortal Combat*, Franklin D. Roosevelt Library.

141 *"at the end of the supply line"*: Knox, Donald, *The Korean War, Vol. I*, p. 10.

141 *"ill equipped and poorly trained"*: Blair, Clay, *The Forgotten War*, p. 93.

141 *"except to fight"*: Fehrenbach, T. R., *This Kind of War*, p. 102.

141 *on the rosy side*: Blair, Clay, *The Forgotten War*, p. 88.

142 *"no combat soldiers, just a cadre"*: James, D. Clayton, *The Years of MacArthur, Vol. III*, p. 84.

143 *was not contagious*: Beech, Keyes, *Tokyo and Points East*, pp. 145–146.

143 *"start riding down the highway"*: Hastings, Max, *The Korean War*, pp. 95–96.

143 *who were true believers*: Ha Jin, *War Trash*.

144 *"Let the gooks kill each other"*: Knox, Donald, *The Korean War, Vol. I*, p. 6.

145 *quickly boarded*: Ibid., p. 17.

145 *"we'll have no difficulty"*: Fehrenbach, T. R., *This Kind of War*, p. 73.

146 *"or bottom to top"*: author interview with Lieutenant Colonel Fred Ladd.

147 *so he could at least take*: Knox, Donald, *The Korean War, Vol. I*, pp. 19–21.

147 *"in Seoul by the weekend"*: Warner, Denis, *The Opening Round of the Korean War*, *Military History* magazine, June, 2000.

148 *"36 miles in 36 hours"*: Ibid.

150 *records would be cleaned*: Knox, Donald, *The Korean War, Vol. I*, p. 33.

150 *get ready for their courts-martial*: author interview with William West.

150 *"It sucked up men from everywhere"*: Fehrenbach, T. R., *This Kind of War*, p. 122.

151 *barely rubbed off*: Appleman, Roy, *South to the Naktong, North to the Yalu*, pp. 214–215.

152 *to attack his command*: Blair, Clay, *The Forgotten War*, pp. 186–187.

152   *"a different and more favorable"*: Ibid., p. 187.
152   *"over here looking for a job"*: Ibid., p. 189. Ridgway oral history, U.S. Army War College Library.
153   *"I couldn't get you out"*: Appleman, Roy, *Ridgway Duels for Korea*, p. 4.

CHAPTER 11

PAGE
154   a two-front war: letter from Mike Lynch to Wilson Heefner, courtesy of Heefner.
154   *"I will not be driven from the Naktong Line"*: Walters, Vernon A., *Silent Missions*, p. 195.
156   released to the Eighth Army: Heefner, Wilson, *Patton's Bulldog*, pp. 159–160.
156   talented, charismatic younger officers: author interview with Sam Wilson Walker.
157   skirmishes on the Mexican border: Heefner, Wilson, *Patton's Bulldog*, pp. 5–13.
158   *"fighting little son of a bitch"*: author interview with Sam Walker.
158   from the Michelin tire advertisements: Thompson, Reginald, *Cry Korea*, p. 235.
159   *"what they're giving me to fight"*: author interview with Frank Gibney.
159   *"George Patton and Douglas MacArthur"*: author interview with Sam Walker.
159   excessive with compliments: Blair, Clay, *The Forgotten War*, p. 35.
159   Ridgway and *"Lightning" Joe Collins*: Blair, Clay, *The Forgotten War*, p. 35.
162   and no sympathy for himself: author interview with Bill McCaffrey.
163   Ned the Anointed: Appleman, Roy, *Escaping the Trap*, p. 45.
163   to designate one's standing with the general: Leary, William (editor), *MacArthur and the American Century*, p. 241.
163   *"instinctive knack of ingratiation"*: Coleman, J. D., *Wonju*, p. 93.
164   you simply could not speak to a superior that way: author interview with Bill McCaffrey.
164   *"on a desert island"*: Blair, Clay, interview with John Chiles, U.S. Army War College.
164   you had to play to his entire team: author interview with Bill McCaffrey.
164   *"Is this Almond speaking"*: Mike Michaelis oral history at U.S. Army War College; author interview with Layton Tyner.
166   albeit in a losing war: author interview with Layton Tyner.
167   *"we will die fighting together"*: Heefner, Wilson, *Patton's Bulldog*, p. 185; author interview with Layton Tyner; Hastings, Max, *The Korean War*, p. 84.
168   *"a defeated Confederate General"*: Goulden, Joseph, *Korea*, p. 201; Lem Shepherd, oral history at Marine Corps History Archive and oral history at Columbia University.
168   *"August is the month of victory"*: Shen Zhihua, Cold War International History Project, Winter 2003, Spring 2004.

CHAPTER 12

PAGE
173   *"direct lineal descendant of FDR"*: Smith, Richard Norton, *Thomas Dewey and His Times*, p. 35.
174   *"It is a crusade"*: Oshinsky, David, *A Conspiracy So Immense*, pp. 49–50.
175   *"now a Republican country"*: Ibid., p. 53.
175   then a traditionally liberal: Ibid., p. 53.
176   *"horses with blinders on"*: Miller, Merle, *Plain Speaking*, p. 164.
177   to $6 or $7 billion a year: Ferrell, Robert (editor), *Off the Record*, p. 133.
179   hurtling over the wires: Collins, Lawton, *War in Peacetime*, p. 39.
179   *"no boats, no votes"*: Christensen, Thomas, *Useful Adversaries*, p. 39.

179   *the rush to demobilize*: Heinl, Robert, *Victory at High Tide*, p. 4.

179   *"it was a rout"*: Ibid., p. 4.

179   *"out of a paper bag"*: Bradley, Omar, with Blair, Clay, *A General's Life*, p. 474.

180   *"kill a horse"*: McCullough, David, *Truman*, p. 738.

181   *as so many of our top strategists*: Myers, Robert, *Korea in the Cross Currents*, p. 79.

183   *"Bring the boys home"*: Isaacson, Walter, and Thomas, Evan, *The Wise Men*, p. 338.

183   *had greatly angered MacArthur*: Rovere, Richard, and Schlesinger, Arthur M., Jr., *The General and the President*, p. 120.

184   *"from his command on April 11, 1951"*: Acheson, Dean, *Present at the Creation*, pp. 126–127.

184   *"on behalf of the big bankers"*: Cumings, Bruce, *The Origins of the Korean War, Vol. II*, p. 45.

185   *"pearls before swine"*: Isaacson, Walter, and Thomas, Evan, *The Wise Men*, p. 465.

185   *" 'You stand for everything that has been wrong for America for years' "*: Chute, David, *The Great Fear*, pp. 42–43.

185   *"You owe it to Truman"*: Isaacson, Walter, and Thomas, Evan, *The Wise Men*, p. 547.

185   *"that little fellow across the street"*: Halberstam, David, *The Best and the Brightest*, p. 332; author interview with John Carter Vincent.

185   *"a constituency of one"*: Isaacson, Walter, and Thomas, Evan, *The Wise Men*, p. 464.

186   *"than they have seen fit to use"*: McLellan, David S., *Dean Acheson: The State Department Years*, p. 383.

187   *"Chiang going out"*: Isaacson, Walter, and Thomas, Evan, *The Wise Men*, p. 475.

188   *"and hang on to our friends"*: Davis, Nuell Pharr, *Lawrence and Oppenheimer*, p. 294.

189   *"worldlier English prototype"*: Cooke, Alistair, *A Generation on Trial*, pp. 107–108.

189   *"come to the brink, like Chambers"*: Halberstam, David, author interview with Murray Kempton, *The Fifties*, p. 13.

190   *too many glitches in Hiss's story*: author interview with Homer Bigart, *New York Times*.

190   *"and could vouch for them absolutely"*: Weinstein, Allen, *Perjury*, p. 37.

190   *"what I have to do"*: Isaacson, Walter, and Thomas, Evan, *The Wise Men*, p. 491.

191   *spoiling for a fight*: author interview with Lucius Battle.

191   *Average Americans would have understood that*: author interview with James Reston for *The Best and the Brightest*.

191   *"a tremendous and totally unnecessary gift"*: Goldman, Eric, *The Crucial Decade*, pp. 134–135.

192   *"I hope they hang him"*: Donovan, Robert, *Tumultuous Years*, p. 133.

192   *"Traitors in the high councils"*: Goldman, Eric, *The Crucial Decade*, pp. 134–135.

192   *"a dead cat around his neck"*: Ibid., p. 134.

CHAPTER 13

PAGE

195   *"when it came to the final responsible"*: Gellman, Barton, *Contending with Kennan*, p. 14.

196   *"its preservation was tremendous"*: Foot, Rosemary, *The Wrong War*, p. 60.

196   *"even I don't make her nervous"*: Isaacson, Walter, and Thomas, Evan, *The Wise Men*, p. 150.

197   *"My voice now carried"*: Kennan, George, *Memoirs 1925–1950*, pp. 294–295.

198   *"a ceremonial Chinese bow and a polite giggle"*: Isaacson, Walter, and Thomas, Evan, *The Wise Men*, p. 477.

199   *"and borders on recklessness"*: Foot, Rosemary, *The Wrong War*, p. 39.

200 *"than with the Secretary of Defense"*: Bradley, Omar, with Blair, Clay, *A General's Life*, p. 519.
200 *"but don't put any figure in the report"*: Isaacson, Walter, and Thomas, Evan, *The Wise Man*, p. 499.
200 *"scaring me out of my shoes"*: Acheson, Dean, *Present at the Creation*, p. 373.
201 at Princeton, *"saved us"*: Isaacson, Walter, and Thomas, Evan, *The Wise Men*, p. 504.

CHAPTER 14

PAGE
203 *"just mild about Harry"*: McCullough, David, *Truman*, p. 493.
203 *"And poor people of the United States"*: Ibid., p. 320.
204 not one of these fancy tractors: Abels, Jules, *Out of the Jaws of Victory*, p. 182.
204 *"clear thinking and forceful"*: Bradley, Omar, with Blair, Clay, *A General's Life*, p. 444.
205 the pages of Sinclair Lewis: McCullough, David, *Truman*, pp. 324–325.
205 *"but did not know what they were getting"*: Phillips, Cabell, *The Truman Presidency*, p. 47.
205 *"of democracy if it works"*: McCullough, David, *Truman*, p. 525.
207 *"Ajax of the Ozarks"*: Abels, Jules, *Out of the Jaws of Victory*, p. 95.
207 *"Truman, Harry Truman"*: Goldman, Eric, *The Crucial Decade*, p. 83.
207 *"a dead Missouri mule"*: Ibid., p. 19.
208 *"neck-and-neck race"*: Manchester, William, *The Glory and the Dream*, p. 465.
208 *"from rocking the boat"*: Abels, Jules, *Out of the Jaws of Victory*, p. 150.
208 *"keep this table vacant"*: Ibid., pp. 12–13.
209 *"as a Washington lawyer and national"*: McFarland, Keith D., and Roll, David L., *Louis Johnson and the Arming of America*, p. 133.
209 got the Defense portfolio: Ibid., pp. 137–139.
209 *"I'll give 'em hell"*: Donovan, Robert, *Tumultuous Years*, p. 16.
209 *"with them and not at them"*: McCullough, David, *Truman*, p. 675.
210 *"smug, arrogant, and supercilious"*: Abels, Jules, *Out of the Jaws of Victory*, p. 141.
210 *"Brownell lamented years later"*: author interview with Herbert Brownell for *The Fifties*.
210 *"I thought I was"*: Smith, Richard Norton, *Thomas Dewey and His Times*, p. 26.
211 *"looking under beds"*: Ibid., p. 507.
211 *"obstinately laboring president"*: Abels, Jules, *Out of the Jaws of Victory*, p. 180.
212 *"let's get on with the job"*: Phillips, Cabell, *The Truman Presidency*, pp. 243–244.
212 why Truman had won: McCullough, David, *Truman*, p. 712.

CHAPTER 15

PAGE
215 not augur well for the future: *Life* magazine, December 20, 1948.
216 as Omar Bradley wrote: Bradley, Omar, with Blair, Clay, *A General's Life*, p. 549.
217 to stay clear of him: Goulden, Joseph, *Korea*, p. 155; Donovan, Robert, *Tumultuous Years*, pp. 260–262.
217 *"stop kicking him around"*: Blair, Clay, *The Forgotten War*, pp. 184–185.
217 *"the communists in China"*: Donovan, Robert, *Tumultuous Years*, p. 261.
218 *"of willpower and courage"*: author interview with Lieutenant General (Ret.) Ed Rowny; Toland interview with Rowny, Franklin D. Roosevelt Library.
218 might exceed battle: Ridgway, Matthew B., *The Korean War*, p. 36.
219 *"great national asset"*: Blair, Clay, *The Forgotten War*, pp. 188–189.

220 *"and its position in the U.N."*: Goulden, Joseph, *Korea,* pp. 161–162.

220 *"worst appointment Truman ever"*: McCullough, David, *Truman,* p. 741.

221 *"does away with the Navy"*: Heinl, Robert, *Victory at High Tide,* pp. 6–7.

221 *"one mental case with another"*: Bradley, Omar, with Blair, Clay, *A General's Life,* p. 503.

222 *"I can't and he's one of the"*: Ferrell, Robert (editor), *Off the Record,* p. 189.

223 as Indigo-China: Cray, Ed, *General of the Army George C. Marshall,* p. 234; Oshinsky, David, *A Conspiracy So Immense,* p. 36.

224 to do the Lord's work: Melby, John, *The Mandate of Heaven,* p. 135.

225 *"with or without Russian aid"*: Rovere, Richard, and Schlesinger, Arthur M., Jr., *The General and the President,* p. 195.

227 *"illiterate, peasant son of a"*: Kahn, E. J., *The China Hands,* p. 82.

227 *"became the Government's chief"*: Tuchman, Barbara, *Stilwell and the American Experience in China,* p. 303.

228 *"without money or influence"*: Ibid., p. 316.

228 *"to try and unify China"*: Kahn, E. J., *The China Hands,* p. 184.

228 most likely quite ill: Melby, John, *The Mandate of Heaven,* p. 55.

229 Marshall quickly answered: Cray, Ed, *General of the Army George C. Marshall,* p. 574.

229 *"how would I extricate them"*: author interview with Walton Butterworth for *The Best and the Brightest.*

230 *"of these boobs"*: Melby, John, *The Mandate of Heaven,* p. 97.

230 *"the largest troop movement"*: Zi Zhongyun, *No Exit?,* p. 25.

230 of some 1.2 million Japanese soldiers: Ibid., p. 27.

231 *"from disregarding my advice"*: Cray, Ed, *General of the Army George C. Marshall,* p. 574.

CHAPTER 16

PAGE

232 *"we will take it away from them"*: Fairbank, John, and Feuerwerker, Albert, *The Cambridge History of China, Vol. 13,* p. 758.

232 *"Uncle Chump from over the Hump"*: Cray, Ed, *General of the Army George C. Marshall,* p. 758.

233 *"smell of corruption and decay"*: Melby, John, *The Mandate of Heaven,* p. 44.

233 *"into campaigns of mobile warfare"*: Fairbank, John, and Feuerwerker, Albert, *The Cambridge History of China, Vol. 13,* p. 764.

234 the wildest of boasts: Payne, Robert, *Mao,* p. 227.

234 *"of feint and deceit"*: Salisbury, Harrison, *The New Emperors,* p. 6.

234 *"doesn't he generalize"*: Swanberg, W. A., *Luce and His Empire,* p. 282.

235 *"whether it is wise to continue to supply his troops"*: Cray, Ed, *General of the Army George C. Marshall,* p. 634.

235 *"our supply officer"*: Salisbury, Harrison, *The New Emperors,* p. 8.

235 *"more of our equipment than the Nationalists did"*: Rovere, Richard, and Schlesinger, Arthur M., Jr., *The General and the President,* pp. 214–215.

235 *"the end is at hand"*: Melby, John, *The Mandate of Heaven,* p. 289.

236 *"almost a fanatical fervor"*: Cray, Ed, *General of the Army George C. Marshall,* p. 634.

236 *"the Yangtze with broomsticks"*: Rovere, Richard, and Schlesinger, Arthur M., Jr., *The General and the President,* p. 214.

236 so he canceled the dinner: Zi Zhongyun, *No Exit?,* pp. 101–102.

236 *"No sir, I do not"*: Koen, Ross Y., *The China Lobby in American Politics,* p. 90.

237 *"greater military power than any ruler"*: Cray, Ed, *General of the Army George C. Marshall,* p. 673.

CHAPTER 17

PAGE

239 *"without even a gesture of assistance"*: Christensen, Thomas, *Useful Adversaries*, p. 70.

241 *the China they knew was dying*: Herzstein, Robert, *Henry Luce and the American Crusade in Asia*, p. 5.

242 *so different and so poor*: Halberstam, David, *The Powers That Be*, pp. 57–58.

242 *"remembered for centuries and centuries"*: Swanberg, W. A., *Luce and His Empire*, p. 186.

243 *"in the early 1950s in the same way"*: author interview with Professor Alan Brinkley.

243 *"on most issues, isolationists"*: Ibid.

244 *"is traceable to Chiang"*: White, Theodore H., *In Search of History*, pp. 176–178.

244 *"to guard against"*: Ibid., pp. 205–206.

245 *"couldn't get a job as dog-catcher"*: Kahn, E. J., *The China Hands*, p. 10.

246 *"the gigantic task ahead"*: Swanberg, W. A., *Luce and His Empire*, p. 266.

246 *"he was too intelligent not to"*: Wellington Koo oral history, Columbia University.

247 *"I know the man"*: Cray, Ed, *General of the Army George C. Marshall*, p. 686.

247 *the Atlantic, the Democratic one*: Rovere, Richard, and Schlesinger, Arthur M., Jr., *The General and the President*, p. 230.

248 *for a changed China policy*: Ibid., p. 213.

248 *"Would you send your own sons"*: Zi Zhongyun, *No Exit?*, p. 260.

248 *"quite another thing to plan resultful aid"*: Phillips, Cabell, *The Truman Presidency*, p. 286.

249 *"The animals," Truman said*: Halberstam, David, *The Fifties*, p. 56.

249 *"pouring money down a rathole"*: papers of Matthew Connelly, Harry S. Truman Library.

249 *"I'll bet you that a billion dollars"*: Lilienthal, David E., *The Journals of David E. Lilienthal: Vol. II*, p. 525.

249 *"I spoke American to him"*: Wellington Koo oral history, Columbia University.

250 *such was reality*: Ibid.

250 *"Back to the mainland!"*: Kahn, E. J. *The China Hands*, p. 247.

CHAPTER 18

PAGE

253 *able to catch their breath*: Appleman, Roy, *South to the Naktong, North to the Yalu*, p. 289.

253 *got to use it first*: author interview with Charles Hammel.

254 *"bleeding to death"*: Fehrenbach, T. R., *This Kind of War*, p. 138.

254 *"then you are asking for trouble"*: Goncharov, Sergei, et al., *Uncertain Partners*, p. 155.

255 *"the forgotten commander of the forgotten war"*: Mike Lynch interview in the Toland papers, Franklin D. Roosevelt Library.

255 *"then we'll stay here until"*: Mike Lynch interview with Clay and Joan Blair, U.S. Army War College Library.

256 *"how many reserves have you dug up"*: Appleman, Roy, *South to the Naktong, North to the Yalu*, p. 335; author interview with Layton Tyner.

258 *that night or the next one*: author interview with George Russell.

258 *or seven football fields*: author interview with Joe Stryker; letter from Master Sergeant Harold Graham to Berry Rhoden, June 29, 1951.

258 *"where the hell anyone else"*: author interview with Erwin Ehler.

258 *"impossible at night"*: Ibid.

260   *"Like millions of ants"*: author interview with Terry McDaniel.

261   *"we were the turkeys"*: author interview with Rusty Davidson.

261   *"to the point of being invisible"*: author interview with George Russell.

263   to try to get his squad out of there: author interview with Berry Rhoden.

265   managed to keep going: letter from Master Sergeant Harold Graham to Berry Rhoden.

266   *"Best thing I ever tasted"*: Ibid.

267   *"and you'll be in Charley Company"*: Knox, Donald, *The Korean War, Vol. II,*
      pp. 62–63; author interview with Joe Stryker.

269   were simply too much for him: Mike Lynch interviews in the Toland papers, Franklin
      D. Roosevelt Library.

269   *"what to do to stop it"*: Ibid.; Heefner, Wilson, *Patton's Bulldog,* p. 220; author
      interview with Layton Tyner.

270   was now extended beyond September 4: Appleman, Roy, *South to the Naktong, North
      to the Yalu,* pp. 462–463; Blair, Clay, *The Forgotten War,* pp. 250–251.

273   *"began to get a very shaky feeling"*: author interview with Lee Beahler.

274   *"Yes, sir," Fry replied instantly*: author interviews with Lee Beahler and Gino Piazza.

275   *"All right, Sergeant, carry on"*: Ibid.; author interview with Charles Hammel.

276   *"I never saw a man so cool"*: Ibid.

278   If the engineers had not been perfectly: author interview with Jesse Haskins.

279   there was no way to save him: author interview with Vaughn West.

279   maybe you should cry: Ibid.

279   spoke with forked tongues: author interview with Lee Beahler.

280   it really was just that bad: author interview with George Russell.

281   *"he had done everything right"*: author interview with Lieutenant General (Ret.)
      Harold G. Moore.

283   the great mass of people: Paul Freeman oral history at U.S. Army War College Library.

283   *"for his own good"*: Ibid.

283   as if he were a member of the board: Ibid.

285   *"do my best as a professional soldier"*: letters of Paul Freeman, courtesy of Anne Sewell
      Freeman McLeod.

287   had been able to forget that moment: author interview with Berry Rhoden.

288   he had received the Silver Star: author interview with Jack Murphy.

290   it seemed like a small miracle: Ibid.

CHAPTER 19

PAGE

293   *"when he was a military genius"*: Perret, Geoffrey, *Old Soldiers Never Die,* p. 548.

294   *"scuddle up to the Manchurian"*: Cumings, Bruce, *The Origins of the Korean War,
      Vol. II,* p. 692.

294   he had ever encountered: Heinl, Robert, *Victory at High Tide,* p. 30.

295   *"and Inchon had all of them"*: Ibid., p. 24.

295   *"solidifying chocolate fudge"*: Ibid., p. 26.

296   *"an ideal place for mines"*: Ibid., p. 27.

296   *"Bradley is a farmer"*: Ibid., p. 10.

297   *"made aware of the details"*: Ibid., p. 40.

298   *"Barrymore and John Drew could hope"*: White, William Allen, *The Autobiography of
      William Allen White,* pp. 572–573.

298   *"I studied dramatics under him"*: Lee, Clark, and Henschel, Richard, *Douglas
      MacArthur,* p. 99.

298   *"So MacArthur went over to the senator"*: Eisenhower, Dwight D., *At Ease,* p. 214.

298 *"as if he hadn't seen her for years"*: Allison, John, *Ambassador from the Plains*, p. 168.

299 *"If I were asked, however"*: Heinl, Robert, *Victory at High Tide*, p. 40.

299 *"breed timidity and defeatism"*: MacArthur, Douglas, *Reminiscences*, p. 349.

300 *"I wouldn't have taken that promise"*: author interview with Bill McCaffrey.

300 *"Once we start ashore"*: Heinl, Robert, *Victory at High Tide*, p. 40.

300 to resist such a great personal: author conversations with Fred Ladd, 1963.

300 *"the Navy will take you in"*: Heinl, Robert, *Victory at High Tide*, pp. 40–42; Manchester, William, *American Caesar*, pp. 576–577; Blair, Clay, *The Forgotten War*, pp. 231–232.

300 *"Spoken like a John Wayne"*: Smith, Robert, *MacArthur in Korea*, p. 78.

301 *"an astonishing course of deceit"*: Blair, Clay, *The Forgotten War*, p. 236.

301 *"you'd best get on with your briefing"*: Goulden, Joseph, *Korea*, pp. 209–210.

302 "What?" *according to John Chiles*: Blair, *The Forgotten War*, p. 229.

302 outside the reach of the Chiefs: author interview with Matthew B. Ridgway.

303 ten months younger than he was: Oliver P. Smith oral histories at Columbia University and U. S. Marine Corps History Division.

303 Marines and Army, in the command: Oliver P. Smith's personal log at U.S. Marine Corps History Division.

303 *"mercurial and flighty"*: Russ, Martin, *Breakout*, p. 17.

303 airpower was another thing: Ibid., p. 208.

CHAPTER 20

PAGE

305 his mind-set, and his personality quirks: author interview with Chen Jian.

305 as the most likely target: Goncharov, Sergei, et al., *Uncertain Partners*, p. 149.

306 *"I have never considered retreat"*: Shen Zhihua, Cold War International History Project, Winter 2003, Spring 2004.

307 *"the stuff of legends"*: Simmons, Edwin H., *Over the Seawall*, p. 23; author interview with Edwin H. Simmons.

307 while relatively few Japanese surrendered: author interview with Edwin H. Simmons.

308 *"that read easier in newspapers"*: Oliver P. Smith oral history at Columbia University.

309 *"I'll see that they are carried out"*: Alexander, Joseph, *The Battle of the Barricades*, p. 19.

309 without confirmation from Division: author interview with Edwin H. Simmons.

309 *"to kill a handful of green troops"*: Toland, John, *In Mortal Combat*, p. 205.

310 *"We have been bastard children"*: Ibid., p. 210.

311 Few people have suffered so terrible: Heinl, Robert, *Victory at High Tide*, p. 242.

311 *"a callous indifference to casualties"*: Ibid., p. 294.

311 *"The public relations brigade"*: Goulden, Joseph, *Korea*, p. 241.

314 *"invite you to all our landings"*: Weintraub, Sidney, *MacArthur's War*, p. 204.

314 *"the greatest conflict of interest"*: author interview with Jack Murphy.

314 was scarier still: author interview with Jack Murphy.

315 its full implications much too late: author interview with Matthew B. Ridgway; Ridgway, Matthew B., *The Korean War*, pp. 46–62.

CHAPTER 21

PAGE

316 senior Chinese Nationalist officials had very good intelligence: author interview with Robert Myers.

317 consequences of such an encounter: Koen, Ross Y., *The China Lobby in American Politics*, p. 83.

317 *"is here in Washington where its lobbyists"*: Zi Zhongyun, *No Exit?*, pp. 243–244.
319 *"a little more friendly to us"*: Ibid., pp. 278–279.

CHAPTER 22

PAGE

324 *"probably more bloodied"*: Foot, Rosemary, *The Wrong War*, p. 103.
325 *"and the Congressional Medal of Honor"*: Halberstam, David, *The Best and the Brightest*, p. 324.
325 *"a shift in the balance of power"*: Foot, Rosemary, *The Wrong War*, p. 52.
326 *"some early affirmative action"*: Ibid., p. 43.
326 *"bigoted influence of the China Lobby,"* Kennan, George F., *Memoirs 1925–1950*, pp. 490–493.
327 *"in a time of despair"*: Ibid., pp. 102–103.
328 *"the more unsound it would become"*: Ibid., p. 488.
329 *"why should we hesitate?"*: Ibid., p. 73.
329 *"up to a surveyor's line and stop"*: Acheson, Dean, *Present at the Creation*, p. 445.
329 *"The Hiss Survivors association"*: Foot, Rosemary, *The Wrong War*, pp. 69–70.
330 *"had adopted a hawkish stance"*: Bradley, Omar, with Blair, Clay, *A General's Life*, p. 558.
331 *"a ratification of actions"*: papers of James Webb, Harry S. Truman Library.
331 *"the neatness of the phrasing"*: Isaacson, Walter, and Thomas, Evan, *The Wise Men*, p. 532.
331 *"to take on the entire Joint Chiefs"*: author interview with Lucius Battle.
331 *"a superhuman effort"*: Isaacson, Walter, and Thomas, Evan, *The Wise Men*, p. 540.
331 *"There is no stopping MacArthur"*: Weintraub, Stanley, *MacArthur's War*, p. 163.
332 *"terrible, terrible defeats"*: author interview with Frank Gibney.
332 *"We love you as the savior of our race"*: Spurr, Russell, *Enter the Dragon*, p. 428.
332 *"wasting your valuable time"*: Weintraub, Stanley, *MacArthur's War*, p. 162.
332 *"without regard to dark hints of possible disaster"*: Ridgway, Matthew B., *The Korean War*, p. 45.
332 *"someone ready to give it a try"*: Ibid., p. 44.
333 *"old and even pitiable without his hat"*: Thompson, Reginald, *Cry Korea*, p. 87.

CHAPTER 23

PAGE

335 just to do ordinary shopping: Panikkar, K. M., *In Two Chinas*, p. 23.
335 *"deportment of a queen"*: Ibid., p. 25.
335 *"for whose culture she had no great"*: Ibid., p. 27.
336 *"what can atomic bombs do there?"*: Ibid., p. 108.
336 *"MacArthur's dream has come true"*: Ibid., pp. 109–112.
337 *"mere vaporings of a panicky Panikkar"*: Isaacson, Walter, and Thomas, Evan, *The Wise Men*, p. 533.
337 their real problem was that long border: Foot, Rosemary, *The Wrong War*, p. 81.
338 was around 60,000 deaths: Chen Jian, *China's Road to the Korean War*, pp. 153–154.
340 *"I will respond with my hand grenade"*: Chen Jian, *China's Road to the Korean War*, pp. 153–154.
342 he knew the population better: author interview with Chen Jian.
342 the half person, he said condescendingly: Ibid.
342 *"a 1,054 page whitewash"*: Foot, Rosemary, *The Wrong War*, p. 44.

343 *and asked for Chinese*: Shen Zhihua, Cold War International History Project, Winter 2003, Spring 2004.

345 *apparently agreed to*: Chen Jian, *China's Road to the Korean War*, p. 161.

CHAPTER 24

347 *136 of 199 division commanders*: Laquer, Walter, *Stalin: The Glasnost Revelations*, p. 91.

347 *"Every crime was possible"*: Djilas, Milovan, *Conversations with Stalin*, p. 190.

348 *"Revolution is not a dinner party"*: Bloodworth, Dellis, *The Messiah and the Mandarins*, p. 62.

348 *"not even a fart"*: Li Zhisui, Dr., *The Private Life of Chairman Mao*, p. 117.

349 *unlikely to invest their military*: Djilas, Milovan, *Conversations with Stalin*, p. 182.

350 *"Chairman Mao will reconsider"*: Goncharov, Sergei, et al., *Uncertain Partners*, p. 29.

350 *"he needed no instructions"*: Ibid., pp. 29–30.

350 *"Long live Comrade Stalin!"*: Ibid., p. 62.

351 *"had never read* Das Kapital": Ibid., p. 88.

351 *"This is feudalism"*: Ibid., p. 105.

351 *Stalin's fiftieth birthday*: Laquer, Walter, *Stalin: The Glasnost Revelations*, p. 179.

351 *"as the starting point of time"*: Ibid., p. 183.

352 *the bodies of potential rivals*: Li Zhisui, Dr., *The Private Life of Chairman Mao*, p. 122.

352 *"to its original greatness"*: Ibid., p. 124.

352 *"served to order, like food"*: Ibid., p. ix.

352 *"neither is as close as Chairman Mao"*: Laquer, Walter, *Stalin: The Glasnost Revelations*, p. 189.

352 *"a needle up his ass"*: Li Zhisui, Dr., *The Private Life of Chairman Mao*, p. 261.

353 *"the head of the Bulgarian party"*: Ulam, Adam B., *Stalin: The Man and His Era*, p. 695.

353 *Again they refused*: Goncharov, Sergei, et al., *Uncertain Partners*, p. 85.

353 *"You know that Chinaman"*: Talbott, Strobe (editor), *Khrushchev Remembers*, pp. 239–240.

354 *"I am here to do more than eat and shit"*: author interview with Chen Jian.

354 *mutual instinct for misunderstanding*: Talbott, Strobe (editor), *Khrushchev Remembers*, p. 239.

354 *"meat from the mouth of a tiger"*: Bloodworth, Dennis, *The Messiah and the Mandarins*, p. 101.

354 *"an abiding hatred of the Soviet"*: Ulam, Adam B., *Stalin: The Man and His Era*, p. 695.

354 *with an urgent request for Chinese troops*: Chen Jian, *China's Road to the Korean War*, p. 172.

355 *the terrible dangers in store*: Ibid., pp. 173–175.

355 *"is nothing to be afraid of"*: Li Zhisui, Dr., *The Private Life of Chairman Mao*, p. 125.

356 *"how can we stand aside"*: Chen Jian, *China's Road to the Korean War*, p. 182.

356 *"and last, as a leader"*: Peng, Dehuai, *Memoirs of a Chinese Marshal*, p. 7.

356 *giving his teeth a greenish pallor*: Li Zhisui, Dr., *The Private Life of Chairman Mao*, p. 99.

357 *"Only our general"*: Ibid., p. 383.

359 *"let alone provide for our parents"*: Peng, Dehuai, *Memoirs of a Chinese Marshal*, p. 161.

360 *or roughly 130,000 men*: Chen Jian, *China's Road to the Korean War*, pp. 195–196.

360 *"How many bombers"*: Ibid., p. 201.

362 *"may cause great harm"*: Ibid., p. 202.

362 *for the majority of battle commanders*: Ibid., p. 207.

CHAPTER 25

364   *"God's right hand man"*: Nellie Noland interview, Harry S. Truman Library.

364   *his staff pressured him to go*: Charles Murphy interview, Harry S. Truman Library.

365   *"king go to the prince"*: Matt Connelly interview, Harry S. Truman Library.

365   *"the attributes of a foreign sovereign"*: Acheson, Dean, *Present at the Creation*, p. 456.

365   *"he was still fighting"*: John Muccio interview, Harry S. Truman Library.

365   *"all American soldiers regardless"*: Walters, Vernon A., *Silent Missions*, p. 204.

366   *"the Chinese are about to intervene"*: interview with Vernon A. Walters, American Masters, WGBH Television.

366   *"the Palace Guard"*: author interview with Frank Gibney.

366   *more smoke blown in his face*: Toland, John, *In Mortal Combat*, p. 241.

367   *no commander in history*: Ibid., pp. 241–242; Blair, Clay, *The Forgotten War*, pp. 346–349; Spurr, Russell, *Enter the Dragon*, p. 159.

368   *"before we get in trouble"*: Dean Rusk interview, Harry S. Truman Library.

368   *"as if they were the heads of different"*: Gunther, John, *The Riddle of MacArthur*, p. 200.

368   *"a different idea of what it was"*: Acheson, Dean, *Present at the Creation*, p. 455.

369   *"luster to his dream of victory"*: Ridgway, Matthew B., *The Korean War*, pp. 37–38; Spurr, Russell, *Enter the Dragon*, p. 158; Blair, Clay, *The Forgotten War*, p. 188.

369   *"honestly believes he's a patriot"*: *New York World-Telegram*, April 8, 1964.

370   *"how completely oblivious"*: author interview with Matthew B. Ridgway.

370   *"obedient, dutiful, childlike, and quick"*: Cumings, Bruce, *The Origins of the Korean War, Vol. II*, p. 97.

370   *was the Chinese commander*: Weintraub, Stanley, *MacArthur's War*, p. 291.

371   *"some old war horse similar to"*: Cumings, Bruce, *The Origins of the Korean War, Vol. II*, p. 103.

371   *fixed, immobile Japanese*: Collins, J. Lawton, *War in Peacetime*, p. 215.

371   *"know your enemy"*: Mike Lynch interview, Toland papers, Franklin D. Roosevelt Library.

371   *to events he did not like*: Perret, Geoffrey, *Old Soldiers Never Die*, p. 551.

372   *for his official file explaining*: Morris, Carol Petillo, *Douglas MacArthur: The Philippine Years*, pp. 204–213.

372   *"An arrogant enemy," he added*: Chen Jian, *China's Road to the Korean War*, p. 148.

373   *"nothing again should ever hurt him"*: Lee, Clark, and Henschel, Richard, *Douglas MacArthur*, p. 166.

373   *"You have a court"*: Acheson, Dean, *Present at the Creation*, p. 424.

373   *"sycophancy was what tripped him up"*: Weintraub, Stanley, *MacArthur's War*, p. 161.

373   *"the dreamworld of self worship"*: Stueck, William, *Rethinking the Korean War*, p. 113.

373   *and arrogant was he*: author interview with Carleton West.

373   *"too much of a Prussian accent?"*: D. Clayton James interview with Roger Egeberg, MacArthur Memorial Library.

374   *"all ideology"*: author interview with Frank Wisner, Jr.

374   *"give England to the Germans"*: Naval Historical Center Colloquium on Contemporary History, June 20, 1990.

374   *"a friend of the United States"*: Kluckhohn, Frank, the *Reporter*, August 19, 1952.

374   *"than the people at the Dai Ichi"*: author interview with Frank Gibney.

375   *"and headed towards Washington"*: Ibid.

376   *"the faceless mob driven by"*: Cumings, Bruce, *The Origins of the Korean War, Vol. II*, p. 106.

377 *"of Communism would trump mine"*: author interview with Joseph Fromm.

377 *"that headquarters to deal with reality"*: Ibid.

377 *"subjugation of the Western world"*: Cumings, Bruce, *The Origins of the Korean War*, Vol. II, p. 112.

377 *eventually passed on to McCarthy*: Ibid.

378 *"had been so outspoken about him"*: author interview with Bill McCaffrey.

378 *"Willoughby falsified the intelligence"*: Blair, Clay, *The Forgotten War*, p. 377.

378 *"where it would have to be acted on"*: author interview with Bill Train.

379 *had not been so deadly serious*: author interview with Carleton Swift.

379 *"that he had made up his mind on"*: Ibid.

380 *anyone higher up about the intelligence*: author interview with Robert Myers.

380 *"the enormous power that Willoughby had"*: author interview with Bill Train.

381 *"to a low point of effectiveness"*: Heefner, Wilson, *Patton's Bulldog*, p. 264.

381 *indicate a serious Chinese presence*: Ibid., p. 272.

381 *"was very much under his shadow"*: author interview with Bill Train.

381 *"was unduly influenced by Willoughby"*: Blair, Clay, *The Forgotten War*, p. 379.

382 *"but not the full armies themselves"*: Heefner, Wilson, *Patton's Bulldog*, p. 272.

382 *"moving into that awful goddamn trap"*: author interview with Bill Train.

383 *"a lot of Mexicans in Los Angeles"*: Tom Lambert interview, Toland papers, Franklin D. Roosevelt Library.

CHAPTER 26

384 *"know Karl Marx from Groucho Marx"*: Bayley, Edwin, *Joe McCarthy and the Press*, p. 68.

385 *"you've got to be a Communist"*: Ibid., p. 73.

385 *"pig in a minefield"*: author interview with Murray Kempton for *The Fifties*.

385 *"only a mucker can muck"*: Oshinsky, David, *A Conspiracy So Immense*, p. 174.

385 *"should proceed with another"*: Patterson, James, *Mr. Republican*, p. 455.

385 *"the most nefarious campaign"*: Oshinsky, David, *A Conspiracy So Immense*, pp. 168–169.

386 *"how things had changed"*: Ibid., p. 178.

386 *"without gaining that of the Chinese"*: Blair, Clay, *The Forgotten War*, p. 400.

389 *his virtual disobedience*: Ridgway, Matthew B., *The Korean War*, p. 65.

389 *"they will get Christmas dinner at home"*: Toland, John, *In Mortal Combat*, p. 281.

389 *he simply said, "Bullshit"*: Ibid., p. 282.

389 *"the first time he smells Chinese chow"*: Ibid., Heefner, Wilson, *Patton's Bulldog*, pp. 281–282; author interview with Layton Tyner; Tyner interviews with Toland, Toland papers, Franklin D. Roosevelt Library.

390 *"hit the jackpot"*: Weintraub, Stanley, *MacArthur's War*, p. 221.

390 *"like Custer at the Little Big Horn"*: Ridgway, Matthew B., *The Korean War*, p. 63.

390 *"the most fitting conclusion"*: Perret, Geoffrey, *Old Soldiers Never Die*, p. 548.

CHAPTER 27

395 *a friendly little tank-shove*: author interview with Jim Hinton.

396 *"to be disappearing into the vast"*: Ibid.

397 *from the very face of the earth*: author interview with Paul O'Dowd.

398 *"less able to support us each day"*: author interview with John Carley.

398   *couldn't get anyone to act on it*": author interview with Malcolm MacDonald.
401   *the time was not quite right to attack*: author interview with Sam Mace.
401   *no one seemed very interested*: author interviews with John Eisenhower and Dick
      Gruenther.
402   "*a phantom which cast no shadow*": Marshall, S. L. A., *The River and the Gauntlet*, p. 1.
402   *The next day the Chinese hit*: author interview with John Eisenhower.

CHAPTER 28

PAGE

404   *bandaged up and wrapped in blankets*: author interview with Sherman Pratt; Pratt,
      Sherman, *Decisive Battles of the Korean War*, pp. 15–20.
404   "*From here I just don't see a solution*": letters of Paul Freeman courtesy of Anne Sewell
      Freeman McLeod and Roy McLeod.

CHAPTER 29

PAGE

408   *beyond their comprehension*: author interview with Alan Jones.
409   *disgrace the Takahashi name*: author interview with Gene Takahashi.
412   *could dry their clothes*: Ibid.
414   *retreating to a higher point on the mountain*: author interview with
      Dick Raybould.
416   *in a moment of total cowardice*: author interview with Bruce Ritter.
418   *and got both Smith and White out*: author interviews with John Ritter, Billie Tinkle,
      and John Yates.
420   *a huge pile of enemy bodies*: author interview with Sam Mace.
422   "*knowing a Chinaman when I see one*": author interview with Charley Heath.
422   *the fear in the air*: author interview with Sam Mace.
423   *in conversation, the Big Ego*: Ibid.; Spurr, Russell, *Enter the Dragon*, p. 193.

CHAPTER 30

PAGE

427   *just as endangered*: Paul Freeman oral history, U.S. Army War College Library.
427   "*because we were set up to fail*": author interview with Dick Raybould.
428   "*MacArthur could do no wrong*": Appleman, Roy, *Escaping the Trap*, p. 47.
428   "*Ned was aggressive*": Blair, Clay, *The Forgotten War*, p. 32.
428   "*can those things float?*": Victor Krulak oral history, U.S. Marine Corps History
      Division.
428   "*always lengthy shitlist*": Russ, Martin, *Breakout*, p. 17.
429   "*enough to form an additional regiment*": Hoffman, Jon T., *Chesty*, pp. 370–371.
430   *the Congressional Medal of Honor*: author interview with James Lawrence.
430   "*if only he would put on a little weight*": Russ, Martin, *Breakout*, p. 186.
430   "*It might take only two*": Sloan, Bill, *Brotherhood of Heroes*, p. 58.
430   *the ten thousand Japanese soldiers*: Ibid., p. 310.
431   "*may have saved the Marine Division*": Alpha Bowser oral history, U.S. Marine Corps
      History Division.
431   *had mounted in Europe*: Ibid.
431   "*Even Genghis Khan wouldn't*": Russ, Martin, *Breakout*, p. 64.

431 *"he got away with it at Inchon"*: D. Clayton James interview with Oliver P. Smith, MacArthur Memorial Library.

432 *or the last time he would use it*: Hoffman, Jon T., *Chesty*, p. 378.

432 *not part of any massive Chinese*: author interview with Bill McCaffrey.

432 *and received the Navy Cross*: author interview with James Lawrence.

432 *"selected dumps along the way"*: Russ, Martin, *Breakout*, p. 52.

433 *Chinese forces on the eastern front*: Lawrence, James, paper on the Chosin fighting he prepared for U.S. Marine Corps Symposium; author interview with James Lawrence.

433 *"still far from our preselected killing zones"*: Simmons, Edwin, *Frozen Chosin*, U.S. Marine Corps Korean War Commemorative Series, 2002, p. 34.

433 *in case the Chinese struck*: Russ, Martin, *Breakout*, p. 71.

434 *"of sick and wounded"* Ibid., p. 72.

435 *"we took 4500 casualties out"*: Frank, Benis, *The Epic of Chosin*, U.S. Marine Corps History Division.

435 *"and a chasm on the other"*: Ridgway, Matthew B., *The Korean War*, p. 65.

435 *"with much the same scenario"*: author interview with James Lawrence. Russ, Martin, *Breakout*, p. 82.

437 *"on where you wanted to measure"*: Russ, Martin, *Breakout*, p. 82.

438 *"and that's what we started to do"*: Simmons, Edwin, *Frozen Chosin*, p. 49.

438 *"an insane plan"*: Blair, Clay, *The Forgotten War*, p. 456.

438 *"the most ill-advised and unfortunate"*: Ibid.

439 *"was the Tenth Corps commander"*: author interview with James Lawrence.

439 *would have tragic consequences*: Blair, Clay, *The Forgotten War*, p. 418.

440 *"What did the general say?"*: Gugeler, Russell, *Combat Operations in Korea*, p. 62.

440 *"What a damned travesty"*: Russ, Martin, *Breakout*, pp. 196–197; Blair, Clay, *The Forgotten War*, pp. 462–464.

440 *"an arrogant, blind march to disaster"*: Blair, Clay, *The Forgotten War*, p. 464.

441 *easy prey for the Chinese*: Heefner, Wilson, *Patton's Bulldog*, p. 295.

CHAPTER 31

PAGE

442 *"were running in all directions"*: Paul Freeman oral history, U.S. Army War College Library.

443 *was blocked by the Chinese*: Ibid.; Blair, Clay, *The Forgotten War*, p. 478.

444 *might well have seen Chinese*: Marshall, S. L. A., *The River and the Gauntlet*, p. 264.

445 *"or just barrel through"*: author interview with Alan Jones.

445 *He had never heard of it before*: author interview with Malcolm MacDonald; MacDonald family memoir.

445 *"Well, come out my way"*: Blair, Clay, *The Forgotten War*, p. 477.

447 *always bad, became even worse*: author interview with Larry Farnum.

447 *"we lost because of it"*: author interview with Harold G. Moore.

448 *and with disabled vehicles*: Blair, Clay, *The Forgotten War*, pp. 478–81.

448 *"so I guess I can run another one"*: author interview with Jim Hinton.

450 *Lucky Charley, he had thought*: author interviews with Sam Mace and Charley Heath.

453 *to die on that road trying*: author interview with Alan Jones.

453 *"on the road to Sunchon, would you?"*: Ibid., author interview with Bill Wood.

CHAPTER 32

PAGE

454   *"I've lost my whole battalion"*: author interview with Malcolm MacDonald.
455   *"Can't any of you do anything?"* Marshall, S. L. A., *The River and the Gauntlet*, p. 319.
456   *an epitaph for the day*: Ibid., p. 320.
456   *"in this godawful country"*: Spurr, Russell, *Enter the Dragon*, p. 193.
458   *"More fucking Chinese!"*: author interview with Paul O'Dowd.

CHAPTER 33

PAGE

460   *"some kind of officer's club"*: author interview with Gino Piazza.
461   *they were stuck with all that*: Ibid.
461   *"commitment to his men made things harder"*: Ibid., author interviews with Larry
      Farnum and Alarich Zacherle.
463   *bore him no animus*: author interview with Alarich Zacherle.
464   *"very few of them made it back"*: author interview with Bob Nehrling.
466   *just how close the Chinese were*: author interview with Hank Emerson.
467   *a kind of death for him as well*: author interview with Charley Heath.

CHAPTER 34

PAGE

468   *Had their communications been more modern*: Alpha Bowser oral history, U.S.
      Marine Corps History Division.
469   *"non-battle injuries, mostly frostbite"*: Hoffman, Jon T., *Chesty*, p. 410.
470   *"preferably one with yellow skin"*: Russ, Martin, *Breakout*, p. 6.
470   *"simply attacking in another direction"*: Alpha Bowser oral history, U.S. Marine Corps
      History Division.
471   *"overly cautious executing any order"*: Simmons, Edwin H., *Frozen Chosin*, p. 35.
471   *"I was never more satisfied"*: D. Clayton James interview with Oliver P. Smith,
      MacArthur Memorial Library.
472   *"You tell General Walker to"*: Marshall, S. L. A., *Bringing Up the Rear*, pp. 181–183.
473   *"Never serve under Tenth Corps"*: Hoffman, Jon T., *Chesty*, p. 417.

CHAPTER 35

PAGE

474   *in the previous six weeks*: Blair, Clay, *The Forgotten War*, p. 468.
475   *"as if the madness were in the room"*: author interview with Matthew B. Ridgway.
475   *"he could not bear to end his career in checkmate"*: Manchester, William, *American
      Caesar*, p. 617.
476   *"omissions of the more unpalatable facts"*: Hastings, Max, *The Korean War*, p. 178.
476   *prematurely triggered the Chinese attack*: James, D. Clayton, *Refighting the Last War*,
      p. 45.
476   *and thus redeem himself*: Bradley, Omar, with Blair, Clay, *A General's Life*, p. 626.
476   *victories of his adversaries not really victories*: author interview with Matthew
      B. Ridgway.
476   *"Whom the gods destroy"*: Acheson, Dean, *Present at the Creation*, p. 518.
477   *"Someone is crazy"*: author interview with Joe Fromm.

477 *"It was disgraceful"*: Bradley, Omar, with Blair, Clay, *A General's Life*, p. 603.
478 *why couldn't we?*: Ibid.
479 *"thereby to unite the forces of Eighth Army and Tenth Corps"*: Ibid.
479 *"one promising front in the war to liberate"*: Herzstein, Robert, *Henry Luce and the American Crusade in Asia*, p. 139.
479 *"Luce wants the Big War"*: Ibid., p. 147.
480 *"to Manhattan's Upper West Side"*: Ibid., p. 136.
483 *"so often been right when everyone else"*: Ridgway, Matthew B., *The Korean War*, p. 61.
483 *"I never afterward had occasion to discuss this"*: Ibid.; author interview with Matthew B. Ridgway.
483 *"the British at Singapore in 1942"*: Hastings, Max, *The Korean War*, p. 170.
483 *"ill-armed and on their feet"*: Ibid., p. 167.
485 *"complete disgrace and of shame"*: author interview with Sam Mace.

CHAPTER 36

PAGE
487 *"a lot sooner in the game"*: author interview with Jack Murphy.
488 *"the last great battle between East and West"*: Blair, Clay, *The Forgotten War*, p. 69.
488 *"we risk disaster"*: Ibid.
490 *"was the same as that on it"*: author interview with Ken Hamburger; Blair, Clay, *Ridgway's Paratroopers*, pp. 138–141.
490 *"not before the Japanese people"*: Matthew B. Ridgway interview, Toland papers, Franklin D. Roosevelt Library.
490 *"very little in the way of blood"*: Ridgway, Matthew B., *The Korean War*, p. 110.
491 *greatest American soldier*: Ridgway, Matthew B., *The Korean War*, dedication.
491 *"stuck to the bone"*: Blair, Clay, *The Forgotten War*, p. 569.
491 *"Do what you think best"*: Ridgway, Matthew B., *The Korean War*, p. 83.
492 *"the most underrated"*: Allen, George, *None So Blind*, p. 96.
492 *"like no other general's in our"*: Bradley, Omar, with Blair, Clay, *A General's Life*, p. 608.
492 *"seldom took advantage of it"*: Ridgway, Matthew B., *The Korean War*, pp. 88–89.
492 *"not in retreat, but in flight"*: Harold Johnson oral history, U.S. Army War College Library.
492 *"You must be ruthless"*: Toland, John, *In Mortal Combat*, p. 378.
493 *"Fight them! Finish them!"*: Ibid.

CHAPTER 37

PAGE
495 *"He wanted to go to war with China"*: Blair, Clay, *The Forgotten War*, pp. 566–567.
495 *"We are fighting the second team"*: Hastings, Max, *The Korean War*, p. 186.
495 *"of what many might call 'appeasement'"*: Ibid., p. 569.
497 *"under which we were fighting"*: Bradley, Omar with Blair, Clay, *A General's Life*, p. 646.
497 *"Even with his penis he was defiant"*: Blair, Clay, *Ridgway's Paratroopers*, p. 111.
498 *wings were going to be partially clipped*: Coleman, J. D., *Wonju*, p. 59.
498 *no longer going to play games*: author interview with Bill McCaffrey.
499 *Jeter was gone, and word*: Blair, Clay, *The Forgotten War*, p. 574.
499 *the smallest details right*: author interview with George Allen.
502 *the beginning of the turnaround*: interview with Mike Michaelis, Clay Blair papers, U.S. Army War College Library.

CHAPTER 38

PAGE

505   *might prove a crisis in itself*: Xiaobing Li, et al., *Mao's Generals Remember Korea*, p. 11.
506   *becoming drunk with success*: Spurr, Russell, *Enter the Dragon*, p. 252.
506   *"if they weren't ours"*: author interview with Walter Killilae, Killilae private memoir.
508   *always treated them*: Spurr, Russell, *Enter the Dragon*, pp. 41–42.
508   *he intended to savor it*: Ibid., p. 167.
508   *"will be a battle of supply,"* Ibid., pp. 80–81.
509   *"who see the conduct of war in dogmatic"*: Ibid.
510   *"and one bite [of] snow"*: Xiaobing Li, et al., *Mao's Generals Remember Korea*, p. 54.
510   *met only a quarter of the army's*: Ibid., p. 18.
511   *weaker than the Chinese Nationalist*: Ibid.
511   *"goals defined by Mao tended to go beyond"*: Ibid.
512   *"had thrown their rifles and pistols away"*: Ridgway, Matthew B., *The Korean War*,
        pp. 93–94.

CHAPTER 39

PAGE

515   *"most of us hated them"*: author interview with John Carley.
515   *more bravado than he felt*: Spurr, Russell, *Enter the Dragon*, p. 285.
517   *everyone hit the ground*: Paul Freeman oral history, U.S. Army War College Library;
        Hamburger, Kenneth, *Leadership in the Crucible*, pp. 92–93.
517   *"and a basin of water"*: Paul Freeman oral history, U.S. Army War College Library.

CHAPTER 40

PAGE

519   *five hundred meters each surrounded it*: Hamburger, Kenneth, *Leadership in the
        Crucible*, p. 98.
520   *and been lucky as well*: author interview with Maurice Fenderson.
522   *of little value for much of the morning*: Hamburger, Kenneth, *Leadership in the
        Crucible*, pp. 99–100.
523   *"This is our only chance"*: Ibid., p. 100; Appleman, Roy, *Ridgway Duels for Korea*,
        pp. 202–203; Gugeler, Russell, *Combat Operations in Korea*, pp. 85–87; author
        interviews with survivors, including Laron Wilson and Richard Fockler.
524   *made him feel he had a lot*: author interview with Laron Wilson.
526   *an American captain in a jeep spotted him*: author interview with Richard Fockler.
527   *it was Private William Stratton*: Gugeler, Russell, *Combat Operations in Korea*,
        pp. 87–90.
528   *for the fourth time and died*: author interview with Laron Wilson; Gugeler, Russell,
        Combat Operations in Korea, pp. 80–90.
528   *"will be with you shortly"*: Hamburger, Kenneth, *Leadership in the Crucible*, p. 103.
529   *"small-unit actions in the Korean"*: Freeman, Paul, *Wonju to Chipyongni*, U.S. Army
        War College Library.

CHAPTER 41

PAGE

531   *"to demonstrate his superiority"*: Coleman, J. D., *Wonju*, p. 91.
531   *was not trusted by his superior*: Ibid., p. 58.

531 *"who often commanded by instilling fear"*: Hamburger, Kenneth, *Leadership in the Crucible,* pp. 89–90.

532 *"murder my regiment"*: Stewart, George, private memoir.

534 *the wisdom of the ages*: Knox, Donald, *The Korean War, Vol. II,* p. 25.

534 *"enemy is close enough to kill"*: Martin, Harold, *Saturday Evening Post,* May 19, 1951.

535 *then returned to Freeman's headquarters*: Stewart, George, private memoir.

536 *pointless rounds into the air*: author interview with Kenneth Hamburger, who had interviewed George Stewart at length.

536 *Then, still in a rage, he drove off in his jeep*: author interview with Sherman Pratt; Pratt, Sherman, *Decisive Battles of the Korean War,* p. 154.

536 *"at the tunnels is doubtful"*: Hamburger, Kenneth, *Leadership in the Crucible,* p. 111.

537 *and soon the French fires*: Paul Freeman oral history, U.S. Army War College Library.

537 *"Let's kill as many Chinese"*: Stewart, George, private memoir.

539 *"bit the stems off three pipes"*: Ibid.

540 *"Like a Hollywood battle"*: Freeman, Paul, *Wonju to Chipyongni,* U.S. Army War College Library.

CHAPTER 42

542 *as they preferred to do*: author interview with Sherman Pratt.

544 *"By order of Scotch"*: Hamburger, Kenneth, *Leadership in the Crucible,* p. 154.

544 *"we are going to stay and fight it out"*: Ibid., p. 176.

545 *"relay answer to me as soon as possible"*: Appleman, Roy, *Ridgway Duels for Korea,* p. 258.

545 *"we can fight well where we are now"*: author interview with Sherman Pratt.

CHAPTER 43

546 *"evoking memories of Almond's operations"*: Blair, Clay, *The Forgotten War,* p. 685.

547 *separate black units*: Coleman, J. D., *Wonju,* pp. 93–94.

547 *Walker relieved of his company command*: Ibid., p. 94.

547 *like a betrayal by a member of his family*: author interview with Bill McCaffrey.

548 *"His racism tainted"*: author interview with J. D. Coleman.

549 *to absorb the heaviest punishment*: Paik, Sun Yup, *From Pusan to Panmunjon,* pp. 125–26.

549 *"and drawn them up himself"*: Coleman, J. D., *Wonju,* p. 95.

550 *who was only a captain would know so much*: Ibid., pp. 103–104.

551 *"had created a gauntlet"*: Blair, Clay, *The Forgotten War,* p. 689.

552 *"NICE GOING HARRY"*: Ibid., p. 740.

554 *"you have to risk the lives of your men"*: author interview with Kenneth Hamburger.

554 *"BUT THE DECISION IS YOURS"*: Stewart, George, private memoir.

555 *"until the gun barrels melt"*: Ibid.

CHAPTER 44

558 *the most vulnerable part of Paul Freeman's regimental defense*: author interview with Paul McGee.

560 *"you should have stayed back home"*: Ibid.

566 *they were going to pull Freeman*: author interview with Dr. Robert Hall.
566 *"stay out of my way"*: Paul Freeman oral history, U.S. Army War College Library.

CHAPTER 45

PAGE

567 *"and I know you'll do it"*: Blumenson, Martin, *Army Magazine*, August 2002; author interview with Martin Blumenson.
570 *"in any event, reach us"*: Hamburger, Kenneth, *Leadership in the Crucible*, p. 205.
571 *"trains or no trains"*: Blair, Clay, *The Forgotten War*, p. 700.
571 *hell for leather to Chipyongni*: author interview with Martin Blumenson.
572 *were not lined up properly*: author interview with Tom Mellen.
573 *"the last strong company gone to hell"*: Hamburger, Kenneth, *Leadership in the Crucible*, p. 200.
573 *"I refuse the order too!"*: Ibid., pp. 200–201.
574 *when it was all over*: Blair, Clay, *The Forgotten War*, p. 707.
575 *the state of the other men*: Hamburger, Kenneth, *Leadership in the Crucible*, pp. 206–207, 213–214.

CHAPTER 46

PAGE

581 *to try to save Inmon's life*: author interviews with Cletis Inmon and Paul McGee.
585 *give him a shot to sedate him*: author interview with Dr. Robert Hall.
585 *doing a giant jigsaw puzzle*: Knox, Donald, *The Korean War, Vol. II*, p. 73.
585 *"I will court-martial him"*: Hamburger, Kenneth, *Leadership in the Crucible*, p. 215.

CHAPTER 47

PAGE

587 *"starting with the victories up along the"*: author interview with Chen Jian.
588 *"can't wait for him to wake up"*: Ibid.

CHAPTER 48

PAGE

592 *"it is a free Asia"*: Blair, Clay, *The Forgotten War*, p. 659.
593 *would use it as an excuse for an intervention*: Truman, Harry S., *Memoirs, Vol. II*, p. 420.
593 *the Russians would send in by train*: Ibid., p. 416.
593 *"did not consider it beyond his own powers"*: Hastings, Max, *The Korean War*, pp. 192–193.
593 *"igniting World War III, and a nuclear"*: Bradley, Omar with Blair, Clay, *A General's Life*, p. 616.
594 *plan a major offensive*: Weintraub, Sidney, *MacArthur's War*, p. 305.
594 *"but had almost forgotten"*: Ibid., p. 616.
594 *"the contingency of 'success'"*: Manchester, William, *American Caesar*, p. 625.
596 *"in Manchuria are contained by"*: Paul Freeman oral history, U.S. Army War College Library.
598 *had nothing to lose by ignoring*: Weintraub, Sidney, *MacArthur's War*, p. 307.

600 *"the most gross indifference"*: Blair, Clay, *The Forgotten War*, pp. 767–768.

600 *"combined disbelief with controlled fury"*: Acheson, Dean, *Present at the Creation*, p. 519

600 *"I wanted to kick him into the North China Sea"*: Truman, Margaret, *Harry S. Truman*, p. 513.

CHAPTER 49

PAGE
602 *"This is outright* treachery*"*: Goulden, Joseph, *Korea*, pp. 477–478.

603 *"but it does not get me anywhere"*: Truman, Harry S., *Memoirs, Vol. II*, pp. 446–447.

603 Lincoln as *"the original gorilla"*: Goodwin, Doris Kearns, *Team of Rivals*, p. 383.

605 *"and my decision alone"*: author interview with George Elsey; George Elsey interview, Harry S. Truman Library.

606 *"We'll let them think so"*: Donovan, Robert, *Tumultuous Years*, p. 355.

606 *"the Emperor of the Far East"*: Truman interviews, Harry S. Truman Library.

606 That was absurd, Almond insisted: Blair, Clay, *The Forgotten War*, p. 788.

606 *"His soldierly qualities were never"*: Goldman, Eric, *The Crucial Decade*, pp. 201–202.

CHAPTER 50

PAGE
607 *"almost a professional little man"*: Swanberg, W. A., *Luce and His Empire*, p. 312.

607 *"to be a fit commander in such a war"*: Hastings, Max, *The Korean War*, p. 207.

608 *"nothing to match it since the Civil"*: Rovere, Richard and Schlesinger, Arthur M., Jr., *The General and the President*, p. 5.

608 *"the adoring crowd that thronged"*: Caro, Robert, *Master of the Senate*, pp. 369–370.

608 *"Would you like me to get out"*: Halberstam, David, *The Fifties*, p. 114.

608 *"into the persona of a great General"*: Goulden, Joseph, *Korea*, p. 507.

609 *"a damn bunch of bullshit"*: Halberstam, David, *The Fifties*, p. 115.

610 *"Thank God that's over"*: Acheson, Dean, *Present at the Creation*, p. 524.

611 for one last try: Goulden, Joseph, *Korea*, p. 498.

611 was a dubious honor: Caro, Robert, *Master of the Senate*, p. 372.

615 *"with parochial interests and knowledge"*: Goulden, Joseph, *Korea*, p. 527.

616 *"the wrong war at the wrong place"*: Bradley, Omar with Blair, Clay, *A General's Life*, p. 640.

616 *"that were run off China in the first place"*: Goulden, Joseph, *Korea*, pp. 534–535.

617 *"destroyed the Truman Administration"*: Acheson, Dean, *Among Friends*, p. 103.

CHAPTER 51

PAGE
621 *"the more he damaged himself"*: author interview with Bill McCaffrey.

622 *"he just did not understand"*: Walters, Vernon A., *Silent Missions*, pp. 209–210.

622 *"in purple splendor"*: Eisenhower, Dwight D., *At Ease*, p. 227.

CHAPTER 52

PAGE
625 *"Why don't you get a red flag?"*: Smith, Richard Norton, *Thomas Dewey and His Times*, p. 591.

626 *"And don't take us down that road"*: Manchester, William, *The Glory and the Dream,* p. 617.

627 *"rather than opposes the White House"*: Caro, Robert, *Master of the Senate,* p. 525.

628 *"little or no effect on them"*: author interview with Harold G. Moore.

629 *"deserves a place in history"*: Marshall, S. L. A., *Pork Chop Hill,* p. 146.

630 *came back with 14*: author interviews with Joe Clemons, Walter Russell, and Harold G. Moore.

EPILOGUE

PAGE

648 *"a Stevenson with balls"*: Halberstam, David, *The Best and the Brightest,* p. 24.

649 *never corrected Kennedy*: author interview with Leslie H. Gelb.

650 *"a profile in caution"*: author interview with Allen Whiting.

650 *"Jackie, we need the Bloody Marys"*: Schlesinger, Arthur M., Jr., *A Thousand Days,* pp. 479–480.

651 *"but dreaming different dreams"*: author interview with Bernard Fall.

652 *"right wingers who had criticized"*: author interview with George Elsey.

652 *"with poor George's marshmallow mind"*: Brinkley, Douglas, *Dean Acheson,* p. 91.

652 *"the poor fellow who comes after me"*: Sorensen, Theodore, *Kennedy,* p. 294.

653 *"except as a practical need to be"*: Geyelin, Philip, *Lyndon Johnson and the World,* p. 17.

654 *"raggedy ass little fourth rate country"*: Halberstam, David, *The Best and the Brightest,* p. 512.

655 *"you can get along fine"*: Ibid., p. 531.

655 *"Right up my ass"*: author interviews with Bill Moyers and George Reedy.

Bibliography

Abels, Jules. *Out of the Jaws of Victory*. Henry Holt & Co., 1959.
Abramson, Rudy. *Spanning the Century: The Life of W. Averell Harriman 1891–1986*. William Morrow, 1992.
Acheson, Dean. *Among Friends*. Dodd, Mead, 1980.
———. *Present at the Creation*. W. W. Norton & Company, 1969.
Alexander, Bevin. *Korea*. Hippocrene, 1956.
Alexander, Joseph. *The Battle of the Barricades*. Korean War Commemorative Series, Marine Historical Center, 2000.
Allen, George. *None So Blind*. Ivan R. Dee, 2001.
Allison, John, *Ambassador from the Plains*. Houghton Mifflin, 1973.
Appleman, Roy. *Disaster in Korea*. Texas A&M University Press, 1989.
———. *Escaping the Trap*. Texas A&M University Press, 1990.
———. *Ridgway Duels for Korea*. Texas A&M University Press, 1990.
———. *South to the Naktong, North to the Yalu*. U.S. Army Center of Military History, 1961.
Armstrong, Charles. *The North Korean Revolution*. Columbia University Press, 2003.
Ayers, Eben A. *Truman in the White House*, edited by Robert H. Ferrell. University of Missouri Press, 1991.

Bain, David. *Sitting in Darkness*. Houghton Mifflin, 1984.
Bardos, Phil. *Cold War Warriors*. Xlibris, 2000.
Bayley, Edwin. *Joe McCarthy and the Press*. University of Wisconsin Press, 1981.
Beech, Keyes. *Tokyo and Points East*. Doubleday, 1954.
Blair, Clay. *The Forgotten War*. Anchor, 1987.
———. *Ridgway's Paratroopers*. Dial, 1985.
Bloodworth, Dennis. *The Messiah and the Mandarins*. Atheneum, 1982.
Bradley, Omar, with Blair, Clay. *A General's Life*. Simon & Schuster, 1983.
Brady, James. *The Coldest War*. St. Martin's Press, 1990.
Breuer, William. *Shadow Warriors*. John Wiley & Sons, 1996.
Brinkley, Douglas. *Dean Acheson*. Yale University Press, 1992.

Caro, Robert. *Means of Ascent*. Alfred A. Knopf, 1990.
———. *Master of the Senate*. Alfred A. Knopf, 2003.
Caute, David. *The Great Fear*. Simon & Schuster, 1978.
Chase, James. *Acheson*. Simon & Schuster, 1998.
Chen Jian. *China's Road to the Korean War*. Columbia University Press, 1994.
Christensen, Thomas. *Useful Adversaries*. Princeton University Press, 1996.
Clark, Eugene. *The Secrets of Inchon*. Putnam, 2002.
Coleman, J. D. *Wonju*. Brassey's, 2000.

Collins, J. Lawton. *Lightning Joe*. Louisiana State University Press, 1979.
———. *War in Peacetime*. Houghton Mifflin, 1969.
Cooke, Alistair. *A Generation on Trial*. Alfred A. Knopf, 1982.
Cray, Ed. *General of the Army: George C. Marshall*. Touchstone, 1990.
Cumings, Bruce. *The Origins of the Korean War, Volumes I and II*. Princeton University Press, 1981 (Vol. I) and 1990 (Vol. II).

Dae-Sook, Suh. *Kim Il Sung*. Columbia University Press, 1988.
Davis, Nuell Pharr. *Lawrence and Oppenheimer*. DeCapo Press, 1986.
Dawidoff, Nicholas. *The Fly Swatter*. Pantheon, 2002.
Dean, William. *General Dean's Story*. Viking, 1954.
D'Este, Carlo. *Eisenhower: A Soldier's Life*. Henry Holt and Co., 2002.
Djilas, Milovan. *Conversations with Stalin*. Harcourt Brace & Company, 1962.
Donovan, Robert. *Tumultuous Years*. W. W. Norton, 1982.
Dower, John. *War without Mercy*. Pantheon, 1987.

Eisenhower, Dwight D. *At Ease: Stories I Tell to Friends*. Doubleday, 1967.

Fairbank, John, and Feuerwerker, Albert. *The Cambridge History of China, Volume 13*. Cambridge University Press, 1980.
Fehrenbach, T. R. *This Kind of War*. Brassey's, 1994.
Ferrell, Robert (editor). *The Eisenhower Diaries*. W. W. Norton & Company, 1981.
———. *Off the Record: The Private Papers of Harry S. Truman*. Harper & Row, 1980.
———, ed. *Truman in the White House: The Diary of Eben A. Ayers*. Columbia: University of Missouri Press, 1991.
Foot, Rosemary. *The Wrong War*. Cornell University Press, 1985.
Fromkin, David. *In the Time of the Americans*. Vintage, 1995.

Gaddis, John Lewis. *We Now Know*. Oxford University Press, 1998.
Gellman, Barton. *Contending with Kennan*. Praeger, 1984.
Geyelin, Philip. *Lyndon Johnson and the World*. Praeger, 1966.
Gibney, Frank. *Korea: A Quiet Revolution*. Walker, 1992.
Goldman, Eric. *The Crucial Decade*. Alfred A. Knopf, 1956.
Goncharov, Sergei, Lewis, John, and Xue Litai. *Uncertain Partners*. Stanford University Press, 1993.
Goodwin, Doris Kearns. *Team of Rivals*. Simon & Schuster, 2005.
Goulden, Joseph. *Korea*. McGraw-Hill, 1982.
Gugeler, Russell. *Combat Operations in Korea*. Office of the Chief of Military History, 1970.
Gunther, John. *The Riddle of MacArthur*. Harper & Row, 1951.

Ha Jin. *War Trash*. Pantheon, 2004.
Haas, Michael. *The Devil's Shadow*. Naval Institute Press, 2002.
Halberstam, David. *The Best and the Brightest*. Random House, 1972.
———. *The Fifties*. Villard, 1993.
———. *The Powers That Be*. Alfred A. Knopf, 1979.
Hamburger, Kenneth. *Leadership in the Crucible*. Texas A&M University Press, 2003.
Hammel, Eric. *Chosin*. Presidio Press, 1981.
Hart, John. *The Making of an Army Old China Hand*. Institute of East Asian Affairs, Berkeley, 1985.
Harvey, Robert. *American Shogun*. Murray, 2006.
Hastings, Max. *The Korean War*. Simon & Schuster, 1987.

Hechler, Ken. *Working with Truman.* University of Missouri Press, 1996.

Heefner, Wilson. *Patton's Bulldog.* White Mane Books, 2001.

Heinl, Robert. *Victory at High Tide.* Lippincott, 1968.

Herzstein, Robert. *Henry Luce and the American Crusade in Asia.* Cambridge University Press, 2005.

Hickey, Michael. *The Korean War.* Overlook, 2000.

Higgins, Trumbull. *Korea and the Fall of MacArthur: A Precis in Limited War.* Oxford University Press, 1960.

Hockley, Ralph M. *Freedom Is Not Free.* Brockton, 2000.

Hoffman, Jon T. *Chesty.* Random House, 2001.

Hoopes, Townsend. *The Devil and John Foster Dulles.* Little Brown, 1973.

Hughes, Emmet John. *The Ordeal of Power: A Political Memoir of the Eisenhower Years.* Atheneum, 1963.

Isaacson, Walter, and Thomas, Evan. *The Wise Men: Six Friends and the World They Made.* Touchstone, 1986.

Isenberg, George. *Korea: Tales from the Front Line.* Worldpro Press, 2001.

James, D. Clayton. *The Years of MacArthur, Volumes I–III.* Houghton Mifflin, 1970.

———. *Refighting the Last War.* Free Press, 1993.

Jones, Alex S. and Tifft, Susan E. *The Trust: The Private and Powerful Family Behind The New York Times.* Little Brown, 1999.

Jung, Chang and Halliday, Jon. *Mao: The Unknown Story.* Alfred A. Knopf, 2005.

Kahn, E. J. *The China Hands.* Viking, 1975.

Karnow, Stanley. *In Our Image: America's Empire in the Philippines.* Random House, 1989.

Kennan, George F. *Memoirs 1925–1950.* Atlantic Monthly Press, 1967.

———. *Memoirs 1950–1963.* Pantheon, 1971.

Kenney, George. *The MacArthur I Know.* Duell, Sloan, 1951.

Klingon, Greta. *The Soldier and General Herbert Powell.* Privately printed.

Knox, Donald. *The Korean War, Volume I.* Harcourt Brace & Company, 1985.

———. *The Korean War, Volume II.* Harvest, 1988.

Koen, Ross Y. *The China Lobby in American Politics.* Harper & Row, 1974.

Laquer, Walter. *Stalin: The Glasnost Revelations.* Scribner, 1990.

Leary, William (editor). *MacArthur and the American Century.* University of Nebraska Press, 2001.

Leckie, Robert. *Conflict: The History of the Korean War, 1950–53.* G. P. Putnam, 1962.

Lee, Clark, and Henschel, Richard. *Douglas MacArthur.* Henry Holt and Co., 1952.

Li Zhisui, Dr. *The Private Life of Chairman Mao.* Random House, 1994.

Lilienthal, David E. *The Journals of David E. Lilienthal: Volume II: The Atomic Energy Years, 1945–1950.* Harper & Row, 1964.

Linn, Brian. *The Philippine War.* University of Kansas Press, 2002.

MacArthur, Douglas. *Reminiscences.* McGraw-Hill, 1964.

Maher, William. *A Shepherd in Combat Boots.* Burd Street Press, 1997.

Mahoney, Kevin. *Formidable Enemies.* Presidio Press, 2001.

Maihafer, Harry. *From the Hudson to the Yalu.* Texas A&M University Press, 1993.

Manchester, William. *American Caesar.* Little Brown, 1978.

———. *The Glory and the Dream: A Narrative History of America, 1932–1972.* Little Brown, 1974.

Marshall, S. L. A. *Pork Chop Hill*. William Morrow, 1956; Berkley Press, 2000.
———. *Bringing Up the Rear*. Presidio Press, 1979.
———. *The River and the Gauntlet*. Battery Press, 1987.
Martin, Bradley K. *Under the Loving Care of the Fatherly Leader: North Korea and the Kim Dynasty*. St. Martin's Press, 2004.
McCullough, David. *Truman*. Simon & Schuster, 1992.
McFarland, Keith D. and Roll, David L. *Louis Johnson and the Arming of America: The Roosevelt and Truman Years*. Indiana University Press, 2005.
McLellan, David S. *Dean Acheson: The State Department Years*. Dodd, Mead, 1976.
Melby, John. *The Mandate of Heaven*. University of Toronto Press, 1968.
Miller, Merle. *Plain Speaking*. Berkley Press, 1973.
Millett, Allan. *Their War in Korea*. Brassey's, 2002.
Moore, Lt. General Harold G. and Galloway, Joseph L. *We Were Soldiers Once . . . and Young*. Random House, 1992.
Morris, Carol Petillo. *Douglas MacArthur: The Philippine Years*. Indiana University Press, 1981.
Mossman, Billy. *Ebb and Flow, November 1950–July 1951: United States Army in the Korean War*. University Press of the Pacific, 2005.
Myers, Robert. *Korea in the Cross Currents*. Palgrave Macmillan, 2001.

Novak, Robert, and Evans, Rowland. *Lyndon Johnson: The Exercises of Power*. New American Library, 1966.

Oberdorfer, Don. *The Two Koreas: A Contemporary History*. Addison-Wesley, 1997.
Offner, Arnold A. *Another Such Victory: President Truman and the Cold War, 1945–1953*. Stanford University Press, 2002.
Oliver, Robert T. *Syngman Rhee: The Man Behind the Myth*. Dodd, Mead, 1954.
Oshinsky, David. *A Conspiracy So Immense: The World of Joe McCarthy*. Free Press, 1983.

Paige, Glenn D. *The Korean Decision, June 24–30, 1950*. Free Press, 1968.
Paik, Sun Yup. *From Pusan to Panmunjom*. Brassey's, 1992.
Panikkar, K. M. *In Two Chinas*. George Allen, 1953.
Paschal, Rod. *Witness to War*. Perigree, 1995.
Patterson, James. *Mr. Republican: A Biography of Robert A. Taft*. Houghton Mifflin, 1972.
Payne, Robert. *Mao*. Talley and Weybright, 1969.
Peng, Dehuai. *Memoirs of a Chinese Marshal*. University Press of the Pacific, 2005.
Perret, Geoffrey. *Old Soldiers Never Die: The Life and Legend of Douglas MacArthur*. Random House, 1996.
Peters, Richard, and Xiaobing, Li. *Voices from the Korean War: Personal Stories of American, Korean, and Chinese Soldiers*. University of Kentucky Press, 2004.
Phillips, Cabell. *The Truman Presidency*. Macmillan, 1966.
Pratt, Sherman. *Decisive Battles of the Korean War*. Vantage, 1992.

Quick, Rory. *Wars and Peace*. Presidio Press, 1999.

Ridgway, Matthew B. *The Korean War*. Doubleday, 1967.
———and Martin, Harold H. *Soldier: The Memoirs of Matthew B. Ridgway*. Harper & Brothers, 1956.
Rovere, Richard, and Schlesinger, Arthur M., Jr. *The General and the President and the Future of American Foreign Policy*. Farrar, Straus and Giroux, 1951.

Russ, Martin. *Breakout: The Chosin Reservoir Campaign, Korea 1950*. Fromm, 1999.
———. *The Last Parallel: A Marine's War Journal*. Rinehart and Co., 1957.

Salisbury, Harrison. *The Long March*. McGraw-Hill, 1985.
———. *The New Emperors*. HarperCollins, 1993.
Sandler, Stanley (editor). *The Korean War: An Encyclopedia*. Garland Publishing, 1995.
Scalapino, Robert, and Chong-Sik Lee. *Communism in Korea*. University of California Press, 1972.
Schlesinger, Arthur M., Jr. *A Thousand Days*. Houghton Mifflin, 1965.
Schnabel, James. *Policy and Direction*. U.S. Army Center of Military History, 1972.
Sebald, William. *With MacArthur in Japan*. Cresset, 1965.
Shen Zhihua, Cold War International History Project. Winter 2003, Spring 2004.
Shu, Guang Zhang. *Mao's Military Romanticism*. University Press of Kansas, 1995.
Simmons, Edwin H. *Over the Seawall: U.S. Marines at Inchon*. Marine Corps Historical Center.
———. *Frozen Chosin*. Marine Korean War Series, 2002.
Singlaub, John. *Hazardous Duty*. Summit, 1991.
Sloan, Bill. *Brotherhood of Heroes: The Marines at Peleliu, 1944—the Bloodiest Battle of the Pacific War*. Simon & Schuster, 2005.
Smith, Richard Norton. *Thomas Dewey and His Times*. Simon & Schuster, 1982.
Smith, Robert. *MacArthur in Korea*. Simon & Schuster, 1982.
Soffer, Jonathan. *General Matthew B. Ridgway*. Praeger, 1998.
Sorensen, Theodore. *Kennedy*. Harper & Row, 1965.
Sorley, Lewis. *Honorable Warrior, General Harold Johnson*. University Press of Kansas, 1998.
Spanier, John. *The Truman-MacArthur Controversy and the Korean War*. Harvard University Press, 1959.
Spurr, Russell. *Enter the Dragon*. Newmarket, 1998.
Stanton, Shelby. *America's Tenth Legion*. Presidio Press, 1989.
Stokesbury, James. *A Short History of the Korean War*. Quill, 1988.
Stone, I. F. *The Hidden History of the Korean War*. Monthly Review Press, 1952.
Stueck, William. *Rethinking the Korean War: A New Diplomatic and Strategic History*. Princeton University Press, 2002.
Swanberg, W. A. *Luce and His Empire*. Scribner's, 1972.

Talbott, Strobe (translator and editor). *Khrushchev Remembers: The Last Testament*. Little Brown, 1974.
Taubman, William. *Khrushchev*. W. W. Norton & Company, 2003.
Terry, Addison. *The Battle for Pusan*. Presidio Press, 2000.
Thomas, Evan. *The Very Best Men*. Simon & Schuster, 1995.
Thompson, Reginald. *Cry Korea*. MacDonald, 1952.
Thornton, Richard. *Odd Man Out*. Brassey's, 2000.
Toland, John. *In Mortal Combat*. Quill, 1991.
Truman, Harry S. *Memoirs, Volume II*. Doubleday, 1956.
Truman, Margaret. *Harry S. Truman*. William Morrow, 1973.
Tuchman, Barbara. *Stilwell and the American Experience in China*. Macmillan, 1971.

Ulam, Adam B. *Stalin: The Man and His Era*. Beacon, 1973.

Walters, Vernon A. *Silent Missions*. Doubleday, 1975.
Warner, Denis. *The Opening Round of the Korean War*. Military History magazine, June 2000. Republished on www.historynet.com.

Weathersby, Kathryn. Cold War International History Project, Winter 1995–96.

Weinstein, Allen. Perjury. Alfred A. Knopf, 1978.

Weintraub, Stanley. MacArthur's War: Korea and the Undoing of an American Hero. Free Press, 2000.

Whalen, Richard. Drawing the Line. Little Brown, 1990.

White, Theodore H. In Search of History. Harper & Row, 1978.

———(editor). The Stilwell Papers. MacFadden, 1948.

———and Jacoby, Analee. Thunder Out of China. William Sloane Associates, 1946.

White, William Allen. The Autobiography of William Allen White. Macmillan, 1946.

Whitney, Courtney. MacArthur: His Rendezvous with History. Alfred A. Knopf, 1956.

Willoughby, Charles. MacArthur, 1941–51. McGraw-Hill, 1954.

Wofford, Harris. Of Kennedys and Kings. Farrar, Straus and Giroux, 1980.

Xiaobing Li, Millett, Allan Reed, Bin Yu (translators and editors). Mao's Generals Remember Korea. University of Kansas Press, 2006.

Zi Zhongyun. No Exit? EastBridge, 2003.

Zimmerman, Warren. First Great Triumph. Farrar, Straus and Giroux, 2002.

Index

Visit **www.panmacmillan.com** to read more about all our books and to buy them. You will also find features, author interviews and news of any author events, and you can sign up for e-newsletters so that you're always first to hear about our new releases.